Foundations of Education

THE CHALLENGE OF PROFESSIONAL PRACTICE

Robert F. McNergney
UNIVERSITY OF VIRGINIA

Joanne M. Herbert
UNIVERSITY OF VIRGINIA

Allyn and Bacon

Boston   London   Toronto   Sydney   Tokyo   Singapore

Series Editor: Virginia Lanigan
Development Editor: Mary Ellen Lepionka
Editorial Assistant: Nicole De Palma
Marketing Manager: Ellen Mann
Production Administrator: Elaine Ober
Editorial Production Service: Schneck-DePippo Graphics
Text Designer: Deborah Schneck
Cover Administrator: Linda Knowles
Composition Buyer: Linda Cox
Manufacturing Buyer: Megan Cochran

 Copyright © 1995 by Allyn & Bacon
A Simon & Schuster Company
Needham Heights, MA 02194

Library of Congress Cataloging-in-Publication Data

McNergney, Robert F.
    Foundations of education / Robert McNergney,
Joanne Herbert
    p.   cm.
Includes bibliographical references and index.
ISBN 0-205-13962-0
1. Teaching—Vocational guidance—United States.
2. Education—United States.   I. Herbert, Joanne.
II. Title.
LB1775.2.M32   1995
371.1'002373—dc20

94-29562
CIP

Printed in the United States of America
10 9 8 7 6 5 4 3 2 1   99 98 97 96 95 94

PHOTO CREDITS

Courtesy of National Teacher of the Year Program: p. 30;
Vanessa Vick/Photo Researchers: p. 36; The Granger
Collection: p. 58, p. 62, p. 80; Courtesy of CBS: p. 86; Bettman
Archive: p. 89 (left); The Granger Collection: p. 89 (right);
Bettman Archive: p. 95; Courtesy of the Chautaugua Institute:
p. 112; National Library of Medicine: p. 145; AP/Wide World:
p. 178; Stephen Shames/ Matrix; p. 219, 237; Bob
Daemmrich/Stock Boston; p. 265; J.D. Schwalm/The Clarion
Ledger: p. 273 (left), Jim Wilson/New York Times Pictures:
p. 273 (right); Erika Stone: p. 290 (top); The Granger
Collection: p. 349; Jim West/ Impact Visuals: p. 353; Courtesy
of Glenn Comeau: p. 382; Doug Plummer/Photo Researchers:
p. 430; UPI/ Bettmann: p. 436; Courtesy of Stuart Garfield &
The Anti-Defamation League: p. 439; Dan Habib/Impact
Visuals: p. 458; Russell Curtis/Photo Researchers: p. 459;

Lori Grinker /Woodfin Camp & Associates: p. 473; Steve
Northup/Black Star: p. 480; Mike Yamashita/Woodfin Camp
& Associates: p. 498: David Butow/Black Star: p. 543; John
Coletti: p. 546; North Wind Picture Archive: p. 40, p. 44, p. 47,
p. 49, p. 55, p. 57, p. 59 (bottom), p. 69, p. 72, p. 90, p. 94,
p. 135, p. 137; Will Faller: p. 22, p. 82, p. 129, p. 144, p. 161,
p. 175 (left), p. 176, p. 246, p. 297 (center), p. 308, p. 333,
p. 376, p. 386; Stephen Marks: p. 1, p. 6, p. 10, p. 175 (center),
p. 186 (both), p. 262, p. 284, p. 286, p. 290 (bottom); p. 311;
p. 371, p. 400; Jim Pickerell: p. 171, p. 227, p. 258 (center &
right), p. 289, p. 315; Brian Smith: p. 258 (left), p. 410, p. 450,
p. 486; Robert Harbison: p. 175 (right), p. 210; p. 290 (center);
Courtesy of Jeffrey P. Harper: p. 523, p. 527, p. 530, p. 533;
Mary Ellen Lepionka: p. 297 (top & bottom)

TO OUR PARENTS

Quentin and Thelma McNergney

AND

Elmore and Arvilla May

WITH LOVE

CONTENTS

CHAPTER 3

Modern U.S. Education History, 1865 to the Present   80

PREFACE

When you first look seriously at a classroom from the other side of the desk, the teacher's side, you begin to sense the challenge of the profession. It is one thing to imagine what it would be like to be a teacher—to experience glimmers of disappointment and exhilaration as you envision yourself working side-by-side with your students. Not until you reflect carefully on what good teachers do, however, can you begin to appreciate the importance of the foundational knowledge underlying their success.

The Plan of the Book

The book's organization reflects our conception of teaching as a profession. To us, professionals possess foundational knowledge others do not possess and are able to apply that knowledge to do things others cannot do. Professionals in all fields can explain why they behave as they do. They also have the capacity to reflect on or evaluate their actions and thus to continue to progress professionally. These abilities set the professional apart from other people.

We have relied on a simple but useful device—a set of five Professional Practice Questions (PPQs)—to guide the selection of material and activities to include in each chapter. These Professional Practice Questions foster our view of professionalism as a set of abilities to perceive, value, know, act, and evaluate. The PPQs suggest not only what you should learn but why.

Professional teachers perceive problems that need to be solved and opportunities to learn as they interact with students. They recognize when their own values and the values of others influence education. Professional teachers know about teaching, about students, about learning, and about content so they can improve their chances for successful practice. Because professional teachers are always reinforcing and extending their foundational knowledge, they can act in timely fashion and evaluate or reflect on their actions to advance their development.

Many people have a stake in our educational systems. Because we have a society of ethnic, racial, religious, and social diversity, we also have a tradition of pluralistic thought and action with respect to educational matters. The book reflects this tradition of working together to make a better place for everyone.

The book contains 14 chapters. These chapters collectively acknowledge the interdependence of knowledge in the disciplines, knowledge in professional education, and knowledge from practice. Chapter 1 communicates the theme of professionalism. Chapter 2 through 4 place the education profession in historical and philosophical contexts. Chapter 5 explores the meaning of the concept of school. Chapter 6 through 8 examine the challenges of meeting people's diverse educational needs. Chapters 9 and 10 describe what is taught and how teaching occurs. Chapters 11 through 13 explore issues of governance, management, and finance of education. Chapter 14 anticipates a future for educators in an increasingly interdependent world.

Aids to Understanding

We have built in a set of features in each chapter to help you recall, understand, and use the material in the book. These include

- **Overview** of information presented in the chapter.

- **Professional Practice Questions** to encourage you (a) to perceive influential ideas, problems, events, issues, and key players in American education; (b) to recognize values that drive personal and professional actions; (c) to become aware of knowledge relevant to professional practice; (d) to apply knowledge, or to hypothesize how you might do so in professional ways; and (e) to evaluate your actions. These questions will help you structure your thinking as you read. More important they will reinforce in your own mind why you are reading—to understand how professionals think and behave and to prepare yourself to think and behave in like fashion.

- **Benchmarks**, a thematic or topical time chart in each chapter.

- **Terms and Concepts** denoted by bold print in the body of the chapter and listed alphabetically at the end of each chapter.

- **Figures and Tables** illustrating current theory, research, and additional background information that elaborate points made in the text.

- **Foundations in Action** features, located in Chapters 5 through 10, that show how concepts are immediately relevant to real teachers in real classrooms across the nation.

- **Cultural Awareness** features that highlight the influences of culture, variously defined, on teaching and learning.

- **Voices** features that are composed of first-hand accounts, reportage, and professional writings that bear on key issues in each chapter. Critical Thinking Questions guide your analysis of these excerpts.

- A **Summary** that reiterates the main points made in the chapter.

- **Student Activities** designed to provide opportunities to perceive and value, know and act, evaluate, and discover information relevant to ideas presented in each chapter.

At the end of this book you will find a Glossary with definitions of terms and concepts and several Appendices that provide in-depth information on selected topics.

This book is accompanied by a student *Study Guide*. The *Study Guide* provides opportunities to apply knowledge through a variety of activities. It also reinforces the importance of key ideas and concepts noted in the text and is useful in preparing for tests.

Acknowledgments

We owe thanks to many people who have helped with the production of this book. The following reviewers provided invaluable comments on various drafts of the manuscript:

Frederick J. Baker
California Polytechnic University

William Britt
University of North Carolina

Patricia Ann Brock
Trenton State College

Joseph Bronars
*Queens College, The City University
    of New York*

Sol Cohen
University of California, Los Angeles

Ruth Doyle
Casper College

Kathleen A. Gormley
Russell Sage College

Mary Harris
Bloomsburg University

W. Scott Hopkins
Cameron University

Richard A. King
University of Northern Colorado

Ava L. McCall
University of Wisconsin

Catherine E. McCartney
Bemidji State University

Leonard L. Mitchell
Evangel College

Joyce C. Ragland
East Tennessee State University

David Schimmel
University of Massachusetts

James Van Patten
University of Arkansas

John Mack Welford
Roanoke College

Harry White
State University of New York, New Paltz

Nancy Forsyth, Editor-in-Chief at Allyn and Bacon, made this project move. Her decisiveness, candor, and good sense have been refreshing. Christine Nelson, Nancy's assistant, has helped us find our way through the Allyn and Bacon system on more than one occasion. Our editor, Virginia Lanigan, is simply the best and the brightest. She has been supportive, demanding, perspicacious, diplomatic, and always present for us. We are extremely lucky to have worked with her. Nicole DePalma, Virginia's assistant, kept us all in touch when it seemed we were moving in different directions. Mary Ellen Lepionka, developmental editor, has been a champion, throwing and taking intellectual punches with gusto and a large sense of humor. She has brought her considerable talent to bear on major issues and minor details from beginning to end—we owe her our gratitude. Leslie Brunetta, copyeditor, improved our writing with skillful wielding of her blue pencil. Deborah Schneck, designer, Susan Duane, photo researcher, and Linda Knowles, cover coordinator, have performed outstandingly. Elaine Ober, production manager, worked magic to make the people and pieces come together to yield a whole of which we can be proud.

Our colleagues were generous with their time and insightful with their suggestions for improvements to the manuscript. At the University of Virginia, Dan Hallahan, Jim Kauffman, John Lloyd, Greta Morine-Dershimer, Jennings Wagoner, Deborah Verstegen, and Don Medley were especially helpful. Betsy Anthony, Nancy Oakey, Kay Cutler at the University of Virginia, JoEllen Vinyard at Eastern Michigan University, and

Fred Beamer at the National Center for Education Statistics responded munificently and quickly to our many requests for facts and figures.

For the past several years, The Hitachi Foundation has supported our work with case-based teaching about multicultural education and with the resulting Foundations-in-Action features in the text. At key times, Felicia Lynch and Laurie Regelbrugge have offered wise counsel about the design, presentation, and evaluation of videocases. Their generosity, professional insight, and friendship have been gifts for which we will always be grateful. We also want to thank filmmaker Ernest Skinner and sound technician Edward Damerel for going well beyond their obligations to apply their creative energies to the project.

The gang at the Commonwealth Center for the Education of Teachers at the University of Virginia summoned incredible energy to help us with tasks larger and small. Mike Coyne, Susan Doyle, Rudy Ford, Jeff Harper, Todd Kent, Bruce McDade, Julie Plum, Colleen Sheehy, and Larry Thursby saved us many times in many ways. We thank them all. Our special thanks go to Denise Huffman. She has been a superb colleague and a friend throughout. We would not have wanted to do the job without her help.

Finally to our families—Maggie, Erin, Carrie, Mary Caitlin, Larry, Jonathan, and Andrew—thank you for your patience. The long hours of work and hazy half-present conversations have been tough, but your understanding has been generous and comforting.

RFM & JMH

Teachers
and
Teaching

This chapter frames a concept of the teacher as professional— a concept that has much in common with concepts of professionals in other fields yet is uniquely suited to the work that teachers perform. We consider both group and individual characteristics of the people who call themselves teachers. We also explore why people choose to become teachers, the routes they take to prepare themselves to enter the classroom, why some decide to leave teaching, and what ultimately encourages most who enter to stay and build careers as professional educators.

This chapter presents information on how to obtain teaching certification, where to find jobs, how much money teachers can expect to earn, and how to understand processes of teacher evaluation and of the distribution of rewards. Because conditions of teaching in schools and processes of educating teachers are changing, we use recent reform proposals to make plausible and realistically optimistic predictions of teaching's future.

1 Who chooses to become a teacher? What credentials must you have to teach?

.... `Perceive`

2 What is it about teaching that attracts and holds individuals in the job? Why do people leave teaching? What kind of status does teaching have in the eyes of teachers, parents, and students?

.... `Value`

3 What do people know intuitively about characteristics of good and bad teaching? What more do professional teachers know about teaching quality?

.... `Know`

4 If you had a chance to earn either a bachelor's degree and a teaching certificate in 4 years of college or a master's degree and a teaching certificate in 5 years, which would you choose? Why?

.... `Act`

5 Which of your teachers do you remember as being especially good or especially poor as teachers? What are the reasons supporting your judgments?

.... `Evaluate`

WHAT DOES IT MEAN
TO BE A TEACHER?

People construct the concept of "teacher" in ways that convey many meanings. Some constructions reflect rather unemotional, linear, technical descriptions of the people who play the role of teacher and of the tasks they are expected to perform. Other constructions are much more lively, warm, multidimensional conceptions of the people who call themselves teachers and of their actions. One need only scratch the surface of the concept of "teacher" to reveal the richness and significance of its meaning.

VOICES

On Teaching as a Moral Endeavor

Teachers have ample opportunity to demonstrate how they think about issues of right and wrong. In doing so, they teach others how to think and behave with regard to moral issues. Professor Gary Fenstermacher believes that to understand the nature of the job of teaching, we must consider its moral dimensions.

What makes teaching a moral endeavor is that it is, quite centrally, human action undertaken in regard to other human beings. Thus, matters of what is fair, right, just, and virtuous are always present. Whenever a teacher asks a student to share something with another student, decides between combatants in a schoolyard dispute, sets procedures for who will go first, second, third, and so on, or discusses the welfare of a student with another teacher, moral considerations are present. The teacher's conduct, at all times and in all ways, is a moral matter. For that reason alone, teaching is a profoundly moral activity.

CRITICAL THINKING

Recall and evaluate an incident in school when a teacher attempted to teach you a moral lesson directly and explicitly. Then recall a time when a teacher influenced your moral reasoning indirectly through modeling. Do you agree with Fenstermacher's conclusions?

Source: Fenstermacher, G. D. (1990). Some moral considerations on teaching as a profession. In J. I. Goodlad, R. Soder, & K. A. Sirotnik (Eds.), *The moral dimensions of teaching* (pp. 130-151). San Francisco: Jossey-Bass.

Teachers Are Models

Teachers are public people. Whether they realize it or not, they are always on display. Teachers serve as models for children and adults as they teach and as they live their lives both inside and outside schools.

In recent years, the model teacher has increasingly been cast by reformers and the media in terms of the bright, liberally educated, street-savvy professional. This model teacher is solidly grounded in one or more disciplines and works intelligently to make knowledge accessible and useful to students. The image this teacher portrays is of a person who can help all students succeed, regardless of their needs, abilities, or circumstances.

It is clear that people look for more in teachers than the abilities to transmit content and to teach skills to students. Through their words and deeds, teachers demonstrate what it means to be enlightened, hard-working, virtuous—indeed, what it means to be an educated person. Teachers both shape and are shaped by this public image.

A Teacher's Work Week, Work World

In some ways, day-to-day life in public and private schools, at least when it comes to how teachers spend their time, is remarkable for its sameness. An analysis by the National Center for Educational Statistics shows that there are few differences in the way public-school and private-school elementary and secondary teachers spend their workweeks. According to responses from 7,991 public- and 4,544 private-school teachers surveyed between 1984 and 1986, teachers put in about 50.2 hours a week, half of which (25.5 hours) were devoted to instruction, as shown in Figure 1.1. The remaining time was spent on planning and evaluation (15.2 hours), extracurricular supervision (2.4 hours), tutoring and counseling (4.4 hours), lunch and free time (2.4 hours), and sick or personal leave (0.3 hours) ("Dimensions," 1990).

In other ways, however, day-to-day life in schools is restricted only by one's powers of imagination. Like the artist Christo, who challenged human sensory experience by draping an island in fabric and filling a hillside with umbrellas, a teacher may invite students to perceive their educational world in unique and personal ways. When this happens, every day in school is figuratively and literally different.

Society's Expectations of Teachers

Society expects teachers to be all and do all—a mission impossible, of course, but one that often has the effect of bringing out the best in those who accept it. Teachers succeed by exhibiting extraordinary commitment to people, to ideals about professional behavior, and to plain old hard work.

As Edward Ducharme (1993) observes, teachers often expect themselves to meet the challenge of doing important work.

> I went into junior high school teaching. An urban, inner-city school. I did it for a weird reason. I had student taught in a suburban school which was close to where I lived. One of my professors told me that this junior high school (the urban school) was one of the two most difficult junior high schools in which to teach in Pennsylvania. My student teacher supervisor's wife taught there. I wanted to try it and see what I could do in that environment. I loved it; and I succeeded.—(p. 28)

FIGURE I.I

The Teacher's Workweek

Redraw this graph to show what, if anything, you would change about the way teachers use their time during a typical workweek. What are your reasons?

(*Note:* from "Dimensions: The Teacher's Workweek" by Education Week, February 7, 1990, Copyright 1990 by Education Week. Reprinted by permission.)

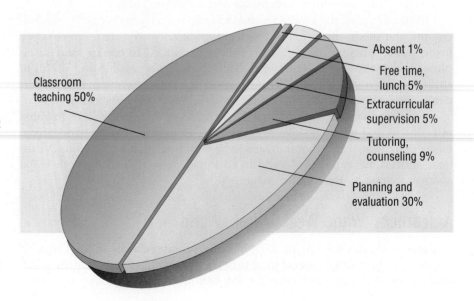

The public attaches uncommon but often tacit importance to teachers' connections to the people they serve. Teachers are held accountable for possessing specialized knowledge and applying it when conditions warrant. Knowing and knowing how, then, are explicit attributes of teachers who are professionals. These are not the only characteristics, however, thought to be significant. The most successful teachers are often perceived as caring deeply about the people they serve and about the work they perform: Passion for learning and for life are characteristics thought to distinguish the best teachers.

Teachers Are Professionals

Teachers are professionals. **Professional teachers** are people who possess specialized knowledge and skills about education. They have been selected to enter professional programs, their knowledge and skills have been evaluated during their general and professional studies, they have met programs for graduation from an institution of higher education, and they have fulfilled requirements for **certification**—recognition by the state that they have met minimum standards for competent practice.

In some ways, however, teaching is different from other professions. Educators hold many opinions about what constitutes the knowledge base—the teaching knowledge, skills, and values that yield student learning. Unlike other professions, teaching lacks consensus on what constitutes the knowledge base. Multiple acceptable opinions are reflected in more than 1,200 institutions of higher education that maintain teacher education programs and in thousands of inservice programs in elementary and secondary schools.

In addition, teachers do not exert control over their own licensing. Physicians, lawyers, accountants, and other professionals control who enters their professions; that is, they set minimum standards for professional practice. People other than teachers typically control decision making in matters of governance and education practice. They hire and fire teachers, decide what teachers must do to continue progressing as professionals, and prepare curricula for students. Teachers often participate in these decisions, but they do not control them. Other professionals often command higher salaries than teachers. Public teachers' salaries and perceptions of teachers' capabilities, however, have shown steady increases in recent years.

Despite these differences, teachers are regarded as professionals in critical ways. They are alert to educational issues and opportunities as they arise in the workplace. They are sensitive to their own and others' values that influence thinking and behavior. Professional teachers also possess specialized knowledge and skills acquired from long, intensive academic and practical preparation—knowledge and skills that inform their actions. And they have the capacity to act—to call up and apply imaginatively what they know when needed and to articulate defensibly the reasons for their actions. Finally, professional teachers are equipped intellectually and emotionally to reflect on their work and develop their expertise over time. Figure 1.2 suggests the complexity of what teachers know and do as professionals.

FIGURE I.2

Foundations of Education: A Teacher's Professional Knowledge Base

Compare the items in this figure with the chapter titles in this textbook.
How will your course on the foundation of education be meaningful to
you as a teacher?

	Education Futures?	
Comparative Education		Self-Knowledge
School Law		Process of Learning
Impact of Social Problems and Political Issues		Historical Foundations of Education
Characteristics of Students		Subject Area Expertise
Cultural Diversity		Curriculum
Teaching as a Profession		Instructional Methods
Schools as Social Institutions		Education Finance
Educational Philosophies		School Governance

The National Education Association   Teachers often join professional associations. The National Education Association (NEA) was organized by 43 people, mainly from institutions of higher education, at a meeting in Philadelphia in 1857 for the purpose of advancing professionalism. It now boasts some 2.1 million members, including college and university students, school secretaries, bus drivers, custodians, guidance counselors, librarians, college professors, school administrators, and, of course, teachers.

The NEA is a diverse organization. The NEA is often referred to as a **teacher union**—a confederation of individuals with a common purpose, in this case education, joined politically to advance their cause. The organization provides members a wide array of services, from negotiations for salaries, through research on a variety of educational issues, to staff development. The NEA is one of the most effective lobbying organizations of any type in the country. Teachers vote. Working as they do in the crossroads of America, the public schools, teachers teach others to vote. NEA representatives are visibly present to state their views on educational matters in Washington, D.C., in state capitals, and in communities across the country.

The American Federation of Teachers   From 1902 to 1916, 20 local groups of teachers in 10 states created unions intent on advancing the grievances of workers in schools. Many of those early teacher unions did not survive, but in 1916 eight locals joined together to form the American Federation of Teachers (AFT). The AFT began with about 3,000 members who immediately affiliated themselves with the American Federation of Labor (AFL). Later the AFL merged with the Congress of Industrial Organizations (CIO). Today, the AFT has about 800,000 members, mostly in cities, who ally themselves with the AFL-CIO. Only in the late 1970s did the AFT admit workers other than teachers.

Organized from the outset as a labor union, the AFT has always taken strong positions on teachers' salaries and working conditions. When leaders have believed occasions called for vigorous action, they have used a variety of strategies. The AFT has promoted **collective bargaining** (negotiation of the professional rights and responsibilities of teachers as a group). The organization has encouraged teachers to "work to rule" (to follow every rule to the letter, performing only those tasks specified in contracts and only during regular school hours). In cases of contract disputes the union sometimes advocates job actions (withholding of professional services through such practices as work slowdowns and sickouts). The AFT has also organized and supported **strikes** (teacher walkouts from schools, designed to halt operations).

Although the AFT and NEA have a long history of competition for members and a record of disagreement on various issues, they have grown philosophically more compatible in recent years. NEA leaders have advocated political action on job issues with increasing frequency, and AFT leaders have spoken out on issues of professional competence. The organizations' leaders and staffs do cooperate on educational projects deemed important to the public welfare, such as the founding of the National Board for Professional Teaching Standards.

The Impact of Unions on Education   Teacher unions are frequently criticized by outsiders for shielding their members from scrutiny and for maintaining the status quo. They are also commended for exercising considerable power for the improvement of public education. Both the NEA and AFT have helped shape conditions of schooling that promote child welfare. Both have fought for and won increases in teachers' salaries and improvements in working conditions. Both have heightened public awareness about the importance of involving teachers in decision-making processes and of cultivating concepts of teachers as professionals.

Mary Hatwood Futrell, the NEA's immediate past president, will assume the presidency of a new worldwide organization—Education International—that will advance issues of quality education and teacher unions. The organization represents a merger of the International Federation of Free Teachers Unions, with whom the AFT has been affiliated, and the World Confederation of Organizations in the Teaching Profession, of which the NEA is formerly a member. The organization will bring together unions and associations representing more than 20 million educators. This occurrence suggests that the ultimate effects of unions are yet to be felt ("Teachers of the World," 1993).

Other Professional Associations for Teachers   A loose coalition of independent educators—the Independent Professional Education Associations—is striving to establish itself as an alternative to the NEA and the AFT. The organization has adopted bylaws and is seeking funding to incorporate. The group's leaders claim between 150,000 and 200,000 educators belong to independent organizations or private schools. Their appeal seems to be their antiunion stance ("A New Voice," 1992, p. 10).

Teachers, counselors, administrators, and others in education often belong to professional associations closely allied with their particular disciplines. These associations offer a variety of services—journals, conferences, action committees—designed to provide opportunities for interacting with others who have similar interests and to promote continuing professional development. A list of subject area and specialty organizations appears in Appendix A at the end of the book.

WHY DO PEOPLE CHOOSE TO TEACH?

Talk with anyone who teaches or has taught or has ever contemplated the idea of teaching and you will get a variety of reasons for their career decisions. Dan Lortie (1975, p. 30) described five themes, or what he called "attractors to teaching," that remain current in the minds of many teachers: (a) the interpersonal theme—feelings of wanting to work with people, (b) the service theme—the desire to perform a special service for society, (c) the continuation theme— the opportunity teaching offers of staying in school, (d) the material benefits theme—job security and steady income, and (e) the time compatibility theme—the attraction of vacations and appeal of on-the-job hours.

Table 1.1 contains more specific information about why people have entered teaching. More teachers are now attributing their original decision to enter the field to the influence of another teacher.

For the most part, the social origins of teachers tend to make teaching a "disproportionately middle class operation" (Warren, 1989, p. 41). This was not always the case. As we shall suggest in Chapters 2 and 3, teaching has been a respectable way to a better life for thousands of Americans.

> "I'm a teacher. It's a profession I loved and still love. It's been my ambition since I was eight years old. I have been teaching since 1937. Dedication was the thing in my day."

TABLE 1.1　Principal Reasons Selected by All Teachers for Originally Deciding to Become a Teacher 1971–1991

Reason	1971	1976	1981	1986	1991
Desire to work with young people	71.8%	71.4%	69.6%	65.6%	65.9%
Value or significance of education in society	37.1	34.3	40.2	37.2	37.2
Interest in subject matter field	34.5	38.3	44.1	37.1	33.6
Influence of a teacher in elementary or secondary school	17.9	20.6	25.4	25.4	26.8
Never really considered anything else	17.4	17.4	20.3	21.0	23.8
Influence of family	20.5	18.4	21.5	22.9	22.7
Long summer vacation	14.4	19.1	21.5	21.3	20.7
Job security	16.2	17.4	20.6	19.4	16.7
Opportunity for a lifetime of self-growth	21.4	17.4	13.1	9.7	7.9

Note. From National Education Association (1992). *The Status of the American Public School Teacher 1990–1991*, Washington, DC: National Education Association, p. 62. Reprinted by permission.

Intrinsic Rewards of Teaching

One survey indicates that 83% of all public school teachers are satisfied with their jobs, but they are displeased with their salary and status as professionals (Feistritzer, 1990). Despite such dissatisfaction, however, many, like Marcia Miller, an elementary teacher, simply like the work.

> This is the best job I could ever have, despite the low salary. I could never sit behind a desk like you do at other jobs. Here I get to work with children, which is fun. It's hard to be in a bad mood when you are with them. Also, my day goes quickly, and I'm never bored. (Herbert & Keller, 1989, p. 25)

Don Campbell, a high school physics teacher, also finds the intrinsic rewards of teaching particularly satisfying.

> But in the long run, it's not the material or current events that count the most. It's the students. One year I was working with this boy who had been a D student all the way through. I could hardly keep him in his seat. He was just a rascally boy. He never stepped over the line completely, but he was a thorn in my side all year long. In the lab he would always do something offbeat. By the end of the year he was coming along in his work OK. I didn't see him after that for 2 or 3 years. Then one day here was this young man coming down the hallway dressed in

Intrinsic rewards of teaching include the satisfaction of making a difference in young people's lives and helping them to achieve their full potential.

a smart business suit...it was that fellow. I said, "Well, what have you been doing?" and he said, "I've been in the Marines and I came back to thank you." I said, "What for?" because I thought I'd never taught that boy any science. And he said, "It's not for the science. It's because you taught me to be honest and to say what I observed. That was really important to me." I'll carry that with me forever. (Macrorie, 1984, p. 147)

Practical Benefits of Teaching

Beyond a desire to develop a career and to help others succeed, there are practical reasons for continuing one's work as a teacher. These reasons often change over time.

Teacher Salaries and Benefits   States and localities have increasingly moved to recognize the close tie between teacher quality and teachers' salaries and benefits. According to a survey reported by the American Federation of Teachers (1993), public school teachers nationwide earned an average of $35,104 in 1992. The average salary was 3.2% higher than in the previous year. Some states showed notable disparities in local pay levels; for instance, in Missouri and Illinois, the highest paid 5% of teachers earned more than twice as much as the lowest paid 5%.

Salary figures for teachers can be found in Table 1.2. The longer teachers stay on the job, the more important financial security becomes to them (National Education Association, 1992).

Teacher Promotions and Tenure   Tenure was originally conceived as protection for good teachers against capricious administrative action, including attempts to fire teachers thought to be too outspoken or too expensive. With tenure, a teacher is afforded a measure of freedom to exercise his or her opinions without fear of being fired. Tenured teachers can only be released when it can be demonstrated that there is just cause. Tenure, sometimes referred to as continuing contract, can be achieved in all states within 2 to 5 years of successful teaching experience.

Although requirements vary from state to state, school boards typically grant tenure to teachers on the basis of principals' and superintendents' recommendations. These administrators base their judgments on numerous criteria, but they often depend heavily on classroom observations of teachers.

The School Calendar   Summer vacation, even though it is unpaid, also appeals to teachers who want to share time with their families and to continue professional studies. Many teachers have learned that they can do a year's work in 10½ months, but not in twelve; that is, the summer vacation refreshes them, allowing them to be more productive than they would be without it. The school calendar also becomes more important to teachers the longer they stay in teaching (National Education Association, 1992).

TABLE 1.2   Average Public School Teacher Pay, 1992–1993

State	Average Salary 1992–93	Percent Change 1990–91 to 1992–93	State	Average Salary 1992–93	Percent Change 1990–91 to 1992–93
Connecticut	$48,918	10.2	Florida	31,172	2.0
Alaska	46,799	7.8	Kentucky	31,115	6.9
New York	44,999	6.9	Texas	30,974	8.2
New Jersey	43,355	12.9	Kansas	30,713	9.0
Michigan	42,256	5.9	Wyoming	30,317	4.6
Pennsylvania	41,515	15.1	West Virginia	30,301	16.7
Rhode Island	40,548	6.1	Maine	30,250	6.1
D.C.	40,228	2.0	Iowa	30,124	7.7
California	39,992	1.2	Missouri	29,421	4.0
Massachusetts	39,245	7.6	Tennessee	29,313	3.8
Maryland	38,753	1.2	South Carolina	29,151	3.0
Illinois	38,701	11.8	North Carolina	29,108	2.9
Nevada	37,360	5.9	Nebraska	28,768	8.2
Wisconsin	36,477	10.3	Georgia	28,758	3.5
Hawaii	36,472	8.7	Arkansas	28,013	17.3
Delaware	36,217	2.8	Montana	27,617	3.1
Oregon	35,883	11.1	Alabama	27,490	2.3
Washington	35,870	8.4	Idaho	27,011	5.9
Vermont	35,328	13.1	Utah	26,997	5.5
Minnesota	35,093	5.9	New Mexico	26,463	2.7
Indiana	35,068	6.5	Oklahoma	26,355	8.1
Ohio	34,100	6.7	Louisiana	26,074	–0.4
New Hampshire	33,931	8.7	North Dakota	25,211	6.9
Colorado	33,541	5.4	Mississippi	24,367	0.3
Virginia	32,896	5.0	South Dakota	24,291	8.6

Note: F. Howard Nelson, *Survey and Analysis of Salary Trends, 1993* American Federation of Teachers: Washington, DC, September, 1993. Reprinted by permission.

Opportunities for Professional Growth Teachers avail themselves of many opportunities to continue their professional development. They do so to maintain their certification, to invest in themselves as professionals and as persons, and for the sheer joy such opportunities provide. Teachers take college courses and in-service courses offered by their schools, teach in alternative education programs in the summers and during the academic year, work at part-time jobs outside education, and participate in an incalculable range of informal development activities—reading, writing, performing, and the like. To be a teacher is to be a learner.

WHY DO PEOPLE LEAVE TEACHING?

According to Louis Harris and Associates (1991), most new teachers (85%) do not plan to leave the profession (see Figure 1.3). For them, education is a long-term career choice. A small group (13%) of beginning teachers does plan to move on to something else. Many more eventually leave, and they do so for various reasons. Low salaries, discipline problems, and low status are often cited as reasons for leaving teaching (Feistritzer, 1990).

Mary Dilworth (1990) argues that salary may be more critical to job decisions made by African- and Hispanic-American women because of economic realities: a greater proportion of their families are headed by women, and African- and Hispanic-American women contribute a larger share to

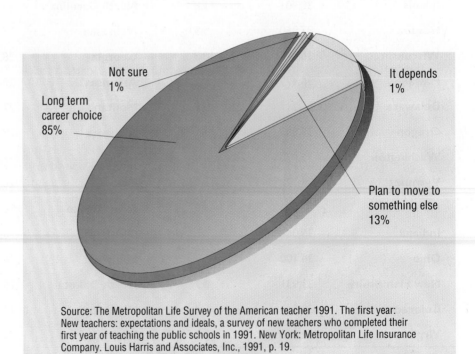

FIGURE 1.3

New Teachers: Do You Plan to Stay in Teaching?

How does this graph support the idea that teaching generally requires a high level of commitment?

Not sure
1%

It depends
1%

Long term
career choice
85%

Plan to move to
something else
13%

Source: The Metropolitan Life Survey of the American teacher 1991. The first year: New teachers: expectations and ideals, a survey of new teachers who completed their first year of teaching the public schools in 1991. New York: Metropolitan Life Insurance Company. Louis Harris and Associates, Inc., 1991, p. 19.

TABLE 1.3 Teachers' Most Important Reasons for Leaving/Not Entering Teaching, by Race/Ethnicity

Reasons	White	African American	Hispanic
Low salaries	73/44%	75/74%	68/62%
Discipline problems	62/23%	75/53%	60/43%
Burnout/exhaustion	44/12%	26/29%	34/30%
Frustration	25/27%	17/42%	28/32%

Note. From *Reading Between the Lines: Teachers and Their Racial/Ethnic Cultures* (p. 32) by M.E. Dilworth, 1990, Washington, DC: ERIC Clearinghouse on Teacher Education and American Association of Colleges for Teacher Education. Adapted by permission.

two-salary incomes than do European-American women. She also suggests that discipline may be more of an issue for prospective minority-group teachers, many of whom have been educated in urban and low-income schools sometimes associated with discipline problems, than for prospective European-American teachers, who often come from and intend to return to smaller or more affluent systems.

Stress and Burnout

Like other professionals, teachers can experience stress in their work. If the stress becomes severe it can lead to low morale, and, in turn, to burnout—a general psychological state of exhaustion affecting those who work too hard and give too much of themselves (Freudenberger, 1975). Teachers who experience burnout often choose to leave their jobs. Sometimes they return reinvigorated, but not always.

In itself, burnout is a serious problem for any teacher who experiences it, but it can also constitute a serious problem for students. "Very simply, if you aren't well you can't teach well" (Gold & Roth, 1993, p. 3). The five most frequently cited reasons for burnout have been reported as: (a) lack of administrative support, (b) lack of parental and community support, (c) workload, (d) low student motivation, and (e) discipline (Raquepaw & deHass, 1984).

When teachers and administrators address such concerns, the problems seem less severe. "Putting it another way, teachers who have stronger coping mechanisms, communication skills, interpersonal relations, are emotionally secure, or feel intellectually stimulated and have a balance in personal and professional satisfaction, are much better able to deal with these same problems" (Gold & Roth, 1993, p. 9).

Other Opportunities

Teachers who leave the profession do so for a variety of reasons. Many leave to have and raise children, and a large proportion of these return later to carry on with their careers. With increasing opportunities in the workplace, many women leave the classroom to acquire more education and to pursue careers in virtually every other field. Men do the same. In reality, a teacher's education is a capital investment in herself or himself, one that can often be developed and invested elsewhere. There is also a constant and natural flow of people out of education due to retirement.

> **Women constitute about 70% of teachers in public schools and about 25% of public school administrators. About 13% of public school teachers are members of minority groups.**

WHO ARE AMERICA'S TEACHERS TODAY?

Teachers are an amazingly diverse group of people. Attempts to character-ize them collectively inevitably mask the rich variation among individuals' values, knowledge, skills, and interests. Nonetheless, it is often useful for individual teachers to develop their professional identities, in part, by think-ing about themselves in relation to others and to the teaching force as a whole.

Characteristics of the Teaching Force

Table 1.4 contains information about the teaching force as a whole and about groups within the profession. It is important to note that certain trends are not apparent in the data. For instance, by the year 2001, it is anticipated that the number of teachers in classrooms across the country will increase to 3.2 million (Ogle, Alsalam, & Rogers, 1991).

Average ages of teachers are listed for the country and for particular regions; you will note that there is great variation from place to place. What implications might these variations have for beginning teachers?

Of the "new" teachers hired between 1985 and 1990 (approximately 28% of the teaching force), about 50% were returning teachers who had taken at least one break from teaching and at least 19% of them had taken two or more breaks. Why might these facts lead people to characterize teaching as a profession with a "revolving door" (Feistritzer, 1990, p. 3)?

Women and Men in the Teaching Force

Table 1.4 also contains information on the men and women in the teaching force. The numbers of men in teaching have increased as sex-role stereo-types have broken down, the status of teaching as a profession has risen,

TABLE 1.4   Teachers as a Group

Number of teachers in U.S.	2,753,000
Number of public school teachers	2,400,000
Number of private school teachers	353,000
Teachers' average age	42
Teachers' average age in Northwest	34
Teachers' average age in West	49
Teachers' average age In South	38
Teachers' average age in Midwest	50
Teachers' average age in inner cities	33
Teachers' average age in small towns and rural areas	42
Percentage of teachers married	75
Public school teachers' average years experience	15
Private school teachers' average years experience	14
Percentage of women who have left teaching and later returned	50
Percentage of men who have left teaching and later returned	25
Percentage of African-American teachers in public schools	5
Percentage of Hispanic-American teachers in public schools	2
Percentage of Asian-American or Pacific Islander-American teachers in public schools	1
Percentage of Native-American and Alaskan Native-American teachers in public schools	1
Percentage of public school teachers who are women	70
Percentage of private school teachers who are women	78
Percentage of elementary school teachers who are women	86
Percentage of junior high school teachers who are women	61
Percentage of high school teachers who are women	47
Percentage of public school administration jobs held by women	25
Percentage of private school administration jobs held by women	52

Note. From *Statistical Abstract of the United States: 1990* by Bureau of the Census, January 1990, Washington D.C.: U.S. Government Printing Office. And from *Profile of Teachers in the U.S.* (p. 11–13) by C.E. Feistritzer, 1990, Washington D.C.: National Center for Education Information. And from *The Condition of Education 1991: Volume I, Elementary and Secondary Education* (p. 235–236) by U.S. Department of Education, 1991, Washington, D.C.: U.S. Department of Education, National Center for Educational Statistics.

and trends in employment have opened doors to women in other careers (Warren, 1989). While women still hold most classroom positions, however, men hold most of the administrative positions in public schools (Ogle, Alsalam, & Rogers, 1991).

Shortage of Minority and Bilingual Teachers

In public schools, 13% of teachers and 29% of students are members of minority groups. The public school teaching force is composed of the following (U.S. Department of Education, 1993):

- 1% Native Americans and Alaskan Native Americans

- 1% Asian/Pacific Islander Americans

- 8% Non-Hispanic African Americans

- 2.5% Hispanic Americans

- 87.5% European Americans

Many teachers belonging to minority groups are located in the southern and western parts of the United States. A large proportion of them teach in large and medium inner cities. Moreover, 95% of new teachers entering the profession between 1985 and 1990 through traditional teacher education programs were European-American. Such data suggest that the trend of a predominantly European-American teaching force will continue unless efforts are made to attract members of minority groups into the profession (Feistritzer, 1990).

At the turn of the 20th century, about 5% of teachers were African American at a time when they composed about 11% of the population. (One in four teachers in the total teaching force were first or second-generation immigrants—6% being second-generation). By 1980, African Americans' representation reached 10%, mainly due to the civil rights movement and the resulting extension of educational opportunities to members of minority groups (Warren, 1989). As in the past, however, the proportion of African-American to European-American teachers remains lower than the proportion of African-American to European-American students. When teacher-education students were asked recently why members of minority groups are less prone to enter the teaching profession, responses indicated that low salaries and discipline problems were major deterrents.

WHERE ARE THE TEACHING JOBS?

The availability of teaching jobs is affected by two interrelated factors: the numbers of properly qualified teachers available and the demand for those teachers. Both supply and demand, in turn, are subject to other influences in society.

Teacher Supply and Demand

Many factors determine demand for elementary and secondary teachers in any school year: enrollment changes, class size policies, budget considerations, changes in methods for classifying and educating special education students, and job turnover due to retirement or attrition. These factors influence decisions about hiring new teachers.

The supply of teachers is affected by a number of factors: salaries, educational and licensure requirements, interest in particular disciplines and in geographical areas of the country, the cost of living in some states, and other quality of life issues. Projections suggest there will be slight fluctuations in the demand for new teachers during the 1990s, but toward the end of the decade demand for teachers will gradually increase (Gerard & Hussar, 1991).

Projected Student Enrollments   Enrollment trends vary for elementary and secondary schools. In elementary schools, student numbers have been increasing steadily since the mid-1980s as a result of the "echo effect"—as the offspring of the baby-boom generation began entering schools. Projections suggest that enrollment in kindergarten through eighth grade will continue to increase to the year 2002. In secondary schools, student numbers began declining in 1976, reaching a low of 12.4 million in 1990. Since that time, enrollment has steadily increased as the baby boomers' children grew. Forecasters project enrollment in secondary schools to increase to 15.2 million by the year 2000 (Gerard & Hussar, 1991).

Between 1990 and 2002, enrollment patterns will look different across regions, states, and communities. Projections indicate the greatest increases in public school enrollment will occur in the northeastern states, particularly New Hampshire and New Jersey. Increases are also likely in the western part of the country—Arizona, California, Hawaii, New Mexico—and in Alaska.

The federal government reports that the student-teacher ratio in the nation's schools is steadily declining (Gerard & Hussar, 1991). In 1989, there were about 18 students per staff member in public elementary schools and 16 per staff member in secondary schools. By 2002, the ratio will be approximately 18:1 at the elementary level and 15:1 at the secondary level. These figures are much lower than actual class size, however, because they are calculated by counting all the adults in schools—including many specialists who do not meet regularly with full classes—instead of full-time teachers. In 1986, for example, when the pupil-teacher ratio was 17.7:1, average class size was 24 (Tomlinson, 1988).

Budget Capacity   As we shall discuss in Chapter 12, "Education Finance," school budgets determine the capacity for hiring personnel. Personnel costs compose the largest category of expenditures in education budgets. Philosophy and mission drive budgets, but, when times are financially lean, boards of education and school administrators often tend to fall back on pocketbook considerations, choosing to eliminate positions through attrition or lay-offs. "Back to the basics" has come to mean more than just concentrating philosophically on the three Rs; the phrase also means cutting jobs in public education that are viewed as "frills." The term "reduction in force," or RIF for short, has become all too familiar to public school employees in recent years.

Teacher Demand by Location and Subject Area   Teacher shortages are felt most acutely in the nation's large cities. Why? The work is challenging, the working conditions often difficult, and teaching opportunities in other more attractive situations often pull teachers away from cities. For example, 56.6% of public school administrators in Washington, D.C., reported difficulty in finding qualified applicants (Choy, Bobbitt et al., 1993). The South and Southwest also have unmet needs for teachers. Population growth in these sections of the United States has increased demand for teachers.

The need to provide bilingual education and special education services can also influence the demand for teachers. This demand varies, sometimes markedly by state. For example, during the 1991–92 school year, the percentage of children ages 6 through 17 receiving special services for all disabilities was 7.98% in Louisiana and 15.11% in Massachusetts (U.S. Department of Education, 1993). The demand for special services can also vary considerably over time. In California, for instance, there were 332,291 children (from birth through age 20) with disabilities receiving special services in 1976–77. By 1991–92, this figure had risen to 469,282 (U.S. Department of Education, 1993). Sometimes these figures, and thus the demand for teachers, are affected by the number of students with disabilities entering and leaving school systems. But at other times, the numbers change due to changes in the criteria used to define a particular disability.

Demand is so great in some areas that school districts have offered cash bonuses, increased salary schedules, and other types of pay increases to attract and hold new teachers (see Table 1.5). These incentives have been designed to attract people into less desirable geographical locations and into particular subject areas that have experienced shortages. Nearly 24% of private school administrators reported general difficulty finding qualified applicants to fill teaching vacancies; about 23% reported difficulty in some fields (Choy, Bobbitt et al., 1993).

Teaching Jobs in Nonpublic and Nonschool Settings

About 15% of the nation's teachers are employed in private schools. These schools can be separated into parochial (sectarian) schools affiliated with religious groups and independent (nonsectarian) schools. Catholic schools employ more teachers than any other type of private school because the Catholic system is larger than any other private system. Private school teachers serve children anywhere from preschool through the 12th grade.

Although states do not require teachers in private schools to meet the same level of certification as public school teachers, most private school teachers are fully certified. Operating without tax support, private schools are free from many state regulations governing curriculum and teaching. At the same time, because private schools are supported by private funds,

TABLE 1.5　Percentages of Public and Private Schools Offering Incentives to Recruit and Retain Teachers

	Less desirable locations			Fields of shortage		
	Cash bonus	Increase in salary schedule	Other pay increase	Cash bonus	Increase in salary schedule	Other \ pay increase
Public	1.1	3.3	1.8	1.1	2.8	1.8
District size						
Less than 1,000	0.9	4.3	2.2	0.7	3.1	2.1
1,000 to 4,999	1.3	2.1	1.3	1.2	2.2	1.1
5,000 to 9,999	1.4	2.4	2.0	1.7	3.1	2.3
10,000 or more	1.9	2.9	1.3	3.6	3.2	2.4
Private				2.4	7.3	5.0
School size						
Less than 150				1.8	4.5	4.3
150 to 499				2.7	9.4	5.4
500 to 749				3.7	9.2	7.6
750 or more				3.2	13.0	4.5

Note. From *America's Teachers: Profiles of a Profession* (p. 38) by S.P. Choy, S.A. Bobbitt, R.R. Henke, E.A. Medrich, L.J. Horn, and J. Liberman, 1993, Washington, D.C.: U.S. Department of Education.

average teaching salaries are far below teaching salaries in public schools. Choy, Bobbitt et al. (1993) report that the average salary for a beginning teacher with a bachelor's degree in religiously affiliated schools was $12,065 in 1987–88. In nonsectarian schools the average was $13,969.

For many reasons, some people with education degrees take jobs outside both public and private school systems. Employers in business and industry and various government agencies hire people with education degrees to perform a variety of tasks—computing, writing, training, selling, buying, evaluating, and so forth. Strong educational programs that combine liberal and professional studies prepare people for a variety of technical and human service positions.

HOW DO PEOPLE BECOME TEACHERS?

Teacher preparation first appeared formally in America in 1839 under the leadership of Henry Barnard and in the form of institutes designed to raise the quality of the teaching force (Stinnett, 1969). The first normal schools also opened in 1839.

Today most teachers obtain a teaching **license**, or certification of minimal professional competence, by completing, at a college or university in the state, a teacher education program approved by the state department of education. Many of these preparation programs are at the undergraduate level, but there is a growing trend to make teacher preparation a 5-year graduate education experience.

> By 1900, there were more than 3,000 agencies in the United States issuing teaching certificates. Today, candidates typically complete a state-approved teacher education program.

Teacher education programs in the United States have typically consisted of the following: a component of general studies, or courses in arts and sciences—some required, some elective; a set of professional studies taken in schools, colleges, or departments of education; and a period of clinical practice or field experience designed to provide opportunities to work in schools. But increased pressure to reform the training of teachers is giving rise to new patterns of education.

Extended Teacher Education Programs

Most institutions of higher education have "upper division" teacher education programs; that is, students are not officially admitted to education programs until their 3rd year of college, and professional studies are taken during the 3rd and 4th years. In these programs, the first 2 years of course work are devoted entirely to general studies.

In recent years, however, some institutions of higher education have begun to institute 5-year programs of teacher education. These programs spread general, professional, and clinical studies across a student's college career. The programs may permit students to earn a bachelor's and/or master's degree upon successful completion. The general philosophy underlying these programs holds that longer study that integrates general and professional studies, including periodic application of one's skills and knowledge in schools, will produce the best teachers.

Some institutions of higher education have 5th-year or 5th- and 6th-year programs of teacher education. Students must earn a bachelor's degree in a discipline and then apply for admission to professional studies. Students take no professional education courses until they are in a master's program, which is completed in 1 or 2 years. In the main, 5th- and 5th- and 6th-year programs are driven philosophically by the perceived need for teachers to be firmly grounded in a discipline before they work with children.

Different program patterns have various strengths and limitations from students' points of view. Four-year programs cost less, students do not lose an extra year or two of earning power, and they remain members of the cohort of students with which they entered college. Longer programs offer opportunities for strengthening one's preparation before assuming a job and often lead to master's degrees, thus allowing graduates to begin teaching at a higher step on a salary schedule. Some people also believe that graduating with a master's degree enhances employability.

Collaborative Internships and Induction Programs

People in institutions of higher education and elementary and secondary schools know that working together to prepare teachers makes more sense than working in isolation. Collaboration often occurs with regard to the structure and delivery of field experiences—classroom observation, student teaching, and internships—for prospective teachers in schools. In-service teachers, school administrators, and college or university faculty all have a stake in new teachers' success, and they recognize with increasing frequency that all should be involved in designing programs for professional development.

One notable example of attention to collaborative field experience for beginning teachers is the concept of an induction program. These programs are structured to provide special assistance, mentoring from experienced colleagues, and feedback on teaching performance to beginning teachers in their first 1 to 3 years on the job. Induction has been recognized as an especially important phase in shaping a teacher's career.

Student Teaching

Student teaching—planning, organizing, and providing instruction to students full time over a period of weeks—typically occurs at or near the end of a preservice teacher's program. To prepare preservice teachers for student teaching, most programs require students to engage in a variety of field experiences. The types of assignments to be completed during these early field experiences are different from program to program, but they are generally structured to help preservice teachers become familiar with various contexts in which teaching occurs.

Preservice teachers may be asked to maintain a journal in which they record information about students' needs and abilities (e.g., reading levels, mathematics proficiencies, personal interests), classroom rules and routines, and the flow of instructional activities. Preservice teachers may also be expected to conduct one-on-one tutoring sessions or to assist the teacher with classroom activities. Such field experiences are usually supervised by the classroom teacher and college instructor to whom the preservice teacher is assigned.

As preservice teachers separate from their previous roles as students and begin their careers as professional educators during student teaching, they often gradually assume classroom responsibilities. They grade papers, teach parts of lessons designed by the classroom teacher (sometimes referred to as the supervising or cooperating teacher), plan for and engage in whole-class instruction for 1 or 2 class periods, and eventually assume responsibility for the whole day's instruction.

Unlike earlier field experiences, student teaching typically occurs in a classroom on a full-time basis for a number of weeks. Depending on college requirements, some student teachers spend the entire semester with the same cooperating teacher while others teach for several weeks in different classrooms over the course of the semester.

While student teaching, preservice teachers are jointly supervised by the classroom teacher and a college supervisor. That is, the classroom teacher

In every state, accredited teacher education programs include on-site practice teaching. Recent wider use of internship and induction programs highlights the importance of on-site support for new and prospective teachers.

and university supervisor offer feedback and support to the student teacher as he or she teaches lessons. The classroom teacher is typically available for such guidance on a daily basis; the college supervisor may visit only once a week, depending on the needs of the student teacher.

Because of the demands of student teaching, preservice teachers seldom enroll in academic courses during their field placements. Many teacher education programs, however, do require student teachers to attend weekly seminars. Such seminars may be held on campus and sometimes in classrooms of student teachers. The seminars offer preservice teachers opportunities to discuss problems and issues of teaching and to share ideas about more and less effective teaching strategies.

Evaluations of Teacher Education Programs

At present, no agency has ever functioned nationally to certify teachers. Since 1927, teacher education programs, however, have been subject to **accreditation**, that is, to processes of program review by outside experts. From 1927 to 1952, the American Association of Teachers' Colleges (forerunner of the American Association of Colleges for Teacher Education, or AACTE) performed this function. The National Council for the Accreditation of Teacher Education (NCATE) now performs this function.

Most states' guidelines for the approval of teacher education programs—the most common route to certification—have been influenced by standards developed by the National Association of State Directors of Teacher Education and Certification (NASDTEC) (Roth & Pipho, 1990). The NASDTEC standards are statements about expectations for course work and experiences that are thought to constitute professionally acceptable programs of teacher education.

National Council for the Accreditation of Teacher Education (NCATE) In recent years, the most visible national organization to accredit teacher education programs has been the National Council for the Accreditation of Teacher Education (NCATE). The mission of this organization is twofold: "(1) to require a level of quality in professional education that fosters competent practice of graduates, and (2) to encourage institutions to meet rigorous academic standards of excellence in professional education" (NCATE, 1992, p.1).

NCATE undertakes to accomplish its mission by judging, according to a set of established standards and accompanying criteria, teacher education programs that voluntarily apply for such review. NCATE's 18 standards and 94 criteria address five categories of educational units—schools, colleges, departments of education, but not particular programs—within institutions of higher education. The five categories are: (a) knowledge bases for professional education, (b) relationship to the world of practice, (c) students, (d) faculty, and (e) governance and resources.

For example, Standard IV.B: Faculty Load reads: "The unit ensures that policies allow for faculty opportunities in teaching, scholarship, and service" (NCATE, 1992, p. 56). One criterion for assessing this standard states: "The teaching load of undergraduate faculty is no more than the equivalent of 12 semester/quarter hours; the teaching load of graduate faculty is no more than the equivalent of nine semester/quarter hours" (NCATE, 1992, p. 56).

NCATE has 500 accredited member organizations; another 57 are in the process of application (A. E. Wise, personal communication, May 13, 1992). Passing an NCATE accreditation review, however, does not ensure public acceptance of a program.

> The adequacy of standards is continually under debate. . . . Prestigious universities have withdrawn from NCATE, apparently with impunity. NCATE accreditation has not been required for either state program accreditation (less than half of the state-accredited programs are accredited by the NCATE). . . . Consequently, non-NCATE institutions are able to retain claims to legitimacy in teacher preparation. (Clark & McNergney, 1990, p. 103)

State Professional Standards Boards All states except South Dakota now have permanent boards or commissions to establish standards for teacher education program approval and to take other professional regulatory actions. However, the makeup of each board, the process of selection for membership, and the authority of board members varies greatly from state to state.

The Alabama State Advisory Committee on Teacher Education and Certification has approximately 30 members representing teachers, administrators, teacher educators, school boards, and the public, but regulations do not stipulate how many representatives must serve from each group. Constituent groups nominate candidates and the state superintendent selects members for a 3-year term. The committee does not have final regulatory authority, but all proposed changes in teacher education or licensure are required to have the committee's approval before being submitted to the superintendent and the State Board of Education (AACTE, 1990b).

In contrast, the Minnesota Board of Teaching has 11 members appointed by the governor. Law stipulates that board membership must include six teachers, one principal, one individual from higher education, and three lay members (two of whom must be local school board members) (National Education Association, 1991). The board has autonomous authority to establish licensure, entry, and exit standards for teachers. It also approves teacher education programs (AACTE, 1990b).

Teacher Certification

Requirements for teacher certification are established and monitored by the states. Certification as the term is typically used in education is granted when teachers have demonstrated minimum teaching competence. A teaching certificate is the conceptual equivalent of a license to practice. Certification is not meant to convey the idea that a teacher is an expert or even exceptionally well qualified. Processes of certification or licensure are controlled by state governments to protect the public from harmful teaching practice backed by false claims of professional expertise.

Teaching certificates are typically granted in two ways: transcript assessment and program approval. The transcript assessment process requires a person to submit his or her college transcript directly to the state education department. The department then compares the transcript to the state requirements and grants or denies the request for certification. The program approval approach requires that teacher education programs be approved or accredited by the state. Once a student graduates from an approved program, the program submits transcripts of all graduates, and the state grants certification.

Reciprocity Agreements   Certification requirements for teachers differ from state to state. When a college or university student graduates from an approved teacher education program, he or she receives certification to teach in the state where the program is located. But many states recognize one another's certification, that is, states have **reciprocity agreements**, or pacts by which licensure in one state makes one eligible for licensure in another state.

Because states sometimes change their own certification requirements, the list of states having reciprocity agreements can change from time to time. Appendix B at the end of the book shows those states having reciprocity agreements good through 1996. It is important to remember, however, that even when one state does not recognize another's certification, the additional requirements to obtain a state's certification can often be fulfilled fairly easily by taking some college course work. If one obtains a job in a state without holding valid certification in that state—a somewhat unusual but not unheard-of occurrence—certification requirements can be completed while teaching with an emergency certificate.

Alternative and Emergency Certifications   In recent years, several states have vigorously promoted the concept of **alternative certification**, or approval to teach without having participated in a traditional, state-approved teacher education program. New Jersey's alternative route into teaching, for example, allows people with college degrees but no formal education training to assume teaching positions and to take education courses as they teach. This alternative certification program offers supervisory assistance to people as they learn to teach on the job.

Emergency certification, allowing yet another avenue into the classroom, has existed in many states for many years. When school superintendents have been unable to find a certified teacher to fill a position, they have petitioned their state education departments to hire an uncertified person on an emergency basis. This strategy buys time for the person to become certified or for the school district to find another teacher who possesses valid certification.

Another example of an alternative route into teaching is represented by the Metropolitan Multicultural Teacher Education Program. In response to the critical need for excellent teachers in inner-city schools, Martin Haberman of the University of Milwaukee has worked with the American Federation of Teachers and several private foundations to develop a program leading to Wisconsin certification. The program emphasizes on-the-job training and careful candidate selection (Gursky, 1992).

CULTURAL AWARENESS

In low-income inner-city schools with high proportions of at-risk students, mismatches between teachers' prior experiences and those of their students are common. Such mismatches can lead novice teachers to disillusionment or to enlightenment.

> My first year was arduous, exhausting, and disillusioning. The progress my class made was not sufficient. My students' environment was the first obstacle I encountered. Poverty dominated their lives: almost all were on welfare, lived in public housing projects and come from single-parent homes. All were African American. . . . Most witnessed violence and drug use in their neighborhoods daily. . . . These problems powerfully affected the children; they came to school angry, upset and scared. . . . (Lach, 1992, p. 151)

> Teaching in these schools is rough. It takes commitment and a deep understanding of why you are doing what you are doing. If you have the drive, direction, endurance, and self-discipline to get through the rough times, you will have the opportunity to reap great personal rewards through achieving your goals. You will also learn priceless lessons about yourself, others, and life itself. (Deck, 1991, p. 7)

Teach For America The program Teach For America (TFA) offers yet another way into the classroom for college graduates who do not have teacher education backgrounds. Wendy S. Kopp's senior thesis at Princeton University stimulated the founding of this national teacher corps in 1989. Early funding from foundations and corporations has enabled recruits to earn from $15,000 to $29,000 as beginning teachers (Lawton, 1991).

In 1990–91, there were 500 TFA recruits nationwide. In 1991–92, TFA had some 1,200 new and returning recruits. Recruits spend 8 weeks in training before assuming teaching responsibilities for at-risk students.

> Some hail Teach For America as a bold and admirable effort that brings a pool of otherwise untapped talent into teaching. . . . Others, however, say the program places pedagogically under prepared teachers in charge of classrooms full of the at-risk students who populate inner-city and rural schools (Lawton, 1991, p. 26).

The National Teacher Examinations (NTE) and PRAXIS

More than 30 states require the **National Teacher Examinations (NTE)**, an examination constructed and marketed by the Educational Testing Service, as a test of teacher competency before granting initial certification. Although most states do not require people to reach minimum scores for certification, Kentucky, New Mexico, Montana, and Rhode Island do require some minimum level of performance on the NTE for initial licensure (Tryneski, 1991).

The surplus of teachers during the 1930s prompted urban superintendents to look for ways to select among certified teachers whose credentials were uneven. At the same time, a general public interest in science and efficiency contributed to the development and use of the NTE for certification purposes. The NTE was first administered in March 1940 (Warren, 1989).

In recent years, the NTE has consisted of a set of separate tests designed to measure general knowledge, communication skills, and professional knowledge. The newly developed **Praxis Series** is an examination battery that purports to assess skills and knowledge at each stage of a beginning teacher's career, from entry into teacher education to actual classroom performance. It concentrates on measuring teachers' basic skills in reading, writing, and mathematics. Praxis also measures professional education and subject matter knowledge. The Praxis battery assesses teaching skills such as planning instruction, teaching, classroom management, and assessment of student learning. (See Appendix C at the end of the book for more information on Praxis.)

HOW IS TEACHING PERFORMANCE EVALUATED AND REWARDED?

Evaluation of teachers is used mainly to help teachers grow professionally or to determine whether they meet minimum levels of competence (Duke & Stiggins, 1990). The first type of evaluation is considered formative and the second summative. The distinction between them is sometimes cloudy.

Excellence in teaching has been recognized via career ladder programs and merit pay plans, defined below. Various public and private organizations give teacher of the year awards, which are often accompanied by monetary rewards and media acknowledgment. Plans for implementing a national certification system that identifies outstanding teachers are also being developed.

> **Professional teachers strive for individual excellence, evaluate themselves, make judgments about how they can improve their teaching, and modify their performance accordingly.**

Formative and Summative Assessments

Formative assessment is evaluation conducted for the purpose of shaping, forming, and improving teachers' knowledge and behavior. Formative assessment is not concerned with making judgments about salary, status, or tenure. Instead, formative assessment has been described as "a helping, caring process that provides data to teachers for making decisions about how they can best improve their own teaching techniques" (Barber, 1990, p.216). Evaluators concerned with formative assessment often concentrate on teachers' in-class performances by collecting data on teacher-student interactions during instruction and by helping teachers perceive what is happening during instruction. According to Larry Barber (1990), the formative evaluation is based on the philosophical belief that

> (a) professional teachers constantly strive for continued individual excellence; (b) given sufficient information, professional teachers can and will evaluate themselves and modify their performance as well as or better than others; and (c) the evaluation procedures provide feedback designed to assist teachers in making judgments about how they can best improve their teaching. (p. 217)

Summative assessments are designed to collect and interpret data to inform summary decisions about teachers—decisions on such matters as hiring, compensation, status, tenure, and termination. Like formative assessments, summative assessments can also be based on in-class performances of teachers. Unlike formative evaluation, however, summative assessments of teachers' strengths and weaknesses are not typically used to improve teachers' knowledge and behavior. For the most part, the teacher is less an active participant in summative evaluation than in formative evaluations (Bacharach, Conley, & Shedd, 1990).

Competency Testing

There are now 48 states that require some form of competency testing for teachers (McCarthy & Cambron-McCabe, 1992). These tests provide perspective on the effects of teacher education beyond that provided by teacher education programs themselves. If teachers do well on competency tests, teacher education programs can claim some of the credit for identifying and developing teaching talent. When prospective teachers perform poorly on these tests, programs must take some of the responsibility.

Control of teacher education through teacher competency tests is subtle but potentially quite powerful. As teachers exit from their professional programs, they are expected to demonstrate the knowledge, skills, and attitudes such tests purport to measure. Teacher education programs will continue to feel pressure to make sure that beginning teachers excel on these tests. In a very real sense, the tests will influence the curriculum of teacher education. The days when states were willing to rely strictly on schools, colleges, and departments of education to provide evidence of program quality are gone. Competency tests provide alternative measure of the effectiveness of teachers and teacher education.

Career Ladders and Merit Pay

Career ladder programs are examples of incentive programs for teachers offering advancement of status, increased responsibility, and extra pay for exemplary teaching practice. In theory, career ladder programs are incentive programs based on the assumption that "the secret to improvement lies in bringing a change of focus into what one is doing," by motivating teachers to scrutinize their teaching, by encouraging them to think about alternative ways of teaching, and by focusing on what students are learning (Brandt, 1990, p 222). Career ladders are usually designed to acknowledge differences in teachers' levels of accomplishment as, for example, between beginners and master teachers.

Like career ladders, **merit pay** was conceived as an incentive program—a program for encouraging teachers to strive for outstanding performance by rewarding such practice. The idea of merit pay for teachers began in the 1920s. Essentially, merit pay plans are intended to augment the lock-step progression of salary increases that characterize typical salary schedules by awarding either bonuses (one-time cash awards) or raises (financial increases added to teachers' base salaries). Various plans for awarding merit pay have been instituted and usually discarded through the years.

Merit pay plans have faltered most often for three reasons. First, processes of identifying meritorious teachers are difficult to design and implement. Second, until recently, the NEA and AFT have opposed merit plans because they believed paying some teachers more would mean paying other teachers less. The unions have dropped their opposition when convinced that new money would be used for merit plans and merit programs would be coupled with efforts to improve all teachers' salaries. Third, in difficult financial times, money has not been forthcoming for merit pay plans.

WHAT REFORMS IN TEACHER EDUCATION HAVE BEEN PROPOSED?

Criticism of education has been described as a "minor industry" in the United States (Ashton & Webb, 1986, p. 1). Often the criticism is leveled directly at teachers. Others argue that the people who select, prepare, and place teachers in schools—the teacher educators—hold the power to

BENCHMARKS

Teacher Education Reform Reports and Reforms of the 1980s

1985	**A Call for Change in Teacher Education,** National Commission for Excellence in Teacher Education of the American Association of Colleges for Teacher Education (AACTE)
1986	**Tomorrow's Teachers,** the Holmes Group
1986	**A Nation Prepared: Teachers for the 21st Century,** Task Force on Teaching as a Profession, the Carnegie Forum on Education and the Economy
1986	**Time for Results: The Governors' Report on Education,** the National Governors' Association (NGA)
1986	**Visions of Reform: Implications for the Education Profession,** the Association of Teacher Educators (ATE)
1987	National Board for Professional Teaching Standards (NBPTS) established
1989	National Goals of Education issued from the White House

improve teachers, teaching, and opportunities for learning, and must therefore change themselves. These same critics would reform teacher education before, or at least at the same time as, they set out to remedy problems in schools.

In some ways, teacher education works remarkably well. It supplies teachers for the schools in predictable fashion and cheaply. At the same time, people worry about programs that produce a bland, homogenous corps of teachers. Although the academic capabilities of many prospective teachers are outstanding, what passes for teacher education in some instances is said to alienate intellectually capable students.

A host of organizations called for the reform of teacher education in the late 1980s, advancing both compatible and competing ideas. Some of the more influential groups pressing for reform included the American Association of Colleges for Teacher Education (AACTE), the Association of Teacher Educators (ATE), the Holmes Group, the Task Force of the Carnegie Forum, and the National Governors' Association (NGA). These reform reports are especially important to young teachers, because they forecast a set of scenarios for the profession.

Tracey Leon Bailey, the 1994 National Teacher of the Year, watches his students conduct an experiment. He was chosen from state candidates for Teacher of the Year, selected annually by each state and commonwealth. Recognition by one's peers for excellence is one reward of professional achievement.

American Association of Colleges for Teacher Education (AACTE)

In 1985, an AACTE commission described its vision of change for teacher education in a document entitled *A Call for Change in Teacher Education.* The AACTE (1985) organized its recommendations around the following five themes.

1. Supply and demand for quality teachers. The AACTE recommended rigorous academic and performance standards for program entry and exit, financial incentives to recruit teachers, and special guarantees to ensure that qualified members of minority groups not be barred from teacher education programs because of financial cost.

2. Programs for teacher education. The AACTE recommended upgrading the quality of the liberal and professional curricula, requiring a 1-year internship of provisional certification, and encouraging experimental models of teacher education.

3. Accountability for teacher education. The AACTE recommended that certification and program approval continue to be state responsibilities, that teacher education programs continue to be located in colleges and universities, and that programs begin to consider national accreditation.

4. Resources for teacher education. The AACTE advocated the establishment of a National Academy for Teacher Education to which promising teacher educators could be nominated for postgraduate traineeships.

5. Conditions necessary to support the highest quality of teaching. Finally, the AACTE tackled the issue of improving the conditions of teaching by recommending, among other things, higher salaries for teachers, staff development opportunities, differentiated staffing, and incentives to pursue additional college work. They also suggested that administrative training programs in higher education be examined and modified to provide for explicit leadership skills in school administrators.

Association of Teacher Educators (ATE)

In 1986, the ATE fashioned its reform report—*Visions of Reform: Implications for the Education Profession*—by examining the Holmes report, the Carnegie report, and *NCATE Redesign,* a description of the reform of teacher education program accreditation from the National Council for Accreditation of Teacher Education. The ATE task force viewed some recommendations for structural change of teacher education with alarm (ATE, 1986).

1. The task force rejected the idea of eliminating 4-year teacher education programs, advanced by Holmes and Carnegie. Task force members reasoned that teachers' salaries and working conditions were not attractive enough to justify the cost of an extra year or two.

2. The task force viewed the National Board for Professional Teaching Standards proposed by Carnegie as problematic for states, local education agencies, and teacher education programs. It thought national certification might increase competitiveness among state colleges and

universities to produce Board-certified teachers. It was also concerned that national certification would stimulate teacher educators to "teach to the test" and homogenize preparation programs.

Among the ATE task force's recommendations were:

1. Establishment of a National Network of States for the Teaching Profession to determine goals and priorities for the teaching profession, set standards for professional practice, and provide direction and support for the profession.

2. Revision of the professional curriculum for teachers based on a strong liberal arts and subject-matter background. The induction phase into teaching would be structured as an internship designed and monitored collaboratively by schools and colleges.

3. Three-tiered licensure: instructor, teacher, career teacher. Certification would be separated for early, middle, and secondary levels.

4. Organization and management of schools that would emphasize collegiality, individualized instruction for students, and more technological support.

The Holmes Group

In 1986, the Holmes Group recommended: (a) making the education of teachers more solid intellectually; (b) recognizing differences in teachers' knowledge, skill, and commitment to education, certification, and work; (c) creating standards of entry to the profession that are professionally relevant; (d) connecting institutions of higher education to schools; and (e) making schools better places for teachers to work and learn.

The Holmes Group advocated the following reforms in teacher education:

1. Establish a three-tier system of teacher licensing: instructors (beginners with nonrenewable certificates); professional teachers (people who had demonstrated their competence through work, examinations, and in their own education); and career professionals (outstanding teachers having promise as teacher educators).

2. Eliminate the undergraduate major in education.

3. Require all teacher education students to complete an academic major and program of liberal studies.

4. Reform undergraduate education to achieve greater coherence and dedication to liberal education.

5. Organize academic course requirements so undergraduate students can understand the intellectual structure of their discipline.

6. Revise educational studies to focus on the study of schooling; knowledge of pedagogy; skills of classroom teaching; dispositions; values, and ethics of education; and the integration of professional studies with clinical experiences.

7. Establish professional development schools where teachers, administrators, and university faculty can collaborate to improve education for prospective teachers.

8. Change the working conditions in schools to make them compatible with requirements of a new profession.

9. Increase the number of members of minority groups in teacher education programs through recruitment, loan forgiveness, retention, and valid evaluations of professional competence (Holmes Group, 1986).

National Governors' Association (NGA)

The NGA made its top priority the definition of the body of professional knowledge and practice that teachers must have in order to be successful. It issued the following 11 recommendations in response to the question, "What do we do to attract and keep the able teachers?"

1. Define the body of professional knowledge and practice that teachers must have.

2. Create a national board to define teacher standards. This board would define what teachers need to know and be able to do, administer a voluntary system to assess professional capacity, and award nationally recognized certificates to qualified candidates.

3. Rebuild the system of teacher education.

4. Redesign the organization of schools to create more productive working and learning environments.

5. Redesign the structure of the teaching career to provide advancement without moving outside the classroom.

6. Recruit able teacher candidates—including members of minority groups.

7. Improve teacher compensation.

8. Align teacher incentives with schoolwide student performance.

9. Improve teacher mobility.

10. Establish a loose/tight approach to state and local regulation of schools. (See Chapter 11, "School Governance and Administration," for an explanation of loose and tight coupling in organizations.)

11. Establish the concept of educational bankruptcy. States should establish a fair, measured process of review against standards, remedial planning, and additional assistance, but with a final recourse to direct state intervention in the school district (National Governors' Association, 1986).

Task Force of the Carnegie Forum

In 1986, the Task Force of the Carnegie Forum issued its report, 1 month after the Holmes Group report. The Task Force placed greater emphasis on reforming schools and processes of schooling than did the Holmes Group. The following eight points of the Carnegie reform proposal are ordered to permit a comparison with similar proposals offered by the Holmes Group.

1. Restructure the teaching force, and introduce a new category of Lead Teachers, teachers who have the proven ability to provide active leadership in the redesign of the schools and in helping their colleagues to uphold high standards of teaching and learning.

2. Create a National Board for Professional Teaching Standards, organized with a regional and state membership structure, to establish high standards for what teachers need to know and be able to do, and to certify teachers who meet that standard.

> **Proposed reforms include academically upgraded liberal arts requirements for teachers, national accreditation of teacher educaiton programs, and national certification.**

3. Require a bachelor's degree in the arts and sciences as a prerequisite for the professional study of teaching.

4. Make teachers' salaries and career opportunities competitive with those in other professions.

5. Relate incentives for teachers to schoolwide student performance, and provide schools with technology, services, and staff essential to teacher productivity.

6. Develop a new professional curriculum in graduate schools of education leading to a Master in Teaching degree, based on systematic knowledge of teaching and including internships and residencies in the schools.

7. Restructure schools to provide a professional environment for teachers, freeing them to decide how best to meet state and local goals for children while holding them accountable for student progress.

8. Mobilize the nation's resources to prepare minority-group youngsters for teaching careers (Carnegie Forum, 1986).

WHAT REFORM INITIATIVES HAVE BEEN UNDERTAKEN?

Since the reform reports were published, there have been some notable efforts to change teacher education and the conditions of teaching, some more visible than others. We describe three on the pages that follow.

VOICES

On Teachers as Agents of Change

Reform reports have called for changes in the way teachers are prepared and schools are run. Yet change is often difficult and slow. Change models tend to succeed or fail on a case by case basis as they are continually reinvented in schools across the country. Often, the role of the teacher as an agent of change is not clear. Yet teachers are in a position to change the life chances of their students. Deborah Meier (1992), educator and founder of the celebrated Central Park East Schools in New York City, addresses these concerns.

Since I began teaching, some twenty-five years ago, I have changed the way I think about what it means to be a good teacher. Today it is clear that since we need a new kind of school to do a new kind of job, we need a new kind of teacher, too.

The schools we need require different habits of work and habits of mind on the part of teachers—a kind of professionalism within the classroom few teachers were expected to exhibit before. In addition, to get from where we are now to where we need to be will require teachers to play a substantially different role within their schools as well as in public discourse. Teachers need to relearn what it means to be good in-school practitioners, while also becoming more articulate and self-confident spokespeople for the difficult and often anxiety-producing changes schools are expected to undertake. If teachers are not able to join in leading such changes, the changes will not take place. . . .

The lessons drawn from sixteen or more years of school experience as a student remain largely intact and dictate the way most people handle their role as teachers. This is hardly surprising.

Many of those who enter teaching hope to do unto others what the teachers they knew and loved did unto them. . . . [I]n most cases the constraints of the job, plus old habits and a kind of societal nostalgia for what school "used to be like," make teachers part of the broader inertia that makes fundamental change hard to implement.

The habits of schooling are deep, powerful, and hard to budge. No public institution is more deeply entrenched in habitual behavior than schools—and for good reason. Aside from our many years of direct experience as students, we have books, movies, television shows, advertisements, and myriad other activities, games, and symbols that reinforce our view of what school is "supposed" to be.

If I could choose five qualities to look for in prospective teachers they would be: (1) a self-conscious reflectiveness about how they themselves learn and, maybe even more, how and when they do not learn; (2) a sympathy toward others, an appreciation of their differences, an ability to imagine their "otherness"; (3) a willingness to engage in, better yet a taste for, collaborative work; (4) a desire to have others to share some of one's own interests; and (5) a lot of perseverance, energy, and devotion to getting things right.

CRITICAL THINKING

According to Meier, why is school reform so difficult? What examples can you give of "habits of schooling" that are reinforced in the media? What new roles does Meier believe teachers must play to bring about change? Do you agree? Do you possess the qualities of a prospective teacher she identifies? Why or why not?

Source: Meier, D. (1992). Reinventing teaching. *Teachers College Record*, 93(4), 594–609. Reprinted by permission.

National Certification and the National Board for Professional Teaching Standards (NBPTS)

The collaborative efforts of many individuals and professional groups concerned about teaching excellence in the public schools formed the National Board for Professional Teaching Standards (NBPTS) in 1987. The goal of NBPTS has been to effect a national process of certification for individual teachers who represent the best and the brightest in the profession.

The NBPTS has been instrumental in reinforcing the distinction between concepts of licensure and certification in teaching. As we noted earlier, when people speak of being "certified" to teach, they typically mean being "licensed." Licensure in all professions except teaching is bestowed upon those who meet minimal professional requirements—requirements set down to protect the public from incompetence. Certification in other professions is reserved for those recognized as outstanding in their field.

The NBPTS is also developing assessments as alternatives to paper-and-pencil tests meant to measure teachers' abilities to apply professional knowledge in their respective fields. These alternative assessments will take the form of teacher portfolios, which may contain a variety of products, such as the tests teachers produce and videotapes of their teaching.

The National Education Goals

When former president Bush and the nation's governors met in the spring of 1989, they crafted and pledged to address what were the first **National Education Goals** for public education. Their intent was to "capture the attention and resolve of Americans to restructure our schools and radically increase our expectations for student performance" (Romer, 1991, p. 1). To make sure that this pledge wasn't an empty gesture, they committed themselves to continual monitoring of progress. The goals and reports on states' progress to achieve them serve as highly visible indicators of the nation's collective response to calls for reform. A summary of the National Education Goals, signed into law by President Clinton in 1994, appears in Figure 1.4.

Since the goals were established, additional curriculum and achievement standards have been developed to amplify public expectations for schooling. In addition, another set of standards devised to maximize fairness and equity for students—called "opportunity to learn" (OTL) standards—are being proposed (Porter, 1993). These standards represent what schools, teachers, and administrators must do to ensure all children have a chance to master appropriate content and to demonstrate achievement.

Andrew Porter (1993) suggests that OTL standards may eventually serve three purposes: (a) to describe with some precision the kinds of opportunities schools provide, (b) to chart the progress of school reform, and (c) to provide information that can offer explanations when student achievement goals are not reached.

In 1992, the National Association of State Directors of Teacher Education and Certification (NASDTEC) proposed altering its own standards for teacher education programs to complement the National

FIGURE 1.4

The National Education Goals

Research and present statistical data that justify each of the 8 National Education Goals.

1 Readiness for School. By the year 2000, all children in America will start school ready to learn.

2 High School Completion. By the year 2000, the high school graduation rate will increase to at least 90 percent.

3 Student Achievement and Citizenship. By the year 2000, all students will leave grades four, eight, and twelve having demonstrated competency over challenging subject matter including English, mathematics, science, history, foreign languages, civics and government, economics, arts, and geography; and every school in America will ensure that all students learn to use their minds well, so they may be prepared for responsible citizenship, further learning, and productive employment in our modern economy.

4 Teacher Education and Professional Development. By the year 2000, the nation's teaching force will have access to programs for the continued improvement of their professional skills and the opportunity to acquire the knowledge and skills needed to instruct and prepare all American students for the next century.

5 Science and Mathematics. By the year 2000, U.S. Students will be first in the world in science and mathematics achievement.

6 Adult Literacy and Lifelong Learning. By the year 2000, every adult American will be literate and will possess the knowledge and skills necessary to compete in a global economy and exercise the rights and responsibilities of citizenship.

7 Safe, Disciplined, and Alcohol- and Drug-Free Schools. By the year 2000, every school in America will be free of drugs and violence, and the unauthorized presence of firearms and alcohol and will offer a disciplined environment conducive to learning.

8 Parental Participation. By the year 2000. every school will promote partnerships that will increase parental involvement and participation in promoting the social, emotional, and academic growth of children.

Source: U.S. Senate-House Conference Report 103-446 Goals 2000 Educate America Act, March 21, 1994.

Education Goals. The new standards NASDTEC leaders envision involve the use of outcomes to assess programs, or demonstrations of teachers' learning contained in portfolios. A **teacher portfolio** is described as "a container for storing and displaying evidence of a teacher's knowledge and skills." (NASDTEC, 1992, p. 15).

Such portfolios, according to the NASDTEC, should contain evidence of teacher education students' abilities to perform in ways that are congruent with the National Goals. Evidence may consist of such things as a teacher's research plan for determining and accommodating the readiness levels of each child; a video showing samples of nurturing a child's stages of adjustment over a prescribed period of time; lessons that contain classroom activities for accommodating the different entry states of academic, physical, and social development; assessments identifying students who are having trouble socializing with other children because of transitioning into formal schooling or transferring into a new school, and the like. NASDTEC would evaluate the efficacy of programs by examining evidence of teachers' success contained in the portfolios (NASDTEC, 1992).

As we shall suggest again at the close of the book, the future as projected in the National Goals and present reforms has its own way of pulling people in directions they never could have imagined. What seems reasonably certain is that teachers' jobs will increasingly demand that they demonstrate broader and deeper knowledge, exercise more skills at higher levels, and be more creative than at any other time in history. Professional teachers will collaborate more closely with one another and with people in the communities they serve to redefine what it means both to teach and to learn. Professional teachers will come to understand how to shape and to be shaped by the contexts in which they live and work.

SUMMARY

1. Teachers are models for others.

2. About half of the 50 hours per week teachers devote to their jobs is spent in classroom instruction.

3. The professional status of teachers is sometimes questioned because of the uncertain knowledge base, the control of licensing and decision making, and salaries.

4. Professional teachers demonstrate their abilities to recognize issues, perceive values, call up and apply knowledge, take action, and reflect on what has occurred to improve their abilities.

5. The National Education Association (NEA) and the American Federation of Teachers (AFT) are unions that represent their members' many and varied interests. There are many professional associations that are more narrowly defined, often along disciplinary lines, that promote their members' professional development.

6. People choose to teach for many reasons including, but not limited to: the desire to work with young people; the desire to perform a special service for society; the opportunity teaching offers for staying in school; the material benefits—job security, steady income; and the attraction of vacations and appeal of on-the-job hours.

7. People also leave education for many reasons: to relieve stress and burnout, for better salaries, to have and raise children, to further their educations, to pursue other careers, and to retire.

8. Generalizations about teachers often hide important differences among them, but broad brush strokes can supply a useful outline of the teaching force. For instance, women constitute about 70% of teachers in public schools and about 25% of public school administrators. About 13% of public school teachers are members of minority groups.

9. Minority and bilingual teachers are in short supply.

10. Many factors affect demand for elementary and secondary teachers—enrollment changes, class-size policies, budget considerations, changes in methods for classifying and educating special education students, and job turnover due to retirement or attrition.

11. The supply of teachers is affected by salaries, educational and licensure requirements, personal interest in particular disciplines and in geographical areas of the country, cost of living and quality of life issues, and other factors.

12. Some geographical areas are experiencing teacher shortages now: inner cities, southern states, the Southwest, and rural areas across the country. Others are likely to face shortages in the future—the Northeast, the Southwest, Alaska, and Hawaii. Some teaching fields are experiencing teacher shortages: selected foreign languages, special education, physical science, vocational/technical education, biology or life science, and mathematics.

13. People enter teaching by completing programs approved or accredited by their state governments. These programs take from 4 to 6 years to complete. The programs may or may not be accredited, or recognized for excellence, by an independent agency.

14. Individual teachers are certified or licensed to practice by state governments. Certification is typically granted automatically upon successful completion of an approved program. In some locales people can, however, become certified through alternative routes and obtain emergency certification while working to complete requirements. Reciprocity agreements allow teachers to move among some states to assume jobs.

15. Teachers are evaluated for two purposes: to help them improve (formative evaluation) and to make summary judgments about hiring, promotion, rewards, and termination (summative evaluation).

16. Teacher competency tests are increasing in use and in sophistication. Examples are the National Teacher Examinations (NTE) and the Praxis Series.

17. Since about 1983, many professional and government groups have called for the reform of public schools and of teacher education. They have recommended focusing greater attention on many aspects of schooling and teacher education, including: needs of minority students and teachers, the curriculum in schools, standards for student performance, teacher accountability, organization and management of schools, and opportunities to learn.

18. Perhaps the most visible fruits of reform have been the establishment of the National Education Goals. The goals are becoming a focal point for state action in education across the nation. Responses include the development of portfolio assessment for teachers.

TERMS AND CONCEPTS

accreditation	merit pay	reciprocity agreement
alternative certification	National Education Goals	strike
career ladder		summative assessment
certification	National Teacher Examinations (NTE)	teacher portfolio
collective bargaining		teacher union
formative assessment	Praxis Series	tenure
license	professional teachers	

STUDENT ACTIVITIES

Becoming a professional teacher affords many opportunities for perceiving, valuing, knowing, acting, evaluating, and discovering. These are the steps that lead to sound professional practice.

Perceive and Value

What factors encourage you to enter the education profession? What worries you most about becoming an educator? In which subgroup identified in Figure 1.3 do you belong? Why?

Know and Act

What does your state require to become certified as a beginning teacher? What period of time will your initial certification last, and what will be required to renew your certification? If you were certified to teach in a particular subject area or for a range of grade levels, what would be required to become endorsed to teach a different subject or another grade level? Begin your inquiries by asking your program advisor, the departmental office, or the office of teacher education.

Evaluate

Reread the sections on the reform reports—AACTE, ATE, Holmes, Carnegie, and NGA. What themes do you recognize, both explicit and implicit, in two or more of the reports? Which theme or single recommendation do you think is most important? Least important? Be prepared to justify your analysis and assessments.

Discover

Contact the National Education Association and the American Federation of Teachers at either the state or national levels. Request information on membership for certified teachers—costs and benefits. Do the same for one or more of the professional associations listed in Appendix A at the end of the book. What do you find appealing/unappealing about joining any of these organizations?

This chapter describes American education from the arrival of European settlers in the 1600s to the end of the Civil War in 1865. The stage is set by noting the influence of European thinkers and events in history that influenced education. This chapter also describes variations in educational opportunities extended to or denied different peoples living in America—opportunities that depended on people's ethnicity, gender, religion, wealth, and geographical location.

For many years, informal education—homeschooling, apprenticeships, and other educational activities outside school walls—were more important and more prevalent than formal processes of schooling. Formal education—schooling—developed unevenly over time and across geographical regions. This chapter examines both the structure and functions of education, broadly defined, in America during this period.

Finally, this chapter describes early reform movements that led to a universal tax-supported system of free schools and increased educational opportunities for women. During this time, people debated what a "good education" should be. As they struggled to define curriculum, people also considered the meanings of educational success and failure.

Historical Foundations of American Education, 1600 to 1865

PROFESSIONAL PRACTICE QUESTIONS

1 Because so few early Americans actually attended schools, and because those who did attended only for short periods of time, most of what people learned was acquired informally. What events influenced the course of people's lives and thus their education during colonial times? What organizations played a part in people's education?

Perceive

2 For what religious, economic, political, and personal reasons did early Americans value education?

Value

3 What do we know about the students whom teachers and schools served? What was to be learned in these schools? How did teaching typically occur?

Know

4 If you had lived in colonial America, or on the American frontier in the early nineteenth century, what might you have done to educate yourself for the future? Why?

Act

5 How did early Americans of different races and ethnic backgrounds judge the success of their education?

Evaluate

WHAT EUROPEAN THINKERS INFLUENCED EARLY AMERICAN EDUCATION?

Although colonists were located far from England and Europe, immigration and overseas trade allowed for the exchange of goods and ideas between America and the larger world. America's formal educational system was influenced heavily by European intellectuals.

Newton

In the late 1600s, Sir Isaac Newton (1642–1727), an English mathematician and physicist, built on the work of Copernicus, Galileo, and Kepler to discover the laws of motion, or the "natural laws" governing the movement of the planets. His experiments with light challenged traditional ways of thinking about humans' place in the world, convincing many that reason was key to understanding the universe and the principles by which the god they believed in governed it. Newton suggested that God was not an arbitrary monarch who predetermined people's fate but a remote and indifferent master craftsmen who had created an intricate world and left it to work on its own (Blum et al., 1989).

Comenius

John Amos Comenius (1592–1670), a Czech theologian and philosopher, viewed education as the primary means for improving society. All children—rich or poor, male or female—were to be instructed "thoroughly" by methodically trained teachers using quality textbooks in schools supported financially by state and city governments and the clergy. Educational programs were to be divided into four distinct "grades": the nursery school (birth to age 6), the elementary or national school (ages 6 to 12), the Latin school or gymnasium (gifted children ages 13 to 18), and the Academy (gifted youths ages 19 to 24). Children in each grade were to meet in a special school for 6 years. For such children, the process of education would be "easy and pleasant" if the following conditions were met: (a) education began early, before a child's mind was "corrupted"; (b) a child's mind was "prepared" to receive instruction; (c) instruction moved from the general to the specific; (d) tasks were arranged from the easy to the more difficult; (e) the number of subjects studied was manageable for children; (f) teachers maintained a reasonable lesson pace; (g) instruction was age-appropriate; (h) everything was taught through the senses; (i) material being learned was constantly before the children's eyes; and (j) a single method of instruction was employed at all times. To attain universal peace and progress, Comenius also advocated universal textbooks and schools, as well as a universal college and a universal language (Edwards, 1972; Ulich, 1968).

Locke

John Locke (1632–1704), an English philosopher, argued convincingly that the human mind at birth is a blank slate (tabula rasa), not a repository of innate ideas placed there by God. He proposed that children should not simply read books but should also interact with the environment using their five senses to accumulate and test ideas. Teachers should tailor instruction to the individual aptitudes and interests of each child; they should encourage curiosity and questions; and they should treat children as "rational creatures." Through reason, people might unlock life's mysteries. These ideas stimulated what came to be known as the Enlightenment, a period of time when application of reason was recognized as a virtue. According to Locke, children learned through imitation; a good teacher taught by example and suggestion, not by coercion (Gay, 1964). Locke's belief in the essential goodness of people foreshadowed the development of a benevolent view of the kind of education children should receive if they were to grow and prosper.

Rousseau

Jean Jacques Rousseau (1712–1778), a Swiss philosopher, criticized educational methods that he believed ignored children's ways of thinking, seeing, and feeling. He contended that schools ignored the natural conditions of a child's growth, imposing books and abstract ideas on minds and bodies not yet ready to deal with such demands.

In *Emile,* Rousseau described the development of a human being from infancy to maturity—one who was educated in the country away from the "vice and error" of contemporary social life. Emile's tutor provided experiences in harmony with natural conditions of Emile's growth. From infancy through age 11, Emile's tutor dispensed a "negative" education, removing any obstacles that might impede development. Emile explored the environment with his senses, learning through trial and error and experiencing joy and pain from naturally occurring experiences. Between ages 11 and 14, Rousseau argued, education should become more intellectual as Emile was introduced to geography, astronomy, and his first book, Daniel Defoe's *Robinson Crusoe.* Emile also learned carpentry, a practical skill that might serve him later in life. During adolescence, Emile began to decenter, comparing himself with others, making abstractions, and probing secrets of the universe. Because his tutor had respected his human nature, removing obstacles that might hinder his development, Emile began to understand the meanings of love, justice, and duty as he entered into a deeper unity with the universe and a greater understanding of divine laws (Boyd, 1962; Ulich, 1968).

> **"At age 5 we make all nature . . . vanish from before their eyes . . . [and] pen them up like sheep, whole flocks huddled together, in stinking rooms. . . ."**

Pestalozzi

Rousseau's ideas contributed to the child-study movement and to efforts to create child-centered schools. Johann Heinrich Pestalozzi (1746–1827), a Swiss educator, tested Rousseau's ideas with teachers and students at two schools for boys established in Germany. Pestalozzi (1898), like Rousseau, decried educational conditions that stifled children's playfulness and natural curiosity:

> At age five we make all nature . . . vanish from before their eyes . . . [and] pen them up like sheep, whole flocks huddled together, in stinking rooms; pitilessly chain them for hours, days, weeks, months, to the contemplation of unattractive and monotonous letters. (pp. 60–61)

Like Rousseau, Pestalozzi believed children passed through a number of stages and that optimal growth occurred only when children fully mastered experiences and tasks of the previous stage. Such learning was facilitated by kind and loving educators who provided an array of sensory

Johann Pestalozzi

experiences when teaching concepts and skills rather than relying heavily on verbal instruction (Gutek, 1968). Pestalozzi wrote about his experiments with teaching and learning so parents and teachers might understand his simple methods for developing the inner capacity of the child. In *How Gertrude Teaches Her Children,* a book written for mothers, Pestalozzi (1898) illustrated why it was important to "always put a picture before the eye":

> It was inevitable, for instance, when [the teacher] asked, in arithmetic, How many times is seven contained in sixty-three? The child had no real background for his answer, and must, with great trouble, dig it out of his memory. Now, by the plan of putting nine times seven objects before his eyes, and letting him count them as nine sevens standing together, he has not to think any more about this question; he knows from what he has already learnt, although he is asked for the first time, that seven is contained nine times in sixty-three. So it is in other departments of the method. (p. 97)

Pestalozzi's "object lessons" served as models for ways to facilitate step-by-step learning of abstract concepts. His ideas challenged educators in Germany and America to rethink methods of instruction that relied on repetition and memorization.

Herbart

Johann Friedrich Herbart (1776–1841), a German philosopher, psychologist, and educational theorist, believed a primary goal of education was to respect a child's individuality while conveying the discipline and consistency necessary to develop moral strength of character. A teacher should cultivate a child's interests while also introducing the child to a variety of human knowledge and experiences necessary for understanding and appreciating fundamental values of civilized societies. Herbart proposed several "steps of instruction" for developing a child's ability to concentrate, retain ideas, and participate in learning: (a) "clearness" (understanding of content); (b) "association" (connecting new ideas with previously learned content); (c) "system" (the analysis of new ideas and their relation to the purpose of the lesson); and (d) "method" (the ability to apply newly acquired knowledge to future problems). By the nineteenth century, teacher education programs stressed Herbart's methods of instruction (Ulich, 1968).

Froebel

Friedrich Froebel (1782–1852), a German philosopher of education, established the first kindergarten in 1837 at Blankenburg. Froebel's kindergarten was not a school in the traditional sense, but a "general institution" where little children could learn through the use of educational games and "occupations" (activities). A large portion of a child's school day was spent on gardening, an activity intended to help children see the similarity in the growth of plants and their own development (Downs, 1978).

Unlike Herbart, who explained the workings of the human mind as either associating or conflicting representations, Froebel viewed mental life as "the outgrowth of the incessant creativeness of the Divine" (Ulich, 1968, p. 287). To Froebel, a person's senses, emotions, and reason were the critical attributes necessary for learning to occur. Quality early childhood experiences that focused on play, music, and art allowed a child to reveal his or her internal nature. Children were not "lumps of clay" to be molded; instead they were like plants and animals which needed time and space to develop according to natural law. Froebel recognized play as an important facet of learning and as the child's first sign of purposeful activity (Downs, 1978).

In 1855, Margaretta Schurtz, a German immigrant and one of Froebel's former students, established one of the first kindergartens in America in Watertown, Wisconsin. Schurtz's kindergarten was conducted in German, as were others founded by German immigrants. In the main, these early kindergartens were meant to ensure that children would learn to speak German and to guarantee the preservation of their German heritage. The first kindergarten to be conducted in English was founded in Boston in 1860 by Elizabeth Peabody. By 1868, the first public kindergarten was opened in St. Louis, Missouri. It was a remarkable success, and thus imitated widely.

Spencer

Herbert Spencer (1820-1903) was an English Social Darwinist. As such, he believed that certain species survived and prospered because they were among the most fit and able—they adapted to conditions in their environments to which other weaker species could not adapt. Spencer pressed for a "utilitarian" education focused on practical objectives rather than on the more general goals proposed by humanistic and classical educators in English schools. He contended that education should prepare people for self-preservation, earning a livelihood, raising children, and participating fully in society. With such an education, Spencer believed, the fittest would triumph while the laggards would disappear.

HOW DID AMERICANS BEFORE THE CIVIL WAR RELY ON INFORMAL EDUCATION?

Society educates in many ways. European settlers who arrived on the shores of the New World in the 1600s had to adapt European ideas to their new environment as they struggled with themselves, with each other, and with outside forces in their efforts to survive and prosper. Education both reflected and shaped peoples' values as they established their settlements along the eastern coast of America.

Education in the Southern Colonies

Then, as now, ideas were the currency of education. People often defined ideas that dominated everyday communication—ideas about right and wrong, good and bad, winning and losing—in simple terms. Their ways of thinking greatly influenced both formal and informal interactions with one another. Those who settled in the southern colonies of Virginia, Maryland, Georgia, and the Carolinas typically lived on large plantations where there were rigid class distinctions. A plantation was like a small community where such crops as tobacco, sugar, or cotton were raised. The owner's home was often at the center of the plantation and surrounded by a kitchen, smokehouse, stable, and sometimes a school where a hired tutor taught the landowner's children. Around the periphery were tobacco fields and barns and cabins in which slaves from Africa and indentured servants from Europe lived. These people were the backbone of plantation life. They were trained as field workers, household workers, and skilled artisans—cobblers, carpenters, tailors, blacksmiths. Plantation owners were powerful people, directing both the lives of these servants and the lives of the numerous small farmers in the South.

Small farmers were isolated. Although they worked for themselves, their livelihood was often affected by plantation owners' willingness to purchase or sell surplus crops, rent their lands, and loan money. Farmers' decisions about where to settle were based mainly on the lay of the land, the quality of the soil, and proximity of water. For these people who struggled to eke out a living from the land, there was no community of any sort; nor were there nearby schools or churches. For the most part, education was informal. Skills boys and girls needed to learn were taught by the family. Families also taught their children to read and often conducted their own worship services until the middle of the eighteenth century, when itinerant missionaries began to minister to people in the backcountry.

Most colonists, particularly in the South, were Protestants who believed the Scriptures were key to understanding God's will. To them, education should help save souls. As early as 1619, Virginia law made religious study on Sunday afternoons standard practice. The Bible was typically the medium for instruction; interpretations of God's will figured prominently in the formative years of the Republic.

Education in the Middle Colonies

People in the Middle Atlantic colonies (New York, New Jersey, Pennsylvania, and Delaware) were more diverse than settlers in the southern colonies. Although most Middle Atlantic colonists spoke English, there were also Dutch-, German-, and Swedish-speaking individuals whose religious orientation varied greatly from one another. Among others, there were Catholics, Mennonites, Dutch Calvin Lutherans, Quakers, Presbyterians, and Jews, all diligent in their efforts to preserve their languages and beliefs. To do so, different groups established their own parochial schools. English, Irish, Welsh, Dutch, and German Quakers, for instance, who settled mainly in Pennsylvania, stressed the importance of formal education focused on religion, mathematics, reading, and writing. They also offered some vocational training to children. Teachers viewed children as inherently good and rejected use of corporal punishment. Their schools were open to everyone, including Native Americans and slaves (Bullock, 1967).

VOICES

On Being an Apprentice

The tradition of **apprenticeships**—practical work experiences under the supervision of skilled workers in trades and the arts—also shaped the development of formal schooling and curricula in Britain's American colonies. Sometimes children as young as 7 years of age were sent to live with masters to learn a particular trade, and where law required it, to learn to read and write. Benjamin Franklin's early experiences as an apprentice in various trades led to his successful apprenticeship as a printer under an older brother:

At ten years old, I was taken to help my father in his business of a tallow chandler [candlemaker] and soap boiler, a business to which he was not bred, but had assumed on his arrival in New England, because he found that his dyeing trade, being in little request, would not maintain his family. Accordingly, I was employed in cutting the wick for the candles, filling the molds for cast candles, attending the shop, going of errands, etc.

I disliked the trade, and had a strong inclination to go to sea, but my father declared against it; but, residing near the water, I was much in it and on it. I learned to swim well and to manage boats; and when embarked with other boys, I was commonly allowed to govern, especially in any case of difficulty; and upon other occasions I was generally the leader among the boys and sometimes led them into scrapes . . .

Through formal apprenticeships the children of early colonists added technical skills to any basic literacy skills they learned at home.

To return: I continued thus employed in my father's business for two years, that is, till I was twelve years old; and my brother John, who was bred to that business, having left my father, married and set up for himself at Rhode Island, there was every appearance that I was destined to supply his place and become a tallow chandler. But my dislike to the trade continuing, my father had apprehensions that if he did not put me to one more agreeable, I should break loose and go to sea, as my brother Josiah had done, to his great vexation. In consequence, he took me to walk with him, and see joiners, bricklayers, turners [a person who uses a lathe], braziers [a person who works in brass], etc., at their work that he might observe my inclination and endeavor to fix it on some trade that would keep me on land . . . . My father determined at last for the cutler's trade, and placed me for some days on trial with Samuel, son to my uncle Benjamin, who was bred to that trade in London and had just established him in Boston. But the sum he exacted as a fee for my apprenticeship displeased my father, and I was taken home again . . .

CRITICAL THINKING

How did masters during Franklin's time judge an apprentice's suitability for a craft or trade? How did Franklin judge his own suitability and the performances of his teachers?

Source: Franklin, B. (1842). *Memoirs of Benjamin Franklin* (Vol. I). New York: Harper & Brothers, pp. 21–25.

Education in the New England Colonies

In the New England colonies of Massachusetts Bay, New Hampshire, and Connecticut, there was less divergence in ideas and values, which made possible the establishment of town schools. Two school laws were instrumental in moving New Englanders in this direction. The Massachusetts Act of 1642 required that efforts of parents and master craftsmen who trained novices be monitored to assure that children were learning to read and understand religious principles. The Massachusetts Act of 1647, sometimes referred to as the Old Deluder Satan Law, required towns to provide for the education of youth so they might thwart Satan's trickery. To produce Scripture-literate citizens, every town of 50 households was required to employ a teacher of reading and writing, and every town of 100 households was to provide a grammar school to prepare youth for study at Harvard University.

Many settlers were Puritans who followed the teachings of John Calvin, a Swiss religious reformer. Calvin believed God was omnipotent and good while human beings were evil and helpless, predestined for salvation or eternal torment. The role of schooling was to produce literate, hardworking, frugal and respectful men and women who might resist the temptations of the world. Children, perceived as savage and primitive creatures, were to be trained and disciplined for a life of social conformity and religious commitment.

Colonists living in northern cities experienced a lifestyle very different from other colonists. Cities were densely populated and built on trade. Merchants, who were key people in the community, made available an array of goods and services not found in other parts of the country. Cities also contained skilled craftsmen, barbers, wigmakers, and an abundance of school teachers better educated than those in the country. Ships arriving at port brought both goods and ideas from England and Europe. This meant city dwellers were among the best informed and sometimes the most influential of colonists. At the same time, city residents faced a number of problems not encountered by other colonists. Among these were increasing numbers of poor and unemployed colonists, fires, vice, and filth that necessitated sewers and sanitation laws (Blum et al., 1989).

Except in the New England colonies, where church, state, and school were closely related, there was generally a separation of church and state. Nonetheless, church leaders greatly influenced people's thinking. Some, like Cotton Mather, were among the most prolific writers in America, and some, like Michael Wigglesworth, enjoyed wide readership. Between 1662 and 1701, Wigglesworth's *The Day of Doom*, an account of the Last Judgment, went through five editions (Blum et al., 1989).

Education for Nationhood

Weekly newspapers and literary and political essays and verse were also popular reading matter. The colonists understood how government worked, but they did not always agree on how it should work. Some colonists argued that they should rip themselves free from England; others counseled

FIGURE 2.1

Some Factors Affecting American Education Before the Civil War

As you read, identify people whose contributions you might add to this figure under the heading "Influential American Educators and Their Ideas."

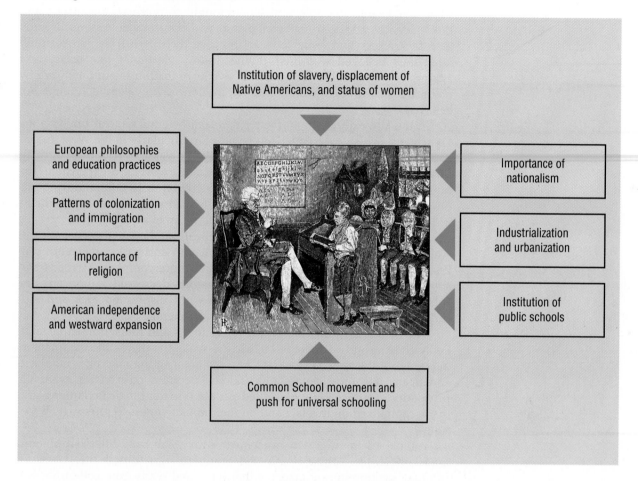

people to reconcile their differences with England and to remain a colony. The struggle for their loyalties, both on and off the battlefield, shaped the talk and writings of the day. By the middle of the eighteenth century, almost every colony had a printing press churning out a daily newspaper containing not only local news and news from abroad but also literary and political essays. Printers also produced almanacs, flyers, and books. Thomas Paine's *Common Sense*—a compelling case for independence—sold 100,000 copies in its first 3 months of publication in 1776 and captured the minds and hearts of the delegates to the Continental Congress and of many others outside Philadelphia (Cremin, 1970). As Figure 2.1 suggests, independence was one of several developments that significantly affected the development of an American system of education.

As the country grew and matured, competing forces continued to shape Americans' views of themselves and others. The plantation owners in the South protected their virtually self-sufficient communities with their permanent labor force, while abolitionists in the North battled covertly and openly to destroy the system of slavery that supported the plantations. The Cherokee, Creek, Iroquois, and others fought to preserve their lands and their physical and spiritual well-being, while European Americans took land by trickery and force so as to improve their own lives and to fulfill what they believed was their divine destiny. Struggles like these were among the more visible "educational" events of the times, but they were by no means the only significant ones that influenced how people thought and behaved.

In the late eighteenth and early nineteenth centuries, conflict with the French and British over American territory, particularly in the West, fueled nationalistic fervor. Between 1800 and 1840, the value of American agricultural products grew remarkably, largely due to westward expansion. The number of farmers increased from about 5 million to 15 million during this time. Only about one seventh of the people lived west of the Appalachians in 1810 whereas one third did so after 1840 (Blum et al., 1989).

Forces of urbanization and industrialization shaped the character of America in the Northeast in the late eighteenth and early nineteenth centuries. After 1830, factories grew larger and more complex. As roads and shipping improved, and as transportation costs decreased, Americans distributed their goods to mass markets. Hard work, inspiration, luck, and education all combined to influence these developments.

The Northeast had waterpower for factories and mills, iron and coal in Pennsylvania, and entrepreneurs ready to make the region the manufacturing center of the nation. The Erie Canal, an engineering marvel, symbolized Americans' technical capabilities and the people's passion for economic prosperity. American law permitted people to patent their inventions, and many capitalized on this fact and on their inventiveness to pursue their fortunes.

As colonists migrated westward into Alabama, Mississippi, and Louisiana, King Cotton dominated Southern agricultural life. Once Eli Whitney's cotton gin—a machine that separated seeds from cotton fibers—was invented in 1793, production jumped from about 10,000 bales to about 500,000 bales in the 1820s (Blum et al., 1989). While the North propelled itself toward industrialization, the South remained rural and dependent on agriculture for its economic well-being.

As described earlier, slavery, more than anything else, made the cultures in northern, Middle Atlantic, and southern colonies different from one another. In the northern states, many people, especially the Quakers, decried human bondage. By the early nineteenth century, antislavery groups produced enough pressure to achieve abolition of slavery in the northern states. In the South, however, slavery continued to flourish. Slavery was recognized by the federal Constitution as a local institution within the jurisdiction of individual states; it was also a profitable fact of life for European-American planters in the South. The practice provided a reliable pool of field hands, miners, craftsmen, and domestics. In the 1850s, nearly half the populations of both Alabama and Louisiana was African slaves; more than half of Mississippi's population consisted of slaves. Most slaves were owned by a relatively few people; three fourths of southern European-American families never owned slaves (Blum et al., 1989).

Nat Turner's bloody rebellion against bondage in South Hampton County, Virginia in 1831 and John Brown's terrorism in support of the abolitionist cause in the 1850s proved harbingers of much greater violence. As Abraham Lincoln and Stephen Douglas debated the nature of slavery and freedom in the United States, the stage was set for civil war.

As perhaps only calamity can, the war forced people to think about education in different ways. People concerned about educating their own children learned that for their own good, they also had to care about educating others' children. The educational system that began to evolve reflected these concerns. Over time, people came to realize they were connected to each other in ways that only few could imagine in earlier times. Education both revealed and strengthened those connections.

HOW DID AMERICANS VIEW THE AIMS OF EDUCATION?

The nation's founders believed that education was the best hope for the Republic. Freedom had to be tempered by the responsibility to maintain social order. Education would prepare good citizens. The virtuous, the disciplined, the intelligent would know how to participate responsibly in a democracy. Noah Webster in Connecticut, Benjamin Rush in Pennsylvania, and Thomas Jefferson in Virginia argued that the ability to read, write, and cipher would make the people and the nation strong. Jefferson (1931) viewed education as the key to advancing civilization:

> Education . . . grafts a new man on the native stock, and improves what in his nature was vicious and perverse into qualities of virtue and social worth. And it cannot be but that each generation succeeding to the knowledge acquired by all those who preceded it, adding to it their own acquisitions and discoveries, and handing the mass down for successive and constant accumulation, must advance the knowledge, and well-being of mankind, not *infinitely*, as some have said, but *indefinitely*, and to a term which no one can fix and foresee. (p. 250)

The Role of Religion

As described earlier, early Protestants believed that God was everywhere in their lives. The ideas of John Calvin (1509-1564), the most famous of Protestant leaders in the seventeenth century, greatly influenced Puritan men and women who settled in New England. Puritans' ideas about people's place in the universe were to influence Americans' thinking for more than 150 years. Like Calvin, Puritans believed that God was omnipotent and good and that mankind was evil. Although they did not know if they were predestined for heaven or hell, they took holy joy in trying to follow God's commandments as given in the Bible (Blum et al., 1989).

The King James Bible and other devotional literature instructed people on how to live and how to die. Written in the 1670s, *The Poor Man's Family Book* taught colonists how to attend to their private duties, family duties, church duties, and duties to rulers and neighbors. Early writers often taught by telling stories and applying religious and moral principles to particular situations. Children's school books reinforced these principles. Educators' methods of writing and teaching, sort of a case-method approach to divinity, was called "casuistry" (Cremin, 1970, p. 45).

In the 1740s, religious experiences were brought to thousands of people in every rank of society when George Whitefield, a traveling English preacher, prompted the Great Awakening with his religious revivals. Whitefield journeyed from the Carolinas to New England teaching the word of God to rich and poor, old and young, educated and ignorant. Whitefield combined Calvinism and showmanship as he dramatized in vivid detail the pain awaiting sinners, urging his audience to confess its sins and submit to God.

Jonathan Edwards, a minister from Northampton, Massachusetts, who was a staunch defender of the Awakening, preached a stricter Calvinism than New England had ever heard. Edwards's Calvinist theology suggested that children were inherently evil and in need of strict discipline. His notions encouraged harsh treatment of children at home and at school (Blum et al., 1989).

> "Education has so cold, so hopeless a sound.
> A treatise on education, a convention on education, a lecture, a system, affects us with slight paralysis and a certain yawning of the jaws."

By the nineteenth century, the hard tenets of orthodox Calvinism began to soften, and Americans adopted more rationalistic and humanistic views. Some began to challenge the traditional methods of education. Transcendentalist philosophers Henry David Thoreau, Bronson Alcott, and Ralph Waldo Emerson were among those who advocated the radical reform of education. They were concerned in particular with the stifling nature of education. According to Emerson (1884),

Education has so cold, so hopeless a sound. A treatise on education, a convention for education, a lecture, a system, affects us with slight paralysis and a certain yawning of the jaws . . . Education should be as broad as man. Whatever elements are in him that should foster and demonstrate. If he be dexterous, his tuition should make it appear; if he be capable of dividing men by the trenchant sword of his thought, education should unsheathe and sharpen it; if he is one to cement society by his all-reconciling affinities, oh! hasten their action! If he is jovial, if he is mercurial, if he is great hearted, a cunning artificer, a strong commander, a potent ally, ingenious, useful, elegant, witty, prophet, diviner,—society has need of all these. The imagination must be addressed. (p. 133)

The Impact of Industrialization

American industrialization in the early nineteenth century led to an increasing emphasis on practical rather than theoretical learning. At the same time, demands for cheap, reliable labor had a direct effect on schools' enrollment. Women and children met the increased demands for labor in the Northeast by working long hours under extremely difficult conditions. Infant schools, a concept devised by a Welsh cotton-mill owner and social reformer named Robert Owen (1771–1858), provided much-needed care for young children of working women. Such schools were designed to meet the mental, physical, and moral development of children not yet old enough to work in the factories. Owen established them to give child factory workers some minimal education. Members of the clergy also opened Sunday schools in the larger cities—New York, Philadelphia, Boston. (The idea behind Sunday schools was developed by Robert Raikes, an English religious leader.) In 1830, the American Sunday-School Union declared that it would have a Sunday school in every destitute place in the Mississippi Valley.

The Education of Slaves

When the Civil War began in 1861, there were some 7 million slaves in the southern and western states. By the time the war ended in 1865, there were about 4 million, about 5% of whom could read and write (Blum et al., 1989). In the early 1600s, when the American slave trade began, English clergy had expressed interest in providing religious training for slaves and had made some progress in achieving their goal. Presbyterians went a step farther, providing formal training to African Americans to prepare them for religious leadership. In 1740, Hugh Bryan, a wealthy and pious Presbyterian, opened his school for African Americans in Charleston, South Carolina. By 1755, Presbyterian schools had extended to Virginia, where slaves were being taught to read and write. In an experiment to test African Americans' abilities to succeed in college, Presbyterians sent John Chavis of North Carolina to Princeton University. Chavis graduated and established a school in the South only to find that European Americans would not allow non-European-American children to attend.

The education of slaves was also augmented by other religious groups. Near the beginning of the eighteenth century, Dr. Thomas Bray of England, organizing the Society for the Propagation of the Gospel, procured the funds and teachers needed to start schools for slaves in Charleston, South Carolina, Savannah, Georgia, and other parts of Georgia. Between 1764 and 1785, southern Quakers established two schools for slaves in Virginia. By 1808, the Quakers had implemented a trustee system that allowed for individualized instruction of slaves on a familial basis, followed by emancipation from slavery. For the most part, these and other formal education programs for African Americans were available mainly to household servants or to free blacks (Bullock, 1967).

European-American missionaries and free blacks established African schools and black academies in the North and the South during the 1800s.

Christopher McPherson, a free black, started a Richmond, Virginia, African school in 1811 to teach other free blacks and slaves. From dusk until 9:30 each night, a European-American teacher he had hired taught English, writing, arithmetic, geography, and astronomy for about $1.25 per month. Flush with success, McPherson ran an advertisement for his school in the newspaper. Southerners in positions of authority were not quite so enthusiastic about his efforts: They closed his school as a public nuisance and sent McPherson to the Williamsburg Lunatic Asylum (Berlin, 1974).

In some southern colonies, such as South Carolina, laws forbade teaching slaves to read and write. Some colonists justified such laws by persuading themselves that slaves were incapable of learning any more than was required to perform their menial jobs. Others believed that education would produce a leadership that would encourage slaves to rebel against a life of bondage. In fact, such leadership did evolve. Denmark Vesey led a group of slaves in Charleston, South Carolina, in an attack on their masters in 1822. David Walker of Wilmington, North Carolina, published his widely read *Appeal*, a spirited attack on slavery, in 1829. Two years later, the educated slave rebel of Virginia, Nat Turner, led a bloody revolt against slave masters (Bullock, 1967).

> "The plan which I mainly adopted, and the one which was most successful, was that of using my young white playmates, whom I met in the streets, as teachers."

As described above, religious groups played a major role in extending educational opportunities to the oppressed. Slave owners and African-American preachers were also sources of education for slaves. Some owners placed their slaves under the tutelage of master craftsmen and even helped slaves establish small businesses to help them buy their freedom. Slaves who did not receive formal education learned informally from their associations with literate European Americans. When assigned to houses, domestic workers might learn to read from the personal libraries of their masters and from studying recipes, music, and the Bible.

Slave children learned from their masters' children as they played school with one another, hidden from public view. Stories were told by former slaves about listening outside schools to lessons being taught. Frederick Douglass, an escaped slave from Maryland, learned the alphabet from his mistress and no doubt would have learned more from her had it not been for his master. When Master Hugh discovered that she was teaching the young slave, he said, "Learning will spoil the best nigger in the world. If he learns to read the Bible it will for ever unfit him to be a slave. He should know nothing but the will of his master, and learn to obey it" (Douglass, 1974). After his mistress's lessons were curtailed, Douglass (1882) was more determined than ever to learn to read:

> The plan which I mainly adopted, and the one which was most successful, was that of using my young white playmates, whom I met in the streets, as teachers. I used to carry almost constantly a copy of Webster's spelling-book in my pocket, and when sent on errands, or when play-

time was allowed me, I would step aside with my young friends and take a lesson in spelling. I am greatly indebted to these boys—Gustavus Dorgan, Joseph Bailey, Charles Farity, and William Cosdry. (p. 2)

Douglass was one of the most eloquent orators against slavery in the United States. In his speeches and his newspapers, he advocated the destruction of slavery in the South and the achievement of voting and other rights for African Americans in the North. To help slaves overcome their lack of formal education, Douglass also ran a Sunday school which he held in barns, in woods, and in the fields. Being African American, Douglass was among the most influential propagandists against the evils of slavery (Bullock, 1967).

Informal, often illegal, education for slaves became a hidden passage to freedom for some African Americans.

In some instances, owners taught their slaves because they simply wanted to protect and enhance their investments; in other cases, efforts to educate slaves came about as a result of respect and caring. Henry Bullock (1967) called these educational activities the **hidden passage** to freedom— they provided the intellectual power for slaves to escape bondage and to make lives for themselves after the Civil War.

Fear about educating slaves mounted in the years just before the Civil War. Well-educated, vocal freed men and escaped slaves were in a position to demand equal rights and privileges. In the 1840s, some fearful citizens went so far as to create a list of "safe" books that reflected the Southern viewpoint. The South Carolina Legislature made it a misdemeanor "to learn a slave to write, subject to fine and imprisonment" (The Sun, 1833a, p. 2). Later safe reading lists included a Confederate edition of the New Testament. Many European immigrants in Northern cities also feared and resented Africans and non-European immigrants, perceiving them as threats to their jobs and way of life.

Education for Native Americans

In Revolutionary times, many settlers believed Native Americans should be "civilized" or taught the ways of European Americans. At one time, Thomas Jefferson believed European Americans should intermingle with Native Americans and become one people. Paradoxically, he also believed African Americans did not possess the mental capabilities to achieve equality with European Americans and should probably be resettled elsewhere. Jefferson wrote of Native Americans in 1803,

In truth, the ultimate point of rest and happiness for them is to let our settlements and theirs meet and blend together, to intermix, and become one people. Incorporating themselves with us as citizens of the United States, this is what the natural progress of things will of course bring on, and it will be better to promote than retard it. (Cremin, 1980, pp. 231–232)

Sequoyah

During the 1780s and 1790s, Native Americans were often portrayed in writing and in speeches as good candidates for assimilation, but, in practice, they were subjugated by European Americans.

Assimilation, integration, and intermarriage with European Americans did not occur to any appreciable degree; nonetheless, some Native Americans who were self-educated in the European manner in turn advanced the European-style education of their people. In 1821, a Cherokee named Sequoyah devised an 86-character phonetic Cherokee alphabet. A press using Sequoyah's type churned out stories, hymns, and even a Bible in Cherokee. A newspaper, *The Cherokee Phoenix*, did much to advance literacy and knowledge among the tribe. Education of this sort, however, did little to insure the Cherokees' welfare.

To characterize Native Americans as one people, as many did in early America, is inaccurate. The tribes, nations, and confederacies varied significantly from one another. Some, like the Iroquois and the Cheyennes, had extended families that traced their descent through their mothers. Social relations were determined in part by the status of women. The Comanche, on the other hand, were patriarchal and practiced polygamy. All Native-American tribes made life revolve around the family. Typically, the women tended the crops, made clothing, and prepared food. Men hunted, fished, and defended the community. Elders taught children by example, explanation, and imitation (Cremin, 1980).

Schooling for Native Americans was a continuation of their education, not a beginning (Barman, Hebert, & McCaskill, 1986). People of the tribe had always guided children into adulthood. Relatives bore the primary responsibility for education, but they assumed this responsibility in ways markedly different from European-American society. Native-American children were surrounded by educators and caregivers—father and mother, grandparents, older siblings, uncles and aunts, other adults, and specialists, such as weavers, potters, warriors, and shamans (Coleman, 1993).

During the early nineteenth century, Protestants and Catholics established schools among the Native Americans to teach English and to inculcate Christianity. One example was Brainerd Mission, established among the Cherokees in Georgia. Brainerd Mission tried to prepare the Cherokees for assimilation into the dominant culture. The schoolmaster even gave each child a new English name. The Mission became a self-sufficient society, producing nearly everything students needed to live. By 1830, there were eight such schools. The Brainerd Mission became the most common model for educating other eastern tribes and nations.

As far as the larger society knew, such schools were the best answer to "the Indian problem." The *Sun* (1833) newspaper carried this report in 1833:

> There is, . . . an Indian School under the superintendence of Col R.M. Johnson, in Scott Co. which has one hundred scholars from the Choctaws, Creeks, Potawatomies, and Miamies, and supported chiefly by their own funds. This interesting school was established at the house of Col. Johnson, by the Choctaws, some years ago. It is very flourishing, and will do good (*The Sun*, 1833b, p. 3).

Cultural Awareness

The roles of observation, practice, and self-discipline in traditional Native-American education are evident in the account of Zitkala-Sa (1921), a Nakota (Yankton Sioux), about learning beadwork:

> Close beside my mother I sat on a rug . . . with a scrap of buckskin in one hand and an awl in the other. This was the beginning of my practical observation lessons in the art of beadwork. . . . It took many trials before I learned how to knot my sinew thread on the point of my finger, as I saw her do. . . . The quietness of her oversight made me feel strongly responsible and dependent upon my own judgment. She treated me as a dignified little individual as long as I was on good behavior; and how humiliated I was when some boldness of mine drew forth a rebuke from her! . . . Always after these confining lessons I was wild with surplus spirits, and found joyous relief in running loose in the open again. (pp. 18–21.)

Education in Spain's American Colonies

The Aztecs and Mayas had highly developed cultures before the Spanish conquistadors came to Mexico in the early sixteenth century. The Mayas had devised a calendar, hieroglyphic writing, and a number system. The Aztecs designed and built the city of Tenochtitlán, an engineering and architectural marvel.

Santa Fe (now New Mexico), was founded by the Spanish in 1609, only 2 years after the English settled Jamestown in Virginia. In 1790, there were about 23,000 Spanish-speaking people in what is now the southwestern United States; they had migrated northward from Mexico. Most were of mixed Native-American and Spanish descent, having a heritage that had come to be dominated by the Spanish language, religion (Catholicism), and social and political organizations. The Church and its missionaries provided what little formal education existed for Hispanic Americans in those early years (Manuel, 1965).

Formal education was basic and heavily religious, conducted mainly by older men for younger men. A notable exception to this rule was a woman named Sor Juana Ines de la Cruz (1648–1695):

Roman Catholic missions and a class system based on racial origins shaped the educational experiences of Native Americans and Africans in the Spanish colonies.

> I was not yet three years old when my mother sent an older sister of mine to be taught to read at a school. . . Moved by affection and a mischievous spirit, I followed her; and seeing her receive instruction, such a strong desire to read burned in me that I tried to deceive the teacher, telling her that my mother wanted her to give me lessons. . . (Hahner, 1976, pp. 22–23)

Juana Ines later studied Latin and took the vows of a nun. She wrote many poems for important occasions of the Church and the state. She has been the subject of many historians (Flynn, 1971). Her intellectual abilities made her a favorite of the Spanish viceroy and his wife in Mexico City and she served as a kind of court poet to them, successfully debating teachers from the university.

Spanish colonization of the Southwest fulfilled more than one purpose. The **mission schools** established by priests were to convert Native Americans to Catholicism, to effect a sort of peaceful conquest of the indigenous people (Fogel, 1988). But the missions also served to capture and hold territory for Spain, while impeding any interests France and Britain might have had in these areas. Junipero Serra, a Franciscan priest, established missions in California territory in the 1770s.

> The missions were far more than religious outposts: They were social institutions, designed to transform the Indians from scattered hunting and gathering peoples into disciplined farmers, ranchers, and cloth weavers clustered around, and faithful to the church. (Fogel, 1988, p. 53)

From the outset, the Spanish-speaking and English-speaking peoples in the Southwest fought for control of the land. English-speaking Texans achieved their independence from Mexico in 1836. The United States, in turn, annexed Texas in 1844. In 1846, the United States and Mexico commenced the Mexican war, which ended 2 years later with Mexico's defeat and the addition of California, Utah, New Mexico, and other western territories to the United States.

Education for Women

As the heads of families, men occupied positions of complete authority. Their duties were clear: They were to govern their families so as to preserve personal, religious, and social stability. They were supposed to live the ideal life of piety and to see that their families did likewise. Women's duties were equally clear: They were to serve men. In so doing, they were to instruct children in ways that made them examples of virtue. Children were to "obey, serve, fear, love, honor, and revere their parents . . . also to follow their good precepts and examples of life and to take correction patiently at their hands" (Cremin, 1970, p. 51). Corporal punishment was to be used to alter children's willful behavior when necessary.

During colonial times, women played a relatively insignificant role in the formal education of children. In just about every colony, however, there are records of at least one or more women having been employed as teachers. Most often, they instructed the younger children, and in many instances, children of the poor in **dame schools**, or schools run by local

Emma Willard

women which concentrated on rudimentary reading skills. Generally, women taught during the summer months (April to September) and men taught during the winter. The Quakers in Pennsylvania did not discriminate against women to the degree other religious sects did. While they were not compensated as well as Quaker schoolmasters, Quaker women accounted for a large proportion of the teachers in Pennsylvania (Elsbree, 1939).

Benjamin Rush's 1787 speech "Thoughts Upon Female Education" marked a turning point in the education of women in the colonies. Rush contended that male heads of families were increasingly occupied with their roles outside the home and thus unable to serve as primary educators of their sons and daughters. Women, who would necessarily assume such roles, were ill-prepared for the task.

Emma Willard was among several educators who developed programs for women that were more academically focused than schools of the past. In her speech to the New York legislature in 1819, Willard advocated the formation of schools that would teach geography, science, domestic skills, music, and other courses to women. Emma Willard opened a school in 1821 in Troy, New York. Her efforts stimulated others, such as Catherine Beecher, Zilpah Grant, Mary Lyons, and George B. Emerson, also to establish institutions expressly for the purpose of educating women (Deighton, 1971).

Catherine Beecher

Education for People with Disabilities

The object of many superstitions, people with physical or mental disabilities were relegated to lives of confinement and idleness or were subjects of scapegoating and exploitation. The first permanent, state-supported school built expressly for the mentally retarded in the United States was opened in Syracuse, New York, in 1854. Clergymen and physicians were among the leaders in providing care and training for the disabled.

"The assumption of the leaders in special education was that *all* handicapped persons could and should be provided with residential care that would cure their behavioral deficits and make them useful and productive citizens or at least improve their condition and skills markedly." (Kauffman, 1981, p. 5).

Although such beliefs can be traced far into history, Lester Mann (1979) and others afford Jean-Jacques Rousseau a distinctive place in the annals of special education as it has become operationalized in modern times. With the publication of *Emile* in 1762, Rousseau asserted that humans are fundamentally good but that society corrupts them. Rousseau championed the idea that people could encourage children to achieve the potential they all possessed inherently. He wrote of the importance of sensory-motor development in young children, followed by higher intellectual development in their later years. His ideas stimulated Jean-Marc Itard (1775–1838) and Edouard Seguin (1812–1880) in France, Pestalozzi in Switzerland, Froebel in Germany, and Maria Montessori (1870–1952) in Italy to fit education to a child's development.

Samuel Gridley Howe and Thomas Gallaudet both left the United States during the early 1800s to study abroad before they established their own programs here to educate children with disabilities. Howe taught Laura Bridgmen, a person without sight, hearing, or speech, and achieved interna-

Thomas Gallaudet

Cultural Awareness

In 1829, Louis Braille adapted a system used by the French army for the exchange of messages by touch in war zones at night. Braille's raised-line system is a code that utilizes a six-dot cell to represent 63 alphabetical, numerical, and grammatical characters. By the end of the nineteenth century, "braille" was the universally accepted means of teaching blind people to read and write.

Grade 1   Braille grade 1 uses full spelling and consists of the letters of the alphabet, numbers, punctuation signs, and composition signs which are unique to braille.

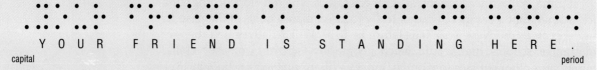

capital   Y O U R   F R I E N D   I S   S T A N D I N G   H E R E .   period

Grade 2   Braille grade 2 is a contracted system much like shorthand, and consists of grade 1 braille plus 189 contractions and short-form words.

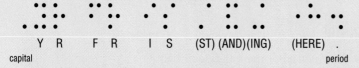

capital   Y R   F R   I S   (ST) (AND)(ING)   (HERE) .   period

Orlansky, M.D., & Rhyne, J.M. (1981). Special adaptations necessitated by visual impairments. In J.M. Kauffman & D.P. Hallahan (Eds.) *Handbook of special education.* Englewood Cliffs, NJ: Prentice-Hall, Inc., 552–575.

tional fame. He also taught Anne Sullivan, who later became the teacher of Helen Keller. Named after the pioneer in education for people with hearing impairments, Gallaudet College for the Deaf in Washington, D.C., is the only college for the deaf in the world (Hewett & Forness, 1984).

Daniel Hallahan and James Kauffman (1994) contend that the development of education programs specially fitted to people's needs is deeply rooted in the past. Many of today's special education practices can be traced to ideas expressed much earlier, including prescribing instruction based on the child's characteristics, carefully sequencing tasks from simple to complex, emphasizing stimulation of the child's senses, and tutoring in functional skills.

HOW DID FORMAL EDUCATION DEVELOP IN AMERICA BEFORE THE CIVIL WAR?

Being a teacher in colonial America was much like being a lawyer; neither required formal training. Academic qualifications of teachers, most of whom were men, ranged from bare ability to read and write to the scholarly attainments of a college graduate. The more rural the school, and the younger the children, the lower were the qualifications for a teaching position. In the North, particularly in Massachusetts, communities at the doorstep of Harvard were more selective, typically giving preference to college-trained men. For the most part, however, communities were not as interested in a candidate's scholastic preparation as in his character and religious orthodoxy. The Quakers of Pennsylvania, for example, stressed morality and membership in the Society of Friends. The Scotch-Irish in Pennsylvania insisted that schoolmasters be intelligent and sufficiently pious to teach the principles of the Calvinistic faith. In 1750, Pennsylvania Lutherans required the following:

> That the schoolhouse shall always be in charge of a faithful Evangelical Lutheran schoolmaster, whose competency to teach Reading, Writing, and Arithmetic, and also to play the organ (Orgelschlagen) and to use the English language, has been proved by the pastor; special regard being had at the same time, to the purity of his doctrine and his life. He shall be required to treat all his pupils with impartial fidelity, and to instruct the children of other denominations, and of the neighborhood generally. He shall not allow the children to use profane language either in or out of school; but shall carefully teach them how, both in church and in school, and in the presence of others and upon the highway, to conduct themselves in a Christian and upright manner, and "not like the Indians." (Elsbree, 1939, p. 39)

The Colonial Schoolhouse

Besides their teaching duties, schoolmasters were expected to perform a variety of duties outside school. In New England, some of the more common tasks were conducting religious services, leading the church choir, sweeping out the meetinghouse, ringing the bell for public worship, and digging graves (Elsbree, 1939). Schoolmasters usually juggled teaching and extra duties with one or more other jobs, ranging from surveying to innkeeping to artisanship. Teaching was often a stepping stone for other careers, particularly the ministry. This meant turnover among teachers was often quite high (Rury, 1989).

Teaching meant making children memorize facts. To do so, children had to sit quietly in their seats until called upon by the teacher to recite. Teachers relied on whole-group instruction and choral responses in mixed-ability classes. The entire system depended on repetition and drill, helped along with a more than healthy dose of punishment (Kaestle, 1983).

When students misbehaved, the teacher punished them swiftly and often severely. Teachers used whipping, ear boxing, hand caning, and other assorted terror tactics to control their charges. Although some educators expressed qualms about such brutality, most defended the use of corporal punishment. Punishment was an extension of authoritarian child-rearing practices and religious dictates.

> Use of corporal punishment was widespread. Eliphalet Nott, who grew up in Connecticut in the 1780s, said, "If I was not whipped more than three times a week, I considered myself for the time peculiarly fortu-

nate." In 1819, six-year-old James Sims was sent to a boarding school in South Carolina where new boys were always flogged, usually "Until the youngster vomited or wet his breeches." (Kaestle, 1983, p. 19)

During the mid-1800s, there was a decrease in such brutality. Historians attribute this change to a number of events: (a) graded schools which separated older children from younger children evolved so that teachers who had once dealt with as many as 100 students now dealt with smaller groups of children; (b) an influx of women into the teaching profession; (c) educators such as Pestalozzi set out to enlighten teachers about the benefits of teaching students to behave in certain ways instead of beating or coercing them into submission; and (d) some school systems, particularly those in the cities, passed ordinances prohibiting harsh punishment. Syracuse, New York in 1867 was one of the first cities to do away with corporal punishment (Elsbree, 1939; Kaestle, 1983).

The Monitorial Method

Children started school at different ages. Abecedarians—beginners at school—often started as young as age three. This meant, of course, that teachers often faced very large groups of students, composed of as many as 40 or 50 children, who differed markedly in abilities (Kaestle, 1983). The Lancasterian or **monitorial method** of teaching provided one response to this challenge.

Before graded schools were established in the cities, there were so many students crowded into a room that a single teacher could not deal with all of them at one time. In the 1820s, Joseph Lancaster, a Quaker, found these urban classrooms to be fertile ground for the monitorial method of teaching used in Europe. In this educational pyramid scheme, the master teacher served as a "silent bystander" and "inspector." He instructed the monitors, and they, in turn, instructed the younger children. The older students also monitored attendance and kept order in the classroom. The approach made reading, writing, and arithmetic available to large numbers of children, and it was cheap. Lancaster also offered extensive and explicit directions on how to teach. If teachers followed his system, Lancaster argued, they could not fail (Reigart, 1969).

When reading was being taught, for example, the school was to be divided into eight classes focusing on different topics: letters of the alphabet, words and syllables of two letters, words and syllables of three letters, words and syllables of four letters, reading lesson of one syllable, reading lesson of two syllables, the Testament, and the Bible. A group of 10 children in the class who were to receive instruction on the alphabet were to be seated at a table equipped with trays of sand. This table faced a large board

Lancaster's monitorial method of instruction addressed the challenge of overcrowded, understaffed, ungraded classrooms in the rapidly expanding cities of the early nineteenth century.

or alphabet wheel that displayed the letters to be studied. Monitors were then to proceed as follows:

> [E]ach scholar has a stick given to him about the thickness of a quill, and four inches long, with which he is to write the letters on the sand. The alphabet is divided into three parts, viz., the perpendicular letters, I H T L E F i and l, form the first lesson; the triangular letters, A V W M N Z K Y X v w k y z and x form the second; and the circular letters, O U C J G D P B R Q S, a b o d p q g c m n h t u r s f and j, form the third class. These are in succession placed before the class, which is under the direction of a monitor, who, with an audible voice, desires them to form the first letter; each scholar now makes his best effort, which, perhaps, is a very awkward one; but the monitor pointing out the defects and occasionally printing the letter for them, teaches them to retrace it; after repeated trials upon the same letter, the class is soon able to form it readily, and with neatness...The monitor then points to the first letter, and asks aloud, "What is that?" The boy at the head of the class answers first, when, if he should make a mistake, the question is put to the second boy, and so on until some one in the class answers aright; in which case the boy takes precedence in the class. This exercise soon perfects them in the knowledge of their letters and is also a pleasing relaxation. (Reigart, 1969, pp. 41–42)

The monitorial system was one of the most successful and widely used educational methods of the first 30 years of the nineteenth century. Cheap, efficient, and easy to use, the monitorial method enabled voluntary associations to extend educational opportunities to increasing numbers of children from low-income families. Reformers concerned with moral training of the poor believed the system might inculcate in these children obedience, industry, and promptness. At the same time, the Lancasterian system's use of monitors allowed for the training of future teachers (Kaestle, 1983).

The American Lyceum

As school programs were expanding, people also began to acquire knowledge formally outside schools in new and varied ways. In 1826, a wealthy Connecticut farmer, Josiah Holbrook, founded the American **Lyceum**, an organization devoted to the advancement of education for both children and adults. Holbrook wanted to provide an economical and practical education to American youth and to encourage the application of science and education in everyday life. People belonged to a lyceum for $1 a year. Some lyceums were reading circles, some debating clubs, and some band concerts. There was even a society devoted to phrenology—the "science" of determining character and temperament by studying the shapes of people's heads.

Millbury, in Worcester County, Massachusetts, had the first branch of the American Lyceum. By 1829, the Lyceum had spread across the country. This first formal adult and community education movement thrived in the late 1820s and 1830s and faded in the years following the Civil War. Ralph Waldo Emerson, a frequent lecturer on the lyceum circuit, called the American Lyceum a new form of education and a broad cultural movement.

The Development of Public Primary Schools

The main goal of education for European Americans was salvation of souls. Schooling began at home with the family. Father laid down the rules, keeping an eye on the King James Bible in doing so, and Mother enforced them. Formal schooling was patterned after English schools. In New England, a few legislatures tried to remind parents of their responsibility for their children's education, but laws were not well enforced. When families and communities organized themselves to provide schooling for their children, they sent them to inexpensive dame schools run by women in the area. Schools were private, although some received town support. Attendance was voluntary. Adult and community education, both of which began to emerge in various forms, were distinctly American.

The term "educated" evolved rather quickly to mean more than learning God's law. People began to view education as a means for personal advancement. Moreover, our government leaders promoted education as a way to develop wise and honest people who would help the fledgling democracy succeed.

Rise of Common Schools   Jefferson believed that it was to society's benefit to educate all its citizens so they might provide leadership and support for the country. As a member of the Virginia Assembly's Committee to Revise the Laws of the Commonwealth from 1776–1779, Jefferson drafted the Bill for the More General Diffusion of Knowledge—a bill he considered one of his finest pieces of work (Cremin, 1980).

The bill proposed the establishment of **common schools**, tax-supported schools for reading, writing, arithmetic, and history where all boys and girls might attend free for 3 years and pay thereafter. The bill also proposed the establishment of 20 grammar schools for the teaching of Latin and Greek, English grammar, and advanced arithmetic. The brightest students from the lower schools who could not afford to pay tuition would attend these grammar schools at public expense. Others who could afford to pay would do so. From the grammar schools, 10 scholarship students would go on to the College of William and Mary for 3 years at public expense. Through such a system of education, Jefferson believed, society could safeguard liberty. Although successful in establishing a public university, Jefferson did not live to realize his dream of publicly supported schools for Virginia's children (Cremin, 1980, 440–441).

Jefferson's friend, the distinguished scientist and signer of the Declaration of Independence Benjamin Rush was also an advocate for the common school. Like his comrades, Rush knew that a fledgling democracy could not survive, let alone prosper, with an ignorant citizenry. He argued that education should be organized to help prepare people to function effectively in a democratic society, which meant, at least in part, that education should encourage public over private interests. Moreover, education should be uniquely American, that is, practical and forward-looking, particularly in its view of the place of the emerging sciences. If America was to be a beacon of liberty, the nation needed an exemplary education system that would teach the world about freedom and the value of learning (Cremin, 1980).

David Tyack's (1967) observation suggests, however, that Rush's notion of liberty as applied to education was somewhat different from its operational definition today:

> . . . Rush believed that the teacher should be an absolute monarch. "The government of schools . . . should be arbitrary," wrote Rush. "By this mode of education we prepare our youth for the subordination of laws, and thereby qualify them for becoming good citizens of the republic. I am satisfied that the most useful citizens have been formed from those youth who have never known or felt their own wills till they were one and twenty years of age. . . ." (p. 88)

Land-Grant Schools

The Northwest Ordinance of 1785 sliced the Northwest Territories (now the states of Ohio, Indiana, Illinois, Michigan, Wisconsin, and part of Minnesota) into townships of 36 square miles each. As depicted in Figure 2.2, a township provided a section of land to be used for education. This first national education legislation established the precedent for financing education through land grants.

The Ordinance constituted what historians typically recognize as the greatest accomplishment of the government under the Articles of Confederation, or the governing principles established by the Continental Congress that preceded the United States Constitution. In fact, fear stimulated passage of the Ordinance—fear on the part of leaders in the East that those who lived in or moved to the Northwest would be less civilized than people on the coast. The framers of the Ordinance wanted to be certain that residents of the Northwest did not undo democracy from their corner of the country. Education meant socialization.

Early Reforms   As schooling itself became more important, schoolhouses became centers of culture and social activity across the land, particularly in rural areas. Meetings, spelling bees, concerts, and contests brought children and adults together at schools on many evenings. Sometimes they came to attend a lyceum conducted by a traveling speaker.

When the common-school reform program began in the 1830s, the complexion of education in the United States began to change. Reformers pressed for a variety of measures: (a) taxation for public education (Horace Mann embarrassed Massachusetts towns into improving funding for education by publishing an annual list of all towns ranked by per-pupil expenditures); (b) longer school terms; (c) a focus on getting particular groups of nonattenders enrolled in schools, particularly those living in urban slums and factory tenements and the children of free blacks; (d) hierarchical school organizations (e.g., state education agencies headed by a superintendent, schools headed by a "principal teacher", graded schools); (e) consolidation of small school districts into larger-scale school units so per-pupil expenditures would be more uniform from district to district; (f) standardization of educational methods and curriculum; and (g) teacher training (Kaestle, 1983).

1 mile

6	5	4	3	2	1
7	8	9	10	11	12
18	17	16	15	14	13
19	20	21	22	23	24
30	29	28	27	26	25
31	32	33	34	35	36

FIGURE 2.2

Under the Northwest Ordinance of 1785, the sixteenth square mile of a township's land grant was reserved for town-supported education.

The Development of Public Secondary Schools

Primary-school enrollment rates increased over time. In the late eighteenth and early nineteenth centuries, school attendance was higher in rural areas than in the cities. More girls began to go to school, particularly in the Northeast (Kaestle, 1983). Signs of literacy—the number of people able to sign their names and the number of newspaper subscriptions—pointed to rapid societal advancement during this period (Cremin, 1970). Another view, however, suggests that what might appear as "advancement" or progress toward some purposeful end would better be described simply as change—change in terms of upward mobility, the spread of literacy, and the empowerment of citizens to exercise some control over their own destinies. From the seventeenth through the early twentieth century, however, no more than 10% of the eligible school-age children ever went beyond elementary school.

Latin Schools

The **Latin grammar school**, or the first formal type of secondary school in the colonies, was established in Boston in 1635. Boys entered the grammar school at ages 9 or 10, if they could read and write English, and attended for 4 to 5 years. Although Latin grammar schools often offered arithmetic, geography, algebra, trigonometry, or rhetoric, their hallmark was the teaching of Latin and Greek and associated literatures. In other ways, the Latin grammar school was a conceptual leap backward to Europe, where money and social status meant power and privilege. The very few students who prepared to enter college went to these schools. There were no girls allowed.

English Academy   By the middle of the eighteenth century, it was clear that an elementary or basic education of reading, writing, and calculating left people unprepared for the demands of daily life. The country needed more and better-prepared workers. Ben Franklin's response to this challenge was to create an English language academy in Philadelphia in 1749 (Best, 1962). Franklin recognized the need to prepare young people for highly skilled occupations and for the world of commerce. The classics were not neglected entirely, but the **English Academy** emphasized the acquisition and application of practical knowledge thought to be most useful to the modern man.

The school originally taught practical subjects such as penmanship, arithmetic, and bookkeeping. Unlike in the Latin grammar school, English was the language of instruction, but students could study other languages related to their needs. Prospective merchants studied French, Spanish, or German. Prospective clergy studied Latin or Greek. Franklin's Academy also taught many other practical skills, such as farming, carving, shipbuilding, carpentry, and printing.

Public High School   The high school emerged in Boston in the 1820s as yet another alternative to the Latin grammar school and the English academy. It did not, however, become important in American education until the late 1800s, when courts ruled that people could raise taxes to support such schools (Krug, 1964). The high school was a public institution that provided an English or a classical secondary education. Lawrence Cremin (1980) described this early high school as one that "reproduced under public auspices the upper reaches of the academy, making available to day students at modest cost or gratis what had formerly been available to boarding students at more substantial cost" (pp. 389–90).

Henry Barnard did much to promote the concept of the public high school. He argued that primary schools were not up to the task of providing the intellectually rigorous education students needed. He also believed that by reaching out for students over a larger geographical area than did private schools, the high school would better serve the public. The high school "must make a good education common in the highest and best sense of the word common—common because it is good enough for the best, and cheap enough for the poorest family in the community" (Barnard, 1857, p. 185).

The Proliferation of Parochial Schools

Although Protestants were the dominant religious group during colonial times, there was great diversity in religious preferences. Of the 260 churches existing in 1689, there were 71 Anglican, 116 Congregational, 15 Baptist, 17 Dutch Reformed, 15 Presbyterian, 12 French Reformed, 9 Roman Catholic, and 5 Lutheran. There were also loosely organized groups of Quakers, Mennonites, Huguenots, Anabaptists, and Jews (Cremin, 1970). Depending on their religious beliefs, different groups had particular ideas about the education of children and so established **parochial schools**, or private schools with religious affiliations.

German Lutherans, for example, wanted to protect their language and way of life. By 1840, there were more than 200 Lutheran parochial schools in Pennsylvania. In 1856, in return for a rent-free house, firewood, a salary of $12 per month, and extra pay for baptisms and marriages, Lutheran minister Edmond Multanowski preached and taught members of his congregation, 6 hours a day, nearly 11 months a year in Carlinville, Illinois (Cremin, 1980).

The Amish and Mennonites, too, typically educated their own children, holding them out of the common schools. Parents were fearful that outside influences might corrupt their sons and daughters.

In the 1840s, Catholic leaders protested the use of the King James Bible in the common schools. They also fought against the religious and ethnic slurs aimed at Irish Catholics in particular in the common schools. The climate was right for the establishment of their own alternative school system—one that has grown to be the largest alternative to public education in the world. John Hughes, Bishop of New York, admonished his parishioners "to build the schoolhouse first, and the church afterwards" (Lannie, 1968). By 1865, Catholic schools were teaching 16,000 students, or about one third of the Catholic school population, in New York (Dolan, 1985).

If these God-fearing parents—the Catholics, the Lutherans, the Amish, the Mennonites, and others—wanted only to protect their children and their ways of life, the general public wanted that and more. Educational reformers during the 1830s and later viewed parochial schools as the greatest possible threat to democracy. In their minds, "the goals of a common-school system—moral training, discipline, patriotism, mutual understanding, formal equality, and cultural assimilation—could not be achieved if substantial numbers of children were in independent schools" (Kaestle, 1983, p. 116).

The Growth of Institutions of Higher Education

The colonists modeled their new colleges on Oxford and Cambridge. Only 6 years after the Puritans landed in Massachusetts, they founded the college that later assumed the name of its first benefactor, John Harvard (see Figure 2.3).

Harvard students studied the liberal arts and sciences: Latin, Greek, Hebrew, mathematics, logic, rhetoric, astronomy, physics, metaphysics, and philosophy. Prospective ministers prepared for their callings only after they had graduated. The other colonial colleges also promoted the idea that higher education prepared young men for lives of leadership.

Teachers typically did not attend college. Most prepared to learn on the job in schools. They served as apprentices to teachers who had instructed them. Occasionally, they would read a textbook or attend a teachers' institute meant to transmit some new bit of scientific knowledge about teaching and learning. The first of these institutes, established by Henry Barnard at Hartford, Connecticut, in the autumn of 1839, provided 6 weeks of instruction focused on instructional strategies and curriculum to 26 young men (Cremin, 1980; Elsbree, 1939).

Seminaries   Initially, private **seminaries**—academies for girls—were the primary means for advancing the educational skills of future teachers. In 1823, Samuel R. Hall opened a seminary with a model school at Concord, Vermont. That same year, Catherine and Mary Beecher, sisters of Harriet Beecher Stowe, opened a seminary for young women in Hartford, Connecticut, that eventually became the Hartford Female Seminary. They taught grammar, geography, rhetoric, philosophy, chemistry, ancient and modern history, arithmetic, algebra, geometry, theology, and Latin (Cross, 1965). In 1827, James G. Carter, with the help of local citizens, established a teachers' seminary at Lancaster, Massachusetts. At about the same time, James Neef founded the New Harmony Community School in Indiana, where he introduced Pestalozzi's ideas about teaching and learning. As one might expect, these and other private institutions did not have sufficient resources to meet the training needs of teachers across the nation (Elsbree, 1939).

In response to the need for more training programs, state-aided seminaries and academies began to evolve. Often this amounted to existing institutions being supported financially by state monies. Gradually private and semi-private institutions gave way to public normal schools.

Normal Schools

The first normal school (from the French *école normale*) was established at Lexington, Massachusetts, in 1839. **Normal schools** were educational pro-

Founding of the Colonial Colleges	
1636	Harvard
1693	William and Mary
1701	Yale
1746	Princeton
1754	Columbia
1755	Pennsylvania
1766	Brown
1766	Rutgers
1769	Dartmouth

FIGURE 2.3

Founding of the Colonial Colleges

grams dedicated solely to training teachers so that they could perform according to high standards, or "norms." Such institutes had existed in Germany for about 100 years and in France and England since the early 1800s. By 1850, there was a handful of normal schools in the United States, mainly in the Northeast, preparing young women to become teachers. The curriculum consisted of courses in the history and philosophy of education, instructional principles, and teaching methodology, and a period of practice teaching (Elsbree, 1939; Kaestle, 1983).

Land-Grant Colleges   Passed in 1862, the Morrill Act provided federal assistance for the establishment of public colleges of agriculture and the mechanic or industrial arts. The Act granted each state 30,000 acres of public land for each of its congressional representatives. The income from the grant went to support at least one **land-grant college** in the state that was devoted to agricultural and mechanical instruction. The Morrill Act emphasized the importance of applied science and made higher education accessible to millions of people in the years that followed. Like the Northwest Ordinance of 1785, it was also a precursor of federal involvement in education.

Leaders in the Movement for Universal Education

Schools and curriculum came together in a universal tax-supported system of free schools in the 3 decades before the Civil War. The Jeffersonian ideal of **universal schooling**, educating all citizens for the common good, came close to reality in the common schools intended to serve all the children in an area. These were forerunners of town-supported public schools. Some leaders, such as Horace Mann and Henry Barnard, left a lasting imprint on the nation's earliest collective concept of public education.

The primary mission of common schools was to teach reading, writing, and arithmetic to young children of any and all social classes. The schools were to give children the skills they would need to get and hold jobs. Common schools were to inculcate a set of values that guided children to get along with one another and to become good, productive citizens.

Even with the advent of the common school, most people of African, Native-American, and Hispanic descent were denied access to formal education. During this time, however, women became the backbone of the American educational system. First through their own schooling and then by assuming roles as teachers themselves, they capitalized on new and socially acceptable opportunities to assert their independence. Women benefited from the chance to fill jobs men, for a number of reasons related to the expanding economy, no longer wanted.

Horace Mann   As Secretary to the Massachusetts State Board of Education from 1837 to 1848, Horace Mann (1796–1859) aggressively promoted public schools for all children. As mentioned above, Mann believed tax support of education was a key to improving school facilities and equip-

Horace Mann

ment needed for quality education. In his mind, the health of society depended on well-educated citizens and citizens had a right to expect good education supported by public funds.

Mann saw the strength of such an education as its reliance on Protestant values—morality, obedience, discipline, and order. While Mann envisioned a nondenominational type of system, he clearly favored the King James version of the Bible—a preference that would rankle Catholic immigrants as they began to fill the schools in the Northeast (Cremin, 1980).

> "There are thousands of females amongst us, who now spend lives of frivolity, of unbroken wearisomeness and worthlessness, who would rejoice to exchange their days of painful idleness for such ennobling occupations [as teaching] . . . .."

Horace Mann was instrumental in the establishment of public normal schools in Massachusetts. In 1837, he convinced a friend, Edmund Dwight, to contribute $10,000 toward teacher training on the condition that the state would provide matching funds. Largely due to Mann's efforts, the state legislature passed a resolution accepting the proposal and the first public normal school in the United States was opened at Lexington on July 3, 1839 (Elsbree, 1939).

In 1844, Mann (1974) also promoted the idea of encouraging women to become teachers, although he did so with somewhat less than a ringing endorsement of their talents:

> There are thousands of females amongst us, who now spend lives of frivolity, of unbroken wearisomeness and worthlessness, who would rejoice to exchange their days of painful idleness for such ennobling occupations [as teaching]; and who, in addition to the immediate rewards of well-doing, would see, in the distant prospect, the consolations of life well spent, instead of the pangs of remorse for a frivolous and wasted existence. (p. 1317)

Henry Barnard   With Horace Mann, Henry Barnard (1811–1900) was a leading proponent of the common school. A journalist by training, Barnard was secretary of the Connecticut Board of Education (1838–1842), state commissioner of the public schools in Rhode Island (1845–49), chancellor of the University of Wisconsin (1858–60), and U.S. commissioner of education (1867–70). He wrote about public education and European educational reformers such as Pestalozzi and Froebel in the *Connecticut Common School Journal* and the *American Journal of Education.*

Barnard extolled the virtue of teaching civic values and basic skills. But to him, the most important subject was the English language. He recognized the need for strong teacher preparation and for paying people enough to get them into teaching and to keep them there. This meant, of course, that he also perceived the importance of building public support for such actions: "The right beginning of this work of school improvement is in awakening, correcting, and elevating public sentiment in relation to it" (Barnard, 1857).

WHAT CURRICULA AND TEXTBOOKS SHAPED A UNIQUELY AMERICAN EDUCATION?

The curriculum, or what was to be learned, was driven by unswerving interpretations of God's preferences and the three R's. The curriculum remained that way until about 1830, when people began in earnest to reform schools.

One of the more important but less obvious reasons for a curricular focus on this common body of knowledge was books, or more to the point, the lack of books. The Old and New Testaments served as the main reading books in the late eighteenth and early nineteenth centuries. These were valued, of course, but they were also available. Arithmetic students learned from what was around them. Dealing with money, for example, reinforced the importance of numeracy skills. Many children studied the books their families sent to school with them—books that were jealously guarded. Sometimes teachers had to contend with as many different books as they had children in their schools (Kaestle, 1983).

Students learned to read by first learning their ABCs. They moved on to memorizing vowel sounds such as "ab, eb, ib , ob, ub," then one-syllable words, and then longer words and sentences. They practiced on slates and worked their way up to quill pens and copybooks.

Hornbooks, Primers, and Almanacs   The **hornbook** served as the first reader for many students. It was a single piece of parchment imprinted with the alphabet, vowels, syllables, the doctrine of the Trinity, and the Lord's Prayer. To increase its durability, the parchment was covered with a transparent sheet of cow's horn and the two were tacked to a board. The hornbook was eventually replaced with more elaborate "books" of several pages.

The *New England Primer* appeared in the late seventeenth century and was the prototype for **primers**—textbooks designed to impart rudimentary reading skills—used widely in the colonies through the eighteenth century. The *Primer* was a collection of rhymes for the letters of the alphabet, adorned with woodcut drawings. Each rhyme, an admonition or prayer, reflected the religious values of the colonies (Ford, 1899).

Benjamin Franklin left his imprint on the curriculum in the eighteenth century, as he did so often on anything in which he took an interest. His *Poor Richard's Almanack* extolled the virtues of thrift, hard work, and creativity. The *Almanack,* which became a mainstay in the classroom, served as a sort of philosophical touchstone for the self-made colonist.

Physical Education   Some educators recognized the importance of attending to the somatic, or physical, aspects of human development as well. The first physical education programs in the United States evolved during the 1820s. Charles Beck of Round Hill School in Northampton, Massachusetts, is recognized as the first official physical education instructor. He based his educational program on the German gymnastics system for building strength and teaching popular sports and games. During the mid-1800s, Catherine Beecher borrowed concepts from Swedish gymnastics to introduce young ladies to calisthenics in order to contribute to their health, beauty, and strength (Steinhardt, 1992).

Geographies, Spellers, and Dictionaries for Americans

Jedidiah Morse provided an opportunity for children to think about their cultural identity when he produced his *Geography Made Easy* in 1784. The book focused on the geographies of the United States rather than on that of Europe or Britain. Much like Franklin's *Poor Richard's Almanack,* it also contained patriotic and middle-class morality themes.

In the late 1700s and early 1800s, Noah Webster promoted a common English language—one that was uniquely American. Webster's *American Spelling Book,* sometimes referred to as the **Blue-Backed Speller**, was first published in 1783; by 1837 some 15 million copies had been sold. His magnum opus, the *American Dictionary,* first published in 1825, became the authoritative source on information about English words. Webster believed that power and prestige as a nation distinct from Britain would never come to the United States until it established its own distinctive vocabulary, spelling, and usage.

> "He that speaks loud in school will not learn his own book well, nor let the rest learn theirs; but those that make no noise will soon be wise, and gain much love and good will."

McGuffey Readers

William Holmes McGuffey, a clergyman, produced his legendary reader in 1836. It was the most widely used reading

FROM THE NEW ENGLAND PRIMER.

The *New England Primer* reflected the grim Puritan outlook and focus on religion as the point of education. Later early American textbooks reflected the importance of moral character and national pride.

book in America in the nineteenth century. **McGuffey readers** taught literacy skills and sought to advance the Protestant ethic through stories and essays. These writings imparted values of thrift, honesty, and diligence. By including speeches of the nation's founders, McGuffey also used his book to promote patriotic nationalism.

HOW WERE EDUCATIONAL SUCCESS AND FAILURE EVALUATED?

Kaestle (1983) argues that before the Revolution and up until about 1840, local communities viewed their schools as quite successful. Because communities still depended on family and church to teach moral values and on work to train young people for occupations, schools did what they were supposed to do: provide rudimentary education in basic skills at low cost.

School is so much a part of American life today that people must remind themselves of how different things were in earlier times. From the arrival of the colonists until the Civil War, few people went to school. Those who attended public schools got a dose of reading, writing, calculating, and the Protestant ethic, and then went their own way. Most acquired the knowledge necessary to survive and prosper from their families, churches, and work.

When the young Frenchman Alexis de Tocqueville came to America in 1831 to see the new democracy in action, he observed that Americans influenced or taught one another informally and routinely through newspapers and voluntary associations. Tocqueville (1840) believed the press in particular had great educational power:

> Nothing but a newspaper can drop the same thought into a thousand minds at the same moment . . . I shall not deny that in democratic countries newspapers frequently lead the citizens to launch together into very ill-digested schemes; but if there were no newspapers there would be no common activity. The evil which they produce is therefore much less than that which they cure. (p. 116)

The narrowly defined and severely delivered education in early America helped those children who attended, most of whom were white, Protestant, and male, to learn the three Rs and to assimilate Protestant or Catholic values. For other young people—Native Americans, African Americans, immigrants, and those living in poor, rural places—schooling, if it existed at all, was at best a mixed blessing. Public schools saved some from illiteracy but simultaneously reinforced the idea that one's worth was measured in terms of race and social class.

As the nation grew, people debated what it meant to be American. As Riesman (1954) observed, in the early days, the idea of America as the melting pot of nations was valuable. It forced people to think about equality and hospitality to culturally diverse peoples. But the early arrivals to our country narrowed the idea to try to produce a uniform variety of American, "freed of all cultural coloring, maladjustment, or deviation" (p. 60). This trend continued and even accelerated in the early twentieth century.

BENCHMARKS

Historical Foundations of American Education, 1600 to 1865

1519–1540	Spanish conquest of Native-American peoples in Mexico, the Caribbean, Florida, Peru, the American Southwest, and southern California.
1600–1620	Dutch, English, and French settlement of the Atlantic seaboard and exploration of the river systems of North America and Canada.
1619	African slaves brought by Dutch traders to tobacco and sugarcane plantations in the southern colonies and the Caribbean.
1620–1630	Puritans and Pilgrims settle in New England, establishing the pattern of education for the New England and middle colonies.
1635–1636	Latin Grammar school established in Boston as a college preparatory school for young men. Harvard College founded.
1642–1647	Massachusetts Act of 1642 makes citizens responsible for the education of their children and sets a precedent for the development of compulsory education. The Massachusetts Act of 1647, known as the Old Deluder Satan, passed.
1788	U. S. Constitution ratified. The framers of the constitution give the power to establish schools and license teachers to the individual states rather than to the federal government.
1803	Thomas Jefferson doubles the size of the United states with the Louisiana Purchase. During the next 100 years, American go west, building one-room schoolhouses across the country to preserve traditions of education.
1810–1811	The Shawnee under Tecumseh establish a confederacy of tribes to preserve their lands and way of life.
1819	Emma Willard asks the New York legislature to extend educational opportunities to women.
1819	First public high school opened in Boston.
1824	Rensselaer Polytechnic Institute opened in Troy, New York.
1824	Federal government establishes the Bureau of Indian Affairs.
1825	First edition of Noah Webster's *The American Dictionary* published.

1826	Josiah Holbrook founds the American Lyceum movement for adult education.
1827	Massachusetts becomes the first state to require every town with 500 or more families to establish a public high school.
1833	First "penny press," the *New York Sun,* makes newspapers available to most everyone. Popular literature aids the spread of literacy.
1836	First of the McGuffey readers published. About 122 million copies of the series sold after this date.
1836–1837	Wesleyan College in Georgia and Oberlin College in Ohio become the first chartered colleges for women.
1837–1848	Horace Mann, secretary of the Board of Education in Massachusetts, calls for sweeping reforms based on the principle of universal free education for all citizens and the belief that teaching is a profession.
1839	First public normal school (teachers college) in the United States established in Lexington, Massachusetts.
1846–1848	In the Mexican War and annexation of Texas, the United States gains former Spanish territories comparable in size to the Louisiana Purchase.
1848	Education issues aired at the Women's Rights Convention in Seneca Falls, New York.
1852	Harriet Beecher Stowe's *Uncle Tom's Cabin* sells 300,000 copies and wins thousands of converts to the antislavery movement.
1852	Massachusetts enacts the first compulsory school attendance law.
1854	Lincoln University, the nation's first college for free African Americans, established in Pennsylvania.
1855	Henry Barnard founds the *American Journal of Education,* the first educational journal in the United States.
1855	First kindergarten in the United States established by Margaretta Schurtz in Watertown, Wisconsin.

BENCHMARKS

Historical Foundations of American Education, 1600 to 1865 (*cont.*)

1857	The National Education Association (NEA) established as a professional organization for teachers.
1857	In the Dred Scott decision, the U.S. Supreme Court rules that African Americans, free or slave, are not citizens.
1860	Elizabeth Palmer Peabody opens the first English-speaking kindergarten in Boston.
1861–1865	Civil War.
1862	Emancipation Proclamation.
1862	Morrill Land Grant College Act passed.
1863	Elizabeth Peabody and Mary Mann publish the first American textbook on the kindergarten.

Heavy immigration from southern and eastern Europe and growing industrialization helped give rise to what Ezra Pound referred to as the "white alabaster cast," or the cultural mold that was used to produce Americans.

When compared to education in other societies, however, education broadly defined in early America was remarkably successful. The nation's literacy rate climbed, industries flourished, people's standards of living increased, and governments usually changed hands peacefully.

SUMMARY

1. Although colonists were located far from England and Europe, America's formal education system was influenced heavily by European theorists such as Newton, Comenius, Locke, Rousseau, Pestalozzi, Herbart, Froebel, and Spencer.

2. Education both reflected and shaped peoples' values as they established their settlements in the northern, middle, and southern colonies along the eastern coast of America.

3. Most colonists, particularly in the South, were Protestants who believed the Scriptures were key to understanding God's will. To them, education should help save souls.

4. Colonists in the middle colonies were more diverse than settlers in the southern colonies. To preserve their language and beliefs, different groups estab-

lished their own parochial schools.

5. In the New England colonies, the similarity of colonists' ideas and values made possible the establishment of town schools. Many settlers were Puritans who followed the teachings of John Calvin, a Swiss religious reformer.

6. Informal education for all people in early America meant learning from the family and from others in social situations and while at work in apprenticeships. People learned from each other as they interacted face to face. As books and newspapers became available, they also learned from one another by reading.

7. As the country became industrialized and the population grew, the strength and diversity of American beliefs forced new meanings on schooling. Schools began slowly to broaden their focus from serving God, family, and narrowly defined communities to preparing greater numbers and more culturally diverse children for secular lives in the new nation.

8. Religious groups played a major role in extending educational opportunities to oppressed groups, for whom individuals such as Frederick Douglass, Sequoyah, Sor Juana Ines de la Cruz, and Catherine and Mary Beecher, for example, were sources of inspiration.

9. Missionaries, freed blacks, religious groups, and slave owners were also a source of education for slaves. The education of Native and Hispanic Americans took place at home and in mission schools established by priests who wanted to convert students to Catholicism. Until the 1800s, when formal schools were established for women, females were mainly educated at home or in dame schools where they learned a variety of rudimentary skills. Clergymen and physicians, including Braille, Howe, and Gallaudet, developed educational programs for people with disabilities.

10. During colonial times, academic qualifications of teachers, most of whom were men, ranged from bare ability to read and write to the scholarly attainments of a college graduate. Most often, teaching meant making children memorize facts. Teachers relied on whole-group instruction and choral responses in mixed-ability classes. In such settings, harsh corporal punishment was frequently administered.

11. In the 1820s, Joseph Lancaster, a Quaker, introduced the monitorial method of teaching, an educational pyramid scheme in which the master teacher served as a "silent bystander" and instructed monitors who in turn instructed small groups of children.

12. The spread of lyceums, common schools, land-grant colleges, Latin grammar schools, English academies, and high schools expanded formal education at the primary and secondary levels. Private parochial schools attracted many colonists who wanted to preserve their languages and their religious and cultural beliefs. Educational reformers during and after the 1830s viewed such schools as a threat to democracy.

13. Within 6 years after the Puritans landed in Massachusetts they founded the first college (Harvard), and by 1769 eight additional colleges had been established to prepare young men for lives of leadership. The Morrill Act of 1862 expanded educational opportunities even further by providing federal assistance for the establishment of public colleges of agriculture and colleges of mechanical or industrial arts.

14. The common-school reform program that began in the 1830s affected greatly the quality of education in the United States. Henry Barnard and Horace Mann were among those who aggressively promoted public schools for all children. Taxation for public education, longer school terms, and the emergence of teacher training programs were among significant outcomes of reform efforts.

15. The Bible served as the main reading book in the eighteenth and nineteenth centuries. Hornbooks, primers, almanacs such as Franklin's *Poor Richard's Almanack*, geographies, and spellers were also used widely. These texts often contained patriotic and middle-class morality themes.

TERMS AND CONCEPTS

apprenticeships	land-grant college	normal schools
Blue-Backed Speller	Latin grammar school	parochial schools
common schools	lyceum	primers
dame schools	McGuffey readers	seminaries
English academy	mission schools	universal schooling
hidden passage	monitorial method	

STUDENT ACTIVITIES

Perceive and Value

How did each of the following events affect the development of education in the United States?

(a) The establishment of slavery in the southern colonies.

(b) The framing of the U.S. Constitution.

(c) Common-school reforms that began in the 1830s.

Draw conclusions from the following letter written by Reverend Colman to his daughter about the aims of education for women in colonial times:

Boston
August 4, 1718

My Dear Child,

I have this morning your letter, which pleases me very well and gives me hope of many a pleasant line from you in time to come, if God spare you to me, and me to you.

I very much long to see your mother, but doubt whether the weather will permit me today. I pray God to bless you, and make you one of his children. I charge you to pray daily and read your Bible and fear to sin. Be very dutiful to your mother and respectful to everybody....Be very humble and modest, womanly and discreet. Take care of your health, and as you love me do not eat green apples. Drink sparingly of the waters except as the day be warm. When I last saw you, you were too shamefaced; look people on the face, speak freely, and behave decently (Caplan, 1965).

Know and Act

If you and your family had lived around the time of the American Revolution, what education would you likely have received? Would you have attended school? Why or why not? What kind of school might you have attended? What would you likely have studied? How would you have been taught? What would have been the aims of your education? What would you have learned outside school? Write a one page, first-person fictional account of your life as a student and your hopes for the future.

Evaluate

Judgments about the success of education depend on determining what kind of education is meant, for whom it is intended, and for what purposes it is delivered. Using these three criteria as the basis for your responses, express a judgment about the educational success of the following schools:

dame schools	land-grant colleges
English academies	lyceums
Latin grammar schools	mission schools

Discover

Build your knowledge about educational life in early America by reading original documents. You could begin by identifying and scanning the oldest newspapers you can find that were available to people in your geographical area. These constitute one of the best sources of knowledge available about informal education. You could also browse through Sol Cohen's *Education in the United States: A Documentary History*. This five volume set is published by Random House and contains copies of original documents.

This chapter describes education in the United States from 1865 to the present. The chapter provides an historical overview of slavery and the reconstruction of the South after the Civil War, of calls for educational and social reform, of the influences of science, philanthropy, and the mass media on education, and of Federal involvement in schooling.

This chapter also discusses the nature of the various types of people who were teachers and students in this society, drawing attention to similarities and differences among these groups. Also noted are the gradual changes in how schools defined themselves and their missions as their leaders faced the demands of progress in its many forms.

Finally, the chapter discusses the evolution of teaching and curriculum. As curriculum and teaching have changed over this time, so too have society's expectations for educational success.

3

Modern U.S. Education History, 1865 to the Present

PROFESSIONAL PRACTICE QUESTIONS

1 As society became more complex in the post-Civil War era, opportunities for education increased dramatically. What factors influenced Americans' abilities to take advantage of these opportunities?

`Perceive`

2 Why have people continued to place such a high premium on education even when they have found education wanting? As a nation, have we grown to expect too much or too little from public education? Why have people through the years been willing to pay for the privilege of sending their children to private schools?

`Value`

3 How do the goals of public education today compare to those of one or two generations ago? If you had to describe schooling in America to a visitor from another country, what would you say?

`Know`

4 If a wealthy benefactor promised to pay for the private education of your child provided you could supply a defensible rationale, what would you ask for and why?

`Act`

5 How have standards for judging the effectiveness of education changed through the years? How are success and failure measured in today's schools?

`Evaluate`

WHAT CHANGES AFTER THE CIVIL WAR AFFECTED THE AMERICAN SYSTEM OF EDUCATION?

The end of the Civil War left people in the North and South seeking ways to build a nation. Slavery had ended and with it a set of social mores that had governed people's conduct. The nature of the Union was settled, but there was no blueprint for how that Union was to be operationalized in everyday lives. Leaders and ordinary citizens defined education by their actions both inside and outside schools. As illustrated in Figure 3.1, several events and reform efforts changed the nature of American education.

FIGURE 3.1

Some Factors Affecting American Education in the Modern Era

End of Slavery

Constitutional Amendments

Landmark Supreme Court Decisions

Progressive Social & Educational Reforms

Research on Human Behavior, Psychology, & Learning

Professionalization of Teaching

Industrialization & Urbanization

New Immigration & Greater Cultural Diversity

Greater Federal Involvement in Education

Developments in Science & Technology

Philanthropy & the Mass Media

Consolidation & Bureaucratization of Schools

Reconceptualizations of Schooling, e.g.:

Preschools

Middle Schools

Comprehensive High Schools

Adult Education

National & International Events, e.g.:

Great Depression

World Wars

Civil & Equal Rights Movements

Space Race & Cold War

Curriculum Reforms, e.g.:

Standardization

Diversification

Innovation

End of Slavery and Reconstruction of the South

Passion for intellectual freedom and civil liberties widened and deepened after the Civil War. The Thirteenth, Fourteenth, and Fifteenth Amendments to the U.S. Constitution changed race relations legally by ending slavery, defining citizenship, and forbidding states to deny the right to vote, but the customs of segregation and discrimination remained entrenched. Northerners moved to reconstruct the South, often by trying to reeducate the vanquished. Not surprisingly, southerners detested and resisted these actions.

The Bureau of Refugees, Freedmen, and Abandoned Lands, commonly known as the **Freedman's Bureau**, established 1 month before the end of the war, provided food, medicine, and seed to destitute southerners. The Bureau secured legal rights for freed slaves and extended educational opportunities to them. Hundreds of northern teachers went south to teach African-American children and adults. Despite opposition, the Freedman's Bureau succeeded in establishing and operating more than 4,000 primary schools, 74 normal schools, and 61 industrial schools for former slaves and, in so doing, strengthened the role of the federal government in education (Degler, 1959).

Anxious to keep "Negroes" in an inferior position, southerners constructed the so-called **black codes** of conduct. These codes, or "halfway stations back to slavery," allowed African Americans to hold property, to sue and be sued, and to marry, but forbade them to carry firearms, to testify in court in cases involving European Americans, and to leave their jobs (Degler, 1959, p. 211).

The end of the Civil War did not end violence toward African Americans. Although precise numbers are impossible to determine, between the end of the war and 1900, there were approximately 2,500 known lynchings, mainly of African Americans. Between 1900 and World War I, more than 1,100 African Americans are known to have been lynched—mostly in the South but also in some midwestern states (Franklin, 1967). As late as in 1933, 28 people were lynched, including 24 African Americans. Although rare, lynchings continued into the 1950s. In 1934, the **National Association for the Advancement of Colored People (NAACP)**, the first nationwide special interest group for African Americans, lobbied for the Costigan-Wagner antilynching bill, which failed. Antilynching bills failed to pass throughout the Roosevelt and Truman administrations.

Calls for Educational and Social Reform

The push for universal education that began in the 1830s and 1840s gained momentum as the country moved toward the twentieth century. Many intellectuals and citizens tried to combat racial, ethnic, and gender discrimination wherever they existed, including in schools. In the main, however, schools tended to sort by social class, race, and gender, thereby reinforcing stereotypes.

Largely as a result of pressure from the National Teachers Association, organized in 1857, Congress created a Department of Education in 1867. President Andrew Johnson appointed Henry Barnard to assume the position of commissioner of education and to run the department. The commissioner collected statistics and facts on education and tried to promote the cause of education throughout the country.

By the beginning of the twentieth century, critics initiated what was to become a sustained attack on public schools, particularly in the cities. Social reformers, sometimes called "muckrakers," bemoaned what they saw as mechanical teaching and learning, administrative ineptitude, and lack of parent interest in their children's welfare. Joseph Mayer Rice (1893), for instance, thought the environment of the New York City schools was nothing short of pernicious:

It is indeed incomprehensible that so many loving mothers whose greatest care appears to be the welfare of their children are willing, without hesitation, to resign the fate of their little ones to the tender mercies of ward politicians, who in many instances have no scruples in placing the children in class-rooms the atmosphere of which is not fit for human beings to breathe, and in charge of teachers who treat them with a degree of severity that borders on barbarism. (pp. 10–11).

Leonard Ayres's *Laggards in Our Schools* (1909) presented what he claimed was scientific evidence that the schools were filled with retarded children, or children who were overage for their grade. He blamed this consequence on the schools for creating programs for unusually bright children and ignoring the slow or average children.

In the early twentieth century, many problems played themselves out in schools: an antievolution crusade, antiimmigration movements, organized campaigns against Roman Catholics, and increases in antisemitism, to mention but a few. Urban poverty and the exploitation of children as cheap labor in the rapidly expanding industrial economy fueled both the development of public schools and the organization of American labor; that is, schools protected children and prepared them for work later in life. In doing so, schools kept children out of the labor market, thus protecting jobs for adults.

Influence of Science and Philanthropy

Education reformers in the early twentieth century placed their faith in science to solve education and social problems. Science had propelled the nation to preeminence in business and industry so why not in education? Frederick Taylor's studies on scientific management, or a system for getting greater productivity from human labor, appealed to businessmen who ran the school boards who hired the superintendents who ran the schools (Callahan, 1962). Spurred on by grants from private foundations, leaders in school administration—including Elwood Cubberley, Frank Spaulding, and George Strayer—encouraged educational specialization and scientific management (Tyack & Hansot, 1982).

The seeds of basic research on teaching and learning also began to take root in American schools at the turn of the century. James Cattell introduced "mental tests" to assess individual differences and encouraged counseling agencies and schools to incorporate such measures as part of their routine procedures. The work of Alfred Binet, Lewis Terman, and later Edward L. Thorndike on the measurement of intelligence was hailed as a great practical advance for schools (Travers, 1983). Psychologist Charles Judd emphasized the importance of viewing teaching and learning as social constructs, that is, as ideas that derive meaning from their use in everyday life. In contrast, John Watson's view of behavior and learning as mechanical phenomena—elements to be manipulated continually by an outside source—prompted a revolution in the way people thought about human behavior. Although strikingly different in philosophical persuasions, these researchers shared a belief in the power of science to improve the human condition.

If, as Walter Lippman argued in the popular press, science was our best weapon against ignorance, others recognized that there was money to be made from applying science to teaching and learning. Survey research and personality assessment centers sprang up in business and industry in the 1930s and 1940s and did much to shape the thinking of adults about what counted in life. For instance, Dale Carnegie (1936) reported that,

> Investigation and research uncovered a most important and significant fact . . . about 15 percent of one's financial success is due to one's technical knowledge and about 85 percent is due to skill in human engineering—to personality and the ability to lead people. (p. 16)

He used this dubious claim to build a case for teaching others how to win friends and influence people. Carnegie sold about 1 million copies of his book in its first 2 years of publication.

From the late nineteenth century on, schools were embedded in a society that demonstrated in many ways the increasing value of education. In the 1870s, fine-art museums first opened—the Metropolitan Museum of Art in New York and the Museum of Fine Arts in Boston. The Library of Congress opened its Jefferson Building in 1897, permitting wide public access to its collection (Cole, 1979). By 1900, there were more than 45 million volumes housed in the more than 9,000 public libraries sited across the country (Blum et al., 1989). Philanthropists such as Andrew Carnegie and Andrew Mellon gave money for promoting public access to books and art and for establishing foundations.

At the turn of the twentieth century, southern educators, ministers, and political leaders joined forces with northern capitalists and philanthropists to upgrade educational conditions in the South. Funding for the Southern Education Board (SEB), a philanthropic agency, was provided by such northern capitalists as merchant Robert Ogden, railroad man William Baldwin, and Standard Oil's John D. Rockefeller.

Influence of the Mass Media

The press grew ever more powerful as an instrument of social education in the twentieth century. Newspapers and magazines no longer served only the educated middle and upper classes: They now catered to the masses. The sensationalism of the "yellow press" of New York City—so called because the front pages of special editions were printed on yellow paper to catch people's eyes—led by William Randolph Hearst and Joseph Pulitzer, shaped American opinion on many matters, including but not limited to its views of foreigners.

In the 15 years preceding the turn of the century, the number of periodicals published increased by 2200. Many focused on trades and special interests, but many more were written for the general public. By 1905, there were twenty 10¢ monthlies having a combined circulation of 5.5 million (Blum et al., 1989). From 1920 to 1940, newspapers and magazines "continued to rival schools and churches as the chief instruments of mass education and the dissemination of ideas" (Link & Catton, 1963, p. 295).

By 1930, Americans were experiencing the throes of an economic depression. At the same time, new communications technology was fast becoming a part of daily life. Motion picture theaters were spread across the country. There were about 23,000 theaters with a combined seating capacity of more than 11 million (Link & Catton, 1963). The entertainment value of the big screen was apparent immediately—the lure of escaping everyday troubles was too powerful to ignore. The more subtle educational influences of the movies—their power to compose the texts by which people lived or wished to live—would become an enduring national issue.

Radio captured the collective imagination of Americans in the 1920s, 1930s, and 1940s. The first broadcast was made in 1920. By 1922, there were 220 radio stations, and, by 1923, there were some 2.5 million sets in the country. Approximately 80% of American families had radios in their homes by 1937 (Link & Catton, 1963). It was almost as if the entrepreneurial spirit that Thomas Alva Edison had established so boldly in the late nineteenth and early twentieth centuries had come alive for everyone who could turn the knob on a set.

Radio, like television after it, educated Americans about culture like no other technological innovation or school system had done before. David Halberstam (1979) writes that:

> Millions of Americans had made radio the focal point of their households, scheduling their day around their favorite programs. When "Amos 'n' Andy" was on the air, the nation simply stopped all its other business and listened. When Pepsodent sponsored "Amos 'n' Andy" its sales tripled in just a few weeks. . . . by 1931 the American Tobacco Company spent $19 million to advertise Lucky Strike on radio. (p. 15)

While radio educated by delivering live voices of famous people into listeners' homes, television added images to those voices. The educational effects of seeing and hearing things that people discussed in school were both profound and trivial and eventually almost constant. By January 1960, there were television sets in 9 out of 10 homes competing with, contradicting, and complementing other sources of information, including teachers and parents. Today, children ages 2 to 17 watch television between 3 and 4 hours a day (Television Bureau of Advertising, 1989). By high school graduation, they have spent more hours watching television than in the classroom.

As a nation, our collective memory is branded with television images of events teachers talked about in schools: of Americans being cross-examined as Communist sympathizers during the "red scare," of a cold war that divided the German city of Berlin with a wall, of children entering segregated schools under police protection, of Neil

Our Miss Brooks and Mr. Conklin

Armstrong setting foot on the moon, of the bodies of young soldiers being dragged out of Southeast Asian jungles and shipped home halfway around the world, of communism and the Berlin wall crumbling, and of Our Miss Brooks outsmarting her stodgy principal, Mr. Conklin. In its own amoral way, television, probably more than any other phenomenon, has educated us while simultaneously reinforcing our ignorance.

Impact of Changes in Federal Involvement

Direct federal involvement in education increased after the 1950s, when the Supreme Court ruled that school racial segregation was unconstitutional. Schools became front-page news in the 1960s as battlegrounds in the War on Poverty, desegregation, and the quest for racial equality. The federal government exerted its influence with money, legislation, and exhortation in many arenas: desegregation, aid to schools serving poor children, legislation guaranteeing racial and sexual equity, new entitlements for students with disabilities, bilingual-bicultural programs, and career education. The compensatory and early intervention programs emanating from Washington, D.C., were aimed at meeting the basic needs of children living in poverty. The most dramatic example of federal involvement was the Elementary and Secondary Education Act (ESEA) of 1965. The ESEA changed the center of policy-making power from states and localities to the federal level. The Act provided funds to alleviate the effects of poverty through a variety of programs. It supported school libraries, the purchase of textbooks and other instructional materials, guidance, counseling, and health services, and remedial instruction. It also established research centers and laboratories to advance educational practice. Changes in how Americans viewed schooling during this period were also shaped in large measure by the civil rights movement—the nonviolent and sometimes violent actions of disenfranchised citizens aimed at gaining access to mainstream American society.

The New Federalism of the 1980s returned to states and localities both the power and financial responsibility for educational programs. As federal support for education shrank in terms of real dollars, the rhetoric of educational reform increased. National, state, and local commissions and task forces issued a spate of reports that called for changes in everything from how public schools are organized and schoolbooks are written to how teachers and students are taught and tested. Joseph Murphy (1990) described these reforms in terms of three conceptual thrusts concerned with: raising performance standards for students and teachers, decentralizing school management, and providing aid such as preschool and nutrition programs to children in poverty areas.

WHO ARE "WE THE PEOPLE"?

Concepts of federalism, or the defining attributes of American unity, have grown richer and more plentiful through the years. America is one nation out of many peoples—*e pluribus unum*. The American people are similar because we are different (Fuchs, 1990). Nearly one in four Americans in the United States is a member of an ethnic or racial minority group.

After the Civil War, the population of the United States grew rapidly, most noticeably in the cities and industrialized areas. In the 1890s, about 30% of the population of 63 million lived in cities; by 1988, three fourths of the country's 245 million people lived in urban areas (U.S. Bureau of the Census, 1990). Although the population of the United States tripled between 1859 and 1914, the number of workers in manufacturing increased 6.5 times. (U.S. Bureau of the Census, 1975).

In 1910, about one half of men and women in the labor force lived in poverty. They worked long hours for meager wages and their children often left school to work in factories. Only one third of the children enrolled in primary schools finished; less than one 10th finished high school. Jacob Riis, a photographer who had an agenda for social reform, found poverty and ignorance wherever he pointed his camera. In one large New York City East Side tenement building reported to house 478 tenants, Riis (1890) wrote, the truant officer could find only 7 children who said they attended school: "The rest gathered all the instruction they received running for beer for their elders" (p. 180).

Young social workers, nearly all of them women, took active roles in improving the deplorable living and working conditions of the poor. Some of these individuals ran charity nurseries, such as New York's Five Points Mission and the Five Points House of Industry. By 1890, it was estimated that 60,000 children had received assistance from these two institutions alone (Riis, 1890).

Other agents of change investigated sweatshops and tenements and lived in **settlement houses** established in poor neighborhoods to help immigrants adjust to life in a new country. The first of these houses was established in 1886 in New York. By 1900, there were 100 such houses. This figure had climbed to 200 by 1905, and doubled again by 1910 (Carlson, 1975). Jane Addams's Hull House in Chicago was among the notable, with its own education program that included playgrounds, a nursery, and a library.

Life was difficult in the rural areas as well, particularly where the tenant farmer population was large. The census of 1930 indicated that tenants comprised 64% of the population in Alabama and 66% in Georgia (Dabney, 1969). James Agee's account of the lives of three tenant farm families in Alabama, accompanied by Walker Evans's photographs, created a classic documentation of the period. Agee (1960) described the families' educational needs:

> They learn the work they will spend their lives doing, chiefly of their parents, and from their parents and from the immediate world they take their conduct, their morality, and their mental and emotional and spiritual key. One could hardly say that any further knowledge or consciousness is at all to their use or advantage, since there is nothing to read, no reason to write, and no recourse against being cheated even if one is able to do sums . . . (p. 268)

Cultural Awareness

Jacob Riis's 1890 photograph (left) shows people crowded into an urban slum in New York City. Walker Evans's 1930 photograph (right) shows children from rural tenant farm families in Alabama. Conditions for many African-American children were as difficult or worse.

As the twentieth century wore on, social scientists and reformers talked about discovering a culture—a way of life shared by many old and young, urban and rural, European and non-European Americans. They called it the culture of poverty.

Native Americans

After the Civil War, military supremacy, the destruction of the buffalo, the expansion of railroads, confinement on reservations, and efforts to encourage individual rather than tribal ownership of land did much to erode the traditional cultures of Native Americans. As Helen Hunt Jackson noted, the official abuse and neglect of Native Americans shaped a *Century of Dishonor*. Writing in the late nineteenth century, Jackson (1880/1977) estimated that there were 250,000 to 300,000 Native Americans in the United States, excluding those in Alaska:

> There is not among these . . . one which has not suffered cruelly at the hands either of the Government or of white settlers. The poorer, the more insignificant, the more helpless the band, the more certain the cruelty and outrage to which they have been subjected...There are hundreds of pages of unimpeachable testimony on the side of the Indian; but it goes for nothing, is set down as sentimentalism or partisanship, tossed aside and forgotten. (pp. 337–338)

Government efforts to educate Native Americans were administered through the **Bureau of Indian Affairs (BIA)**. Off-reservation boarding schools were meant to insure Native American survival, but were also instrumental in their destruction. These federal boarding schools took children away from their families and attempted—by way of food, dress, regimented schedules, religion, and job and language training—to impose on them the values and customs of the dominant European-American culture. Students were compelled to learn English and to "breathe the atmosphere of a civilized instead of a barbarous or semi-barbarous community" (U.S. Bureau of Indian Affairs, 1974, p. 1756). One such school, the Carlisle Indian School, established in 1879 by a young army officer named Richard Henry Pratt, educated approximately 4,000 children over a period of 24 years.

Boarding schools immersed Native-American youngsters in the ways of a culture totally foreign to them.

> The first thing to do was to clean them thoroughly and to dress them in their new [military] attire. . . . [then] everything except swallowing, walking, and sleeping had to be taught; the care of person, clothing, furniture, the usages of the table, the carriage of the body, civility, all those things which white children usually learn from their childhood by mere imitation, had to be painfully inculcated and strenuously insisted on. In addition to this, they were to be taught the rudiments of an English school course and the practical use of tools. (U.S. Bureau of Indian Affairs, 1974, p. 1749)

Reservation schools had similar aims, which many Native Americans of the time accepted as valid. In the late nineteenth century, Princess Sara Winnemucca founded a school in California for Piute children. She taught them to spell, read, write, and calculate in English. She also taught drawing and sewing. The parents were sorry they could not pay to have their children board at the school in the summer, because the children were so much happier than when they attended the reservation's government school (Peabody, 1886).

The Dawes Act of 1887 undermined tribal authority by breaking up reservation land into smaller parcels and allotting them to individual Native Americans. These land allotments—most unsuitable for farming, particularly by people who had not been farmers—were initially held in trust and later transferred to individuals. Four out of five individuals were bilked of their property or lost it in other ways (Blum et al., 1989).

Some historians have marked the conclusion of the Indian Wars at 1890 with the massacre at Wounded Knee, South Dakota. Among the Sioux, there had a been a revival of ghost dancing

Indian Boarding Schools were conceived as a humanitarian way to help Native American children assimilate, but they often imposed cruel hardships. Students were expected to reject and despise their identities as Indians, their families, and their way of life.

VOICES

On Assimilation

In the late 1800s, the responses of Native-American peoples to schooling on federally administered reservations varied widely. Some resisted, but many had come to believe—and were supported in that belief—that the dominant European-American culture was superior to their own. In a letter to the school trustees of Inyo and to Dr. Lyman Abbot, editor of the *Christian Union*, Sarah Winnemucca appealed to Piutes to send their children to school to address the need for self-determination in the face of perceived cultural inadequacy:

Hearing that you are about to start a school to educate your children, I want to say a word about it. You all know me; many of you are my aunts or cousins. We are of one race,—your blood is my blood,—so I speak to you for your good. I can speak five tongues,—three Indian tongues, English, and Spanish. I can read and write, and am a school teacher. Now, I do not say this to boast, but simply to show you what can be done. When I was a little girl, there were no Indian schools; I learned under great difficulty. Your children can learn much more than I know, and much easier; and it is your duty to see that they go to school. There is no excuse for ignorance. Schools are being built here and there, and you can have as many as you need; all they ask you to do is send your children. You are not asked to give money or horses—only to send your children to school. The teacher will do the rest. He or she will fit your little ones for the battle of life, so that they can attend to their own affairs instead of having to call in a white man. A few years ago you owned this great country; today the white man owns it all, and you own nothing. Do you know what did it? Education. You see the miles and miles of railroad, the locomotive, the Mint in Carson, where they make money. Education has done it all.

CRITICAL THINKING

Winnemucca's letter contains six arguments for education. What are they? Why might Piutes have rejected the idea of formal schooling? What assumptions does the letter reveal about the power of education to change people's lives? How might Native Americans respond today to the viewpoint the letter expresses?

Source: Peabody, E.P. (1886). *Sara Winnemucca's practical solution of the Indian problems: A letter to Dr. Lyman Abbot of the "Christian Union"*. Cambridge, MA: John Wilson and Son, pp. 5–6.

(collective dancing that was supposed to bring back to life all the dead warriors and kin and all the dead buffalo and wild horses). Viewing these dances as a sign of resistance, the Army was ordered to arrest and imprison any fomenters of disturbances. On December 15, a Native American policeman killed Chief Sitting Bull and on the 29th, the cavalry surrounded Chief Big Foot at Wounded Knee Creek and slaughtered between 150 and 300 Sioux men, women, and children. All openly hostile Native-American resistance was crushed.

Native Americans were not considered citizens of the United States until passage of the Citizenship Act of 1924. At about the same time, the Meriam Report—a study conducted by the Brookings Institute—revealed the poor condition of education programs provided by the Education Division of the Bureau of Indian Affairs.

The 1930s and early 1940s were a period of gain for Native Americans. John Collier, commissioner of Indian affairs for Franklin Roosevelt, began to encourage preservation of Native American culture by permitting reservation schools to offer instruction in Native-American languages and culture. Collier also promoted the idea of local self-government, hired Native Americans in his agency, and channeled millions of dollars into improving Native-American lands. Passage of the Indian Reorganization Act of 1934 returned self-government to Native Americans, eliminated allotment policies that had reduced tribal land holdings, and prompted the study of ways to improve the poor economic, health, and social conditions of Native Americans.

Coinciding with the onset of World War II, reduced funding for educational programs and a resurgence of assimilationist policies had a deleterious effect on the struggle for Native-American autonomy. The National Congress of American Indians, founded during the war, was aggressive in its efforts to improve the lot of Native Americans. The American Indian Movement of 1968—composed mostly of militant urban Native Americans—resorted to violence. As Native Americans continued to press their case, Congress reversed its decision to terminate federal reservations and in 1975 passed the **Indian Self-Determination and Educational Assistance Act**.

Native-American cultures are tremendously diverse. As a group, however, Native Americans are statistically trailing others in terms of income, life expectancy, and level of education. Unemployment is much greater than that for the total population and poverty is rampant—particularly among widowed, divorced, and aged women (Goodman, 1985).

European Americans

After the Civil War, the population of the United States grew increasingly heterogeneous due to immigration. From 1880 to 1924, the majority of immigrants came from southern, central, and eastern Europe. Many settled in American cities and took jobs in industry. In Chicago in 1910, for example, 75% of the residents were immigrants or the children of immigrants (Cremin, 1988). In the 1930s and 1940s, people from northwestern and central Europe fled the totalitarian regimes of Italy and Germany for the freedom and safety of the United States, and after them in the 1950s followed survivors of the Holocaust. The impact of new immigration on education was twofold: schools were required to provide basic education to more people and to socialize these new arrivals to American ways. **Assimilation**, therefore, became a major goal of education.

> **"Give me your tired, your poor, Your huddled masses yearning to breathe free . . . ."**

As the population increased, then, it also diversified by religion and ethnicity. Differences in language and culture among the new arrivals, and between the immigrants and native-born Americans, made assimilation slow, difficult, and sometimes seemingly impossible.

From 1892 to 1954, some 12 million immigrants from many middle and eastern European countries entered America under the gaze of the Statue of Liberty in New York harbor. Emma Lazarus's (1883) poem "The New Colossus," inscribed at the base of the statue, welcomed all who arrived:

> Give me your tired, your poor,
> Your huddled masses yearning to breathe free,
> The wretched refuse of your teeming shore.
> Send these, the homeless, tempest-tost to me,
> I lift my lamp beside the golden door.

Lazarus's belief in the power of religious and ethnic tolerance, shaped in part by her own Jewish heritage, did not, however, convey the nation's long-standing ambivalence between accepting and rejecting foreign nationals. Many new immigrants met with the hostility of those who had preceded them. Nativism—formal policies and informal actions designed to favor the existing culture in opposition to immigrants—flourished. For example, a committee of the Fiftieth Congress appointed to investigate immigration viewed many immigrants with disdain:

> They are of a very low order of intelligence. They do not come here with the intention of becoming citizens; their whole purpose being to accumulate by parsimonious, rigid, and unhealthy economy a sum of money and then return to their native land. They live in miserable sheds like beasts; the food they eat is so meager, scant, unwholesome, and revolting that it would nauseate and disgust an American workman, and he should find it difficult to sustain life upon it. Their habits are vicious, their customs are disgusting, and the effect of their presence here upon our social condition is to be deplored. (Lodge, 1891, p. 33)

Although many immigrants have retained their ethnic identities through the years, many others have willingly and unwillingly shed these identities. Based on a carefully selected sample of 524 households, Richard Alba (1991) found almost no ethnics were fluent in the language of their group. About 2% had ever received help in business endeavors from other members of their group. Only 2% were members of ethnic social clubs, while 1% ate ethnic foods daily, and 11% lived in neighborhoods having concentrations of their own ethnic group.

African Americans

After the Civil War, African Americans began to take advantage of the citizenship they had gained via the Fourteenth Amendment by participating more fully in society, including attending public schools. In 1860, less than 2% of all school-age African-American children were enrolled in school; by 1900 the figure had risen to 31%. Furthermore, illiteracy dropped from 82% in 1870 to 45% in 1900 (U.S. Bureau of the Census, 1990). As noted earlier, this progress was due in no small measure to the work of the Freedman's Bureau.

Emancipated slaves and European Americans established Sunday schools and universal public education during Reconstruction. Churches and ministers in African-American communities often formed the nucleus

Booker T. Washington

from which such campaigns spread. By 1868, the African Methodist Episcopal Church had already enrolled 40,000 pupils in Sabbath Schools; by 1885, there were 200,000. African-American teachers offered almost all the instruction. At its height, the Freedman's Bureau operated over 4,000 primary schools, 74 normal schools, and 61 industrial schools for African Americans. Northern European Americans who tried to teach in such schools were sometimes subject to violent attacks by European American southerners (Degler, 1959), yet thousands of "Yankee school marms" ventured south to teach in needy established schools for African Americans.

Booker T. Washington was among the many African Americans who flocked to normal schools to gain an education that would enable them to be effective leaders of their people. Washington became a teacher in 1875 and a teaching assistant at Hampton Normal and Agricultural Institute in Virginia. In 1881, he went to Macon County, Alabama, to become principal of the newly created state normal school for African Americans in the town of Tuskegee.

> **"Mental development is a good thing. Gold is also a good thing, but gold is worthless without an opportunity to make itself touch the world of trade."**

Through Washington's leadership, the Tuskegee Institute became a national model for educating African-American teachers, farmers, and industrial workers. Washington believed that vocational or industrial education was the best way for African Americans to gain financial self-sufficiency and better their lives. According to Washington (1907):

> Mental development is a good thing. Gold is also a good thing, but gold is worthless without an opportunity to make itself touch the world of trade. (p. 77)

The development of Washington's ideas about the need for practical rather than academic education is evident in his autobiography, *Up From Slavery*. In response to his own times and experiences, he discouraged African Americans from seeking education as lawyers, doctors, or politicians. He believed that achieving respectability as a trained worker contributing to the economy was the key to advancement, not upsetting the social order. Washington was working in a time when African Americans were perceived as inferior in ability, and an educated African-American citizenry was perceived as a potential threat to white supremacy.

An opposite view was taken by Washington's severest critic, W.E.B. Du Bois—an African-American sociologist with a PhD from Harvard. Du Bois (1904) argued that African Americans would never achieve civil and political equality with industrial education alone and instead advocated a more academic approach to "train the best of the Negro youth as teachers, professional men, and leaders" (p. 240).

Du Bois advocated political activism and challenged the ideas of both African and European Americans, helping to found the civil rights movement that continued through the 1970s. As editor of *The Crisis,* the journal of the National Association for the Advancement of Colored People, Du

Bois helped formulate the educational policy of that body, which was that all American children and youth should have equal opportunity to an education.

Individuals such as Mary McLeod Bethune were also instrumental in pushing education. Bethune believed, as did other African-American leaders of the time, that education was the means to better lives for her people. As an educator concerned with practical training for upward mobility and as a political activist, Bethune may be seen as representing a combination of the views of Booker T. Washington and W.E.B. Du Bois.

Mary McLeod Bethune

In 1904, Bethune founded the Daytona Normal and Industrial School for Training Negro Girls, which was expanded in 1923 to become Bethune-Cookman College. During the Depression and World War II eras, she served in the administrations of Franklin Roosevelt and Harry Truman as director of the National Youth Administration and advisor to the United Nations.

The efforts of leaders such as Du Bois and Bethune gave rise to the Civil Rights Movement that grew over the next 50 years and beyond, for in the early twentieth century, despite the efforts of the new leadership, education did little to improve economic opportunities or to create political and social equality. Because of segregated housing and voting districts, schools for African Americans and schools for European Americans were funded from separate tax bases, and African Americans' comparative poverty (on average) meant that their schools were usually underfunded.

In 1896, in *Plessy v. Ferguson*, the Supreme Court ruled that public facilities for European and African Americans could be separate but equal, which served to legalize school segregation. By 1917, the discrepancy in financial resources for European-American and African-American schools had jumped to four:one in favor of European Americans. In some rural areas, schools for European Americans received 15 times more support. In Georgia in 1928–1929, for example, 99% of the money budgeted for teaching equipment went to European-American schools even though African Americans composed 34% of the population (Bond, 1934).

By 1900, African Americans outnumbered European Americans in several southern cities, including Charleston, South Carolina, Savannah, Georgia, and Shreveport, Louisiana. They had few opportunities for employment. Jim Crow—the colloquial name for laws and customs supporting racial segregation—sharply restricted opportunities.

In the South in the 1890s, salaries of all teachers were pitifully low. But by 1907 in Alabama, for example, European-American teachers were allotted roughly five times more money than African-American teachers. Patterns of financial support like this held for years because Jim Crow laws had disenfranchised African Americans, preventing them from fighting inequality at the ballot box.

At the same time, southern states spent an average of $9.72 per pupil in 1900 compared to $20.80 per pupil in the north-central states. Publicists such as Walter Hines Page admonished southerners for such inequities and urged citizens to support increases in state and local taxes to narrow the gap between educational conditions for European Americans and African Americans. Political leaders and members of philanthropic organizations such as the Southern Education Board also lobbied for better funding of schools. Although such efforts did not equalize funding for schools, between 1902 and 1910 appropriations for schools in the South doubled, enrollment of European American students increased by almost a third, and school terms increased from 5 to 6 months. Illiteracy among European Americans declined from 11.8% in 1900 to about 5.5% in 1920; during the same time period, illiteracy among African Americans 10 years of age or older declined 44.5% to about 22.9% (Link & Catton, 1963).

Poverty forced many African Americans to live in squalor. As industrialization advanced in the post-Civil War period, many African Americans migrated northward hoping to find work and to avoid what they perceived as a trend toward economic reenslavement in the South. For instance, after the Civil War, around 6,000 freed slaves left Louisiana, Mississippi, and Texas for Kansas in what was called the "Kansas Fever Exodus." These "exodusters" and other African Americans leaving the South prized education and sought educational opportunities as well as land in Kansas, in the West, and in northern cities (Painter, 1977).

Despite hardships, freedom in northern cities brought a burst of creativity. In New York City following World War I, a group of African-American writers, artists, jazz and blues musicians, and performers shaped what became known as the Harlem Renaissance, a period of artistic expression that celebrated African-American culture and protested against social and economic injustices. Among the leading writers were James Weldon Johnson, Countee Cullen, and Langston Hughes.

African Americans continued to struggle for equality and were heard. President Harry Truman acted to integrate the armed forces in 1948 and 1949. Many members of minority groups capitalized on their opportunities to go to college paid for by the G.I. Bill. Thurgood Marshall of the NAACP argued constitutional cases, including the landmark *Brown v. Board of Education of Topeka, Kansas* in 1954. In **Brown v. Board of Education**, the Supreme Court ruled that segregation of students by race is unconstitutional and that education is a right that must be available to all Americans on equal terms.

Martin Luther King, Jr., taught civil disobedience through nonviolent protest to win civil rights. King was awarded the Nobel peace prize in 1964, just 4 years before he was assassinated. Malcolm X, at first affiliated with the Nation of Islam, which advocated racial separatism, later rejected this idea and worked a brief time before his assassination in 1965 to promote unity among the races.

Because of these and other developments, the economic, political, social, and educational conditions of African Americans have improved over the years. Although the physical separation of African-American students is not legally sanctioned today as it was before *Brown v. Board of Education*, some argue that the public schools are being resegregated by economic and demographic factors, particularly in America's cities (Bates, 1990). In Detroit's schools, between 1975 and 1984, for example, African-American enrollment increased from 71% to about 90% (Harris, 1984). In 1979, Linda Brown-Smith, who was 5 years old when her father filed the historic *Brown* case on her behalf, went back to court on behalf of her own child to charge that the Topeka, Kansas, public schools remained segregated—a consequence that years of forced busing to promote integration has not cured, as we shall suggest again in Chapter 7 ("Cultural Diversity").

Today, many African Americans still remain at the lower end of the economic scale, have more health problems, have a shorter life expectancy, and are statistically more prone than European Americans to youth unemployment, teenage pregnancy, drug use, and violence. And, although the college-going rates of African Americans are increasing after a low between 1977 and 1983, the percentage of high school graduates enrolling in college has consistently remained lower than that for European Americans. In 1988, 49.7% of African-American students enrolled as opposed to 59.2% of European-American students (U.S. Department of Education, 1991).

Access to education, natural abilities, and new opportunities in society have produced a new generation of African-American leaders. Andrew Young served as ambassador from the United States to the United Nations. Patricia Harris served as a U.S. cabinet member. Shirley Chisholm served seven terms in the United States House of Representatives. Guion S. Bluford was selected as an astronaut. Colin Powell served as chairman of the Joint Chiefs of Staff. Douglas Wilder served as governor of Virginia.

Hispanic Americans

Hispanic Americans constitute the fastest growing ethnic group in America. The term **Hispanic** means having Spanish colonial origins or being Spanish-speaking. Hispanics include people of Native-American, African, and European descent. People from Puerto Rico, Cuba, Central and South America, and Mexico have come to the United States to work and in some cases to find a haven from war and political repression.

Some groups in the American Southwest prefer the name Latino (feminine: Latina) or Chicano (feminine: Chicana) to Hispanic, which originally described immigrants to urban areas of the eastern United States. Most Cubans arrived in the United States as political refugees after Fidel Castro overthrew the Cuban dictatorship of Fulgencio Batista in 1959. Puerto Ricans, on the other hand, have migrated freely between the United States and Puerto Rico since 1917, when Puerto Rico became a possession of the United States with commonwealth status and its citizens became U.S. citizens. As pointed out in Chapter 2, Mexican Americans were absorbed into the United States through conquest and later through annexation of their lands. For decades, Mexican nationals have attempted border crossings to the more affluent United States in search of economic opportunities. Today, Hispanic peoples—Mexican Americans, Mexican nationals, Puerto Rican Americans, and Central Americans—comprise over 70% of the migrant work force, which is made up mainly of farm workers (Bennett, 1990).

Like other immigrant groups, Hispanic Americans have had to struggle to overcome prejudice and discriminatory practices directed against them. Their struggles for civil rights and political representation during the 1960s resulted in four Mexican Americans winning election to Congress. By the 1980s, Hispanic Americans were seen as an emerging political force as they elected members of Congress, a governor in New Mexico, and mayors in Denver, San Antonio, Miami, Tampa, and Santa Fe.

In some states, such as California, Texas, and Florida, Hispanic Americans constitute the majority of public school enrollees. Overall, educational levels of Hispanic Americans have ranked somewhat lower than those of other groups. Comparisons of drop-out rates indicate that while only 10.8% of European-American and 12.4% of African-American 14- to 24-year-olds dropped out of school in 1988, 29.7% of Hispanic-American youths failed to complete school (U.S. Bureau of the Census, 1990). Income levels for Hispanic Americans averaged slightly higher than those of African Americans in 1987, but 70% of Hispanic-American children under the age of 18 lived in poverty (U.S. Department of Education, 1990, Vol. 1).

Some Hispanic and non-Hispanic Americans, including educators, have pushed for bilingual education, insisting that children be taught in their native tongue as well as in English. In Congressional hearings that preceded passage of Title VII of the Elementary and Secondary Education Act of 1965 (ESEA), Ravitch (1983) observed that four "assumptions" dominated discussions:

> . . . first, that Hispanic children did poorly in school because they had a "damaged self-concept"; second, that this negative self-appraisal occurred because the child's native tongue was not the language of instruction; third, that the appropriate remedy for this problem was bilingual instruction; and fourth, that children who were taught their native language (or their parents' native language) and their cultural heritage would acquire a positive self-concept, high self-esteem, better attitudes toward school, increased motivation, and improved educational achievement. (p. 272)

The ESEA extended to Hispanic-American students the same consideration that had been extended to African-American children in *Brown v. Board of Education.*

Bilingual education has been hotly contested. Some argue that bilingual education only retards assimilation. These fears fueled an unsuccessful movement to make English the official language of the United States.

Asian Americans

Chinese immigrants began entering the United States in large numbers during the 1850s, many of them settling in the American West, where there was an acute labor shortage. They labored in gold mines and helped build the first transcontinental railway. Most of these early immigrants, typically men who planned to better their lot and then return to China, often lived in Chinatowns, where they continued their traditional customs and cultural practices. Attempts by Protestant and Catholic missionaries to Americanize the Chinese were unsuccessful and prompted others to use forceful means— burning Chinatowns and cutting off the customary long braids of Chinese men—to try to destroy their "clannish" ways (Carlson, 1975).

Although these immigrants who seemed so resistant to assimilation composed less than 1% of the total population in 1870, Americans grew increasingly distrustful of them, particularly as union leaders began to paint the Chinese as "part of a diabolical plot to deprive white Americans of their rightful jobs and bleed the West of its wealth" (Brown & Pannell, 1985, p. 203). Congress passed **exclusion acts** based on race to stop unwanted immigration.

The Chinese Exclusion Act was passed in 1882 , and Japanese immigrants stepped readily into a number of agricultural jobs in California and Hawaii. Despite the fact that the Nipponese Empire of Japan and the United States were allies at the turn of the century, by 1924 the flow of Japanese into this country was halted with the passage of the Oriental Exclusion Act. With the onset of World War II, Asian immigrants—particularly those of Japanese descent—suffered the ire of Americans: more than 100,000 Japanese Americans were driven from their homes and placed in temporary assembly centers, relocation centers, and internment camps and their property was confiscated. Many believed that this was our worst wartime mistake, but it was not until 1990 that the federal government officially apologized and offered Japanese Americans restitution for the internment.

Since the Korean and Vietnam wars, many immigrants from Korea and Southeast Asia have made America their home. Vietnamese Americans, one of the larger Asian groups to enter our country recently, represent only 8.4% of the total Asian population (U.S. Bureau of the Census, 1990). The first arrivals "were generals and peasants, schoolteachers and spies, physicians and fisherman, . . . [who] became in America a poignant symbol of the refugee's will to succeed" (Efron, 1990). Making up about one third of the current Vietnamese-American population, these early Vietnamese immigrants have generally done well by American standards. By 1980, their household incomes equalled the U.S. average and, for the most part, their children were quite successful in American schools. Vietnamese immigrating since the fall of Saigon in 1975, however, have not fared so well. The majority live in poverty, are poorly educated, and have less upward mobility than their predecessors (Efron, 1990).

Cambodians, Laotians, and Thais have also immigrated to the United States, but not in so many numbers as the Vietnamese. These tribal peoples, who were deeply affected by the war in Vietnam, have had to face physical separation from their homelands. They have also had to contend with a society that relies on the power of science and technology to solve human problems, educational and otherwise—a society that is truly foreign or alien in character to that which they left behind.

In the 1950s, the United States government began to lift restrictions on immigration by race. In 1965, Congress abolished the quota system that based annual numbers of people allowed to enter the United States on the basis of the proportion of their relatives already here.

Other Americans

People from Africa, the Middle East, and the Indian subcontinent are among more recent immigrants who are also part of the population of the United States. Events and conditions of the 1940s through the 1990s, such as the partition of India, the creation of the state of Israel, the Iran-Iraq War, the Persian Gulf War, and widespread drought and famine have brought Indians, Pakistanis, Palestinians, Egyptians, Lebanese, Persians, Chaldeans, Saudis, Ethiopians, and many others. Among the largest groups are Arabs—people from around the world who have their cultural origins in the Arabian Peninsula and the Arabic language. This group includes Muslim,

Christian, and secular Arabs. Between 1948 and 1958, more than 330,000 Arabs immigrated to the United States (Orfalea, 1988). Barbara Aswad (personal communication, January 30, 1991) estimates that in Detroit alone there are today between 150,000 and 200,000 Arab Americans.

Exceptional Learners in America

Efforts to meet the educational needs of students with exceptional abilities or disabilities did not begin until the 1800s. The majority of such efforts were directed toward helping people with disabilities (Kauffman, 1981). Physicians, clergymen, educators, and social reformers such as Dorothea Dix were leaders in this movement. Between 1817 and the Civil War, their crusade resulted in the establishment of residential schools for people who were deaf, blind, mentally retarded, or orphaned.

After the Civil War, many of these schools were deemed unsavory places—overcrowded, impersonal, and sometimes quite inhumane. At about the time reformers were calling for an end to such institutions, several states began to include special classes for students with disabilities in their public schools, and a number of professional organizations were formed to improve the care and treatment of children with disabilities.

Although programs for the disabled improved, by the end of the nineteenth century there was a concerted effort to institutionalize the mentally retarded and, in the early twentieth century, to sterilize them because people believed that the "intelligence" of a whole society was determined solely through heredity. People with abnormalities of behavior were seen as deviant, regardless of the causes. Behavioral traits, such as intelligence, were thought to be strictly inherited but were also linked to concepts of moral worth. In the early twentieth century, therefore, many state laws prohibited mental and social "deviates" from marrying, and compulsory surgical sterilization became widespread. People with mental retardation and seizure disorders such as epilepsy were sterilized along with convicted prostitutes and criminals.

The early twentieth century also saw an upsurge in the scientific study of children, the scientific classification and measurement of types of disabilities, the establishment of the Children's Bureau in 1912, an increase in public school classes and resource programs for exceptional learners, and the emergence of new professional organizations and training programs for teachers. At the same time, the widespread institutionalization of people with disabilities in isolated special-care facilities led to social isolation and abuses, which sparked humanitarian reform movements in the 1950s and civil rights reform movements in the 1970s and 1980s.

Through federal involvement in the 1960s, a Bureau for the Handicapped was added to the United States Office of Education, which is now the Office of Special Education and Rehabilitative Services in the U.S. Department of Education. Federal legislation and additional information on exceptional learners, including students with disabilities and students identified as gifted or talented, and issues in special education are discussed again in other contexts in Chapters 7 and 8.

American Women

Women's place in society in the early twentieth century remained restricted and confused. Some, following in the footsteps of Emma Willard—touted as having done more in the nineteenth century for the education of women than anyone in America—were determined that women should enjoy the privilege of education no less than men (Raven & Weir, 1981). These women and others fought for and won an amendment to the U.S. Constitution granting women the right to vote in 1920. The suffragettes, as they were called, included Susan B. Anthony, a teacher; Elizabeth Blackwell, the first woman in the United States to qualify as a physician; Margaret Fuller, a teacher and foreign correspondent for the *New York Tribune*; and Elizabeth Cady Stanton, one of the organizers of the 1848 Seneca Falls Women's Rights Convention.

> **"No person . . . shall, on the basis of sex, be excluded from participating in or be denied the benefit of . . . any education program . . . receiving federal financial assistance."**

Women did not participate fully in society simply by virtue of winning formal recognition. During the Depression of the 1930s, they were often laid off from their jobs before men were, had greater difficulty finding jobs, and were rarely considered for supervisory positions. When World War II created a labor shortage, women were suddenly pulled into previously male-dominated jobs, and were just as suddenly discouraged from having careers when the war ended and the men came home.

After Congress passed an equal employment act in 1964, many types of job discrimination against women were eliminated. In the 1960s, 1970s, and 1980s, this created new opportunities in the workplace and women moved out of what had become traditionally female-dominated jobs of teaching and nursing and into nearly all professional and occupational roles, including those traditionally held by men, such as firefighting, law enforcement, and military combat. In 1970, women accounted for approximately 5% of law school graduates; in the late 1980s, they represented about 40% (Blum et al., 1989). Title IX of the Education Amendments Act, passed in 1972, guaranteed that "no person in the United States shall, on the basis of sex, be excluded from participation in, be denied the benefits of, or be subjected to discrimination under any education program or activity receiving federal financial assistance." The greatest impact of Title IX has been on school athletic programs, in which girls may not be excluded from any sport and must be given equal access to coaching and equipment.

The **Women's Educational Equity Act (WEEA)** of 1974 was a comprehensive attack on sex discrimination in education and had far-reaching impact on curriculum and instruction in the nation's schools. The law expanded programs for females in mathematics, science, technology, and athletics; mandated nonsexist curriculum materials; implemented programs for increasing the number of female administrators in education and raising the career aspirations of female students; and extended educational and career opportunities to minority-member, disabled, and rural women.

The Women's Educational Equity Act (WEEA) of 1974 expanded opportunities for female students in math, science, and technology.

The struggle for equal rights for women continued through the feminist movement and efforts to amend the Constitution. Meanwhile, women were nominated for vice-president of the United States, elected as mayors, governors, state legislators, and members of Congress, and appointed as ambassador to the United Nations, heads of cabinet posts, and heads of federal agencies. At the same time, sex discrimination and sexual harassment suits against corporations and government agencies have increased, and education researchers in the 1990s have reported the widespread persistence of subtle gender bias in classroom interaction on the part of both male and female teachers. Issues pertaining to gender and education are further elaborated in Chapter 8.

Many women continue to battle poverty. Indeed, there appears to be what some have referred to as a "feminization of poverty." Between 1960 and 1980, the number of female-headed households increased twofold. By 1985, approximately 10 million children lived in such homes; about 6 million of them were with mothers whose incomes were less than $10,000. On average, women earn about 67¢ for every $1 earned by men (U.S. Department of Education, 1988).

HOW DID TEACHING CHANGE AFTER THE CIVIL WAR?

Following the Civil War, most teachers were young, poorly paid, and rarely educated beyond elementary subjects. Teaching was not considered a desirable job, and the turnover of teachers was high.

Discourse on teaching often reflected the traditional image of the teacher as a mentor, model of virtue, and disciplinarian whose principal concern was the character of his or her pupils. Efforts to professionalize teaching began during the nineteenth century as expectations of teachers broadened to include less subjective qualifications. By the twentieth century, teachers were supposed to be scientific experts having a mission to educate.

By 1920, 86% of teachers were women. As thousands of immigrants streamed into urban schools in the late nineteenth century, teachers sometimes found themselves with classes of 70 pupils speaking dozens of different languages. The children were poor, often unbathed, and hungry (Tyack & Hansot, 1982).

VOICES

On Teaching in the Late 1800s

A. P. Marble, an educator from Maine who between graduation from college in 1861 until his death in 1905 served as a classroom teacher, college professor, principal, assistant superintendent, and superintendent of schools, described teaching as a job not meant for the faint of heart:

Teachers are employed for purposes "vastly great." They must teach the science of health with all the learning but without the pay of the doctor; they must inculcate the principles of morality with all the impressive sincerity but without the sectarianism of the minister; they must be altogether more patient and discreet than God Almighty himself, for He was "wroth" when He punished the wicked, whereas, if a teacher punishes in anger, he is guilty of an assault and battery; they must invent schemes to invert human nature, and make every good thing and thought enticing and every bad thing and thought abominably disgusting . . . they must tenderly moderate the zeal of the too ambitious, and inspire the dullest blockhead with a manly thirst for fame and knowledge; the incorrigibly uncouth and vicious, they must endow with the tastes, the instincts, and the manners of the refined and virtuous. And in short, they must turn all from the thousand paths that lead to indolence, ignorance, and folly; and prepare them to find infallibly all the ways of pleasantness and all the paths of peace.

CRITICAL THINKING

Which teaching conditions and expectations of teachers that Marble describes do or do not apply today? Give examples to support your conclusions. Marble's comments portray teaching as a balancing act. How might you rewrite his description to reflect present-day realities of teaching to help preservice teachers understand the notion of teaching as a balancing act?

Source: Elsbree, W.S. (1939). *The American teacher: Evolution of a profession in a democracy.* New York: American Book Company.

Shifts in the Status of Teachers

Men controlled public education, but in the early 1900s, women began to protest publicly about administrative edicts and the effects of decision making on life in schools. Women teachers fought for better working conditions and for pay that was equal to that received by men teachers.

Women such as Margaret Haley and Catherine Goggin, leaders of the Chicago Teachers Federation (CTF), an all-female teacher organization founded in 1897, drew attention to discrepancies in salaries between administrators and teachers. They also challenged the old male guard in the NEA and tried to force the association to focus on concerns of women teachers who made up the majority of the teaching profession. Ella Flagg Young, a brilliant scholar and leader in the women's movement, spoke against the psychological control that scientific management exerted on teachers, in a sense treating them like "mere workers at the treadmill" (Tyack & Hansot, 1982, p. 181).

Margaret Haley

Although women gained positions as teachers during this time, they lost positions as school administrators. Decisions about who might be the best candidates for various administrative positions were less often based on performance records than on gender. Women, at the mercy of all-male boards, were generally appointed to posts men did not desire to fill. The absence of requirements for special credentials for school administrators continued until the 1930s.

Women became increasingly forceful in their efforts to reform schools as time went by. Margaret Haley challenged the male old guard in the National Education Association (NEA), seeking responsiveness to women's concerns (Tyack & Hansot, 1982). The NEA reacted by offering symbolic gains, such as appointing a female president every other year.

Marriage was typically a liability for women in education but an asset for men. Most women in public schools have been young and single—in 1900 only 10% were married, and in 1940 only 22%. In 1928, the NEA found about three fifths of urban districts prohibited hiring married teachers, and half forbade married teachers from continuing in their jobs. The situation grew worse during the Depression, as thousands of districts passed new bans against employing married women.

The Progressive Movement

Between 1920 and 1945, educators were influenced by the progressive movement in American politics and social life. **Progressivism** called for the application of human and material resources to improve the American's quality of life as an individual. Applied to education, progressive ideals meant that the needs and interests of students rather than of teachers should be the focus of everything that happens in schools. Progressive teachers relied more on class discussions, debates, and demonstrations than on direct instruction and rote learning from textbooks. Teachers also experimented with individualized instruction and curricula that involved students in practical experiences and relevant learning outside the classroom. Students were responsible for maximizing their own potential with the teacher's role that of a helper and guide.

As progressivism took hold, individuals crafted different types of programs to try to make education relevant to students' lives. In 1921, to encourage creativity, decision making, and independent thinking in boys and girls alike, Helen Parkhurst implemented what was to become known as the Dalton Laboratory Plan in Dalton, Massachusetts. The Dalton Plan organized the school day into subject labs. Students from 5th through 12th grades set their own daily schedules. Officials turned off the bells, eliminated schedules, and disbanded traditional classrooms. The Plan gave students some control over their learning and relied on their interests to promote learning (Edwards, 1991; Parkhurst, 1922).

The greatest proponent of progressive education, however, was John Dewey (1859–1952), whose Laboratory School at the University of Chicago scientifically tested child-centered curricula and instructional approaches. As will be discussed in the next chapter in connection with educational philosophy, Dewey wanted to avoid teaching subjects in isolation, favoring the idea of integrating them during social activities, such as cooking, sewing, or building a playhouse, so that students might learn about cooperation among human beings (Kliebard, 1986).

Teachers practicing progressive techniques were not united by a single cohesive educational philosophy. After 1945 and until about 1960, critics expressed dissatisfaction with progressive education because it lacked a common set of principles and a body of knowledge. Some said that progressivism risked pandering to individual happiness at the expense of intellectual rigor and placed Americans at a disadvantage in international competition. Nevertheless, the concept of child-centered education remained and has been revived again in educational reforms of the 1990s.

John Dewey

Cycles of Change in Educational Reforms

Despite the progressive movement, from the late nineteenth century through World War II most instruction remained traditional and teacher-centered: teachers did most of the talking, and teachers controlled the time, the activities, and classroom space. Innovative instructional ideas emerged, but as the old saw goes, something often got lost in translation; that is, sooner or later innovation was abandoned for more traditional instructional behavior.

As Lawrence Cremin (1988) notes, industrial education, for example, was supposed to help students appreciate the philosophy and methods at the heart of industrial society; instead it rapidly became vocational education, concentrating on transmitting skills. Activities intended to make learning concrete soon became substitutes for academics.

Contemporary critics claim that teachers and teaching have been, and continue to be, virtually impervious to change. Larry Cuban (1984) writes:

> I have been in many classrooms in the last decade. When I watched teachers in secondary schools a flash of recognition jumped out of my memory and swept over me. What I saw was almost exactly what I remembered of the junior and senior high school classrooms that I sat in as a student and as a teacher in the mid 1950s. This acute sense of recall about how teachers were teaching occurred in many different schools. How, I asked myself, could teaching over a forty-year period *seem* . . . almost unchanged? (p. 1)

Cuban suggests there are at least three reasons for the durability of teacher-centered instruction: (a) schools are a form of social control and sorting; (b) the organizational structure of the school and classroom drives teachers to adopt instructional practices that change little over time; and (c) the culture of teaching itself tilts toward stability and a reluctance to change.

Education in the National Interest

World War II caused an exodus of men and women from teaching. By 1945, more than one third of the teachers employed in 1941 had left for more lucrative professions in business, industry, and government. Approximately 109,000 individuals employed on emergency certificates assumed some of those positions. Some schools were closed completely or open only for short terms. Some subjects had to be eliminated from the curriculum because there were no qualified staff to teach them.

David Brinkley (1988) describes life in the Washington, D.C., public schools during World War II as a difficult and somewhat unprofessional situation:

> The District School Board ordered its teachers to serve as wardens to protect their school buildings at night. But no one was sure what the buildings were to be protected from or what to protect them with. One teacher was ordered to remain in the school all night and maintain communication with her principal through a telephone inside a locked closet to which she was denied a key. The buildings being unheated at night, the teachers were told to report for duty with blankets and heavy coats. One teacher spent the nights in a chair on the front steps of Eastern High School bundled in blankets, a shotgun in her lap and a German shepherd lying on each side. Another, ordered by her principal to report for duty, agreed and politely asked what she was to do. His response, in tones of some tough drill sergeant he must have seen in the movies: "This is war. It is not the time for subordinates to ask questions." (p. 98)

From 1940 to 1960, many critics expressed dissatisfaction with American education by focusing on progressive education techniques which generally attempted to make education "practical" and related to daily life. Walter Lippmann, for instance, argued that progressive education had no common principles, no common body of knowledge, and no common moral and intellectual discipline. The Soviet Union's launch of its satellite Sputnik in 1957, before the United States could launch such a satellite, was taken as evidence of our intellectual and moral flabbiness and led to intensified efforts to beef up education in the United States. Schools, critics charged, simply had not been teaching students to think. What we needed was greater emphasis on mathematics, science, and foreign languages. The American mindset for a century had been, "We're the best. We're number one. If we didn't invent it, we improved it." President John Kennedy used the Cold War competition to push the space program, and ultimately to put an American on the moon.

If, as some believed, education was foundering at state and local levels, the **National Defense Education Act (NDEA)**, passed in 1958, signaled that the federal government was taking the lead in improving schools. The NDEA provided funds for upgrading the teaching of mathematics, science, and foreign languages, as well as for the establishment of guidance services. It also provided low-interest, forgivable loans to college students. Not since the establishment of the National Science Foundation in 1950 had the federal government moved so decisively in education policy. The passage of the NDEA marked the beginning of a pattern of federal leadership in education.

In various ways, the Vocational Education Act (1963), the Elementary and Secondary Education Act (1965), the Higher Education Act (1965), the Education Professions Development Act (1967), and other federal legislation and programs emphasized our national commitment to progress in education. These pieces of legislation provided more federal aid directly or indirectly to public schools and to institutions of higher education.

In 1979, President Jimmy Carter and Congress split the Department of Health, Education, and Welfare into two federal departments: Health and Human Services and the Department of Education. Carter appointed Shirley M. Hufstedler as the first secretary of education, thus raising the Department of Education to the cabinet level. One might have anticipated a future of vigorous federal leadership in education given these actions. But as early as 1983, President Ronald Reagan was already trying to dismantle the Department of Education, and in particular the National Institute of Education. As an avowed political conservative, Reagan aimed to curtail the involvement of the federal government in education matters he believed were better left to states and localities.

Presidential candidate George Bush promised, if elected, to be the Education President. His education summit, planned and carried out in cooperation with the National Governors' Association, set the federal course in education early in his first term. The summit and the rhetoric of his first secretary of education, Lauro Cavazos, signaled that public education was to be largely a state, not a federal, matter.

HOW DID SCHOOLS CHANGE DURING THE MODERN ERA?

The number of schools rose dramatically after World War I, but resources for funding schools rose and fell with the economy. The early depression years (1929–1932) had a profoundly negative effect on funding for schools and colleges. By 1933–34, school expenditures had dropped more than 30% in many states. School funding in Michigan and Mississippi fell 41 and 52% respectively. This meant that some rural schools' budgets were reduced by one fifth to one half. Teachers' salaries were cut, and some were even paid in 4-year-maturity state bonds rather than by cash or check.

Colleges and universities were also hurt by the Depression, particularly state-funded institutions, whose funding was cut by about one third. Between 1931 and 1934, total enrollment in higher education declined by 8.5% (Link & Catton, 1963).

Consolidation and Bureaucratization

Most schools were small and rural until a program of consolidation began after World War II. Typically, one teacher taught all ages of students in the same room, and each student progressed at his or her own pace. Rural one-room schools were ungraded until about the 1920s. These one-room schools began to fall by the wayside as school districts were combined to concentrate resources and centralize administration. The number of separate school districts was reduced from about 130,000 in 1930 to fewer than 16,000 in 1988 (U.S. Department of Education, 1989). This consolidation meant students had to be bused to central locations, such as huge regional high schools, often over long distances.

As consolidation increased in rural areas, bureaucratization became the hallmark of urban schooling. Boston, Massachusetts, and New York City developed complex networks of schools having distinct roles and rules, standardized curricula and procedures for each grade level, and administrative ideologies bent on efficiency, rationality, precision, and impartiality. Large cities patterned their school systems on the factory model: the single superintendent with a few foremen to supervise hundreds of operatives. This put a great deal of power into the hands of a few people who had little or no management training (Tyack & Hansot, 1982).

Many people within the system struggled against bureaucratization. Leonard Covello, teacher and principal in New York's East Harlem, worked from before World War I until 1956 to connect schools to communities. He was among the pioneers of bilingual education, storefront schools, community advisory committees for schools, multicultural education, programs to prevent school dropouts, school-based community service, and political action programs. He also criticized the misapplication of IQ tests on culturally different populations (Tyack & Hansot, 1982).

New Links Between Schools and Communities

A sociological view of connections between schools and communities gained credence in the 1960s and 1970s. A survey conducted in the fall of 1965 by James S. Coleman, then of The Johns Hopkins University, and Ernest Q. Campbell, of Vanderbilt University, suggested that the disparity between academic achievement scores of European Americans and members of minority groups was due more to the racial composition of a school than to school facilities, teacher salaries, and per-pupil expenditures. Coleman also served in an advisory capacity for a study by the Civil Rights Commission in 1965 which revealed that 75% of African-American urban elementary students were in all-African-American schools while 83% of European-American urban elementary students were in all-European-American schools. Among other findings was that African-American students performed better in desegregated schools than in those that were "racially isolated" (Cremin, 1988). Christopher Jencks (et al., 1972) and his colleagues used data from a variety of sources to argue that economic and social equality in adult society had little relation to educational opportunities in schools; if minorities were to become part of the mainstream in society, school reform alone would not accomplish this end.

Schools were embedded in communities, but as Marcus Foster demonstrated in the mid-1960s and 1970s, relationships between the two could be both nurturing and calamitous. Foster was a teacher and principal in Philadelphia, Pennsylvania, and then superintendent of the Oakland, California, schools. An African American, Foster worked with militant community leaders to try to make schools more responsive to the needs of the communities in which he served. His success in helping others succeed was legendary. Foster instituted honors courses with scholarships for college-bound students, expanded vocational courses and tied them to employment, sponsored the first course in Philadelphia in Afro-American history, built an educational and recreation center in the community, and generally mobilized people to get involved with their schools. On November 6, 1973, as he left the weekly meeting of Oakland's Board of Education, Foster was murdered. The Symbionese Liberation Army (SLA), a small radical organization, claimed credit for the shooting. They sent a letter to a radio station claiming they "executed" Foster because he had supported a controversial student identification program (McCorry, 1978).

> **"Large numbers of American children are in limbo—ignorant of the past and unprepared for the future."**

As technological progress accelerated, people perceived more links between schools and society, or more specifically between schools and the world of work. In 1986, the Carnegie Forum on Education and the Economy argued that weak schools threatened America's ability to compete in world markets: "Large numbers of American children are in limbo—ignorant of the past and unprepared for the future. Many are dropping out—not just out of school but out of productive society" (p. 2).

Those schools that worked—which, if one listened to the rhetoric of reform of the 1980s, were few in number—were thought to be alike in several ways. They had climates that were safe and free of disciplinary problems. Teachers expected that students could achieve and communicated these expectations publicly. The schools emphasized basic skills with plenty of time for students to work. School personnel monitored and evaluated student progress. Successful schools also had strong principals who served as program leaders (Bossert, 1985).

By 1987, 39 million students were enrolled in elementary and secondary schools and more than 12 million in institutions of higher education. As in the past, the majority of these students were enrolled in public schools. It is worth noting, however, that within the private-school sector there remained a large and complex system of schools operated by the Roman Catholic Church. In 1987, approximately 2.6 million students were enrolled in such schools, which constitute the largest single group of private schools (U.S. Department of Education, 1989).

Rise of Preschools

The preschool movement began anew in the United States in the 1920s and rapidly diversified. The American version of the nursery school, patterned on the earlier experiences of the British, stimulated interest in educating the whole child instead of simply providing custodial care. Inspired by the work of Rachel and Margaret McMillan in England, some farsighted teachers, such as Patty Smith Hill of Columbia Teachers College, created a few models that would guide the development of more schools.

By the depths of the Depression, the country needed good child care, and unemployed teachers needed jobs. Financial support from the federal government in the early 1930s stimulated the formation of many more nursery schools throughout the nation. By 1937, the Works Progress Administration (WPA) was responsible for 1,472 nursery schools with an

Preschool education and federally funded compensatory preschool programs for children from low-income families expanded during the 1970s.

enrollment of 39,873 children. At the same time, the WPA sponsored 3,270 parent education classes with an enrollment of 51,093 (Cremin, 1988).

During World War II, the WPA programs were phased out and replaced by programs that were more oriented to child care than to education. By 1946, the majority of these child-care centers closed when federal funds were withdrawn. As women continued to enter the workforce, the need for child care prompted the establishment of many private preschools. Today, enrollment in private prekindergartens continues to exceed that in public preschool programs.

When President Lyndon Johnson launched his war on poverty during the 1960s, education programs such as Head Start were the weapons he chose. Head Start had a dual focus—to stimulate the development and academic achievement of 4- and 5-year-olds from low-income families, and to involve parents in the education of their children. Although Head Start serves only one in five eligible children, it still remains one of the largest and most popular preschool programs (Reed & Sautter, 1990).

The growing interest in early childhood education and the success of experimental public kindergartens prompted many school districts to establish programs for 5-year-olds. At the beginning of the twentieth century, there were 225,394 kindergartners in the United States, 58% of whom were in public schools (Cremin, 1988). By 1987, about 2.5 million 5-year-olds were enrolled in public schools and 378,000 were enrolled in private schools (U.S. Department of Education, 1990).

The Middle School Movement

The housing of grades kindergarten through 8 in elementary school, and grades 9 through 12 in secondary school, or the 8-4 pattern, was for many years the most common organizational scheme for schools in the United States. During the early 1900s, however, some school systems began to experiment with other ways of grouping their students. Although several organizational patterns were tested, the 6-3-3 pattern, or clustering of grades 7 through 9 in a "junior" high school—first tried in the cities of Columbus, Ohio, and Berkeley, California—proved to be quite popular in the years following World War I. By the 1950s and 1960s, many school districts began moving 9h-graders back into high schools and replacing their junior high schools with "intermediate" or "middle" schools (Cremin, 1988). Today, many school systems continue to group 9th-graders with high school students in a 4-4-4 pattern. But their "middle" group of students (5th- through 8th-graders) are clustered in a variety of ways with both the primary and high school grades. The middle-school movement has resulted in significant changes in curriculum and instruction for students in transition between late childhood and early adolescence.

Comprehensive High Schools

After the 1870s, private academies declined in number and were replaced by public high schools. A court case in Kalamazoo, Michigan, validated the right of school districts to establish and support public high schools with tax monies. By 1890, about 203,000 students were enrolled in public high schools, and 95,000 were enrolled in private academies. Together, these two groups made up less than 6% of the population of students 14 to 17 years of age, yet they constituted the entire potential pool of college entrants. In contrast, by 1987 more than 92% of young people were enrolled in secondary schools. Twelve million were enrolled in public secondary schools and more than 1 million in private schools (U.S. Department of Education, 1989).

Although every high school is unique, each shares with other schools a common feature—a multiplicity of course offerings for a student body having diverse needs, interests, and abilities. These schools are designed to be comprehensive in their offerings. Arthur Powell, Eleanor Farrar, and David Cohen (1985) liken the comprehensive high school to a shopping mall "governed by consumer choice" (p.309). They see high schools wanting to maximize their holding power by satisfying consumers. In this metaphor, teachers are salespeople, classrooms are stores, students are customers. This outlook has led to a variety of course offerings, or "specialty shops" for high achievers, students with special needs, troublemakers, students with vocational and technical interests, athletes, and others.

Homeschooling

An educational process reminiscent of colonial times, homeschooling is an alternative to on-site public education. Most states allow children to be taught at home, but as will be explained in Chapter 13, such arrangements are regulated in various ways. Typically, parents must demonstrate that the education their children receive at home is equivalent to what they would receive in the public schools in terms of the books used, tests given, and time spent on studies.

Like private schools, home schools have grown in number for both pedagogical and ideological reasons. Estimates of the numbers of students served in such environments range from 200,000 to 300,000. The majority of these students tend to be from middle-class European-American families located in the western and southern parts of the United States. The curriculum services used by homeschoolers indicate that the majority of families exercising the homeschool option do so for religious reasons (Kohn, 1988).

Adult Education

Adult education took many forms in industrial America. Factories taught safety. Settlement houses taught immigrants and their children English and the skills needed to survive in a foreign culture. And beyond the cities, agricultural extension agents helped farmers improve their methods of growing crops and raising livestock.

The **Chautauqua movement** was the preeminent adult education movement of its time. What began as a Methodist Sunday School Institute in 1874 at Lake Chautauqua, New York, flourished as a secular educational institution through World War I. It was not "a single, unified, coherent plan, developed and directed by one man or a group of men. It was, fundamentally, a response to an unspoken demand, a sensitive alertness to the cravings of millions of people for 'something better'" (Gould, 1961, p. vii). Through the years, the Chautauqua movement pioneered the establishment of civic music associations, correspondence courses, lecture-study groups, youth groups, and reading circles. It responded to a vast need for adult education, particularly in rural areas of the United States. The movement may also have been, however, yet another indication of the American preoccupation with self-fulfillment and social advancement.

Public schools and adult education also became intertwined at the turn of the century. Progressives strengthened the philosophical and practical connections between community and school, perhaps most notably via the Gary Plan. After 1907, William Wirt, a school administrator in Gary, Indiana, worked to make public schools the centers of life in Gary neighborhoods. His intent was to unify the general, vocational, intellectual, and moral education of youth. By adhering to a "platoon system" of organization, students could be at gymnasiums, playgrounds, and assembly halls, as well as at schools. Gary schools could then accommodate twice as many students as traditional schools (Cremin, 1988). By 1929, the Gary Plan had spread to more than 200 cities in 41 states. The Plan faded when people opposed it as a form of cheapened education for their children.

More important than progressive philosophy, the hard times of the 1930s forced people to use every resource at hand to help young and old alike work their way out of the Depression. Many programs made it appropriate for adults as well as children to congregate at school. The federally funded community education project associated with the Tennessee Valley Authority (TVA) in the mid-1930s, for example, tried to improve life in the rural TVA area by providing "lifelong educational opportunities that directly related to community needs, and that served the entire community not just its youth" (Minzey & LeTarte, 1979, p. 7). This meant helping adults learn basic literacy and job skills.

During the 1940s, the Alfred P. Sloan Foundation supported efforts in Kentucky, Florida, and Vermont to determine if "school curriculum and particular instructional materials could improve the economics of living in homes and communities touched by schools" (Decker, 1972, p. 54). In the 1950s and 1960s, the Mott Foundation and the Kellogg Foundation, both in Michigan, promoted rural community health programs, school camping programs, and continuing education throughout the Midwest. These foundations encouraged local schools to work cooperatively with other agencies to create systems for all the people in a community.

Today's growing demand for adult education can be traced, for example, to the Chautauqua movement of the late nineteenth and early twentieth centuries.

The Economic Opportunity Act of 1964 further extended educational opportunities through the establishment of Adult Basic Education (ABE) programs for individuals 18 or more years old. Although ABE funds were initially limited to school districts, by 1978 both public and private nonprofit agencies were deemed eligible for financial assistance. The Office of Economic Opportunity also included Job Corps for school dropouts ages 16 to 21 and Volunteers In Service To America (VISTA)—essentially a domestic Peace Corps.

Adult education will likely become more important as we move into the twenty-first century. In the private sector, more and more corporations offer incentives for job-related education and for postsecondary adult education. Volunteer efforts such as Literacy Volunteers of America and Reading Is Fundamental also underscore the importance of adult education. As Lamar Alexander, President George Bush's second secretary of education, declared,

> The largest number of undereducated and underskilled people in America are the parents, not the children. Helping the grownups go back to school might be a way not only to get our work force in better shape more immediately, but it might help the adults of America understand the urgency of what should be done for our children. (Cooper, 1991, p. 49)

HOW DID OPPORTUNITIES FOR HIGHER EDUCATION EXPAND?

On-going pressures of industrialization in the North, the need for postwar development in the South, and the Morrill Act of 1862 combined to stimulate higher education in America. The higher education system offered a variety of alternatives for people who wanted to continue their education beyond high school. Technical training produced graduates for occupations and trades, while colleges and universities educated people for the professions, research, business and industry, and virtually every field people would want to explore.

Technical and Professional Schools

The applied sciences and agriculture accounted for much of the program growth in the latter part of the nineteenth century even though agriculture did not attract many students compared to the twentieth century, when semi-vocational majors such as economics, political science, and psychology also increased dramatically. Although higher education remained largely a man's world, by 1890 about 2,500 women a year were graduating from college, often prepared to fill roles not open to them.

The ideal of research was extremely influential in the development of such institutions as Johns Hopkins, Harvard, and Stanford. As these research universities grew to become knowledge producers, the disciplines within them became increasingly specialized and esoteric. Simultaneously, the utilitarian forces driving industrialization in the United States stimulated the development of colleges that concentrated on problems of agriculture and mining, including the large multipurpose state-supported institutions such as the University of Wisconsin and some private universities such as Cornell.

The desires of the growing middle class for upward mobility stimulated colleges and universities to produce "experts," specialists, and managers having greater skills and more degrees. Consequently, new professional schools—in dentistry, architecture, business administration, engineering, mining, forestry, education, and social work—emerged alongside the older but reforming professions of law, medicine, and theology.

Private and State Colleges and Universities

The formation of the Association of American Universities in 1900 marked the beginning of nationwide efforts to raise academic standards in postsecondary education. There were slightly fewer than 1,000 colleges and universities in 1900 with 238,000 students. By 1920, there were 1,041 institutions of higher education but enrollment had more than doubled to nearly 600,000 students. The prosperity of the 1920s saw increases in state aid to public universities, colleges, and junior colleges, which made possible improvements in facilities for graduate and specialized training and technical education. Private institutions such as the Massachusetts Institute of Technology also helped set the stage for the beginning of an important adult education movement (Link & Catton, 1963).

The years 1940 to 1960 yielded phenomenal growth in higher education. Enrollment increased from 1.5 million students to about 3.5 million. During World War II, however, enrollments plummeted. After the war, with the passage of the Servicemen's Readjustment Act of 1944 (G.I. Bill of Rights), enrollment increased once again. Overcrowding was a problem. But issues of academic freedom concerned people as much if not more. The McCarthy Era—so named for Senator Joseph McCarthy of Wisconsin—was a modern witchhunt for communists and presumed communists. People's careers and lives were destroyed by rumor, innuendo, and accusations. In some places, educators, like people in other fields, were forced to swear allegiance to the United States: if they did not, they were branded as communists or communist sympathizers.

Dissent and progressivism were identified with anti-American persuasions. In 1948 and 1949, many states imposed loyalty oaths on teachers and established committees to examine textbooks for subversive materials. Kansas, Massachusetts, and Pennsylvania authorized schools to dismiss teachers for disloyalty. Maryland, New York, and New Jersey forbade teachers to join certain organizations thought to be subversive. Only native-born citizens could remain on the University of Oklahoma staff. Charges and countercharges had chilling effects on institutions of higher education. The often bitter and sometimes destructive debate over what William Ebenstein (1954) called "today's isms"—communism, fascism, socialism, and capitalism—cast a pall over higher education.

Many Americans took advantage of higher education in the 1970s, 1980s, and 1990s. Enrollment increased by a third between 1967 and 1972 and by another third between 1972 and 1982. Between 1971 and 1988, the share of degrees in business and other technical/professional fields almost doubled, increasing from 24% in 1971 to 42% in 1988. In contrast, the share of degrees in education fell from 22% to 9% (U.S. Department of Education, 1990, Vol. 2).

The ratio of average annual earnings of college graduates to high school graduates indicates that postsecondary education remains a good investment. For both men and women, the earnings premiums of college graduates increased dramatically in the last 20 years (U.S. Department of Education, 1990, Vol. II).

With the expected retirement of many faculty during the next decade, colleges and universities face a potential shortage of qualified replacements, particularly in the sciences. Between 1971 and 1976, the number of doctoral degrees granted in the natural sciences declined precipitously. The U.S. share of those degrees also fell. In 1988, foreign students earned 45.5% of all U.S. doctoral degrees in computer science and engineering (U.S. Department of Education, 1990, Vol. II).

WHAT ISSUES AROSE IN CURRICULUM DEVELOPMENT?

Advocates for common schools after the Civil War tried to encourage citizens to send their children to public schools. But deep divisions along class, religious, and ethnic lines made the task difficult. No single philosophy seemed broad enough to permit the integration of all Americans into the schools. Social changes in the late nineteenth century—the growth of cities, popular journalism, and railroads—forced previously isolated, self-contained communities to live in a bigger world. As we shall discuss in Chapter 9, these conditions stimulated the struggle for control of American curricula.

Standardization of the Curriculum

In 1893 the **Committee of Ten on Secondary School Studies** (established by the NEA in 1892) attempted to standardize high school curricula. Chaired by Charles Eliot, president of Harvard University, the Committee of Ten prescribed four different academic courses of study for high school students: classical, modern languages, English, and Latin-scientific. The committee urged high schools to provide 4 years of English and 3 years each of history, science, mathematics, and a foreign language. Although the avowed intent of the curriculum was to put modern academic subjects and classical ones on an equal plane, not to sort students, the report elicited condemnation. Critics viewed it as a program for failure for all but the college-bound student. From about 1870–1910, colleges exerted considerable influence over the typical high school curriculum.

The **Committee of Fifteen** took on the curriculum of elementary schools in 1895. Chairman of the committee, William Torrey Harris, U.S. Commissioner of Education, while appearing to be more sensitive to forces of social change than Eliot, expressed strong belief in the value of a curriculum focused on "the five windows of the soul"—grammar, literature and art, mathematics, geography, and history. Harris recommended that knowledge of Western cultural heritage be transmitted to students via standard literary works. He viewed the role of school as an efficient transmitter of cultural heritage through a curriculum that was graded, structured, and cumulative. Harris had established the first successful public school kindergarten in St. Louis in 1873 and gave America the graded school (Kliebard, 1986).

Diversification of the Curriculum

School curriculum at the turn of the century became a battle ground. While some educators were out to safeguard tradition, others, such as G. Stanley Hall, pressed the case for making curriculum responsive to human stages of development and to the nature of learning. Social efficiency experts—David Sneddon, Ross Finney, and Franklin Bobbitt—advocated training for specialized skills, much like industrial training. Social meliorists such as Lester Frank Ward viewed curriculum as an instrument for producing social change.

Still others, such as John Dewey, were not aligned with any one group, but identified with "progressive education." The progressive movement waxed and waned during the twentieth century, but for the most part it was characterized by several factors: expanded, differentiated curricula; individualized school programs; and the use of schools to solve various social and political problems, such as those of racial, ethnic, class, and gender equality (Cremin, 1988).

Progressivists' concerns were fueled by studies that suggested that the standard curricula did not fit the needs of increasingly heterogeneous classrooms. For instance, in 1906, Susan M. Kingsbury reported that of approximately 25,000 children in Massachusetts between the ages of 14 and 16 who had dropped out of school, five sixths had not completed an eighth-grade education and few had attended high school (Massachusetts Commission on Industrial and Technical Education, 1906).

As the curriculum diversified, students took different courses and different programs depending on their abilities. Schools assumed more responsibilities for students' health and home lives and for vocational training.

President Woodrow Wilson's signing of the Smith-Hughes Act in 1917 promoted job-skill training in public schools. The bill permitted federal funds to be used to train and pay teachers' salaries in agricultural, trade, industrial, and home economics subjects. Some saw Smith-Hughes as a natural link to the world of work. But Dewey, Harris, Du Bois, and others argued that courses of study might be predetermined for students, short-circuiting their choices and their natural potential.

Cultural Diversity in the Curriculum

Dewey and others looked for a middle ground between separation and assimilation of people by calling for "pluralism" in curricula. This meant all were to learn a common culture, but other cultural views were to be both accepted and encouraged. Public school leaders, however, were often more willing to compromise on ethnic differences than on religious ones. Some public schools offered bilingual instruction, usually English and German. In the late 1880s, eight states had statutes permitting bilingual instruction in public schools. In 1872, Oregon legalized monolingual German schools (Tyack & Hansot, 1982).

Americanization began to intensify in 1914 at the start of World War I and continued into the early 1920s. Schools treated southern and eastern European Americans much as they did African Americans—as a special group requiring a special, nonacademic education. Such education emphasized American government, home economics, and vocational training. During World War I, German was eliminated from the curriculum, and schools began to give report card grades not just for academic achievements but also for students' behavior. Citizenship grades were thought to be a "measure of [students'] dedication to the creation of a happy harmonious America" (Carlson, 1975, p. 123).

The NEA's Commission on the Reorganization of Secondary Education in 1918 set a new direction for high schools. Their Cardinal Principles of Secondary Education called for "comprehensive" institutions that served all social groups and trained for many occupations (Commission on the Reorganization of Secondary Education, 1918). High schools were no longer to be just for the college-bound.

Core Curricula and Censorship

As curriculum increasingly focused on progressivists' concerns with developing life skills, more people began to take the school curriculum to task for its lack of coherence. Robert Maynard Hutchins, president of the University of Chicago from 1929 to 1945, for example, advocated a core curriculum emphasizing grammar, rhetoric, logic, and mathematics. He also encouraged the study of the great books of the Western world so as to provide a common core of knowledge to students. This theme of a "common core," while attracting only a small following at the time, is one that would resurface periodically throughout the century in debates over what schools should teach.

Was God or Charles Darwin to be part of the common core? William Jennings Bryan led an antievolution crusade in the 1920s. Bryan was concerned about the possibility of atheistic evolutionists posing as teachers in public schools and undermining the Christian faith of American school children (Link & Catton, 1963). The 1925 Scopes trial in Dayton, Tennessee, upheld the right of states to ban the teaching of evolution. Although the forces of science would prevail in transmitting this Darwinian concept, to this day the teaching of evolution in the public schools remains a contentious issue.

Curriculum reformers in the 1930s disliked what they perceived as colleges' domination of the high school curriculum, a curriculum heavy on traditional academic subjects. The Progressive Education Association launched the Eight-Year Study to examine what was being taught in high schools. This investigation, directed by Ralph Tyler, involved 3,600 students in matched pairs from 29 high schools. The results were published in 1942 and 1943 and suggested that students in experimental secondary schools (those having a more progressive or "functional" orientation) achieved as well in college as did students from traditional high schools. This study stimulated educators to modify the core curriculum so as to prepare students for what they saw as the duties of life. It also encouraged the use of behavioral objectives (statements describing what students should know or be able to do at the end of a lesson) when developing curricula. Such objectives were to have "a lasting and profound effect on the future course of curriculum development" (Kliebard, 1986, p. 220).

Innovation and Reaction

By the 1950s, critics grew vitriolic in their attacks on education in America, and particularly on professors of education. Arthur Bestor's *Academic Wastelands* (1953) decried the antiintellectualism he associated with "life adjustment" education promulgated by some education professors. He advocated intellectual training for the masses, not just college-bound students (Kliebard, 1986).

Life adjustment education and other progressive strategies were blamed for America's intellectual failures, which seemed so apparent to some after the USSR's launch of Sputnik. Critics such as Vice-Admiral Hyman G. Rickover, credited with the development of the atomic submarine, attacked what he believed was the neglect of the gifted and talented students in America. Rickover saw education going soft intellectually and thus failing to help the country win the Cold War. He continued to disparage public education freely and widely until his death in 1986.

> "[Only] by the maintenance of high academic standards can the ideal of democratic education be realized— the ideal of offering to all the children . . . the privilege of receiving . . . the soundest education that is offered any place in the world."

The 1960s and 1970s spawned a host of innovative curricula and instruction methods: School Math Study Group (SMSG), Man A Course of Study (MACOS), Physical Science Study Committee (PSSC), Harvard Project Physics, Biological Science Curriculum Study (BSCS), Chemical Education Materials Study (CHEM Study), Project English, audio-lingual language laboratories, and many more. Most of these efforts tried to involve students actively in their own learning by deemphasizing teacher-centered instruction while concentrating on methods of inquiry.

Despite the creativity of many such programs, they often seemed to stall at the classroom door. (An interesting exception to this rule was BSCS—the only innovative curriculum that repaid more in publication royalties to the U.S. Treasury than was given in grant money.) Students—particularly poor and minority students—appeared to be learning less in school year-by-year, while various estimates of the dropout rate climbed. As the country flirted with the possibility of becoming a second-rate economic power in the 1980s, everybody seemed to offer proposals for reform. The National Commission on Excellence in Education (1983) warned of a "rising tide of mediocrity." There were so many reform reports and proposals offered to fix public education that it is difficult to imagine there was a good idea, or for that matter a bad idea, that failed to surface.

HOW DO PEOPLE TYPICALLY MAKE JUDGMENTS ABOUT EDUCATIONAL SUCCESS AND FAILURE?

Despite the fact that continual education reform seems to imply continual failure, American education has improved dramatically over the years. Schools today educate and provide a variety of services to millions of children every year. Progress has been uneven across regions of the country and across time, but there is no doubt that schools are better today than they were at the turn of the century.

Typically, judgments about educational success and failure have been guided by three factors: (a) the inputs into education, or in a sense the raw materials from which educated citizens are produced; (b) what occurs in schools and classrooms, or the processes of education; and (c) some measures of student learning.

People have not always considered all these factors at once when judging education, or always used these terms, but they have relied on the concepts as indications of educational quality for a long time. For instance, the person who says something like the following is concentrating on inputs: "We have a good school. We built a new building, paid big salaries to hire the best teachers, and bought the newest books and equipment." One who evaluates education in terms of processes might say: "The teachers and students in our school work together as inquirers. The curriculum is geared toward helping them identify important problems, collect information, and propose solutions. Teachers are always doing interesting things; it is a great school." And the person who extols the virtues of schools because of "students' high test scores, winning football teams, and students' affection for the teachers" is judging success by outputs.

There are many ways to define these attributes of schools. In 1896, Kratz asked 2,411 students grades 2 through 8 in Sioux City, Iowa, to judge their teachers. Students across the board ranked "personal appearance" as the most important characteristic of teachers. The teachers of Sioux City in turn might have argued with some justification that teaching went well when the students were bright and interested. Indeed, students' characteristics, like those of teachers, constitute another important input into the system.

BENCHMARKS

Modern U.S. Education History, 1865 to the present

1865	Thirteenth Amendment to the Constitution abolishes slavery; Freedman's Bureau established.
1868	Fourteenth Amendment grants citizenship to African Americans and guarantees that, "No state shall make or enforce any law which shall abridge the privileges or immunities of citizens of the United States; nor shall any state deprive any person of life, liberty, or property without due process of law; nor deny to any person within its jurisdiction the equal protection of the laws."
1869	Wyoming becomes the first state to grant women the right to vote.
1870	Fifteenth Amendment grants African Americans the right to vote.
1874	*Kalamazoo,* Michigan, case establishes that states may establish and support public high schools with tax funds, contributing to the secondary school movement and eventually to compulsory high school attendance laws.
1881	Booker T. Washington named head of Tuskegee Institute in Alabama.
1890	Massacre of Sioux men, women, and children by the U.S. Cavalry at Wounded Knee, South Dakota, breaks Native American resistance to forced assimilation.
1893–1895	The Committee of Ten on Secondary School Studies and the Committee of Fifteen on Elementary School Studies attempt to standardize public high school and elementary school curricula.
1896	In *Plessy v. Ferguson,* the Supreme Court rules that states can provide separate but equal public facilities, legalizing racial segregation.
1898–1900	Period of American imperialism and statecraft in which Cuba, Puerto Rico, the Philippines, Hawaii, Alaska, and Pacific islands such as Midway, Guam, and Samoa become possessions of the United States.
1901	First public junior college established in Joliet, Illinois.
1909	First junior high schools established in Berkeley, California, and in Columbus, Ohio.
1909	The NAACP founded through the efforts of African-American leaders such as W. E. B. Du Bois.

1910	Ella Flagg Young, PhD, the first female superintendent of schools of a large city (Chicago), becomes president of the National Education Association (NEA).
1914–1918	World War I and revolutions in Russia swell the rank of immigrants to American cities and schools from western, central, and eastern Europe.
1916	American Federation of Teachers formed as a labor union for classroom teachers.
1917	Congress passes the Smith-Hughes Act, which provides federal matching funds for vocational education in public high schools.
1919	Progressive Education Association established to promote the educational philosophy of John Dewey and his followers.
1920	Nineteenth Amendment grants women the right to vote.
1925	Trial of John Scopes in Dayton, Tennessee, known as the Monkey Trial, upholds the right of states to ban the teaching of Darwin's theory of evolution.
1929–1936	Stock market crash precipitates the Great Depression; Franklin Roosevelt's New Deal provides federal aid for education of the unemployed and for school construction.
1939–1946	World War II era; citizens of Japanese ancestry dispossessed of their property and confined to relocation camps. Holocaust survivors and other war refugees come to the United States from southern and eastern Europe and from countries around the globe touched by war.
1944	GI Bill provides financial aid for veterans to attend college.
1946–1953	The McCarthy Era, Korean War, and beginning of the Cold War period; the House Un-American Activities Committee (HUAC) abridges academic freedom and blacklists artists and intellectuals seen as communist sympathizers.
1950	National Science Foundation founded.
1954	The Supreme Court rules in *Brown et al. v. Board of Education of Topeka, Kansas,* that separate but equal schooling is unconstitutional on the grounds that segregated schools generate feelings of racial inferiority and are inherently unequal.

BENCHMARKS

Modern U.S. Education History, 1865 to the present (*cont.*)

1957	President Eisenhower orders federal troops to Little Rock, Arkansas, to enforce the Supreme Court's ruling against school segregation.
1957	The Soviet Union's successful launch of Sputnik I, the first artificial satellite, sparks a race for space and a movement for curriculum reform in the United States.
1958	National Defense Education Act (NDEA) provides federal funds to improve the teaching of science, mathematics, and modern foreign languages, and to help schools provide guidance services.
1959–1961	Communist revolution in Cuba brings new wave of immigration; President Kennedy and Soviet Premier Khrushchev bring the world to the brink of nuclear war over the Cuban Missile Crisis and the Berlin Wall.
1963	President Kennedy assassinated in Dallas, Texas.
1964	The Civil Rights Act of 1964 authorizes the federal government to compel compliance with school desegregation through lawsuits and through the withholding of federal funds from school districts that continue to discriminate. The era of busing to end racial segregation begins. President Johnson's War on Poverty begins to increase federal funding for school programs.
1965	Elementary and Secondary Education Act (ESEA) and subsequent amendments provide federal funding to aid students from low-income families through programs such as Title I (Chapter I); the Economic Opportunity Act of 1965 creates Head Start as a compensatory education program.
1965–1973	Vietnam War Era brings new waves of immigrants from Southeast-Asian countries; the antiwar movement leads to the "Kent State Massacre" in 1970 and profoundly affects curriculum and instruction in schools and on campuses across the United States.
1968	Dr. Martin Luther King, Jr., and Robert F. Kennedy assassinated.
1968	Bilingual Education Act enacted into law to address the special needs of students whose first language is not English.
1969	American Neil Armstrong becomes the first person to walk on the moon.
1972	Title IX of the Education Amendments and Civil Rights Act prohibits sex discrimination in schools receiving federal funds.

1972	Indian Education and Self-Determination Act gives Native Americans more control over their schooling.
1974	Richard M. Nixon resigns the presidency of the United States as a consequence of the Watergate scandal.
1975	Education of the Handicapped Act (EHA) increases federal commitment to the education of children with disabilities and establishes a basis for subsequent special education legislation.
1979–1980	Department of Education established; the U.S. Secretary of Education becomes a cabinet-level post.
1981	Educational Improvement and Consolidation Act (EICA) gives states greater power in allocating federal funds through block grants.
1983	National Commission on Excellence in Education issues a report, *A Nation at Risk*, which leads to new calls for educational reform to eliminate illiteracy and raise SAT scores.
1984	Perkins Vocational Education Act upgrades vocational programs in the schools.
1989	Carnegie Foundation's report, *Turning Points: Preparing American Youth for the Twenty-First Century*, calls for the elimination of tracking and creation of learning communities in the schools.
1989	Presidential Summit Conference on Education held in Charlottesville, Virginia, attended by President Bush and the 50 governors, who agree that, "Good education makes good politics, good business, and good sense."
1992	Chris Whittle announces his Edison Project, a plan to create 1,000 for-profit schools to compete with the public schools system.
1992	Supreme Court rules that officially sanctioned prayers or invocations in public schools are unconstitutional.

Processes of schooling have most commonly been characterized in terms of curriculum and courses offered. The more academic, more relevant, more practical, more intellectually challenging, and the like, the better the processes of schooling. As we shall discuss in Chapter 9 ("Curriculum"), social scientists near the end of World War II began stretching beyond curriculum to describe and quantify teaching behavior. This permitted researchers to relate processes of instruction to both inputs and outputs. These relationships guided further judgments about more and less effective teaching.

The quintessential measure of educational output is the standardized achievement-test score. Joseph Rice developed the first educational achievement test in the United States in 1895. His spelling test consisted of 50 words, and he administered it to more than 16,000 pupils in grades 4 to 8. Stone's arithmetic reasoning test and Thorndike's scale for evaluating pupils' handwriting followed quickly. The Stanford Achievement Test, referred to as a "test battery," was published in 1923. It was designed as a group of survey tests in different content areas standardized on the same elementary school population. The Iowa High School Content Examination was published in 1925. Other test batteries, such as the Metropolitan and the California, followed shortly thereafter.

The 1930s are sometimes referred to as the period of Dustbowl Empiricism. Large state universities of the Midwest led the development of a range of tests used to assess all aspects of the educational enterprise from input of student aptitudes to the output of student achievement. "If it moved, measure it! If it didn't move, measure it!", some joked, became the rallying cry of many who would judge educational success and failure. Such tests have had both positive and negative effects on children, teachers, and schools. They have offered cheap, seemingly objective ways for making judgments about abilities and achievements. They have also created previously unavailable opportunities for some poor children to demonstrate their capabilities.

At the same time, critics have charged that standardized tests by their very nature limit students' chances to demonstrate their true abilities. They also argue that such tests provide only the illusion of a meritocracy while masking inherent cultural biases. A test, too, can control or drive the curriculum, thus becoming less an indication of quality and more an instrument of instruction or curriculum control.

To ask if some aspect of education works well is a useless question until one also asks: "Compared to what?" In the 1980s and 1990s, there has been renewed interest in comparing people and schools and communities in order to assign some relative value to what goes in, what goes on, and what comes out of schooling. Secretary of Education William Bennett, for example, instituted what became known as "wall charts," or summaries of key statistics to facilitate comparisons over time. The **National Assessment of Educational Progress (NAEP)**—a battery of achievement tests administered nationwide—has received renewed interest as a means of charting progress, or the lack thereof, state by state.

Any serious effort to understand educational quality must look at a bigger picture, or consider how schools affect and are affected by societal contexts. With the rapid development of modern society have come expectations that schools will improve the income, status, and social and personal discipline of all who attend. It is clear, however, that some places and some people have more talent, more money, more opportunities, and more luck than others. These contextual factors exert powerful influences on education and on later success in life. They are not readily dismissed in the quest for educational quality (Jencks et al., 1972).

SUMMARY

1. Passion for intellectual freedom and civil liberties increased greatly when the Civil War ended. Passage of constitutional amendments changed race relations legally by ending slavery, defining citizenship, and forbidding states to deny the right to vote. Nonetheless, the customs of segregation and discrimination remained entrenched. Intellectuals and ordinary citizens led organized efforts to combat racial, ethnic, and gender discrimination wherever they existed, including in schools.

2. After the Civil War, the population of the United States grew rapidly, most noticeably in the cities and industrialized areas. As Fuchs (1990) observed, because America was meant to be inclusive of all, the country became a kaleidoscope of race, ethnicity, and civic culture. Schools were supported to shape the pieces into a coherent social design—a design that included Native Americans, European Americans, African Americans, Hispanic Americans, Asian Americans, other Americans, exceptional learners, and women.

3. Following the Civil War, most teachers were young, poorly paid, and rarely educated beyond elementary subjects. Teaching was not considered a desirable job, and the turnover of teachers was high. Efforts to professionalize teaching began during the nineteenth century as expectations of teachers broadened to include less subjective qualifications. Teachers also gained a measure of economic independence. At the same time, they lost managerial and curricular control of schools and schooling.

4. "Civilization" spread across the frontier in the form of one-room schools. As time passed and communities grew, people expected schools not only to eradicate ignorance but also to minimize differences among people and to ameliorate the effects of poverty and discrimination. Schooling was viewed as a way to get ahead.

5. Rapid industrialization in post-Civil War America created immense demands for workers who were willing and able to produce goods cheaply and quickly and to offer services efficiently. Public school teachers and school administrators taught immigrants, members of minority groups, and those from impoverished circumstances skills of literacy and numeracy as they transmitted the work ethic.

6. From the late nineteenth century on, schools were embedded in a society that demonstrated in many ways the increasing value of education. The increasing availability of newspapers, books, and magazines stimulated and supported people's desires to learn. The development of radio, motion pictures, television, and other forms of mass communication made informal or out-of-school education more pervasive than ever before.

7. By the beginning of the twentieth century, critics initiated what was to become a sustained attack on public schools, particularly in the cities. Increasingly educators looked to science for answers to their problems, engaging in research on teaching and learning and using techniques of scientific management to run the schools.

8. Wars and economic depressions have had dramatic effects on both the adults and the young in schools. Prior to World War II, for example, one teacher taught all ages of students in the same room, and each progressed at his or her own pace. These one-room schools began to fall by the wayside as school districts were combined to concentrate resources and centralize administration. Consolidation meant students had to be bused to central locations, such as huge regional high schools, often over long distances in the Midwest and West.

9. The concept of school developed continually over time. Preschools acknowledged the special needs of young children. Middle schools were structured to help young people make the transition between childhood and early adolescence. Comprehensive high schools were established to meet the diverse needs, interests, and abilities of older students.

10. Between 1920 and 1945, educators were influenced by the progressive movement. Progressive teachers served as helpers and guides, relying more on class discussions, debates, demonstrations, and individualized learning than on direct instruction and rote learning from textbooks. Nonetheless, from the late nineteenth century through World War II, most instruction remained traditional and teacher-centered: teachers did most of the talking, teachers controlled the time, the activities, and classroom space.

11. In the 1960s, schools served as battlegrounds in the War on Poverty, in desegregation, and in the quest for racial equality. The federal government exerted its influence to end segregation, to support the needs of children living in poverty, to promote racial and sexual equity, to secure entitlements for students with disabilities, to promote bilingual-bicultural programs, and to provide career education opportunities. The New Federalism of the 1980s returned to states and localities both the power and financial responsibility for educational programs.

12. With technological advances, people have perceived more links between schools and the world of work. The 1986 Carnegie Forum on Education and the Economy argued that weak schools threatened America's ability to compete in world markets. Schools that worked were described as places that were safe and free of disciplinary problems. Teachers expected that students could achieve and communicated these expectations publicly. The schools emphasized basic skills. School personnel monitored and evaluated student progress. Successful schools also had strong principals who served as program leaders (Bossert, 1985).

13. School curriculum has often reflected the nation's moods and values as well as its knowledge. Public schools, as defined in terms of teachers and curriculum, have been criticized routinely for trying to be and to do too much. Efforts to standardize the curriculum, to diversify course offerings, and to integrate different cultural views in course materials have been among major concerns.

14. Higher education has grown continually, providing increasingly varied access to adults. Institutions of higher education provide technical training in occupations and trades and academic preparation in the professions, research, business and industry, and a variety of other fields.

15. Those having responsibilities for regulation and control of public education have come to view educational success and failure in terms of what goes in, what goes on, and what comes out of schools.

TERMS AND CONCEPTS

assimilation
black codes
Brown v. Board of Education
Bureau of Indian Affairs (BIA)
Chautauqua movement
Committee of Fifteen
Committee of Ten on Secondary School Studies
Elementary and Secondary Education Act

exclusion acts
Freedman's Bureau
Hispanic
Indian Self-Determination and Educational Assistance Act
National Assessment of Educational Progress (NAEP)

National Association for the Advancement of Colored People (NAACP)
National Defense Education Act (NDEA)
Plessy v. Ferguson
progressivism
settlement houses
Women's Educational Equity Act (WEEA)

STUDENT ACTIVITIES

If Americans live in the present with one eye on the future, they are surely defined in large measure by their past. Take a few moments to explore some connections among the past, present, and future as they relate to education.

Perceive and Value

A pattern of the ebb and flow of reform emerges in this period of American educational history; that is, individuals and groups push for change in public education, the change is accepted and institutionalized, or tabled, or it dies, sometimes only to reappear in another decade. *Identify* one concern about schooling that has stimulated reform, *describe* that concern from the points of view of those who were for and against the change, and trace the outcomes of actions taken to address it.

Know and Act

In this chapter, science, philanthropy, and mass media were identified as being among the important factors that shaped education in the United States in the generations following the Civil War. In what ways were these factors important? To what extent are they still important today? In shaping education, are these factors important in the same or in new ways? Find out and write about how developments in science, philanthropy, or mass media may affect you and your students in the classroom. In your essay or journal, outline a specific plan for using this influence in ways that benefit you as a teacher and your students as learners.

Evaluate

Why do you think educational reform movements tend to overlap in repeating cycles over time? Develop a hypothesis that might explain this phenomenon, and test your hypothesis against the historical evidence presented in this chapter. Then, work with classmates to intuitively develop a list of conditions or criteria, which, when satisfied, may indicate that a given educational reform is successful. Use a concrete example from history to illustrate your findings.

Discover

As a team project, contact education interest groups, political action groups, or lobbies to collect literature and learn their agendas for school reform. Also, find out what education bills are presently slated for consideration in the U.S. Congress and what reform issues they address. For each current issue you discover, identify its precedents in the past, and then predict the possible outcomes. What do you think will be the impacts or implications of these outcomes in the future of education in America?

4

Philosophical Foundations in Action

Philosophies live in people's minds and hearts and are made evident through their behavior. Although people rarely stop to notice, philosophy saturates their personal and professional existences. This chapter provides an overview of major philosophies that have influenced thought and behavior through the ages and that have special relevance for educators.

Francis Fukuyama (1992) has contended that people in the Western world have reached "the end of History," or the point at which all the really big philosophical questions have been settled. While communism is in decline and liberal democracy enjoys popularity, the increasingly complex problems and opportunities that present themselves in everyday life clamor for philosophical attention. No less than those who have preceded them, people seek to understand who they are and who they might become.

Besides describing classical thought that is relevant to teachers and teaching, this chapter focuses on ways philosophies are reflected in schools and through teachers. The chapter also explains why it is important to understand how people think about the means and ends of education and provides specific examples of ways different views have been defined through personal and social action. Finally, the chapter explains how you may begin to articulate your own personal philosophy of education and to shape it over time.

1 What ancient philosophical beliefs underlie present educational practice? How are these views of life similar and different from one another?

`Perceive`

....

2 People behave as they do for many reasons. Why may teachers vary in the ways they think about teaching and learning?

`Value`

....

3 How do the roles of teachers and students and methods of instruction compare in educational systems influenced by existentialism, behaviorism, pragmatism, perennialism, essentialism, and social reconstructionism?

`Know`

....

4 Describe your personal philosophy of education. What outcomes would you want students to attain? By what means might you help them reach such goals? What roles might teachers and students play in the classroom?

`Act`

....

5 How might you determine what beliefs influence a teacher's classroom behaviors?

`Evaluate`

....

WHAT IS PHILOSOPHY AND WHAT DOES IT HAVE TO DO WITH YOU AS A TEACHER?

When people define philosophy as the pursuit of wisdom, the classic dictionary definition, do you conjure up a set of stereotypical images—people strolling through gardens in togas, deep in erudite conversation, and slightly seedy, disheveled professors who misplace their car keys? The word *philosophy* has strange effects on people, somewhere between the ridiculous and the sublime. In the dictionary, *philosophy* does not begin to communicate the beauty, the complexity, or the power of the ideas behind the word.

Philosophy Defined

Philosophy can be characterized as a set of ideas about the nature of reality and about the meaning of life. Ideas about being, knowledge, and conduct have evolved over time as philosophers have pondered such questions as: What is basic human nature? What is real and true about life and the world? What is the nature of knowledge? What is worth knowing or striving for? What is just, good, right, or beautiful? Whether he or she realizes it, every individual has some notion about the answers to these questions, about the world and the nature of the people who inhabit it.

In the preface to a collection of essays, G.K. Chesterton, nineteenth- and twentieth-century author, poet, social and literary critic, wrote:

> There are some people—and I am one of them—who think that the most practical and important thing about a man is still his view of the universe. We think that for a landlady considering a lodger it is important to know his income, but still more important to know his philosophy. We think that for a general about to fight an enemy it is important to know the enemy's numbers, but still more important to know the enemy's philosophy. (cited in James, 1907, p. 17)

As Chesterton suggests, there are some practical reasons why philosophy is important. If we know a lodger's or a general's or a teacher's philosophy, then we have some indication of how he or she will behave and why. It is the propensity for action inherent in one's philosophy that gives it practical importance. John Dewey (1916) was more direct when he argued that, "Whenever philosophy has been taken seriously, it has always been assumed that it signified achieving a wisdom which would influence the conduct of life" (p. 378).

The Place of Philosophy in Education

Philosophy influences daily educational life in many ways. Parents may choose or reject schools for their children because they believe schools' philosophies will be translated into desirable or undesirable educational experiences. Principals run schools in keeping with their thoughts about managing people and administering programs—sometimes like businesses or factories, sometimes like churches, sometimes like colleges, sometimes like football teams. Teachers plan lessons, interact with students, and judge students' performances according to their views of knowledge, which may depend heavily on their memories of being a student and their idealized conceptions of the role of teacher. A professor requires teacher education students to learn a particular set of instructional methods to use with pupils in classroom settings based on his or her view of acceptable professional practice. Philosophy shapes the writing of curricula, the preparation and scoring of tests, and the architecture of school buildings.

The Importance of Putting Educational Philosophies in Perspective

The potential for conflict in this philosophical potpourri is great. And from time to time, some person or some group tries to claim hegemony—the philosophical upper hand, the one best way to view the universe. But the one-best-way people do not seem to last long in public education. Public schools appeal to the general public for support. Sooner or later, extreme ideas are recognized as falling outside the latitude of acceptance of the majority of people the schools are meant to serve.

Philosophies, or one's principles, as Nel Noddings (1984) warned in her treatise on caring, can be wielded as bludgeons:

> Wherever there is a principle, there is implied its exception and, too often, principles function to separate us from each other. We may become dangerously self-righteous when we perceive ourselves as holding a precious principle not held by the other. The other may then be devalued and treated "differently." (p. 5)

Philosophical wars in education have become almost routine. People who rigidly adhere to philosophies often neglect to reexamine their views in light of changing conditions. Actions become habitual, out of touch with the present, and limited as expressed visions of the future.

For example, we build educational systems with a view of the "typical," "average," or "ordinary" person in mind, and then put considerable resources and energy into maintaining these systems while they are becoming populated by "extraordinary" people. Martin Haberman (1987) argued persuasively that the education of inner-city children and teachers in the United States has suffered from this phenomenon. Colleges and universities are guided by philosophies fitted to suburban America as they recruit, select, and educate teachers to teach the nation's children. These philosophies, however, are radically out of line with life in urban schools and communities.

> "The pretension to dogmatize about ['isms'] . . . is the root of most human injustices and cruelties, and the strain in human character most likely to make the angels weep."

There are other reasons the study of philosophy is important. A philosophy, particularly that which is different from one's own, forces a person to examine his or her thinking in a new light. Someone who calls herself an "idealist," cannot help but grow from a serious consideration of a "realist" view, and vice versa. There is almost always some room to change one's mind, but change is unlikely if people are unaware of the options. Big minds have room to consider more than one point of view; they are not constricted by real or imagined pressure to be "philosophically correct." Many educators, for example, favor eclecticism—they select what appears to be the best from various doctrines, methods, or styles. Others are more pluralistic, that is, they are guided at different times by different philosophies based on their perceptions of learners' needs and educational goals.

WHAT ARE THE ROOTS OF AMERICAN EDUCATIONAL PHILOSOPHIES?

A number of philosophies, or systems of ideas, have developed through the ages. As will be described below, efforts to address life's questions have informed thinking about the education of children. By understanding how these educational philosophies translate into practice, teachers can form their own personal philosophies about teaching and learning.

The Classical Branches of Philosophy

Western philosophies originated with the classical Greeks who used a systematic method for addressing life's questions. Figure 4.1 shows how Greek thinkers divided philosophy into three branches:

1. **Metaphysics** and its two corollary areas deal with the study of reality. *Ontology* explores issues related to nature or existence or being, while *cosmology* is concerned with the nature and origin of the cosmos or universe.

2. **Epistemology** is concerned with the nature of knowledge or how we come to know things. We develop knowledge of truth through thought from observations, and from logic—by reasoning deductively from a general proposition to a particular case, and inductively from a set of particulars or facts to a general principle. We also develop knowledge from scientific inquiry, intuition, and our senses.

3. **Axiology** seeks to ascertain what is of value. More specifically, **ethics** explores issues of morality and conduct while **aesthetics** is concerned with beauty.

The philosophies described in the following sections have influenced education in our society.

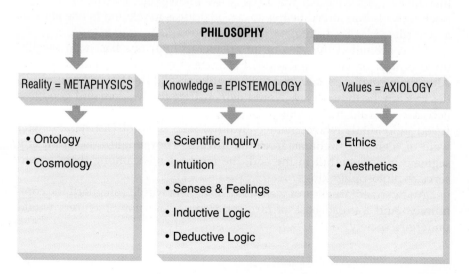

FIGURE 4.1

Summary of Branches of Philosophy

How is each branch of philosophy embedded in your role as a teacher?

Idealism

Idealism is a philosophy that suggests ultimate reality lies in consciousness or reason. The progenitor of idealism, Plato (427?–347 BC), student of Socrates and citizen of Athens, imagined a society driven by the pursuit of knowledge. To search for truth, justice, and beauty in the world was to seek meaning in one's own life and in the collective life of the community. Plato envisioned this exploration as a shift of the mind away from the immediate physical world of what we can see, feel, smell, hear, and taste and toward a world of enduring ideas. Plato believed it was the place of philosophy and philosophers to help people think clearly about these important ideas and to aid people in governing themselves wisely. Perfect knowledge of the ideal resided outside humans as an absolute, or as God.

In his writings, Plato explained his vision through imaginary conversations between Socrates and his students. These discussions or dialogues were written as poetry, science, and philosophy. They have guided thought and action in Western civilizations since the fourth century AD, when Socrates died from drinking hemlock at about age 60. He had been convicted of corrupting the young and of not believing in the gods.

In these dialogues, Socrates asks questions of students that force them to examine critically their notions about life, truth, beauty, and justice. As they interact with Socrates, students discover the errors in their thinking and formulate clearer, more accurate ideas about life's questions. The **Socratic method**, then, is one of teaching through inquiry and dialogues in which students discover and clarify knowledge.

The Republic is Plato's most celebrated dialogue. In it he described his ideal society—how people were to think, to value, to behave, to teach, and to organize and govern society. Plato knew this utopia was unattainable. Yet for him, and for the idealists who have followed, such visions of perfection are to serve as goals toward which we should strive in our own lifetimes and as benchmarks against which we should judge human progress over many lifetimes.

Plato, like Socrates, believed that people were born with knowledge and that the task of the teacher was to elicit this knowledge. The dialogues were teaching tools that forced people to consider ideas in relation to one another and to some idealized state.

Plato promoted the idea of an aristocracy, not one based on wealth, brute power, or family influence, but instead on wisdom and goodness. Although he believed men and women alike should be afforded opportunities to learn, he thought few would demonstrate the wisdom and goodness necessary to rule their fellow citizens. In Plato's utopia, those tried and tested individuals who remained healthy, who thought clearly, and who were of high moral character would govern. They might arise from any segment of society, but in the end, the most talented among them would serve as philosopher kings.

An intermediate class of well-trained soldiers would safeguard the community. And a broad base of farmers, traders, and manufacturers would undergird society.

In short, the perfect society would be that in which each class and each unit would be doing the work to which its nature and aptitude best adapted it; in which no class or individual would interfere with others, but all would cooperate in difference to produce an efficient and harmonious whole. That would be a just state. (Durant, 1961, p. 32)

For Plato, then, education was the vehicle of social mobility. It was also the key to creating and perpetuating the ideal society. Philosophers would train people to think clearly, and processes of education would screen people for their assignments to social classes. Plato's curriculum for this idealized society was straightforward, rigorous, and in some ways lifelong. He advocated physical education in the early years, followed by the study of music. He also envisioned a kind of moral education that would make citizens realize they had responsibilities to one another. At various points in one's development, a person would test his or her progress in the crucible of real life.

Realism

Realism is a philosophy that suggests objects of sense or perception exist independently of the mind. Aristotle (384–322 BC), student of Plato, differed from his teacher in philosophical views. Plato, the idealist in search of truth had turned away from the physical world toward the world of ideas. Aristotle sought truth by investigating the real world around him. His work reflected the philosophical orientation called realism.

Aristotle established a vast library of manuscripts, a collection of zoological and botanical specimens, and a school, or lyceum, in Athens, where he taught many young scholars. A staff of assistants helped him record raw observational information and synthesize the knowledge of the day. Despite the lack of scientific equipment and basic knowledge of the laws of nature, Aristotle pushed science forward by acting on the belief that the study of matter would lead to a better understanding of ideas. Much of the intellectual spadework for Mendel's genetic theory, Darwin's theory of evolution, the science of embryology, the disciplines of biology and psychology, and the study of aesthetics was performed by Aristotle and his students.

For Aristotle, Plato's ideals were real only in so far as they were actualized in material objects. He believed everything sought to fulfill its potential or to take the form of what it was meant to be. He characterized this movement from potential to actual as involving four causes. If marble (material cause) as determined by the sculptor to be a statue of a woman (formal cause), and was shaped by the sculptor (efficient cause) to take the form of a woman (final cause), then the potential of the marble would be actualized. This same progression of causes, according to Aristotle, held for the development of humans.

Aristotle believed that humans learn through their senses. As individuals experience the world, they develop and refine concepts about objects. They do so through direct experience. Unlike idealists, for whom truth resides within an individual waiting to be discovered, realists believe

Aristotle

knowledge exists independent of human knowing. The role of education, then, is to teach students about the world in which they live.

Aristotle believed happiness is the ultimate goal in humans' lives. Unlike Plato, he believed that goodness and wisdom were means to this end, not ends in themselves. People traversed the path to true happiness by stretching their minds to the fullest of their capabilities. "Virtue, or rather excellence, will depend on clear judgment, self-control, symmetry of desire, artistry of means" (Durant, 1961, p. 60). People were thought to demonstrate virtue through the achievement of experience; they did not simply possess virtue because of their intent or innocence.

But if excellence is desirable, excess is taboo. Aristotle counseled people to seek the middle ground, or Golden Mean, in matters of life ". . . between cowardice and rashness is courage; between stinginess and extravagance is liberality; between sloth and greed is ambition . . ." (Durant, 1961, p. 60). Indeed, to Aristotle, the middle ground was fertile territory where training could make excellence flourish. As people practiced thinking and behaving in productive ways, they developed habits that would lead them to excellence.

Like Plato, Aristotle believed in government by an aristocracy of talented people. A government-run education system would emphasize balance in assigning people to the work of society and teaching responsibility to the state. Education would serve these purposes.

Thomism

Thomism is a philosophical orientation that relies on faith and reason as complementary sources of truth. Thomism may rightfully be considered the religious form of realism (O'Neill, 1981). Named after Saint Thomas Aquinas (1225–1274), a Dominican theologian who taught at the University of Paris, Thomism is based on the belief that there is a knowable independent reality that is the creation of God, Christianity's supreme power. Like Aristotle, Aquinas believed that human beings use their senses and reason to understand the world. Aquinas also believed that all people have a soul, and that the ultimate goal in life is to experience eternity with God. Truth, then, is both natural and spiritual. Natural truth is knowledge about the physical world gained through reason. Attainment of spiritual or supernatural knowledge is also dependent on reason:

> Supernatural knowledge is *nonrational*, but it is not *irrational*. Ideally, the teachings of faith should be presented through reason, as a logical inference from the known. When this is done, the supernatural pronouncements of faith become convincing beyond all doubt, because (a) they are the logical outgrowth of man's innate powers of rational inference and (b) they reflect a vision of reality that is so overwhelmingly meaningful as to be rationally irresistible. (O'Neill, 1981, p. 164)

To grasp truth, people combine reason with faith in the perfect knowledge that comes directly or indirectly from divine revelation or from the authority of the Church. The role of education is first and foremost to train individuals to understand religious truths necessary for spiritual salvation.

Secondary aims are to develop the intellectual, social, religious, and physical skills that will enable students to be effective and contributing members of society. Most often this is achieved through direct rather than indirect instructional methods; that is, information is conveyed through drill, lecture, recitation, teacher-directed questioning, and highly structured discussions. Catholics have used catechisms to teach students to reach their goals.

Although Thomism is the historical and philosophical foundation of Roman Catholic education, according to Nancy Lesko (1988), many Catholic schools today do not adhere strictly to the principles of Thomism. They have turned their attention instead to secular issues common to the middle class:

> [R]eligious training is becoming secondary in Catholic schools; that is, these schools have become centrally concerned with preparing Catholic youth for contemporary life, i.e., facilitating their educational and social mobility. Catholic school administrators and board members are also prompted to emphasize the academic side of their schools as they develop strategies for the schools' economic survival. (p. 18)

Humanism

Humanism is a philosophy that, in terms of education, calls for respect and kindness toward students and developmentally appropriate instruction in liberal arts, social conduct, and moral principles. This orientation is grounded in the writings of Erasmus (1466?–1536), Martin Luther (1483–1546), and Jean Jacques Rousseau (1712–1778).

During the Renaissance in Europe, Erasmus advanced an enlightened view of the essential goodness of children. He advocated that the young be taught with kindness and gentleness. Children were to be nurtured, not scolded and abused.

Rousseau enriched this humanistic perspective on the needs of children and the dictates of education. He suggested children not be viewed as blank slates, or as miniature adults, but as individuals possessing natural goodness and needing continual support (see Chapter 2).

Luther and others associated with the Protestant Reformation inspired the idea of public-supported education—education meant to prepare people to take responsibility for their own lives—so that people could read and interpret the Bible for themselves. As people defined the ways they would worship God, then, they also began to define how they would educate for character. Education was an essential ingredient in stimulating and sustaining both the Reformation and the Renaissance. Education empowered people to make their own decisions, thereby to determine their own destiny on earth and thus in the afterlife.

Jean Jacques Rousseau

In the 1950s, 1960s, and 1970s, humanistic psychologists, including Alfred Adler, Carl Rogers, Paul Goodman, and Abraham Maslow, extended humanist philosophy to education and schooling. They wrote and spoke often about the assumptions upon which a humanistic education should be based. Students were not to be forced to learn; the humanists believed students would learn what they needed and wanted to know. Processes of learning were thought to be as important if not more so than the acquisition of facts and skills. Students were assumed to be capable of evaluating themselves and so did not need to be judged by teachers or other adults. Students' emotional well-being was of critical importance in the learning process. Schools must be free from threat

> "[The] safety and strength of a city reside above all in a good education, which furnishes it with instructed, reasonable, honorable, and well-trained citizens."

FIGURE 4.2

Philosophies on Which Western Education Is Based

How might teachers who are idealists, realists, Thomists, and humanists differ in their philosophies of education, relationships with students, and approaches to teaching?

	IDEALISM	REALISM	THOMISM	HUMANISM
Philosophers	Plato	Aristotle	Thomas Aquinas	Erasmus
Metaphysics	Reality is an unchanging world of perfect ideas and universal truths.	Reality is observable events, objects, and matter independent of human knowing.	Reality is an ordered world created by God that people can come to know. People strive for eternity with God.	Reality is also humanity's creation. People strive for personal meaning in their experience and interpretation of life on earth.
Epistemology	Knowledge is obtained when ideas are brought into consciousness through self-examination and discourse.	Knowledge is obtained when students are taught ideas that can be verified and skills that enable them to know objects they encounter.	A combination of reason and faith enables students to acquire and use bodies of knowledge.	Exploration, questioning, and critical thinking enable students to discover or construct and use knowledge.
Axiology	Wisdom of goodness; discipline, order, self-control; preservation of cultural heritage of the past.	Self-control; clear judgment and rational thought; personal excellence; balance and moderation.	Knowing, loving, and serving God.	Knowing and loving God; serving humanity.

if students were to take responsibility for their learning and to enjoy what they did.

The work of Paulo Freire, a Brazilian educator, swept the developed world in the 1960s and 1970s. He was instrumental in encouraging the teaching of illiterate, indigent workers in the developing world. With the abilities to read and write, Freire believed, people would become aware of their own essential humanness and their social situation. Education, Freire (1970) wrote, would empower people to better their own lives and the lives of others:

> [W]hile both humanization and dehumanization are real alternatives, only the first is man's vocation. This vocation is constantly negated, yet it is affirmed by that very negation. It is thwarted by injustice, exploitation, oppression, and the violence of the oppressors; it is affirmed by the yearning of the oppressed for freedom and justice, and by their struggle to recover their lost humanity." (p. 28)

Through the years, idealism, realism, Thomism, and humanism have made their effects felt in classrooms. Each philosophy, as can be seen in Figure 4.2, reveals itself in educationally recognizable ways.

WHAT MODERN PHILOSOPHIES INFLUENCE WESTERN EDUCATION?

Some philosophies are relatively new or young compared to idealism, realism, and humanism. Yet they too have influenced American education.

Existentialism

Sören Kierkegaard (1813–1855) is considered the father of **existentialism**, a philosophy that emphasizes the subjectivity of human experience and the importance of individual creativity and choice in a nonrational world. Friedrich Wilhelm Nietzsche (1844–1900), Martin Heidegger (1889–1976), Jean-Paul Sartre (1905–1980), Albert Camus (1913–1960), Paul Tillich (1886–1965), Martin Buber (1878–1965) and others have developed existentialist thought by attempting to describe reality not as separate from or beyond the comprehension of humans, but instead as the result of individual passion and life experience.

Existentialists believe that the physical universe has no inherent meaning apart from human experience. The world and forces of nature exist, but they are not ordered in some grand scheme in which humans play their appropriate part. Human life, too, exists; we are here, but we are only what we make of ourselves. In Sartre's (1947, p. 28) often quoted phrase, "existence precedes essence." We owe our existence to nature, but we define ourselves through our actions.

Nietzsche (1924, 1961) revealed the dark side of this view. He characterized life as a grim battle in which one requires strength, pride, and intelligence just to survive. Sensitivity, kindness, and consideration were signs of weakness. There was no god of mercy who ruled benevolently and rewarded the worthy with eternal life in heaven. Indeed, there was no God at all. And if there ever had been, He was surely dead.

Nietzsche would have restructured ideas of morality and theology to reflect evolution theory. He believed that we should strive not to better the majority of people, who were mostly worthless, but to promote genius and to develop superior personalities. From an aristocracy of talent and power—one cultivated by those who choose to restrain and discipline themselves—would arise the superman.

For existentialists, choice is a critical concept. People choose whom they will be. Some allow others to decide for them, but exercising this default option is also a kind of choice. Although existentialists do not reject morals or norms of behavior, they repudiate habitual adherence to them. Existentialists encourage people faced with a difficult conflict of values to concentrate seriously on their own situations and to choose what is right for them. When we are cut loose from restrictions, we assume responsibility for our own actions. We cannot simply rely on what we are told to do or on what some scripture directs us to do. And when we are free to choose our directions, we prize that freedom for others.

Martin Buber, existentialist and Hasidic Jew, assailed theologians' talk about God and their pretensions about knowing God. In *I and Thou* (1937), Buber did not try to prop up religion or to argue that God was present in all things. Instead, he raised the possibility that life without religion lacked an important dimension (Buber, 1970). Buber proclaimed that the secular was sacred, and that God is present when people encounter one another in honest dialogue. Human relationships are central in creating meaning in our lives. Buber and other existentialists influenced the development of humanistic psychology, in which relationships, free thinking, and action lead to self-actualization or personal fulfillment.

A.S. Neill's Summerhill in England is a famous application of existential/humanistic philosophy to schooling. Under Neill's direction, teachers encouraged students to philosophize about life using their personal experiences as bases for examining individual choice making. Through dialogue with peers and instructors, students learned to perceive and solve problems. The goal was to help students become cognitively equipped "authentic" individuals having a deep commitment to the creation of a better world.

Marxism

Marxism is a philosophy based on the belief that the human condition is determined by forces in history that prevent people from achieving economic freedom and social and political equality. Karl Marx (1818–1883) was an historian, philosopher, and social theorist born to Jewish parents in Germany. In the main, his work was not taken seriously until after his death.

As a university student, Marx was influenced greatly by the idealist Georg Wilhelm Friedrich Hegel (1770–1831), who at the time was the grand master of German philosophy. Although Marx grew to reject Hegel's political philosophy, he was influenced greatly by Hegel's thought, particularly his development of the concept of the dialectic.

Hegel referred to the process by which human thought and human history progresses as a dialectic. The dialectic was a constant intellectual

VOICES

On the Existentialist Teacher

George F. Kneller, philosopher of education formerly at the University of California at Los Angeles, argued that if teachers were to adopt an existentialist view, their choices would be important and difficult and their pedagogical strategies would be clear.

If we accept [existentialism as a world view] . . . as free men and free teachers we must seek to expose and combat all those forces in culture and society that tend to dehumanize men by denying their freedom. We must repudiate the subordination of the person to economic "laws," the tyranny of the majority over the dissenting minority, and the stifling of individuality by social conformism. We must urge our students to recognize and fulfill the freedom that is theirs as persons. What we urge we must also practice by respecting their freedom as we value our own.

Most choices we make are admittedly trivial and inconsequential—choice of a necktie, choice of a restaurant, choice of a movie. A serious choice is a choice between actions involving fundamental values. It calls for deep concentration, a looking into oneself. However, I must not be content merely to apply an abstract moral principle. This is a weak choice, reliance on a rule rather than on myself. I should choose the course of action that seems uniquely right in this particular situation. I should seek not the way but my way. The hardest choices to make are often those between alternative goods. Two courses of action seem to have an equally good claim on us—which course do we take?

If I am an existentialist teacher, I urge the student to take responsibility for, and to deal with, the results of his actions. To act is to produce consequences. He must accept that these consequences are the issue of his choice, but at the same time he must not submit to them as unalterable, for this is to assume that freedom is exhausted in a single act. Freedom is never exhausted, and each

consequence poses the need for further choice. I would teach him that his life is his own to lead and that no one else can lead it for him. It is pointless to blame his failures on environment, family, temperament, or the influence of others. These conditions are for choice to challenge. Whatever may have happened to the student in the past, the future is his to make.

Does this attitude lead to a ruthless disregard for others, to my fulfillment at the expense of yours? Not at all. True freedom implies not egoism but communion. The egoist is driven by a narrow self-interest. With him choice is not self-fulfillment but self-limitation. Freedom, open and dynamic, longs for other centers of freedom, other persons. It does not calculate but gives. The fulfillment of freedom is communion with others.

If as a teacher I assume the style and gestures for which convention calls, I may touch only surfaces of my students' lives. I must go beyond familiarity and open myself to them. I must come top them unreservedly, creating the trust from which springs communion and true self-fulfillment.

CRITICAL THINKING

How might a classical idealist such as Plato respond to Kneller's declaration? How might a classical realist such as Aristotle respond? What examples of "dehumanizing" and "stifling" conditions in school cultures might Kneller accept as evidence of his claim? To what teacher "styles" and "gestures" might Kneller refer when he suggests teachers risk touching only the "surfaces of students' lives"? How might teachers "open themselves" to students to create communion or mutual participation in educational life? How might "schools without walls" and "democratic classrooms" reflect values implicit in the philosophy of existentialism?

Source: Kneller, G.F. (1971). *Introduction to the philosophy of education* (2nd ed.). New York: John Wiley & Sons, pp. 72–76.

movement from thesis, to antithesis, and finally to synthesis. Movement in thought occurred, for example, when one played the thesis or the idea against its opposite, which for Hegel was the reality of nature. Thought moved along a continuum by way of the dialectic process to richer, more complex syntheses. He argued that ultimately this process would reach the Absolute Idea, or an idea that bore close resemblance to idealists' conceptions of truth. Hegel rejected the realist view that truth is independent of our minds. People become and remain alienated, according to Hegel, until they understand they are thinking beings and that truth is a function of this self-realization.

The process, Hegel maintained, worked also for history. Civilization progressed along a continuum toward richer, more complex syntheses. Culture moved forward, building on what had come before.

Marx recognized the value of science as a way to acquire knowledge. For Marx, human perception is based on the sense experience of the material world, and this perceptual experience shapes one's knowledge. The social order, therefore, is not fixed. Human nature is malleable—people and social institutions can be shaped and formed. A person's social class is a matter of education and circumstance rather than a matter of some preordained right. Marx meant to arrange these factors to produce human progress; that is, he meant to revolutionize society.

Marx thought of the dialectical process as a clash of economic forces in which the capitalist system exploited the worker. The ruling class seized workers' productive capacities and offered money in return, making workers subservient to the system.

Within this context, Marx saw progress as a mixed blessing. In capitalist society, the forces of production continually increase. Simultaneously, people create a more oppressive social organization in that society becomes characterized by unequal classes. Capitalists, Marx contended, accumulate great wealth, but they create inequalities and dehumanize people. Marx thought that in time the exploited would rise up and overthrow the ruling class. The aim of Marxism, then, is to change the material conditions of society. When these conditions change, consciousness changes; when consciousness changes, ideology changes, and the perfect, classless, communistic society will result.

There have been many varieties of Marxism over the years, but in the twentieth century, Marxism has been articulated and developed intellectually most notably by people referred to as the Frankfurt School—a school of thought based on Marxist assumptions about the social world. Max Horkheimer, (1895–1973), Theodor Adorno (1903–1969), Herbert Marcuse (1898–1979), and Jürgen Habermas (born 1929) have written about the nature of knowledge and human interest to describe how they think the world works and have projected how people might proceed to improve the human condition.

Habermas in particular has exerted considerable influence on social and educational theory. As a philosopher and sociologist, he is respected as one of the most influential thinkers in Germany over the past decade (Ewert, 1991). Critical theorists such as Habermas attempt to reveal the covert values in schooling and society. They claim that schools alienate students and "de-skill" them by establishing the goals of education instead of encouraging students to set their own goals. The process of schooling, then, is characterized as one that breeds dependency on authority, promotes top-down communication, and advances a distorted view of history (Apple, 1982). Many of the negative attributes of schools have been identified and attacked by modern education reformers who are not Marxists, but who nonetheless recognize the debilitating effects of maintaining the status quo.

Behaviorism

Behaviorism is a philosophical orientation based on the belief that human behavior is determined by forces in the environment that are beyond our control rather than by the exercise of free will. Behaviorism stands in stark contrast to **cognitivism**, a philosophical orientation based on the belief that people actively construct their knowledge of the world through experience and interaction rather than through behavioral conditioning. Several names are associated with the development of behaviorism—Ivan Pavlov (1849–1936), John Watson (1878–1958), and E.L. Thorndike (1874–1949)—but none is more prominent than that of B. F. Skinner (1904–1990). His influence on the field itself and on modern education is incalculable.

Skinner was a psychologist who concentrated on scientific experimentation and empirical observation. Although he made his reputation with tightly controlled laboratory experimentation, he could let his mind roam freely over complex social problems. Skinner (1971) viewed our failure to solve social problems as a failure of the knowledge of human behavior:

> Physics and biology have come a long way, but there has been no comparable development of anything like a science of human behavior. Greek physics and biology are now of historical interest only . . ., but the dialogues of Plato are still assigned to students and cited as if they threw light on human behavior. Aristotle could not have understood a page of modern physics or biology, but Socrates and his friends would have little trouble in following most current discussions of human affairs. And as to technology, we have made immense strides in controlling the physical and biological worlds, but our practices in government, education, and much of economics, though adapted to very different conditions, have not greatly improved. (pp. 5–6)

Skinner would have placed science in the hands of those who would work for a peaceful and more just world. Science could be used to shape morality. To behaviorists, education conditions people to behave in more and less civilized ways.

Behaviorism is sometimes characterized as an "empty organism" theory of behavior; that is, behaviorists view the immediate world in terms of stimuli and responses to these stimuli without acknowledging what, if anything, happens in a person's mind. Watson was extremely influential in this regard. In some of his experiments, he conditioned his son to fear small animals and then deconditioned him. Watson repudiated completely the value of introspection in psychology. He thought that because people could not measure free will in a human being, free will did not exist.

Behaviorists believe that if something exists, it can be measured. Like other realists, then, they rely on knowledge derived from the physical

B. F. Skinner

world, the world around them. To understand this world in relation to human behavior, they examine patterns of environmental influences on patterns of human responses to these influences.

The educational applications of behaviorism to enhance both achievement and to improve conduct are many and varied. Schools use programmed instruction, both computer-based and print materials, to teach mathematics, reading, and other subject matter. These curricula are organized into discrete, sequentially ordered units of study, accompanied by unit tests, opportunities for feedback on performance, and chances to practice skills. Educators also advocate the use of behavioral contracts or contingency management schemes to influence student behavior. These are organized as if . . ., then . . . agreements between teachers and students: If you do your homework correctly, then you can spend the end of the class period working in the library.

Beyond curricula, the behavioristic school of thought has permeated life in education in more subtle ways. The language of education is rife with behavioral terminology—reward, punishment, contingency, reinforcer, shaping, fading. Teachers speak of "reinforcing desirable behavior." They try "to ignore inappropriate behavior." People want student motivation "to become intrinsic" rather than "extrinsic," and so forth. Many educators use the words and phrases of behavioral engineering. They have incorporated the ideas, the language, and some of the practices into their own professional repertoires without abandoning strongly held beliefs about such things as the importance of students' thoughts and feelings (Cohen & Hearn, 1988).

When students are not learning, behaviorists think there must be something wrong with the educational program. The way to solve the problem is to break the program down into its component parts and to fix the pieces that are broken, or to scrap the program altogether and try a new one. The challenge, then, is to engineer environments that produce desired results. This outlook has influenced both the lay public's and educators' perceptions of educational problems and solutions.

Alternatives to the behaviorist outlook take a variety of forms loosely called cognitivism, from cognition—the process of thinking and knowing. On the basis of research on thinking, cognitive psychologists assert that people are not passively conditioned by the environment but rather are active learners. They mentally construct their knowledge of the world and beliefs about reality through their own direct experiences and interactions, and then they act upon those constructs. Cognitivists therefore focus on thought, which cannot be observed directly, while behaviorists focus on behavior that is observable and measurable.

Education that emphasizes thought processes and encourages students to construct meaningful knowledge through real experiences expresses a philosophical orientation known as cognitivism or cognitive-constructivism.

Like behaviorism, cognitivism is a philosophical orientation having implications for education. Educators who favor teaching models based on cognitivism often choose student-centered learning experiences. They aim to assist students by teaching them study skills, thinking skills, and problem-solving skills. They try to provide conceptual **scaffolding** upon which students construct meaning or make sense of information for themselves. In education, the movement to modify curriculum and instruction to reflect the cognitivist outlook is called constructivism.

Pragmatism

Pragmatism is a philosophical method that defines the truth and meaning of ideas according to their physical consequences and practical value. An Englishman, Charles Sanders Pierce (1839–1914), is acknowledged as the originator of modern pragmatism. But pragmatism is so readily equated with the quality people refer to as "common sense" that many would claim it as the unofficial American philosophy. In the last 100 years or so, William James (1842–1910), John Dewey (1859–1952), and, most recently, Richard Rorty (born 1931) have used pragmatism to try to strike a philosophical balance between the realism of the natural sciences and the beliefs of idealists as expressed in art, religion, and politics (Rorty, 1991).

Like other philosophers, early pragmatists concerned themselves with the dualism of mind and matter: a subjective reality exists in our minds, an objective reality exists in the physical world around us. They agreed with the realists that a world exists and is not merely a figment of our imagination. For the pragmatist, the important distinction in the objective/subjective dichotomy, however, is that objective reality has meaning only insofar as people ascribe such meaning based on the consequences of the object. The goal of pragmatists, then, has been to seek wisdom, or truth, by examining the consequences of holding particular beliefs and acting on them.

William James emphasized the right of individuals to create their own reality. He described (James, 1955) the pragmatic method as a way to settle metaphysical disputes that otherwise might be continual:

> Is the world one or many?—fated or free?—material or spiritual?—here are notions either of which may or may not hold good of the world; and disputes over such are unending. The pragmatic method in such cases is to try to interpret each notion by tracing its respective practical consequences. What difference would it practically make to any one if this notion rather than that notion were true? If no practical difference whatever can be traced, then the alternatives mean practically the same thing, and all dispute is idle. Whenever a dispute is serious, we ought to be able to show some practical difference that must follow from one side or the other's being right. (p. 42)

Other pragmatists have argued that the correspondence between human beliefs and physical objects is unimportant. If we believe with good reason that something is true, and there is some gap between our beliefs and truth, we can always improve our beliefs as new evidence becomes avail-

William James

able. Truth is what is good for us to believe (Rorty, 1991). For all practical purposes, if something works, it is true.

Arguably the most important American philosopher ever to consider educational problems, John Dewey, linked pragmatism on many occasions and in many ways to educational preparation for life in a democracy. When people were educated democratically, Dewey argued, they were prepared for life. And when education concentrated on real-life problems, that education prepared people for living fully and effectively in a democracy. Dewey believed ordinary people possessed the intelligence to govern themselves and to direct their own actions; the function of education was to enhance human potential.

> "Cease conceiving of education as mere preparation for later life, and make of it the full meaning of the present life."

The educational implications of pragmatic thought are many and varied, but several are obvious. Pragmatists believe children should be encouraged to learn to make difficult decisions by considering the likely consequences their actions would have on others. Because democracy is the one kind of social organization that permits people to consider multiple points of view, pragmatic action and democracy complement each other. Education never ends—it is a process that continues throughout one's lifetime.

People are instruments of change, capable of experiencing, experimenting, and testing their beliefs. Dewey believed people can interpret the practical consequences of their actions; democracy demanded as much. And "pragmatism was the logic of this new conception of intelligence. . . ." (Westbrook, 1991, p. 149).

Dewey criticized American public education as mechanical, mindless, and practically irrelevant—as little more than indoctrination. His progressive views (see Chapter 3) led him to argue for education that helped students realize their capacities to engage in activity that called for genuine thinking and problem solving. According to Robert Westbrook (1991),

> The youngest children in [Dewey's] school, who were four and five years old, engaged in activities familiar to them from their homes and neighborhood: cooking, sewing, and carpentry. The six-year-olds built a farm out of blocks, planted wheat and cotton, and processed and transported their crop to market. The seven-year-olds studied prehistoric life in caves of their own devising while their eight-year-old neighbors focused their attention on the work of the seafaring Phoenicians and subsequent adventurers like Marco Polo, Magellan, Columbus, and Robinson Crusoe. Local history and geography occupied the attention of the nine-year-olds, while those who were ten studied colonial history, constructing a replica of a room in an early American house. The older groups of children . . . [focused on] scientific experiments in anatomy, electro-magnetism, political economy, and photography. The search of the debating club formed by the thirteen-year-old students for a place to meet resulted in the building of a substantial clubhouse, which enlisted children of all ages in a cooperative project. . . . (pp. 101–102)

Perennialism

Modern educational philosophers have looked backward through history and forward in time to shape a school of thought about the goals and processes of education called **perennialism**. Perennialists exalt the great thoughts and accomplishments of Western culture for their own sake, but also for what they believe the accomplishments of Western culture as expressed in classical writings can offer to future generations. Perennialists believe that the purpose of schools is to develop students' intellectual capabilities.

Perennialists contend that there are principles of education so important, so central to the development of culture that they cannot be ignored. These principles—the universality of truth, the importance of rationality, and the power of aesthetics and religion to encourage ethical behavior—recur again and again in efforts to advance knowledge and to extend civilization. Perennialists believe, much like realists, that such principles exist in the physical world and demand the attention of teachers and students. Culture is not relative, perennialists argue; that which is rational and intellectually self-disciplined is most desirable.

This philosophical view of what is important in education has been articulated most notably by Robert Maynard Hutchins (1899–1977) and Mortimer Adler (born 1902). They have argued that humans are rational beings and that, in every important way, people are basically the same, regardless of where they live and who they are. If so, the argument goes, there must be constancy in the way humans are educated—they need the same basic education, despite the fact that everywhere change is a virtual constant in modern society. This education should consist of a fundamental grounding in history, language, mathematics, science, literature, and the humanities.

Hutchins and Adler introduced perennialism in the 1930s in reaction to progressive educational approaches that stressed the importance of change in society and the dynamism of teaching and learning. Progressivists thought education should be tailored to the times, the people, and the places it was offered. They advocated such things as active learning, child-centered teaching, and problem solving as opposed to knowledge acquisition.

The perennialists have contended that people are rational animals having free will who learn to exercise self-control when their minds are disciplined by basic education. Education implies teaching, teaching implies knowledge, knowledge is truth, truth is the same everywhere: therefore education should be the same everywhere (Hutchins, 1936).

Schools are supposed to prepare students by putting them in touch with the classics of Western culture. A contemporary curriculum that disregards the classics does students and society a disservice. One must know the past if one is to be prepared to participate fully in the present and to contribute in the future. This view led to the development of the Great Books program at the University of Chicago in the 1950s.

Mortimer Adler's *Paideia Proposal* (1982), a more recently developed perennialist recommendation, calls for a one-track system of public schooling. This single track would promote the same three learning objectives for all students. The first deals with mental, moral, and spiritual self-improvement. The second concerns civic education. The third addresses adults' needs to earn a living. In Adlerian language, these objectives are translated into goals. The goals and the means to their achievement are described in Figure 4.3.

The practical implications of perennialism for schooling are numerous. Perennialists prefer teacher-centered education; the teacher is the authority who must possess both the knowledge and responsibility necessary to educate young people. Moral education, including Bible study, is important for what it communicates about self-control and social responsibility. Concepts of academic tracking and gifted education are acceptable to perennialists. The curriculum is defined by a Eurocentric core.

Essentialism

Essentialism is a philosophical orientation that acknowledges the existence of a body of knowledge that all people must learn if they are to function effectively in society. Like perennialists, essentialists acknowledge the timeless quality of great work, but they do not base their views on realist princi-

FIGURE 4.3

Adler's Recommended Course of Study

What might be some advantages and disadvantages of Adler's curriculum for a one-track system of public schooling?

	A	B	C
Goals of Education	Acquisition of organized knowledge	Development of intellectual skills and skills of learning	Enlarged understanding of ideas and values
	by means of	*by means of*	*by means of*
Means to Goals	Didactic instruction, lectures and responses, textbooks and other aids	Coaching, exercises, and supervised practice	Socratic questioning and active participation
	In three areas of subject-matter	*In the operations of*	*In the*
Areas, Operations, and Activities	Language, literature, and the fine arts	Reading, writing, speaking, listening	Discussion of books (not textbooks) and other works of art and
	Mathematics and natural science	Calculating, problem-solving, observing, measuring, estimating	Involvement in artistic activities e.g., music, drama, visual arts
	History, geography, and social studies	Exercising critical judgment	

Note: From *The Paideia Proposal: An Educational Manifesto* (p. 8) by M. Adler, 1982, New York: Macmillan. Copyright 1982 by the Institute for Philosophical Research. Reprinted with the permission of Macmillan Publishing Company.

ples. Moreover, they do not agree on what constitutes the "essentials" educated people should know. They are bound to each other by the idea that such essentials exist, and that they ought to be represented in the curriculum. Essentialists typically rely on a Eurocentric curriculum, for which they have been criticized by those who do not assume this view.

Essentialists want students to study great works so they may be better prepared to solve contemporary problems. Traditionally, essentialists have viewed the sciences as particularly useful and central to the process of knowing and improving one's world. But increasingly, essentialists have concentrated on encouraging students to master other disciplines as well.

William Bagley (1874–1946) founded the Essentialistic Education Society as a reaction to progressive, pragmatic trends in education. Like the perennialists at the end of World War II, Bagley and his colleagues feared what they saw as an erosion of moral and intellectual standards in the young. To remedy this situation, they advocated that schools transmit a common essential core of knowledge to all students.

Admiral Hyman Rickover (1900–1986), often referred to as the founder of the nuclear navy in the United States and frequent education critic, has been called an essentialist. Rickover (1963) wrote,

> . . . there are innumerable virtues I should like to see inculcated in American youth. But the one thing which I believe will be of the greatest importance for the future of our Nation and of the free world, the one indispensable thing, is to bring all our children to markedly higher intellectual levels. (p. 307)

Essentialist Arthur Bestor (1879–1944) also criticized American education. Bestor (1985) wrote,

> To put the matter bluntly, we regard schooling as a mere experience, delightful to the recipient but hardly valuable to society. The school or college has become, to our minds, merely a branch of the luxury-purveying trade. Like the club car on a passenger train, it dispenses the amenities of life to persons bound on serious errands elsewhere. (p. 2)

In contrast to perennialists, essentialists such as Rickover and Bestor place less emphasis on learning for learning's sake. They would concentrate instead on the power of knowledge for solving contemporary problems and for preventing such problems from arising in the future.

"animism, Babbit, covalent bond, xenophobia, You can't make a silk purse out of a sow's ear, Zionism"

How would essentialists encourage societal progress? They would have teachers instill in students the value of old-fashioned discipline, self-control, and hard work. Because essentialists view children as incapable of directing their own learning, teachers would direct it by structuring and pacing students' mastery of subject matter. Because much knowledge is abstract, practical problem solving or "learning by doing" will not apply. Essentialists might well argue that details get in the way of seeing the big picture (Clive, 1989).

Essentialist curricula are rarely as specific as the recommendations of E. D. Hirsch (1987; Hirsch, Rowland, & Stanford, 1989). He argues that society cannot function properly without communication among its members, and communication cannot occur in the absence of literacy. But true literacy, Hirsch contends, is more than mechanical performance of the skills of reading and writing; it depends on people's shared information, or common knowledge of their culture.

Hirsch developed his concept of **cultural literacy** into an elaborately prescribed curriculum for students. He delineated what he believed children need to know by the end of sixth grade in such categories as literature, religion and philosophy, history, geography, mathematics, science, and technology. Hirsch (1987) stated that,

> Unquestionably, decisions about techniques of conveying traditions to our children are among the most sensitive and important decisions of a pluralistic nation. But the complex problem of how to teach values in American schools mustn't distract attention from our fundamental duty to teach shared content. (p. 25)

Cultural Awareness

A criticism of Hirsch's work and that of perennialists and essentialists generally is that it is Eurocentric—that is, it is centered on the history and cultures of Europe. Such a curriculum is said to consist mainly of works by "dead white males." "Cultural literacy" becomes an exclusionary concept, one that does not include knowing the history and culture of non-European peoples. Defenders of essentialism, such as Allan Bloom in his book *The Closing of the American Mind* (1987), say that this is as it should be: "One should conclude from the study of non-Western cultures that not only to prefer one's own way but to believe it best, superior to all others, is primary and even natural— exactly the opposite of what is intended by requiring students to study these cultures" (p. 36). In the United States, members of minority cultures are among those who bitterly oppose the essentialist interpretation of what is worth knowing. The countermovement of Afrocentrism makes the history and cultures of Africa and African Americans the focus of the curriculum.

Social Reconstructionism

Social reconstructionism is a philosophy based on the belief that people are responsible for social conditions and can improve the quality of human life by changing the social order. Theodore Brameld (1904–1987) and George Counts (1889–1974) were instrumental in articulating **social reconstructionism**—a philosophy that advocates education as a means of preparing people to create a new society. Stimulated by progressivism, Brameld, Counts, and others pushed for change further and faster and wider throughout society to effect a new world order. Where the progressivists and pragmatists of Dewey's day were politically moderate, urging gradual change, the reconstructionists were provocative in advocating systemic change.

For example, reconstructionists might attack the governance structure of schools to reorganize the decision-making power, as they did in Chicago in the 1920s (Counts, 1928). They argued that every major legitimate interest in the city should be represented on the school board and that teachers should prepare themselves professionally to meet their responsibilities and guard their right to perform professional functions. Counts (1928) and other reconstructionists argued that reconstructing public education was not going to be easy, but that it was possible with courageous leadership and modern science:

> Unless the profession can develop a superior type of social leadership, a leadership at least equal in intelligence, courage, and power to the leadership in other fields of interest with which it must contend, the profession will find itself unable to incorporate in the systems of public education the findings of educational science. (p. 361)

The same kinds of arguments made by early social reconstructionists are advanced today to restructure schools and redesign professional education for teachers.

From the 1930s to the 1960s, reconstructionists saw a world where confusion and crisis reigned. The Great Depression, World War II, the Nuclear Age, and the Cold War era stimulated and sustained concerns about world order. Rather than bemoan world conditions, reconstructionists sought to define opportunities to build a good and just society. People could not sit comfortably in their safe homes holding tightly to the good life, reconstructionists argued, while others less fortunate sit on the outside looking in. People have to face forward, to move ahead, and to bring the have-nots into a better society.

Brameld thought the future could be bleak or promising: the choice belonged to all. People can take control of their lives and behave in ways that improve the human condition. But the education system itself would need to be reconstructed as a tool for transforming individuals' lives and shaping a new social order. The optimism of early reconstructionists was based on faith in the power of science to solve human problems, a faith others criticized as unjustifiable.

Like the Platonists, reconstructionists were utopian. As Theodore Brameld (1950) noted,

> The common denominator of [reconstructionism's] beliefs is a passionate concern for the future of civilization. It centers attention, therefore, upon clear-cut cultural goals, which, because they are idealizations of human and especially social potentialities, are in the historic stream of utopian philosophy. (p. 407)

The spirit of reconstructionism has been nurtured in the United States over the years by individuals and groups intent on creating change. Even though they did not call themselves reconstructionists, these problem

	Goal of Education	Role of Students	Role of Teachers	Teaching Methods	Subjects Studied
Existentialism	Develop authentic individuals who exercise freedom of choice and take responsibility for their actions.	Develop independence, self-discipline; set challenges and solve problems.	Encourage students to philosophize about life and to recognize and fulfill personal freedom.	Discussion and analysis, examination of choice-making in own and others' lives.	Drama Art Literature Social Sciences History
Marxism	Shape people and institutions; change material conditions of society, producing classless society.	Live and work harmoniously with others, acquire and use knowledge that will enable them to transform natural and social world.	Lead and advocate change	Scientific methodology, practical activity (problem solving).	Emphasis on science and history
Behaviorism	Engineer environments that efficiently maximize learning.	Respond to environmental and behavioral stimuli; become self-regulated.	Manipulate the learning environment and present stimuli, using conditioning and social learning to shape student behavior.	Programmed instruction that provides feedback on performance behavioral contracts, reinforcement.	Learning tasks in which behavior can be directly observed, measured, and evaluated.
Cognitivism	Develop thinking skills for lifelong self-directed learning.	Construct meaningful knowledge through experience and interaction.	Stimulate cognitive development; mediate student learning and monitor thought processes.	Use of manipulatives and real-life learning opportunities relevant to students' prior experiences.	Integrated curricula; emphasis on thinking and critical thinking skills, study skills, and problem solving skills.
Pragmatism	Develop and apply practical knowledge and skills for life in a progressive democratic society.	Active learning and participation.	Teach inductive and deductive reasoning, the scientific method, and the powers of observation and practice.	Hands-on curricula; group work; experimentation.	Emphasis on citizenship, knowledge and skills applicable to daily life, and career or job preparation.
Perennialism	Acquisition of timeless principles of reality, truth, and value; learning for the sake of learning.	Receive knowledge and academic skills.	Guide to the classics; teach basic skills.	Teacher-centered direct instruction.	Emphasis on Great Books and core curricula in the arts and sciences.
Essentialism	Acquisition of culture; cultural literacy for personal benefit.	Receive knowledge; demonstrate minimum competencies.	Deliver a standard curriculum.	Subject-centered direct instruction.	Uniform curriculum for all students that emphasizes the essence of traditional American culture.
Social Reconstructionism	Solve social problems and create a better world.	Inquire, apply critical thinking skills, and take action.	Ask questions; present social issues and problem solving challenges; serve as organizer and information resource.	Stimulate divergent thinking and group investigation.	Emphasis on social studies, social problems, global education, and environmental issues.

FIGURE 4.4

Philosophical Orientations in Education Today

What combination of philosophical orientations best matches your own beliefs and values?

solvers and radical social activists saw education as a means to effect full participation in society. The work of Saul Alinsky (1909–1972), Ivan Illich (born 1926), and others, while not confined exclusively to issues of education, embodies the spirit of self-determination common to reconstructionists.

President Lyndon Johnson's Teacher Corps in the 1960s and 1970s represented an institutionalized, officially sanctioned brand of reconstructionism. By the time the Teacher Corps was dismantled in the late 1970s, there had been federally supported, locally organized groups of "change agents" in areas of poverty all across the country. The interns, who had little or no professional educational training, and the in-service teachers with whom they worked were picked for their commitment to educational innovation. The rhetoric of change associated with the Teacher Corps's educational and community projects, combined with the Federal government's commitment to direct intervention in local schools and communities, marked the program as a unique effort to transform education for the poor in America.

Social reconstructionists of the late twentieth century press for schools to address many societal problems. For example, the crisis in teen pregnancy and the spread of AIDS have driven activists to develop and implement sex education programs in the schools. Such programs often view these problems as emanating from a variety of interrelated causes; that is, problems occur because of ignorance, poverty, lack of educational and employment opportunities, and the like. This multiple-causation view of problems dictates a multifaceted approach to solving them. Reconstructionists conceive of education, then, not so much as a linear response to a particular need but more as support to address an interdependent set of intellectual, emotional, personal, and social needs.

This same view of the interrelatedness of problems and solutions can be seen in recent educational reform efforts. In the minds of the new social reconstructionists, changes in school organization and governance will yield little if school administrators, teachers, and parents remain unprepared to relate to one another in new ways. If students are to develop new technological skills and to recognize the importance of such skills for the future, they must have access to new equipment, and teachers must be prepared to assist them. And so on. Social reconstructionists' views of the interconnectedness of problems and solutions and of people's responsibility to society shape educational programs for young and old alike.

WHAT NON-WESTERN PHILOSOPHIES INFLUENCE AMERICAN EDUCATION?

Eastern and Middle Eastern philosophies, religions, and cultures are gradually beginning to influence schools in the United States as the number of people having roots in Eastern and Middle Eastern countries grows. In cities across the country, there are many first-, second-, and third-generation American and foreign national public school students who have Asian and Middle Eastern backgrounds. Groups such as Buddhist-Vietnamese

Americans in Los Angeles, Islamic-Arab Americans in Detroit, and Hindu-Indian Americans in New York often maintain private schools and educate children and adults through cultural festivals and religious celebrations.

Some nonsectarian private schools guide students in an exploration of world religions. Students are encouraged to develop secular spirituality, a personal ethical system, and inner peace. Multicultural curriculum materials provide access to past and present ideas and expressions of spirituality. In these alternative private schools, non-Western philosophies generally play a significant role, as F. Robinson (1990) reports about a school in the affluent community of Chevy Chase, Maryland:

> The Oneness school in Chevy Chase is one of a handful of non-sectarian schools in the metropolitan area whose curriculum includes a "spiritual" component . . . In what seems like a modern version of the one-room schoolhouse, 6-year-olds and 11-year-olds interact easily and help each other with schoolwork. A copy of the Koran sits on a book case in front of a poster celebrating the fourth centenary of the death of Teresa of Avila. Nearby were Native American sand paintings used by medicine men, statues of Shiva, Buddha and St. Francis, crucifixes from South America and a wooden plaque of the Virgin Mary from Yugoslavia. (pp. 9–10)

In general, Western ways encourage people to look outward toward what they hope lies ahead in their personal and professional lives. One's sense of progress is rooted in work and one's place in society. Attendance at church or temple, the latest self-help book, or some traumatic event prompts people to think about "meaning" in their lives, but introspection may occur all too rarely for many. Non-Western philosophies can remind people that a long, focused gaze inward, often undertaken with the help of a spiritual guide or teacher, is essential if a life is to be fully lived.

Hinduism

Hinduism is a religion, a philosophy, and a way of life:

> Hinduism is a spectrum of beliefs and practices ranging from the veneration of trees, stones, and snakes in villages scarcely out of the Stone Age to the abstract metaphysical speculations of sophisticated urban intellectuals whose attainments have been recognized [widely]. (Organ, 1974, p. 1)

Major Hindu writings began to appear in the form of hymns and chants, or mantras, about 1200 BC to AD 200. The three basic Hindu texts—the Vedas, the Upanishads, and the Epics—reveal a way of life that has evolved to guide believers through the years.

The Vedas present a vision of the universe consisting of the earth, the atmosphere, and heaven. Vedic believers worship many gods, ascribing human characteristics to nonhuman things. Varuna, for example, is thought to control the changes in seasons.

The Upanishads, or secret teachings, recognize a single god, Brahman, and established laws to govern conduct. These laws laid down rules for personal conduct and promoted the caste system. This system of social hierarchy, now outlawed, put the Brahmin, or priests, teachers, and other thinkers, at the top and relegated the Sudras, or "untouchables," to the bottom.

The Epics, which contain among other writings the Bhagavad-Gita, were written between 200 BC and AD 200. The Bhagavad-Gita is a poem of more than 700 verses that depicts a compassionate god who opens salvation to all devoted, dutiful souls. The Bhagavad-Gita also describes yoga as a means of uniting one's soul with the Absolute. Through yoga's teaching of right posture, correct breathing, and control of the senses, one learns to concentrate so as to free the mind and to attain enlightenment.

Perhaps more visibly than any other modern Hindu, Mohandas Gandhi, known as the Mahatma (the Great), influenced thought in the Western world. His advocacy of nonviolence as a means to social reform is conspicuous in the writings and actions of Martin Luther King, Jr., during the struggle for civil rights in America. King (1964) wrote about the use of Gandhian nonviolent political action during the bus boycott in Montgomery, Alabama: "For Gandhi love was a potent instrument for social and collective transformation. It was in this Gandhian emphasis on love and nonviolence that I discovered the method for social reform that I had been seeking for many months" (p. 79).

To characterize Hindus as a single group having a monolithic set of beliefs is inaccurate and misleading. "Diversity is perhaps the first and most important feature of Hindu worship to be noted" (Rambachan, 1992). The beliefs, customs, and religious practices of Hindus vary widely from sect to sect and place to place. The life of a Bengali woman in rural India, for instance, can differ markedly from that of a Hindu woman in Calcutta, and even more so from the life of a Hindu woman in New York.

Buddhism

Having its roots in Indian Vedic culture, Buddhism is meant to help people recognize truth for themselves:

> Buddhism is not a fundamentalist religion. Its teachings are not dogmas or articles of faith that have to be blindly accepted at the cost of suspending reason, critical judgment, common sense or experience. Quite the contrary, in fact; their basic aim is to help us gain direct insight into the truth for ourselves. (Snelling, 1987, p. 51)

Buddha, or the Enlightened One, was born as Siddhartha Gautama (563–483 BC) to wealthy parents in Nepal. Although Gautama enjoyed a sheltered, opulent existence until age 29, tradition teaches that his life was immutably altered by three events. He saw an old man bent over a walking stick, a diseased man suffering with fever, and a corpse being carried to a funeral pyre. These experiences compelled him to seek a spiritual inner peace with which to face the ravages of old age, sickness, and death.

Gautama left his wife and son and lived an austere life of study concentrated on human suffering and its cure. The doctrine, or dharma, he taught consisted of four truths: life is full of suffering and dissatisfaction; suffering emanates from desire; suffering will cease when desire stops; and the cessation of desire can be accomplished through eight steps. These eight steps are: right views, right aspirations, right speech, right conduct, right liveli-hood, right effort, right mindfulness, and right contemplation.

Buddhists think of life as a flowing stream. They believe in Hindu reincar-nation, that is, rebirth in which people assume a new physical form and status depending on the quality of their deeds (*karma*). They also believe that with progress along the path marked by the

> "Learning without thought is labor lost; thought without learning is perilous." (Confucius)

Enlightened One, people will reach *nirvana*, or a state of serenity and wisdom from which they will not be reborn. Although Buddha did not believe in an Absolute or god, after his death he became revered as a god. As time passed, other Buddhas, or people who followed, were given divine status.

Zen, a sect of Buddhism, took root in Japan in the twelfth century. In feudal, patriarchal Japanese society, Zen stressed the dignity of physical labor. Zen monks creatively coordinated the human needs and political needs of the state by helping to build economic relations with China. They also influenced the arts, swordsmanship, and the tea ceremony by empha-sizing stern discipline, selflessness, and spontaneity. Zen beliefs and rituals became integral to Japanese culture.

Shinto is another important sect or cult within Buddhism. Shinto has been defined as a generic name for ideas and institutions existing in Japan before the introduction of Buddhism and Confucianism (Holtom, 1922). It has also been defined through practices of worshipping nature and Japanese ancestors. In Shinto philosophy, God is viewed as an assimilation of natural events or objects and events in human society. As a system of thought, Shinto encourages feelings of reverence and loyalty toward important persons, both dead and alive.

Islam

Islamic philosophy can be viewed as the work of thinkers belonging to a religious community who relied on the writings of the Koran (Quran). The Koran is the holy or sacred book of Muslims.

Muslims believe that the word of God, or Allah, was revealed to Muhammad by the angel Gabriel. Abū-Bakr, Muhammad's father-in-law, collected Muhammad's words in the Koran. Muhammad (570–632), then, was a prophet who described Allah's will. He foretold of a world where Allah would come on the Last Judgment to appraise all souls by their abili-ties to live according to Allah's will. To those who succeeded, eternal reward would be granted in paradise; those who failed would be con-demned to suffer the pain of eternal fire. The religion of Islam was thus rooted in both Judaism and Christianity (Corbin, 1993; Fakhry, 1983).

Al-Kindī (died after 870), an Arab and an early important Muslim philosopher, thought of God as an absolute and transcendent being. Like the great Muslim philosophers who would follow, he believed that revealed truth (that which emanated from philosophy and religion) and rational truth were the same thing.

Al-Fārābī (875–950), a Turk, developed a full-scale view of Muslim philosophy with God at the top undergirded by descending levels of intelligence. In Al-Fārābī's scheme, the goal of humankind was to attain immortality through education or the development of one's intellect.

The most important Muslim philosopher, however, is generally thought to be ibn-Sina or Avicenna (980–1037). He described concepts of matter, form, and existence in a way that allowed for a Necessary Being or God who was distinct from the world. For him, the prophets were teachers who used religion as philosophy for the masses to reveal symbolic truth—a kind of truth that helped people approach absolute truth or God.

Islamic faith dictates that Muslims believe in no God but Allah. They must pray five times each day—at sunrise, noon, midafternoon, sunset, and nightfall. They must fast between sunrise and sunset during the month of Ramadan (the 9th lunar month in the Muslim calendar). Muslims are required to perform acts of charity. And they must make a pilgrimage to the holy city of Mecca at least once in their lives.

Cultural Awareness

During the 1960s, Islam gained large numbers of converts in the United States among African Americans, particularly among urban African-American males. The principal reason is that Islam is non-racist. The Koran, which includes both Judaic and Christian writings in addition to those of Muhammad and his disciples, expressly forbids discrimination in thought or deed on the basis of race. Submission to Allah and strict adherence to Islam's five pillars of faith guarantee automatic brotherhood and equality. In 1965, Malcolm X (1965), an influential "Black Muslim," wrote bitterly about the need for Islam at a time when many African Americans felt disappointed that the civil rights acts of the late 1950s and early 1960s had not yet made much of a difference in people's lives.

> I am in agreement one hundred per cent with those racists who say that no government laws ever can *force* brotherhood. The only true world solution today is governments guided by true religion—of the spirit. Here in race-torn America, I am convinced that the Islam religion is desperately needed, particularly by the American black man . . . (p. 369)

African and Native-American Philosophies

According to M.K. Asante, African and African-American philosophies are different from European philosophies in important ways. Western thought is rational (I think, therefore I am), whereas African thought is based on feeling and sociality (I feel, and I relate to others, therefore I am) (Asante, 1987). Likewise, Christine Sleeter and Carl Grant (1993) describe a "synergetic" way of thinking among some African Americans as a preference for working cooperatively rather than independently and a desire to integrate personal relationships into learning tasks (p. 54).

Such a joining of people and ideas is expressed often by the African writer Chinua Achebe. While no single scholar can claim to represent the African perspective, Achebe's *Things Fall Apart* (1968) has been translated into 50 languages and sold 50 million copies. He has "held fast to an African vision of the role of art, one that rejects the Western tradition of seeing the artist apart and alienated from society. In Africa's communal culture, 'art is intended to help society . . . .'" (Winkler, 1994, p. A9).

Asante (1992) writes of the importance of understanding an African-American philosophy and its bearing on educational life in America. He advocates an Afrocentric approach to curriculum, that is, an approach that puts African history and culture at the center of the curriculum. In doing so, he implies the power of emotion associated with such a perspective.

> The African-American children in your classrooms are not a black version of white people. They have different cultural and historical experiences that must be looked at and examined in a different way. To give an obvious example, African-Americans did not come to America on the Mayflower. We recognize the Mayflower as part of the American experience, but our experience was different: We crossed the ocean packed in boats with as many as 1,000 other people, with only 18 inches of space between us and the deck above, and chained from neck to ankle. (p. 21)

Traditional Native-American thought also emphasized nonrational being and social relations. Reason and logic, for example, are not seen as superior to nonrational explanations of events. Like African traditions, Native-American traditions encourage spiritualism based on animism—belief in the presence of active supernatural forces in the natural world—and on the ideal of harmonious coexistence with nature. Truth comes not from great books or scientific inquiry but from personal introspection, oral traditions, and the values and knowledge handed down from ancestors.

Native-American philosophies stress personal dignity and moral responsibility and the mutual interdependence of all the people in a society or group. Group identity and well-being take precedence over individual needs and abilities. Traditional social values encourage silent reflection over verbalizing, cooperation over competition, stability over change, and continuity over "progress" (Banks, 1994).

African and Native-American thought, like the religious and secular philosophies of the Middle East, India, and Asia, influence the development of educational philosophies in the United States in two main ways: They broaden people's minds and they enlighten changes in curriculum and instruction that are designed to meet the needs of all students in our culturally diverse society.

AS A TEACHER, HOW CAN YOU DEVELOP YOUR PERSONAL PHILOSOPHY OF EDUCATION?

Western and non-Western philosophies have influenced what educators value. Such philosophies have also shaped how educators think and behave with regard to their professional practice. Individual educators draw upon various philosophies, both purposefully and casually, to fashion their own unique views of teaching and learning.

Since the mid-1970s, educational researchers and cognitive psychologists have explored teachers' beliefs, judgments, and decisions for clues to the "mental lives of teachers" (Clark & Peterson, 1986, p. 255). Overtly, much of the work has been aimed at portraying the psychology of teaching so as to guide policymakers, curriculum developers, and teacher educators; but in so doing, research on teachers' thought processes has also revealed the philosophies and habits of mind that shape and are shaped by life in classrooms.

The most revealing studies of teacher thinking, and also the most difficult to do, are those that are conducted in real classrooms where teachers are interacting with their students. In contrast to tightly controlled laboratory investigations, such studies are useful because they try to account for the complexities of real life. But they are troublesome methodologically because real life is subtle, uncontrollable, and just plain messy; that is, children and teachers carry their own unique histories into the classroom, and these influence the way they think and behave.

Teachers' Theories and Beliefs

Clark and Peterson (1986) offer a model that attempts to account for the relationships between teachers' thought and action. In Figure 4.5, the first circle depicts what goes on inside teachers' heads, the unobservable. In this circle the terms "preactive," "postactive," and "interactive" refer respectively to thoughts before, after, and during teaching. Teachers' theories and beliefs refer to fairly explicit propositions about the way teachers think about the nature of children as learners (metaphysics), ways of knowing (epistemology), and right content and conduct (axiology). The second circle—teachers' behaviors, students' behaviors, and indications of students' achievements, such as test scores—represents the observable in classrooms. This circle is the domain where teaching actually occurs.

Note in particular the position of the arrows forming the first circle. They are meant to suggest interaction among thoughts: teachers' theories and beliefs affect their planning and their thoughts during teaching, which in turn, affect their theories and beliefs. Teachers understand objects, events, and people in certain ways, psychologists argue, because of their accumulated knowledge. While some of this knowledge is fairly simple, some is

FIGURE 4.5

Teachers' Thought Processes in Relation to Teachers' Actions

In what ways might teachers' thought processes constrain teachers' actions? In what ways might teachers' thought processes provide opportunities for enhancing the effects of teachers' actions?

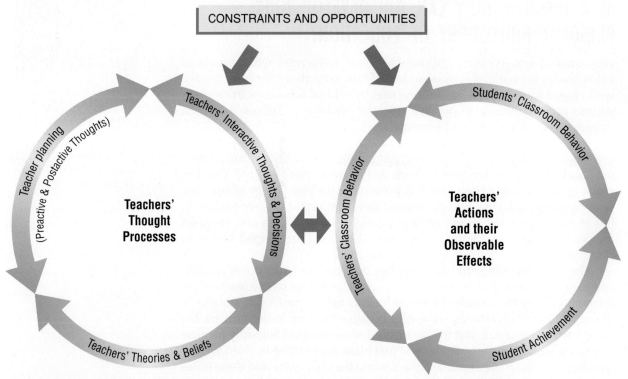

CONSTRAINTS AND OPPORTUNITIES

Teacher planning (Preactive & Postactive Thoughts)

Teachers' Interactive Thoughts & Decisions

Teachers' Thought Processes

Teachers' Theories & Beliefs

Teachers' Classroom Behavior

Students' Classroom Behavior

Teachers' Actions and their Observable Effects

Student Achievement

Source: From "Teachers' Thought Processes" by Christopher M. Clark and Penelope L. Peterson. Reprinted with permission of Macmillan Publishing Company from *Handbook of Research on Teaching*, Third Edition, Merlin C. Wittrock, Editor. Copyright 1986 by the American Education Research Association.

organized into fairly elaborate structures upon which teachers rely either explicitly or tacitly to make sense out of the world around them.

Some teachers are more predisposed than others to look for meaning in events of teaching and learning. They are open-minded and sensitive to new ideas. They resist simple explanations for complex problems and try instead to understand acts in the contexts in which they occur. They might be said to be more philosophical or theoretical than other teachers; they might also be said to be more practical.

How do teachers develop their habits of thinking, their personal philosophies? Although there are no simple answers, David Hunt (1987), an instructional psychologist at the Ontario Institute for Studies in Education, has provided some intriguing leads.

Hunt observes that most new ideas in philosophy, psychology, education, and social sciences are presented in orthodox fashion by making cases for them based on research results or on theoretical grounds. Teachers, for instance, take college courses designed to present them with the latest research and thinking on human behavior. They, in turn, are supposed to translate this knowledge into action with their students. Most of the time, then, teachers begin with someone else's ideas and try to make sense out of them in their own situations, a logical progression from philosophy to practice.

Hunt argues, however, that viewing the development of knowledge this way cuts people off from their own experiences. In effect, they must take information from outside themselves and try to integrate it or to put it inside themselves. Hunt believes people should begin constructing their philosophical and professional knowledge by examining their own personal beliefs. For teachers this means making explicit their beliefs and values about teaching and learning. This means considering such things as their ideals about the nature of children as learners, what is worth knowing, and the purposes of education.

Developing a philosophy of education involves self-knowledge based on both personal life experiences and professional learning. Teachers are guided by beliefs and values, for example, about human nature and the purpose of education.

Teachers' Personal Life Experiences

Personal life experiences profoundly affect a teacher's educational philosophy. Gerber (1992) investigated the life of a teacher with learning disabilities, TJ, as he spent his first year on the job. TJ's assignment was as a resource room teacher—a special education teacher who works with students in small groups. This role was new to the rural school district where TJ taught, so he faced the additional challenge of helping others understand how resource teachers function.

The way he decorated his classroom walls was an indicator of TJ's beliefs about people with learning disabilities:

> From the first moment that one enters TJ's classroom several messages become abundantly clear. They are—it is okay to have a learning disability, and you must work hard in order to succeed. Moreover, when you are learning disabled you are entitled to basic rights granted to persons with disabilities. An article complete with pictures from *Psychology Today* informs the reader that George Patton, Auguste Rodin, Leonardo Da Vinci, Albert Einstein, Tom Cruise, and Stephan Cannell (television writer and producer) were learning disabled. The LD Bill of Rights is thumbtacked next to it. It states that when one has a learning disability certain accommodations are permitted such as extended time limits for testing, tests read by a reader, presentation of material so it can be understood, access to a resource room, and the right to an appropriate education. (p. 219)

TJ's student teaching experience was fraught with problems. His university supervisor even suggested he would not "make it as a teacher." The negative feedback "made him feel like he wasn't worth a plug nickel" (p. 17). When Gerber observed TJ in the classroom, however, he saw a very different teacher—one who was self-confident and supportive of his students.

Estimates of teacher attrition vary from 20% to 40% during the first 5 years on the job, yet this very unusual young teacher was still there at the end of the 1st year and planned to return the next. TJ's philosophy of teaching, realistically formed by collecting information from both sides of the teacher's desk, weighted the importance of success and personal satisfaction heavily:

> The satisfaction of witnessing the learning of his students is exhilarating. As TJ explained, "My experiences have really helped me with the students. If I had to do it all over again, I'd do it all over again. Because when I feel I'm with my students and things are clicking—that's a great high. . . ." (p. 224)

Teacher Reflection and Problem Solving

Researchers have explored how teachers think on the job. As illustrated in Figure 4.6, Greta Morine-Dershimer (1990) has noted that teachers think about teaching in a variety of ways.

First, some teachers base their thoughts on organized structures of knowledge that represent relationships among concepts. For example, sometimes they think in terms of "scripts" that summarize typical classroom routines. They envision "scenes" to organize information about people and objects in recurring classroom events. They also formulate propositions to summarize factual knowledge about students, subject matter content, and teaching strategies. Morine-Dershimer (1990) believes this line of work "provides a very positive image of the mental functioning of teachers" (p. 5). Studies of experts and novices indicate that experienced teachers have acquired and systematically stored much useful information. They have the ability to access this information when they need it (Clark & Peterson, 1986).

Second, teachers' thinking has been characterized in terms of artistry, or as reflecting in and reflecting on action. Reflection in action has been compared to having a conversation with a situation (Schon, 1987). During *reflection,* a teacher perceives a problem, thinks about other past similar events, interprets the problem in light of this past knowledge, and takes action. The problem "talks back" by yielding information that causes the teacher to reframe the problem and to make another move. And so on. In contrast, reflection on action is after-the-fact analysis. That is, once an event has occurred, a teacher might think back on what he or she might have done differently and what effects such action might have produced. Such reflection is disconnected from present action. Because there is no need for a quick response, reflection on action is a more analytical process.

Vivian Paley (1979) demonstrated this type of thinking after a colleague accused her of reinforcing stereotypes. She reported, in *White Teacher,* how a middle-aged, Jewish woman learned to think about her own thinking as she interacted with her African-American kindergarten students:

FIGURE 4.6

Comparing Conceptualizations of Teacher Thinking

Conceptualizations	**Types of information emphasized**	**Notable transformations of information**	**Ideal State**	**Possible use in teacher education**
Thinking through schemata	Routines/scripts Classroom organizations/scenes Activity Structures	Reorganization of new information according to existing schemata	Teacher manages flow of information in order to track pupil understanding of lesson content	Prospective teachers learn classroom routines
Reflecting in/on practice	Classroom events recalled from prior situations "Backtalk" of pupils in immediate situation	Reframing an ambiguous or problematic situation	Teacher reconceptualizes the situation and resolves the problem	Prospective teachers acquire experience in a variety of settings
Formulating pedagogical content	Subject matter content Pedagogical processes Pupils' common misconceptions of subject matter Pupils' real life experiences related to subject matter	Transforming subject matter for presentation to pupils	Teacher uses appropriate analogies and varied examples to develop pupil understanding of concepts, and relates topic to pupils' own experiences	Prospective teachers learn many alternative analogies and examples appropriate for use with basic concepts
Perceiving practical arguments	Experiential knowledge (situational premises) Propositional knowledge (principals of practice; empirical premises) Normative knowledge (value premises)	Recognizing "subjectively reasonable beliefs" and reformulating to arrive at "objectively reasonable beliefs"	Teacher's actions are consistent with objectively reasonable beliefs (research and "warranted practice")	Prospective teachers explore own beliefs in relation to research

Source: From *To Think Like a Teacher*, by G. Morine-Dershimer, 1990, Vice Presidential address presented to the annual meeting of the American Education Research Association, Boston. Reprinted with permission.

. . . "the black girls" were, in fact, five separate girls who played together and copied each other a great deal. I could name five white girls who played together, but I did not call them "the white girls." I was starting to realize, with help of a good friend, that thinking of Ayana, Rena, Karla, Joyce, and Sylvia as "the black girls" kept me from seeing them always as individuals. (p. 135)

BENCHMARKS

Developments in Western Intellectual Thought and Their Influence on American Education

The Classical Period 500 BC–500 AD	Greeks and Romans define the branches of philosophy and basic ideas on which Western intellectual thought is based. Socrates and Plato define idealism, Aristotle, realism. Quintillion establishes the Roman school system from which the American school system is descended.
The Middle Ages 500 AD–1300	Arab scholars preserve the Greco-Roman intellectual traditions after the fall of Rome. Arab mathematicians, geographers, physicians, and scientists, such as Ibn-Sina (Avicenna), Ibn-Rushid (Averroes), and Ibn-Battuta contribute to Western learning.
	In Charlemagne's empire, Alcuin establishes a prototype curriculum of seven "liberal arts." The first universities are established in medieval Spain, France, and England.
	Thomas Aquinas formalizes scholasticism, later known as Thomism, an educational philosophy based on the logical study of beliefs of the Church. Thomism becomes the basis of Roman Catholic parochial education.
The Renaissance and Reformation 1300–1700	Humanism revives the classical philosophies of human nature. The humanist philosopher Erasmus calls for respect and kindness toward students and developmentally appropriate instruction in liberal arts, social conduct, and moral principles.
	Developments in printing-press technology increase the availability of books and public demand for literacy. To the curriculum of humanism, Johann Comenius adds the study of science and the use of textbooks written specifically for students.
	Martin Luther launches the Protestant Reformation, a reaction against some of the teachings of the Roman Catholic Church based on the idea that people should read and interpret the Bible for themselves. Luther and other Protestants call for universal state-supported liberal education.
	Ignatius of Loyola founds the Society of Jesus (Jesuits) and Jean Baptiste de la Salle founds the Brothers of the Christian Schools, teaching orders devoted to furthering the cause of the Church and counteracting the Protestant Reformation.
	In *Essay Concerning Human Understanding and Some Thoughts on Education*, John Locke expresses the realist view that reality and thought are separate. He describes a child's mind as a blank slate (tabula rasa) on which teachers must imprint an education.

The 1700s	In *Emile*, Jean Jacques Rousseau expresses a humanistic view of education in which children are not blank slates but possess natural goodness and freedom which must be nurtured so that individuals can express their greatest potentials. Educator Johann Pestalozzi puts Rousseau's theory into practice.
	The writings of Voltaire and Descartes help to popularize scientific inquiry and spread commitment to rationalism and empiricism as philosophical orientations to education.
	In his *Critique of Pure Reason*, Immanuel Kant reflects classical idealism in his definition of knowledge as the interaction of reason and experience. German idealist Georg Wilhelm Friedrich Hegel describes reality as a dialectic between thesis (idea), antithesis (nature), and synthesis (mind or spirit).
The 1800s	Karl Marx transforms Hegel's dialectic between ideas, nature, and mind into a dialectic between economic or material conditions and human choices. Dialectical materialism becomes the basis of the political philosophy known as Marxism.
	Educators Johann Herbart and Friedrich Froebel develop Rousseau's philosophy into teaching methods that spread to the United States.
	Charles Darwin's 1859 *On the Origin of Species* focuses attention on heredity, evolution, and natural processes of adaptation and change. His work stimulates the scientific movement and influences the philosophers and educators who come to be known as the pragmatists. Herbert Spencer's theory of Social Darwinism becomes the basis of a movement calling for utilitarian education.
Around the Turn of the Century	Charles Peirce and William James express the philosophy of pragmatism, based on the idea that the purpose of thought is to produce action. Practical knowledge and applied skills become a focus of educational reform.
	Maria Montessori develops an educational philosophy in the humanist tradition that continues today through a system of private schools.
1920s and 1930s	John Dewey extends the philosophy of pragmatism in education. His views—that ideas must be tested through experimentation, that people learn best through questioning and hands-on experiences, and that the needs of the child are most important— become known as progressivism. Progressivism becomes the most influential educational philosophy in America until the 1950s.

BENCHMARKS

Developments in Western Intellectual Thought and Their Influence on American Education (*cont.*)

1920s and 1930s (*cont.*)	Influenced by events of the Great Depression, Theodore Brameld and George Counts develop the philosophy of social reconstructionism, in which the aim of education is to reform the social order, fulfill democratic ideals, and improve the quality of human life.
1940s and 1950s	Progressivism underlies Jean Piaget's studies of children's cognitive and social development.
	Opposing Dewey and progressivism, Robert Maynard Hutchins and Mortimer Adler promote the philosophy known as perennialism. They develop Great Books of the Western World, the study of selected classics to uncover enduring basic truths. Other perennialists call for reserving general education for the gifted and including character training and Bible study in the curriculum.
	Other critics of progressivism, such as William Bagley and Arthur Bestor, promote essentialism, calling for a common core of essential knowledge that changes with the times and rigorous teacher-centered instruction in basic skills so that people can lead productive lives.
	Influenced by events surrounding World War II, existentialist writers and philosophers such as Sören Kierkegaard, Albert Camus, and Jean-Paul Sartre popularize the idea that reality resides within the individual, that we are free to search for our own meaning in the world, and that we are what we choose.
	Behavioral psychology emerges from experiments by Ivan Pavlov, John Watson, and others. B. F. Skinner improves this earlier work and develops principles based on the idea that behavior is determined by environment and that people are best motivated by rewards and punishments.

Third, Morine-Dershimer notes that Lee Shulman (1987) has suggested that teachers possess a unique form of knowledge that lies at the intersection of content knowledge and knowledge of teaching or pedagogy which he calls "pedagogical content knowledge." Shulman's work has explored how teachers transform content and pedagogy by reading, discussion, observation, and practice into knowledge that is adapted to the abilities of students. TJ, the teacher of learning-disabled students, for example, uses himself as an

1960s and 1970s	In *Walden Two*, B. F. Skinner shows how behavioral engineering—the scientific control of the educative process—might lead to the creation of a utopian society. Behaviorism widely influences educational practice.
	Humanistic psychology develops from the work of Alfred Adler, Carl Rogers, Abraham Maslow, and others, partly as a reaction against behaviorism, and influences the open school movement. Experimental curricula, such as A. S. Neill's Summerhill, express the humanistic and existentialist views that the aim of education is to promote personal freedom and expression and individual self-fulfillment.
	Eastern philosophies derived from Hinduism and Buddhism influence curriculum in the United States and educational movements based on existential and reconstructionist philosophies.
	Social reconstructionism based on Marxist assumptions about the world is expressed in the writings of Herbert Marcuse, Jurgen Habermas, and others.
1980s and 1990s	In *Paideia Proposal*, Mortimer Adler extends the educational philosophy of perennialism that he and Hutchins developed earlier in the century, calling for one course of study for all.
	The Back to Basics movement, the Essential Schools movement developed by Theodore Sizer, and E. D. Hirsch's curriculum for cultural literacy revive interest in essentialism.
	Constructivism and multiculturalism as educational movements have combined roots in the philosophies of humanism, progressivism, existentialism, and reconstructionism.

analogy for his students, adjusting his teaching to meet the needs of students whom he perceives to be much like himself.

And fourth, teachers' thinking about their work has been characterized in terms of Aristotle's concept of "practical argument"; that is, an argument ending in action related to the logic of one's initial proposition. Tom Green (1976) suggested that good teachers can perceive the practical arguments of students. For instance, when students are incorrect or unreasonable, the teacher determines why students think as they do, then helps them reexamine their beliefs so as to formulate better responses. Gary Fenstermacher (1986) also suggests that research on teaching can be used to influence teachers' beliefs, in a sense, to strengthen their practical arguments.

When teachers understand, articulate, and act on their philosophies, they cultivate their own "literacy of thoughtfulness" (Brown, 1991, p. 35). By example, then, they encourage students to do the same. These consequences, some would argue, are enough to justify the study of philosophy for its own sake. But a teacher's philosophy serves other purposes as well. Philosophy provides the foundation upon which teachers construct knowledge about teaching and learning. Philosophy guides the professional rationale that supports reasoned and reasonable action. Philosophy helps teachers evaluate their work and thus assists them in their pursuit of personal and professional excellence.

SUMMARY

1. Philosophy is a set of ideas about the nature of reality and about the meaning of life. Both ancient and modern philosophies influence education today.

2. The three main branches of philosophy are (a) metaphysics, which deals with the study of reality; (b) epistemology, which is concerned with the nature of knowledge; and (c) axiology, which seeks to determine what is of value.

3. Idealists are concerned with goals against which people can judge their own progress and the progress of civilization. Platonian idealists believe education is the key to creating and perpetuating a society in which talent rises to the top.

4. Realists seek to discover truth in the world around them via methods of direct observation and scientific inquiry. Aristotle believed excellence would flourish as one sought the middle ground between life's extremes.

5. Thomists believe there is an independent reality knowable to man that is the creation of God. A combination of reason and faith enable people to discover truth.

6. Humanists reform people's perceptions of themselves in relation to teaching and learning. They also express their beliefs in the inherent goodness of children.

7. Existentialists believe people are free to define their lives as they choose. As such, existentialist educators prize individuality and resist social conformism.

8. When Marxists view public schools in the United States, they see evidence of the ruling elite, or the haves, in a capitalist society dominating the have-nots. This evidence, they contend, is often veiled by a curriculum that assumes the values of the ruling elite are viable for all.

9. Behaviorism explicates relationships between the environment and behavior. In America's schools, both curriculum and teaching reflect behavioristic philosophy in the use of conditioning and modeling techniques.

10. For pragmatists, experimentalists, and progressivists, truth is relative or determined by science or by function. According to their philosophy, people are capable of experiencing, experimenting, and testing their beliefs, changing them if need be.

11. Perennialists and essentialists assert that there are some recurring principles of education so important that they should be learned for their own sake. Because people are basically the same, there must be constancy in the way they are educated. Essentialists also believe that some principles must be taught to all students so they can solve contemporary problems. For essentialists, science is central to societal progress.

12. Social reconstructionists seek change in society. They would use education to reform not only schools but also the communities in which schools are embedded.

13. Non-Western philosophies present alternative views of life and learning that can influence students and educators to think and behave in ways that are different from expectations expressed in Western philosophies.

14. Philosophy influences daily educational life by lending direction to the educational activities of individuals and organizations.

15. Teachers hold personal philosophies that are influenced by their backgrounds and interactions with students and others and that, in turn, drive teachers to behave in certain ways.

TERMS AND CONCEPTS

aesthetics	existentialism	pragmatism
axiology	humanism	realism
behaviorism	idealism	scaffolding
cognitivism	Marxism	social
cultural literacy	metaphysics	reconstructionism
epistemology	perennialism	Socratic method
essentialism	philosophy	Thomism
ethics		

STUDENT ACTIVITIES

Perceive and Value

1. How are idealism and realism made evident in today's discussions of education reform?
2. Why might a principal with a pragmatic outlook on schooling choose to spend her money on developing programs to make parents and community members part of school activities instead of on sending teachers to staff development conferences?

Know and Act

Compare and contrast the data in Table 4.2 (Philosophies on which Western Education is Based) on educational goals. What similarities and differences do you observe among the various philosophies? Which philosophies appeal to you the most, and why? Describe in your own words your philosophy of education.

Evaluate

How would a behaviorist and a cognitivist judge the relative success of schooling and what different sorts of evidence might they consider?

Discover

Heighten your awareness of the philosophical underpinnings of arguments. Select a broad, controversial issue in education and construct a questionnaire about it with the aim of finding out the underlying philosophies on which your own and others' views are based. Use the information in this chapter to help you frame your questions. If your issue was mainstreaming or multiculturalism, for instance, what kinds of questions would you ask to determine if views reflect a philosophy of social reconstructionism? Of perennialism? Of existentialism? And so on. Frame questions carefully or refine them as you proceed so that answers will tell you what you want to know. Ask your questions of a number of respondents, including yourself, and write or record what people say. Then analyze the responses to identify any consistent patterns that point to the philosophical stances described in the chapter.

5

Schools

The emergence of the common school marked the beginning of public education in America. Many, like Horace Mann, viewed the common school as a great equalizing force having the potential to eliminate poverty, crime, and ignorance. Although schools have fallen short of these goals in many ways, Americans continue to pin their hopes for a better world on a place called "school."

This chapter describes some of the ways schools differ from one another and what makes some schools more appealing to one group of people than to another. Also presented is the research on more and less effective schools, which focuses on a number of attributes that seem to make a difference in students' performance and their attitudes toward school.

HOW IS THE SCHOOL A SOCIAL INSTITUTION?

The school is first and foremost a social **institution**; that is, an established organization having an identifiable structure and a set of functions meant to preserve and extend social order. Schools are structured to operate as relatively self-contained units, loosely coupled to other schools within a system. Schools have "personalities" that characterize daily life within their walls. Sometimes these personalities are visible in written mission statements, but more often than not they emerge in interactions with the members of the organization.

As a social institution, a school's primary function is to move young people into the mainstream of society. The curricula, teaching, processes of evaluation, and relationships among people reinforce a "public image" to which young people are expected to aspire. This image is concerned with preserving our heritage, adapting to social change, and making change happen where it is needed.

In public schools, the *unum* of *e pluribus unum* is defined more clearly and visibly than in any other place in society. That is not to say that schools aim for homogenization, or the repression of individuality. The oneness promulgated by public schools seeks to ensure tolerance of differences among people, and, indeed, in some schools, to celebrate our diversity.

More and more people are recognizing the power of the school as a social institution. Recent reform efforts have tried to capitalize on the fact that schools are the places where all our people come together and stay together for an extended period of time in their lives. In such settings, educators work with parents, children, and outside agencies to insure the psychological and physical well-being of students and to foster academic success. They also work collaboratively to build understanding and acceptance of others.

School districts vary widely in size. Many have only one school. A few have as many as 500 schools.

School Districts

A **school district** is a state-defined geographical area assigned responsibility for public instruction within its borders. During the 1990-91 academic year, there were 84,538 public schools serving a total of 41,223,804 students in grades prekindergarten through 12 (National Center for Education Statistics, 1992). Sizes of school districts vary from place to place, but generally the largest can be found in the eastern third of the United States. As illustrated in Table 5.1, the largest districts

TABLE 5.1   Public School Districts and Enrollment by Size of District, 1990–1991

Enrollment size of district	Number of districts	Percent of districts	Percent of students
Total	15,358	100.0	100.0
25,000 or more	190	1.2	28.7
10,000 to 24,999	489	3.2	17.7
5,000 to 9,999	937	6.1	15.9
2,500 to 4,999	1,940	12.6	16.6
1,000 to 2,499	3,542	23.1	14.1
600 to 999	1,799	11.7	3.4
300 to 599	2,275	14.8	2.4
1 to 299	3,816	24.8	1.2
Size not reported*	370	2.4	

*Includes school districts reporting enrollment of 0.

Note. From *Digest of Education Statistics, 1992* (p. 95) by National Center for Education Statistics, 1992. Washington, DC: U.S. Department of Education, Office of Educational Research and Improvement.

TABLE 5.2   Variation in Racial/Ethnic Composition of Student Populations in Six Districts, in Percent

School District	Hispanic	African American non-Hispanic	European American non-Hispanic
Dade County, FL	43	33	23
Dallas, TX	29	49	20
Fort Worth, TX	25	36	36
Austin, TX	32	20	46
Denver, CO	37	23	36
Boston, MA	19	48	25

Note. From *Characteristics of the 55 largest public elementary and secondary school districts in the United States: 1987–88* (p. 6) by National Center for Education Statistics, 1989, Washington, DC: U.S. Department of Education, Office of Educational Research and Improvement.

serve more than 28% of the total elementary and secondary population in the country, yet they account for only 1% of all school districts. New York City school district, the largest in the country alone, has 993 schools, 53,000 teachers, and 939,900 students (National Center for Education Statistics, 1989).

Big school districts are very different from one another in a number of ways. In Gwinnett County, Georgia, for instance, 3% of the students are eligible for free lunch while 73% of those in Orleans Parish, Louisiana, qualify for the program. Racial/ethnic compositions of school districts also show considerable variation. At least 91% of students in the District of Columbia are African American while 95% in Jefferson County, Colorado, are European American. In Hawaii, 72% are Asian/Pacific Islander American while 71% in El Paso, Texas, and 80% in San Antonio, Texas, are Hispanic American. As noted in Table 5.2, six large school districts, three of which are in Texas, have student bodies composed mainly of three racial/ethnic categories.

Types of Schools

Many students have little choice about where they go to school. For the most part, assignment to particular schools is based on where students and their parents live. In some instances, students may be assigned to a school because they have violated a public school's standards for behavior or because they have social, emotional, or academic needs not being met by the public schools.

For an increasing number of students, educational opportunities are less restricted, that is, they are free to exercise "school choice." The concepts of school choice—as well as of "tuition tax credits" and "vouchers"—mechanisms to encourage school choice—will be described in detail in Chapter 12 ("Education Finance"). For now, it is sufficient to understand that sometimes choices of schools are extended to students because parents are willing to pay out of pocket or to apply for government-provided subsidies, vouchers, or tuition tax credits to enroll their children in particular public, private, or parochial institutions. School choice may also be a matter of public policy. In Minnesota, for example, students may attend any public school, even across district lines.

Children in the United States have access to many types of public and private schools. (See Figure 5.1). There are, of course, schools designed for different ages of students—preschools, elementary schools, middle- and

PUBLIC SCHOOLS	PUBLIC ALTERNATIVE SCHOOLS	PRIVATE SCHOOLS
Kindergarten (K)	Head Start	Nursery Schools & Preschools
Elementary School (K/1-6 or K/1-8)	Prekindergarten Programs	"Concept School" Alternatives
• Primary (K-2)	Laboratory Schools	• Montessori Schools
• Intermediate (3-6)	Nongraded Schools	• Waldorf Schools
Middle School (5-8)	Magnet Schools	• Steiner Schools
Secondary Schools	Charter Schools	"Ethnic School" Alternatives
• Junior High School (7-8 or 7-9)	Accelerated Schools	• Afrocentric Schools (Black Academies)
• High School (7-12, 9-12, or 10-12)	Cluster Schools	• Reservation Schools
Post-Secondary Schools	Vocational-Technical Schools	Parochial/Religious Schools
• Community Colleges	Professional Development Schools	• Catholic Schools
• State Colleges	Government-Run Schools	• Christian Academies
• State Universities	• Department of Defense Dependents Schools	• Hebrew Schools
	• Native-American Schools	• Islamic Schools
	• Career Academies	College Preparatory Schools
	• Job Corps	
	Home Schooling	Trade Schools
		Military Academies
		Junior Colleges
		Colleges & Universities
		Adult Education Centers

FIGURE 5.1

Examples of the Structure and Types of Schooling in America

As you will learn as you read this chapter, it is difficult in many cases to draw solid lines between the three columns in this chart. Develop a hypothesis that you think might explain this difficulty.

junior-high schools, high schools, junior colleges, and colleges. In many public school settings, there are magnet schools, charter schools, alternative schools, and vocational or trade schools. There are also rural schools, suburban schools, and urban schools. The various schools often differ in structure (organization) and function (programs and services).

An analysis of more than 14,000 parental responses to a survey conducted by SchoolMatch, a data-based information and counseling service in Columbus, Ohio, suggests that many parents think about several things when selecting a school. Among respondents, however, low pupil-teacher ratios was the one attribute of schools having universal appeal. The majority (62.7%) wanted "small" or "very small" classes for elementary-aged children and 57% indicated "average" classes were suitable for junior- and senior-high school students. With regard to rigor, only 28.3% wanted their children in schools with the highest range (81st to 99th percentile) of composite scores on standardized tests; 53.2% wanted a school system in the second highest range (61st to 80th percentile). Data suggest that parents want their children to attend school where they can be successful rather than where students have the highest scholastic ranking (Bainbridge & Sundre, 1992).

HOW IS EARLY CHILDHOOD EDUCATION ORGANIZED IN THE UNITED STATES?

Many of the first early childhood programs were in day nurseries funded by philanthropic organizations and associated with settlement houses. Enrollees in these programs were most often children from low-income families whose mothers worked, children who were neglected by their parents, and immigrants seeking to be "Americanized." These first day nurseries were mainly custodial in nature (Williams & Fromberg, 1992).

Today, preschool programs are more diversified and are supported by both public and private interest groups and sponsors. Project Head Start, infant intervention and enrichment programs, nursery schools, public and private prekindergartens and kindergartens, college and university laboratory schools, church-sponsored preschools, and parent cooperatives offer a variety of educational programs for young children. Although enrollment in such programs has gradually increased over time, 4- to 5-year-olds are more likely to receive some type of education on a regular basis than 3-year-olds. (Nonminority group children also participate in such programs at higher rates than minority group children.) The majority of students receiving preschool services are enrolled in nursery schools and other types of organized group programs such as prekindergarten and Head Start (National Center for Education Statistics, 1993a).

For economic as well as educational reasons, the demand for child care and public preschools has grown rapidly in the United States during the last decade.

With so many agencies sponsoring preschool programs, there is much variation in the types of services offered and in the types of families served. While some preschools offer full-day educational or custodial care, others offer only half-day programs. Preschools may also be restricted to children from low-income families, to children of adolescent parents, or to children with disabilities. Among the different preschools, program goals and philosophies about teaching and learning also vary considerably.

The professional preparation of early childhood education staff and the quality of programs vary greatly. This fact has fueled ongoing debates about whether early childhood programs should be school-based or community-based. Qualitative differences in programs have also spurred the **National Association for the Education of Young Children (NAEYC)**, one of the largest professional associations for early childhood educators, and the National Association of Early Childhood Specialists in State Departments of Education (NAECS/SDE) to develop guidelines that could be used to ensure quality education of 3- through 8-year-olds (NAECS & SDE, 1991).

Cultural Awareness

At their 1992 annual meeting, the NAEYC showcased methods used in Reggio Emilia, Italy, to illustrate how preschools may be structured appropriately to cultivate problem-solving, creativity, and cognitive skills in young children. These included projects that can take days or months—open-ended explorations that are generated by questions or experiences of children, provoked by natural phenomena or events, or conceived by teachers to address particular cognitive or social needs. The Italian teachers also attempt to integrate art into the curriculum and to use alternatives to print media to assess student learning. To Italian educators, collaboration among children, parents, and teachers is critical. (Cohen, 1992)

While many tout the importance of philosophy and curriculum in preschool settings, others contend that increased funding for public preschool programs is crucial. In 1992, child care teachers with bachelors degrees earned only $6.53 per hour, or $13,600 per year. Such low wages make it difficult to attract and retain qualified staff—and it is staff who ultimately make the difference in what children experience at school (Schweinhart, 1992).

Head Start

Head Start was launched under the auspices of the Johnson administration in 1965 with the enrollment of 561,359 children in 11,068 centers across the nation (Washington & Oyemade, 1987). The first major early childhood program subsidized by the federal government, Head Start represents a national effort to provide comprehensive services to low-income 3-and 4-year-olds and their families. Head Start uses a multifaceted approach to improve children's social, physical, mental, and affective development. Besides offering such services as dental and physical exams, the program provides field trips and in-class experiences for young children to stimulate learning readiness. Not all Head Start program directors advocate the same instructional methods or philosophy about teaching and learning, but they do recognize the importance of parents in the education process. Parents are encouraged to assist in the classroom so they can reinforce educational experiences at home. Knowing that extenuating circumstances, such as a child's family being evicted from its home, will interfere with a child's attention to classroom routines, staff members support families by providing them with a variety of health, nutrition, and social services.

Some Preschool and Early Elementary Alternatives

Montessori preschools are less diversified philosophically than Head Start programs; they focus mainly on the development of children's perceptual, motor, intellectual, and social skills. Programs are based on the ideas of Maria Montessori (1870–1952), a physician who developed preschool teaching methods in the early 1900s focused on students' maturation levels and readiness to learn particular skills. Teachers trained in Montessori methods use a curriculum centered around particular materials designed to help children discover the physical properties of objects. As students interact with materials, such as the "pink tower" (blocks of graduated size), learning is self-directed rather than teacher-directed. Teachers act as observers, assisting indirectly by asking questions or providing materials to optimize learning. Given that most instructional materials are graded and self-correcting, students experience "liberty within structure" in such settings.

Montessori schools do not necessarily restrict themselves to teaching preschool children. At Sands Montessori Elementary School in Cincinnati, Ohio, classes are divided into overlapping age-group combinations: 3 to 6, 6 to 9, and 9 to 12. Often teachers organize their curriculum around a theme, such as "workers in the neighborhood," so children of different ages and abilities can work as a group as well as practice skills at different levels. When doing a theme-related project, for example, "an eight-year-old may write down a story dictated by a six-year-old, type it, and bind it into a book illustrated by the nonreader, then give it back to the nonreader, who can use it to practice reading his own work" (Cushman, 1990, p. 32).

At the other end of the philosophical spectrum, Waldorf educators oppose a focus on the

Maria Montessori's ideas have become generally incorporated into public school early childhood and elementary programs, including the idea of giving children developmentally appropriate materials and learning challenges.

acquisition of particular learning skills. Waldorf education has its roots in the spiritual-scientific research of Rudolf Steiner (1861–1925), an Austrian scientist and educator. According to Steiner's philosophy, young children learn primarily through their senses and respond in the most active mode of knowing: imitation. In Waldorf preschools, creative play is viewed as the critical element in a child's development. Waldorf teachers believe that to draw the child's energies away from creative play to meet intellectual demands will rob the child of the health and vitality he or she will need in later life. They argue that in the end, premature intellectual demands weaken the powers of judgment and practical intelligence the teacher wants to encourage (Barnes, 1991).

WHAT IS THE STRUCTURE OF PUBLIC SCHOOL EDUCATION?

By the time children in the United States reach kindergarten age, nearly 85% enroll in one of the more than 59,000 public elementary schools (National Center for Education Statistics, 1991). Enrollees are often classified as primary (kindergarten through grade 2) and intermediate (grades 3 through 6) students. In some instances, students in grades 7 and 8 are designated as upper-elementary students, but more often they are classified as junior-high school students.

In elementary schools, there is similarity in teachers' credentials (most are certified to work in grades kindergarten through 8) and the types of programs offered to children. Not all students spend the same amount of time in school, however. While the number of students attending kindergarten on a full-time basis has quadrupled since 1969, only 40% of 5-year-olds experience full-time programs (National Center for Education Statistics, 1991).

Kindergarten

In some instances, children old enough to enter kindergarten programs are placed in one of two tracks, the regular kindergarten or a "junior kindergarten." Those in junior kindergartens go to school for 1 year before being promoted to a regular kindergarten. This experience is supposed to help get them "ready" for kindergarten.

Placement in either setting is usually determined by students' performance on a variety of screening tests. Although screening policy and practice vary from district to district, low-income males have a tendency to score poorly on screening tests and thus are more likely to spend two years in kindergarten (Walsh, Ellwein, Eads, & Miller, 1991). Boys' lower scores may be due in part to the fact that they develop more slowly than girls in the early years and also that some cultures' expectations for young boys are not geared toward the development of attributes measured by such tests. Even extra time in kindergarten, however, often fails to improve achievement or to eradicate students' inadequate school readiness (Smith & Shepard, 1989).

In some kindergarten programs, teachers are oriented to an academic curriculum which often means extensive time spent in whole-group settings, didactic instruction, use of worksheets, and few opportunities for small-group, individualized, or hands-on activities. Other kindergarten teachers use a curriculum that is more student-centered, or "developmentally appropriate," which usually means students are expected to acquire skills and abilities at their own pace, doing so through exploration and free play.

Although states may differ, many kindergartens focus on academics. A 1988 survey of 103 public kindergartens randomly selected from different regions of North Carolina revealed that only 20% of kindergarten classes used a developmental approach. Type of instruction seemed unaffected by region of the state, size of the school, or per pupil expenditure. Researchers hypothesized that, among other things, differences might be attributed to kindergarten teachers' and principals' beliefs about best practice, parent and community values, and attitudes of and pressures from first- and second-grade teachers (Bryant, Clifford, & Peisner, 1991). While there are certainly regional variations, North Carolinians are like many other citizens with respect to their emphasis on academics.

Elementary Classrooms

There are physical differences in buildings housing elementary students, but in the main the schools they attend are stunningly similar. Often there are 20 to 25 students working in a self-contained classroom with a teacher and sometimes, particularly at the primary level, with an aide. Classroom teachers usually focus on language arts, mathematics, science, social studies, and health while specialist teachers offer instruction in art, music, physical education, and special education.

Despite many similarities, there are a number of curricular and instructional variations within and among elementary schools. Sometimes students are grouped homogeneously by ability or achievement for instructional purposes. Such grouping can occur within a classroom or across classrooms. In other settings, students work in **nongraded classrooms**, where they are grouped heterogeneously, sometimes with students of various ages. Nongraded programs, also referred to as multiage, multigrade, or family grouping programs, are most prevalent in primary schools.

The popularity of multigrade or nongraded programs has waxed and waned through the years. During the 1950s and 1960s, nongrading was practiced in more than 7% of the schools. The popularity of the concept declined, however, when "back to basics" ideas took hold during the mid-1970s. Recently, concerns about the strong correlation between retention in grade and subsequent dropout of a growing number of students have stimulated some elementary schools to revert to the one-room schoolhouse notion of multiage groupings of students. One state, Kentucky, mandates that every school provide nongraded instruction through the third grade (Willis, 1991).

Ideally, nongraded programs provide developmentally appropriate curriculum—curriculum that may be tailored to differences in students' stages of intellectual, emotional, physical, and/or social development—that allows for individualized, continuous progress for young children. Purportedly, this means that, while there are standards of performance to be reached by students, the time taken to reach those standards and methods for doing so will likely vary from student to student. Any grouping for instruction is said to be "flexible" and based on "abilities, interests, and needs" of students. In such programs, there is no formal promotion from one grade to the next. Instead, a student stays with a group of students until she or he has mastered necessary skills.

Such educational settings exhibit

> . . . a range of techniques loosely linked by a developmental, child-centered philosophy of learning but otherwise as idiosyncratic as American education itself...Many teachers work in teams, but just as many classes are self-contained. Some mixed-age groupings take place for as little as an hour of shared time a day; others keep the mixed group together only for certain subjects; and some keep them together all day. (Cushman, 1990, pp. 28, 30)

Research on nongraded elementary schools suggests they can be quite effective when nongrading is used as a grouping method rather than as a means for individualizing instruction. Positive effects are greatest in situations where students are grouped across age lines in just one subject (usually reading) or in multiple subjects, with students receiving direct instruction for the majority of a class session. Experts agree that groupings should not be stagnant, however. They should be reassessed frequently and changed when student performance indicates a mismatch in instruction and achievement (Gutiérrez & Slavin, 1992).

Junior High Schools and Middle Schools

In the fall of 1909, Columbus, Ohio, opened a new 3-year intermediate school, calling it a "junior high school." This was the first mention of such a school. In 1910, Berkeley, California, opened two 3-year intermediate schools and called them "introductory high schools"—a name that never caught on (Til, Vars, & Lounsbury, 1967). Junior high schools have been an important part of our education system since the 1930s. Junior high school programs are meant to help students make the transition from elementary to high school by concentrating on academic subjects and by exposing students to careers and occupations.

In the 1960s, there were about 1,000 middle schools nationwide. Today there are more than 12,000.

Although there are variations in enrollment patterns for junior high schools, most include students who are in grades 7 through 9. As in elementary schools, instruction occurs mainly in self-contained classrooms. Curriculum at the junior high school level, however, is usually more diversified, that is, there are more types of courses offered. Like their colleagues at the senior high school level, junior high school teachers generally specialize in the content and teaching of a particular subject area. Junior high schools typically use six class periods per day; instruction is usually teacher-directed.

Middle schools, which emerged in the 1960s, aim to provide an educational environment less imitative of high school and better suited to the needs of 10- to 14-year-olds. By the 1970s, the number of middle schools (usually grades 5 to 8 or 6 to 8) had surpassed the number of junior high schools. Despite their continued popularity, particularly in the suburbs, middle schools for many years have been criticized for tailoring programs similar to the ones they were designed to replace. A survey of 2,400 schools conducted in 1988 by the Johns Hopkins Center for Research on Elementary and Middle Schools indicated that middle school students often experienced six-period days rather than the recommended eight-period day. In the majority of schools surveyed, there was also little evidence of team teaching, flexible scheduling, or interdisciplinary programs. As in junior high schools, lecture-style instruction was still the norm (Cuban, 1992).

Are the middle grades the "forgotten years," as some have claimed? During the middle-school years, adolescent problems begin to flare up and can be manifested in outcomes such as dropping out of school, teenage pregnancy, and drug and alcohol abuse. Critics assert that middle schools, often quite large, leave students feeling disconnected. Of particular concern is the fact that many of these adolescents have little opportunity to establish relationships with a trusted adult or to receive individual counseling (Kolman, 1992).

Advocates for middle schools argue that the special needs of young adolescents require a school that is not so juvenile in its structure and approach as an elementary school and not so impersonal and demanding of independence as a high school. In a middle school, they contend, students will have a chance to mature before being thrust into the high school environment.

More educators and parents alike maintain that **tracking**, a process of segregating students by ability, which often occurs in middle schools, contributes to problems experienced by youngsters in their early adolescent years. More often than not, students in middle schools are grouped homogeneously by ability for at least one subject (Mansnerus, 1992). At Lanier Middle School in Houston (as in all Houston, Texas, schools), students are placed into one of two tracks—the Vanguard program for gifted and talented students or the "regular program." The two groups of students meet only during lunch, gym, and elective classes (Suro, 1992). We shall discuss concepts of ability grouping more fully in Chapter 8 ("Students and Learning") and of tracking in Chapter 10 ("Instruction").

There are exceptions to such programs. At Louis Armstrong School in Queens, New York, a middle school for grades 6 through 8, students of different abilities have more opportunity to interact. Tracking occurs only in some eighth-grade math and English classes because of state mandates. Otherwise, students work in heterogeneous groups, each classroom taking on the aura of a microcosmic society. Louis Armstrong is the only middle school in New York City, however, that follows the heterogeneous model (Newman, 1992).

Evelyn A. Hanshaw Middle School in Modesto, California, offers another example of a learning environment different from the more tradi-

VOICES

On Freedom With Responsibility

Long-time observer of schools Gene I. Maeroff, formerly of the *New York Times*, now a senior fellow at the Carnegie Foundation for the Advancement of Teaching, sees possibilities for motivating students among the most difficult to reach—young adolescents. His account of Shoreham-Wading River Middle School, located at the eastern end of Long Island and recognized as an exemplary middle school, raises interesting questions about issues of student freedom, student responsibility, and the role of the school in building and maintaining a sense of community.

Early one morning a few months ago, at an hour when most students had not yet arrived at school, three of the booths in the bagel shop down the road from Shoreham-Wading River Middle School were taken by students deep in conversation with the teachers sitting opposite them. This scene, a youngster swigging cold orange juice and a teacher sipping hot coffee—the pair of them munching doughnuts or buttered bagels—was a typical "advisory" meeting. At least it was typical as anything can be at a school that is decidedly untypical.

"It blew me away when I moved here in time for the sixth grade," said Mike D'Arrigo, an articulate 13-year-old now in the eighth grade, who has found his niche in drama activities. "In my old school it was like being in prison, but this school is comfortable. It's like being at home. The teachers get to know you well, and there's enough happening to keep you busy all the time. I really like it here."

Shoreham-Wading River is a school in which team teaching is the norm, experiential learning is a hallmark, cooperative learning is widely practiced, teacher participation in decision making is extensive, and teachers lunching with their students is a daily event. Community service is part of the curriculum, the school has its own small farm on which students work, youngsters take frequent trips to explore career options, almost all classes are heterogeneously grouped, and students almost never cut school.

Shoreham-Wading River enrolls students in grades 6 through 8, and a team approach ensures that in each grade a core group of 40 to 45 children is taught the four main subjects by a team of two teachers. This reduces by half—as compared with the typical middle school—the number of adults with whom a student must deal. Twice as much time with each of two teachers instead of half as much time with any of four teachers means that teachers and students get to know each other better.

The idea of freedom with responsibility is mentioned frequently at Shoreham-Wading River, and some students have been trained in conflict resolution so that they can help peers resolve disputes. The school exemplifies John Dewey's contention that a sense of community—what Dewey called "the moving spirit of the whole group"—can lead to order when everyone has a chance to feel a part of the enterprise.

The extent to which this approach could be replicated with youngsters who have less self-control is an open question. So inclined to good behavior are students at Shoreham-Wading River that the school psychologist has encountered only three cases of hard-core drug use by students in 15 years.

CRITICAL THINKING

How do schools create environments that feel like "home" to students? How important do you think it is for teachers "to get to know their students" and what does this phrase mean to you? How might schools be organized to provide students "freedom with responsibility?" Do you think it is possible to replicate the kind of environment that seems to exit in Shoreham-Wading River in other communities where students have "less self-control"?

Source: Maeroff. G. I. (1990) Getting to know a good middle school: Shoreham-Wading River. *Phi Delta Kappan*, 71 (7), 504–511. Reprinted by permission.

tional junior high and middle schools. Hanshaw serves a population of 800 students, many of whom live in communities plagued by drug dealing and violence. Three fourths of the students are Hispanic Americans, most of whom qualify for free lunches and few of whom speak English at home.

Hanshaw, built in 1991, consists of five attractive buildings surrounding a central grassy courtyard, each connected to the next by column-lined walkways. Inside these buildings, seventh graders experience two interdisciplinary 88-minute core classes, one covering mathematics and science, the other dealing with English and social studies. Eighth graders attend 44-minute classes in the four core subjects, but their teachers try to make connections between content areas. Both groups also complete an "exploratory wheel" which includes courses in such areas as arts and crafts, chorus, industrial technology, and teen issues.

As in other middle schools, students work in teams of 60 to 100 students with 4 to 5 teachers. Each team, or "house," is named after a California State University campus which students have a chance to visit at least once during their stay at Hanshaw. The curriculum is centered around projects and themes (e.g., independence, justice, wellness, social structures), with almost no reliance on textbooks. Within each house, cooperative learning, mixed-ability grouping, and team teaching are the rule as teachers try to build a "sense of community" to encourage students to stay in school and avoid falling into menial farmworker jobs so prevalent among South Modesto's Hispanic-American population (Gursky, 1992).

Similar schools can be found in Massachusetts, where the state department of education implemented a "carrot and stick" approach for encouraging school districts to implement heterogeneous, or mixed ability, grouping at all grade levels. Believing that homogeneous grouping (tracking) was widening the gap between high and low achievers and segregating students by race, gender, language, and disability, the department in 1990 began awarding and denying state drop-out prevention and remedial education money to schools based on whether they use such grouping procedures (Schmidt, 1993).

High Schools

High schools, or secondary schools, usually include grades 10, 11, and 12 or grades 9 through 12. In some states, such as California, Illinois, and New Jersey, where 4-year high schools are the rule, the high school may function as a separate entity, having its own board of education. For the most part, however, the trend has been to combine elementary, middle, and high schools into a unified district.

High schools vary greatly in size, with enrollment in alternative schools as low as 200 and enrollment in large "comprehensive" high schools as high as 4,000. As noted in Chapter 3, comprehensive high schools—large high schools having a full range of programs—evolved over time from experimentation with concepts of the Latin grammar school, the academy, and the high school that emerged in the late nineteenth century. The comprehensive high school, largely as it exists today, was popularized in the late 1950s through the efforts of James B. Conant, former Harvard University president.

Large high schools are "comprehensive" in their educational offerings and also in their social mission. These institutions assemble under one roof many students who differ in race, ethnicity, religion, and economic background. They educate in the general sense, they prepare young people for the world of work and for college, and they fulfill the civic mission of working toward the maintenance of a sense of community.

But comprehensive high schools are not without critics. They are depicted by some as unpleasant places where students are easily lost in the shuffle:

> The coldness and impersonality of such surroundings is heightened by the huge size of many schools . . . In such schools, students are merely so many numbers in a computer and the principal is only a voice heard over a public-address system or a face glimpsed amongst the crush of bodies during "passing period" between classes. (Toch, 1991, p. C2)

Critics argue that the sense of alienation and purposelessness that plagues minority and other disadvantaged students, particularly those in urban areas, is only deepened in huge and impersonal school settings. They point to high dropout rates, absenteeism, and classroom disorders as indications of the failure of large schools. (Toch, 1991). School size may not cause such problems, but the difficulties of individual students are more difficult to identify in large schools and thus resistant to remediation.

In recent years, several school districts have reduced the size of their secondary schools. In Columbus, Ohio, educators reorganized several of their 17 high schools, creating "houses" of 250 students, each with an administrator, a team of teachers, and a guidance counselor who stay together throughout students' high school careers.

In New York City, Community School District 4 subdivided Benjamin Franklin High School, a crime-ridden, one-building school, into a progressive elementary program for 220 youngsters, a junior-high for 250 advanced seventh and eighth graders, and a high school for 1,300 students with average or above-average academic performance (Toch, 1991). Other school districts have created magnet programs, or schools within schools, to create a more personal environment. Many high schools in New York City, for example, include "clusters," or groups of programs in related career areas such as business, communications, law, and technology education.

Comprehensive schools can offer a wide variety of curricula fairly economically. They typically provide an array of courses to prepare students for vocational or technical areas and for college, but they also offer other experiences. Besides expecting students to have a certain number of credit hours in core courses, some, like Missouri's Pattonville High School, require students to spend 50 hours performing community service to graduate. To fulfill the requirement, students at Pattonville must work without pay in nonpolitical organizations.

Depending on their academic needs, some high school students take courses at nearby colleges. In Minnesota, where state policy in 1985 made it possible for high school juniors and seniors to earn both high school and

Regional vocational-technical schools and county agricultural schools are examples of specialized or alternative public high schools. These schools serve the interests and needs of particular students and localities.

Parents who teach their children at home must comply with state and school district guidelines and standards. A national organization for home schoolers exists to help parents succeed at this difficult and often controversial task.

college credits at state expense, the line of distinction between the two institutions has become somewhat blurry. In 1992, about 650 students of high school age and younger took classes at the University of Minnesota (Olson, 1992b).

High school students typically start their day about 8:00 a.m. and finish in midafternoon. In some situations, however, educators have moved from a daytime to evening schedule to meet the needs of at-risk high school students. Manhattan Comprehensive Night High School in New York City is an academic, accredited, diploma-granting high school that opened in February 1989 and runs from 5:00 p.m. to 10:45 p.m. Monday through Thursday, with Sundays from noon to 6 p.m. devoted to athletics and cultural enrichment activities. Applicants must have completed 1 year of high school and be reading at a seventh-grade level to gain admission.

During the 1991 academic year, 450 students ages 17 to 22 enrolled in Manhattan Comprehensive. Most worked full- or part-time jobs. Seventy-five percent received some type of public or private assistance, about 40% had children or were pregnant, 45% were Hispanic American, and another 40% were African American. Some had been in trouble with the law, were homeless, or were living in nontraditional situations. Although students at Manhattan Comprehensive meet every criterion for being at-risk, they earned academic diplomas, rather than General Educational Development certificates (Lawton, 1991).

Some high schools are "specialized" institutions, focusing on science, art, or performing arts. There are also vocational technical high schools and alternative high schools. In many instances, programs are "screened," meaning students are accepted on the basis of an audition, written exam, or school records. In New York City, regardless of whether students desire to attend one of these specialized schools or remain in their neighborhood schools, they must make formal application to attend high school.

WHAT IS THE STRUCTURE OF HIGHER EDUCATION?

In many ways, the structure of higher education shapes the structure of high schools, just as high schools influence junior high schools. Because parents and school leaders want high school students to go on for more education, high schools try to prepare students to move up the academic ladder.

The first colleges in the United States were typically small in size and attended by upper-class males. Established by religious denominations, these exclusive institutions of higher education generally offered a curriculum centered around liberal arts courses, with an emphasis on Greek and Latin—courses necessary for the education of future clergymen. Over time, federal land grants changed the complexion of postsecondary education as state-supported colleges and universities began to spring up across the country. These publicly controlled schools offered a diverse curriculum that allowed individuals to select from a number of scientific rather than classical courses.

With time, the makeup of college populations also changed. By the 1970s, the proportion of women and men attending college directly from high school was roughly the same. Between 1976 and 1988, minority-group students increased from 15 to 18% and nonresident aliens from 2 to 3% of total enrollment. By 1988, African Americans accounted for 9%, Hispanic Americans 5%, Asian Americans 4%, and Native Americans 1% of the total college enrollment.

Two- and Four-Year Colleges

As the student body changed, so too did the structure of higher education. Two-year junior or community colleges began to evolve offering transitional programs to 4-year colleges and universities and providing technical and vocational education. Between 1972 and 1990, except for a brief period during the early to mid-1980s, enrollment in these institutions increased more rapidly than enrollment in 4-year public and private colleges. By 1990, there were 1,548 public and 1,953 private institutions of higher education in the United States with enrollments ranging from under 200 students to 30,000 or more (Editors of the Chronicle of Higher Education, 1993). As Figure 5.2 depicts, public institutions at that time accounted for over three fourths of higher education enrollment. Students in 2-year public colleges claimed 36% of total enrollment (National Center for Education Statistics, 1992).

Curricular offerings in 2- and 4-year colleges are somewhat different. Two-year colleges typically offer basic undergraduate liberal arts and science courses while providing a wide range of vocational, technical, and adult education programs. Colleges and universities generally offer a full undergraduate course leading to a bachelor's degree as well as first-professional and graduate programs leading to advanced degrees.

Within such programs, special classes have been added to meet the needs of an increasingly diverse student body. A survey conducted by the National Center for Education Statistics during fall 1989 revealed that three out of four institutions offered at least one remedial course during the fall

FIGURE 5.2

Higher Education Enrollment, by Type of Institution, Fall 1972–Fall 1990, by Percent of Total Enrollment

On the basis of information in this graph, make one generalization about higher education enrollments, one about enrollments in two-year versus four-year schools, and one about enrollments in public versus private colleges and universities.

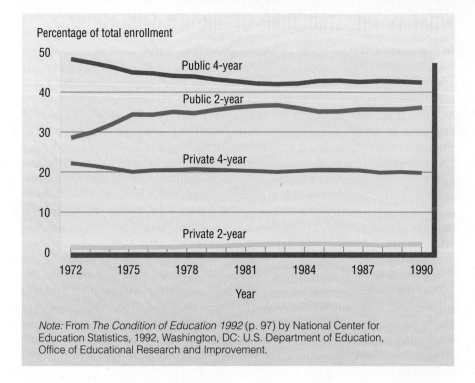

Percentage of total enrollment

Public 4-year

Public 2-year

Private 4-year

Private 2-year

Year

Note: From *The Condition of Education 1992* (p. 97) by National Center for Education Statistics, 1992, Washington, DC: U.S. Department of Education, Office of Educational Research and Improvement.

semester. Sixty-eight percent offered mathematics, 65% writing, and 58% reading. At least 30% of college freshmen enrolled in such a course, with 21% taking remedial mathematics, 16% writing, and 13% reading (National Center for Education Statistics, 1991).

As noted earlier in the chapter, some institutions of higher education affiliate in some way with the public schools. Bethany College has had a partnership with Bethany Primary and Middle Schools in Bethany, West Virginia, since 1989. College students have taught swimming lessons at the college pool, offered one-on-one and in-class tutoring, and helped high school students with fund raisers. College faculty have worked directly with high school teachers to support efforts to upgrade instruction. During the 1992 academic year, one Bethany College faculty member taught Japanese language and customs on a weekly basis in a kindergarten classroom (Appalachia Educational Laboratory, 1992). The concept of the **professional development school**—a school where university and public school people work together in a teaching laboratory—is another indication of the mutual interdependence of schools at all levels.

Adult Education

As described in Chapter 3, adult education programs have allowed many citizens to return to school. The increasing numbers of younger and older adults participating in such programs illustrate the possibilities for lifelong learning in our society. Many people enroll in college courses while others attend university lectures and audit classes. Adult education classes offer opportunities for young and old alike to develop interests and talents and to increase their literacy skills. According to the first report from the National Adult Literacy Survey, adults with higher literacy skills are more likely to work full time, to earn high wages, and to vote (National Center for Education Statistics, 1993b).

Study groups, like those at New York's New School for Social Research, have flourished over time. In existence for more than 30 years, the New School is a unique program that brings together people from all walks of life who want to continue to learn. Enrollees such as Mrs. Schwelb, a 90-year-old woman with a PhD in German studies from the University of Prague, design their own courses and teach one another.

> A former cleaning contractor and a former high school principal jointly teach sculpture. A retired nurse who teachers a popular offering on James Joyce is preparing another course on fairy tales. A retired bookstore owner offers a tour of black feminist literature. A former medieval scholar teaches advanced word processing. . . (Martin, 1991, p. 23)

Elderhostels also provide educational opportunities for people aged 60 and older. A network of some 800 institutions of higher education in the United States sponsors a wide variety of travel and study opportunities in every state and in many foreign countries. Students live in dormitories and study in college classrooms and conference centers. Even though elderhostels do not give college credit, the offerings can be quite demanding. Topics range from oceanography to space science with everything in between. The relatively low cost of elderhostels boost their appeal.

WHAT ARE SOME SCHOOLING ALTERNATIVES?

An **alternative school** is any school operating within the public school system that has programs addressing the specific needs or interests of targeted student groups. Some alternative schools are self-contained structures; others are organized as schools within schools. As will be described later in the chapter, a number of alternative schools, such as accelerated schools and charter schools, are the result of recent efforts to reform schools.

Magnet Schools

Magnet schools are alternative schools within a public school system that draw students from the whole district instead of drawing only from their own neighborhoods. Magnet schools emerged in the 1970s, primarily as a means to desegregate schools. The intent was to avoid the divisiveness of mandatory busing by developing schools so appealing that a racial cross-section of students would be drawn voluntarily to the schools. Today, there are more than 1,500 magnet schools and programs in the United States. Despite the fact that many enrollees have to travel long distances for a longer and somewhat harder school day than they might have in typical public schools, the appeal of magnet programs is strong enough that schools usually have long waiting lists for enrollment (ERIC Clearinghouse on Urban Education, 1991).

Magnet schools typically have three distinct features: (a) an enrollment policy that opens the school to children beyond a particular geographic attendance zone, (b) a student body that is present by choice that meets variable criteria established for inclusion, and (c) a curriculum based on a special theme or instructional method (Dentler, 1991). Built into any level from preschool to senior high school, magnet schools may organize their curricula around mathematics and computers, the arts, the sciences, foreign language, or general academics such as college preparation and honors courses.

> **Today, there are more than 1,500 magnet schools and programs nationwide, including 24 "micro-society" schools.**

There are more than 24 "micro-society" magnet schools in elementary and middle schools around the country that are trying to make schooling more relevant to students' lives. To cultivate the skills students will need to be good citizens, micro-society schools operate

> miniature civilizations complete with all the trappings of the real world: a legislature, courts, banks, post offices, newspapers, a host of entrepreneurial businesses, and even an Internal Revenue Service. Students hold jobs and are paid salaries in an ersatz currency, which they use to pay simulated taxes and tuition and to purchase a variety of goods and services at the school's marketplace. (Sommerfeld, 1992, p. 14)

Vocational-Technical Schools

As the name implies, vocational-technical high schools provide an education for students who wish to enter the trades or to develop technical skills for future employment. They offer programs in cosmetology, food production, management, and service, law enforcement, horticulture, automotive repair, tool and machine operation, air conditioning and refrigeration, building construction, masonry, graphic and commercial arts, drafting, electronics, data processing, a variety of health-related fields, child care, and many other areas.

Although vocational-technical high schools are designed to prepare people to assume jobs upon graduation, students who attend these schools may go on to community colleges or 4-year institutions. Vocational-technical schools that integrate academic work with technical training are thought to provide the best opportunities for continued development.

There are three general approaches to encouraging such integration (Grubb, 1991). Some schools simply exhort vocational instructors to use more reading, math, or writing in their courses. This is the least effective strategy. Other schools operate as academies, aligning the content of both types of courses so that they reinforce each other. Such approaches are fairly common in Philadelphia, Pennsylvania, and California, and appear to increase enrollments and decrease drop-out rates. The third approach is to organize and deliver academic courses to clusters of related occupations. For example, a manufacturing cluster might include mathematics and writing instruction relevant to future engineers, machinists, and production-line workers.

Dauphin County Technical School in Harrisburg, Pennsylvania, operates on the cluster approach by integrating basic skill training with vocational education. While studying a trade, ". . . in their four years of English, students will work on everything from basic writing skills and comprehension through literature to American literature, job applications, writing of business and personal letters, and development of the resume and cover letter" (Penkowsky, 1991/1992, p. 67).

> **"I'm not trying to make the statement that schools are bad. . . . . I'm just trying to make a choice that works for our family and works for our kids. . . ."**

Home Schools

It is estimated that about 300,000 primary and secondary students in the United States study at home, or in "home schools," rather than in public or private schools. As described in Chapter 3, the majority of these students are children of ideologists who want to ensure their religious doctrines are an integral part of daily lessons and values. People educate their children at home to avoid what they perceive as lock-step learning practices sometimes used in schools. David Guterson, a homeschooling parent in Bainbridge Island, Washington, whose son didn't learn to read until he was 7 years old, describes his beliefs about homeschooling:

> I'm not trying to make the statement that schools are bad and home-schoolers are good. I'm just trying to make a choice that works for our family and works for our kids . . . Why did he need to read at 5? . . . We don't worry about comparisons to other kids or to the established norms of each grade. They're not relevant to our thinking. But I certainly would start to be concerned if . . . [my children] got to be about 10 or 11 and they weren't interested in learning to read. It's really great when a kid says . . . [he wants to read] as opposed to school, where it maybe gets rammed down their throats and some kids aren't ready. (Hill, 1993, pp. 16, 21)

Schools for Special Student Populations

Although not run as military schools, the **Department of Defense Dependents Schools (DoDDS)** provide education for the children of many U.S. military personnel as well as for U.S. Government civilian personnel on official overseas assignments. In 1991, when the DoDDS system was at its largest, it included nearly 270 schools that served more than 115,000 students around the world (Department of Defense Dependents Schools, 1991). In 1993, after the reduction of armed forces in Europe, the system enrolled approximately 100,000 students in 208 schools (V. Addison, Personal Communication, October 22, 1993).

Like many other schools in the United States, these schools are accredited by the North Central Association of Colleges and Schools. About one third of DoDDS teachers are hired in the United States; the other two thirds are hired overseas, with preference given to DoDD military and U.S. Government civilian personnel. The curriculum of DoDDS appears almost identical to many U.S. public schools stateside, with the possible exception of "intercultural instruction" which introduces students to unique offerings of schools' host nations.

In 1992, as part of President George Bush's defense-adjustment plan, the Department of Defense and the Department of Education provided an educational option for troubled students when they created **Career Academies**. One academy is housed in Phelps Career High School in Washington, D. C.; 10 other academies are located in sites around the country. Career Academies combine the disciplined environment of the military with academic and vocational requirements of schools. Target students are those with behavior problems and youngsters who are returning dropouts. Besides learning mathematics and science on computers provided by the military, enrollees must choose a vocational track such as auto mechanics, digital communications electronics, or robotics. Class instructors include retired Army staffers and Junior Reserve Officers Training Corps personnel (Figueroa, 1992).

Job Corps, a program more than 30 years old, is the only federally supported residential education and job training program for adolescents who need multiple support services (e.g., medical and dental care, social skills training, parenting education, counseling, and job placement). The program is tuition-free and reaches more than 66,000 students per year. It is also supported by business, labor, volunteers, and a variety of advocacy organizations nationwide. Education and training take place in empty federal government properties, including former Army bases. More than 69% of program graduates become productive citizens, completing their education, attending college, joining the military, or entering the workforce (Office of Job Corps, 1992).

Children with serious health problems also have educational options. In Montgomery County, Maryland's only one-room school is located on the 10th floor of the National Institutes of Health. Children's School has been in operation for more than 40 years and serves the needs of gravely ill children who frequent the Bethesda Hospital, some of them for months at a time. Elementary students get 1 hour of instruction per day; older students receive half an hour in each subject. Teachers' goals are to keep students optimistic and to help them keep up with work during their absence from their regular school. Students' illnesses also influence content of instruction. One teacher, for example, avoids reading the book *Charlotte's Web* to her students: "The spider dies at the end. I don't want this child at that point to think of death" (Goldstein, 1991, p. C1).

Students living in remote areas of the country experience a variety of education programs. While some are far removed from modern technology, other students attend schools where technology is at the center of the educational program. In 1990, Chapter I students, migrant students, and students with limited English skills from the remotest areas of Alaska, Idaho, Montana, Oregon, and Washington were the target of an attempt to broaden educational opportunities through state-of-the-art technology. In more than 400 schools, satellite dishes, computers, and modems allowed students not only to view math, science, and technology classes on television, but also to interact with television teachers by phone during lessons. This growing phenomenon is referred to as "distance learning." At-risk students who were part of the Northwest Star Schools project received feedback on homework assignments and tests within 24 hours by way of data transmission over phone lines (Northwest Regional Educational Laboratory, 1992).

Increasing numbers of adult students are taking advantage of distance learning. Jeff Sun, director of the National Distance Learning Center, a federal clearinghouse, estimates that there are 25,000 students working toward a college degree by taking distance learning classes. A growing number of well-regarded colleges, such as the University of Maryland and George Washington University, grant college credit and degrees for courses taken through television (Jordan, 1992).

HOW ARE PRIVATE SCHOOLS DIFFERENT FROM PUBLIC SCHOOLS?

Private, or independent schools, are nonprofit, tax-exempt institutions governed by boards of trustees and financed through private funds, such as tuitions, endowments, and grants. Some are religious-affiliated while others are secular. All are accredited by state departments of education, must meet state and local health and safety rules, and must observe mandatory school attendance laws.

> The distinction between public and private education has become increasingly fuzzy.

As alternatives for schooling have increased, the distinction between public and private education has become increasingly fuzzy. Although not a prevalent practice, the use of public revenues to fund private education has done much to blur the definition of a private school: "Public vouchers are being used to pay for private education, and private firms are operating public schools. Some corporations are underwriting design efforts to transform the public schools; others are investing in for-profit enterprises to compete with them" (Olson, 1992a). Other actions obscuring the division between public and private education include: (a) state loans of secular textbooks to church schools, (b) state reimbursement of funds for transportation to church schools, and (c) public funding for mandated standardized testing and scoring and for diagnostic, therapeutic, and remedial services in private and parochial schools.

There are approximately 26,807 private elementary and secondary schools in the United States (National Center for Education Statistics, 1992). The line demarcating public from private schools has traditionally been drawn in the expenditure of funds and in the proscription of religious activity. That line, however, has continually been challenged. Although the number of initiatives to transform schools is small, the acceptance of new ideas about structuring schools seems to be growing. Those proposing private and quasi-private alternatives anticipate that the use of market forces and competition will do for public schools what regulation and exhortation have not done (Olson, 1992a).

Those who oppose a blurring of the line between public and private schools, particularly as public funds are spent, raise several arguments. First, the Constitution prohibits the establishment of a religion; giving public funds to religiously affiliated schools might constitute such an establishment. Second, members of minority groups and children from impoverished households would be put at a disadvantage in such a situation; for a variety of reasons, not simply money, they lack access to private schools. Third, if funds flow away from public schools to private schools, public schools will be left to serve those most in need and will be diminished in their capacity to do so. Fourth, to separate children by race, ethnicity, religion, and/or socioeconomic status—as public-private mergers might do—is to deprive children of opportunities to learn from and about each other. Ultimately, ignorance of others leads to many undesirable outcomes for society as a whole.

Despite their similarities, public schools differ from private schools in several ways: (a) public schools are tax-supported while, in the main, private schools are not; (b) private schools can set their own admissions requirements while public schools must accept all those who come for an education; (c) private school students are enrolled by parental or student choice, while, in the main, public schools serve only students in their districts; and (d) private schools have the freedom to craft philosophies that appeal to particular groups of people; public schools are driven by inclusivity.

Cultural Awareness

By 1990 there were some 835 one-room schools in America, and Old Order Amish accounted for about 80% of those schools (Leight & Rinehart, 1992). Most of these are in rural Pennsylvania and Ohio.

At Meadowbrook School, one of several hundred Old Order Amish schools in the United States, 30 children in eight grades sit in a sunny schoolroom heated by a potbellied coal stove.

> Four second-graders are at the recitation bench taking turns reading aloud as the other children work quietly at their desks. The teacher listens to each child read and then, while the third grade comes up to the recitation bench, she calls on the students whose hands are raised . . . . [m]ethods and materials differ little from those of two generations ago. . . . The pupils have no catechism, but together with their teacher they pray the Lord's Prayer and sing hymns. . . . On the walls . . . there are posters and pictures... with moral messages that support cooperative attitudes rather than competitiveness. Absent from the school curriculum are books on science, physical education, computer instruction, and sex education. Also absent are organized sports, clubs, career education, guidance counseling, and television. (Hostetler & Huntington, 1992, pp. 1–2)

Parochial Schools

As described in Chapter 2, private schools that are maintained and operated by religious organizations are called **parochial schools**. Parochial schools vary in terms of their underlying philosophies, their structures, and their programs.

Catholic Schools   Although their enrollments have declined over the years, Catholic schools account for the largest number of parochial-school students. The majority of these students attend schools in New York, Pennsylvania, California, Illinois, and Ohio. There are, however, other areas of the country where Catholic schools are prominent, such as New Orleans, Louisiana, and Detroit, Michigan. Most experts would agree that a Catholic education today is different from the kind of experience depicted in the movies of Bing Crosby and Barry Fitzgerald in the 1940s and 1950s. Sociologists have described the Catholic school as contributing heavily to the middle-class mores of our society. It taught "respectability, cleanliness, conformity, ambition, patriotism" (Fichter, 1958, p. 451).

Many Catholics began to think about Catholicism differently after the Second Vatican Council or Vatican II. This reexamination of belief and practice, initiated by Pope John XXIII, occurred between 1962 and 1965 and was meant to "bring the church up to date" (Dolan, 1985, p. 424). It had the effect of changing how Catholics prayed, how they related to others, and how they educated their young. Nancy Lesko (1988) contends that Catholic schools have turned their attention to secular issues common to the middle class:

> Religious training is becoming secondary in Catholic schools; that is, these schools have become centrally concerned with preparing Catholic youth for contemporary life, i.e., facilitating their educational and social mobility. Catholic school administrators and board members are also prompted to emphasize the academic side of their schools as they develop strategies for the schools' economic survival. (p. 18)

Reinterpretation of church doctrine, economic forces, and a raising of social consciousness throughout the country combined to change the size and character of Catholic schools in America. In 1965-66, about 5 million children attended Catholic elementary and secondary schools (Hunt & Kunkel, 1984) compared to about 2.5 million in 1991. In 1967, about 60% of teachers in Catholic schools were religious brothers and sisters (Bryk, Holland, Lee, & Carriedo, 1984). By the 1990s, that changed to about 10 to 15%. By 1992, according to a study by the National Catholic Educational Association (NCEA), about 15% of high school students were non-Catholic, nearly 25% were members of minority groups, about 25% came from families with annual incomes of less than $25,000, and about 5% were on welfare ("Survey Tracks," 1993).

According to the NCEA survey, Catholic schools have a relatively high success rate with students, sending about 90% of high school graduates to college. Students at-risk for academic failure are among those who fare well in Catholic high schools. In New York City, the Roman Catholic Archdiocese of New York educates 50,000 disadvantaged youth a year. According to a national study published by the Brookings Institute in 1990, during a 4-year period such students gain more than 1 full year in academic achievement over their counterparts in public schools. One explanation for their success is that Catholic schools are generally small, so it is difficult for students to fall through the cracks. Another reason may be that everyone—principal, teachers, and students—has chosen to be part of a particular school. This is quite different from zoned inner-city schools where principals are assigned to a school, central office determines the curriculum, teachers are appointed, and students are required by law to attend (Flanigan, 1991).

Jewish Education   According to the Commission on Jewish Education in North America (1991), about 40% of American Jewish children are currently enrolled in Jewish schools. Supplementary schools, which for years have reached the largest number of Jewish students in the United States, meet at the end of a full day of secular school. Curricula often include instruction in Hebrew or Yiddish, Bible, Rabbinic literature, prayer, religious ritual procedures, and Jewish history, lore, and law (Brown, 1992). Day schools, attended by about 12% of the total Jewish population, generally integrate the secular and religious worlds of American Jews (Commission on Jewish Education in America, 1991).

Chabad-Hebrew Academy is a parochial Jewish dayschool that focuses on Hebrew and secular studies. The academy was founded in 1969 in Westminster, California. During the 1992 academic year, 400 students were enrolled in nursery-level through twelfth grade classes. Classes at the academy are coeducational through the ninth grade; classes in grades 10 through 12 are for girls only. According to Rabbi Moishe Engel (personal communication, July 23, 1993), vice-principal of the academy, boys in the upper grades either attend public schools or they enroll in yeshivas, private boarding schools that have a more religious atmosphere and a greater emphasis on Hebrew.

Christian Academies   Other parochial schools, in particular fundamentalist Christian schools, are growing in number more quickly than other private schools, in large measure because of the popular appeal of their philosophies and curricula. Melinda Wagner's 1990 study of nine Christian schools in the southeastern United States suggests why this may be so. In examining the schools' philosophies, Wagner found that conservative Christians attempt to create an "ideal" culture to serve as a "crucible of change" for altering the inadequacies and evils in existing culture (p. 20). Curriculum decisions reflect this goal:

> Dells Christian School teachers had used a variety of secular textbooks, including Economy Readers, and were neither dissatisfied with them nor concerned that using these books made their school any less a Christian school: "Our teachers are different [from public school]." But that changed when the sponsoring church's new pastor, who had children in the school, became interested in the school's curriculum. He read . . . [a] report on the content of public school textbooks, and he had heard people say, "If you're going to use the same stuff as public schools, then what's the difference?". . . . And so the DCS staff began to

look at materials for teaching reading designed especially for Christian schools. . . . They discussed "story content." The administrator wanted to see traditional portrayals of families, and not one-parent families. "I know that a lot of families are one-parent families [including children in the Christian schools]. But maybe we can change the frame of thinking. If kids are taught [about the traditional family form], maybe things will change. Because I know a lot of people go into marriage thinking—well, if it doesn't work out I can always get out of it . . ." (p. 172)*

Independent Non-sectarian Schools

There are a number of nonsectarian private school options in the United States. These schools vary in focus, structure, social organization, and size. Some, such as military schools, emphasize self-discipline while encouraging academic study. Others, such as elite college preparatory schools, place an unusually high premium on academic achievement. Some schools are less easily classifiable, developing their own unique personalities.

Since the 1970s, many military schools have became co-educational institutions that send the bulk of their graduates to higher education rather than to service academies such as West Point. Today there are fewer than 50 military schools in the country, seven of which are located in Virginia. Fork Union Military Academy in Fork Union, Virginia, is the largest all-male military school in the United States, having an enrollment of 640 students. Due to its affiliation with the Baptist General Association of Virginia, Fork Union also offers Bible classes for cadets. In addition, Fork Union uses a "one-subject plan" which allows upperclassmen to focus on a single academic subject each 7-week term (Goodrich, 1993).

Phillips Exeter Academy is a residential boarding and day school in Exeter, New Hampshire, that has an enrollment of 996 students between the ages of 14 and 18. Exeter is an elite college preparatory institution, both in terms of admission requirements and cost. Exeter stresses academic excellence via small-group instruction. Using what is termed the Harkness Plan, faculty conduct class in a seminar mode, sitting at a table with 12 to 15 students and encouraging active participation in class activities and discussions (Sargent, 1993).

Distinctions among Private Schools

Important differences set private schools apart from public schools and from one another. A school's unique identity, image, and offerings ideally attract enough students to keep the school going. In a comprehensive and creative set of investigations, Eric Bredo and Mary Henry (1989) studied nine private elementary schools in a single city in a southern state to determine what kinds of schools existed. They also investigated how schools were related to and different from one another, what approaches to teaching and learning they advanced, and the roles these schools played in the more broadly defined society.

*From *God's Schools: Choice and Compromise in American Society* by Melinda B. Wagner, Copyright 1990. Reprinted by Rutgers University Press, The State University.

The schools they studied drew from a common pool of potential students. Collectively, they spanned the continuum of a student's education from kindergarten through high school. The schools advertised themselves as representing certain social values, and they promoted, both explicitly and implicitly, particular philosophies or ideologies. Bredo and Henry described clusters of schools in terms of their views on religion, their senses of community or social outlook, and their technical values.

Religious Orientation   St. Catherine's, according to Bredo and Henry, is the prestige school in the community. It has Episcopalian origins, a resident minister, and requires chapel once a week. In tradition, the school is much like an English boarding school—well organized and more secular than evangelical in its approach. The school is viewed as good, firmly established, and somewhat pretentious. Teachers know they are supposed to stretch students to the highest levels of performance.

At Holy Trinity, religion figures more prominently. The families who patronize the school are mainly middle-class. They value order and appreciate teachers who speak their minds on religion. The school is organized to offer students from kindergarten to high school a version of a "great books" curriculum. Students must attend classes on the Bible and biblical history. The school also holds special seminars on the Bible for parents.

Social Orientation   The Togetherness school is largely middle-class and not so selective or academically oriented as St. Catherine's. Its philosophy suggests that the school fosters a close rapport between teachers and students, but not at the expense of mutual respect. Togetherness tries to unite freedom and responsibility in young people to promote intellectual and ethical growth. The school emphasizes a sense of community among teachers and students.

The Steiner School is a Waldorf school based on Rudolf Steiner's anthroposophy, or humanistic philosophy. Many parents are openly religious, some Christian and some non-Western (e.g., Sikh, Sufi). As a result, the school evinces a sort of mystical quality. In keeping with Steiner's beliefs, teachers teach by moral authority, and students are expected to respect that authority.

Parents run the Country School and try to maintain a sense of community for those living in the surrounding area. The main goal is for the children to receive an outstanding education in an environment that is intellectual and caring. Country School, according to Bredo and Henry, is progressive and pragmatic in its approach, not doctrinaire. The school is neither pushy about academics nor prepared to offer very much in the way of remediation.

Technical Orientation   The Montessori School, like other schools based on Maria Montessori's work, emphasizes scientific and mathematical tasks of teaching and learning. Teachers concentrate heavily on academics by encouraging children to choose tasks that "fit" their stages of development. They also encourage, but less so, the creative or aesthetic side of learning.

The Dyslexia Center focuses on learning problems by bringing to bear a clinically scientific version of education—one that refers to "processing problems," "behaviors," and "tactile-kinesthetic" approaches. The Center's goal is to help students who have difficulty learning but are not characterized as unintelligent. It is the most expensive of all the schools. Most students stay only 1 or 2 years and then, it is hoped, go on successfully to other schools.

The Genius School is for "bright" students who are having difficulty in other schools. It also concentrates on remediating problems of dyslexia. Bredo and Henry characterize the Genius School as driven by a philosophy that is part science and part religion—a sort of "mom and pop" enterprise that operates at less than half the price of the Dyslexia Center.

There is, of course, a broad range of variation within these and other ways of categorizing independent schools. However constituted and run, nonsectarian and parochial schools clearly serve the special interests and perceived needs of particular groups.

WHAT MAKES SOME SCHOOLS MORE EFFECTIVE THAN OTHERS?

Research on schools suggests that students perform best in settings where principals serve as strong instructional leaders and teachers think positively about students' abilities to succeed, set high but reasonable standards for student performance, and maximize students' chances to succeed. Good schools have a strong academic focus exemplified by clear goals, a coordinated curriculum, staff commitment to meeting goals, and an assessment system that matches instruction and gives teachers information about student progress. Effective schools are safe and orderly (Odden, 1985).

Positive School Environments

Interviews with 54 students (selected for diversity with respect to gender, achievement level, and ethnicity) from four comprehensive high schools in two California school districts suggest that students' views of positive school environments match those of contemporary theorists. Student measures include: the level of visibility and accessibility of the principal, the amount of support students receive from teachers and staff members, perceived degree of personal safety, types of interactions between student groups, student behavior in general, availability of extracurricular activities, the physical condition of the school, and the degree to which students can speak their native language in informal settings and the availability of at least one staff member who shares the same language (Phelan, Davidson, & Cao, 1992).

Students' opinions about schools are particularly strong when they have attended more than one high school or when their experiences in middle school are quite different from those in high school. One student who had recently moved to California described vividly how the environment in her former high school compared to her new one:

> They didn't really care if you were in the classroom, they didn't care what you were doing...Only one teacher in the high school had a personal thing with any of the students. It was a very large school, maybe that's why. There were real large classes, but [the teachers] were very distant from everybody, so they didn't know me. I could have done anything. They had no idea who I was.
>
> I did very bad in that school. I came here, and I was failing. It was so easy not to do anything. I mean it was, well they don't care, so why should I?
>
> And then I got here and the teachers that I met, the first day they had my name right. "Wow, this is cool! You know who I am." I was tardy to class once, a couple of minutes late, and that day they called my house to talk to my parents.
>
> Oh, this is great . . . You go in and you're not there for a day and they notice and say, "Hi, are you tardy?" And they care. (Phelan, Davidson, & Cao, 1992, p. 702)

Effective schools, defined commonly as those schools that can demonstrate student learning, have substantial staff development time, some of which takes place during the regular workday. In these schools, improvement goals are sharply focused, attainable, and valued by staff members who receive in-class guidance and support from specialists. School needs guide staff, not standardized forms and checklists. Methods for reaching goals are often based on techniques and materials that have proven successful in similar situations. Furthermore, a "judicious mixture" of autonomy for participating faculties and control from central office permeates improvement programs in particularly effective schools (Levine, 1991).

Others contend that the most successful schools are also those that serve families "that have some hope, some income, and some health care . . . Families with those characteristics are in less stress and they take control of their neighborhoods" (Berliner, 1992, p. 59). For schools to work effectively, then, some reformers argue that it is more important to help parents find employment so they can live with dignity than to try to "fix" the schools. Bracey (1991) contends that the schools do amazingly well and may need less fixing than many seem to believe.

School Reform Initiatives

There is an unfortunate tendency to enter the discussion on school reform in the present moment, with little or no sense of what has preceded. As Chapters 2 and 3 suggest, schools have evolved rather dramatically over time. Change has come, as it often does, in fits and starts. It has occasionally been embraced, has often met with resistance, and has even more often gone unnoticed.

An analysis of local, state, and national education systems by the Sandia National Laboratories, Albuquerque, New Mexico, suggests that today's schools are successful. When Sandia evaluated student performance on the

National Assessment of Education Progress (NAEP) and the Scholastic Aptitude Test (SAT), for instance, they found that student scores have steadily improved over time, and that gains have not been at the expense of advanced skills. The supposed decline in test scores is due not to decreasing student performance but to the fact that more students in the bottom half of their class are taking the exam today than they did in years past. Although every ethnic group taking the test performs better today than it did 15 years ago, minority-group youth still lag behind their European-American colleagues on standardized measures (Carson, Huelskamp, & Woodall, 1991). To be sure, standardized test scores are not the only criteria for determining success and failure of schools and students, but they are important indications.

Over the years, dissatisfaction with public education has stimulated a number of efforts to overhaul American schools. Heterogeneous grouping, small-group cooperative learning activities, school-based management, management of schools by for-profit firms, parental involvement in school governance, and connections with community agencies for health and social services are among commonly discussed ideas for altering schools. An examination of such efforts reveals, however, that schools attempting to restructure often make changes in teaching techniques, but few alter school governance and collaboration between schools and community (Center on Organization and Restructuring of Schools, 1992).

One effort to restructure schools has involved changing factors such as class schedule and class size. Colorado's Wasson High School has altered class schedules so students have four class periods instead of seven. It now takes only half a year instead of a full year to complete a course. Parents, students, and teachers have responded positively to 90-minute classes. Data suggest that there are fewer discipline problems and greater enthusiasm for learning than there were in the existing system (American Political Network, 1992).

Ewell S. Aiken Optional School, a school in Alexandria, Louisiana, serving 300 students aged 14 and older who need help in grades 5 through 12, has also drastically changed the typical school day to try to help its at-risk enrollees. Classes are held in 4-hour blocks, with a maximum of 15 students per class. Instruction is computer-assisted and self-paced. The school also provides day care for students who have young children.

While fiscal woes prevent some school districts from running schools for more than 7 months, others provide **year-round schools** for their students—or educational programs that run through the summer months as well as during the academic year. In some instances, such programs are used to relieve space and budget concerns. In others, year-round schools are viewed as a means to improve pupil performance. Some 1.58 million students in 2,048 public and private schools attended school year-round during the 1992-93 academic year. States having the largest year-round enrollments were California, Utah, Texas, Florida, and Nevada. According to a survey by the National Association for Year-Round Education, the majority of schools having year-round programs operated on a single-track calendar rather than on overlapping multitrack schedules typically used to save money (Harp, 1993).

In California's Oxnard Elementary School District, year-round schools have been in place for 17 years. Norman R. Brekke, superintendent of the district, notes that the year-round program has had a variety of effects over time: teacher and student burnout are less evident, staff-development efforts have expanded, and innovative between-session programs designed to challenge students and help address learning problems have been put in place. Student achievement scores have also improved in the past 9 years. However, students have yet to reach the average state achievement scores in most categories (Harp, 1993).

Accelerated Schools   Forty elementary and middle schools have joined the **accelerated schools movement**—a national movement for speeding up the learning of economically disadvantaged students. Accelerated schools run counter to conventional practice. Disadvantaged students have most often been removed from class for remediation or placed in slower-moving classes. In accelerated schools, they remain in regular classrooms where they are grouped heterogeneously for instruction. Instead of relying on flash-card drills and worksheets to strengthen skills, teachers encourage students to build on strengths, much like teachers do when teaching "gifted and talented" students. This means engaging students in stimulating conversations with their peers and thinking of ways to challenge them rather than thinking of them as pupils who need to be "repaired."

Based on the ideas of Henry M. Levin, a Stanford economist, the accelerated schools movement promotes a philosophy about teaching and learning. Levin prescribes no specific process for meeting program ideals, no specific curriculum, and no particular methods for assessment. When a school staff decides to join the project, however, 75% of the school staff must agree to it. The Stanford team then offers a 1-week training session in which staff members set goals and learn ways to implement a governance system in which curriculum, instruction, and resource allocation decisions can be made by the school as a whole. This means teachers, administrators, students, and parents have some say in the workings of the school. Although the program requires a substantial time commitment from teachers, there is evidence that students' test scores, morale, and behavior, as well as teachers' and students' attendance rates, have improved (Rothman, 1991).

Essential Schools   Boston's Fenway Middle College High School is an active member of Theodore Sizer's **Coalition for Essential Schools**, alternative high schools serving targeted students through school-based educational reform initiatives. The school was established in 1983 as an experimental program inside the walls of another school, Boston's English High School. Fenway, an educational program for 10th- through 12th-grade students, has since been relocated to Bunker Hill Community College, about 100 steps from a subway stop on the border of Boston's industrial side. The 160-member student body housed in a small wing of the community college is a mix of African-, Hispanic-, European-, and Asian-American students. Many, but not all, are considered at-risk. According to Mary Koepke (1992), "Concern, support, and respect are as visible in this high school as athletic trophies are in others" (p. 22).

Classes are small and are longer than the standard 50-minute high school period. Every other day, there is an advisory period so students and teachers can talk about personal and social concerns. Scheduling is flexible, adjusted as needed to maximize teaching and learning. The curriculum is issue-based, with the entire student body focusing on the same theme to allow for extended dialogue and interdisciplinary application. Portfolios and exhibitions of student work rather than standardized tests are the norm in student-progress assessment procedures.

A collaborative project with Boston's Children's Hospital allows Fenway students to complete a full-term internship in an area of interest (e.g., radiography, pharmacology, nursing). On-the-job experience is complemented by in-school courses that teach skills necessary for success in the field. The collaboration allows students to shadow hospital staff members, write about their work, and then to complete a scientific research project using hospital staff as a resource. Although some students drop out of the program, about 75% graduate, 70% of whom go on to 2- or 4-year colleges. Two years ago, one graduate returned to Fenway as a teacher (Koepke, 1992).

Charter Schools   Charter schools are independent public schools supported by state funds but freed from many regulations and run by individuals who generally have the power to hire and to fire colleagues and to budget money as they see fit. Like other reform initiatives, charter schools are meant to be innovative—to reach out to those not being served by the public schools. Metro Deaf School, a charter school in Minnesota, teaches all subjects in American Sign Language to students who are deaf or hard-of-hearing. City Academy, a charter school housed in a local recreation center in St. Paul, Minnesota, has a staff of four teachers, two volunteers, and two teachers' aides delivering individualized and small-group instruction to 30 former dropouts.

In 1991, Minnesota became the first state to approve the concept of charter schools. According to Minnesota law, only certified teachers can contract with local school boards to create charters. While the board has a say in what outcomes charters must meet, it maintains a hands-off posture in their day-to-day operation (Olson, 1992b).

In Philadelphia, funding from the Pew Charitable Trusts allowed for the establishment of several charters in neighborhood schools, many of which were considered troubled institutions. Charters serve heterogeneous groups of 200 to 400 children. In some instances, groups stay with the same teachers for 4 years. Parents are encouraged to be active participants in the program and are paid stipends for attending planning and staff-development meetings. Evidence suggests that such programs are paying off; students in charters have better attendance records and lower drop-out rates than those in regular programs. There has been an increase in the number of students repeating ninth grade, a phenomenon officials say reflects the fact that students are choosing to return to school rather than dropping out (Bradley, 1992).

America 2000 Schools   As part of the Bush administration's America 2000 initiative, the New American Schools Development Corporation (NASDC), a private, nonprofit, tax-exempt organization formed by American business leaders and the Bush administration, spon-

BENCHMARKS

The Development of American Schools

1600s and 1700s	Latin Grammar Schools founded as college preparatory secondary schools. Private colleges, such as Harvard College, founded for the preparation of Protestant ministers. Lutheran parochial schools established in the middle colonies. Publicly funded education for literacy first mandated in Massachusetts. American Academies founded as private secondary schools.
1800–1860	Elementary schools using the monitorial method opened in New York City. Roman Catholic parochial schools established in the United States. English Classical School established in Boston as the first state-supported public high school. Normal schools open as the first public teachers' colleges in the United States. Compulsory education laws lead to the spread of elementary and secondary common schools. Kindergartens established.
1860–1900	Vocational agricultural and industrial schools established through federal legislation. Chautauqua Movement in New York creates demand for opportunities for adult education. Laboratory schools for putting progressive ideas into teaching practice opened in Chicago.
1900–1960	Junior High Schools established. Federal funding granted for vocational programs in public high schools. New private alternative schools founded, such as Waldorf and Montessori schools. National Science Foundation and government-school collaboration in the study of science and technology established in response to the launch of Sputnik and the space race. State colleges and universities established.
1960–1995	Project Head Start, Job Corps, and other federal programs established. Private Christian academies and African-American academies established. Private and public preschool education greatly expanded. Middle schools and community colleges created. Magnet schools, charter schools, for-profit schools, essential schools, and accelerated schools founded.

sored a national competition in 1991 for "break the mold" schools. These newly conceptualized schools were to serve as models that would lead the nation into the twenty-first century and restore American education to world preeminence.

In July 1992, NASDC selected 11 out of 686 design teams' proposals for further refinement, field testing, and upon approval, nationwide implementation between 1995 and 1997. One plan, "Roots and Wings," is based in four elementary schools in Lexington Park, Maryland. The brainchild of researchers at Johns Hopkins University, officials in the Maryland Department of Education, and teachers and administrators, the plan calls for students to engage in problem solving, hands-on activities, and teamwork. Work in groups will be based on abilities and interests rather than age.

Those who have trouble keeping up with their school work will not be retained; rather they will be given tutoring, family support services, and other help to master content. Special "World Lab" projects, simulations rooted in "real world" contexts, will be used to encourage students to work collaboratively to solve a variety of problems. Designed to take the place of existing science and social studies curricula, projects are intended to be long-range and multidisciplinary, drawing heavily on use of computers and other technologies (Olson, 1993).

Reform of public education, then, is neither a new idea nor a unidimensional one. It has not been limited to a particular time in history, although as Chapters 2 and 3 indicate, some periods have witnessed greater change than others. In later chapters, we shall return to the concept of reform and consider its curricular, governance, and financial dimensions.

SUMMARY

1. Schools are social institutions; that is, they are organizations having an identifiable structure and a set of functions. Their primary function is to move young people into the mainstream of society. Educators work with parents, children, and outside agencies to insure the psychological and physical well-being of students and to foster academic success. They also work collaboratively to build understanding and acceptance of others.

2. Schools differ in size, structure, and function. Their student populations are also quite diverse in terms of socioeconomic status and racial/ethnic composition.

3. Although many students have little choice about where they go to school, vouchers, tuition tax credits, and sometimes public policy have provided an increasing number of students with opportunities to attend many types of public and private schools. For some parents, decisions about where their children go to school are determined by such variables as class size and a school's scholastic ranking.

4. There are many types of preschools in the United States, and the professional preparation of staff and the quality of programs vary greatly. Although enrollment in these schools has increased over time, only about 34% of 3- to 4-year-olds attend prekindergartens; 67% of these children are enrolled in privately funded schools.

5. About 89% of children in the United States attend public elementary schools. Across settings, there is similarity in teachers' credentials (most are certified to work in grades kindergarten through 8) and types of programs offered to children. At the same time, there are instructional and curricular variations within and among schools.

6. Junior high and middle schools are meant to help students make the transition from elementary school to high school by concentrating on academic subjects and exposing students to careers and occupations. Some critics claim, however, that existing schools are too imitative of high schools and inappropriate to the needs of adolescents.

7. There are many types of high schools; some are "specialized" institutions, focusing on science, music, art, or performing arts. There are also vocational

technical high schools and alternative high schools. Sizes of high schools vary, with enrollment in alternative schools being as few as 200 and enrollment in large "comprehensive" schools—high schools offering a full range of programs—being as many as 4,000. Some programs are "screened," meaning students are accepted on the basis of a written exam, audition, or school progress records.

8. In 1988, three fourths of enrollees in institutions of higher education were enrolled in public colleges. Students in 2-year public colleges claimed 36% of the total enrollment.

9. There are a number of notable alternative programs that provide educational opportunities for people in the United States. Among these are magnet schools, home schools, one-room schools, military schools, religious schools, Job Corps, and schools for retirees.

10. As alternatives for schooling have increased, the distinction between public and private education has become increasingly fuzzy. Despite their similarities, public schools differ from private schools in several ways: (a) public schools are tax-supported, while, in the main, private schools are not; (b) private schools can set their own admissions requirements; (c) private school students are enrolled by parental or student choice; and (d) private schools have the freedom to craft philosophies that appeal to particular groups of people. A study of nine private schools in a southern state revealed that school philosophies varied in terms of their religious, social, and technical orientations.

11. There are several factors that make some schools more effective than others. Students seem to do better, for example, in schools where principals serve as strong instructional leaders and teachers think positively about students' abilities to succeed, set high but reasonable standards for student performance, and maximize students' chances to succeed.

12. Dissatisfaction with schools has waxed and waned over the years. Among commonly discussed ideas for "fixing" schools are heterogeneous grouping, cooperative learning, school-based management, management by for-profit organizations, parental involvement in school governance, Job Corps, charter schools, accelerated schools, essential schools, and a multitude of connections with community agencies for health and social services.

TERMS AND CONCEPTS

accelerated schools movement
alternative school
America 2000 schools
Career Academies
charter schools
Coalition for Essential Schools

Department of Defense Dependents Schools (DoDDS)
Head Start
institution
magnet schools
National Association for the Education of Young Children (NAEYC)

private schools
professional development school
school district
nongraded classrooms
tracking
year-round schools

STUDENT ACTIVITIES

Perceive and Value

Two concepts—success and involvement—characterize much of the modern writing on schools in the United States. Most everyone wants more of both. But often definitions of these terms vary, as do recommendations for how we might boost school success and how we might involve people in school activities. How would you define a successful school? (Describe both the attributes of a successful school and the meaning of success in relation to other schools.)

Know and Act

Team with other classmates to list and analyze forces that blur the distinction between private and public schooling. What are the advantages and disadvantages of these trends for students? For parents? For teachers? For school administrators? For school districts? Be prepared to debate your conclusions.

Evaluate

Assess the statement that public schools are not as bad as they have been portrayed by critics. Be prepared to explain your reasoning. What would you change about public schools and why?

Discover

Can anyone choose to keep their children at home and educate them there? What, if anything, must parents or guardians do to be able to engage in homeschooling in your state? Do requirements vary from state to state?

Is it possible for children in your public school district to attend public school in another district? If so, must students pay tuition to the school outside their own district?

What private schools exist in your immediate area? What do you know about their philosophies? Why do people choose to send their children to these schools? What restrictions does your state place on the establishment of private schools?

Foundations

In Action

Mary Anne Reed-Brown is a second-year teacher working with a culturally diverse group of twenty pupils in an open-spaced classroom.

Schools vary in structure and in the emphasis they place on the development of particular knowledge, skills, and attitudes. The ways such programs are translated into practice, however, are shaped in part by teachers' perceptions of their roles in the schools and the personal and professional challenges they face as teachers. What teachers' roles and challenges can you infer from the three views presented here? In each case, how might school structure and mission shape teachers' perceptions?

Mary Anne Reed-Brown is a 2nd-year teacher in an open-space fifth-grade classroom in a Northern Virginia elementary school. As she describes the challenges of planning for instruction, Reed-Brown explains how her own values influence her behavior in the classroom.

This is my 2nd year teaching, and I just love it. I cannot imagine doing anything else. I look forward to Monday mornings. Many evenings, I stay in my classroom until 6 or 7 o'clock to prepare for the upcoming day. I must be ready.

Growing up, my parents wanted us to be the best we could be. They did not pressure us to become professionals—teachers, doctors or lawyers—but to grow up to be what we wanted to be. They expected us to speak intelligently and to demonstrate good manners. To my parents, these abilities made us desirable to be around. Today, parents seem too tired to teach these values. Maybe the humdrum of "making it" causes parents to let down.

Do we teach values in school? I think we do. We model certain behaviors, and we have rules in our classroom that reflect respect for one another. It is important for all my Asian- and African-American students, as well as my other students, to see me as a role model. My responsibility as a role model is to be the best teacher I can be and to help my students be the best they can be too.

208

Laura Saatzer
teaches in a self-contained third-grade classroom in Roosevelt Elementary School in St. Paul, Minnesota.

Peter Flaherty
teaches fourth grade at Hans Christian Andersen School in Minneapolis, Minnesota.

Laura Saatzer teaches in a self-contained third-grade classroom in Roosevelt Elementary School, a magnet school in St. Paul, Minnesota, that focuses on reading, writing, listening, speaking, and critical thinking skills.

This is my 6th year of teaching. I consider myself a professional. A lot of schooling and time go into becoming a teacher. I try to dress and present myself professionally, because the children and the parents deserve to see someone who is trying her best to help students learn.

In a classroom there are always challenges everyday, every minute, every second. One special challenge is the number of students with limited English proficiency. We can all learn from each other, but many times the language gets in the way. Much as I want to appreciate diversity and to help students hold onto their language and cultural beliefs, we need to find a way to communicate. I strongly encourage my students to practice English, because that is why they are in school. At the same time, it is important for them to strengthen their native language.

The most difficult challenge is to deal with the emotional side of teaching. My students have more problems at their young age than I will ever know. My husband says, "Come on, you're at home, leave the problems at school," but the problems tug at my heart. Some days I am not so patient as I would like to be. I tell myself to think about these students' home lives, because many are crying out for help.

Peter Flaherty teaches fourth grade at Hans Christian Andersen, a multicultural gender-fair demonstration school in Minneapolis, Minnesota. Midway through his 1st year of teaching, Flaherty described some of the personal and professional challenges he faces on a daily basis:

I am from Maine, a state with a homogeneous population. I came to Minnesota in part to be exposed to a different culture.

I ask my students to call me Mr. Flaherty. The surname sounded formal to me at first, but I realized I need all the respect and authority I can get. A year ago I would have hated to use the term "authority," but if being Mr. Flaherty will help me, then I'm Mr. Flaherty.

What scares me most right now is planning my lessons. As a 1st-year teacher, I am still learning what to do and where I am going with my lessons. I am afraid of waking one morning and discovering I have run out of ideas.

I also have difficulty deciding whether I am succeeding with students. Success often comes in such little steps, and success can be defined in so many ways. If I do not look for success, I might not see it. Success also seems to come so slowly. In my case, a lot of students' progress has been in social skills and behaviors such as listening and following directions. Earlier in the year, classroom management was my biggest problem. I had to work to get students in place so I could teach them.

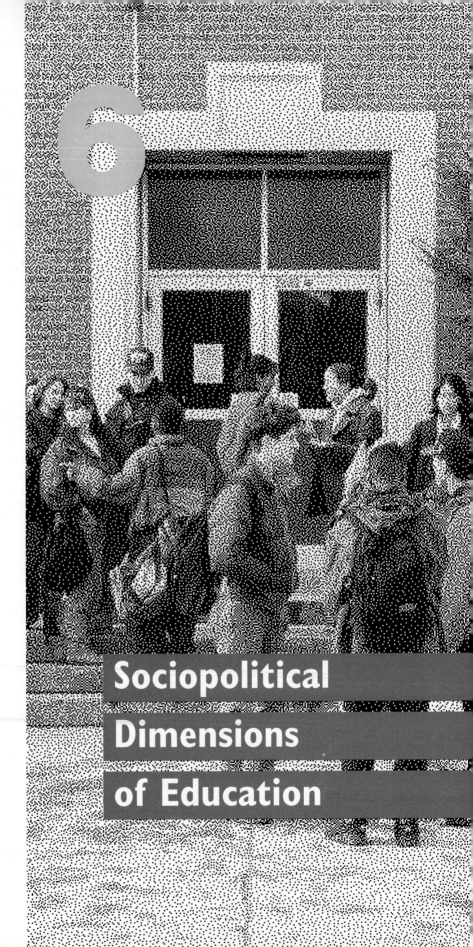

People are social beings. They live in communities, form interdependent relationships, and interact with one another in significant and trivial ways from cradle to grave. People are also political beings. While low voter turnout suggests that Americans may be perilously detached from the formal politics of ruling at the federal and state government levels, they get deeply involved with each other over the control of many issues in their own communities. Social interactions create power by helping people build their knowledge about each other. Political involvements allow people to exercise this power to effect or resist change in their individual and collective lives. Nowhere are these facts more evident than in the debate about schools' attempts to solve students' problems.

Maybe because young people's problems are both acute and chronic, and maybe because of the technological ease with which people are made aware of these problems, many are becoming increasingly concerned about a variety of social pressures on today's youth. This chapter explores some of society's most urgent problems and considers how they impinge on children. Also described are some of the ways schools have stretched beyond their traditional missions to involve parents, social agencies, and private enterprise in efforts to counter threats to young people's lives.

6

Sociopolitical Dimensions of Education

1 What are the critical challenges schools face in light of the social problems encountered by children? How do these problems intrude on life in schools?

`Perceive`

2 Why are schools expected to respond to any and all problems of the young?

`Value`

3 What are some of the particular school programs designed to address serious social problems?

`Know`

4 If you knew young people who were exhibiting signs of depression, what might you do?

`Act`

5 What evidence would you accept as an indication that schools have been successful in involving parents, social agencies, and private enterprise in addressing young people's problems?

`Evaluate`

WHAT ARE SOCIETY'S EXPECTATIONS FOR SCHOOLS?

For many children, the years they spend in school are the best years of their lives. They are with people who care about them and for them—people who do whatever they can to help children learn, to feel good about themselves in the process, and to nurture young people's hopes for the future.

In recent years, however, some have argued that efforts to counter children's social problems while also trying to meet their academic needs have created for our schools what amounts to a blueprint for failure. Students attending school from the beginning of kindergarten to the completion of 12th grade will have spent only about 9% of their total time on earth in the classroom (Finn, 1991). Nonetheless, expectations for schools have usually exceeded the "9% limit" as people have increasingly looked to schools to solve some of society's most difficult problems. (See Figure 6.1.)

FIGURE 6.1

Some Sociopolitical Aspects of Education

Think of other items that could be added to this figure. Why might they be regarded as sociopolitical dimensions of education?

PUBLIC EXPECTATIONS OF SCHOOLS
- Social problem solving
- Implementation of reform initiatives
- National goals of education

SOCIOECONOMIC PROBLEMS OF FAMILIES AND COMMUNITIES
- Family distress
- Poverty and homelessness
- Violence and crime

EDUCATION OF STUDENTS AT RISK
- Early intervention
- Compensatory education
- Dropout prevention
- Parental and community involvement

HEALTH AND SAFETY OF CHILDREN & YOUTH
- After-school care
- Child abuse and neglect
- Substance abuse
- Teen pregnancy
- AIDS and other diseases
- Suicide
- Motor vehicle accidents

EDUCATION OF ALL STUDENTS IN A DIVERSE SOCIETY
- Bilingual education
- Special education

Why is it that schools are expected to accomplish so much? Chester Finn (1991) says it well:

> The temptation is obvious: Schools are the only institutions susceptible to public policy that everybody passes through—and at an impressionable age. . . . [T]hey have been asked to shoulder responsibilities that go far beyond their historic mission and present-day capabilities. Educators nearly always consent to these additional assignments, out of a sense of duty or the sincere belief that they can help. Certainly most would like to. These are the compassionate men and women, glad to do what they can to assist a needy child. (pp. 25–26)

Of particular concern to schools is the growing population of **"at-risk" students**. "*At-risk* appears to be the latest semantic label American educators have attached to several groups of students who have experienced difficulty or, in fact, failure in their careers as learners" (Presseisen, 1988, p. 19). Common definitions of at-risk children include those who (a) are unlikely to complete high school, (b) have failed one or more grades, (c) are enrolled in special education classes, (d) speak a language other than English, and/or

(e) are affected adversely by life- and health-threatening factors such as poverty, disease, abuse and neglect, substance abuse, teenage pregnancy, and physical violence (Waxman, 1992). As these definitions suggest, students may be at risk for failure academically and socially due to intrinsic and/or extrinsic factors. For example, children may be unlikely to complete high school because of their mental disabilities or because their home and community environments do not foster academic accomplishment.

Eventually, many students at risk drop out of school altogether. As will be explained in Chapters 11 and 12, communities across the country have advanced a variety of political initiatives to meet the challenge presented by school dropouts. School choice plans try to stimulate educators to make schools places where students will want to stay. In some states, the act of redrawing school attendance zones ("redistricting") is an attempt to prevent some schools from being marked as way stations where students pause briefly before assuming a permanent spot on the streets. Efforts to equalize funding for public schools are also undertaken to erase the stigma of school failure associated with a high dropout rate.

HOW DO SCHOOLS INTERVENE TO HELP STUDENTS AT RISK?

When young people have problems, society has problems. Typically, the plight of children is addressed by different agencies, the school being preeminent. Because the public supports schools with tax dollars, those educators who benefit directly from this support are expected to prevent and solve children's problems. While children's problems vary—a poor child is more likely to be both at risk for dropping out of school and subject to disease and other threats—responses to such problems are often unidimensional. We recognize a particular problem, and we create a program intended to address it.

> "No magic. But the seeds. Two funny old ladies, two funny little seeds."

Counselors, once reserved for high schools, are gradually making their way into elementary classrooms. By 1990, 12 states required school systems to have elementary school counselors. In general, counselors try to enhance self-esteem, but many also foster career awareness and offer support groups for children affected by divorce or who need work on study skills or social skills. High school counselors tend to focus on college or job counseling. Sometimes they intervene with troubled youths (Cohen, 1990).

For many children, these and other school-based interventions can make a profound difference in their lives. Patsy Walker, a high school dropout with a family history of abuse and neglect, incest, prostitution, drugs, and incarceration abandoned a lucrative career as a prostitute, got a job cleaning a store, completed high school, and at age 26 entered graduate school. Patsy Walker described the secret to her amazing turn-around:

My secret was not so much liking everything we did in school . . . but I did like some of it, and a few of the teachers. Not a lot of them, but you don't need a lot of them. Fact is you only need a few. . . . 'Cause what they both were telling me was, okay, you want to make a secret out of it, that's cool. But we could either forget you and let you fall away like everybody else, or we can, like I say, plant a little seed in you.

That's what both of them did, too, plant little seeds. Took a long, long time for those seeds to grow into something, but they did. . . . What they were telling me, see, was you can play the game, but we want to tell you we'll support you playing a whole 'nother game if there ever comes a time you feel you might be ready. Maybe they were daring me. And the school, see, it stunk like it always stunk. Nothing changed. Wasn't like the day after they spoke with me everything was perfect again, and my mother was all good and my father flew out of prison. No magic. But the seeds. Two funny old ladies, two funny little seeds. So school didn't fail out like everything else. (Garbarino, Dubrow, Kostelny, & Pardo, 1992, pp. 132–133)

Educators cannot help young people avoid and face problems if they are not in school. Simply trying to determine who is not there and why are major challenges for school officials. Some districts count as dropouts students who have died, left school to get married, taken a job, gone to vocational school, entered the armed forces, gone to jail, or been expelled. The federal government uses three measures to calculate dropouts: an event rate, or the proportion of students who drop out in a single academic year; a cohort rate, or the number of students who drop out of a particular grade level; and a status rate, or the percentage of people in a certain age range who are not enrolled in school.

Regardless of the confusion, educators are expected to keep students in school, at least through 12th grade, ultimately turning out literate, responsible, productive citizens. **Holding power**, or the ability to keep students in school until they receive a high school diploma or an equivalency certificate, has increased over the decades as youth have spent more and more years in school. Despite this positive trend, by 1989 more than 12% of students between the ages of 16 and 24 failed to complete high school (Office of Educational Research and Improvement, 1991).

Results from a study of 25,000 10th graders followed for 2 years by the Department of Education indicate a large proportion of American students become dropouts before they reach high school. According to statistics gathered in the spring of 1990, 6.8% of target students had left school before reaching the 10th grade. Among this group were some 10.2% African Americans, 9.6% Hispanic Americans, 5.2% European Americans, 4.0% Asian and Pacific Islander Americans, and 9.2% Native Americans. More males (7.2%) than females (6.5%) left school early. Students from inner-city schools were also more prone to drop out before 10th grade than were students attending suburban schools (Kaufman & McMillen, 1991).

Providing Mentors and Tutors

There are no easy answers to the dropout problem, but the statistics have stimulated a variety of efforts to keep students in school. Some programs are aimed at enhancing academic success and self-esteem of at-risk students. For example, each semester since the fall of 1987, Donovan Steiner, Director of Teacher Education at Eastern Mennonite College, has selected and assigned preservice teachers to serve as mentors of freshmen at Broadway High School in Rockingham County, Virginia. The goals of the **mentoring program** are to help at-risk students stay in school, to improve their academic skills, and to build interpersonal communication skills and self-esteem.

High school students, whose participation is voluntary, work with their assigned mentors twice a week over a 10-week period. At the end of the school year, a day-long outdoor education program brings mentors, their students, and Broadway teachers and administrators together for a series of activities requiring problem solving, persistence, helping behaviors, group interaction, and risk taking. Success has been documented in terms of improvements in students' grades and a lower dropout rate (Steiner, 1990). Such team approaches to reducing the incidence of dropping out are being recognized increasingly as advantageous (Sarkees-Wircenski, 1991).

In other programs, educators have tried to lower the dropout rate by assigning students special roles in the school program. In San Antonio, Texas, the Valued Youth Partnership Program identifies Hispanic-American middle-school students considered dropout risks and trains them to tutor kindergarten-through-third-grade children. Since its inception, the Coca-Cola sponsored **cross-age tutoring** program has reduced the dropout rate among Hispanic-American high school students and resulted in improved skills and self-esteem for potential dropouts ("Hispanic Students," 1990).

Providing Remedial After-school Programs

Sometimes schools provide after-school help for students who are at risk for failure. As part of Kentucky's Education Reform Act, $21.4 million was earmarked for use during 1990–91 (the amount more than doubled the next year) to provide extended school services to students needing extra help. The idea behind this action was to intervene before students lost enthusiasm and self-confidence in their abilities to succeed in school. In one county, after-school programs established in November 1990 served approximately 300 students per day by offering help through direct instruction, tutoring, computer-assisted instruction, and counseling services. Library aides were also hired with some of the reform money so the library could be kept open for use by those staying after school (Appalachia Educational Laboratory, 1991).

Offering Incentives and Disincentives

Other tactics used to encourage academic success include **incentive programs**. These programs offer outside incentives—rewards for good attendance and good grades. Students at Detroit's Western High School who have been in class 95% of the time may earn as much as $40 for each report card, depending on their grade-point averages (Russell, 1991). In about 1500 schools across the nation, students' grades determine their eligibility for a range of discounts on clothing. This incentive program, "Grades for Fashion," is sponsored by Merry-Go-Round Enterprises Inc. (Bratt, 1992).

Some incentive programs are available only to those who graduate from high school. In 1981, Eugene Lang, New York industrialist-philanthropist, promised 59 African- and Hispanic-American sixth graders he would pay for their college education if they finished high school. Lang also funded a support system for the disadvantaged youth to boost their chances of remaining in school (Schorr & Schorr, 1988).

In 1988, in an effort to help young people with little hope of going on to college, Patrick F. Taylor, a Louisiana oil man, guaranteed college tuition and fees for 183 seventh and eighth graders at New Orleans' Livingston Middle School who could meet demands of a rigorous precollege curriculum. By 1991, 126 "Taylor Kids" were still in school, working hard to qualify for Taylor's program. Taylor was also instrumental in getting the state legislature to agree in 1989 to pay tuition at state universities for any Louisiana student completing a college-preparatory core curriculum, maintaining a 2.5 grade average, and scoring at least 20 out of 36 on the Enhanced American College Test (Mitchell, 1991). By 1993, 11 states (Arkansas, Florida, Georgia, Indiana, Louisiana, Maryland, New Mexico, Oklahoma, Tennessee, Texas, and Virginia) had passed similar bills.

> **One state penalizes school dropouts by revoking their driver's licenses.**

Such inducements, however, are not uniformly successful. Business leaders in Boston withdrew from the Boston Compact, a highly publicized reform program rewarding jobs to students who stayed in school and in class, when statistics showed a steady increase in the dropout rate between 1982 and 1986 (Mathews, 1991).

In some instances punitive measures have been employed to reduce the dropout rate. Arkansas penalizes students with excessive unexcused absences and school dropouts by revoking their driver's licenses. Since the establishment of Wisconsin's controversial Learnfare program in 1987 and passage of the Family Support Act of 1988, several states impose penalties on parents who do not demonstrate "responsible" behaviors, including the completion of school. While the Family Support Act makes welfare payments contingent on parents' efforts to obtain education, training, and employment necessary for breaking the cycle of welfare dependency, Learnfare-type programs such as those in Wisconsin, Maryland, and Oregon cut welfare payments to parents whose children are truant or drop out of school (S. A. Riedasch, personal communication, January 19, 1994).

Other programs, such as Ohio's Learning, Earning, and Parenting (LEAP) program, blend penalties and rewards to encourage teenage parents to stay in school. Depending on their attendance patterns, parents get a $62 bonus or $62 deduction from their monthly welfare grants. Preliminary findings from a study of LEAP's effectiveness suggest that the program has been somewhat successful in keeping students in schools but relatively unsuccessful in changing the behavior of long-term dropouts (Cohen, 1993a).

Linking Home, School, and Work

Other efforts have tried to tighten the links among home, school, and the workplace to influence parents' and children's commitments to education.

In 1990, John Freeman—vice chairman of the Danville, Virginia, school board—formed the Industry in Education group to involve local business and industrial leaders in the promotion of educational excellence. The group of about a dozen plant managers and executives uses a variety of means for stressing the value of education. At Goodyear Tire and Rubber Company, the public relations manager devotes one page of the plant's monthly newsletter to accomplishments of employees' children and to other educational issues. Plant employees also work on a volunteer basis in the public schools, speaking to classes, participating in Parent-Teacher Association activities, and tutoring students at the middle-school level (P. Thompson, personal communication, October 22, 1991).

In some instances, businesses and other institutions have actually set up and run public schools to try to meet the needs of students who are struggling in traditional schools or who have already dropped out:

> Rich's Academy has operated for nine years in the Atlanta store of Rich's, part of Campeau Corp.'s Federated Department Stores subsidiary. The teachers, employed by the Atlanta school system, instruct students in math, science, history, and English. The store provides the space, some funding, employees who serve as mentors and tutors, and part-time jobs for students under a work-for-credit program. Cities in Schools, Inc., a nonprofit agency that forms partnerships to operate schools, brings in health workers, drug counselors and other social-service professionals to work with the students, many of whom had trouble in the city's traditional schools. (Stout, 1991, p. B1)

Providing Alternative Curriculum and Instruction

Many of the students who are struggling in school are young and male. And for them, as Larry Cuban (1991) has observed, has come a remedy anchored in despair: the all-African-American, all-male public school. The despair is born not only of young African-American men dropping out of school, but of the violence and death that often befall them on the streets. The concept of all-African-American, all-male academies has received considerable support. For a short time, such academies existed in Detroit until a U.S. District Court judge ruled that the intentional creation of a race-segregated school or class violates existing federal civil rights laws.

The idea for such an academy is based on the notion that African-American males are more likely to counter hostile forces in the environment and become independent, responsible, and productive citizens if they experience an educational program that fosters confidence in themselves. Among proposals for achieving this end is to offer an **Afrocentric curriculum** taught by African-American males who, it is argued, would be able to provide strict discipline and would serve as positive role models for young boys. The Afrocentric curriculum would place African culture and history at the center of what students are expected to learn, illustrating the important role that Africa has played in the development of Western civilization (Asante, 1991).

New programs and proposals for changing how schools serve African-American boys and youth borrow from these ideas but vary from one another in several ways. Some, like those in Milwaukee, Wisconsin, and Minneapolis, Minnesota, are all-day programs in Afrocentric curricula open to both boys and girls (Walsh, 1993). Others are a single class during or after school hours. Some modify the entire academic curriculum for African-American students, others simply add a component on African-American culture, and still others attempt to enrich the curriculum for all students with Afrocentric materials (Ascher, 1991).

Some schools that offer programs for African-American males circumvent legal problems by conducting activities after school. Helping Hands, a program that pairs African-American educators, including teachers, counselors, and administrators, with 11- and 12-year-old African-American male students, was initiated in 1988 in North Carolina's Wake County public schools. Selected educators ("personal models") spend at least 20 after-school hours a month with 8 to 10 students doing such things as visiting students' homes and helping students with academic tasks. After students have been in the program for a year, they spend 12 hours monthly with a successful community member. A 3-year evaluation of this program suggests that Helping Hands improves students' behavior, grades, and attendance and suspension rates (Ascher, 1991).

Other alternative curricular and instructional models are being implemented in schools throughout the nation. As Chapter 10 notes, cooperative learning strategies are aimed at encouraging students to work together for a variety of outcomes. These strategies include, for example, Students Teams-Achievement Divisions (STAD), Teams-Games-Tournament (TGT), and Learning Together. In STAD, the teacher makes a presentation, and then groups of four to five students work together on learning activities. To assess individual learning, teachers administer quizzes and tests. Individual scores are based on improvement over previous scores, and team performances are recognized. Teams-Games-Tournament (TGT) is similar to STAD, except that no quizzes are administered. Instead, students are grouped with classmates of similar achievement levels from other teams, and they are given a set of questions to answer. Students compete to earn points for their own team by answering as many questions as possible. Learning Together capitalizes on small-group work to encourage interdependence. Teachers promote the idea that groups sink or swim together, and students spend time developing their social skills. In all instances of cooperative learning, teachers plan team formation carefully to encourage not only mastery of subject matter but also understanding and acceptance among students.

HOW DOES POVERTY PLACE STUDENTS AT RISK OF SCHOOL FAILURE?

Educational researchers and practitioners have known for years about the positive relationship between **socioeconomic status (SES)**—a combination of one's income, occupation, values, education, and lifestyle—and learning.

Conditions of poverty or lower SES are strongly and consistently related to school failure.

The rate of poverty in the United States is higher than that in other industrialized nations and almost three times as great as in most other economically advanced nations. Children, one in five of whom go to bed hungry, sick, or cold, are among those hardest hit by the effects of poverty (Reed & Sautter, 1990). In 1989, about 19% of all children and 51% of children in female-headed families in the United States lived in poverty. Poverty rates were particularly high among minority groups, with 43% of all African-American children and 36% of all Hispanic-American children living in poverty (Office of Educational Research and Improvement, 1991).

The rate of poverty is higher in rural areas than in inner cities. Regardless of setting, about two-thirds of the poor in the nation are white, and most live in families with a wage earner.

Although poverty is usually associated with inner-city settings, fewer than 9% of poor Americans live in "core" cities. The rate of poverty is much higher in rural areas, with rates sometimes equaling or exceeding 50%. Even affluent suburban communities have their share of poverty, with 28% of their inhabitants struggling to make ends meet. Regardless of social setting, two thirds of the poor are European-American, and most live in families with a wage earner (Reed & Sautter, 1990). Approximately 50% of poor children live in families that receive no welfare payments and about 50% of their mothers were at least 20 years old when they had their first child. Thus only about 1 in 56 poor children matches the stereotype (Taylor, 1991).

For the 100,000 low-income children who are homeless on a daily basis, life is especially grim. One of the most severe problems they face is the red tape they must cut through to register in school. Movement from school to school and district to district has traditionally slowed the transfer of records required for admission to school. Recent studies conducted by Stanford University researchers suggest that new enrollment procedures meant to correct this problem have in fact done so. The researchers concluded that despite severe transportation problems and less than ideal environments for study, 90% of homeless children are in school (Flax, 1991).

> **"[T]he average reading proficiencies of students from advantaged and disadvantaged urban communities differed by nearly 40 points. . . ."**

In terms of academics, effects of poverty can be devastating for children. Poor children often begin kindergarten less prepared than their peers, have difficulty staying on grade level in succeeding years, and are at greater risk of dropping out of school than students whose families have economic security (Hewlett, 1991). A 1988 study by the National Assessment of Educational Progress (NAEP) indicated "the average reading proficiencies of students from advantaged and disadvantaged urban communities differed by nearly 40 points at grade 4, a gap that increased by as much as 14 points at grades 8 and 12" (Langer, Applebee, Mullis, & Foertsch, 1990, p. 14).

An examination of students' in-school experiences reveals that poorer students sometimes miss out on courses that would prepare them for high-school-level work. Findings from the National Education Longitudinal Study of 1988 indicated that, among eighth graders, wealthier students were more likely to be enrolled in algebra courses than poorer students (National Center for Education Statistics, 1990).

Predictably, the students most at risk for failure in school are often the ones attending schools that are understaffed, overcrowded, and ill-equipped to help students learn:

> Last spring, the rain began leaking into the rooms on the fourth floor of Public School 94, an elementary school in the North Bronx. Then last fall, about an hour before parents' night began, huge pieces of the ceiling fell down covering the classroom floors with debris. But a crumbling sixty-year-old building is not the worst problem at PS 94. Overcrowding is. Every day 1,300 students pour into a building designed for half that number. To make more room the school has had to give up its gymnasium and its library. There are English classes in the hallway, speech classes in a stairwell, and science classes in what is supposed to be a locker room. (Hewlett, 1991, p. 57)

Poor schools only reinforce the cycle of poverty. Children in poor neighborhoods live in crowded households that may lack ample heat and hot water or pose lead and electrical hazards. What disadvantaged students need is a quality environment where they can get the special attention they need to improve both their education and their overall chances for success in life.

HOW CAN SCHOOLS RESPOND TO THE PROBLEM OF POVERTY?

The most obvious response to the problem of poverty is to provide money directly to those who need it via some type of cash grant, tax credit, housing assistance, or food stamps. While such assistance can be aimed at families with dependent children, it is difficult to measure how much of the aid touches children directly. The next most obvious approach is to provide assistance indirectly through social or educational services. In many parts of the country, however, schools themselves are so poor that they are virtually unable to compensate for the disadvantages of poverty.

As people realize that problems facing the young are interrelated and are largely environmental, more are advocating the development of comprehensive integrated approaches to reduce the exposure of young people to high-risk settings. According to the Panel on High Risk Youth (1993), "Reducing the risks generated by these settings is virtually a precondition for achieving widespread reductions in health- and life-compromising behavior by adolescents" (p. 235).

Early Intervention

For years, **early intervention** has been considered key to equalizing opportunities for success in elementary school and beyond. This position was reiterated when in 1991 the National Commission on Children recommended that "all children, from the prenatal period through the first years of life, [should] receive the care and support they need to enter school ready to learn—namely, good health care, nurturing environments, and experiences that enhance their development" (National Commission on Children, 1991a, p. 187). The reasoning for such action emanates from a set of facts that make evident the old adage: an ounce of prevention is worth a pound of cure.

There are many testaments to the value of early intervention. The Perry Preschool Program, begun in 1962 by David P. Weikart in Ypsilanti, Michigan, provided a preschool and home-visit program to 3- and 4-year-olds from economically disadvantaged families. The program captured public attention with results from a follow-up study of its students and a matched comparison group. Data collected over a 30-year period revealed that, in comparison to the control group, 27-year-old adults born into poverty who participated in the program made more social gains than adults from similar backgrounds who did not receive preschool services.

Program participants had committed fewer crimes, had better-paying jobs, had been married longer, and were more likely to own their homes than those in the control group. Out-of-wedlock births were high for both groups, but less prevalent among program females (Cohen, 1993b). Some question the generalizability of findings from a study of 123 individuals, 58 of whom received preschool services in a model program led by highly trained and closely supervised teachers. Nonetheless, the project remains a unique long-term study of preschool effects.

A number of programs are currently in place to help disadvantaged students enter school ready to learn. Data collected by the Bureau of the Census in 1987 and 1988, however, reveal that lack of federal funding prevents such programs from reaching large numbers of children. Only 30.1% of 3- and 4-year-old children from families earning less than $20,000, as opposed to 56.1% of children from families whose incomes were above $35,000, attended preschool programs (Bureau of the Census, 1990).

Project Head Start, a federally subsidized preschool program established during the summer of 1965, was developed to give an extra boost to 3- and 4-year-old children from low-income families. In some places, Head Start programs are operated not only by churches and other community centers but also by the public school system. These programs try to provide a curriculum fitted to students as well as to deliver health, nutrition, and social services to their families.

Head Start also promotes parental involvement. Parents participate in program governance and parenting classes, and they also have opportunities to do volunteer work or to be hired as staff members in Head Start classrooms. Despite evidence that Head Start has long-term positive effects on students, federal funding allows only one in five eligible students to participate in the program (Reed & Sautter, 1990). President Bill Clinton, an advocate of Head Start, proposed in 1993 that funding for the program be increased by $10 billion dollars over a 5-year period so as to reach all eligible youngsters.

Compensatory Education

A number of programs have been established to provide children from low-income families with additional educational opportunities beyond those offered in a school's standard program. These **compensatory education programs** attempt to compensate for important educational factors (e.g., teachers, curricula, time, and materials) that may be missing in young people's lives.

Chapter I   Title I, one of the largest federally funded education programs for at-risk elementary and secondary students, was begun in 1965 as the first bill of President Lyndon Johnson's War on Poverty program. Referred to as **Chapter 1** since 1981, the program has provided more than $80 billion to meet the educational needs of low-income, low-achieving students. Currently, about 70% of students receiving Chapter 1 services are found in elementary schools (U.S. Department of Education, 1993). For the most part, academic assistance to Chapter 1 students occurs in **pull-out programs**. That is, Chapter 1 children most often receive their services outside the regular classroom. Instruction usually lasts for 30 to 35 minutes and focuses mainly on reading, mathematics, and language arts. While the majority of the nation's school districts receive federal monies for such assistance, there is not enough money to fund instruction for all children who qualify for extra help under Chapter 1 guidelines. In 1990, about half of eligible students were served, down from 65% in 1980–81 (National Education Association, 1991).

Critics argue that Chapter 1 needs a dramatic overhaul. In the final report emanating from the 1992 National Assessment of Chapter 1 Act (P.L. 101-305), an Independent Review Panel noted a number of flaws in program design and operations that diminished program effectiveness. One concern was that the Chapter 1 program, while intended to be supplemental, contributes little additional learning time for students enrolled in the program. Only 9% of Chapter 1 programs offer before- or after-school classes; about 15% offer summer school classes. Furthermore, when children leave their regular classrooms to receive Chapter 1 help, about 70% of classroom teachers report that Chapter I students miss some regular instruction.

Other program faults cited include:

- An emphasis on what the "disadvantaged" students lack in knowledge, intellectual facility, or experience rather than an emphasis on the knowledge or skills students bring to school.

- A curriculum that teaches mainly low-level skills rather than complex thinking skills.

- Heavy reliance on teacher-directed instruction, sometimes by aides who have less than a bachelor's degree.

- The rigidity of grouping arrangements for Chapter I students, most often determined by students' academic achievement or ability (U.S. Department of Education, 1993).

Success for All   Success for All, a program for preschool and elementary children, organizes resources to ensure that every student in a Chapter I school will be at or near grade level in reading and other skills by the end of third grade and will continue to achieve in later grades. Among elements of the program are one-on-one tutoring for students who are unable to keep up with their peers in reading, daily 90-minute reading periods, frequent assessments, and a family support program that involves parents in the education of their children. Research suggests that Success for All students in grades 1 through 3 out-perform matched control students. The program also seems to reduce grade retention (keeping students at the same grade level for more than one year) and special education placements (Slavin, Madden, Karweit, Dolan, & Waski, 1992).

Upward Bound   Many older children also need all the help they can get. Upward Bound, a federally funded program, is structured to improve the academic performance and motivational levels of low-income high school students. Participants in the program receive tutoring, counseling, and basic skills instruction. The intent is to encourage students to finish high school and win acceptance into college. At the end of the school year, students participate in a summer residential program focusing on the improvement of study skills and content knowledge. Established in the 1960s, Upward Bound programs continue to operate across the nation.

HOW CAN SCHOOLS SUPPORT LATCHKEY FAMILIES?

Every day, as many as 10 million school children ages 6 through 13 come home to an empty house because their parents are at work (Zigler & Lang, 1991). These **latchkey children** may be without adult supervision for several hours each day.

During the past 20 years, women have entered the work force in increasing numbers, with the sharpest increases being among married mothers of young children. By 1990, 58% of mothers with children under age 6 and 74% of women with children between the ages of 6 and 13 were employed or looking for employment. Among employed mothers, at least 70% who had children under 6 and more than 74% who had school-age children worked full time (National Commission on Children, 1991b).

With more women in the workforce, and thus unable to stay at home with their children, traditional roles and responsibilities of parents have changed. In some two-parent families, fathers assume child care responsibilities. In others, parents change their work schedules so one or the other can be home with their children during the day. As illustrated in Figure 6.2, working mothers of children between the ages of 5 and 14 most often hire someone to provide care in the child's home. Although most children under age four have some type of supervised care, this care is often provided outside the home by nonrelatives (Schorr & Schorr, 1988). Some argue that existing child care services, particularly for people with limited incomes, have been shaped by "costs and other political considerations, not the well-being of children" (Beardsley, 1990, p. 138).

FIGURE 6.2
After-School Care

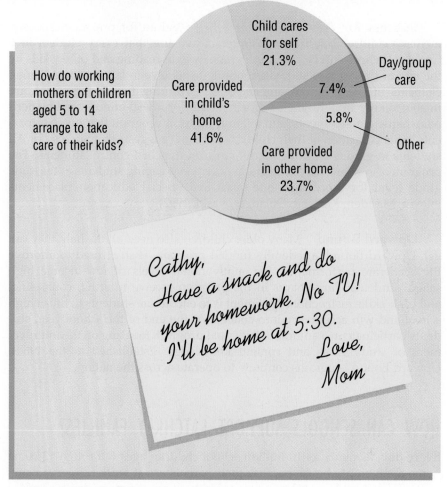

Note. From "After-School Care" by the National Education Association, 1990, *NEA Today*, 8, 9, p. 26. Copyright 1990 by the National Education Association.

Cultural Awareness

According to the U.S. Census Bureau, 3.2 million children in the United States live with their grandparents. That is an increase of some 40% in the past 10 years. Some estimate, however, that even this dramatic increase is an underestimate. About 4% European-American children and 12% of African-American youngsters live with grandparents. At least half of the grandparents are single women who receive less than one third the financial support available to foster families: The national average is $109 per child per month for grandparents who are sole care givers, compared to $371 per child per month for foster parents (Creighton, 1991).

Once they reach school age, more than 20% of children between the ages of 5 and 14 are on their own after school hours (National Education Association, 1990). Concerns about the potentially negative effects of self-care, "from physical danger—vulnerability to crime, fire, and injury, for example—to psychological damage," have spurred efforts in nearly every state to provide appropriate before- and after-school care programs for children (Zigler & Lang, 1991, p. 125). In many instances, such programs have been integrated into the schools.

School Supervision

Schools respond to needs for child care in many different ways. Buses transport children to school in the morning and home in the afternoon. Some children arrive early enough each day to receive a hot breakfast they would not get otherwise. For too many, national school lunch and breakfast programs offer the best meal of the day.

After-school programs offer opportunities for study and play for younger children, sports programs provide older students supervised outlets for pent-up energy, and bands and choruses and clubs of every kind operate in the late afternoons and evenings and weekends all over the country. These offerings are billed as services, extracurricular activities, or enrichment programs, but they also amount to forms of child care. Unless schools provide transportation and equipment for such events, however, low-income children in particular are unlikely to benefit from after-school programs.

Full-Service Programs

Other efforts to improve child care are broader-based. The School of the 21st Century, created by Yale psychologist Edward Zigler, is an example of formal attempts to provide full-service programs that bring child care and family services under the aegis of the school. Their "family support" program, either delivered in or administered by schools, is coordinated by an early childhood education specialist and staffed with individuals trained in child development.

"Developmentally appropriate care" in Zigler's school consists of year-round child care for preschoolers from age three to kindergarten-entry and before- and after-school child care and vacation care for children in grades kindergarten through 6. Outreach services may include a network of licensed or registered family day-care providers (trained by program personnel) and a resource and referral system to help parents find quality care for children with special needs or to help connect them with agencies offering such services as health care. In some instances, home-based parent education programs and screening for devel-

> **"Kids don't need better curriculum, they need better childhoods."**

opmental problems in youngsters are offered to individuals with children under age three. Several school districts in Missouri, Wyoming, Connecticut, and Colorado have in place some version of the School of the 21st Century model (Zigler & Lang, 1991).

Some, like principal Jack Currie of Eustis, Florida, have moved informally in the direction of family support programs by creating what he calls a **full-service school**.

> As the need has arisen, Currie has given showers to students with poor hygiene, cut the hair of shaggy boys, persuaded local merchants to donate children's clothes and stocked a school "food locker" for needy families. He has arranged free medical care from local doctors and taken students into his home during family emergencies. He also has made frequent "home visits" in his blue pickup, counseled families on child-rearing and even telephoned lax parents at night to remind them when to put their children to bed. (Cooper, 1991, p. A1)

When asked about his full-service school, Currie (personal communication, July 7, 1993) explained the rationale for his actions:

> I think we are in a changing society. Sam Sava [executive director of the Elementary School Principals Association] says kids don't need better curriculum, they need better childhoods. Kids learn better when they have full stomachs, when they are clean, and well clothed. More and more of these responsibilities are falling on schools. Somebody has got to raise the kids. Many times we have to help parents do it.

The success of these and other efforts to provide quality child care depend on the ability of teachers, families, and specialists to work together to provide for children the best academic, social, and emotional environment possible. As indicated below, the strength of such connections are one determinant of a child's success in school.

HOW CAN SCHOOLS GET PARENTS INVOLVED IN THEIR CHILDREN'S EDUCATION?

Parents are teachers, too, but sometimes they do not ask the kinds of questions that will lend direction to their actions. How much television is Johnny watching? How much does he read? What should I do to help him with his homework? Is Johnny getting enough sleep? What does he eat? Parents can make a home to school connection an important factor in their son's or daughter's success. When the link is weak or nonexistent, students' chances for healthy, productive academic lives are diminished.

When schools are able to encourage parents to get involved in their children's education, there can be high payoffs.

> There is clear evidence that family concern for education can become practical support for children and for schools, that low educational attainment of a parent need not be a barrier to the parent's providing effective support, and that the more far-reaching the parental involvement—the more roles there are in a school for parents to play—the more effective it will be. (Schorr & Schorr, 1988, p. 229)

Research and common sense support this notion, but surveys indicate that many students lack the parental involvement needed to succeed in school. The 1990 National Assessment of Educational Progress (NAEP) focusing on mathematics skills of 4th, 8th, and 12th graders indicated a relationship between math performance and school attendance, outside reading, homework, and television viewing (activities parents can control). Students watching 6 or more hours of television per day, for example, scored significantly lower than students spending less time in front of the television set (Langer, Applebee, Mullis, & Foertsch, 1990).

Schools support latchkey families through school supervision, such as after-school care, and through parental involvement programs and other services.

The National Education Longitudinal Study of 1988, which focused on 24,599 American eighth graders, their parents, teachers, and principals, revealed a communication gap between parents and students and between parents and schools. There was a mismatch, for example, between students' and parents' perceptions of the frequency with which they discussed school experiences. About 86% of the 9,800 students said they discussed school with their parents regularly, but less than half of their parents agreed with them. There was also disagreement about the frequency with which parents and students were warned about grades. Some 1,500 students reported that their parents were warned by school officials two or more times about their grades. Only 42% of these parents agreed with their children that they had been warned about grades two or more times; about 25% of the parents said they were never warned about grade problems (National Center for Education Statistics, 1991).

Parental Involvement Programs

It is important to recognize that for some parents, school involvement may seem like a luxury. As Figure 6.3 suggests, parents in poverty worry so much about making money to support their families that they may have little emotional energy left to devote to school activities. This is neither an indictment nor an excuse, it is a simple but hard fact of life for some people.

Schools have always tried to involve parents in the education of their children, but their efforts seem to have increased in recent years. Common and visible attempts are parent-teacher conferences, school open houses, and parent-teacher associations and organizations (PTAs and PTOs). PTAs and PTOs vary in size and level of participation. Their goal is to bring parents into school activities to tackle virtually every kind of problem imaginable. In many instances, their fund-raising efforts allow schools to purchase classroom materials and equipment. PTA-generated funds also provide educational opportunities such as field trips and theatrical performances.

One of the more visible efforts to enhance parental involvement in schools has been guided by James Comer (1986). In 1969, Comer and his col-

FIGURE 6.3

Percentage of Parents Who Worry "All the Time" That Their Family Income Will Not Be Enough, By Family Income

Make one generalization based on the information in this graph about the relationship between income and worry.

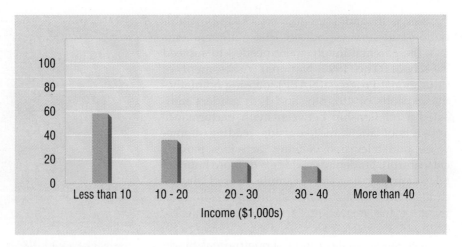

Note. From *Speaking of Kids: A National Survey of Children and Parents* (p. 23), Washington, DC: National Commission on Children.

leagues began working with an elementary school ranked 32nd out of 33 schools in terms of academic achievement in New Haven, Connecticut. With no appreciable shift in student socioeconomic status or ethnic mix, by 1986 the school ranked 3rd. Comer attributed much of the gain to increased parental involvement.

Erwin Flaxman and Morton Inger (1991) contend that there are a few general principles for involving parents in school activities that apply across the board:

- The most effective parental involvement is that which is well organized and long-lasting.
- Parental involvement that concentrates on preventing problems rather than on curing them is most effective.
- It is important to involve parents of students in high school as well as parents of younger students.
- Parents do not have to be well educated to be usefully involved in school activities.
- Students from low income minority-group families have the most to gain from parental involvement (p. 5).

Adult Education Programs for Parents

Some schools facilitate parental involvement by offering adult education programs. As described later in the chapter, some parent education programs are structured specifically for pregnant and parenting teens. Missouri's Parents As Teachers combines parent education with an early childhood program. In all 543 Missouri school districts, the early childhood component provides periodic screening for developmental problems in children through age 4 as well as educational programs for 3- and 4-year-olds who are developmentally delayed (Reed & Sautter, 1990).

The Accelerated Schools Program in California and Missouri attempts to raise parents' expectations for what their children can do in school. By empowering parents with educational skills and by helping them to adopt high expectations, program leaders hope that parents will take more interest in what their children are doing at school and become more involved in their education (Reed & Sautter, 1990).

While some parent education programs are school-based, others are home-based. Greensville County Public Schools in Emporia, Virginia, use a mobile van to deliver workshops to parents. The program, Family School Partners in Education, teaches parents how to tutor their children using a variety of learning materials and strategies. About 60% of low-income parents have been trained, with follow-up progress logs indicating parent participants are doing such things as taking their children to the public library more often, checking homework on a daily basis, and reading with their children each day (Lee, 1992).

Parental involvement figures heavily in efforts to reorganize schools. Concepts of parental choice, for example, are based on the idea that when parents can exercise some control over where their children attend school, schools will become more responsive to consumers. Other strategies of school restructuring and school-based management draw upon parental participation in governing councils to bring about change in school systems.

Sometimes increased parental involvement is a serendipitous byproduct of some other action. In Plainfield, Indiana, for example, when the middle school instituted a no-cut policy with regard to student membership on clubs and teams—anybody who shows up makes the team—parental interest jumped right along with student participation. With 72 cheerleaders and anyone who wants to play football suiting up for games, parents have volunteered their assistance and bought tickets to games in record numbers (Wheeler, 1991).

HOW CAN SCHOOLS REDUCE RISKS THAT THREATEN CHILDREN'S HEALTH AND SAFETY?

Although medical advances and extensions of health-care coverage have resulted in better health and life expectancy for many Americans, today's children have not fared so well:

> Every year, nearly 1 million infants start life at a disadvantage because their mothers did not receive early prenatal care. More than 250,000 babies are born at low birthweight, needing advanced medical technology to survive, and often still are left vulnerable to a lifetime of disabilities. And 40,000 infants die each year. . . . (Children's Defense Fund, 1992, pp. 1–2)

At every age, among all races and income groups, and in communities throughout the nation, the well-being of young people is further threatened by a variety of factors. Some of the more successful responses to the serious threats to life and health of children are multifaceted; that is, they attempt to address complex conditions that usually accompany the most grievous problems.

The challenges of dealing with students who have a variety of health problems have also prompted the establishment of **school-based health centers** in a number of states. These centers allow schools to coordinate health care with health curricula emphasizing preventive care. Full-care clinics provide such services as physical examinations, weight and drug counseling, treatment of illness and minor injuries, and testing for pregnancy and sexually transmitted diseases. The first of these full-care centers was established in Dallas, Texas, in 1970. By early 1990, there were 162 such centers in 33 states (Marriott, 1991).

Preventing Child Abuse and Neglect

Many youngsters can suffer from physical, emotional, and sexual abuse, and many more may be the victims of neglect by their parents or guardians. In 1974, Congress passed the **Child Abuse Prevention and Treatment Act** to provide financial support to states that implemented programs for identification, prevention, and treatment of child abuse and neglect. Nationally, there are about 3 million reported cases of such abuse each year. Some contend that the poor treatment of "throwaway" children—or children no one appears to value—is the nation's "secret scandal" (Reynolds, 1993).

In the majority of states, teachers are among those required by law to report instances of suspected child abuse. When teachers fail to do so, one or more things may happen: (a) they may be fined from $500 to $1,000, (b) they may be given prison terms of up to 1 year, (c) civil suits may be brought against them, and (d) they may be disciplined (e.g., demoted or dismissed) by their school systems (McCarthy & Cambron-McCabe, 1992).

Problems of child abuse and neglect cut across all socioeconomic strata. According to the National Commission on Children (1991a), however, financial problems may be the greatest contributor to the plight of children:

> A recent analysis of the factors that place children at risk of maltreatment suggests that only family income is consistently related to all categories of abuse and neglect. When other factors, such as single parenthood and race, are controlled for income, there is no positive correlation with heightened risk of abuse or neglect. In fact, this analysis suggests that when the same resources are available to families headed by single mothers as to two-parent households, children are actually at lower risk of maltreatment. While poverty does not always or automatically lead to child abuse and neglect, it can contribute to stress and lack of emotional control that can result in violence or an inability to meet a child's basic daily needs. (p. 284)

Because the physical and mental health of parents bears directly on the health and well-being of their children, many community-based programs try to provide parents with the skills and knowledge needed to cope more effectively with everyday stress and to care for and nurture their children. Parenting programs can help increase parents' involvement in their children's lives and also teach parents, particularly young, inexperienced ones, how to take care of themselves and their children. It is not uncommon for schools to sponsor parenting programs within their own buildings. Some provide day care for infants and preschool children of high school students so the parents can complete their own high school programs and avoid the stunningly cruel conditions of life which breed child abuse and neglect.

Preventing Substance Abuse

As seen in Figure 6.4, surveys conducted between 1975 and 1989 reveal that high school seniors' reported use of tobacco, alcohol, and drugs over a 30-day period has declined somewhat over the past few years. Nonetheless, the fact that 28.6% of those surveyed reported use of cigarettes, 60% use of alcohol, and 19.7% use of illicit drugs during the 30-day time frame indicates that many youth are engaging in practices considered detrimental to health and safety (Office of Educational Research and Improvement, 1991). These numbers would be even higher if young people living in institutions, the homeless, and runaways were included in the count.

A variety of school based programs attempt to curb substance abuse. Project ALERT, a curriculum developed by the RAND Corporation, and Drug Abuse Resistance Education (DARE), a program that began as a joint effort between the Los Angeles Unified School District and the Los Angeles Police Department, are two examples of programs designed to help elementary and junior high school students resist peer pressure to experiment with drugs and alcohol. Among program goals are to help students learn to make their own decisions, learn drug and alcohol facts, understand peer pressure,

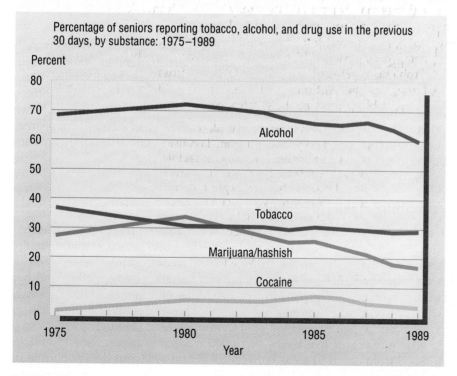

Note. From *Youth Indicators*, 1991 (p. 113) by U.S. Department of Education, 1991. Washington, DC: Author.

FIGURE 6.4

Tobacco, Alcohol, and Drug Use Among High School Seniors

Describe the trends indicated on this graph.

and develop positive self-esteem. While such programs enjoy widespread use, some educators have created their own health education programs to meet their students' needs.

Cultural Awareness

In Hollow, West Virginia, local teachers and instructors from West Virginia University in Morgantown collaborated to create a "culturally relevant" curriculum for rural kindergarten through third grade youngsters. In one lesson designed for third graders, many of whom have tried snuff at least once, teachers deal with the hazards of chewing tobacco.

When carrying out this lesson, classroom teacher Kathy Fawcett begins with a song: "Smoking's not for me; I hope it's not for you; it causes lung cancer and emphysema, too," sings Fawcett.

Then the class chimes in: "I won't smoke, I won't chew. Tobacco's not for me, I want my body to be well and live to one-O-three!"

Fawcett then shows children an oversized plastic jaw called Mr. Grossmouth. Students moan when they see that it is speckled with black cancer growths (Portner, 1993a). Effectiveness of the newly implemented program in West Virginia has not been determined.

Well-designed drug prevention programs have had positive effects. A 7-year study indicated that seventh and eighth graders in 30 schools in California and Oregon who were taught the Project ALERT curriculum reduced their use of illegal drugs, particularly marijuana, by as much as 50% while enrolled in the program. Cigarette smoking was also curbed. Once students left the program, however, positive effects had all but disappeared. Such results suggest prevention programs are most effective if they are continued at the high school level (Portner, 1993b).

Preventing Teen Pregnancy

Teenage childbearing is of particular concern because it is highly correlated with lower educational attainment, low income, and nonparticipation in the labor force. Statistics indicate that for teens "having a child out-of-wedlock is a virtual guarantee of living in poverty for the young mother and her child or children" (Wetzel, 1989, p. 26). Many children of teenage parents wind up as teenage parents themselves, thus perpetuating the cycle of poverty and hopelessness (National Commission on Children, 1991b).

The number of live births per 1,000 women between ages 15 and 19 declined from about 91 to 54 between 1955 and 1988, but the proportion of unmarried teenagers having babies rose dramatically. In 1955, there were approximately 15 births per 1,000 unmarried teenagers while in 1988 there were about 37 such births (Office of Educational Research and Improvement, 1991). Although out of wedlock births occur in all ethnic groups, it is more common in the African-American community, where one out of three mothers is an unwed teenager. About one third of these young women have a second child during their teenage years (Hewlett, 1991).

The high dropout rate among young mothers and, in many instances, the poor health of their babies, have encouraged many school systems to alter their programs to meet the needs of adolescent parents and parents-to-be. In addition to its standard curriculum, the New Futures School in Albuquerque, New Mexico, offers health care, parenting education for fathers as well as mothers, child care services, and vocational training. Comparisons of students enrolled in the New Futures School with those in other school settings indicate that New Futures students are more likely to stay in school and much less likely to have a second child during their teenage years or to end up as welfare recipients (Hewlett, 1991).

Some programs try to involve parents directly in educating children about sexuality. In Howard County, Maryland, educators, PTA officials, and the Governor's Council on Adolescent Pregnancy developed a program for parents of elementary and high school students. School officials offer orientation sessions to parents to suggest more and less effective ways to talk about sex with their children. A county-wide Parents and Children Talking (PACT) Night has also been initiated to encourage parents to take the first step toward opening the lines of communication with their children by taking time to discuss issues related to sexuality (Buckley, 1991).

The World Health Organization estimates that about 60% of HIV transmission is through heterosexual relations.

Sex education, the most controversial of health topics, varies greatly from one school district to another. While some 90% of the American public support some form of sex education in schools, there is a great deal of disagreement about the appropriate content of such education (Sanderson & Wilson, 1991). The overwhelming majority of states encourage some type of sex education in schools, but the content and method of courses vary widely. Instruction runs the gamut from advocating abstinence from sexual contact to distributing condoms even within the same school.

Preventing the Spread of AIDS and Other Communicable Diseases

Students engaging in sexual relationships and students abusing drugs are especially susceptible to sexually transmitted diseases, including Acquired Immune Deficiency Syndrome (AIDS). According to the Center for Population Options, one in every six sexually active teens has a sexually transmitted disease. Although there are no precise figures on the prevalence of AIDS, health officials suspect that the number is dangerously high ("Teenagers & AIDS," 1991).

While AIDS has often been characterized as a disease confined mainly to homosexual men and intravenous drug users, it has rapidly become a disease transmitted largely through heterosexual intercourse. The World Health Organization estimates that about 60% of HIV (Human Immuno-deficiency Virus) transmission is through heterosexual relations, and that this figure could increase to 80% by the turn of the century (WHO, 1991).

Douglas Tonks (1992/1993) counsels educators to remember two important facts when developing programs to prevent HIV transmission. First, many students experiment with drugs as young as age 12. Sexual experimentation also begins at an early age, even though this may not include intercourse. Second, some students at every grade level and in every class are already at risk of HIV infection while others are not. HIV prevention programs, therefore, must begin in elementary school and continue through high school; they must also be flexible enough to meet the needs of all children.

Tonks also argues that while there is little evidence about how best to conduct HIV education programs, other successful health education programs provide some direction. Teachers should focus on risk behavior. Students should not be taught simply to recognize HIV-risk behavior; they also need opportunities to acquire and practice refusal and communication skills. They need to learn how to recognize high risk situations and how to avoid them, too.

Many parents, including a growing number of middle-class parents, cannot afford or do not have access to adequate health care for their children. Often, their children have not received preschool vaccinations on time and therefore enter school most vulnerable to disease. Given that the United States has seen a resurgence of such preventable diseases as measles, mumps, pertussis (whooping cough), and rubella, these children are particularly at risk for contracting diseases that will interfere with their opportunities to learn and achieve in school (Children's Defense Fund, 1992). More recently, the emergence and spread of drug resistant strains of tuberculosis also threaten the well-being of children. Those who do not receive adequate health care or who do not take prescribed medication according to a prescribed schedule are most at risk for contracting and spreading the disease (Groopman, 1993).

To stem outbreaks of childhood diseases, public health officials have expanded outreach programs to ensure the timely immunization of children. They have also increased several immunization requirements for school-age children. To enable all children to meet these requirements, many districts offer school based clinics for youngsters.

Preventing Suicide and Accidental Injury or Death

Suicide is one of the leading causes of death among children and adolescents in the United States. Data indicate that the number of students contemplating suicide has doubled in the last 30 years (Koop & Lundberg, 1992). Between November 1990 and January 1991, researchers surveyed 1,152 randomly selected teenagers between the ages 13 and 17 to solicit information about teenage suicide. Of the total sample, 15% indicated that they had come close to committing suicide; 6% reported that they had actually attempted suicide. More commonly cited factors that had led them to consider or attempt suicide were family problems or problems at home (47%), depression (23%), problems with friends/peer pressure/social relations (22%), low self-esteem (18%), boy/girl relationships (16%), and feelings that no one cared (13%) (Gallup Organization, 1991).

Cultural Awareness

Some groups of students are more prone to suicide than others. Data suggest that homosexual adolescents are two to three times more likely to attempt suicide than their heterosexual peers (Green, 1991). Among ethnic groups, the suicide rate in 1988 for Native-American youth was nearly twice that of European-American youth while suicide rates for Hispanic, African, and Asian Americans were much lower than for European Americans (Department of Health and Human Services, 1990).

Addressing potentially suicidal students, and acquaintances of suicide victims, requires special attention to young people's concepts of themselves. Single suicides can stimulate imitation, or what some have referred to as "cluster suicides." School based programs on suicide prevention and suicide curriculum advocate careful training for teachers who offer such programs. For example, the California State Education Department has developed a program of worksheets, quizzes, and simulation games to address directly the threat of suicide. Other programs in other locales also address suicide more indirectly via drug education programs.

As John Davis and Jonathan Sandoval (1991) note, most suicide prevention programs are conducted in public schools, beginning as early as kindergarten or as late as the 11th grade. In these programs, adults and students may be taught to understand the myths, signs, facts, and symptoms of suicide. They may also concentrate on identifying feelings of students at risk, thinking of ways to help students cope with stress and depression, and learning how to respond to a suicide crisis. Figure 6.5 includes some of the warning signs of suicide and possible responses to troubled students.

Motor vehicle accidents are the leading cause of death among teenagers 15 to 19 years old (Office of Educational Research and Improvement, 1991). Many fatalities are alcohol related. Moving the minimum drinking age up to 21 in states where it was lower has resulted in a decline in arrests for driving while intoxicated among teenagers.

High schools offer driver education programs that precede the granting of a license to operate a motor vehicle. Insurance companies offer incentives to students for high scores in driver safety and for students who do well in academic courses. In combination with health education, driver education

FIGURE 6.5

Warning Signs of Suicide and Possible Responses

WARNING SIGNS:

- Changing eating and sleeping habits
- Withdrawal from friends, family, and regular activities
- Violent or rebellious behavior
- Running away from home
- Unusual neglect of personal appearance
- Radical change in personality
- Persistent boredom, difficulty concentrating, or a decline in the quality of schoolwork
- Frequent complaints about physical symptoms often related to emotions, such as stomachaches, headaches, or fatigue
- Loss of interest in previously pleasurable activities
- Inability to tolerate praise or rewards

POSSIBLE RESPONSES:

- "I'm here for you."
- "I want to hear about what's bothering you."
- "I really care about you."
- "Let's talk and figure out how to make things better."
- "If I can't help you, we'll find someone who can help."
- "No one and nothing is worth taking your life for."

Note. From "Counselors Can Make a Difference" by L. Peach and T.L. Riddick, 1991, *The School Counselor*, 39, p. 107–111. Copyright by ACA. Reprinted with permission. No further reproduction authorized without written permission of the American Counseling Association.

has the potential for lowering the lethal risks of drinking and driving. Nonetheless, when school budgets are tight, driver education courses are among the first to be dropped.

The psychological and physical well-being of many students, particularly adolescents, is also threatened by preoccupation with body image. A growing number of females from all races and socioeconomic groups is particularly vulnerable to anorexia nervosa (self-starvation) and bulimia (binging and purging). Such eating disorders not only harm students physically but also contribute to underachievement, interpersonal difficulties, and emotional instability (Phelps & Bajorek, 1991). Among young males, preoccupation with body image more often manifests itself through use of anabolic steroids. In 1988, Herbert A. Haupt, a St. Louis orthopedist, asserted that some 250,000 to 500,000 male high school seniors under the age of 18 had used or were currently using steroids (Buckley, Yesalis, & Friedl, 1988).

Schools address such problems in a variety of ways. School counselors and school psychologists, though facing serious time constraints, may be involved in the assessment of at-risk behaviors. They may also provide direct intervention with at-risk and borderline cases through individual and group therapy sessions. Health education programs in schools offer instruction on nutrition and drug, tobacco and alcohol abuse prevention as well as on personal hygiene, eating disorders, relationships, and human sexuality.

Many threats to the health and well-being of students are so common they often escape attention. For example, schools must routinely examine science laboratories to insure proper ventilation and fire prevention procedures. Fire drills are a regular part of every school calendar. Inspectors must monitor schools' attention to building codes, check for the use of asbestos building materials, and investigate sanitary conditions of food services. As we note in Chapter 13, teachers bear responsibilities for making students aware of school safety rules.

Preventing School Violence

Assault, homicide, vandalism, and related violent acts committed by and against young people are on the rise. Among all 15- through 19-year-olds, firearm homicide is the second leading cause of death. For African-American teenage males, it is the leading cause of death, claiming close to 1,000 lives annually (Fingerhut, Ingram, & Feldman, 1992). "They occur as the result of violent arguments among people who know each other, and they generally do not occur in public" (Rosenberg, O'Carroll, & Powell, 1992).

Some assaults against young people result from gang warfare, an unfortunate fixture of American life. While gangs are not confined to urban areas, big cities in particular have experienced growth in gang membership and gang violence in recent years. In 1985 in Los Angeles County, for example, there were about 400 gangs and 45,000 gang members countywide. Today, there are about 800 gangs with about 90,000 members (Cantrell & Cantrell, 1993). Much of the gang-related violence that seeps into schools results from struggles between gangs for drug selling "turf."

While some gang and individual acts of brutality appear random and baseless, others are the cold and calculated manifestations of hate against "people who are different." "Different" can be defined in terms of religion, sexual preference, race, age, or virtually any characteristic. Attacks are aimed at specific people or perceived types of people.

The central issue for educators is how to ensure children's safety. A number of efforts, many school based, aim to change the odds for children at highest risk.

Children's shocking violence toward other children, including hate crimes and firearm homicides, came to greater national attention during the 1990s.

In-School Intervention   To deter crime and violence on buses and at school, some localities have turned to metal detectors and video cameras. Some schools employ police officers, sometimes referred to as resource officers, to help maintain order and to prevent people from coming into schools from the streets. Many schools also have educational programs designed to enlist students' cooperation in preventing violence.

FAST Track—for Families and Schools Together—is an 8-year project funded by the National Institute of Mental Health aimed at preventing violent behavior in young people. During 1992, the first year of the project, participants were 480 first grade children from Nashville, Tennessee; Durham, North Carolina; Seattle, Washington; and Pennsylvania who came from low-income families and displayed aggressive behavior in school and at home. About 75% of this first cohort were boys, 50% were African American, and 45% European American.

Besides receiving instruction in a regular classroom placement, FAST Track students are offered "social-cognitive" skill training in small group settings; that is, they learn how to think and behave in social settings. Students also receive academic tutoring in reading and special phonics-based classes that meet three times a week for 30 minutes. These activities are coordinated by a team of school administrators, social workers, counselors, researchers, and parents. Parents, most of whom are single mothers, are paid $15 a week for attending sessions designed to alter such parenting behavior as harshness of disciplinary methods and lack of warmth between parent and child.

A follow-up of 1992 FAST Track students indicated that, at the end of second grade, 75% of the participants were better behaved in class and on the playground. Peer interviews also suggest that participants were better liked by their classmates (Lawton, 1993).

With increasing incidence of conflict, which often involves racial and cultural differences, educators have also worked with older students to teach them ways to solve problems constructively in their personal lives at home, at school, and in the community. At Cleveland High School in Reseda, California, such efforts have resulted in better relations between the school's 2,200 culturally diverse students. Students who have learned to use conflict resolution techniques help stop fights before they begin. Carlos McGhee, a student who helped lead his gang (the Bloods) into a riot that exploded at the school in 1991, is one of several gang leaders, athletes, and student body leaders who now help train other students to be conflict managers (Merina, 1993).

Community Programs   In some communities, families and businesses have collaborated to create safe environments for children. Helping Hand programs, first initiated in Indianapolis, Indiana, in the 1960s, are designed to protect children while they are traveling to and from school. Citizens who participate in the program display in the windows of their homes and businesses placards depicting a large handprint. Children learn at school and through community education programs that buildings displaying "helping hands" are places they can go for help if they are teased,

VOICES

On the Effects of Media Violence

Analyses of a number of short-term studies suggest that exposure to media violence results in a significant increase in children's aggressiveness. According to Dr. Brandon S. Centerwall, when exposure is long-term, the effects may be more serious:

Long-term childhood exposure to television is a causal factor behind approximately one half of the homicides committed in the United States, or approximately 10,000 homicides annually. Although the data are not as well developed for other forms of violence, they indicate that exposure to television is also a causal factor behind a major proportion—perhaps one half—of rapes, assaults, and other forms of interpersonal violence in the United States. . . .

To say that childhood exposure to television and television violence is a predisposing factor behind half of violent acts is not to discount the importance of other factors. Manifestly, every violent act is the result of an array of forces coming together—poverty, crime, alcohol and drug abuse, stress—of which childhood exposure to television is just one. Nevertheless, the epidemiologic evidence indicates that if hypothetically, television technology had never been developed, there would today be 10,000 fewer homicides each year in the United States, 70,000 fewer rapes, and 700,000 fewer injurious assaults.

CRITICAL THINKING

In 1993, television network officials agreed to air parental warnings on shows they considered violent. What are the pros and cons of using such a method to curb children's viewing of violent television programs? Are there ways a teacher might influence children's television viewing habits?

Source: Centerwall, B.S. (1992). Television and violence: The scale of the problem and where to go from here. *Journal of the American Medical Association, 267* (22), 3061.

---

attacked, or intimidated. By necessity, such programs have evolved to include careful security checks of adult volunteers. As Helping Hand programs have expanded, informal evaluations suggest children encounter fewer problems on the streets and are therefore less anxious about their walks to and from school (Goldstein, Harootunian, & Conoley, 1994).

Curbing Violence on Television   Many professional groups, such as the American Medical Association, the American Psychological Association, and the American Academy of Pediatrics, have asserted that television violence threatens the health and welfare of young people. A number of studies conducted since the late 1960s suggest that television plays an integral part in making America a violent society.

There are factors other than social problems that place students at risk for school failure. These include limited English proficiency and disabilities or impairments that interfere with learning. These threats are discussed in Chapters 7 and 8.

BENCHMARKS

Equal Opportunity for Women, Members of Minority Groups, and Low-Income Individuals: Selected Legislation

1946	National School Lunch Act subsidizes school lunches using federal funds. The School Milk Program was enacted in 1954.
1962	Migration and Refugee Assistance Act. In 1975, the Indochina Migration and Refugee Assistance Act extended educational services to refugees from countries affected by Vietnam.
1964	Civil Rights Act calls for desegregation of the schools and prohibits racial discrimination in the schools.
1965	Economic Opportunity Act creates early childhood compensatory education programs, including Operation Head Start.
1965	Elementary and Secondary Education Act (ESEA) funds Title I educational programs for economically disadvantaged students (with amendments in 1966, 1968, and 1970).
1968	Bilingual Education Act mandates bilingual education for students whose limited English proficiency interferes with learning.
1972	Title IX of the 1972 Amendments to the Civil Rights Act prohibits sex discrimination in schools receiving federal funds. Funding for the education of females is extended in 1974 through the Women's Educational Equity Act.
1975	Indian Self-Determination and Education Assistance Act gives Native Americans the right to establish and control their own schools. In 1978, these rights are extended through the Tribally Controlled Community College Assistance Act.
1981	Title I of ESEA becomes Chapter 1 of the Educational Consolidation and Improvement Act (ECIA), which expands compensatory education programs for low-income and at-risk students.
1984	Public Law 98-558 creates teacher education scholarships and continues funding for Head Start and Follow Through. Public Law 98-377 funds science and math programs, magnet schools, and equal access to public schools.
1990	National Assessment of Chapter 1 Act (Public Law 101-305) calls for a reassessment of the effectiveness of Chapter 1 programs in light of national educational goals.

SUMMARY

1. Americans have turned increasingly to schools to solve some of society's most difficult problems, many of which have devastating effects on children.

2. Children's problems tend to vary—a poor child is also likely to be at risk for dropping out of school, susceptible to disease, and subject to other threats—but responses to such problems often address only a single issue.

3. Some successful responses to the serious threats to children's lives and health are cooperative ventures among school, home, and community and are attuned to special cultural needs. Many of these focus on preventing children from dropping out of school.

4. Educators are increasingly expected to help children face many serious threats to their health and well-being: poverty and homelessness, infectious diseases, automobile accidents, lack of parental supervision during non-school hours, lack of parental involvement in their children's education, suicide, eating disorders, drugs and alcohol, teenage pregnancy, and physical violence.

5. Schools offer a variety of programs to meet the challenges facing youth. These include: parent education, peer mediation, family life education, special education, and gifted education. Schools also offer counseling services, health clinics, before- and after-school programs, and day care for infants and preschool children of high school parents.

TERMS AND CONCEPTS

Afrocentric curriculum
at-risk students
Chapter 1
Child Abuse Prevention and Treatment Act
compensatory education program

cross-age tutoring
early intervention
full-service school
holding power
incentive programs
latchkey children

mentoring program
pull-out programs
school-based health centers
socioeconomic status (SES)

STUDENT ACTIVITIES

Perceive and Value

What should be expected of schools?

Below you will find a list of functions for the public schools. Take the list and rank the functions according to the importance you attach to each, with "1" being most important, "2" being next most important, and so on.

Now join with four or five classmates and negotiate a group ranking. You may vote to settle disagreements, but do not opt for this procedure before discussing the function thoroughly. Is there consensus among your group members about the importance of a function or functions? What functions generate the most disagreement?

Public School Functions

Your rank	Group rank	
_____	_____	Schools should provide breakfast and lunch for students who cannot afford to buy these meals.
_____	_____	Schools should provide birth control for students who request it.
_____	_____	Schools should teach students of different races and cultural backgrounds how to get along with one another.
_____	_____	Schools should provide before- and after-school care for students.
_____	_____	Teachers should go into homes to seek greater parental involvement.
_____	_____	Schools should see that children are adequately clothed.
_____	_____	Schools should provide compensatory programs for at-risk students.
_____	_____	Schools should offer all students more help with academic subjects.
_____	_____	Schools should offer education programs on drugs and alcohol, tobacco, guns, and auto safety.
_____	_____	Schools should include sex education in the curriculum.
_____	_____	Schools should provide education for all students about homosexuality.
_____	_____	Schools should provide individual and group counseling.
_____	_____	Schools should offer child care for their students' infants and preschoolers.

Know and Act

Use information in this chapter to justify your top three choices in the previous activity. As a classroom teacher, for the grade level you plan to teach, how would you plan to carry out these three sociopolitical functions with your students?

Evaluate

Develop a list of at least three criteria you would use to judge whether a particular school program is addressing adequately what you perceive to be the most pressing problem young people face. You may want to consider factors such as money for program start-up and maintenance, the skills of people running the program, the kinds of activities offered in the program, and/or the results of the program as measured in a variety of ways. Discuss why the criteria you identify are important.

Discover

Read the same newspaper each day for 7 days. Clip every article you find on problems facing young people and/or on programs designed to address such problems. What if any pattern do you perceive in the articles? What might few or no articles on young people's problems indicate?

Foundations In Action

Across the nation, millions of teachers begin each school day with administrative tasks and strategies for helping students make the transition between home and classroom. At such times, teachers are often closest to concerns about students and their lives outside school, concerns that reflect some sociopolitical dimensions of education. In the following cases, what strategies have the teachers developed for starting the day and addressing concerns about the well-being of their students?

As students enter the classroom on Monday morning, teacher Mary Anne Reed-Brown greets them, shows Joshua, the new student, where to sit, and reminds students to begin morning work (called Early Bird): "Class, while you are working on your Early Bird activity, please raise your hands if you are buying lunch tickets. Okay. I have buying lunch tickets: Enny, Crystal, Alvie, Kamila, Eric, and Joshua. Now, let me introduce to you a new student. This is Joshua. Be kind to him today. This is a new school for him and we're glad to have him. Okay, we need to leave for gym."

Every morning, we are scheduled to go to gym within 10 minutes after students' arrival. I must check to see which students need lunch tickets. About 45% of my students are on free lunch and about 10% are on reduced-price lunch. The first 10 minutes, then, are taken up with taking roll, doing a lunch count, and filling out forms. The more I hurry, the longer it takes. While I complete these tasks, I have work, or Early Bird activities, for students to do at their desks.

On Monday a new student, named Joshua, arrived. I learned Friday evening that I would have a new student. When Joshua arrived, I knew absolutely nothing about him. Joshua was accompanied by the secretary, who introduced him to me and gave me a copy of his entrance form.

"I want all my students to understand our classroom is a place where they belong. . . ."

"I see problems every day. When I can, I intervene to help solve them."

As students enter Laura Saatzer's classroom, they talk quietly with one another. Several students gather around Saatzer and talk with her, too. Saatzer reminds everyone to put their popsicle sticks with their names on them in either the "hot lunch" can or the "cold lunch" can.

I try to be at the classroom door to greet my students every morning—just to say hello and ask them how they are doing. After I greet them, students put their sticks in either of two cans at the front of the classroom. I use the sticks to take attendance and to determine how many students need a hot lunch. Thus, students have responsibility for taking attendance and for establishing the lunch count, which I believe teaches them responsibility.

Lots of teachers have tasks for their students to do as soon as they arrive, but I like my students to visit in the morning and to get to know each other. The school day is so busy, it is important to use this time to make connections with one another.

Some students are very quiet. It is difficult to determine what they are thinking. I find at the beginning of the year these children need more space, and they need to establish a comfort level with me. I try to give them an extra boost to help with their self-esteem. I want all my students to understand our classroom is a place where they belong, where they are appreciated.

Peter Flaherty moves among his students as they prepare for the breakfast program. Some of his students count on getting breakfast at school, others eat breakfast at home or on the way to school. Flaherty greets individuals, asks about homework, and answers students' questions. He reinforces the idea that school is a place to learn. Flaherty values regular attendance and participation. He is also concerned about teaching appropriate social behavior. When Flaherty sees three boys entering the classroom, he moves quickly toward them and speaks to them about a concern:

Flaherty: Gentlemen.

Student 1: We didn't try to beat up Carlos!

Flaherty: Okay, I just wanted to find out what was going on. That's why I called you guys last night. Okay? Let me talk to you for a second. Jonathan? Carlos is very nervous that you guys were after him last night. I want to talk with you about this problem.

I see problems every day. When I can, I intervene to help solve them. In most instances I listen before I take action. This morning a boy told me his parents had gotten into a fight last night, and the father had been thrown out of the house. The events upset him. Today his classroom behavior may be affected.

I try to greet students as they come in the classroom, especially those who often miss school. I want to make sure they know I have noticed them, and that I appreciate their presence.

This chapter explores concepts of diversity in society and speculates about what differences and similarities among the nation's people mean for education. The assumption upon which the chapter is based is that how people view society depends greatly on where they stand; thus the chapter positions readers to perceive different conceptions of the influence of culture on education.

This chapter draws attention to the confusion in language used to describe concepts of diversity and speculates on some of the practical implications of this language for schools and society. Americans have developed some unique ways of living with their diversity, as the chapter notes. It also describes the more prominent ways multicultural education has been defined theoretically and in practice.

Rarely, if ever, has an education concept been surrounded by more contentious debate than has multicultural education. This chapter explores reasons for this state of affairs; it also explores the challenges of evaluating multicultural education programs fairly and thoroughly.

7

Cultural Diversity

1 How do culture and educational opportunities relate to one another?

.... | Perceive |

2 Why do some people strive to become part of an "American main-stream," however real or imagined, while others resist assimilation into such a group?

.... | Value |

3 What do the terms "culture," "ethnicity," and "race" mean?

.... | Know |

4 How might you use knowledge of cultures to teach tolerance of differences among students?

.... | Act |

5 How might you determine if attending to cultural influences in one's teaching makes any difference in how students think and behave?

.... | Evaluate |

WHAT IS THE LANGUAGE OF DIVERSITY?

What do people mean when they speak of the influence of "culture"? To what characteristics does one's "ethnicity" refer, and how is ethnicity different from one's "national origin," if at all? Is "race" a concept with many connotations or only those limited to physical characteristics? When educators mention "minorities," do they intend to refer only to the human attributes of race and ethnicity, or do they also mean gender, sexual orientation, disabilities, giftedness, and social class?

The language of diversity is perplexing because the concepts are defined largely in terms of variable attributes, not critical attributes. A variable attribute is a characteristic of a concept that may or may not be present for an example to be classified as a member of the concept class. For instance, horses can have long legs, a graceful presence, and they can run like the wind. But not all horses have these attributes, and not all animals with these characteristics are horses. The attributes of long legs, graceful presence, and speed, then, are said to be variable—they may be present in a member of the class of horses or they may not be. Although variable attributes do not provide clear and precise definitions, they do help people communicate.

In contrast, critical attributes—characteristics that must be present in order for an example to be classified as a member of the concept class—are much more difficult to define. People rely most often on phenotypes, or physical characteristics, as critical attributes to classify living things. If an animal looks like a horse and runs in races organized for horses, the animal is said to be a horse. Even critical attributes, however, can be elusive. It is not difficult to imagine that on some distant high plain in some remote part of the world there are people who look at horses and gazelles and see them as slight variations of the same animal they call a horse. They may even race them once a week on a day our society calls Saturday. Just as our culture has done, these people have constructed the meaning of the concept of horse.

There are some variable and a few more or less critical attributes used to define the bewildering array of terms that compose the language of human diversity.

Race

Race is defined most often by physical characteristics. People with the same or similar skin color can be classified as being members of the same race. For example, in the United States, if it is known or acknowledged that a person has African ancestry, he or she is classified by census takers as black. The terms *black*, *African American*, and *black American* are typically used interchangeably in common speech, but writers seem to be moving toward the use of African American (Banks & Banks, 1993; Nieto, 1992). In Puerto Rico, however, if a person has some African ancestry but looks completely Caucasian, that person would be considered white (Banks, 1993). One's racial classification is not typically chosen but instead assigned by others.

Ethnicity

The concept of **ethnicity** is used to refer to a group with a common tradition and a sense of identity that functions as a subgroup within the larger society. An ethnic group may have its own language, its own religion, and its own customs. These characteristics distinguish members of the ethnic group from other members of society (Theodorson & Theodorson, 1970).

The most important identifying characteristic of an ethnic group is the members' feelings of identification with the group (Banks, 1993). Because membership in an ethnic group is largely a matter of self-identification, people can cease their membership in the group—by speaking a new language, changing religion, or dropping old customs and adopting new ones.

Culture

Culture can be used in an inclusive or "macro" sense to refer to the sum of the learned characteristics of a people—language, religion, social mores, artistic expression, sexual behavior, etc. In some cases a culture may be tied to a geographical region, while in other cases a culture exists largely irre-spective of geography.

Culture can also be used in a "micro" sense to describe more conceptu-ally discrete groups of people—cultures within cultures, subcultures, or microcultures. Users of illegal drugs are said to be part of the "drug culture" or "drug subculture." Some people with hearing impairments choose to be part of the "Deaf culture." Some women consider themselves to be members of the "feminist culture."

> **To ignore or misunder-stand students' cultures is to risk teaching at cross-purposes with them.**

Culture is an important concept for educators to understand because it influences students' lives. Culture teaches; it shapes learners' identities, beliefs, and behaviors. Understanding students' cultures is a prerequisite to enlisting the force of culture as an instructional ally. To ignore or misunder-stand students' cultures is to risk teaching at cross-purposes with them. In recent years, social scientists have begun to explore critically the influence of culture in classrooms.

Educational and psychological research used to be conducted routinely on the American "mainstream"—the dominant ethnic and cultural group, typically composed of Anglo-Saxon Protestant males from middle or higher social classes. When results suggested certain educational approaches were more or less effective, these results were translated into educational materi-als and programs for all students, including females, African Americans, and others. These approaches, however, often worked better with Euro-pean-American males than with females, people of other racial groups, and students from different cultures. Now, instead of assuming research find-ings hold up across genders and cultural groups, researchers investigate how such differences among people affect learning and teaching.

Minority Status

The term *minority status* or *minority* carries both a quantitative, or statistical, meaning and a political connotation. Those groups or subgroups in society who are identifiably fewer in number than another group are said to be in the minority. This is a relative term, however. Nationally, African Amer-icans are a minority compared to European Americans. In some states and cities, however, African Americans constitute a majority of the population.

Minority is also used to describe perceptions of the relative political power or influence that a group exerts in society. For example, because women do not hold public office in the same proportion as their number in the population, women are said to be a minority, that is, they are perceived to exert less formal influence on the operation of government than do men. The term *minority*, then, is defined comparatively.

Some groups are minorities for more than one reason. Because the lan-guage of commerce, government, and education in the United States is English, and because most people speak English, those who do not speak English are members of language minority groups. They are fewer in number than the majority English-speaking culture, and they are perceived to exert less influence in society. It is important to note that minority status is not equivalent with concepts of social or socioeconomic status (SES).

WHAT ARE SOME IMPLICATIONS OF THE LANGUAGE OF DIVERSITY FOR SCHOOLS AND SOCIETY?

Three important facts emerge immediately from a dispassionate examination of terms such as *race*, *ethnicity*, and *culture*. First, as Webster observes, these classification systems are arbitrary—established capriciously or by convention, or left generally ill-defined. Moreover, people might, and indeed do, think of many other ways to classify people—by interests, by height, by weight, by religion, by knowledge, by income, and so on. Such classifications may or may not coincide with classifications of race, ethnicity, and culture.

Second, and often less apparent, there may be as much or more variation within a group as there is between or among groups. For example, Matute-Bianchi (1991) found that "Mexican-descent students" as a group are quite diverse in terms of their school performances. Thus the group requires more precise definition to explain the differences among students relevant to their educational achievement. Mexicans tend to perform relatively well in school and in many cases outperform nonimmigrant Mexican-American students. A simplistic classification scheme can mask important differences among people. When this happens teachers may be "pulled" to behave in ways that are consistent with that scheme but out of line with students' needs.

A nonschool example may help further illustrate the importance of within-group variation. Assume, for instance, a person is trying to sell a 1957 Chevrolet. She has studied photos of the crowds at concerts of the Beach Boys and identified a group of people she thinks might be potential buyers. She labels this group "European-American men about age 50" and intends to concentrate her advertising budget on this group.

Although she would be wise to be sensitive to everyone in the group— good sales technique and simple decency dictate as much—each man in the group may hold a markedly different opinion about the value of owning a 1957 Chevrolet. The salesperson's classification system reveals nothing about the strength of the individuals' desires to recapture lost youth, to buy Hondas, to risk financial loss for the pure pleasure of expressing one's deepest desires, and the like. There is, of course, also the possibility that concentrating her sales strategy on this group will cause her to overlook an affluent woman with a penchant for old Chevrolets. While the characteristics of the potential group of buyers has helped the salesperson shape her strategy, if she is insensitive to within-group variations, she may fail to reach her ultimate goal.

The third fact that emerges from a consideration of the language of diversity, as Brian Bullivant (1993) observes, is that people can define themselves, or others from outside the group can describe them. "The subgroups within a pluralist society can be distinguished by outsiders, or they can distinguish themselves because of the characteristics their members share" (p. 36). Different perspectives, not surprisingly, often yield dissimilar concepts. When people behave in accordance with their differing expectations, as people often do, misunderstanding and conflict can arise.

Even the process of self-definition, while seemingly a reasonable way out of the semantic maze, can be problematic. For example, census takers ask people to supply information about their race by designating themselves as (a) American Indian or Alaskan Native, (b) Asian or Pacific Islander, (c) black, (d) white, or (e) of Hispanic origin. The federal government defines "American Indian or Alaskan Native" as, "A person having origins in any of the original peoples of North America, and who maintains cultural identification through tribal affiliation or community recognition" (Office of Federal Statistical Policy and Standards, 1978, p. 37). People must define for themselves the meaning of "origins" and "maintains cultural identification. . . ."

One's origins or ancestry and one's identity, however, are not necessarily the same. People can have mixed origins but identify with only part of their ancestry. Alba (1990, p.61) points out that people of mixed Irish ancestry are three times more likely to call themselves Irish than they are some other part of their background. Among people of mixed English ancestry, the ratio is reversed. We can only wonder about the confusion of the Native American born to Native-American parents who no longer attends tribal meetings and lives far from a Native-American community as she or he responds to a census item about race.

Figure 7.1 shows the 1991 census data for Americans defined by race. Looking across the nation, much as a demographer might, yields a patchwork of racial, religious, and educational diversity. There is considerable variation of such factors within and between regions of the country.

The labels attached to people can be useful administrative devices—in the case of special education, for example, labeling schemes have made it possible to designate money for children who merit special support. The labels themselves, however, rarely imply how best to meet people's needs, they often tend to obscure more important characteristics, and they may rule in and out of consideration for preferred treatment some deserving people at the edges of the labels. Nieto (1992) suggests that one's choice of terms to describe people be based on (a) what people in question want to be called and (b) what is the most precise term.

At times, the language of diversity has created problems for schools. The general imprecision and carelessness in use of concepts of race, ethnicity, culture, minority status, and related terms have contributed to a sense of confusion among both adults and students. In some cases, this confusion has fueled prejudice—unfavorable attitudes toward a group without regard for the facts—and hardened stereotypes held by members of majority groups about members of minority groups, and vice versa.

Grouping and labeling, when done inappropriately, may also have fostered self-fulfilling prophecies for some students. For instance, if someone is designated "handicapped," he or she may become trapped in a downward

FIGURE 7.I

Population Distribution By Race and Region*

MIDWEST
Population: 59,668,632—24% of the nation

	Total	White	Black	Asian	Hispanic (of any race)
Region	100%	87%	10%	1%	3%
Nation	24%	26%	19%	11%	8%

Projected Minority H.S. graduates, 1995: 11.13%
Percent Completed 4 yrs. of H.S. or more, 1991: 80.8%
Percent of Population Church/Synagogue Members:

Nation: 69%
Region: 72%

NORTHEAST
Population: 50,809,229—20% of the nation

	Total	White	Black	Asian	Hispanic (of any race)
Region	100%	83%	11%	3%	7%
Nation	20%	21%	19%	18%	17%

Projected Minority H.S. graduates, 1995: 17.1%
Percent Completed 4 yrs. of H.S. or more, 1991: 80.4%
Percent of Population Church/Synagogue Members:

Nation: 69%
Region: 69%

WEST
Population: 52,786,082—21% of the nation

	Total	White	Black	Asian	Hispanic (of any race)
Region	100%	76%	5%	8%	19%
Nation	21%	20%	9%	56%	45%

Projected Minority H.S. graduates, 1995: 20.67%
Percent Completed 4 yrs. of H.S. or more, 1991: 80.1%
Percent of Population Church/Synagogue Members:

Nation: 69%
Region: 55%

SOUTH
Population: 85,445,930—34% of the nation

	Total	White	Black	Asian	Hispanic (of any race)
Region	100%	77%	19%	1%	8%
Nation	34%	33%	53%	15%	30%

Projected Minority H.S. graduates, 1995: 30.64%
Percent Completed 4 yrs. of H.S. or more, 1991: 74.4%
Percent of Population Church/Synagogue Members:

Nation: 69%
Region: 74%

Note. From *Educational Attainment in the U.S.* (pp. 77–79), *Census of Population and Housing* (p. 59), and *Statistical Abstract of the U.S.* (11th Ed.) (p. 55), all by U.S. Department of Commerce, Census Bureau, 1991, Washington, DC: Author. Also from *A Demographic Look at Tomorrow* (p. 4) by H.A. Hodgkinson, 1992, Washington, DC: Institute for Educational Leadership.
*Many of the tables and figures in this chapter are based on census data. Census Bureau data are self-reports. The term "white" denotes e.g., Canadians, Germans, Italians, Lebanese, Near-Easterners, Arabs. The term "black" denotes, e.g., African Americans, black Puerto Ricans, Jamaicans, Nigerians, West Indians, and Haitians.

spiral of decreasing self-esteem and diminishing performance. The difficulty may not be with the labels themselves, but with people's reactions to the labels (Hunt & Sullivan, 1974). A label sets up expectations in the minds of those who label and those who are labeled; behavior flows from these expectations.

It is **discrimination**—differential treatment associated with labels—that gives rise to conflict. People too often report and interpret information about groups as though all members conform to some mythical image of sameness, some average that, in turn, drives educational action. This tyranny of "average thinking" overwhelms good sense about the real people who are assigned to these groups. Understandably, when this happens individuals in the groups become offended.

HOW HAVE AMERICANS LEARNED TO LIVE WITH DIVERSITY?

As Chapters 2 and 3 suggest, Americans, like no other social experimenters in history, have cursed and tolerated and ignored and celebrated their diversity in virtually every way imaginable. As Table 7.1 indicates, when diversity is defined in racial terms, numbers only hint at the richness of our culture.

Thoughts about culture in the United States have been dominated by the metaphor of the melting pot. Immigrants, like ingredients, were to be added to the great cauldron (public education) and simmered over low-intensity educational fire until a perfectly blended soup was achieved in which characteristics of the individual ingredients disappeared.

TABLE 7.1   Race and Hispanic Origin for the United States: 1990

Are figures lower, higher, or about the same as you would have estimated?

United States	Number	Percent
Total Population	248,709,873	100
White	199,686,070	80.3
Black	29,986,060	12.1
American Indian, Eskimo, or Aleut	1,959,234	0.8
Asian or Pacific Islander (Chinese, Filipino, Japanese, Asian Indian, Korean, Vietnamese, Hawaiian, Samoan, Guamanian, and other Asian or Pacific Islander)	7,273,662	2.9
Other Race	9,804,847	3.9
*Hispanic Origin (Mexican, Puerto Rican, Cuban, and other Hispanic)	22,354,059	9.0

Note: Percentages total more than 100% due to rounding error and interaction of race (white and black) and Hispanic origin.
*Spanish origin and race are distinct; thus, persons of Spanish origin may be of any race.

Note. From *Census Bureau Releases 1990 Census Count on Specific Racial Groups*, CB91-215 (p. 4) by U.S. Department of Commerce, Census Bureau, 1991, Washington, DC: Author.

The melting pot metaphor has come under attack, however, by proponents of cultural pluralism, who call for the preservation, even celebration, of Americans' cultural diversity. In the pluralist salad bowl (or salsa) metaphor, people in all their crisp, colorful, tangy ways, while tossed together, retain their unique identities and essential differences.

Such metaphors can be useful devices for thinking about problems and potential solutions in creative ways and for communicating social ideals. But a metaphor can become a hindrance when it is used as a prescription for practice. Although public education has in fact educated the public in remarkable fashion, it has not completely met the demands of the melting pot, the salad bowl, or the mosaic, nor is it likely to do so anytime soon. Who Americans are as a people, and who Americans wish to become, are ideas too complex to be fully described by any metaphor. As a society, we seek a sense of **cultural pluralism**; that is, a state in which people of diverse ethnic, racial, religious, and social groups maintain autonomous participation within a common civilization.

> **In the pluralist salad bowl metaphor, people in all their crisp, colorful, tangy ways, while tossed together, retain their unique identities and essential differences.**

How then are educators to view our sprawling, complex society to perceive the talents and needs of the people? There is no fail safe plan, but the urgency to "decenter," to see and understand society from different points of view, is compelling. For the alternative is to be locked in an **ethnocentric** power struggle for the societal upper hand—a struggle based on the belief of the superiority of one's own ethnic group or culture.

The Roman poet and satirist Juvenal understood these simple truths well. For some unknown reason his experiences obliged him to push people to examine the world through others' eyes. He did so not as a revolutionary throwing caution to the wind, but judiciously as a man who feared he might offend the emperor and be tortured and killed for his impertinence. He might have looked the other way when he saw corruption and injustice, or he might simply have kept quiet. But after "staring furiously at all the vices and crimes of Rome" he could not stop himself from writing (Highet, 1954). Through the ages, scholars have recognized Juvenal as the master at viewing society from different perspectives. In doing so nearly 2,000 years ago, Juvenal raised his voice in a way that can still be heard today, reminding people to resist the complacency of defining life only from their own perspective. The following sections of this chapter apply Juvenal's framework for viewing society from different positions.

Viewing Society from a Position of Advantage

As Ernest Hemingway once observed, the very rich are different from the rest of society: they have more money. One implication of this observation is that were it not for what people can buy, it would be difficult to tell them apart. As Pierre Bourdieu and Jean Claude Passeron (1977) have suggested, however, that it is not simply one's affluence that is important, but how one's resources are invested. People often distinguish themselves by accumulating "cultural capital" much as they would purchase other assets such as real estate or stocks and bonds. Education can be a form of cultural capital.

Baltzell (1964) emphasized the importance of acquiring an appropriate college preparatory education for the solidarity of America's upper class. "Appropriate" he defined in terms of a group of 16 socially elite boarding schools on the East Coast: Phillips (Andover) Academy (Massachusetts), Phillips Exeter Academy (New Hampshire), St. Paul's School (New Hampshire), St. Mark's School (Massachusetts), Groton School (Massachusetts), St. George's School (Rhode Island), Kent School (Connecticut), Middlesex School (Massachusetts), Deerfield Academy (Massachusetts), The Lawrenceville School (New Jersey), The Hill School (Pennsylvania), The Episcopal High School (Virginia), and Woodberry Forest School (Virginia).

Carolyn Percell and Peter Cookson (1990) examined how this group of schools provided advantage to those who attended, noting in particular the later admission of their students to highly selective colleges. They concluded that, "Elite boarding schools are part of a larger process whereby more privileged members of society transmit their advantages to their children" (p. 41). Factors such as parental wealth, preference for children of alumni, advanced placement (AP) coursework, and ability in sports such as ice hockey, crew, or squash influence college admission in the Ivy League, and so too do social background, SATs, and attendance at one of the 16 schools. These factors combine so that "both individual ability and socially structured advantages operate in the school-college transition" (p. 41). Occasionally attendance at one of the 16 schools helps some low SES students with high SATs gain admission to highly selective colleges—a result of what Percell and Cookson call the "knighting effect."

Humorist Calvin Trillin (1983), with tongue in cheek, described a position of privilege as an incredible burden to bear, particularly as it is visited upon some little boys in school:

> Every American child—at least every male, white, Christian American child—is told that, this being the land of opportunity, he could grow up to be the President of the United States. What they don't tell him is that he doesn't have to be the President of the United States if he doesn't want to be. There are other respectable callings. It is obvious, in fact, that a young man who showed promise at being able to slice up an enzyme or put together an inspired clam chowder would be wasting his talents as President. The second-grade teacher never talks about that part of it. . . . (p. 91)

While some affluent private schools provide a view of society unseen by most, some in public education occasionally have an advantageous perspective themselves. Viadero (1991) described one such school in Kansas City, Missouri. Central High School has an Olympic-size swimming pool, an indoor amphitheater, a 42,000 square feet fieldhouse which will accommodate basketball and track practice at the same time, a six-lane, one-10th-mile indoor track, weight-training facilities, racquetball courts, and a gymnastics room with a spring floor exercise mat. A stadium across the street from the school will include four tennis courts, an outdoor track, and football, soccer, and rugby fields. The school also contains 1,000 networked computers, sophisticated electronics equipment, robotics facilities, and computer aided drafting programs. Governor John Ashcroft has called the building the Taj Mahal—a fact that has not escaped wary taxpayers.

Central is really two magnet schools under one roof—the nation's first classical Greek magnet school, designed for the scholar-athlete, and a computer science school. The Greek program requires students to take philosophy, Greek, and Latin, and 5 days a week of physical skills training. The computer program provides the equivalent of a major in computer science. Central High is the showpiece school in Kansas City's court-ordered effort to desegregate its schools.

Central High School was constructed on the site of the city's oldest and most difficult to desegregate school. Under federal order, school leaders are aggressively promoting the facilities and programs to recruit European-American students, and with some success. In 1987, every student in the school was African-American. As of 1993, 70% were African-American (W. Mahone, personal communication, January 8, 1993). Attending Central High may not be quite the same as looking down from Mount Olympus, but according to one teacher, students say, "this is a beautiful building, and they're wanting to come to school everyday" (Viadero, 1991, p. 7). What is unclear, however, is the degree to which this kind of support has made a difference in the lives of the children who attend Central.

While educational resources can enable some people to rise above the fray, others view life from atop their academic accomplishments. One function of public education has traditionally been to create such opportunities for young people, regardless of their origins. Some of these successful children may be "gifted" or be "at promise in any domain where intelligences figure" (Gardner, 1993, p.54). But others achieve with the assistance of powerful family support.

Viewing Society from Behind Barriers

There are many barriers in society that obscure one's vision of America. Some, like poverty, surround people. Others, such as prejudice, reside in people's minds and hearts and are as real as obstacles that can be seen and touched.

Barriers of Poverty   As Chapter 6, "Sociopolitical Dimensions of Education" noted, there is a basic link between poverty and learning. Low-income communities mean underfunded school districts and poorer schools on virtually every index of quality. High-poverty schools have diminished capacities to create educational opportunities for students. As Figure 7.2 indicates, students in high-poverty schools have test scores markedly lower than their counterparts in more affluent schools.

The concept of "family" when viewed from behind the barrier of poverty reveals some simple, powerful facts about children's cultures. Most

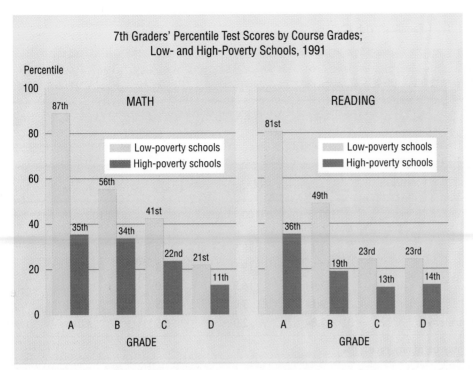

7th Graders' Percentile Test Scores by Course Grades; Low- and High-Poverty Schools, 1991

Note. From Exhibit 49: "Seventh Graders' Grades and Percentile Test Scores: Low- and High-Poverty Schools, 1991" by Abt Associates, 1993, *Reinventing Chapter 1: Final Report of the National Assessment of the Chapter 1 Program* (p. 199) Washington, DC: U.S. Department of Education.

FIGURE 7.2

Poverty and Performance

According to this graph, how does school poverty appear to relate to student academic achievement?

children will grow up knowing two parents. As Table 7.2 indicates, however, the percentage of children living in two-parent households varies greatly across different racial groups. Many single parents perform admirably, but the demands they must face can be formidable. Moreover, those parents most in need of child care are least likely to be able to afford it. In 1987, for example, families below poverty level spent 25% of their weekly income on child care, while more affluent families spent only 6.3% of their weekly income on child care (U.S. Department of Commerce, Census Bureau, 1991, p. 376).

Conditions of life for many low income families can be depressing. But these conditions are by no means characteristic for all minority group members. It has been estimated that some 36% of African-American families and 40% of Hispanic-American families have incomes of $25,000 or more (U.S. Department of Commerce, Census Bureau, 1991). There are many more European-American than minority group children in the United States living in poverty. Within minority groups, however, percentages of children from low-income families are higher. Socioeconomic status cuts across all group distinctions.

Generally speaking, the sooner a child starts school, the longer he or she stays, and the greater the financial reward in later life. (The positive relationship between education and earnings is described further in Chapter

TABLE 7.2   Household Data, 1991 Families With Children

Why might family configurations vary across racial groups?

Why might so few one-parent families be headed by fathers?

	All Races	White	Black	*Hispanic
Family groups with children under 18 years living with:	100	100	100	100
Two parents	71.1	78.5	35.9	66.3
One parent	25.5	19.5	57.5	29.8
Mother only	22.4	16.5	54.0	26.6
Father only	3.1	3.0	3.5	3.2
Other relatives or nonrelatives	2.8	2.0	6.5	4.0

*Persons of Hispanic origin may be of any race.

Note. From *Marital Status and Living Arrangement—Current Population Reports* (p. 8) by U.S. Department of Commerce, Census Bureau, 1991, Washington, DC: Author.

12.) The social conundrum inherent in this statement is that the more afflu-ent parents are, the sooner their children are likely to go to school, and the longer they are likely to stay in school. Table 7.3 demonstrates the disad-vantage minority group children face in this regard.

Looking from the wrong side of a line drawn to designate poverty, one can feel the despair of having to eke out a day to day existence. According to the federal government, the poverty line in 1990 for a family of two adults and two children was $13,360—a figure calculated as three times the cost of a diet that would meet minimum nutritional requirements, or $9.15 for food a day for each family member. That figure does not include other living expenses, such as housing, transportation, and health care.

If one manages to edge just across the poverty line, it is possible to see millions of others working for meager wages. These people, regardless of their ethnicity or race, are more alike, by virtue of work and worry, than they are different from one another. Harold Hodgkinson (1992) and others have argued that the most important differences among people are not racial or ethnic, but economic. The culture of poverty demands much from its members and does much to shape their outlook on the world:

Bernadette Green and her children, Chuckie, 15, and Crystal, 9, live in a run-down neighborhood in Baltimore. Chuckie goes to an academically exclusive public high school—a challenge and an honor, but he is strug-gling. Crystal is a happy, good student in the fourth grade—a member of the safety patrol. At age 36 Bernadette has never made more than $4.50 an hour. She was laid off about a year ago from her last job as a packer at a bagel shop. The three of them live on $280 a month, food stamps, and help from the children's father who lives nearby and just got laid off. Their third-floor room in a drug-infested neighborhood is a safe, clean haven from the world. (Asayesh, 1992, p. 17)

Caste Barriers   Anthropologist John Ogbu has offered a controversial theory on the differences between immigrant minority groups in the United States (Ogbu, 1991). He describes "castelike minorities," or involuntary nonimmigrant minorities, as people who live in the United States as a result of slavery, conquest, or colonization. Ogbu contends that involuntary minorities experience discrimination from the dominant European-American culture, but they also defeat themselves through feelings of inferiority.

When Ogbu and colleague Signithia Fordham studied bright African-American students in Washington, D.C., they found that the students did not live up to their potentials. Ogbu and Fordham explained this phenomenon in terms of the students' fears of being accused by their peers of "acting white"—speaking standard English; listening to certain radio stations; spending a lot of time in the library studying; going to museums, opera, and ballet; camping and hiking; doing volunteer work; and the like (Hill, 1990). Critics denounced the findings as blaming the victims for their failure.

TABLE 7.3   School Related Data, 1991

Although within-group variation is not apparent from these figures, why might such variations exist; that is, why might Hispanic Americans, for example, differ on these measures?

	*Total	White	Black	Hispanic
Percentage of 3- to 4-year-olds enrolled in pre-elementary school	36.5	40.3	31.4	21.0
Percentage of seventh graders 13 years old or older	29.7	25.5	40.7	40.0
**Status dropout rate	14.3	10.7	16.9	35.9
Percentage of 19- to 20-year-olds completing 12 or more years of school	81.4	87.0	72.5	55.4
Percentage of persons 18 years and over who completed 4 or more years of college	20.3	21.5	11.4	9.2

*Included in the total are individuals who are not Hispanic, white, or black; most of these individuals are Asian and some are American Indian.
**The status drop-out rate is the percentage of 19- to 20-year-olds who were neither high school graduates nor still enrolled in high school.

Note. From *The Condition of Education* (pp. 58, 162, 165) by the Office of Educational Research and Improvement, 1993, Washington, DC: U.S. Department of Education. Also from *The Digest of Education Statistics* (p. 290) by the Office of Educational Research and Improvement, 1993, Washington, DC: U.S. Department of Education.

Ogbu contends that immigrant minorities see education as a remarkable opportunity to get ahead, and they do not equate success in school with losing their culture. Their parents emphasize the value of education. Ogbu argues that as members of involuntary minorities, many African Americans see education as a "subtractive process" that forces them to lose their own cultural identity if they are to succeed.

Particularists create separate courses and programs to educate children about cultures so as to avoid "diluting" or "compromising" the strength of a particular culture. In Atlanta, Georgia, for example, nearly all schools and 80% of teachers are using "Afrocentric curricula" (Cooper, 1992). Definitions of such curricula vary. Afrocentric education often means learning more about Africans and African Americans in the making of our nation. It can also mean purging what is viewed as bias in books and curricula that are viewed as **Eurocentric** or that depict Europe as the cradle of Western culture. African-centered educators like Asa Hilliard may infuse academic material with cultural examples meant to build both knowledge and pride in students. Teachers may work with students to solve math problems in Swahili, read African folk tales, or teach African and African-American history. Making a specific minority culture the focus of a curriculum is not unique to African Americans. Native Americans and others, too, have given increased attention to their own cultures.

Cultural Awareness

Some 12,000 students nationwide now enroll in colleges controlled by Native-American tribes. About 90% of Native Americans who leave reservations for college drop out. But 35% who graduate from tribal colleges transfer to 4-year colleges.

Education, once viewed by many Native Americans as a means of cultural genocide, now builds Native-American pride. Besides general academic courses, tribal colleges offer traditional American Indian history, language, music and philosophy. "Lots of people here have viewed education as the white man's thing," says Janine Pease-Windy Boy, president, Little Big Horn College, which enrolls 300 students. "We've redefined what education is." (Kleinhuizen, 1991, p. 4D)

As we noted in Chapter 6, "Sociopolitical Dimensions of Education," among the more controversial examples of particularist multiculturalism have been the efforts to establish single-sex classrooms and single-sex schools or academies for African-American males. The Matthew A. Henson School in Baltimore, Maryland, formed a single-sex classroom in 1989 so that an African-American male teacher "could be a positive role model for black boys who may come from female-headed households and may know black men only as drug dealers and idlers on the street corners . . ." (Cooper, 1990). Attempts in Milwaukee, Wisconsin, and Detroit, Michigan, to start whole schools for African-American boys met with charges that they were throwbacks to the days of institutionalized racial segregation and sexual inequity.

Mary Hatwood Futrell, former president of the National Education Association, expressed grave reservations about the Baltimore experiment. "It's not simply black males. What about the other kids who aren't getting a quality education? I don't want black males to feel they have to be treated differently to get a quality education" (Cooper, 1990).

Language Barriers   Language can be a formidable barrier in American society. Interpreting life as a language-minority person might do is something most monolingual, English speaking Americans never contemplate. Relatively few monolingual English speakers ever find themselves in situations where someone else does not also speak English. But many students who are categorized as **Limited English Proficient (LEP)** or qualified for instruction in **English as a Second Language (ESL)** view life in American society from behind a language barrier.

When students who do not speak English receive special help, it usually comes in the form of **bilingual education**, or instruction in both English and their native language. Bilingual programs vary in the amount of support they provide. Some offer instruction to students in both English and their native language and culture as long as they are in school. Other programs help students make the transition from their native language to English by offering ongoing, intensive instruction in ESL. Yet other programs remove students from regular classes to receive special help in English or in reading in their native language. And some programs immerse non-English speaking students in English, sometimes providing an aide who speaks the native language, then place students in English-speaking classes.

Teachers of ESL generally try to adjust their instruction in various subject matters to students' levels of English proficiency (Schmidt, 1990). Few strategies for assimilating minority-group students into the American mainstream have been more controversial than bilingual education. Passing the federal Bilingual Education Act of 1968—Title VII of the Elementary and Secondary Education Act—which funded bilingual education programs, did not settle long-standing differences of opinion.

Some believe that teaching non-English-speaking children in their native language, the language they hear most at home, while easing them gradually into English, is the only reasonable way to move these children into the mainstream. Make them "competent in two languages" argues Raul Yzaguirre, director of the National Council of La Raza in Washington, D.C., an umbrella group of several hundred Hispanic organizations (Bernstein, 1990, p. 44). The most prominent concern of bilingual-education advocates is retention of cultural identity.

Others believe that teaching children in their native language is bad for them and bad for the country. They contend that bilingual programs hold children back by doing a substandard job of teaching children in either their native tongue or in English. "Bilingual education, they argue, is more likely to prepare minority children for careers in the local Taco Bell than for medical school or nuclear physics" (Bernstein, 1990, p. 44). There are strong historical trends that have linked public schools with the transmission of a common American culture (see chapters 2 and 3).

Proponents of bilingual-bicultural education advocate that students become equally proficient in both English and the language of the home. This view mirrors that of proponents of language study, who advocate that English-speaking students become equally proficient in at least one other language.

Claims for and against the efficacy of bilingual education are complicated by feelings of ethnic pride. Some Hispanic Americans, for example, argue that a "white, Anglo" education damages students' feelings of self-worth. Others worry that bilingual education emphasizes differences in language, thus pushing people further apart when they need to come together as Americans. It is important to recognize that European and Hispanic Americans can be found on both sides of the argument.

Independently of such disputes, schools often have great difficulty delivering bilingual services. There is a shortage of qualified bilingual teachers. Most are needed for Spanish/English, because most LEP students are Hispanic American. But increasingly, teachers are needed with combined skills in English and other languages. Fewer capable professionals mean higher chances for misdiagnosing learning problems as special education concerns and lower capacity for teaching students with language needs.

Culture is embedded in language and communication. People with hearing impairments have reminded the hearing community that systems of communication that are unspoken and unheard are also culture. People who identify themselves as members of the Deaf culture advocate the use of sign language rather than aids to entry to the hearing world. Some argue that mechanical hearing devices, particularly those that are surgically implanted, rob deaf people of their self-respect and their group identity. They would instead teach hearing-impaired children to communicate fully and happily by signing. Others spurn the legitimacy or value of a Deaf culture and would opt for any chance to help children be more like their hearing peers. Some discourage signing, advocate the use of technology to boost children's chances to hear, and encourage speech therapy for all children with hearing impairments.

> **"Sign language is my language. My eyes are my ears and my hands are my voice."**

Shannon Merryman, a 16-year-old hearing-impaired student from Bristol, Rhode Island, identifies with the Deaf culture. She challenged the Veterans of Foreign Wars to be allowed to enter their national Voice of Democracy speech contest. The contest requires students to submit audiotapes of their speeches on democratic themes, but Merryman's deafness makes her speech difficult to understand. She asked for the right to submit a videotape of herself making a speech in sign language, but the VFW thought that might give her an unfair advantage. Instead she was permitted to have an interpreter make an audiotape. "'Sign language is my language,' she said. 'My eyes are my ears and my hands are my voice'" (Viadero, 1992).

Barriers of Disabilities   The term **exceptional learners** is used to denote students who require special education and related services if they are to realize their full human potential (Hallahan & Kauffman, 1994). Within this group are gifted and talented students (individuals who excel in some way compared to a group of other children of the same age), and students with disabilities (individuals with physical, sensory, cognitive, emotional, or communication abilities that limit task performance). Both groups need educational support. Among those who have learning disabilities, certain issues trigger special concern. Lawrence Gorski (1992) asserts that society must regulate and fund accessible, inclusionary education in neighborhood schools, not segregated institutional environments isolated from children's nondisabled peers. He also points to the need for expanded job training and for decent job opportunities.

The 1975 Education for All Handicapped Children Act (Public Law 94-142) recognized the rights of students between the ages of 5 and 18 to **equal educational opportunity**, or access to resources, choices, and encouragement so they might achieve to their fullest potential. Education programs were to be fitted to students' individual needs and were to be carried out in the least restrictive environment. The 1990 **Individuals with Disabilities Education Act (IDEA)** amended Public Law 94-142 by changing the term *handicapped* to *with disabilities* and by extending a free and appropriate public education to every individual between 2 and 21 years of age, regardless of the nature or severity of his or her disability.

Some are quick to point out, however, that despite strong legislation, "special education students" still have not been included in processes of general education as fully or completely as they should be. Reformers propose to create a "new, inclusive system of education for all students" (NASBE Study Group on Special Education, 1992, p. 5). An inclusive system is meant to move beyond mainstreaming, which is the practice of educating exceptional learners in the regular classroom for as much time as possible.

To effect full inclusion of students with disabilities into general education classrooms, the National Association of State Boards of Education Study Group recommends three courses of action:

1. State boards of education must create a new belief system and vision for education in their states that includes ALL students. Once the vision is created, boards must provide leadership by clearly articulating goals for all students and then identifying the changes needed to meet those goals.
2. State boards should encourage and foster collaborative partnerships and joint training programs between general educators and special educators to encourage a greater capacity of both types of teachers to work with the diverse student population found in fully inclusive schools.
3. State boards, with state departments of education, should sever the link between funding, placement, and handicapping label. Funding requirements should not drive programming and placement decisions for students. (NASBE Study Group, 1992, p. 5)

As we shall discuss again in Chapter 8, **full inclusion**—teaching students with disabilities in regular classrooms throughout the day in their neighborhood schools—like busing to end racial segregation, is controversial. Experts in favor of full inclusion argue that present practices of special education do not work and are costly (Gartner & Lipsky, 1989). On the other side, experts argue that to restructure special education would threaten existing support for students with disabilities and would place an unbearable burden on an already overstressed general education system (Kauffman, 1990).

Over 4 million children ages 6 to 21 now receive educational services for a variety of disabilities. Almost half are classified as having specific learning disabilities. Other high incidence disabilities include speech or language impairments (22.9%), mental retardation (11.6%), and serious emotional disturbance (8.4%). Students with multiple disabilities, hearing and vision impairments, orthopedic impairments, or other health impairments account for only 6.7% of students with disabilities (U.S. Department of Education, 1993).

A large percentage of students with disabilities experiences mixed success in school and is significantly more likely to drop out of school than are students in the general population. Males, African Americans, and students from low-income families are particularly at risk for being categorized as having disabilities. Among all students with disabilities who left high school during the 1985–86 and 1986–87 school years, 32% dropped out, 56% graduated, 8% exceeded the school age limit, and 4% were expelled. Those who failed a course in their most recent school year were almost three times more likely to drop out of school than were students who had not failed a course. Students with certain kinds of disabilities who were enrolled in occupationally oriented vocational training had better attendance records and higher rates of school completion (U.S. Department of Education, 1992).

The Glass Ceiling   Some people are held down in society by an invisible barrier, a "glass ceiling," that limits opportunities to rise to the levels of excellence of which they are capable. This ceiling can be self-imposed, constructed by others, or some combination of both, but the effects are comparable. People who live under it are inhibited, restrained from being themselves.

The glass ceiling also serves to limit economic development and professional advancement. For instance, in many jobs and professions, women have traditionally been paid less than men even though they performed the same work. Also, women have had fewer opportunities to learn and progress in their work and thus have risen to positions of leadership in organizations less often than have men.

As we suggest in Chapters 8, 9, and 10, there have been many highly visible efforts to address issues of gender equity, but some efforts, such as the creation and maintenance of all-girl schools, are often less obvious. Susan Chira (1991) noted that Roman Catholic girls' high schools, particularly those in poor, inner-city neighborhoods, provide a kind of all-female academy that supports girls in their efforts to be themselves. Said one female student of Josephinum High School in Chicago, Illinois, "Here you can say whatever you want to say. . . . Because this is an all-girls' school, they promote leadership for women, which you don't see too often in the big world. They show you anything is possible" (Chira, 1991).

Viewing Society from Within

Who views society from within? Over the years, politicians have identified "middle Americans" as the bedrock of society—the people who make the system work, the people who are fully employed and who pay taxes on the money they earn. Traditionally, the majority of these people have been European Americans because most of the people in the nation have European roots; minority-group working populations, however, are growing at a much faster rate. The working people of the United States are the largest group of any in our country.

Middle Americans as a group are changing. Barbara Vobejda (1991) of the *Washington Post* described how life in a Kansas town has evolved in recent years with the arrival of many non-English-speaking immigrants eager for work in the local meatpacking industry.

> On the dusty streets outside the diner, their town has a new look and feel: Tornado warnings are posted in three languages, Vietnamese, Spanish and English. The police department is under pressure to hire Hispanics, and farmers look forward to the Asian dragon dance at the Cinco de Mayo parade. The old-timers can't pronounce the name of the new Vietnamese restaurant, Pho-Hoa, but they know they like No. 38 (barbecue pork and noodles). (p. A1)

This social restructuring, historically most constant and visible on the east and west coasts of the United States, is occurring throughout the country. When Al Kamen (1991) looked out at Lowell, Massachusetts, through the eyes of Cambodian refugees, he saw people working like those who had come before them to make the United States their home. From 1983 to 1991, the Cambodian population in Lowell grew from 150 families to more than 10,000 persons. Social services, jobs, and housing attracted the Cambodians to Lowell, and helped them get a start, but the two Buddhist temples and some 100 Cambodian-owned businesses formed the spiritual and economic center that kept them there.

Nathan Caplan, Marcella Choy, and John Whitmore (1991) described compellingly the combined power of cultural factors and education in their discussion of "the children of the boat people." In 1981, these researchers began studying Vietnamese, Chinese, and Laotian immigrants to the United States and found among the children "high levels of achievement at the very outset of their formal education in America" (p. 20). Even when they attended poor, inner-city schools, their standardized achievement test scores were uniformly high. Kindergarten teachers' anecdotal records showed that the children were eager to learn and took pleasure from their work even before they entered first grade.

Why were these children so successful? The researchers attributed success on scholastic and economic measures to three factors they called "culturally based values, family life-style, and opportunity" (p. 88). The refugee children most

Research shows that cultural values and family practices that strongly support education increase students' achievement motivation and academic success.

broadly successful are those who:

> (1) have the strongest respect for their past and its relevance to the present, that is, their cultural heritage; (2) are most willing to face the formidable challenge of seeking out new paths and means of adapting to the demands of different settings; and, having arrived stripped of belongings and lucky to be alive, (3) now are most desirous of physical well-being and freedom from danger." (p. 90)

Interestingly, while researchers usually find that the more children there are in a family the less successful are those children, in this study just the opposite was true. The more children in a family, the more successful they were.

Do Americans need to rethink the importance of the role of the family and culture in public education? Many people think so. Caplan and his colleagues advocate recognition of the potential of the family and its culture to foster many kinds of achievement in children. Columnist William Raspberry (1993) put it this way:

> Other equally important learning takes place outside the academic setting. Two of the most important lessons children can learn are that they matter and that they are counted on. Schools can reinforce these lessons, but they are best taught in real-life settings—by parents and neighbors who insist upon the privileges but who also assume the duties of membership in the community. (p. A4)

Some argue that as people, particularly immigrants, succeed, they move onward and upward, forgetting where they came from. "Those who migrate compete for jobs with those already standing in line, often causing resentment" (Ray, 1992). The 1992 annual Kappan poll of the nation's attitudes toward education suggests, however, that middle-class citizens are willing to increase their own taxes to improve public education—a visible sign they are willing to help those in society who need help as well as to help themselves (Elam, Rose, & Gallup, 1992).

Some who have a relatively comfortable place from which to watch life unfold fear that others less satisfied pose a threat to their economic security. This fear is long-standing, and it helped propel the development of the common school (see Chapter 2). The fear is often expressed in racial prejudice. A recent Gallup poll of 511 African Americans, however, challenged "the white myth" that African Americans blame everyone but themselves for their problems. Only one in four African Americans believed government should do a better job of addressing their problems. In contrast, two out of three thought life would improve if they tried harder to solve their communities' problems themselves, or bettered themselves and their families (Thornton, Whitman, and Friedman, 1992).

Viewing Society from Outside

Imagine standing on your porch on a chilly fall evening and peeking inside the house. The lights are on in the kitchen and somebody is cooking dinner. The fog on the inside of the glass says it is warm in there, and some people are laughing—they are involved in one of those not-too-terrible arguments about whose turn it is to set the table. How would it feel if the people inside said you did not belong in that house?

Those who view society from the outside include new immigrants. Some 2 million immigrant children enrolled in American schools in the 1980s—more than at any other time since the early years of this century.

"Don't let them see you cry."

New immigrants are concentrated in cities in California, New York, Florida, Texas, and Illinois. Lorraine McDonnell and Paul Hill (1993), a researcher for the RAND Corporation, has described how these newcomers are "teaching" educators about the need for changes in the schools. For example, many immigrant children have had no formal education but are the ages of sixth, seventh, and eighth graders in U.S. schools. These immigrant children are altering the familiar concept of "student" held by educators in these situations.

Because some people are segregated from society—isolated by formal and informal means—they feel frightened, alone, and yet defiant. Nine teenagers experienced these feelings in the fall of 1957, when they entered Central High School in Little Rock, Arkansas, accompanied by 22 troopers from the U.S. Army's 101st Airborne as 350 more surrounded the building. Hand-picked by the Board of Education, these young people put an end to the era of school segregation.

When one African-American girl showed up at Central High the first day of school alone, unaware that she and the other students were to have stayed home that day, she was met by a screaming mob of white supremacists. National Guardsmen with bayonets sent by the governor supposedly to protect people, turned her away from the school. The girl walked slowly to a bus stop where she sat on the bench with tears running down her cheeks. "A white woman who had viewed the scene with growing horror sat down next to her, put her arms around her, and said softly, 'Don't let them see you cry'" (Edwards and Polite, 1992, p.32).

People learned to steel themselves against the injustice of legalized segregation, but informal separation of the races proved also to be insidious and painful. Legally sanctioned segregation of the races ended in 1954 with *Brown v. the Board of Education*, but informal or de facto segregation continues to place some people outside the mainstream culture.

American culture teaches that almost anyone who has been excluded, for no matter what bizarre or repugnant reason, may work his or her way back into the larger society with the aid of education. Studs Terkel's (1992) description of C. P. Ellis, former Exalted Cyclops of the Durham, North Carolina, chapter of the Ku Klux Klan, demonstrates the kind of thinking that leads to racial prejudice and the ever-present potential for changing one's attitudes toward others.

Ellis told of growing up in abject poverty and quitting school in the eighth grade so he could go to work when his father died. The degrading poverty was fertile ground for hate, and hate is the grist for the Klan:

"I began to say there's somethin' wrong with this country. I really began to get bitter. I tried to find somebody. I began to blame it on black people. I had to hate somebody. Hatin' America is hard to do because you can't see it to hate it. You gotta have somethin' to look at to hate. [Laughs.] The natural person for me to hate would be black people, because my father before me was a member of the Klan. As far as he was concerned, it was the savior of the white people. It was the only organization that would take care of the white people. So I began to admire the Klan." (p. 272)

Through the years, Ellis grew to believe he and other people like him were being used as pawns by white businessmen. His confrontations with an African-American woman named Ann Atwater, and his eventual willingness to sit and talk with African Americans under the auspices of a federal program designed to solve racial problems in the schools, led gradually to a change of heart.

"One day, Ann and I just sat down and began to reflect. Ann said, 'My daughter came home cryin' every day. She said her teacher was makin' fun of her in front of the other kids.' I said, 'Boy, same thing happened to my kid. White liberal teacher was makin' fun of Tim Ellis's father, the Klansman, in front of other peoples. He came home cryin'.' At this point"—[He pauses, swallows hard, stifles a sob.]—"I begin to see, here we are, two people from the far ends of the fence, havin' identical problems, except her bein' black and me bein' white. From that moment on, I tell ya, that gal and I worked together good. I begin to love the girl, really." [He weeps.] (pp. 275–276)

WHAT IS MULTICULTURAL EDUCATION?

There is much confusion about the meaning of the term **multicultural education**, yet there is general agreement on some identifying attributes of the concept.

. . . there is an emerging consensus among specialists that multicultural education is a reform movement designed to bring about educational equity for all students, including those from different races, ethnic groups, social classes, exceptionality, and sexual orientations. We need to create a school environment that is equitable and just; then in our discussions and classrooms, honestly try to search for a balance of views, and present them as fairly as possible. (Banks, 1992, p. 21)

James Banks (1992) further characterizes the challenge as one of seeking common ground for all people without imposing the one on the many.

People on the margins must participate. We must validate their dreams and struggles, and they must participate in shaping the *unum*. So many blacks don't feel a part of this country, so many Hispanics, so many poor whites. Yet all of our fates are tied together. We talk about kids who are at risk, but I think we are all at risk if we don't create a society that is united within a framework of shared values, like democracy and equality. And that is what multicultural education is all about. It's really an education for freedom, freedom for all of us. (p. 23)

Christine Sleeter and Carl Grant (1993) have noted five general educational approaches to multicultural education, shown in Figure 7.3: (a) "teaching the culturally different" involves attempts to assimilate people into the cultural mainstream using transitional bridges in the regular school program; (b) "human relations" tries to help students of differing backgrounds understand and accept each other; (c) "single group studies"

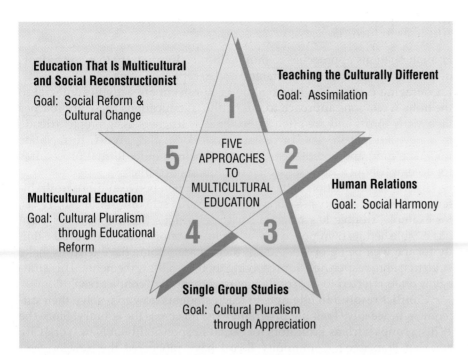

FIGURE 7.3

Five Approaches to Multicultural Education

Think of one clear example of each of the five approaches identified in this figure.

encourage cultural pluralism by concentrating on the appreciation of the contribution of individuals and groups; (d) "multicultural education" promotes pluralism by reforming whole educational programs—altering curricula, integrating staffs, and affirming family languages; and (e) "education that is multicultural and social reconstructionist" promotes active challenge of social inequality. We examine each general approach in turn below.

Teaching the Culturally Different

This approach involves attempts to assimilate people into the "cultural mainstream" using transitional bridges in the regular school program. These attempts may take the form of organizational or instructional changes in programs meant to accommodate culturally different or exceptional students.

For years, this was the preferred approach to multicultural education. As immigrants arrived in this country, they were placed in programs designed to transmit the knowledge, skills, and attitudes deemed appropriate for successful life in American society. As we note in Chapter 9 ("Curriculum"), such programs often made their goals explicit. For example, students were to learn to read and write English, to master American history, to adopt American social customs, and so on.

Programs and processes of teaching the culturally different, however, have also been characterized by their implicit demands. Teachers' expectations for appropriate behavior subtly pull students to behave in certain ways. Whether teachers realize it or not, they often act in ways that they believe will help students to become assimilated into society.

Human Relations

Human relations approaches to multicultural education try to help students of differing backgrounds understand and accept each other.

Encouraging cooperation and building self-esteem are activities integral to the human relations approach to multicultural education. These approaches take many forms and are often as informal as teachers assigning a "friend" to a new student in class or assigning work or play groups to facilitate understanding and acceptance. They also include quite formal procedures for accomplishing such goals as the resolution of conflict.

Interpersonal friction between students—often between those from different races and cultures—seems to plague some schools. In El Paso, Texas, for example, trouble has reached such proportions that the school system has established its own police force. While educators must take responsibility for the well-being of students in their charge, some have tried to make students more responsible for resolving their own disagreements. This strategy is often referred to as "conflict management" or "conflict resolution."

Conflict resolution attempts to teach students how to resolve their differences peaceably. Training programs exist all across the country. Since the 1970s, groups such as Educators for Social Responsibility in New York City and San Francisco's Community Board have pioneered the development and use of conflict resolution strategies with young people (Meek, 1992). In an interesting twist, at Cleveland High in California's San Fernando Valley, gang leaders are learning how to be peacemakers (National Education Association , 1993). Although program goals are the same, the means for teaching students to reach these goals can differ.

David and Roger Johnson, for example, advocate that teachers provide opportunities for students to practice skills involved in negotiating and mediating differences among themselves. The Johnsons' approach proceeds through three steps (Johnson, Johnson, Dudley, & Burnett, 1992). The first step involves negotiation. Here teachers try to "overteach" all students the skills for negotiating constructively. The intent is to keep these skills from being swamped by emotion when they will be most needed. Students learn to: (a) state what they want; (b) state how they feel; (c) state the reasons for their wants and feelings; (d) summarize their understanding of the other person's wants, feelings, and reasons; (e) invent three optional plans to resolve the conflict; and (f) choose one plan and shake hands.

The second step is to teach all students how to mediate the conflicts of their peers. This means asking students if they want to solve the problem, and not proceeding until both say yes. Then the mediator explains that: (a) mediation is voluntary, (b) the mediator will not try to decide who is right or wrong, only to help solve the problem, and (c) each party will have the right to air his or her side of the problem. The parties to the dispute must agree to solve the problem, not to call each other names, not to interrupt, to be as honest as possible, to abide by agreement if it is reached, and to keep confidential what is said in mediation.

In step three, the teacher chooses two official mediators each day, rotating the assignments throughout the class. Any conflicts students cannot resolve themselves are referred to the mediators. The Johnsons advocate booster sessions from time to time to ensure that the skills are a natural part of a student's social repertoire. Peacemaking in this fashion may just help young people learn to settle differences without resorting to violence.

The connection between legal action and education aimed at ending racial strife and promoting understanding has been forged with remarkable clarity by the Southern Poverty Law Center in Montgomery, Alabama. The Center publishes and distributes for free *Teaching Tolerance*, a magazine that describes resources and ideas "to help promote harmony in the classroom" (Southern Poverty Law Center, 1992, p. 4). Center staff led by Morris Dees are also at the front of the legal battle against hate groups.

Single-Group Studies

Single-group studies promote cultural pluralism by concentrating on individual and group contributions. They emphasize the importance of emulating the lives of outstanding people in various cultures. The intent is for young people to study the history of oppression, to feel proud of their heritage, and to recognize that human accomplishment transcends racial and cultural barriers.

Examples of individual and single-group contributions abound. The history curriculum could highlight the work of George Washington Carver, Sojourner Truth, Martin Luther King Jr., Malcolm X, and others, to name only African Americans. Social studies could highlight the influence of immigrant groups from Italy or Norway or Czechoslovakia.

Single-group approaches often address affective objectives (objectives aimed at influencing feelings, attitudes, or values), fostering appreciation and respect for other ways of life or sometimes promoting the value of cultural relativism. In the simplest or most traditional approaches, students present or participate in activities that feature ethnic foods, dress, and customs. Sometimes single-group studies emphasize differences among groups to the extent that pluralism is celebrated over unity. Some curriculum reformers, for example, have taken a centrist, separatist, or particularist tack by emphasizing each of the primary ethnic/racial groups in America in separate courses. Others have advocated pluralist or infusion approaches by integrating information on these groups into all courses at all grade levels (Quality Education for Minorities Network, 1991).

These single-group or single-case strategies try to reform educational programs. They do so by revising curricula, integrating school staffs, and acknowledging the importance of family languages. Sometimes, however, they do so in radically different ways.

Multicultural Education

Multicultural approaches aim to reform education by revising curricula, integrating school staffs, and acknowledging the importance of family languages.

Robert Moses, for example, concentrates on transmitting the academic skills young people need to open society's doors. Moses, a civil rights activist and leader in Mississippi in the 1960s, has returned to the Delta to teach algebra to African-American students. "It's our version of Civil Rights

1992," Moses says (Jetter, 1993). Founded more than 10 years ago, the Algebra Project has touched some 9,000 children from coast to coast. Moses believes that, without mathematics literacy, children will be forced to relive the lives of sharecroppers and serfs.

Moses teaches by drawing on examples from people's everyday lives. For instance, he may teach the often mysterious concept of ratios to students by contrasting rhythms of African drumbeats or having students construct their own recipes. Or he may teach the concept of negative numbers by riding a make-believe subway and labeling the stops on the line—Kleinfeld (1995) calls this the "A Train approach" to teaching mathematics after the A train on the New York subway. Moses also gets students to talk about experiences that illustrate mathematical concepts.

The A Train approach is appropriate for classrooms containing any mix of ethnic groups. The basic method, drawing on children's background knowledge, incorporating it into the curriculum, and creating concrete experiences for students to think about, is universal (Kleinfeld, 1995).

Education that is Multicultural and Social Reconstructionist

This general approach to educate for diversity actively challenges social inequality and seeks to restructure educational institutions for the ultimate purpose of changing society.

Marva Collins is a successful African-American teacher and administrator often held up as an example to others in single-case approaches to multicultural education. Her educational approach, however, is an example of education that is multicultural and social reconstructionist. Collins, an articulate spokesperson for her own private school, has put intellectual rigor at the top of her list of priorities.

> Many attribute Ms. Collins' success to factors typically associated with effective teaching, such as high expectations for the students, high rates of time on task, and active teaching behaviors. . . . [U]nderlying this success is Ms. Collins' ability to establish cultural congruence between teaching activities and the experiences of the students at home and in their communities. (Villegas, 1991)

Marva Collins's classroom is organized like a traditional African family, in which the members cooperate with one another, assume collective responsibility for their actions, and are governed by strong adult leadership (Hollins, 1982). Students cooperate instead of compete with each other as in many American public school classrooms. Collins takes charge of curriculum and teaching, but students function autonomously within the structure she provides, knowing the potential consequences of their actions.

Ana Maria Villegas (1991) contends that Collins links home and school through the use of interaction patterns found in the African-American church. She promotes choral and responsive reading, audience participation, the use of analogies, and the derivation of morals from readings. In so doing, she fosters what might be characterized as "culturally responsive pedagogy."

Robert Moses's culturally responsive instructional methods are characteristic of public education that is multicultural.

Marva Collins's special curriculum and Afrocentric school illustrate education that is multicultural and social reconstructionist.

In many ways, the most radical social reconstructionist move to promote multicultural education has been forced busing of children to end racial segregation in the pubic schools. With *Brown v. the Board of Education* in 1954 came the legal dictum that separate education could never be equal education. Busing children became the mechanism for ending segregated schooling.

Brown did not automatically end segregation or immediately result in massive busing. In Richmond, Virginia, for example, busing did not begin until 1970. From 1954 to 1989, the Richmond public schools went from 57% European-American students to 88% African-American students (Pratt, 1992). Busing plans have been and continue to be formulated today. Philadelphia has only recently ordered more busing to desegregate schools.

The final chapter on busing has yet to be written. Through the years, court-ordered busing plans have signaled the nation's moral resolve to end de jure and de facto segregation. At the same time, many European Americans have fled city schools, or the targets of busing efforts, for the suburbs. Others have moved their children from public to private schools. One thing is clear: busing alone will not solve the problems of racial division that exist in America.

Racial segregation also continues in higher education. In late December 1992, the U.S. District Court ruled that Louisiana can no longer operate separate all-African-American state colleges. When Judge Charles Schwartz ordered the state to merge its traditionally African- and European-American colleges, he argued that the concept of "separate but equal, . . . is an anachronism that our society no longer tolerates" (Marshall, 1992).

WHY IS MULTICULTURAL EDUCATION SO CONTROVERSIAL?

The debate about multicultural education is neither new nor faddish. It is part of the larger, continuing dialogue about the meaning of *e pluribus unum*. As one country composed of many states and many peoples, the nation continues to struggle to define itself. How is America to conceptualize and deliver a public education that is appropriate for all its people? This question arises in many forms and many languages in political forums, churches, social organizations, and schools across the country.

> **The debate about multicultural education is neither new nor faddish. It is part of the larger, continuing dialogue about the meaning of *e pluribus unum*.**

One of the more visible and controversial attempts to alter whole programs has been undertaken by the State of New York. The New York State Social Studies Review and Development Committee (1991) was charged by the New York Commissioner of Education to develop criteria for review of the social studies curriculum, to examine curriculum models showing special promise, and to assess existing syllabi for effectiveness and recommend changes in content, form, or emphasis. Once this was accomplished, the committee was to assist the state education department in the development of changes in syllabi, instructional materials, and staff development.

Upon review, the committee found the syllabi ". . . to contain insensitive language, to draw upon too narrow a range of culturally diverse contexts, and to omit content specific to some groups and areas of the world . . ." (p. 7). They advocated what amounted to a complete overhaul of the social studies curriculum to remedy what they viewed as a series of related needs. These included needs for multiple perspectives; for understanding indigenous social, political, economic, and technological structures and the precolonial histories of indigenous peoples; for viewing effects as bidirectional instead of unidirectional (with the European participants as the actors); for eliminating language insensitivity; for expanding the range of examples used in teaching; and for encouraging educationally appropriate assessment.

Some committee members dissented vigorously with the overall report, characterizing it as divisive. Kenneth Jackson, for example, conceded that all cultures may well be created equal in the abstract, but argued that, "Within any single country, one culture must be accepted as the standard" (p. 81). Arthur Schlesinger (1991) maintained that the republic had survived and grown because of the balance between our differences and our common interests; here, however, he perceived an overemphasis on the *pluribus* at the expense of the *unum*, with the *unum* defined largely in terms of our European antecedents.

Cultural Awareness

Education news headlines feature debates about the limits of multiculturalism. New York's Rainbow curriculum is a case in point.

> Community school board in New York City has rejected a curriculum guide designed to teach 1st graders respect for homosexuals. The board of Community School District 24, which serves 27,000 students in Queens, voted recently to ban the use of "Children of the Rainbow," a 432-page guide that includes a two-page section urging teachers to be aware of the growing number of children raised by homosexual couples. ("Across the Nation," 1992, p. 3)
>
> New York City Schools Chancellor Joseph Fernandez . . . suspended a Queens school board because of its refusal to adopt a multicultural curriculum. . . . The suspension is the result of "seven months of rancorous opposition" (from the board) to "Children of the Rainbow.". . . Mary Cummins [board president] "reiterated her belief that Mr. Fernandez was forcing views on homosexuality on the district under the guise of multicultural education." . . . "I will not demean our legitimate minorities, such as blacks, Hispanics and Asians, by lumping them together with homosexuals in that curriculum." (Myers, 1992, p. 12)
>
> Fernandez's conflict with the Board of Education and local community and parent groups led to a request by the board that he resign. Fernandez honored the request.

One particularly controversial innovation in the New York City system was the establishment of the Harvey Milk School in 1985—the first and only high school so far for gay and lesbian youth. The school is jointly funded by the board of education and the Hetrick-Martin Institute, a nonprofit organization offering counseling and other services to homosexual youth. Named for Harvey Milk, the gay San Francisco supervisor murdered in 1978, the school is fully accredited and run through the board's Alternative High Schools and Programs division (Green, 1991). The school is meant to provide an environment that is free from violence where gay and lesbian youth can work and learn with adults and peers who will not judge them by their sexual orientation.

Initiatives like the Harvey Milk School have been perceived by some people as responses to narrow and partisan interests in society. African-American historian Shelby Steele (1990) argues that a power base, a "new sovereignty," has been organized around the grievances of some interest groups. In higher education, for example, according to Steele, African Americans, women, Hispanic Americans, Native Americans, Asian Americans, gays, and lesbians press their agendas as "victims" of a racist,

VOICES

On Passion

Passions underlying the debate about culture in our nation can be volatile and dangerous; at the same time, they can stimulate genuine human understanding where little or none has existed before. If passion can ever be said to be proper, philosopher Maxine Greene of Teachers College, Columbia University, reaffirms its correct place in the dialogue about American cultural diversity.

There have always been newcomers in this country; there have always been strangers. There have always been young persons in our classrooms we did not, could not see or hear. In recent years, however, invisibility has been refused on many sides. Old silences have been shattered; long-repressed voices are making themselves heard. Yes, we are in search of what John Dewey called "The Great Community"; but, at once, we are challenged as never before to confront plurality and multiplicity. Unable to deny or obscure the facts of pluralism, we are asked to choose ourselves with respect to unimaginable diversities. To speak of passions in such a context is not to refer to the strong feelings aroused by what strikes many as a confusion and a cacophony. Rather, it is to have in mind the central sphere for the operation of the passions: "the realm of face-to-face relationships." It seems clear that the more continuous and authentic personal encounters can be, the less likely it will be for categorizing and distancing to take place. People are less likely to be treated instrumentally, to be made "other" by those around.

No one can predict precisely the common world of possibility, nor can we absolutely justify one kind of community over another. Many of us, however, for all the tensions and disagreements around us, would reaffirm the value of principles like justice and equality and freedom and commitment to human rights; since, without these, we cannot even argue for the decency of welcoming. Only if more and more persons incarnate such principles, we might say, and choose to live by them and engage in dialogue in accord with them, are we likely to bring about a democratic pluralism and not fly apart in violence and disorder. Unable to provide an objective ground for such hopes and claims, all we can do is speak with others as eloquently and passionately as we can about justice and caring and love and trust.

We want our classrooms to be just and caring, full of various conceptions of the good. We want them to be articulate, with the dialogue involving as many persons as possible, opening to one another, opening to the world. And we want them to be concerned for one another, as we learn to be concerned for them. We want them to achieve friendships among one another, as each one moves to a heightened sense of craft and wide-awakeness, to a renewed consciousness of worth and possibility.

CRITICAL THINKING

Why might people who interact face to face continually and in authentic ways be less likely to categorize one another and to hold each other at a psychological distance? How might we use information we acquire about others not to understand them but to construct conceptions of whom we believe them to be?

Source: Reprinted from *Freedom's Plow: Teaching in the Multicultural Classroom* (1993), by permission of the publisher, Routledge, New York.

sexist, homophobic society to their own and to others' detriment. Separate dormitories, preferential admissions, campus study centers, fiscal aid policies, and faculty hiring quotas, Steele argues, make people concentrate on attributes such as skin color or sexual orientation first, before they take stock of the content of their own or others' characters.

Diane Ravitch, assistant secretary of education under President George Bush, worried about the kind of separatism Steele described occurring in elementary and secondary schools:

> If educators see multi-culturalism as a way to teach victims' history, then it will become a tool to stir racial hatred. In victims' history, children are taught to identify psychologically with their ancestors and to hate those who are the descendants of their oppressors. (Ravitch, 1990)

While those for and against multicultural education wage rhetorical war, some have opined that "multiculturalism" is a "middle-class movement" that is largely irrelevant to life in inner-city schools. According to these opponents, the middle class and privileged have the luxury to consider such issues because they do not have to suffer the indignities of a life unprotected by money: ". . . [A]dvocates who put their faith for saving the schools in a multicultural social studies program are as mistaken as those who think multiculturalism means the end of Western Civilization. . . . What most teachers need, more than workshops on diversity, are basic supplies— glue, paper, crayons" (Mosle, 1993). And so goes the debate, often with little regard for the many ways multicultural education is defined in practice.

HOW MIGHT MULTICULTURAL PROGRAMS BE FAIRLY EVALUATED?

Multicultural education, however it is defined, is subject to the same assessment questions that any educational approach must answer: What does it cost? That is, what human and material resources are devoted to multicultural education efforts? What happens during the conduct of educational activities? And what are the outcomes of multicultural efforts?

Answers to these questions are judged acceptable or unacceptable by comparing them to program claims, to some other competing program, and/or to some standards that describe what might be expected of any educational program. Useless answers come in response to the inappropriate question, "Is multicultural education effective?" Useful answers about the overall worth of multicultural education, those that can be fairly judged, come in response to the appropriate question, "Are multicultural programs effective compared to other programs and compared to the goals they were designed to achieve?"

It is common to rely on standardized test scores to judge educational programs, and through the years, minority-group students have not fared so well on such tests as have majority-group students. There has, however, been considerable within-group variation, and overall, the scores of

TABLE 7.4   Changes in SAT Scores, by Racial/Ethnic Group

Which two groups showed the greatest improvement in SAT scores between 1975 and 1991?

SAT composite (verbal and math) scores			
Group	1975	1991	Point difference
African Americans	686	737	+51
Native Americans	808	837	+29
Asian Americans	932	945	+13
Mexican Americans	781	797	+16
Puerto Ricans	765	772	+7
Whites	944	933	−11
All students	903	899	−4

Note. From *Digest of Education Statistics* (29th ed.) (p. 126) by National Center for Education Statistics, U.S. Department of Education, Office of Educational Research and Improvement, 1993, Washington, DC: Author.

members of minority groups have increased. As Table 7.4 indicates, members of minority groups have begun to capitalize on educational opportunities in ways many had not in the past. And their continued participation is key to learning.

There are many other outcomes, however, that could usefully be examined to judge the efficacy of multicultural programs. These may or may not be as conveniently and inexpensively acquired as test scores, and they can be extremely useful. For example, high quality paper-and-pencil measures of student satisfaction with programs and with school generally can be obtained and tracked over time. These can be supplemented with interviews of students, parents, and staff to determine what they do and do not like about multicultural offerings. One could also examine figures on school attendance, dropouts, and participation in extracurricular activities to infer program efficacy.

Evaluation reveals the educational and social significance of the debate about multicultural approaches. For the issues with which it deals are central to the mission of public education. Evaluation has forced educators to reconsider what constitutes a proper mix of educational means and ends. If educators equalize the means for all students to achieve, they seem forced to accept inevitable differences in outcomes; that is, students with greater needs require more support to perform satisfactorily. If, however,

BENCHMARKS

Peak Immigration of Selected Groups as Sources of American Cultural Diversity

Precolonial Period	Native Americans
Colonial Era & Early Republic	Spanish, French, English, Dutch, Portuguese, African slaves
1800–1860	Germans, Irish, African slaves, English, Swedes, Danes, Norwegians, Dutch, Belgians, Swiss, French. Peak immigration of people from western and northern Europe. 1 million Irish immigrate to the United States between 1847 and 1860. In 1854, Germans composed 50% of all immigrants
1860–1880	Chinese, Poles, Russians, Hungarians, Serbs, Austrians, Scandinavians, Italians, Greeks, Canadians. By 1880, 4 of 5 New Yorkers are foreign born or first generation American.
1880–1900	Japanese, Italians, Poles, Russians, Slovaks, Magyars, Czechs, Croats, Greeks. 4.5 million Italians and 4 million Russians and Poles immigrate to the United States between 1880 and 1900.
1900–1930	Mexicans, Latin Americans, Canadians, Italians, Russians, Poles. Period of peak immigration from eastern and southern Europe. Puerto Ricans become U.S. citizens in 1917.
1930–1960	Cubans, Mexicans, Koreans. Period of peak relocation of Puerto Ricans. In the 1940s and 1950s, 3.5 million refugees come to the United States from all countries affected by World War II.
1960–1990	Vietnamese, Cambodians, Laotians, Thais, Central Americans, Haitians.

educators provide different levels of support to students to encourage parity in outcomes, educators risk offending students and parents who get less; this is especially troubling when resources are limited. The intellectual and practical challenge facing evaluators is to find some reasonable middle ground.

Multicultural education forces a reconsideration of the place of the individual in society. Like no other educational movement in recent times, multicultural education promises to stimulate a reexamination of the American social contract. As Thomas Jefferson wrote in the Declaration of Independence, "We hold these truths to be self-evident; that all . . . [people] are created equal; that they are endowed by their creator with certain unalienable rights; that among these are life, liberty and the pursuit of happiness."

SUMMARY

1. The language of diversity is characterized by terms, such as *race, ethnicity, culture,* and *minority status,* that are often defined ambiguously.

2. There can be as much variation among members of groups as there is variation between groups.

3. Cultural groups can be formed voluntarily and involuntarily. Labels can be useful devices for assigning educational services to certain groups of learners. Labels can be harmful devices when they fuel discrimination and negative, self-fulfilling prophecies.

4. Various metaphors have been used to explore conceptions of culture in America—the melting pot, the salad bowl, and the mosaic. Through the years, each has been both educative and limiting in its own way.

5. The perspective from which one views American society—from a position of advantage, from behind barriers, from within, from outside—can influence one's perceptions of society and of oneself. "Decentering," or viewing society from multiple perspectives, encourages people to consider their own position in relation to others and to society as a whole.

6. There is much confusion about the meaning of multicultural education, yet there is emerging consensus among specialists that multicultural education is a reform movement designed to bring about educational equity for all students from different races, ethnic groups, social classes, abilities, and sexual orientations.

7. Multicultural educational approaches have been defined in action in five ways: (a) teaching the culturally different; (b) human relations; (c) single-group studies; (d) multicultural education; and (e) education that is multicultural and social reconstructionist.

8. Multicultural education is controversial because people disagree on both the means by which students will be educated and the ends toward which students will strive.

9. Multicultural educational approaches have encouraged reconsideration of *e pluribus unum.* These approaches will be judged as are all other educational approaches—by comparison to their goals and to other programs on dimensions of input, process, and outcomes. Outcomes of interest will include both formal and informal measures, such as test scores, surveys of attitudes, and measures of participation in school activities.

TERMS AND CONCEPTS

bilingual education
conflict resolution
cultural pluralism
culture
discrimination
English as a Second
  Language (ESL)
equal educational
  opportunity

ethnicity
ethnocentrism
Eurocentric
exceptional learners
full inclusion
Individuals with
  Disabilities Act
  (IDEA)

Limited English
  Proficient (LEP)
mainstreaming
minority status
multicultural education
race

STUDENT ACTIVITIES

Perceive and Value

Hopelessness breeds frustration and despair. As the nation learned, an incident like the beating of African-American motorist Rodney King in Los Angeles by European-American policemen can serve as a catalyst for widespread violence.

Following the riots, the *Los Angeles Times* ran its own poll, asking people how they thought the city should begin the healing process. Interestingly, the two most unpopular courses of action were "more government financial aid" and "crackdown on gangs, drugs, and lawlessness." The most popular action was to "renew efforts among groups to communicate [with] and understand each other" (Thornton, Whitman, and Friedman, 1992, p. 41).

What central issues or problems may have stimulated people to identify a renewal of communication as a preferred action?

Know and Act

What aspects of multicultural education and bilingual education are issues in your state? What is your position on these issues? In a teaching context, what strategies or approaches discussed in this chapter might you use to promote social harmony and the acceptance of people's differences?

Evaluate

In what ways does your teacher education program prepare you to teach in culturally diverse schools? How might you determine if such preparation makes any difference in how teachers think and behave?

Discover

How do you define yourself in terms of the categories of diversity discussed in this chapter? Make a list of characteristics and groups you identify with that are part of your social and cultural identity. Then interview classmates to learn others' self-definitions of membership in various racial, ethnic, religious, cultural, or other groups. From this investigation, what conclusions can you draw about the language of diversity in American life?

Foundations

In Action

"I try to capitalize on students' experiences, so new material will connect to what they already know."

How teachers deal with issues of diversity varies considerably from school to school. How do the teachers in these cases try to take advantage of opportunities to reinforce positive attitudes about cultural diversity? How can knowledge of the students, knowledge of the curriculum, and planning skills help teachers successfully integrate multicultural approaches into the fabric of classroom life?

During a typical day, Mary Anne Reed-Brown teaches some classes that are heterogeneous and others that are homogeneous with respect to students' cultural backgrounds. She tries to encourage students to share their backgrounds in class by using different techniques. In one social studies lesson, Reed-Brown asks students to compare an Egyptian folktale to other folktales they have heard:

Reed-Brown: What story have you heard that you can relate to the folktale I just read to you?

Nhung: I know a Vietnamese story about how the world was made. There was a dragon that married an angel. They had 100 children, half boy, half girl so that's how . . . (student recounts folktale to the other class members).

Reed-Brown: That was a Vietnamese folktale? Okay. Any others?

After I read several folktales, I selected one that complemented what we were studying in social studies. I wanted to determine what my students would learn from the folktale that might relate to our study of Egypt.

Because we are team teaching, I teach social studies to both fifth grade classes, and my team-mate teaches all the science. My homeroom class is predominantly Hispanic. The other fifth grade class is more diverse culturally. In both social studies sections I try to capitalize on students' experiences, so new material will connect to what they already know. Today when I asked who had heard a story similar to the Egyptian legend I read to them, I hoped to solicit many different kinds of stories.

"If something is different . . ., does it make it bad?"

Sue Neeser teaches fourth graders about cultural diversity at Hans Christian Andersen School in Minneapolis, Minnesota.

Laura Saatzer announces a change in the lunch menu. The special menu was planned by a resource team of which Saatzer was not a member. The team wanted to expose students to Southeast-Asian culture by serving special foods in the cafeteria.

Saatzer: We're going to be having a Southeast-Asian lunch today. You will have cabbage soup with ham, stir fry, white rice, corn pudding, and tangerine and milk. Now, I see a lot of you making faces. If something is different from what you usually eat, does that make it bad?

Students: No.

Crystal: No, because if you taste something new, you might like it.

Andy: I ate that stuff, that food, when we had that program for parents and stuff and it's good. I ate it.

Saatzer: Right. Those of you who came to the PTA dinner in the fall will remember that parents from different cultures brought food for the pot luck supper. I admit I was a little nervous about eating some of the food, but it was very good, very good.

I did not learn about the Southeast-Asian lunch until just before we were to leave for the cafeteria. If I had had more time to prepare, we might have done some brainstorming to identify ethnic foods we typically eat. My lack of prior knowledge about the special lunch left me unprepared, and the discussion just didn't click for me.

Sue Neeser asks students what the blue color on maps and globes represents. The class names some of the different bodies of water on the globe at the front of the classroom. Then Neeser gives students balloons, magic markers, and maps to create their own "globes." Neeser suggests that cultural studies are not unique to American schools. She tries to broaden students' view of culture by exposing them to ideas about life around the world.

Our team has taught with a thematic approach this year. We have tried to cover many areas of the curriculum: conservation of natural resources, water use around the world, differences and similarities among indigenous cultures, racial characteristics, land forms, to mention but a few. I have tried to integrate content all year long. For example, when we read a story from China, I point out China on the map. We discuss values and knowledge in Chinese culture in relation to values and knowledge in our cultures.

Children's self-esteem is important. I try to remember this fact when I teach about cultural diversity and about disability awareness issues. One of my goals is to build on the idea that each of us is unique. This idea is central to a harmonious society. I want students to learn that being unique or different from someone else is acceptable—our uniqueness is something to celebrate.

283

It takes more than ideas, enthusiasm, and love of children to be a successful educator. To create educational environments that work, teachers need to understand young people in ways that inform teaching. This means teachers must study students—read about, think about, and discuss what others have written about students, and perhaps most important, listen to the students themselves.

In Chapters 6 and 7, the types of problems students face and the influence of culture on their lives have been considered. This chapter focuses on ways students are alike and different. Specifically, students are described in terms of intelligence, cognitive development and academic achievement, moral development, physical development, and "habits of mind"—the shared skills, attitudes, and values transmitted by custom or convention from one generation to the next.

Each person is unique yet like all others in many ways. Successful teachers understand this maxim and try to learn as much as they can about their students. If teachers want students to make sense of the world around them, to begin to construct knowledge for themselves as they are compelled to do in life, they must try to understand the needs of students both generally and individually. Students often suggest, in their own voices, how teachers can be most helpful.

8

Students

and

Learning

PROFESSIONAL PRACTICE QUESTIONS

1 Learners can be described in many terms. If you listened as a group of eighth graders described themselves as learners, what do you think they would say?

Perceive

2 Why do experts believe "intelligence" is an important factor to consider when making judgments about how a person will do in school and on the job? If there is so much disagreement about the definition of intelligence and the use of test scores, why do people continue to rely so heavily on measurements of intelligence to predict success?

Value

3 What do students know about intelligence, moral development, and habits of mind that could influence how teachers teach?

Know

4 If you were charged with the responsibility of reporting to parents about the utility of describing students in terms of their intelligence or their moral reasoning abilities, what would you say and why?

Act

5 If you were observing a math lesson, how might you decide if instruction was well matched with students' learning capabilities?

Evaluate

HOW DO STUDENTS' INTELLECTUAL ABILITIES INFLUENCE LEARNING AND TEACHING?

As Figure 8.1 shows, intelligence is one of several characteristics of students as learners. An analysis by Robert Sternberg and Douglas Detterman (1986) of 24 descriptions of intelligence by leading experts in the field suggests that there are competing ideas about the nature of intelligence. Among other things, intelligence has been defined as a hypothetical construct, a unitary trait, a multidimensional trait that varies from time to time and from situa-

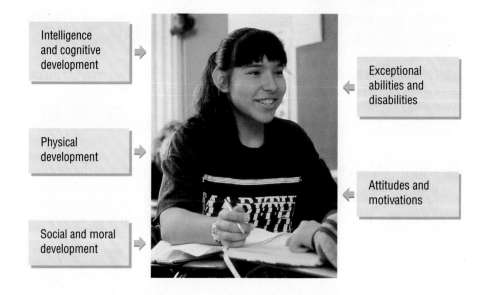

tion to situation, "error-free transmission" of information through the cortex, one's repertoire of intellectual knowledge and skills available at a particular point and time, and the combination of cognitive skills and knowledge demanded, fostered, and rewarded by one's particular culture.

Psychometric Perspective

Those who view the human intellect from a **psychometric perspective** believe that intellectual aptitude can be measured with tests. Measurement is conducted by administering a number of tasks, observing responses to these tasks, and inferring intellectual capabilities from examinees' performances. Efforts to quantify aptitudes in this fashion began in the late 1800s when Sir Francis Galton (1822–1911) devised a series of tests of reaction time and sensory acuity to assess adults' mental ability. By the early 1890s, Alfred Binet (1857–1911) and Theophile Simon (1873–1961) of France had developed intelligence tests designed to discriminate between more and less able students. Test items assessed intellectual abilities such as attention, verbal comprehension, and reasoning.

When Binet's tests were brought to the United States, translated, and revised for use with American children and adults, his detailed profiles of performance across a variety of measures were replaced with a single score, or **intelligence quotient (IQ)**. IQ scores were calculated by dividing an individual's mental age by his or her chronological age and multiplying the result by 100. Thus, IQ test scores compared individual mental ability to average mental abilities for others of the same age.

What do intelligence tests measure, a single, general capacity, or a combination of multiple abilities? Charles Spearman (1927) studied intelligence tests and determined that there was a "general factor," or g that all tests shared. He defined g as a general ability to form abstract relationships.

More recently, J.P. Guilford (1988), Howard Gardner (1993), and Robert Sternberg (1988) have argued that there are many cognitive abilities, each slightly different from the next, that constitute one's intellectual ability. Guilford suggests that mental operations (ways of thinking), contents (what people think about), and products (results of thinking) define more and less intelligent people. Gardner contends that individuals possess **multiple intelligences** that include seven types of capacities and abilities: linguistic (verbal), logical-mathematical, musical, spatial, bodily, knowledge of self, and understanding of others. Sternberg, in his triarchic theory of intelligence, argues that intelligence is determined by the degree to which individuals demonstrate three processes: metacomponents (mental processes used to plan), performance components (processes used to execute a task), and knowledge-acquisition components (processes used to learn how to solve problems). All three theorists contend that people differ in the strength of these intelligences and in the ways the multiple intelligences are invoked and combined to perform tasks and to solve problems.

Is intellectual ability a result of one's biological inheritance or the product of one's environment? In other words, are people born with their intellectual abilities (endowed with them by nature), or are such abilities nurtured (developed by education and life's experiences)? Although it is impossible to answer the question with certainty, most experts agree that intellectual ability is a product of both nature and nurture.

For instance, one of the simplest and most powerful methods for separating the effects of environment from the effects of genetics on human characteristics has been the study of twins who have been reared apart. Researchers at the University of Minnesota have studied 100 sets of reared-apart twins or triplets since 1979. They have concluded that although genetic factors are strong predictors of intellectual functioning, other influences on intellectual ability, such as parenting and education, cannot be ignored (Bouchard, Lykken, McGue, Segal, & Tellegen, 1990). Also, while popular opinion holds that one's place in the family, or "birth order," influences personality, intelligence, and achievement, differences among first-born children and their siblings may be due less to birth order than to differences in parental behaviors toward children or to societal or cultural norms emphasizing the rights of firstborns.

Intellectual ability is certainly critical to one's academic success, but even intellect is influenced by money. Family income is a powerful determinant of intellectual ability, particularly among young children. An analysis of longitudinal data from the Infant Health and Development Program, an eight-site study of low-birthweight babies launched in the 1980s, found that family income correlates more strongly with IQ at age 5 than do such factors as mothers' education, child's ethnicity, or the fact that a child lives in a home headed by a woman. Among the sample of 900 low-birthweight children studied, those living in persistent poverty from birth had IQs about 9 points lower than those who were not poor during their first few years of life (Cohen, 1993).

Intelligence test scores, estimates of scholastic aptitude, and measures of general ability are widely considered good predictors of success in school and in the workplace; yet some contend that test scores tell us relatively little about intelligence and even less about a person's creativity, wisdom, and intellectual style (Sternberg, 1988). They argue that tests unfairly restrict opportunities for growth and advancement (Hilliard, 1990). Employers who have worked with individuals with IQ scores below 100, for example, have found that low-scorers' abilities extend beyond what IQ scores predict (Ceci & Ruiz, 1993).

Young People's Thoughts about Intelligence

Interviews with 71 first, third, and sixth graders suggest that young children think of intelligence as something we are born with while older children believe experiences are a major determinant of intelligence. Many children also think it is the amount of knowledge people have that makes the difference between more and less intelligent people (Yussen & Kane, 1985). Other studies indicate that young people conceptualize ability as either fixed or fluid. Those who think intelligence is fixed are vulnerable to learned helplessness, especially when their confidence is low. Those who think intelligence is changeable are more willing to take risks and are more resilient when unsuccessful at tasks (Elliott & Dweck, 1988). Such beliefs may be modified through instruction (Bempechat, London, & Dweck, 1991).

> **When teachers treat students as intelligent people, students often rise to the occasion.**

Intelligence, however defined, is an important concept in the minds of young people of all ages. Teachers' perceptions of mental ability and the learning environment they create can greatly affect students' attitudes about themselves as learners and their success in school. Teachers who think of intelligence as a fixed entity may characterize children as "fast" or "slow" learners based on test scores, feedback from their other teachers, or their performance in class. Those who fall into the "slow" track may find it difficult to climb out. Even if they show improvement on learning tasks, these children may not receive recognition for their achievements and may give up on school work.

Teachers who view intelligence as a multifaceted, malleable capacity use estimates of it not only as predictors of success but also as ends of instruction; that is, intelligence can be viewed as a dynamic capacity to be changed. Teachers having such a view are more likely to use multiple methods of assessing intelligence rather than to rely on standardized tests and normative comparisons of students. When teachers treat students as intelligent people, students often rise to the occasion.

HOW DOES STUDENT COGNITION INFLUENCE LEARNING AND TEACHING?

Through the years, other theorists and researchers have rejected the study of intelligence and concentrated instead on cognition. Cognitive theories try to explain not what people think or how intelligent they are but how people think. Some cognitivists believe that thinking develops in identifiable stages while others do not.

Developmental perspective

Theories about **cognitive development**, or changes in children's mental functioning over time, suggest that teachers need to be aware of the ways young people make sense of the world. While there are different opinions about how intellectual functioning from infancy to adolescence can best be facilitated, developmental theorists agree that there are qualitative differences in children's behavior as they grow older.

Notions about the timeliness of instruction are based in large part on the work of Jean Piaget (1896-1980), a Swiss psychologist whose lifework was understanding how children at different ages perceive the world around them. Unlike early educators who postulated that intelligence was fixed at birth and quantitative (they labeled children as fast or slow learners), Piaget believed that children were born with the potential to develop intellectually. His systematic observations of children (including his own three children) from birth to adolescence suggested that the increasing complexity of children's thinking over time is due in part to the unfolding of internal structures, or maturational changes in the nervous system, as a child interacts with the physical world and engages in social experiences. Equally important to changes in intellectual development is a child's ability to adjust his or her ways of thinking when old ideas (perceptions) do not match new information and experiences.

To explain how children perceive and structure reality at different points in their development, Piaget categorized children's ways of thinking into four qualitatively different stages: sensorimotor (0–2 years), preoperational (2–7 years), concrete operational (7–11 years), and formal operational (11–16 years). (See Table 8.1.) According to Piaget, children may progress through the stages at different rates, but the order in which they do so remains constant.

The development of cognitive skills from one stage to another is dependent on a child's interaction with the environment. To aid growth, teachers should act more as facilitators than directors. This means providing opportunities for children to manipulate things, to manipulate symbols, and to discover and learn by reconciling findings at one time with findings at another time and comparing ideas with those of peers. Thus, students are directed more by useful materials than by teachers.

If children develop mentally as Piaget suggests, teachers must provide **developmentally appropriate instruction**. Learners who are in the concrete stage, for example, will likely be more successful developing theories and skills when

Swiss psychologist Jean Piaget explained how children perceive and structure reality at different stages in their development. According to Piaget's theory, these young children are likely in the second, or preoperational, stage of cognitive development.

TABLE 8.1   Piaget's Stages of Cognitive Development

Age	Stage	Characteristics
0–2	Sensorimotor	Learn primarily through the senses and strongly affected by the immediate environment. Begin to follow objects with eyes (visual pursuit). Begin to realize objects still exist, even though they are out of sight. Movement from reflex actions to goal-directed activities.
2–7	Preoperational	Vocabulary development, especially the ability to understand and use words, increases. Tendency to talk at rather than with others. Ideas begin to replace concrete experience. Have difficulty realizing the reversible nature of relationships.
7–11	Concrete Operational	Ability to solve problems logically through the use of hands-on materials. Understand reversible nature of relationships. Can classify objects according to color, size, etc. Can arrange objects in sequence according to such attributes as size and weight. Literal minded.
11–16	Formal Operational	Solve abstract problems in logical fashion. Able to hypothesize. Can reflect on their ways of thinking. Aware that people see and think about situations and ideas differently.

Note. From *Educational Psychology: A Developmental Approach, Fifth Edition* (pp. 102–113) by N.A. Sprinthall & R.C. Sprinthall, 1990, New York: McGraw-Hill, Inc. Used with permission of McGraw-Hill.

physically manipulating objects or mentally manipulating ideas emanating from in-class experiences than when receiving direct verbal instruction. Decisions about where a child is on the developmental continuum cannot be based solely on age, however. A major criticism of Piaget's stage theory, one he recognized, is that children demonstrate inconsistencies in thinking. That is, a child may demonstrate one level of thinking in one situation and a more or less sophisticated level of thinking in another. Pupils may also experience a lag between stage of development in one content area and another, particularly when not receiving stimulation in a particular area of study. A high school student, for example, may be at the formal operational stage in science and concrete operational stage in English.

Cultural Awareness

Piaget's stage theory does not account for the effects of individual differences such as gender, personality, intelligence (as measured by IQ tests), or culture on students' cognitive processes. Although Piagetians contend that the four developmental stages are universal, there is evidence that formal operations, the highest level of thinking, is attained by few adolescents, college students, or adults in the United States, Africa, or Europe (Mwamwenda, 1992). In some non-Western cultures that do not focus on abstract thinking, formal operational thought is virtually nonexistent. How quickly children move through the different stages also varies by culture, depending on environmental conditions. Children in Martinique, an island in the West Indies where the culture is Francophone, were 4 years later developing operational thought than their counterparts in Francophone Switzerland. In Tehran, the capital of Iran, children developed similarly to children in Switzerland, but in the villages of Iran, there was a 2-year delay. (Sutherland, 1992)

Contextual Perspectives

Lev Semenovich Vygotsky, a Russian psychologist (1896–1934), suggested that mental development depends greatly on environmental effects. In other words, culture influences what and how children learn. This perspective grew in part out of a concern that theories of intellectual development, such as Piaget's stage theory, were too limiting (Berg, 1992).

While Piaget minimized the importance of systematic teaching, Vygotsky considered concept formation by a child in cooperation with an adult or an advanced student critical to development of higher mental functions. Moreover, Vygotsky believed that children needed to talk with and

VOICES

On Ways of Knowing

Harvard psychologist Jerome Bruner, a noted cognitivist, argues that there are two kinds of cognition. One is scientific, logical, and objective, undertaken to discover truth. The other is intuitive, emergent, and subjective, meant to interpret and construct life. Both have implications for teaching:

Let me begin by setting out my argument as baldly as possible. . . . There are two modes of cognitive functioning, two modes of thought, each providing distinctive ways of ordering experience, of constructing reality. . . . Efforts to reduce one mode to the other or to ignore one at the expense of the other inevitably fail to capture the rich diversity of thought.

Each of the ways of knowing, moreover, has operating principles of its own and its own criteria of well-formedness. They differ radically in their procedures for verification. A good story and a well-formed argument are different natural kinds. Both can be used as means for convincing another. Yet what they convince of is fundamentally different: arguments convince one of their truth, stories of their lifelikeness. The one verifies by eventual appeal to procedures for establishing formal and empirical proof. The other establishes not truth but verisimilitude. (1986, p. 11)

These two modes of thought, as Bruner observed, have different implications for education:

Much of the process of education consists of being able to distance oneself in some way from what one knows by being able to reflect on one's own knowledge. In most contemporary theories of cognitive development, this has been taken to mean the achievement of more abstract knowledge through Piagetian formal operations or by the use of more abstract symbolic systems. And it is doubtless true that in many spheres of knowledge, as in the sciences, one does indeed climb to "intellectually higher ground" (to use Vygotsky's phrase) by this route. One does indeed come to see arithmetic as a special case when one reaches the more abstract domain of algebra. But I think it is perilous to look at intellectual growth exclusively in this manner, for one will surely distort the meaning of intellectual maturity if one uses such a model exclusively.

The idea that any humanistic subject can be taught without revealing one's stance toward matters of human pith and substance is, of course, nonsense.

[T]he language of education, if it is to be an invitation to reflection and culture creating, cannot be the so-called uncontaminated language of fact and "objectivity." It must express stance and must invite counter-stance and in the process leave place for reflection, for metacognition. It is this that permits one to reach higher ground, this process of objectifying in language or image what one has thought and then turning around on it and reconsidering it (pp. 128–129).

CRITICAL THINKING

How do you think teachers might invite reflection and encourage students to create culture? Give some specific examples.

listen to others to develop intellectually (Sutherland, 1992). Vygotsky contended that when children are provided with opportunities to learn, and supported in those efforts by capable adults and more able peers, intellectual growth is more likely to occur. This scaffolding, or assistance to learners, may range from the use of probing questions and hints to the provision of specific strategies for solving problems.

Vygotsky's notions about maximizing instruction in combination with Piaget's ideas about how students think have implications for how teachers teach. Effective teachers are attuned to students—listening to them and watching how they attack problems—thereby to determine children's capabilities. When making decisions about content and methods of instruction, teachers try to find appropriate ways to challenge students and to move them toward sophisticated understanding of concepts and issues. During instruction, teachers try to strike a balance between teacher-directed tasks and instructional activity initiated and directed by students.

Information Processing Theory

Information processing theory offers yet another perspective on cognition, focusing on *how* information is received, analyzed, stored, and used. As these terms suggest, information processing theorists have their roots in the physical sciences, systems theory, and computer technology.

The term *information processing* can usefully be thought of as a synonym for *thinking*. In this case, however, thinking deals with how people think (what kinds of strategies they use to approach tasks and the mental effort that goes into tasks) more than what people think. Although most information processing theorists do not use stages of development to explain how thinking skills change over time, they assume that humans develop increasingly complex cognitive structures that represent and organize their knowledge. These theorists make judgments about the inner workings of the mind by observing behavioral effects. That is, they analyze mental processes in terms of observable behaviors such as reaction times, verbal recall, and verbal recognition of various stimuli (e.g., a series of numbers, a list of names).

Information processing theory emphasizes the importance of helping learners to acquire bodies of useful information and to develop thinking skills that will allow them to learn on their own. Because learners construct knowledge in different ways, logic and theory suggest that teachers may have to teach in different ways—ways that accommodate differences in students. As we suggest in Chapter 10, teachers who are mindful of individual differences use a variety of teaching models to reach specific goals. Often they also teach students **metacognitive skills**, or methods for monitoring and controlling their own thinking. Teachers help students develop and use metacognitive skills by, among other things, teaching them memory strategies, self-questioning activities, and procedures to follow when they have difficulty comprehending written material.

Stanley Pogrow, a faculty member at the University of Arizona, works with educators to develop special programs to improve students' thinking skills. The result of Pogrow's efforts is Higher Order Thinking Skills (HOTS), a compensatory program for disadvantaged students in grades 4 through 7. HOTS replaces drill and practice exercises such students usually experience with computer- and teacher-led activities meant to help them understand how to understand. Groups of no more than 15 students meet with specially trained teachers 35 minutes a day, 4 days a week, for 2 years. During lessons, teachers follow carefully scripted plans, called "learning dramas," loaded with probing questions. For the most part, teachers are pleased with their results:

> "Before I learned about HOTS," says Donna Uebler, describing her Chapter I classes, "I had the mindset that I was dealing with remedial kids, and therefore I felt I had to work on skills to bring them 'up' to the level of other children. I did some drill-and-practice, though I hated it. We did a lot of reading of books, but it wasn't exciting. With the advent of HOTS, the program itself is so intellectually stimulating that I'm constantly reevaluating my teaching. I am much more patient because I've had to learn to wait for answers and give children the time to think. I don't allow 'I don't know' anymore, so they have to respond to me. Now, I'm challenging children to be creative with their thinking." (Shore, 1992, p.25)

HOW DO PHYSICAL AND PSYCHOSOCIAL DEVELOPMENT AFFECT CHILDREN'S LEARNING?

The ancient Greeks recognized the symbiotic relationship between the *psycho* (the mind) and the *soma* (the body). A change in one can and often does affect the other. In healthy individuals, both the mind and the body develop together and over time, but not always at the same rate. Different people quite obviously develop in different ways. Nonetheless, there are identifiable patterns of physical and mental development from birth to death. These patterns of development have important implications for education.

Physical Development

Once children reach preschool age, their physical development is fairly steady; however, height, weight, and motor coordination may vary from child to child. Children who are larger than their agemates are sometimes more advanced in their motor coordination and in their academic and social skills. Genetics, a stimulating home environment, nutrition, and a healthy physical environment are among possible reasons for such differences.

Between the ages of 2 and 5, preschoolers' control of their large and small muscles improves greatly. Teachers of young children optimize development of large muscles by providing a variety of activities that improve agility, strength, endurance, balance, rhythm, and speed. They also incorporate diverse materials and activities such as small-block play, sand play, clay manipulation, puzzles, and Lego blocks to develop fine motor skills and to improve hand-eye coordination.

Some children develop abnormally because of the environments in which they live. One of the most insidious threats—lead—is present in the paint in many homes. Children are poisoned by lead-contaminated dust from lead-based paint simply by playing and eating.

> Lead poisoning, long known to be a hazard, now is recognized as one of the most common and devastating housing-related diseases among children—one that can cause lasting developmental and health problems and, in extreme cases, comas, convulsions, mental retardation, even death... Nationwide, an estimated 12 million children younger than seven live in homes that contain lead paint, and 3 million to 4 million children have unsafe levels of lead in their blood. (Children's Defense Fund, 1992, pp. 37–38)

Children experience a rapid increase in both height and weight that begins at about age 8 or 9 in girls and age 10 or 11 in boys. Though boys are often taller and heavier than girls at age 10, by age 13 girls usually surpass boys in height and weight. By age 16, however, this trend reverses and boys are once again taller and heavier than girls. The growth spurt young people experience during early adolescence is accompanied by a series of changes in all parts of the body as they begin to develop sexually.

Poverty figures prominently in young people's health profiles. Although much of the timing and duration of the preadolescent growth spurt is dependent on genetic makeup, it, too, is influenced by environmental factors, such as proper nutrition. Adolescents from low-income families experience lower rates of achievement in school and higher rates of poor physical health, mental disorders, and depression (Brindis, Irwin, & Millstein, 1992).

Physical health is also influenced by one's level of physical activity. Studies of children's health profiles suggest that up to 25% of young people are obese (Rosenbaum & Leibel, 1989). This, in combination with studies of children's fitness, suggests that today's youth are fast becoming "fully cooked couch potatoes" ("Youth Sports," 1992, p.1).

Although children begin their school careers very interested in sports, a survey of 10,000 young people indicates that there is a sharp decline in desire to participate in sports between the ages of 10 and 18 (Athletic Footwear Institute, 1990). Vern Seefeldt, Martha Ewing, and Stephen Walk (1991) of the Youth Sports Institute at Michigan State University argue that one reason young people's enthusiasm wanes with age is due to the emphasis placed on winning. The keen competition it takes to produce champions drives off the majority of young people who also need opportunities to learn about fair play and chances to practice teamwork skills.

Physical Development and Psychological Well-Being

As children grow and change, their body types influence developmental task achievement, self-image, and self-satisfaction. Students who are attractive and athletic are typically popular with adults and peers and better adjusted than unattractive students, particularly those who are overweight. Some studies indicate that teachers and school counselors expect higher achievement and better social skills from students who are attractive (Clifford, 1975; Lerner & Lerner, 1977).

Adolescents are particularly sensitive about their physical appearance and often have unrealistic expectations for physical attractiveness. Often **self-esteem**, or the value or sense of worth an individual places on his or her own characteristics, abilities, and behaviors, is affected by such expectations. In particular, girls who are dissatisfied with the way they look are often self-conscious and may suffer from low self-esteem (Abramowitz, Petersen, & Schulenberg, 1984; Brooks-Gunn & Petersen, 1983). As we noted in Chapter 6, many teenage girls who are unhappy with their bodies develop eating disorders. Girls who mature early exhibit more eating problems than average- or late-maturing girls. Early-maturing girls are also at greater risk for depression (Rosso, in press; Rierdan & Koff, 1991).

It is essential that adults be sensitive to what children do about weight and say about body image. Young people's comments and actions can provide valuable clues about their psychological well-being as well as about their physical health. But one must be careful when reading these clues. For example, what may appear as laziness in the behavior of students may in fact be a manifestation of poor nutrition. School nurses, counselors, and physical educators are often most knowledgeable about nutrition and physical regimens that will bring harmony to mind and body.

Psychosocial Development

Young people's **psychosocial development**, or changes relating to age and intelligence in the way an individual's social and emotional needs are met through relationships with others, is affected in large part by the people around them. While infants are most influenced by immediate family members, older children are influenced by family, peers, adults at school and in the community, and people in the media. Personal growth is not random but proceeds somewhat systematically. Erik Erikson (1902–1994) proposed that individuals have the potential for proceeding through eight stages of personal development, five of which occur during schooling. (See Table 8.2.) Each stage involves a central developmental crisis; how well an individual deals with each crisis determines progress through succeeding stages.

From birth to 6 years, or childhood, personal development includes three stages: trust versus mistrust (birth to 24 months), autonomy versus shame/doubt (2 to 3 years), and initiative versus guilt (3 to 6 years). During the first stage, feelings of trust or mistrust are influenced by the quality of care and affection babies experience. Those who experience a world that is dependable and warm have a good chance of resolving the conflict between trust and mistrust.

During the second stage of development, autonomy versus shame, children develop a number of skills. Their autonomy, or ability to stand on their own two feet and not experience shame or doubt, is dependent on the

TABLE 8.2   Erikson's Stages of Psychosocial Development

Birth to age 2:
   Trust versus mistrust

Ages 2 to 3:
   Autonomy versus shame and doubt

Ages 3 to 6:
   Initiative versus guilt

Ages 6 to 12:
   Industry versus inferiority

Adolescence:
   Identity versus role confusion

Young adulthood:
   Intimacy versus isolation

Ages 25 to 60:
   Generativity versus stagnation

Full maturity:
   Ego integrity versus despair and disgust

Note. From *Identity and the Life Cycle* (pp. 51–107) by E. H. Erikson, 1980, New York: Norton. Reprinted with the permission of W.W. Norton & Company, Inc. Copyright 1980 by W.W. Norton & Company, Inc. Copyright 1959 by International Universities Press, Inc.

degree to which parents talk with their children, allow them to initiate activities, support rather than criticize their early language skills, and ask questions that allow children to express their ideas and think for themselves.

The last stage of childhood, initiative versus guilt, is a time when children learn what kind of people they are, mainly with regard to gender. According to Erikson, children at this stage need to be allowed to express themselves without a lot of censoring, which may evoke guilt. Because this is also the "play age," children need to be encouraged in their efforts to manipulate things in the environment and to make plans of their own rather than be constrained by adult-imposed, highly-structured educational activities.

From 6 to 12 years (the juvenile period), personal and emotional development turn outward as children enter the fourth stage of personal development—industry versus inferiority. During this stage, home remains an important base of operation, but children spend many more hours away from home than ever before. Neighborhood and classroom cliques (almost always composed of all boys or all girls) become major socializing agents.

Besides being faced with the demands of learning many school oriented skills, youngsters develop a sense of personal mastery as they engage in a number of new games and activities. When not encouraged in their efforts to master their environment, children's sense of personal industry may turn to personal inferiority.

The fifth stage of personal development, identity versus confusion, occurs during adolescence. Young people at this stage of development go through substantial physiological and psychological changes. The main issue with which they contend is the development of an identity, or sense of self, that will provide a firm basis for adulthood. As adolescents begin to think about self and identity, they can differentiate between feelings and emotions in self and others, distinguish between objective and subjective reality, see things from another's perspective, and distinguish between literal

> "Adolescence is almost like entering a foreign country without knowing the language, the customs, or the culture . . ."

and symbolic meaning (Sprinthall & Sprinthall, 1990). Ironically, when adolescents first enter this stage, they become quite egocentric in their thinking. They also become self-conscious and vulnerable to peer pressure, particularly at the junior high school level.

Resolving the crisis of personal identity is a difficult task for adolescents. They have to cope with internal and external changes at the same time. And they must do so while shedding their previous identity. "Adolescence is almost like entering a foreign country without knowing the language, the customs, or the culture; only it's worse because the 'voyagers' don't even have a guidebook" (Sprinthall & Sprinthall, 1990, p. 157).

When sense of self is weak, young people develop what Erikson calls a "diffuse identity." Having no firm direction, they wrestle mentally with who they are and what they want to do with their lives. Young people who do not have satisfying social relationships may experience different degrees of loneliness. A study that examined relationships between loneliness and adolescent health behaviors in a sample of approximately 1,300 senior high school students revealed that extreme loneliness has adverse effects on young people's health. Lonely adolescents, for example, are more prone to use marijuana than those who are not lonely. Boys who are lonely tend to engage in fewer physical activities and are more likely to watch television for longer periods of time than are boys who are not lonely. Among females, loneliness is often associated with cigarette smoking, binge eating, purging, and crash diets (Page, 1990).

The sixth through eighth stages of personal development occur beyond the school years and center on human relations. Intimacy versus isolation, which occurs during young adulthood, is a time when young people must have resolved earlier crises successfully and feel secure with themselves so they can learn to relate to another person on a deep level. During middle adulthood, roughly ages 25 to 60, people enter the stage of generativity versus stagnation. At this point, the challenge is to remain productive and creative in all the activities of life. The last stage of personal development, ego integrity versus despair, occurs during late adulthood. Those who have gained full maturity by resolving earlier stages possess the integrity to deal with such things as the loss of former roles, such as employee or coach. They can also face death with a minimum of fear.

HOW DOES STUDENTS' MORAL DEVELOPMENT INFLUENCE LEARNING AND TEACHING?

Moral development, or changes relating to age and intelligence in the way an individual makes reasoned judgments about right and wrong, has always been a concern of public schools. Despite disagreement over the meaning of the term, educators' goal has been to produce good Americans. Programs have been structured to help students to assume a kind of American character—the particular variety of which was described early on by Horace Mann in terms of "veracity, probity, and rectitude" (Cremin, 1957, p. 100).

Regardless of the particular virtues being advocated, teaching itself is a

> ... fundamentally moral enterprise in which adults ask and require children to change in directions chosen by the adults. Understanding teaching in this light confronts a teacher with potentially unsettling questions: By what authority do I push for changes in the lives of these children? At what costs to their freedom and autonomy? Where does my responsibility for these young lives begin and end? How should I deal with true moral dilemmas in which it is simply not possible to realize two goods or avoid two evils? How much pain and discomfort am I willing to endure on behalf of my students? How are my own character flaws affecting the lives of others? (Clark, 1990, p. 264)

Stages of Moral Development

As teachers have begun to understand how their students think about moral issues, character development and moral education have grown less absolute, less propagandistic, and more aligned with students' development. Beginning with his doctoral studies at the University of Chicago and proceeding through his career on the faculty at Harvard, Lawrence Kohlberg (1927–1987) shaped modern thinking about moral development and moral education. Much as Piaget described intellectual development, Kohlberg described moral reasoning in terms of stages—six in all, each distinct from the other.

Kohlberg reasoned that, given opportunities, people's moral character grows more complex and more comprehensive over time. By studying how people thought about moral questions, he recognized that simplistic terms such as *right* and *wrong*, *good* and *bad* did not reflect the full range of people's capacity to judge moral issues. As illustrated in Table 8.3, people at stages 1 and 2, or what Kohlberg called a preconventional level of morality, make

TABLE 8.3   Kohlberg's Theory of Moral Development

Preconventional Morality

Lawrence Kohlberg

Stage 1: Punishment-Obedience Outlook. Decisions are made on the basis of power. People behave in ways that indicate a desire to avoid severe punishment.

Stage 2: Personal Reward Outlook. Actions are taken to satisfy one's own personal needs. People make trades and exchange favors but try to come out a bit ahead in the bargain.

Conventional Morality

Stage 3: Social Conformity Outlook. People make moral judgments to do what is "nice" and what pleases others.

Stage 4: Law and Order Outlook. People believe laws are right, and they are to be obeyed. They believe people should respect authority and maintain order.

Postconventional Morality

Stage 5: Social Contract Outlook. Morality is governed by a system of laws based on socially accepted standards. Judgments are not based exclusively on the situation or on a particular rule but viewed in relation to the system.

Stage 6: Universal Ethics Outlook. Behavior is judged on principles, not necessarily written, of justice, of concern for human rights, and of respect for human dignity.

Note. From *Lawrence Kohlberg's approach to moral education* (pp. 8–9) by F.C. Power, A. Higgins, & L. Kohlberg, 1989, New York: Columbia University Press. Reprinted with permission of the publisher.

decisions based on their own needs. Those at stages 3 and 4 (conventional morality) weigh social mores and laws as they make judgments. And those who are most complex (stages 5 and 6, a level of postconventional morality) consider moral issues in keeping with abstract, largely personal principles. Kohlberg and others have noted that stages 5 and 6 are difficult to separate from each other because both systems are based on similar concepts.

The stories Kohlberg and his colleagues have used to assess stages of moral development are presented in the form of moral dilemmas—problems that force choices between unsatisfactory alternative courses of action. People's responses to these problems can be categorized into distinct types that represent the six stages in Kohlberg's theory. The following is an example of a dilemma used for assessment and educational purposes:

> Before the junior class trip the faculty told the students that the whole class had to agree not to bring or use alcohol or drugs on the trip. If students were found using drugs or alcohol, they would be sent home. The students knew that without faculty approval they would not be able to have their trip. The students said in a class meeting that they all agreed to these conditions. On the trip, several students ask Bob, a fellow student, to go on a hike with them to the lake. When they get to the lake, they light up a joint and pass it around. (Power, Higgins, & Kohlberg, 1989, p. 247)

Some social scientists have criticized Kohlberg for what they perceive to have been his bias in favor of males (Gilligan 1982; Gilligan and Attanucci, 1988). Carol Gilligan argued that Kohlberg's scoring system penalized females and that his level of postconventional morality excluded a dimension of human caring—a dimension upon which she believed females would excel. Although researchers (Walker, de Vries, & Trevethan, 1987; Walker, 1989) have found no evidence of bias against a response/care orientation to moral decision making by Kohlberg's theory, Gilligan's claims have sensitized others to the importance of compassion as a dimension of morality.

If you had a summer job in a restaurant, would you consider it dishonest to give free fries to friends?

Critics of Kohlberg have also focused on the absence of an explicit relationship in the theory between moral judgment and moral action (Sockett, 1992). Simply because people reason at higher levels of development does not guarantee that they will behave in moral ways.

Most stage theorists, like Kohlberg and Piaget, hold that people only progress to higher stages when forced to confront situations that are slightly more complex than those with which they are prepared to deal. Generally, teachers who wish to encourage development try to understand how their students reason and to create learning opportunities that gently stretch them to consider new possibilities.

Students' Views on Moral Development

Some ministers cheat. Some teachers lie. Some students steal. Should anyone have been surprised when 126,000 youths, ages 13 to 18, responded as they did to this survey question: If you had a summer job in a restaurant, would you consider these things dishonest? Giving free fries to friends (27% said no). Eating as much as you want, despite limits on free food (16% said no). Taking home a gallon of ice cream (9% said no). Borrowing $10 overnight (9% said no) (Ansley & McCleary, 1992).

Surprise is not the appropriate reaction to these responses, but skepticism and concern are in order. These responses came from write-in volunteers, not from a scientifically selected sample. Moreover, both researchers and casual observers have known for a long time that what people say about morality and how they behave often bear slight or no resemblance to one another (Hartshorne, May, & Shuttleworth, 1930). Nonetheless, the problems posed in the survey are real enough. And the level of interest and the variation in responses was sufficiently high to make adults pause and listen more closely to what students say about the real moral issues they face.

Young people confront moral questions regularly. If asked to do so, many can describe such confrontations vividly. When raised to the level of myth, and taken literally as facts that apply to many people, such stories can be grossly misinterpreted, and even serve as prescriptions for mischief disguised as "education." But when understood as ruminations about intensely personal problems, students' stories can lend direction to teaching. Nona Lyons (1993) provides one such example in her discussion of a high school sophomore, Rebecca.

> I just thought, I just went through a stage where I thought that anyone who came here and violated a rule should be kicked out of school because they couldn't handle it. They couldn't come there and totally stay within the rules, you know. And then I went through the thing: Is it possible to go through here four years without breaking a fundamental rule? And I asked someone, who said, "I don't think so." So, that is something I am going to have to deal with in the future. (p. 147)

As Lyons points out, Rebecca articulates a complex view of rules and their meaning in her life and in her relations with others. If she maintains and exercises her power to choose, this view may continue to evolve, influencing her values and sense of integrity.

Even when confronted with hypothetical moral issues, younger children, too, display remarkable capacities to reason about justice and compassion. Experimenters in New England studied reactions of children ages 5 to 13 to two fables—the "Porcupine and the Moles" and the "Dog in the Manger." The "Porcupine and the Moles" fable presents a family of moles who invite a porcupine to share the warmth of their cave. Unfortunately, the porcupine is so large that his sharp quills make the moles uncomfortable. When they courteously ask the porcupine to leave, he declines, because he likes the cave. The "Dog in the Manger" fable describes a hungry ox who returns to his stall after a hard day at work. There he finds a dog on the hay refusing to move aside so the ox can eat. The investigators asked the children how the animals should solve their problems.

Boys and girls tended to reason in similar fashion. As indicated in Figure 8.2, when asked for the best solution to the fables, children preferred what were called "care-oriented responses." Children's ability to see more than one moral orientation depended on their abstract reasoning skills.

While not everyone agrees about what students should be taught to think, many agree that learning how to reason effectively about moral issues should be a high priority. People may favor contemporary moral orientations or prefer traditional values, but teaching children to handle the power to choose falls increasingly to schools and teachers.

FIGURE 8.2

Children's Responses to Fables

JUSTICE-ORIENTED RESPONSES

If there's a whole messload of dogs and a whole messload of oxes, they should have a big war to see who gets the hay.
(Boy, age 8)

They should put out a sign and it has a circle and a cross on it and a porcupine in the middle. And maybe they write in red on it that says "No porcupines allowed."
(Boy, age 6)

The porcupine should move because they [the moles] were there first, and if they left it wouldn't be fair, because they were there first. And the porcupine should move because they could hurt him, you know, really bad like that and stuff, and its their home.
(Girl, age 10)

If you want to be treated nicely, you got to treat the other person nice, too.
(Boy, age 12)

CARE-ORIENTED RESPONSES

The porcupine could make a wall across the cave. 'Cause then they'd both have a home.
(Boy, age 5)

They should cooperate. Maybe like if there was more rock they could try and blast out some more, and they would all help. And a few of 'em, maybe, ought to take care of the babies if they have some.
(Girl, age 6)

They should all go on an expedition for marshmallows on the porcupine's quills and then the moles will really, really, really not get pricked. Then the porcupine would be happy because he could live in the moles' house that suited him just fine and the moles could have tasty tidbits as well as a warm home because of the porcupine's body heat... and all would be happy
(Boy, age 8)

The moles could dig another home for the porcupine. It would be generous of them, and they could make another friend if they did that. The more friends you have usually is the better.
(Girl, age 12)

HOW DO STUDENTS' HABITS OF MIND INFLUENCE LEARNING AND TEACHING?

Students' intellectual capacities and their abilities to reason morally influence both teaching and learning, but so too do what James Rutherford and Andrew Ahlgren (1990) call students' **habits of mind**—the shared skills, attitudes, and values transmitted by custom or convention from one generation to the next. Many people other than teachers try to affect students' habits of mind by writing and selecting curricula, by funding or denying funding for educational programs, by creating employment opportunities for graduates, and by setting college admissions standards. Influencing students' habits of mind is serious business, for this complex of values, attitudes, and skills "all relate directly to a person's outlook on knowledge and learning and ways of thinking and acting" (p. 172).

Formal and Informal Influences on Habits of Mind

The habits of mind deemed important by parents, leaders in government and business, professors, and many other often self-anointed experts appear in written documents. The National Goals, for example, contain direct and indirect references to skills, attitudes, and values that various people consider essential. But in many ways the less visible, informal, often implicit habits of mind held by both extraordinary and ordinary people are those that shape the ethos of a community. They may be thought of as the attributes of the more abstract concepts that bind us together as one people. These beliefs are communicated and reinforced in many ways.

When people discuss education, and what needs to be done to improve it, talk sooner rather than later turns to students' attitudes, or their mental postures toward various people, ideas, and events. These days, two fall at or near the top of many lists of attitudes characterized as socially desirable: cooperation and competition. Students, it is argued, need to cultivate the temperament to cooperate with one another. When they possess cooperative attitudes, and the concomitant skills needed to work together effectively, they will be prepared to compete in the great game of life with our economic rivals. From reports by national commissions on the condition of education to conversations over coffee in diners across the country, one can find evidence that "cooperation and competition" has become a slogan imprinted on our collective consciousness.

Almost as soon as young people realize that cooperating and competing involve some personal risks—working with and against others inevitably means not always getting your own way and maybe losing more often than winning—their outlook on coping becomes critical. The "winning-is-everything" attitude, promoted most visibly in the sports world, simply cannot work for everyone all the time. In fact, striving for success, failing, and coping gracefully yield an uncommon dignity that is widely admired. Arthur Ashe (Ashe & Rampersad, 1993) described how his experiences on the tennis court helped him cope with the certain loss of his life from complications associated with AIDS:

As I settled deeper into this new stage of my life, I became increasingly conscious of a certain thrill, an exhilaration even, about what I was doing. Yes, I felt pain, physical and psychological; but I also felt something like pleasure in responding purposefully, vigorously, to my illness. I had lost many matches on the tennis court, but I had seldom quit. I was losing, but playing well now. . . . Experience as an athlete had taught me that in times of danger I had to respond with confidence, authority, and calm. So many looming defeats had turned strangely, sometimes even miraculously, into victories. . . . (p. 251)

Ashe's situation readily evokes another attitude thought to be essential in a civilized society—compassion. Ashe was a relatively young man, and an articulate, admirable man who had suffered injustice because of his race and overcome the odds to succeed. It was easy for people to empathize with him. But the feelings of kindness and compassion people directed toward him are attitudes decent people show in many situations. Teachers encourage children to be kind to one another not because the school mission statement or curriculum suggests people are supposed to be kind but because civilized people expect as much of each other.

Rutherford and Ahlgren (1990) point to some skills associated with science, mathematics, and technology that most knowledgeable people believe students need to master if they are to participate fully in society. These include calculating skills, skills of manipulating and observing, communication skills, and critical response skills.

Every day, particularly on the job, people need to be able to calculate. Simple paper-and-pencil arithmetic skills used to be sufficient for most situations, but with the introduction of inexpensive electronic calculators, the workplace is changing. Operators must be able to read and follow step-by-step instructions in calculator manuals; construct simple algorithms for solving problems; determine what the unit (seconds, square inches, dollars per tankful) of the answer will be from inputs; round off answers; and judge whether an answer is reasonable by comparing it to an estimated answer. Each of these skills, in turn, involves other problem-solving skills (Rutherford & Ahlgren, 1990).

Mathematically and technologically literate people must also possess skills of manipulation and observation. These skills include: distinguishing between observations and speculations; storing and retrieving computer information using standard computer software; using appropriate instruments to measure length, volume, weight, time, and temperature; troubleshooting common mechanical and electrical systems; and comparing consumer products.

Skills of reading, writing, and speaking have traditionally served as the hallmarks of literacy. The skill of listening—always crucial for learning but magnified in importance with the growth of modern technology—must be added to the list. People cannot take advantage of opportunities or advance their position in society without strong communication skills. Our "information society" demands ever-increasing levels of communicative sophistication.

The skills and attitudes society requires are worth little if young people do not develop a set of values. As we have noted elsewhere, some have

argued that public schools have reinforced values of obedience and conformity in order to protect the status quo. One can certainly make a convincing
case that this has been in part the public education agenda, planned or
unplanned. Such skepticism expressed about educational intent is itself a
very American and widely accepted value. But the results of schooling as
measured in bright, productive people who have emerged from the system
stand as testament to the abiding importance of curiosity and openness to
new ideas. When coupled with motivation or drive, it is difficult as the old
adage goes, to keep a good person down.

The habits of mind valued by society are not always transmitted in ways
that some children are used to seeing and hearing. The style of communication to which they are accustomed is not congruent with that which they
find in school. A study of Native-American children, for instance, revealed
that much of the formal learning that took place at home was nonverbal in
nature. That is, children learned skills and values not from verbal instruction but from observing and sharing directly in the activities of others.
While learning through observation and imitation is common across all cultures, Native Americans' predisposition to use this method of learning puts
them at a disadvantage in schools where teaching socially desirable habits of
mind means telling (Henry & Pepper, 1990).

How Do Students View Habits of Mind?

"'I'm bored,' says Christina Saffell. 'I don't have my book, so it is not very
thrilling for me.' . . . 'You know [the teacher] doesn't care about the homework. She never checks it, just goes over the answers . . .'" (Leff, 1992, p. A1).
Just another day in the life of a student at Bethesda-Chevy Chase High
School, Montgomery County, Maryland. The vast majority of Bethesda-
Chevy Chase students go on to college. Still, here, as in many other schools
across the nation, a group of students
"in the middle" have chosen to cruise
mentally, or to work just enough to get
by. They can meet teachers' expectations without overexertion, and they
are not sufficiently self-motivated to
challenge themselves.

> If teachers expect stu-
> dents to be motivated
> and to master content,
> then students should
> expect no less from
> teachers.

Investigators at the Center for
Research on the Context of Secondary
School Teaching (CRC) at Stanford
study high schools that stretch students to challenge themselves. They have
discovered that when students speak up, they have much to tell teachers
about the skills, attitudes, and values that should be transmitted in schools.
Students often agree with teachers about habits of mind that foster teaching
and learning and about those that get in the way.

Nobody wants to be just a number. Students appreciate an orderly,
organized environment, but not at the expense of their identities. One
student describes a class in which the teacher fails to connect with individual students: "The class I'm getting an F in, he seems like he doesn't really

actually pay attention to anybody in particular in class, it's just a whole class, and this is math. . . . So I don't know what he really actually means. He doesn't look at me. . . ." (Phelan, Davidson, & Cao, 1992, p. 696).

Students want to learn, or more to the point, they want to be taught according to one student:

> "I think if the teacher does something more than just taking things out of the book or something. . . . It's really boring if it's just out of the book. If she includes the students in everything, I think that's really fun. Like what I was thinking about my science teacher, he never does anything new, and it's just all by the book. You just read your chapter, you go on and do the questions. And it's not very interesting, and he doesn't explain about it much." (Phelan, Davidson, & Cao, 1992, p. 699)

If teachers expect students to be motivated and to master content, then students should expect no less from teachers.

Shaping habits of mind that will serve students well has never been a simple matter of being entertaining or of making students feel good about themselves. Teachers must take the subject matter seriously if they expect students to do the same, another student says: "I don't like the teacher—it seems like I end up teaching myself calculus. . . . He seems to just leave you on your own because he doesn't—I don't know if he really knows what he's teaching that well" (Phelan, Davidson, & Cao 1992, p. 701).

Cultural Awareness

A musician from Chicago, Billy Branch, and his band, Sons of Blues, made the importance of commitment to one's discipline, to cooperation, and to competition abundantly clear in Charleston, South Carolina, where they ran a program called Blues in the Schools (Kuralt, 1992). When a local businesswoman read about Branch's program in Chicago, where it originated, she helped bring it south to a predominantly African-American middle school in one of Charleston's poorest neighborhoods. For 2 hours a day for 3 weeks students studied the blues. They played and sang the blues, studied the history of the blues, and wrote their own songs.

Branch: Anybody remember any of the people I mentioned that recorded Willie Dixon tunes?

Unidentified Student #1: Bo Diddley.

Branch: Who?

Student #2: Elvis Presley, Led Zeppelin, The Rolling Stones and Koko Taylor.

Branch: See, somebody took notes. Yes. Right! (p. 13)

(continued)

As a schoolteacher of the blues, Branch does not simply talk about his subject, he jams with his students, teaching them in a demonstrable way how to play together harmoniously and encouraging them to push each other to reach for the best sounds they can produce. Branch listens to students' musical and verbal expressions, which he interprets as indications of their ability to "feel the feel of the blues."

Students "tell" teachers that the knowledge that matters must be rich and varied—be it calculus or the blues—if it is to be taken seriously. They teach teachers that the skills, attitudes, and values that adult society holds dear are not foreign to young people. When teachers are masters of the content, when they do not lock students into traditional modes of communication, and when they appear to care about other people, teachers model productive habits of mind.

WHAT INFLUENCE DOES GENDER EXERT ON LEARNING AND TEACHING?

Girls consistently outscore boys on tests of reading and writing (Mullis, Owens, & Phillips, 1990). Even though girls and boys are approximately equal in measured academic ability when they enter school, by age 12, girls perform less well than boys in such areas as higher-level mathematics and measures of self-esteem, although the gender differences are declining in some areas such as mathematics (AAUW Educational Foundation & National Education Association, 1992). Such differences may be due in part to **gender bias**, discriminatory treatment, often subtle or unconscious, that unfairly favors or disfavors individuals because they are females or because they are males.

Girls receive less attention from teachers than do boys, and the quality of attention boys get is better (Sadker & Sadker, 1993). The literature also suggests that teachers are prone to choose classroom activities that appeal to boys' interests and to use instructional methods that favor boys. Teachers foster competition, for example, despite the fact that many studies suggest that girls, and many boys, experience greater academic success when they work cooperatively (AAUW Educational Foundation & National Education Association, 1992). Teachers also ask boys more challenging questions, and encourage them to work to get a correct answer, offer them more praise and

Research suggests that teachers of both sexes may unintentionally favor the intellectual development of male students through the quality and amount of their interaction with students in their classrooms.

VOICES

On Single-Sex Schools

Some California public schools have experimented with segregation of students by gender within classes. They have done so to combat what they and others perceive as the conditions of schooling that shortchange girls. Jane Gross wrote in the *New York Times* of these purposefully formed single-sex classes.

In Laura Gamb's high school mathematics and science classes last year, the boys would make fun of her if she said million when she meant billion, and she learned to deflect their ridicule by saying, "Just kidding," or "Never mind."

In Amber West's middle school math class, she was so afraid of sounding stupid when she didn't understand something that she swallowed her questions, whispered them to a teacher between periods or waited until she got home and asked her mother.

And in Cara Raysinger's high school math class, she often couldn't concentrate or get the teacher's attention because there were so many rowdy boys jumping out of their seats and throwing pencils across the room and making noises like airplanes.

But Laura, Amber and Cara don't feel embarrassed, intimidated, distracted or ignored anymore because now they are learning math and science in all-girl classrooms in three California

schools. The schools have adopted segregation as a way of solving the widely acknowledged problem of girls lagging behind boys in math and science from middle school onward. . . .

The three experiments are too new to have yielded hard and fast results. At Marin Academy, which is furthest along, the girls have yet to take any standardized tests, and Mrs. Flory said grades were a poor measure because four teachers were involved. Last year, the school interviewed students in all-girl and coed algebra classes and found that far more girls from the all-girl class would take math if it was not required. . . .

California education officials said the all-girl classes are permissible under state law because they are technically open to boys, even though none have enrolled. But Federal officials said they doubted that the classes would survive a more rigorous constitutional challenge because there were alternative ways to improve the educational environment for girls.

CRITICAL THINKING

What might be the advantages and disadvantages for girls (and for boys) of establishing single-sex classes within public schools?

Source: Gross, J. (1993, November 24). To help girls keep up, girls-only math classes. *New York Times*, p. A1.

---

constructive criticism, and acknowledge their substantive achievement more than they do girls (Sadker & Sadker, 1993).

Are boys also victims of bias in the schools? Studies indicate that teachers consider boys in general to be significantly more active, less attentive, less dexterous, and more prone to have behavioral, academic, and language problems than are girls. A study of 152 preservice teachers at the University of Minnesota during the 1990–1991 academic year revealed that the majority of teachers surveyed attributed disparities in academic achievement between boys and girls to society (87%) and school (71%). Other explanations for differences included family (25%) and genetics (21%) (Avery & Walker, 1993).

When schools identify children with learning disabilities, mental retardation, and reading disabilities, boys are typically identified more often than girls. In a longitudinal study of boys and girls in Connecticut public schools, researchers found that identification and placement for learning disability may be based less on discrepancy between a child's ability and achievement than on behavioral problems. Researchers' assessments of a sample of 215 girls and 199 boys in second and third grade classes revealed no significant differences in the prevalence of reading disability in boys and girls at either grade level. An examination of school identifications of boys and girls with reading disabilities in grades 2 and 3, however, revealed that more boys than girls in each grade had been identified (Shaywitz, Shaywitz, Fletcher, & Escobar, 1990).

HOW DOES STUDENT EXCEPTIONALITY INFLUENCE TEACHING AND LEARNING?

Children have similar needs, interests, and ways of knowing. However, about 1 in 10 students also has special abilities or disabilities that set him or her apart from other children (Hallahan & Kauffman, 1994). As we noted in Chapter 7, **exceptional learners** may possess one or more attributes that greatly affect the experiences they have at home, at school, and in the community at large.

Common Exceptionalities

While there is widespread agreement that some children deviate from the norm, there is not always consensus about what the norm is. Normal is defined within the context of a particular culture. Those who deviate from cultural expectations may possess one or more of the following attributes:

Giftedness   **Giftedness**, like other types of exceptionality, has been defined in several ways. According to the 1972 Marland definition (Public Law 91-230, Section 806), gifted and talented students are those children capable of high performance who excel in one or more of the following areas: general intellectual ability, specific academic aptitude, creative or productive thinking, leadership ability, ability in the visual or performing arts, and psychomotor ability. Traditionally, however, children have been labeled as gifted if they score above a certain level on an IQ test. A recent national survey indicated that 73% of school districts have adopted the Marland definition, yet few schools use the definition to identify and serve any area of giftedness other than high general intelligence as measured on IQ and achievement tests (U.S. Department of Education, Office of Educational Research and Improvement, 1993).

As noted earlier, some contend that intelligence is not a general characteristic but instead a combination of several capacities and cognitive abilities that cannot all be measured through the usual types of testing (Gardner & Hatch, 1989). Joseph Renzulli (1982) argues that giftedness is determined by high ability, high creativity, and high levels of motivation and task completion. Giftedness has also been described as "a sign of biopsychological potential in whichever domains exist in a culture" (Gardner, 1993, p. 51).

Mental Retardation   As indicated in Table 8.4, mental retardation is one of several categories of disability. According to the American Association on Mental Retardation (AAMR), **mental retardation** manifests before age 18 and greatly limits personal capabilities. It is characterized by

> significantly subaverage intellectual functioning [an IQ standard score of 70 to 75 or lower], existing concurrently with related limitations in two or more of the following applicable adaptive skill areas: communication, self-care, home living, social skills, community use, self-direction, health and safety, functional academics, leisure, and work. (American Association on Mental Retardation, 1992, p.5)

Despite their limitations, those with mental retardation who receive appropriate support over a sustained period will generally demonstrate improvement in their life functioning.

Hearing Impairment   **Hearing impairment** is a term used to describe degrees of deafness. While individuals who are hard of hearing can usually, with the use of a hearing aid, process oral language, those who are deaf are unable to do so. Educators who work with hearing impaired youngsters are concerned with when in a child's development hearing impairment occurred. They may describe hearing-impaired youngsters as "congenitally deaf" (born deaf) or "adventitiously deaf" (acquiring deafness sometime

---

TABLE 8.4   Some Categories of Disability

Mental retardation

Sensory impairment
>   Hearing impairment
>   Vision impairment

Physical disability
>   Orthopedic impairment
>   Health impairment
>   Seizure disorder

Communication disorder
>   Speech impairment
>   Language disorder

Emotional behavioral disorder

Attention deficit disorder

Learning disability

after birth). The main concern is the degree to which speech and language are affected by hearing loss and how best to facilitate communication skills (Hallahan & Kauffman, 1994).

Visual Impairment   A child who has **visual impairment** may be classified as "legally blind," "partially sighted," or "educationally blind." According to the American Medical Association, a person is considered blind when visual acuity in his or her better eye does not exceed 20/200 with corrective lenses or when the person's field of vision is limited at its widest angle to 20 degrees or less. Those who are partially sighted have better visual acuity (greater than 20/200 but not greater than 20/70 in the better eye after correction.) Children with educational blindness depend on senses other than sight; typically they use braille when reading (Wolf, Pratt, & Pruitt, 1990).

Orthopedic Impairments and Other Health Impairments Individuals with orthopedic and other health impairments include those with neurological impairment, or damage to their central nervous system, skeletal and muscular disorders, and congenital malformations. About half of the children with physical impairments in the United States have cerebral palsy, a neurological impairment characterized by weakness, lack of coordination, and/or motor dysfunction. Other neurological impairments include epilepsy (recurrent seizures), spina bifida (an improperly developed spinal cord that often causes paralysis of the lower body), and spinal cord injuries that occur when the spinal cord is traumatized or severed. Skeletal and muscular disorders include arthritis, a disease that causes inflammation around the joints, and muscular dystrophy, a degenerative disease that causes the breakdown of muscle tissues. Congenital malformations are malformations of any part of the body, such as the heart or the extremities, present at birth.

Speech and Language Disorders   Children with **speech impairments** may have fluency disorders (such as stuttering), articulation disorders (abnormality in the production of sounds), or voice disorders (such as hoarseness or hypernasality—too many sounds produced through the nose). Some children may exhibit delayed speech; that is, they use communication patterns like those of someone of a much younger age (e.g., pointing at something they want rather than verbalizing what they want). Children with **language disorders** may have receptive, expressive, or language processing problems, as well as combinations of these. In some instances, they also have difficulty with the meaning of words (semantics), with the sequential organization of words according to their relationships to each other (syntax), or with the purpose or uses for language (Palmer & Yantis, 1990).

Emotional and Behavioral Disorders   Among terms used to describe those who have emotional, social, and behavioral problems are *behavioral disordered*, *socially maladjusted*, *emotionally disturbed*, and *emotionally/behaviorally disordered*. These problems may manifest as such behaviors as phobias or depressions that are seemingly directed inward or by behaviors that are directed more at others (Wolf, Pratt, & Pruitt, 1990). The federal definition of "seriously emotionally disturbed" is:

The term means a condition exhibiting one or more of the following characteristics over a long period of time and to a marked degree, which adversely affects educational performance: (1) an inability to learn which cannot be explained by intellectual, sensory, or health factors; (2) an inability to build or maintain satisfactory relationships with peers and teachers; (3) inappropriate types of behavior or feelings under normal circumstances; (4) a general pervasive mood of unhappiness or depression; or (5) a tendency to develop physical symptoms or fears associated with personal or school problems. The term includes children who are schizophrenic . . . The term does not include children who are socially maladjusted, unless it is determined that they are seriously disturbed. (U.S. Department of Health, Education, and Welfare, 1977, p. 42478)

Attention Deficit Disorder   Attention deficit disorder (ADD) is sometimes referred to as attention deficit disorder with hyperactivity (ADDH) or attention-deficit hyperactivity disorder (ADHD). One of the most common disorders of childhood, ADD accounts for half of all child referrals to outpatient mental health clinics (Lerner & Lerner, 1991). Manifestations of the disorder include difficulty in staying on task, focusing attention, and completing work. Children with ADD appear not to listen or not to have heard what they have been told. They may also display age-inappropriate hyperactive behavior, be easily distracted, and produce sloppy and careless work (Lerner & Lerner, 1991).

Learning Disabilities   The National Joint Committee on Learning Disabilities, a group of representatives from eight national organizations that have a major interest in **learning disabilities**, defines the term as follows:

> **Learning disabilities** is a general term that refers to a heterogeneous group of disorders manifested by significant difficulties in the acquisition and use of listening, speaking, reading, writing, reasoning, or mathematical abilities. These disorders are intrinsic to the individual, presumed to be due to central nervous system disorder, and may occur across the life span. Problems in self-regulatory behaviors, social perception and social interaction may exist with learning disabilities but do not by themselves constitute a learning disability. Although learning disabilities may occur concomitantly with other handicapping conditions (for example, sensory impairment, mental retardation, serious emotional disturbance) or with extrinsic influences (such as cultural differences, insufficient or inappropriate instruction), they are not the result of those conditions or influences. (Hammill, Leigh, McNutt, & Larsen, 1988, p. 217)

Educational Programs for Gifted and Talented Students

Programs for gifted and talented students have enjoyed varying levels of support over the years. Such events as the launching of Sputnik in 1957 and the publication of *A Nation at Risk* by the National Commission on Excellence in Education in 1983 stimulated Americans to put more emphasis on programs for the brightest students. Between the 1960s and 1970s, however, issues of equity often forced gifted education to take a backseat as educators switched their attention to the needs of below-average and disadvantaged students; with increasingly limited resources for public education, people often chose to curtail or eliminate programs for gifted and talented students.

Currently, in every state and in many school districts there are gifted and talented programs. Gifted and talented students who remain in general education classrooms may be placed in accelerated curricula. They may be pulled out of the general education classroom for special instruction in a resource room. Sometimes gifted and talented students may attend self-contained classes for talented students. They may also skip a grade in school.

When students are selected for gifted and talented programs, studies suggest that economically disadvantaged students are significantly underserved. In 1988, only 9% of students in gifted and talented programs were in the bottom quartile of family income, while 47% were from the top quartile of family income (U.S. Department of Education, Office of Educational Research and Improvement, 1991). Studies also indicate that disproportionately fewer limited English proficient (LEP) students are included in gifted and talented programs. Although schools provide instructional assistance to these students, many people argue that educational programs do not teach the language or higher order skills students need to perform well on placement tests and that many LEP students therefore end up in lower-level classes (Schmidt, 1993).

As noted in Chapter 7, there is sometimes a stigma involved in being labeled a high-achieving student. In a survey of students in three midwestern high schools, students said they wanted to do well in school, but not exceptionally well because they were afraid they would be associated with the "brain crowd" rather than the "in crowd" (U.S. Department of Education, 1993).

The story of one high school student reveals some of the reasons why being bright may be somewhat difficult. In 1993, when Elizabeth Mann was a senior at Montgomery Blair High School in Silver Spring, Maryland, an article in *The Washington Post* bumped her status from "brilliant" to "legendary." (See Finkel, 1993). Elizabeth scored 1570 out of a possible 1600 on the SATs, 800 (out of 800) on her achievement test in math and 800 on her achievement test in physics. Several themes emerged in the story, among them the teachers' near veneration of Elizabeth's talents. The guidance counselor spoke of the "burden" Elizabeth bore because teachers were "absolutely charmed by her" (p. 13) "They are in awe of her. They have set her up as a paragon in their minds, and, I think, in the minds of her peers, which has made her road that much harder."

"I wish teachers wouldn't single out people."

Some spoke of Elizabeth as likely to be among history's greatest mathematicians or among the smartest people of all time. All of which caused Elizabeth to cringe:

From what I've heard and what I can see, you get the general impression they're all overly enamored of me . . . I guess in and of itself, that's nice. I mean, you can't ever be upset that people like you. So that's fine. The consequences of it are what make me uneasy. (p. 22)

It is not difficult to see why Elizabeth feels this way when a fellow student discusses what he perceives as her favored status:

If you look at what's happened to Elizabeth in her four years in the magnet, there isn't one example of her being disadvantaged. . . . I have a hard time complaining. I've gotten a lot out of the magnet program. But no one has gotten as much out of it as she has. Let me make it clear. Nobody has gotten as much attention out of the program as her. (p. 22)

Elizabeth's closest friend, Valerie Wang, also offered her perspective: "No one dislikes her, because she's not dislikable, but I think there's a lot of resentment" (p. 22).

After finishing third behind two of her classmates in a highly competitive science fair, Elizabeth sat outside her house the next day and expressed her doubts and dreams:

I wish I had beautiful hair. . . . I wish I were better at physics and math than I am. I wish I could stay awake 24 hours a day. I wish I had a car. I wish I could figure out why I've lost so much respect from Josh [a fellow student], and what I could do about it, and what I'm doing wrong. I wish teachers wouldn't single out people. I wish I could be respected for my mind and yet liked as a person regardless of what my mind is like. I wish, well, this is a hard one. I wish people knew about my insecurities, so they wouldn't think I'm conceited, as apparently they do. (p. 27)

Educational Programs for Students With Disabilities

As noted in Chapter 7, present law assures individuals with disabilities a right to a free, appropriate education in the least restrictive environment. This means that students with disabilities are to be educated in regular classrooms whenever possible. During the 1989–90 school year, 93% of 6- to 21-year-olds with disabilities were served in regular school buildings alongside students without disabilities. Most often, students with disabilities were placed in regular, resource, or separate classroom environments. Those in regular classes received special services outside the regular classroom for less than 21% of the school day. Students in resource rooms spent 21 to 60% of their school day away from nondisabled students, and those in separate classes spent more than 60% of the school day outside the regular classroom (U.S. Department of Education, 1992).

Mainstreaming laws require that students with disabilities receive free, appropriate educational and support services in the least restrictive environment.

Cultural Awareness

Hispanic students with disabilities are "doubly segregated" in American high schools. They are more likely than European-American and African-American special education students to be placed in special classrooms for disabled students and least likely to spend time in regular classrooms. Furthermore, they get fewer opportunities to receive vocational services, counseling, or job-skills training (Viadero, 1992).

There is debate about how educational programs for students with disabilities should be structured (see Chapter 7). In the main, this debate has centered on whether special services should be delivered in separate or in integrated settings. The words used almost as shorthand to capture the essence of the argument are the *Regular Education Initiative* or *REI* and *inclusion*. Some people advocate and some oppose taking the initiative to move special services out of self-contained settings and into regular or general education classrooms. In other words, advocates of the REI want students with disabilities who are taught with one another to be included fully in general education classrooms with nondisabled children. The resolution of this debate could have striking implications for both general and special education teachers.

Several empirical studies have examined the effects of full-inclusion programs on children with and without disabilities. A 4-year study of children attending a midwestern suburban elementary school where all children worked together in regular education classes focused on academic and social ramifications of full inclusion. Pre- and postassessments of a sample of 100 students including children with disabilities, children considered at-risk for academic failure, and children without disabilities revealed that:

> [(1)] students' achievement levels did not increase consistently to the extent that might be expected; (2) students' self-concept did not improve, as intended, but rather stayed the same; (3) students' social skills did not improve, as intended, but rather stayed the same; and (4) special education students' time in the mainstream classroom did increase, as intended; [however] the increase primarily reflected a change in where special education services were provided. (Ysseldyke, Christenson, & Thurlow, 1993, p. ii)

Results from multiyear studies conducted by researchers at the University of Pittsburgh, Vanderbilt University, the University of Minnesota, and the University of Washington also suggest that current efforts to implement full-inclusion classrooms do not improve and sustain outcomes for all students (Jenkins, Zigmond, Fuchs, Fuchs, & Deno, 1993). The issue of full inclusion is taken up again in Chapter 10.

BENCHMARKS

Equal Opportunity for Americans with Disabilities

1973   Vocational Rehabilitation Act (Public Law 93-112, Section 504): people with disabilities cannot be discriminated against in any way in any federally funded program.

1974   Educational Amendments Act (Public Law 93-380): Federal funds provided to the states for implementing programs for exceptional learners, including the gifted and talented. Rights to due process granted to children with disabilities and their families in special education placement.

1975   Education of the Handicapped Law (Public Law 94-142, Part B, known as the Mainstreaming Law): A free and appropriate public education must be provided for all children with disabilities ages 5 and above. Education must be planned through an individualized education program (IEP) and carried out in the least restrictive environment.

1986   Education of the Handicapped Act Amendments (Public Law 99-457): A free and appropriate education extended to all children with disabilities ages 3 to 5, and early intervention programs established for infants and toddlers with disabilities.

1990   Americans with Disabilities Act (ADA, Public Law 101-336): national mandate to end discrimination against people with disabilities in private-sector employment, in public services, public accommodations, transportation, and telecommunications.

1990   Individuals with Disabilities Education Act (Public Law 101-476): the Education of the Handicapped Act renamed the Individuals with Disabilities Education Act (IDEA), special education services extended to children with autism and traumatic brain injury, and rehabilitation and social work services included in the definition of special education.

Regardless of where children with disabilities are placed in schools, regular and special educators will need to work with parents and other professionals to plan an **individualized education program (IEP)** for each child. A child's IEP includes such things as current level of performance (strengths and limitations), long- and short-term goals, criteria for success, methods for assessing mastery of objectives (e.g., observation, testing), amount of time that will be spent in regular or general education classrooms, and beginning and ending dates for special services. Two pages from a 19-page IEP appear in the Appendix at the end of this chapter.

In some instances, teachers will have students in their classrooms who share many of the attributes of exceptional children but who, for one reason or another, are not identified as such. Although teachers are not required to create IEPs for these children, they are obligated to create a learning environment that enables all children to maximize their potentials.

When implementing plans, good teachers will seek ways to increase students' achievement and to foster positive social relationships between children with disabilities and their nondisabled peers. Just as gifted and talented students may have difficulty winning acceptance by their peers, children with disabilities may also experience social problems. Richard Waller, a 33-year-old from Muskogee, Oklahoma, recalled some of the personal challenges he faced as a student (Orlansky, 1981):

> When I first started to school, I had a speech problem. I went to first grade twice and second grade twice because of it. Then I went straight through school to the fifth grade. Halfway through fifth grade, I went to a school they had here in town, called Jefferson, went to their special education for a year and a half. Then I went from there to the seventh, the eighth, and ninth, and that was the only years I went to school. The ninth grade. Then I started to work at my dad's garage, as an auto mechanic with my dad. I enjoyed that and I'm still an auto mechanic. (127)
>
> . . . I am a slow learner at some things, and it takes me a while to learn, but some other things I can do kind of fast. Like tune a car up, a six-cylinder in thirty minutes.
>
> In school, they found out if I had any handicap, which I did. They put me close to the front, where they could listen to me, so they could understand what I was saying. I felt like I was a privileged person at that point, sitting up in the front. I liked it until the last two years of school. The kids started picking on me, called me a baby and all that stuff. I felt kind of low. (pp. 127–128)

As we noted in Chapters 6 and 7, educators can use such strategies as conflict resolution and cooperative learning to improve interpersonal relationships and to enhance self-esteem. Chapter 10 will describe in particular the utility of cooperative learning for helping to change negative stereotypes and for integrating children with disabilities into the mainstream classroom.

SUMMARY

1. There are competing ideas about the meaning of intelligence. While some experts view intelligence as a unitary trait, others define it as a multidimensional trait that varies over time and from situation to situation. Yet others view intelligence as knowledge and skills deemed important for a particular culture. Young people also view intelligence in different ways, including as a static entity impervious to change and as a dynamic entity that can be affected by teaching.

2. Psychometricians develop tests to assess intelligence. Measurement is conducted by administering a number of tasks and inferring intellectual capabilities from examinees' performances. Scores are used widely to predict success in school and work.

3. Intelligence is sometimes characterized in terms of stages of development, each more complex than the last. Stage theorists suggest that teaching must fit students' levels of development in order to be successful.

4. Theorists with a contextual perspective suggest systematic teaching can and does influence intellectual development. Vygotsky and others with this outlook recommend that teachers actively intervene to shape intellectual growth rather than assume that such growth will occur merely by placing students in educational environments with certain materials.

5. Theories of information processing describe how information is received, analyzed, stored, and used.

6. In healthy individuals, both the mind and body develop together and over time, but not always at the same rate. Different people develop in different ways. Nonetheless, there are identifiable common patterns of physical and mental development from birth to death that have important implications for education.

7. Differences in physical development may be caused by such factors as genetics, amount of stimulation from caretakers, nutrition, and the quality of a child's physical environment.

8. Lead poisoning is one of the most common and devastating housing-related diseases. It can cause severe developmental and health problems for children.

9. Poverty figures prominently in young people's health profiles. Adolescents from low-income families experience lower rates of achievement in school and higher rates of poor physical health, mental disorders, and depression.

10. As children grow and change, their body types influence developmental task achievement, self-image, and self-satisfaction.

11. Young people's personal and social (psychosocial) development proceeds somewhat systematically and is affected in large part by the people around them.

12. Moral development can be described in terms of developmental stages that have implications for how students are taught. Reasoning becomes more complex, less egocentric, and less absolute at each successive stage.

13. Despite claims to the contrary, males and females appear to make judgments about moral issues in much the same way.

14. The most powerful habits of mind (the shared skills, attitudes, and values transmitted by custom or convention from one generation to the next) may be the less visible, informal, implicit ones held and modeled by teachers and by members of a community.

15. Differences in students' achievement may be due in part to what students are taught (or not taught), and how they are treated in the classroom.

16. Although children have similar needs, interests, and ways of knowing, some individuals have special abilities or disabilities that set them apart from other children. These "exceptional" children may possess one or more attributes that greatly affect the experiences they have at home, at school, and in the community at large.

TERMS AND CONCEPTS

cognitive development
developmentally appro-
    priate instruction
exceptional learners
gender bias
giftedness
habits of mind
hearing impairment
individualized educa-
    tion program (IEP)

information processing
    theory
intelligence quotient
    (IQ)
language disorders
learning disabilities
mental retardation
metacognitive skills
moral development

multiple intelligences
psychometric
    perspective
psychosocial
    development
self-esteem
speech impairments
visual impairment

STUDENT ACTIVITIES

Educators can learn much about the students they teach by listening to what students say about life in schools and by observing students' actions. Understanding students is a prerequisite to meeting their needs and capitalizing on their talents. Teachers may fail to understand their students if they are unaware of or do not value the information students can provide about themselves. These activities are designed to accomplish several purposes: (a) to help educators examine their own thinking about themselves in relation to students, (b) to gather information about students from students and to apply it to formulate some directions for teaching, and (c) to judge the efficacy of one's own efforts to acquire and use student information.

A cautionary note is in order about the activities related to observing and talking with students in general. People cannot observe and interview students without the express permission of school authorities. Students and their parents have legal and moral rights to privacy. Information gathered about students must be collected for educational purposes in accordance with school policies and used by proper authorities for educational purposes.

Perceive and Value

List labels that you and your classmates use to describe yourselves as learners. According to your discussion group, what attributes, attitudes, skills, and values are associated with academic success? What conclusions can you draw from your discussion? As a teacher, how might you respond effectively to those differences?

Know and Act

As a teacher, exactly what should you know about your students' levels of physical, cognitive, psychosocial, and/or moral development before teaching, for example, the following topics or skills: using scissors, reporting rule violations, multiplying fractions, playing team soccer, learning the concept of liberty, or giving an oral report? In each case, use information presented in this chapter to develop specific examples showing how your knowledge of developmental issues, individual differences, and exceptionalities could help you teach more effectively.

Evaluate

Reflect on your experiences and observations throughout your school years as a female or a male student. In your opinion, did gender affect academic learning experiences, choices, and degree of success for you and your peers? In what ways were any effects generally positive or negative for you as a student? How will gender issues affect you as a teacher?

Discover

Conduct a survey or interview students on ethical or morally defensible conduct—for example, in researching and writing term papers and in preparing for and taking tests. Ask respondents to justify the conduct they report. Then analyze the behavior and justifications in terms of information in this chapter about stages of moral development. What do you conclude about levels of moral reasoning? What is the relationship between moral reasoning and action?

Foundations

In Action

Teachers act in ways they believe will help students learn, and they also respond to students as unique individuals. Responding effectively to the great array of individual differences and needs typically present in any classroom, however, can be daunting. In the cases that follow, how does student variability challenge teachers to develop strategies for meeting both individual and collective needs?

"I felt I needed to know what they were thinking."

Mary Anne Reed-Brown is meeting with three students she thinks are not achieving as they should. She hopes to increase her knowledge of them as individual learners. As the students read and discuss stories they have written, she listens to learn more about their abilities, attitudes, and motivations. She may need different strategies to encourage greater achievement and better conduct in each child.

Reed-Brown: James, why don't you read your story to us? You did not get to share it yesterday.

James: On Thanksgiving I had a dinner. Albert came over to eat, and I went over to his house to eat, too. Then I played Nintendo. I went to the Grand Canyon on Rad Racer, and I watched a football game—Cowboys against Pittsburgh. Dallas won. I was happy again. Then I stayed up all night watching rap videos. I played Nintendo again. I played a game called Metroid, then I went back outside about 3:00 a.m.

Reed-Brown: At 3:00 a.m.?

Tony: Yeah, in the morning we played football.

Reed-Brown: At 3:00 a.m.?

James: Yeah.

The three boys sitting with me all have difficulty settling down and completing work. I felt I needed to know what they were thinking. Also, listening to one another as they read their work aloud strengthens their skills and their confidence to be better students.

Douglas participates in an English as a Second Language pull-out program and does well, except in writing. The written language is difficult for most of my bilingual students, and it shows up in their testing. James is a natural-born leader. I had some difficulty with him this morning, and I needed to understand why. Tony has a hard time in class. I can't pinpoint his problem, so it has been difficult to address his needs.

"[There] are so many children with so many needs. . . . I remind myself constantly to be patient with them."

"I want them to know that in school they have someone there to listen and help them."

Laura Saazter gathers her students in one corner of the room to explain procedures for recording information from student presentations on famous people. While doing so, Saazter has to simultaneously respond to Brenda, a mainstreamed special education student who at this moment is lying on the floor, refusing to move. How can Saazter balance Brenda's need for individual attention and other students' needs to complete a learning activity in the available time?

Saatzer: In this packet, find paper number one. Brenda, give me this. You're going to find number one and write the name of the famous person. Brenda, sit up! After you have written the person's name, you need to write down one fact you learned about that person. Brenda, come on or I will have to call the office and they might have to call Dad. All right, everyone. Go quietly to your places, and I will give you your packets. Brenda, get up. Are you going to act like a third grader? Then stand up, now.

My class is very challenging this year. Sometimes the students exhaust my patience because there are so many children with so many needs. Knowing their home lives, I remind myself constantly to be patient with them.

One of my students receives special services because she is classified EBD (emotionally/behaviorally disordered). She can be a real challenge at times. Many times I know she is acting out anger that she is unable to handle by herself. Fortunately, I have a backup system. I just buzz the office and our behavior management aide will come. My heart goes out to Brenda, so I don't mind her behavior so much, but it does disrupt class, and it does take time away from other students' learning.

Peter Flaherty has integrated Native-American cultural studies into his math lessons. The students make calculations using Aztec and Mayan calendars and solve problems based on individual classmates' actual experiences. He hopes to teach students about their individuality and commonality while they are learning math.

Flaherty: Heads up front, please. Most of you have mastered some of the counting skills in the Ojibwa language. We are going to practice some multiplication problems using the Ojibwa numbers. The first one: *niizhtana* times *naanan*. What's *niizhtana*?

Students: Twenty.

Flaherty: What's *naanan*?

Students: Five.

Flaherty: What is 20 times 5?

Students: A hundred.

Flaherty: And what is the Ojibwa word for 100?

Students: *Ningodwaak.*

Flaherty: Try this next one, please. Remember, figure it out in numbers and then write it in Ojibwa.

There are times when I really separate myself from the students. I try to be the teacher in the classroom, up in the front, leading the lessons. There are other times when I try to be a different kind of leader and get closer to the students. Because too many of them do not have parents who care. So I want them to know that in school they have someone there to listen and help them.

APPENDIX TO CHAPTER 8

Sample Pages from an IEP

CURRY PUBLIC SCHOOLS
Department of Pupil Personnel Services
1417 Broadway, Curry, Virginia 23234
(804) 666-9876

INDIVIDUALIZED EDUCATION PROGRAM

Name **Amy North**   DOB **7-7-83**   Grade **2**

Parent/Guardian **John/Sandra North**   School **Eugene Field**

Address **1400 Perth Road 23456**   Phone: HOME **945-4546**   WORK **886-1234**

Handicapping Condition(s) **mild mental retardation**   Most Recent Eligibility Date **1-24-91**

IEP Purpose: _____   Initial Placement **✓**   Continued Placement _____   Dismissal from _____

PRESENT LEVEL OF EDUCATIONAL PERFORMANCE:

Amy reads stories of approximately 100 words on first grade level using phonics skills to decode unfamiliar words. She answers factual comprehension questions. She does not copy from the board but completes reading seatwork legibly. She spells C-V-C words from dictation but does not write stories using inventive spelling. In math she solves horizontal & vertical addition & subtraction problems and knows no. facts plus-1, plus-0, plussing numbers to 10 (10 + 4 = □). Her math seat work is more accurate when she remembers no. facts than when she uses manipulatives. She has some difficulty with some self-help skills: buttons & zippers. She eats her lunch independently opening her juice & applesauce. She independently negotiates her school environment and participates in regular P.E. w/adaptations as needed. Amy tends to be telegraphic in responses & spontaneous responses are often inappropriate. It is very difficult to evaluate her language abilities. She indicates a higher level of expressive language during creative play. She is non-compliant frequently. Amy is mildly delayed in manipulative skills & mild-to-moderately delayed locomotor and balance skills. Successfully participates in regular P.E.

Communication Severity Rating Scale: N/A 1 2 3 4 5 ⑥

Name **Amy North**   School **Eugene Field**   Page 3

EDUCATIONAL PROGRAM / SPECIAL EDUCATION AND RELATED SERVICES:

Insruction/Service	Amount of Time in Instructional Week	Percent of Instructional Week	Projected Date for Initiation of Service	Anticipated Completion Date
Speech/Language	3 x 30 min.	5%	9-8-92	6-16-93
self-contained MiMR	27 hours	71%	9-8-92	6-16-93
physical therapy	consult as needed		9-8-92	6-16-93
occupational therapy	1 x 25 min.	2%	9-8-92	6-16-93
adaptive phys. ed.	1 x 30 min.	2%	9-8-92	6-16-93

Unless otherwise noted, the services listed above will be provided within the Charlottesville Public Schools by school personnel or qualified personnel contracted by the school division

Transportation: **✓**   Regular _____   Special: _____

EDUCATIONAL PROGRAM / GENERAL EDUCATION:

_____ All educational options, except those listed above, provided with non-handicapped students

Academic/Non Academic/ Extracurricular Activities	Amount of Time in Instructional Week	Percent of Instructional Week
art	1 x 45 min.	3%
physical education	2 x 30 min.	3%
music	2 x 30 min.	3%
library	1 x 45 min.	3%
soc. st./science/health	3 x 45 min.	8%
lunch, recess, assemblies		

FAMILY LIFE EDUCATION:

✓ Provided in general education setting with the following adaptations/exclusions:

_____

_____ Provided in special education setting with the following adaptations/exclusions:

_____

_____ No Participation

Name _____ Amy North _____   School ____ Eugene Field _____   Page 5

Annual Goal ___ Reading – To demonstrate growth in reading as measured by informal reading inventories

Short Term Objectives	Evaluation Procedure and Criteria	Review Schedule	Completion Date
① will read following sounds in isolation & in words on her reading level: ă, ā, b, c, ĕ, ē, f, g, h, ĭ, ī, k, l, m, n, ŏ, ō, p, r, s, t, u, v, w, sh, th, ch	teacher observation of oral reading – 100%	daily	
② will read following sounds in isolation & in words: ing, er, ar, al, ou, y, oo, j, ȳ	teacher observation of oral & written responses – 90%	daily after presentation	
③ will answer oral & written comprehension questions seeking concrete information about stories on her level (Who is in the story? What happens? When? Why?)	tchr. observation of oral & written responses – 90%	daily	
④ will predict outcomes suggested in reading stories	teacher observation of oral responses	daily	
⑤ will sight-read stories on her level at 60 words/min.	teacher observation of oral responses – no more than 2 errors per reading	weekly after 1/93	

Annual Goal ___ Math – to demonstrate growth in math skills as measured by teacher-made tests

Short Term Objectives	Evaluation Procedure and Criteria	Review Schedule	Completion Date
① will solve simple horizontal & vertical addition & subtraction & missing addend problems	teacher observation of written responses – 90%	daily	
② will solve 2-digit addition without regrouping	tchr. observ. of written responses–90%	daily after present'n 10/92	
③ will add a column of 3 numerals	tchr. obs. of written resp. – 90%	daily – 12/92	
④ will state & write addition facts: plus-1, plus-2, plus-3, plus-4, plus-5 to numerals 1-9	teacher observation of written & oral responses – 90%	daily	
⑤ will translate a simple fraction into an oral statement, represent/write a fraction that describes a picture	teacher observation of oral & written responses – 90%	weekly after presentation	
⑥ will solve word problems written on her level	tchr. ob. of oral & written resp. – 90%	daily	
⑦ will tell time on the hour & half hour	tchr. ob. of oral responses – 90%	daily	

White Copy: Dept. of Spec. Ed/Student Services   Yellow Copy: School   Pink Copy: Parent

Source: From *Exceptional Children: An Introduction to Special Education*, 6th Edition (pp. 36–38) by D. P. Hallahan and J. Kauffman, 1994, Boston: Allyn and Bacon. Copyright 1994 by Allyn and Bacon. Reprinted by permission.

Curriculum is generally thought of as what is taught in school. The word *curriculum*, however, encompasses so many ideas that it defies simple description. This chapter discusses some of the more prominent ways curriculum has been defined through educational practice and explores some of the effects of curriculum on student learning. The chapter also examines the forces influencing curriculum content and the aims underlying the curriculum—aims that may be stated explicitly or left implicit, emphasized or ignored. Finally, the chapter considers how the curriculum is planned, organized, and evaluated.

Curriculum

PROFESSIONAL PRACTICE QUESTIONS

1 What forces have shaped curriculum in American schools and classrooms through the years?

Perceive

....

2 How are people's values and philosophies reflected explicitly and implicitly in various curricular programs? How do your beliefs about what students should learn and how teachers should teach compare to the values underlying various curricula?

Value

....

3 Are there some things every person should know if he or she expects to be a fully functioning member of this society? If so, what might be included in "core" knowledge and skills?

Know

....

4 How might you use what you know about formal, school-based models of curriculum to adapt the informal curricula of newspapers, magazines, and television to the teaching of a particular subject?

Act

....

5 How might public standards influence people's assessments of the value and effectiveness of curricular programs?

Evaluate

....

WHAT IS CURRICULUM?

Most people define **curriculum** in terms of what is taught in school. Books are curriculum. Study guides are curriculum. Movies, newspapers, computer programs, board games, animals, and songs can be curriculum. Curriculum, in the vernacular, is what schools are supposed to be held accountable for helping students master.

Ronald Doll (1986) notes that curriculum has been defined as "the accumulated tradition of organized knowledge contained in school and college subjects. . . . the modes of thinking and inquiring about phenomena of our world. . . . [and] experiences of the race" (p. 6). Indeed, "the experiences of the race," "the race course," "the course to be run" come close to reflecting the original meaning of the word as the Romans used it. The *curriculum* was the Roman word for the track around which they raced chariots. The curriculum can be, however, a racecourse or field that "lacks clean boundaries" (Vallance, 1983).

Peter Oliva (1992) observes that *curriculum* has been used to convey a variety of ideas:

- Curriculum is that which is taught in school.

- Curriculum is a set of subjects.

- Curriculum is content.

- Curriculum is a program of studies.

- Curriculum is a set of materials.

- Curriculum is a sequence of courses.

- Curriculum is a set of performance objectives.

- Curriculum is a course of study.

- Curriculum is everything that goes on within the school, including extra-class activities, guidance, and interpersonal relationships.

- Curriculum is that which is taught both inside and outside school, directed by the school.

- Curriculum is everything that is planned by school personnel.

- Curriculum is a series of experiences undergone by learners in school.

- Curriculum is that which an individual learner experiences as a result of schooling. (Oliva, 1992, pp. 5–6)

A survey of articles in professional journals, agenda for school board meetings, and public opinion expressed through the mass media reveals that Americans have a variety of conflicting conceptions about what constitutes curriculum, and thus about what children should or should not be taught in classrooms. So great is the political stress surrounding curricular decisions that "every tension within the polity, argument about the culture and division in the population descends upon the operating room whenever the curriculum undergoes surgery" (Finn, 1991, p. 46).

The tensions, arguments, and divisions arise in large measure because the population is heterogeneous and rapid socioeconomic change routinely makes curriculum decisions controversial. Because education is a power reserved to the states, states and localities are left to define the curriculum. Beyond some rather vague agreement on the need for students to read, write, and compute, there is considerable variation in people's desires and expectations for what the curriculum should deliver.

Moreover, curriculum can be contextually bound; that is, where a person lives can constrain how curriculum is defined. For instance, a comparative study of community offerings in an inner-city, low-income, largely African-American community and an affluent, largely European-American, suburban community in metropolitan Chicago revealed differences in how curriculum is defined in community programs (Littell & Wynn, 1989). Many after-school resources available to inner-city children were aimed at personal support or tutoring, whereas those in the suburban area included arts activities, clubs, sports, and social and civic events.

People in this country have cared deeply about curriculum for a long time. In colonial days, as we noted in Chapter 2, the curriculum was simple—God and the three Rs. Nonetheless, it aroused strong emotions among those who delivered it and those who received it. Much later, in the 1890s, organized curriculum development grew from a "preoccupation of a handful of educational statesmen operating within a relatively cloistered setting to the concern of a virtual army of specialists and a matter of national concern" (Kliebard, 1979, p. 191). When the National Education Association provided a public forum in the 1890s for the discussion of education, debate was heated. They could not agree on how much curriculum should be altered to prepare students for the new industrial age (Kliebard, 1979).

Like many other past controversies in education, the great curriculum debate of the 1890s rages on today. People have yet to reach consensus on what should be taught and how it should be offered. Perhaps William Schubert (1986, p. 8) put the best face on the situation when he noted that there is a "productive uncertainty" of ideas about the content and aims of school programs.

It is important to remember that curriculum is an operative concept outside school as well as inside. Business, industry, churches, prisons, and other organizations provide out-of-school training in topics as diverse as dog obedience, home sales, and natural childbirth. Curriculum is at issue when the agricultural extension agent drops by the rural farmhouse, when children watch Sesame Street and attend Scout meetings, and when people study for a real estate license. This fact underscores the idea that education is not the exclusive province of the schools.

Explicit Curriculum

The curriculum contained in policy statements, manuals of procedure, instructional materials, books, and other printed matter that explicate what and how students are to learn constitute the **explicit curriculum**. Descriptions of programs, courses, and objectives of study specifically reveal for public consumption the educational expectations held for both teachers and students. Teachers are supposed to teach the explicit curriculum, students are supposed to learn it. The explicit curriculum, then, is that curriculum for which schools are held publicly accountable.

Implicit Curriculum

If the explicit curriculum dominates the public view, another side of the curriculum is unvoiced and often unintended. This side reveals itself in the way teachers present subject matter and the classroom atmosphere they establish. Philip Jackson (1990, p. 33) has called this curriculum the "hidden curriculum." Elliot Eisner (1985, p. 89) has used the term **implicit curriculum** for essentially the same idea.

Based on observations of teacher-student interactions in elementary classrooms over a period of 2 years, Jackson (1990) perceived a number of institutional expectations (the hidden curriculum) that seemed key to a student's success in the classroom. "Trying" was one such expectation taught implicitly, rather than explicitly, through school experiences. If a student "does his homework (though incorrectly), he raises his hand (though he usually comes up with the wrong answer), [and] he keeps his nose in the book during free study period (though he doesn't turn the page very often)," he will likely gain the teacher's approval and be labeled a "model" student (p. 34). What this suggests to students is that mastery of content is not the only road to success in the classroom. Students who understand this seem particularly adroit at "apple polishing" and hiding behaviors from the teacher.

There has been much debate about the effects of routines and rituals of schooling. Such teacher behavior as calling on students with hands raised while ignoring those who verbalize opinions without permission is but one of the subtle ways teachers convey what are considered largely middle-class values. Some contend that the middle-class version of "hidden" curriculum prepares students to function effectively in society; others question the effect on students from the lower, working, and upper classes (Schubert, 1986).

Another type of implicit curriculum relates to teachers' value orientations and to the subject matter they teach. In case studies of four high school teachers (two English teachers and two history teachers), Sigrun Gudmundsdottir (1991) found that teachers' values seeped into the curriculum in at least two ways: through personal interpretations of subject matter and through teaching methods.

> **What do students learn from the implicit and null curricula to which they are inevitably exposed?**

For example, when English teachers were dealing with *Huckleberry Finn*, one teacher viewed the book as an illustration of "an individual rebelling against conventions" while the other considered it "a book about relationships [between Huck and Jim]" (p. 48). In presenting the book, each teacher selected passages for discussion representative of these ideas, thus creating different "texts" for their students. Dialogues between teacher, student, and text were also influenced by teaching methods. One teacher focused more on the content of the text while the other focused on the relevance of content to students' lives. Even though both teachers dealt with the same book, then, their value orientations likely resulted in different outcomes for their students.

Null Curriculum

Consequences of school programs are similarly affected by what Eisner (1985) refers to as the **null curriculum**. This is the curriculum that is *not* taught. Our silence on many matters is purported to have a variety of ramifications, not the least of which is a negative effect on students' ability to examine critically all sides of an issue and to make informed decisions. The intellectual processes and subject matter areas emphasized and neglected by teachers are prime contributors to this condition.

Christine Sleeter and Carl Grant argue that textbook content in particular "withholds, obscures, and renders unimportant many ideas and areas of knowledge" (1991, p. 97). Their picture and story-line analyses of textbooks published between 1980 and 1988 and used in grades 1 through 8 revealed that attention to inequality based on race, sex, disability, and social class left much to be desired.

Social class, for example, was rarely dealt with in textbooks. Sleeter and Grant contend that the version of reality presented did not reveal social stratification as it exists in the United States today; instead, textbooks conveyed an image of a largely middle-class society, devoid of poverty and without great wealth. According to Sleeter and Grant, this tendency to ignore issues of gender, social class, poverty, and disability has the potential for "producing citizens with a shallow social consciousness and narrow sense of history and culture, and alienating from school lower-class children and children of color" (p. 101). Others hypothesize that such curriculum practices reproduce and legitimize existing social-class hierarchies (Apple & Beyer, 1988).

Cultural Awareness

When the New York State Board of Regents set out to shape social studies curriculum for the public schools, its committee acknowledged the contributions of many cultures to the formation of core American values (New York State Social Studies Review and Development Committee, 1991). The Regents appointed a committee of 24 college, university, and public school teachers to review and modify existing social studies syllabi. Their task was to create "a plan for increasing all students' understanding of American history and culture, the history and culture of the diverse groups which comprise American society today, and the history and culture of other peoples throughout the world" (Sobol, 1991, p. 1). In its final report to the board, the committee asserted how social studies curricula should be structured so as to fill what they perceived as the void in the curriculum:

> Social studies should not be so much concerned with "whose culture" and "whose history" are to be taught and learned, as with the development of intellectual competence in learners, with intellectual competence viewed as having as one of its major components the capacity to view the world and understand it from multiple perspectives. Thus the position is taken that a few fundamental concepts should be the focus of the teaching and learning of the social studies, with applications, contexts and examples drawn from multiple cultural sources, differing perspectives and diverse identity group referents. Multicultural knowledge in this conception of the social studies becomes a vehicle and not the goal. Multicultural content and experience become instruments by which we enable persons to develop their intelligence and to function as human and humane persons. (New York Social Studies Review and Development Committee, 1991, p. 13)

Yet another way teachers convey hidden messages to students is through time schedules for different classes and locations for instruction. Time devoted to the arts, for example, is substantially less than time devoted to such courses as science and math and communicates to students "what counts" in schools (Eisner, 1992). Moreover, the fact that art teachers are often "floaters"—moving from classroom to classroom—suggests to students that the arts are less permanent and perhaps less important than other courses. In some schools, the art and music teachers may find themselves teaching in the cafeteria.

The arts and imaginative expression of all sorts are often brought up when people discuss the null curriculum. When money is tight, programs in the arts are often first to take the brunt of cutbacks. Certainly, the teachers in these areas are affected directly and immediately by the ebb and flow of funding for the arts, but society is also affected over the longer term. If even one generation of students grows up ignorant of architecture, music, paintings, theater, sculpture, dance, poetry, drawing, photography, and graphic and landscape design, the record of human achievement is in jeopardy.

Fearing this possible consequence, the American Council for the Arts and the Music Educators National Conference assembled representatives from 25 national organizations on March 24, 1986, in Philadelphia, Pennsylvania (Wilson, 1991). These representatives drafted and signed a resolution that among other things urged every elementary and secondary school to offer a balanced, sequential, and high quality program of instruction in arts disciplines—to move the arts from the null to the explicit curriculum. What was to become known as the Philadelphia Resolution also advocated that the arts be taught by qualified teachers and strengthened by artists and arts organizations. The arts, they argued, must be viewed as an essential component of the curriculum.

Extracurriculum

In many schools, there is a well-developed **extracurriculum**, or curriculum that has arisen in and around the core of a student's studies (Berk, 1992). By definition, this extracurriculum is not credit bearing—it is extra or over and above the required curriculum. Yet it can exert considerable power over students. Students' feelings of self-efficacy, their desire to come to school, their need to belong or be part of a group, and even their performance in other basic curricular areas can be influenced greatly by extracurricular activities.

Sports, band, clubs of all kinds, study groups, school plays, cheerleading, dance, etc. may fall under the rubric of the extracurriculum. In some schools, these activities may be considered "cocurricular" and weighted equally with other academic offerings. In the main, however, most of these activities are viewed as being outside the typical curriculum.

Nevertheless, people make conceptual and policy ties between the curriculum and the extracurriculum. For example, if a student performs poorly on the required curriculum, someone is sure to argue the student should not be allowed to participate in the extracurriculum, at least until there is improvement in his or her grades. Others will argue the opposite—were it

Research suggests that participation in the extracurriculum and life of the school is a critical factor in students' academic success.

not for the appeal of extracurricular activities, a student with academic problems might be a dropout.

Researchers at the U.S. Department of Education's Office of Research and Improvement (OERI) began investigating the connection between extracurricular activities and academic performance and came up with interesting results. Generally, extracurricular participation rates rose with socioeconomic level, enrollment in an academic curriculum, and attainment of a B+ or better average. The positive relationship between participation in extracurricular activities and academic performance was reinforced again in a study of ninth graders (Gifford & Dean, 1990). When OERI researchers studied the possible effect of what strict enforcement of a C average (2.0 GPA) standard would have done to extracurricular participation in athletics they found:

- 85 percent of the varsity athletes and 81 percent of the other students had at least a C average.

- More of the young women athletes than of the young men had a GPA of 2.0 or above.

- 64 percent of the African-American male athletes and 68 percent of the Hispanic male athletes met the 2.0 requirement.

- 88 percent of the participants in extracurricular activities met or exceeded the requirement, while only 72 percent of nonparticipants did. (McNergney & Haberman, 1987, p. 21)

WHAT FORCES AND CHANGE AGENTS AFFECT CURRICULUM CONTENT?

In public education, there is a profusion of interests at work to shape the curriculum. Historically, some interests have operated closely to and directly on the school itself. Others have exercised their power indirectly and from a distance, both conceptually and physically; yet they, too, have wielded considerable authority over what is to be taught and learned. As Figure 9.1 suggests, the forces at work on curriculum are varied.

Business, Industry, and Science

By the end of the nineteenth century, Americans realized that an education system focusing on the 3 Rs and classical studies was out of sync with an emerging industrialized world. People had to learn to work in factories, to

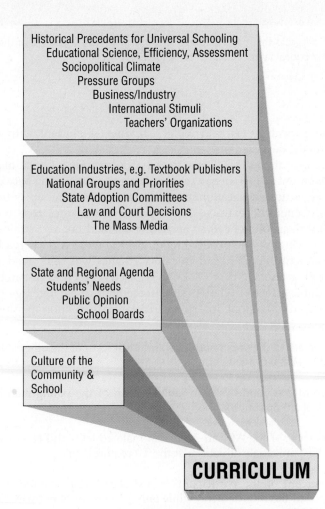

FIGURE 9.1

Forces That Shape the Curriculum

Which forces and groups are most influential in shaping the curriculum in your community's schools?

lay railways, and to construct roads. Progress required technology for managing the vast railroad network, for handling trade, and for maximizing production. Citizens of the United States had to be innovative if they were to address the many economic, social, and practical problems of developing an industrialized base. Increasingly, citizens looked to the schools to "take over many functions that parents, police, and priests had once performed" as they prepared children for their respective places in the new industrial economy (Blum et al., 1989, p. 446). Through the years, many people have operated on the premise that what had been good for American business would surely be good for American education.

During the early part of the twentieth century, many curricular theorists looked to science for the answers to teaching and learning. Researchers such as Edward L. Thorndike believed that experiments would reveal laws of learning that would enable teachers to engineer success in the classroom. Such ideas led to interest in developing a scientifically efficient curriculum to prepare individuals of different mental capacities for different and "proper" places in society. Educators viewed Americanized versions of Alfred Binet's intelligence test as the means for sorting and selecting students for their "destined" roles in society; curriculum was fitted to these roles (Kliebard, 1986).

The view of curriculum development as a scientific process fostered comparative studies to determine the efficiency of educational programs. The NEA's Committee on the Economy of Time in Education, appointed in 1911, was charged with the task of eliminating waste from programs in elementary schools and determining the minimum skills elementary students should possess. Basing it on a study of cookbooks, factory payrolls, advertisements, and hardware catalogs, committee members constructed a mathematics curriculum that would help students learn to solve arithmetical problems likely encountered on a daily basis by housewives, wage earners, merchants, and consumers (Cremin, 1961).

This view of curriculum has its roots in a technological notion of what teaching and learning ought to be. Franklin Bobbitt, an early advocate of social efficiency in education, was an influential proponent of this view. He conceived of curriculum as a way to promote **remediation**, or a process beginning with an analysis of society to determine what students needed to know to function in the workplace (based on laboratory analysis of tasks carried out in the real world), assessing students' "imperfections, errors, [and] shortcomings," and specifying objectives for "directed training" (Bobbitt, 1918, p. 44). Curriculum, in this sense, then, is supposed to remediate students' deficiencies.

National and International Stimuli

There are numerous historical examples of how sociopolitical and socioeconomic forces have influenced curriculum. For instance, between 1890 and 1917, immigrants from southern, central, and eastern Europe poured into the nation's cities in unprecedented numbers. They increased competition for jobs and were perceived as threatening the social order by settling in self-contained ethnic neighborhoods where they continued the life and customs of the old world. Rapid assimilation called for removing all elements of "foreignness" from a curriculum designed to Americanize the new immigrants (Banks, 1988).

World War I, World War II, and the Cold War also affected the curriculum. The need for trained soldiers and workers strengthened vocational education and the teaching of basic skills. Concerns about the security and prosperity of the United States, and persistent claims that the schools lacked rigor, also resulted in efforts to upgrade curricula in physics, biology, and chemistry, financed in large part by the National Science Foundation (NSF).

> **Federal involvement in the science curriculum began after the Soviets launched the first space satellite in 1957.**

With the Soviet launch of Sputnik in 1957, the federal government added its financial support to scientists' efforts; "[W]hat followed were two decades of federal involvement in science teaching and the development of an approach to science education that was focused on the logical structure of the disciplines and on the processes of science" (DeBoer, 1991, p. 147).

Social issues continually spark curriculum reform initiatives. Concerns about biased views of history led educators in Portland, Oregon, for example, to develop an Afro-centric curriculum. Students view the past through the eyes of African Americans.

> School officials in the Oregon city commissioned scholars to write "baseline essays" on the contributions of African and American blacks in six fields of study: art, language arts, mathematics, science, social studies, and music. Teachers are now expected to "infuse" that information throughout their teaching. (Viadero, 1990, p. 11)

Other recent reforms include the development of **multicultural curriculum**, or curriculum that reflects contributions of many cultures to American society.

Government and the Courts

Federal laws have profoundly affected the school curriculum. Passage of the Environmental Education Act (Public Law 91-516), for example, stimulated the modern environmental education movement (DeBoer, 1991). Vocational education (Smith Hughes Act of 1917), preschool education (Economic Opportunity Act of 1964), and expanded school access for students with disabilities (Education for All Handicapped Children Act of 1975 and Individuals with Disabilities Education Act, 1990) are funded through federal laws.

State laws—many prompted by special interest groups—routinely affect curriculum content. State mandates aimed at overhauling secondary school curriculum have resulted in prescribed graduation requirements, an array of state achievement tests, and, in many instances, new textbooks selected to match assessments and graduation requirements (Cuban, 1992).

State Agenda   State agencies—state education departments and state superintendents—have traditionally been influential in shaping the public school curriculum. Robert Buser and William Humm (1975) studied 32 states and found that the following practices had the most effect on local school curricula: (a) providing financial reimbursement to programs and projects; (b) granting or denying school accreditation; (c) tying state financial aid to accreditation; and (d) enforcing education laws.

While federal involvement stimulated curriculum development in the 1960s and 1970s, since the 1980s, states have asserted their authority. Governors and state education leaders have assumed primary responsibilities for formulating and implementing curriculum reforms.

Each state government is influenced by political action committees, networks of parents, professional education organizations, civic organizations, and religious groups, and all these groups develop their own array of education reform agendas. A state may prescribe essential elements for all curricula in all grade levels for all public schools. Some states, Texas for example, issue essential elements for all subjects taught in grades kindergarten through 12 (Armstrong, 1989).

State Textbook Adoption Committees   Textbooks play an important role in student learning, and people who select them play an important role in shaping the curriculum. Various conservative and liberal watchdog organizations routinely urge people to get involved in textbook selection in their states and communities. Nearly half the states have processes by which curricular materials are evaluated and endorsed at the state level. A state-level endorsement in populous states that keep a tight rein on selection—Florida, Texas, California—can be the difference between success and failure for a particular text, and, indeed, for its publisher (Apple, 1993).

State textbook adoption policies have influenced the shape of curriculum for years. According to Michael Apple (1993), these policies originated for several reasons. First, they have been an effort to ensure that school districts purchase books at the lowest possible prices. Second, the state has attempted to protect children from being exposed to poor textbooks by relying on experts to make selections. Third, uniformity among texts at the state level enables the establishment of a minimum and standard curriculum throughout the state.

School Boards and Local Communities   School board members often reflect the communities they serve in terms of their occupations, religions, ethnic origins, and beliefs about the value of education. As representatives of the community, board members are responsible for the governance of the schools. They are supposed to be informed about curriculum and its relationship to school goals. They may be involved as new curricula are proposed and pilot-tested. And they may be involved again when a decision must be made to adopt or reject a new approach (Ornstein & Hunkins, 1988). But their actions may also be only symbolic, especially when the new approach is controversial:

> When a legislator, school board member, or school administrator takes a position in favor of a specific approach to bilingual education, he or she is often articulating a particular constituency's interest on the issue or trying to gain the support of a constituency by articulating a position. (Elmore & Sykes, 1992, p. 187)

At times, a political alliance outweighs the practical importance of a curricular decision.

Some boards take only a macroview of their responsibility, approving and disapproving budgets and hiring and firing superintendents who set the schools' curricular course. Others, however, take a microview of their responsibility, and involve themselves deeply in the identification, evaluation, and selection of curriculum.

Allen Ornstein and Francis Hunkins (1988) argue that school boards may be losing some of their control over curricular decisions: "In some cases, control has been taken away by the actions of legislatures defining just what basic education is. In other cases, special-interest groups have gone to court to alter board policies if such policies are found unacceptable" (p. 216). With the changing landscape of public education, some school boards may find themselves playing a less decisive role in curricular decisions than they have in the past.

Teachers and Students

Teachers themselves affect the selection and transmission of curriculum content. Their habits and dispositions exert powerful influences on what is taught and learned—influences that may be either conservative or boldly innovative.

When teachers stick to familiar tools, content, and activities, they operate as conservative, and some believe negative, forces on curriculum (Cuban, 1992). Some curriculum designers have tried to counteract such influences by creating what are often referred to as **teacher-proof curricula**, or curricula that minimize the role of those who transmit them to students (Grobman, 1970).

> "The evidence of teachers sticking to familiar tools, content, and activities mounts."

Teachers' creative influences on curriculum are many and varied. In language arts or literature-based instruction, for example, teachers with a **constructivist orientation** guide students to define knowledge for themselves, using curricula as stimuli for innovative thinking. These teachers help students select material and act within a social context that molds knowledge but does not determine absolutely what constitutes knowledge (Applebee, 1991; Langer & Applebee, 1986). Teaching in these instances is

VOICES

On the Teacher as Curriculum Maker

Curriculum researchers D. Jean Clandinin and F. Michael Connelley perceive the teacher as a curriculum maker—a collaborator with students and researchers in what is to be learned, not a purveyor of knowledge established by someone else.

This literature of teachers' stories and stories of teachers provides an important avenue for conceptualizing the work of teachers as curriculum makers. Learning to listen to the stories teachers tell of their practice is an important step toward creating an understanding of the teacher as curriculum maker. However, we see our task as researchers as moving beyond this step to a second: to create with teachers a story of teachers as curriculum makers. We see this task as a collaborative one in which we participate with teachers in their classrooms and together live out and construct a story of the teacher as curriculum maker and, in this endeavor, imagine the possibility of curriculum reform. . . . (p. 386)

The collaborative living out of researchers', teachers', and children's stories in the classroom changes the curriculum. . . . In their collaborative endeavor, researcher and teacher see the unfolding plots of the stories and observe them closely. When they tell their mutually constructed story of the teacher as curriculum maker to other teachers and researchers, it invites others to see and examine their stories' plots, scenes, and characters closely. Thus we see the potential for change and growth as other teachers work in their classrooms. To fulfill this agenda calls for not only the creation of a literature that records these stories but also the construction of a method of working with current and prospective teachers and researchers to educate them to the imaginative possibilities of reading this literature. (pp. 392–393)

CRITICAL THINKING

If the concept of teacher as curriculum maker is invigorating and empowering, how may it also be limiting?

Source: Clandinin, D.J., & Connelly, F.M. (1992). Teacher as curriculum maker. In P.W. Jackson (Ed.), *Handbook of research on curriculum* (pp. 363–401). New York: Macmillan.

---

not a matter of transmitting some objectively formed body of knowledge; it is more a matter of helping students construct and interpret knowledge for themselves. There is a shift from encouraging students to acquire content to helping them develop processes that will facilitate understanding (Applebee & Purves, 1992). Such examples, of course, are not limited to language and literature; teachers in many disciplines strive to define curriculum in like manner.

In other intricate ways, teachers shape what is to be learned by bringing their own personal histories with them into the classroom (Clandinin & Connelly, 1992). Their personalities, their formal academic preparation, and their experiences are all lived out with students through continual interactions. Teachers, and in turn students themselves, become the "texts" for study.

Children's needs can and must dictate the nature of some curricula. Indeed, as students' problems increase in number and/or severity, the standard curriculum may well be reduced or modified to make room for special offerings. Traditionally, these curricula and the programs organized to deliver them have been designed for two slightly different but complementary purposes: to compensate for student deficiencies that cannot readily be changed and to remediate particular student needs. The key difference is that the curricula are organized to fit the students instead of the other way around.

Cognitive behavior modification and its special application of **cognitive behavior monitoring** (Lloyd, Landrum, & Hallahan, 1991) is an interesting case in point. Cognitive behavior monitoring is defined by a set of materials and activities designed to teach students with short attention spans to monitor their own attending behaviors in any number of subject matter areas and to increase their attention when need be. It is in effect a curriculum designed to compensate for and remediate a student's inability to pay attention. A student's lack of ability to concentrate is compensated for by the use of an audiotape player with a prerecorded set of beeps. The student learns that a beep is a signal to ask the question: "Was I paying attention?" and records his or her answers on a check sheet. The teacher later reviews the record and works with the student to remediate attention problems.

Students also influence curriculum by the work they prefer to do and do well. Teachers and curriculum developers recognize the power of the aphorism that success breeds success. When a curriculum stimulates and holds student attention, it is likely to be copied, extended, promoted, adapted, and used with other students. In noticeable ways, students influence teachers to behave in certain ways in the classroom; that is, students encourage teachers to emphasize or deemphasize various aspects of the curriculum (Hunt & Sullivan, 1974).

Education Industries and Publishers

Commercial textbook publishers influence the curriculum through the authors they hire and the books and materials they produce. Publishers argue that in fact they do not influence the curriculum as much as do the people who buy the books. In their attempt to read the market, publishers simply provide what they believe people will buy. And buy they do—textbooks gross nearly $2 billion a year (Squire & Morgan, 1990).

Some curriculum experts think that textbooks exert the most powerful influence on curriculum of all (Morrison, 1993). They worry about this circumstance for several reasons:

1. Textbooks may constitute as much as 70% of the curriculum; thus, texts essentially determine the curriculum.

2. To achieve the widest possible sales at any grade level, publishers may encourage textbook authors to teach to the "lowest common denominator" or to "dumb down" the curriculum.

3. To avoid any potential controversy, publishers may produce materials that are bland or devoid of controversial material, for example, material about religious beliefs.

4. Some texts, such as reading series, are constructed according to formulas that result in "skill-drill" approaches and the absence of good literature.

5. Textbooks too often teach inaccurate and erroneous information.

> In an episode that angered educators, scrutiny by an advocacy group in Texas led to the discovery of thousands of errors in the latest U.S. history textbooks...Among the gaffes: One book said President Truman "easily settled" the war in Korea by dropping "the bomb," although nuclear weapons weren't used in Korea, and Eisenhower was president when the armistice was signed. Another said Napoleon won at Waterloo . . . (Putka, 1992, p. B1)

Protests about textbooks can erupt into community squabbles. Parent groups in Canadian and U.S. schools, for example, protested the use of a grades kindergarten through 6 elementary reading series that uses themes such as Halloween to present fiction, nonfiction, and poetry by well-known English, American, and Canadian authors. Curricula based on Halloween are offensive to fundamentalist groups, who contend that they teach children witchcraft (McConaghy, 1992). When such interest group protests are reported by the mass media, they affect the way textbooks are written.

Mass Media and Public Opinion

Connections between the mass media, both print and electronic, and the public are strong and pervasive. The relationship between the press and public opinion is reciprocal; that is, the press reports what happens in education, but in so doing it also shapes the course of events. If there is an educational problem out there, sooner or later, people read about it in the newspaper or see a story about it on television.

The Education Writers Association (1987) describes the challenge:

> Potentially, the education beat is the best there is. No other assignment sweeps across people's lives from infancy to old age. In most communities, education is a major industry. In most states, it consumes the largest share of tax dollars. A reporter or other journalist writing on education will cover everything from budgets to blustery encounters over values, from threatened local law suits to U.S. Supreme Court rulings, from clever products by students in woodworking to the role of education in competition for global markets, from back-to-school features to assessments of the worth of a college degree. (p. ix)

Despite the contention that the press may not always be well informed (McNergney, Hallahan, Keller, & Crowley, 1992), or that it oversimplifies and concentrates on sensational aspects of problems (Weiss & Singer, 1988), the media wield enormous influence over the course of educational events, including, on occasion, the school curriculum.

Beyond serving informational and public oversight functions, the media are involved directly in producing their own curriculum. Educational programming on public television represents one of the most visible and readily accessible forms of instruction. The hour-long Public Broadcasting Service (PBS) documentary entitled "On Television: Teach the Children," first aired in 1992, criticizes television as teacher.

> The primary courses within the TV curriculum, analysts assert, teach expensive lessons in consumption, larded with images of sex, violence, and anti-intellectualism. On occasion, television enhances classroom learning, but TV programming in the U.S. ordinarily consists of "entertainment" fare. (Magee, 1992, p. 9)

Other examples of media-designed and delivered curricula abound. Chris Whittle's media empire beams Channel One into high school classrooms to educate students about current events and simultaneously to hawk commercial products. *Newsweek* magazine's "Education Program" edifies young readers about national and world events and implicitly teaches young people to value information offered by national news magazines. "Visions Exploration," developed by *USA Today* and the National Aeronautics and Space Administration (NASA), and funded by McDonnell Douglas Foundation, teaches elementary and middle school students about explorers of the past and helps them "analyze social and technological issues of the 21st Century using space as the motivating factor" (*USA Today*, 1992).

> Television is the "central nervous system of the body politic. . . ." "Kids think that in going to school they are in a sense interrupting their education."

HOW DOES THE CURRICULUM RELATE TO THE AIMS OF EDUCATION?

As Elliot Eisner and Elizabeth Vallance (1974, p. 2) note, for those trying to make sense of the field of curriculum, "the richness of issues and values . . . provides an arena that can be either a dynamic and stimulating resource or a conceptual jungle difficult to define and almost impossible to manage." They identify five basic orientations to defining the goals, content, and organization of curriculum: (a) development of cognitive processes; (b) academic realism; (c) personal relevance; (d) social adaptation; and (e) mastery of learning objectives. Although a curriculum seldom fits neatly into any one of these categories, the differing perspectives illustrate how the curriculum can be related to the goals of education. Figure 9.2 shows how each type of curriculum relates to aims of education.

FIGURE 9.2

Five Orientations to the Development of Curriculum

Curriculum Orientation	Aims of Education	Roles of Students and Teachers	Examples of Curriculum Content	Examples of Instructional Approaches
Development of Cognitive Processes	Teach students how to learn.	Student-centered: Students think and interact about academic tasks and construct meaningful knowledge in relationship to prior experiences. Teachers mediate and facilitate students' learning.	Thinking skills; study skills; problem-solving skills	Scaffolding; guided discovery
Academic Rationalism	Impart culture to students.	Teacher-centered: Students receive instruction and demonstrate competencies.	Great ideas; great works of art; literary classics; basic skills	Direct instruction
Personal Relevance	Help students find self-fulfillment.	Student-centered: Students and teachers collaborate to create or match curricula to individual and group interests and needs. Teachers provide opportunities for student reflection and self-evaluation.	Values clarification; opportunities for personal expression	Individualized instruction
Social Adaptation & Change	Help students become well-adjusted citizens capable of changing the social order.	Teacher-centered: Teachers present facts, issues, problems, and learning challenges for students to act upon or apply in life.	Citizenship; communication skills; environmental & social issues	Questioning; cooperative learning
Curriculum as Technology	Give students the tools they need to master subjects; deliver instruction efficiently.	Subject-centered: Teachers preestablish developmentally appropriate learning goals, outcomes, objectives, and criteria for assessment for a subject area. Students demonstrate minimum competencies.	Traditional subjects; basic skills	Direct instruction; mastery learning

HOW IS THE CURRICULUM PLANNED AND ORGANIZED?

If a teacher or curriculum designer knows his or her destination—the aims of education and goals of the curriculum—there may be more than one way to reach the destination. Curricular plans can be constructed in different ways, using models that are linear, outcome-based, or processing-based, or that focus on a common core of knowledge, on themes, on personal growth, or on social change.

Linear Models of Curriculum Planning

Step-by-step or linear models have been in use since the early 1900s. Ralph Tyler (1949), for example, proposed a linear model of curriculum planning consisting of a series of four steps: (a) specifying objectives in behavioral terms; (b) selecting learning experiences; (c) organizing learning activities; and (d) planning for evaluation of student learning.

Another enduring example is the work of Benjamin Bloom (1956), who believed that students could be taught to think at more complex cognitive levels. Teachers following Bloom's model select objectives that traverse a hierarchy of simple to complex thought processes (recall, comprehension, application, analysis, synthesis, and evaluation). Bloom's taxonomy of learning objectives guided the development of many curriculum packages. Table 9.1 shows Bloom's taxonomy and the kinds of tasks teachers must undertake if they are to encourage students to accomplish the objectives.

Behavioral Objectives   In the 1960s and 1970s, Robert Mager (1962) taught educators to write instructional **behavioral objectives**—goal statement, conditions under which learning will occur, and criteria for success. Teaching objectives, and later learning objectives, became the backbone of curriculum development, particularly in subject areas in which learning can be measured in quantifiable terms. Statements about what students should know or be able to do after completing a unit of study form the basis of what is taught and how success is judged. As the following example illustrates, outcomes specify the intended result or product of instruction instead of the actual process of instruction.

An Instructional Behavioral Objective in Mager's Terms

Conditions of Performance:	Given a definition and examples of adjectives as a part of speech,
Behavior:	students will identify adjectives in sentences
Criteria for Assessing Performance:	in at least 8 of 10 instances.

A Textbook Example   A linear planning strategy would (a) map all there is to be learned in a particular domain of knowledge, (b) diagnose what students do and do not know, (c) prescribe instruction to fill in the gaps, and (d) evaluate students' mastery of new material. Many major text-

TABLE 9.1 Bloom's Taxonomy of Educational Objectives

Level	Learner Objectives	Teacher Tasks
1.00 Knowledge	To define, distinguish, acquire, identify, recall, or recognize various forms of information.	To present and/or elicit facts, conventions, categories in ways that enable learners to demonstrate knowledge.
2.00 Comprehension	To translate, transform, give in own words, illustrate, prepare, read, represent, change, rephrase, or restate various forms of information.	To present and/or elicit definitions, words, phrases, relationships, principles in ways that enable learners to demonstrate comprehension.
3.00 Application	To apply, generalize, relate, choose, develop, organize, use, transfer, restructure, or classify various forms of information.	To present and/or elicit principles, laws, conclusions in ways that enable learners to apply what they have learned.
4.00 Analysis	To distinguish, detect, identify, classify, discriminate, recognize, categorize, or deduce various forms of information.	To present and/or elicit elements, hypotheses, assumptions, statements of intent or fact in ways that encourage learners to critically analyze information.
5.00 Synthesis	To write, tell, relate, produce, originate, modify, or document various forms of information.	To present and/or elicit structures, patterns, designs, relationships in ways that encourage learners to form new structures of knowledge.
6.00 Evaluation	To judge, argue, validate, assess, appraise various forms of information.	To present and/or elicit from learners different qualitative judgments.

Note. From *Teacher Development* (p. 57) by R. F. McNergney and C. A. Carrier, 1981, New York: Macmillan.

books and basal series express this strategy through a scope and sequence chart illustrating the range of concepts and skills to be addressed over the course of study. Figure 9.3 shows one version of a scope and sequence chart—from a remedial reading series—which illustrates a prescribed order of instruction on consonants.

Success in this and similar reading programs is often measured in terms of students' scores on reading achievement tests. Publishers often provide unit skills tests, mid-book, and end-of-book tests to assess particular reading skills. For teachers interested more in whole language approaches, there are also unit process tests that can be used to monitor a student's progress.

Outcomes-Based Education

Outcomes-Based Education (OBE)—also known as "outcomes-driven developmental model" (ODDM) and "goal-based education" (GBE)—is also an example of a linear model of curriculum planning. This model is supposed to encourage students to achieve outcomes that have real-life applicability. According to William Spady (1986, p. 3), director of the High Success

FIGURE 9.3

Scope and Sequence Chart for Teaching Consonants

GRADE	K	R	PP	PR	1	2/1	2/2	3/1	3/2	4	5	6	7	8
Identifies Words (Decoding)														
Uses phonics														
Consonants														
Initial consonants														
Auditory discrimination	T													
Letter-sound relationships														
b/b/;g/g/;m/m/;s/s/;l/l/	(T)	T	T											
c,k/k/;r/r/;p/p/;d/d/;t/t/			T											
f/f/;h/h/;j/j/;w/w/;n/n/				T										
v/v/;y/y/;z/z/						T								
c/s/;g/j/						T								
kn/n/;wr/r/;qu/kw/								T						
Final consonants														
Auditory discrimination														
Letter-sound relationships														
p/p/;d/d/;t/t/				T										
b/b/;m/m/;s/s/;g/g/;l/l/;n/n/					T									
k,ck/k/					T									
x/ks/														
s/z/										T				
Double final consonants								T						
Medial consonants								T						
Consonant blends														
Initial blends						T	T	T	T					
Final blends						T								
Consonant digraphs														
Initial digraphs					T			T						
Final digraphs					T			T						
Consonant substitution														
Consonant variability principles														
A consonant sound is represented by different consonant letters.														
A consonant letter represents different sounds.														

Key: ■ Instruction   ■ Review, reinforcement, extension   T Tested in Quarter Test only
■ Instruction (optional)   ■ Maintenance   **T** Tested in Quarter Test and End-of-Book Test
(T) Tested in End-of-Book Test (Optional)

Note. From *Focus: Reading for Success, Scope and Sequence* (p. 4, 5) by R. L. Allington et al, 1985. Copyright 1985, Scott, Foresman and Company. Reprinted by permission.

Network on Outcome Based Education, such programs have the following characteristics:

1. A clear focus on the outcomes expected.

2. Close articulation of the curriculum with these outcomes.

3. Realistic challenge for students to attain outcome standards.

4. Instructional delivery timed and organized to match student learning levels.

5. Adequate opportunities for students to reach outcome standards.

6. Rewards and grading linked directly to improved performance on outcomes.

7. Support systems for students requiring special assistance.

Note that OBE is linear in reverse, beginning with outcomes and using a kind of "backward-planning" to plan instruction. "Specifying outcomes and setting high performance targets, the thinking goes, would free teachers and administrators to take charge of their schools, envision new strategies for meeting the higher standards, and find innovative ways to guide more children to knowledge and success" (Harp, 1993, p. 19). But outcomes-based education is proving to be about as controversial as nearly every other reform proposed in recent years, particularly when parents disagree with the outcomes. In Pennsylvania, for example, ex-teacher Peg Luksik has organized opposition to the state OBE plan in large measure because it appeared to reach beyond what some considered its purview. Vocal parents opposed the state plan because it focused attention on student attitudes and values (Harp, 1993).

Processing Models of Curriculum Planning

Curriculum may also be planned to correspond to thought processes, especially to the way people process and remember information. The process of learning becomes in itself a curriculum goal. Teachers use instruction to intervene directly or indirectly to affect not what students think but how they think.

Processing models of curricula are often based on the assumption that if students are going to become independent lifelong learners, they must be encouraged early on to think for themselves and to be responsible for their own learning. This is translated into curricula that involve the use of manipulatives, such as objects for counting or comparing, and opportunities for discovering knowledge. As an example, Figure 9.4 shows a screen from the Geometric Supposer, a series of software programs developed at the Education Development Center, an organization that develops curricula that foster discovery learning. The Supposer has no explicit instructional agenda; that is, it is not programmed to ask questions that will lead students to discover proofs to problems. Instead, students explore the realm of Euclidean plane geometry through problem posing and problem solving. A learner using the Supposer can draw, erase, label, measure angles, perimeters, and areas, change scales, bisect angles, compare angles, repeat figures,

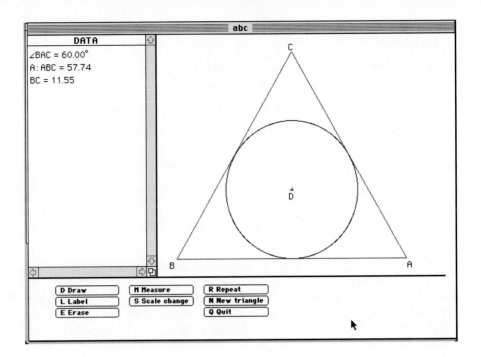

FIGURE 9.4

Screen Display for the Geometric Supposer

In what three ways might a computer program such as the Supposer complement a standard mathematics textbook?

Note. From *The Geometric Supposer: Triangles,* Pleasantville, NY: Sunburst Communications, Inc. Copyright 1991 by Sunburst Communications, Inc.

make new figures, and so forth. Teachers and students "learn to listen carefully to and assess the quality of one another's arguments," working collaboratively to "make" mathematics (Schwartz, 1989).

Process planning models with a focus on problem solving often stress real-life applications with academic content that is more relevant to students' potential work lives. This is accomplished by deemphasizing divisions between academic and vocational content. For instance, the Center for Occupational Research and Development (CORD), in Waco, Texas, and the Agency for Instructional Technology (AIT), in Bloomington, Indiana, have developed and tested curricula for three courses that try to foster cognitive development vis-a-vis the acquisition of practical skills: CORD and AIT's Principles of Technology (applied physics), CORD's Applied Mathematics, and AIT's Applied Communication. These courses set the stage for others (e.g., Applied Chemistry and Biology and Materials Science Technology) that emphasize concrete manipulations and on-the-job reasoning. Figure 9.5 shows an activity in applied mathematics, based on real-life concerns.

Core Curriculum Models

Courses of study based on the idea that all students should be exposed to the same selective knowledge are called **core curriculum**. The idea of teaching all students in U.S. schools a common core of knowledge arouses strong passions because people do not agree on what the core curriculum should contain. People also do not agree on the relative importance of specific content over the learning process itself.

As you will recall from Chapter 4, E.D. Hirsch's (1987) controversial book *Cultural Literacy* criticized schools' tendency to emphasize content-neutral skills (e.g., critical thinking and higher-order thinking skills) at the expense of a body of prescribed knowledge. Hirsch and others have criti-

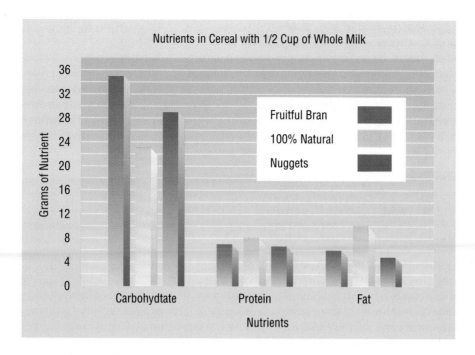

Nutrients in Cereal with 1/2 Cup of Whole Milk

Legend:
Fruitful Bran
100% Natural
Nuggets

Y-axis: Grams of Nutrient (0, 4, 8, 12, 16, 20, 24, 28, 32, 36)

X-axis categories: Carbohydtate, Protein, Fat

X-axis label: Nutrients

FIGURE 9.5

Applying Mathematics to Solve Everyday Problems

Which cereal with milk will have the most protein?

Note. From CORD *Applied Mathematics: Teacher's Guide,* Unit 4, Activity 2: Comparing Breakfast Cereals (pp. 33, T-21). Waco, Texas: Center for Occupational Research and Development, 1988. Used by permission.

cized texts used for teaching reading and writing because they tend to be "screened not for the information they convey but for their readability scores and their fit with the sequence of abstract skills that a child is expected to acquire" (p. 112). Hirsch argued that all students need instead to master a common core of reading materials based on factual information and traditional lore. He therefore promoted a core curriculum that specified, grade by grade, what students must learn. With such a common core of knowledge, Hirsch believed, students will compete in society on equal footing.

Cultural Awareness

One fact possessed by culturally literate people in the United States: . . . the fictional characters Tweedledum and Tweedledee from *Through the Looking-Glass* by Lewis Carroll. They are pictured as fat twins who are identical in speech, attitude, and appearance. Figuratively, any two people or positions that have no real difference are said to be "like Tweedledum and Tweedledee." (Hirsch, Kett, & Trefil, 1988, p. 136)

Others bridle at any effort to impose conformity on what is taught in public schools as an effort to create a national curriculum. Such a curriculum, they believe, might communicate a sameness of values that we do not share. And who is to say what is in this core of knowledge? A core curriculum is short-sighted, these critics argue, because it would be dominated by the most politically powerful group in society. Even if it were fairly representative, such a curriculum would not work—Americans are too independent to attend to it, and knowledge is changing so rapidly that it would be out of date as soon as it was established.

WHAT ARE SOME CURRENT TRENDS IN CURRICULUM DEVELOPMENT?

While some curricula endure, many come and go, almost as fads or fashions. The needs underlying them, however, most often remain. In recent years these needs have stimulated the development of curricula in character education, minimum competency development, gender sensitivity training, environmental conservation, and family life education.

Character Education

Clarifying or teaching values, sometimes referred to as **character education**, may be described as a curricular approach driven by personal relevance. It is an approach that has become highly controversial. "Protesters have taken special exception to the book *Values Clarification* [Simon, Howe, and Kirschenbaum, 1972], ostensibly because the program that it proposes allows students to express their own views on personal problems" (Oliva, 1992, p. 558).

Professor Thomas Lickona of the State University of New York at Cortland contends that the values clarification teaching of the 1960s and 1970s ". . . led students to believe whatever values they had were O.K., as long as they were clarified, even if it was shoplifting or Satanism" (Viadero, 1992, p. 12). He notes that because teachers often opened a lesson on values by saying that there was no right or wrong answer, students were misled. Lickona argues instead that teachers ". . . need to say there may be more than one answer and be prepared to support your answer with your best moral reasoning" (Viadero, 1992, p. 12).

While it has detractors, the movement to return values to the standard curriculum is gaining momentum. As various societal problems appear to be increasing, more educators, politicians, and members of the lay public are pushing for a curriculum that teaches the difference between right and wrong.

The Minimum Competency Movement

If school is designed for all society's children, is there not some common body of knowledge and minimum level of learning that can and should be expected of all children? An affirmative answer to this question has given

VOICES

On Moral Aspects of the Curriculum

Hugh Sockett, Professor of Education, George Mason University, contends that teachers help students think about right and wrong and how to be behave ethically through example. But how teachers do so is largely a mystery.

Surprisingly we do not know what teachers now do by way of moral education in their classrooms. . . . We do not know the ways in which teachers generally confront such basic issues as racial prejudice and sexism or what their curriculum strategies look like. We do not know the extent to which teachers are more or less influenced by their religious persuasions when they teach, nor the precise extent to which state mandates or local community values inhibit moral teaching. Nor do we know to what extent teachers feel their integrity is compromised by any conflict between

their world view in moral terms and the practices of the school in which they work. . . .

In all curriculum subjects there is a complex transition as the child moves from elementary to secondary education. Yet, much more significant for the child's moral education is the difference in mores between schools, the effect of this transition on the child's moral development, and what schools might do to ease that transition. The transition is not merely a move from one set of official school mores to another but also a shift to the mores of a youth culture. (pp. 562–563)

CRITICAL THINKING

Do you believe teachers should intervene in students' lives by providing moral or character education? If so, how? If not, why?

Source: Sockett, H. (1992). The moral aspects of the curriculum. In P.W. Jackson (Ed.), *Handbook of research on curriculum* (pp. 543–569). New York: Macmillan.

---

impetus to what are often referred to as **minimum competency** programs, or curriculum and instruction geared toward the successful completion of "minimum competency" tests.

Beginning in the 1970s and continuing through the present, the minimum competency movement has been both reactive and proactive in nature. It has been a response to what some have perceived as a diminished emphasis on content and academic rigor in schools. It has also been a reaction against the practice of social promotion—promoting children through the grades to keep them with their age-mates even if they cannot keep pace academically—and against decreasing accountability for the use of public funds to produce learning, which is defined in terms of outcome measures of basic **literacy** (reading and writing abilities) and abilities to calculate.

> **Minimum Competencies: What do they look like?**

On the other hand, the minimum competency movement has been proactive by pushing an agenda for educational and social change. By concentrating on the "minimums" in curriculum, proponents hope also indirectly to raise maximum standards (Lerner, 1991). The movement promotes curriculum, instruction, and evaluation purportedly designed to prepare children for the future; that is, an emphasis on the role of technology in the workplace is often coupled with the concentration on basic skills.

Why do advocates believe minimum competence to be so critical? The reasoning underlying the minimal competence movement is a curious blend of politically conservative and liberal points of view. Minimum competence is promoted as a means of helping children from poverty areas who, shortchanged by poor schools, will finally receive the preparation they need to build a future—a future in which they will be employed at something other than menial jobs and thus will be able to exercise at least some self-determination in their lives. Minimum competence is also portrayed as the only hope the country has of preparing a workforce that will be able to operate computerized information and production systems, to employ computerized defense systems in the armed forces, and to otherwise enable people to support themselves so they, in turn, can pay taxes and support the rest of society.

Many states have developed lists of minimum competencies for students. Arizona, for example, has developed lists of skills in seven subjects for the 8th and 12th grades. The first 5 in the list of 87 skills in health for eighth-grade students are:

1. Identifies personal care practices. Example: washing hands before eating, brushing teeth.

2. Communicates symptoms of his/her physical illness.

3. Lists some of the ways communicable diseases are transmitted.

4. Identifies and describes a variety of foods.

5. States the importance of eating breakfast and describes a healthful breakfast (Oliva, 1992, pp. 240–241).

Critics have argued that the minimum competency movement has created a virtual industry of testmakers who control the curriculum by producing "high stakes tests"—tests that are used to evaluate school performance, and upon which students' futures depend heavily because they determine grade promotion, graduation, and entrance to and exit from particular fields of study. The movement and the tests it has fostered, they argue, have also limited what is to be taught and learned to simplistic ideas and material, created a trickle-down effect on teaching in the lower grades, and forced from the curriculum other more stimulating and potentially more important material (Madaus & Kellaghan, 1992).

Civic Responsibility and Volunteerism or Service Learning

As the nation attempts to reform public education in the core areas of English, mathematics, science, history, and geography, R. Freeman Butts has been the psychological pebble in society's shoe reminding people not to forget civic education. He claims that:

> . . . the primary purpose and overarching goal of universal, free, public schooling in the United States is its civic mission, that is, to prepare informed, rational, humane, and participating citizens committed to the constitutional values and principles of American democracy. (Butts, 1991, p. 36)

If a democracy is to function successfully, citizens must demonstrate a collective sense of civic responsibility. Civic or social responsibility, then, may constitute part of any core curriculum. One of the most ambitious kindergarten through 12th grade curriculum projects with respect to the study of government, public policy, and citizenship in recent years is a document entitled *Civitas* (Quigley & Bahmueller, 1991). The word *civitas* has its origins in Latin and is defined two ways:

Integrated service learning is rapidly becoming a part of science and social studies curricula in innovative programs nationwide.

the functioning body of persons and institutions constituting a politically organized community or state; and the concepts and values of citizenship that impart shared responsibility, common purpose, and sense of community among the citizens of the political order. *Civitas* represents an attempt by educators, public leaders, scholars, and national associations to address civic literacy in the United States. Its intent is to outline core values, concepts, and principles of the American community.

The principal goal of the program is to suggest directions for civic education programs in public and private elementary and secondary schools. The framers view it as a curriculum that will promote civic competence and responsibility and encourage youth participation in social and political life in their communities and in the nation. Butts emphasizes the importance of the document as a common core of knowledge, values, and skills—one that outlines ". . . a desirable school learning environment appropriate for students holding a diversity of beliefs and outlooks and reflecting an expanding plurality of ethnic, racial, linguistic, and religious communities in the United States" (Butts, 1991, p. xix). The curriculum is structured according to topics, objectives, and frames of reference (which include conceptual, historical, and contemporary perspectives).

For communities to "work" properly, individuals must be willing to sacrifice some of their personal autonomy for the good of the group. People forfeit their membership in a community figuratively or literally when they are no longer willing to care about the rights of other community members:

> That people need to help and care for one another is an idea as old as the first human communities and equally valid for a modern mass society. But too many Americans, especially the young, feel a debilitating sense of powerlessness in the face of large national and world issues that affect their lives but elude their control. (William T. Grant Foundation Commission, 1988, p. 79)

Psychologists and sociologists tend to agree that one of the obvious manifestations of these feelings of powerlessness is crime. Frustrated people, particularly frustrated, young, immature people, sometimes assault others physically or verbally and sometimes strike out indirectly through acts of vandalism. The less obvious indications of young people's lack of ability to balance their personal needs and desires with those of others are greed, insensitivity, and self-indulgence.

To give students a sense of belonging and to encourage them to participate in the responsibilities of community, state, and nation, a number of schools have developed volunteer curricula for high school youth to encourage volunteerism or **service learning**. In most instances, volunteer groups such as the 300-member service club at Fallston High in Harford County, Maryland, perform their services outside school hours and receive no credit, awards, or certificates of appreciation from their school. They do, however, benefit in a variety of ways from the experience.

Individual service projects, such as tutoring peers or younger children or working with residents in nursing homes, foster communication and intergenerational understanding. Group service projects, such as repairing bleachers or cleaning up the local park, help students learn to plan and cooperate with others to get a job done. Students who volunteer also seem to become more responsible and to develop more favorable attitudes toward the people they work with than other young people do.

Those curricula of volunteerism most likely to succeed have several things in common. Students' involvement and satisfaction with civic work will be enhanced if they are not made to compete with similar community programs. They must be valued by school authorities; if not, the activities do not compete successfully for students' attention against more standardized curriculum. Volunteer programs can and do succeed without involving everybody, but the best ones reach out to less affluent students who do not normally get involved (McNergney & Haberman, 1990).

Beyond volunteerism, civic education has begun to reassert itself as an important aspect of schooling:

> . . . We're told that our work force must be better prepared. Yet in the drive to improve the schools, and to make students more proficient in mathematics and science, another urgent question has been neglected: How can we adequately educate our students to become good citizens and to make responsible decisions that will sustain our country and advance the quality of life, both nationally and internationally? (Boyer, 1991)

Gender Sensitivity Training

Through the years, when issues concerning gender have been reflected in the curriculum they have clustered around several questions: "Should females be educated at all? If they should be educated, should they have the same education as males? Is the presence of female teachers and students educationally harmful for boys?" (Noddings, 1992, p. 659).

In recent years, however, more people have asserted that if sex-role development is to progress in a healthy way, both personally and socially, adults must intervene early in children's lives through **gender sensitivity**

training. This has meant developing curricula that avoid sex role stereotyping and creating opportunities for girls and women to take advantage of all their possibilities for education. Standard history textbooks now draw attention to women's contributions. Educators routinely encourage girls to take and to master mathematics and sciences courses in the early grades and to continue these patterns throughout their educational careers. Education texts avoid the generic use of male terms. The *Civitas* curriculum offers the following objectives for gender sensitivity training.

> The citizen should be able to:
> 1. explain the similarities and differences between men's and women's political participation through American history.
> 2. explain how the changing roles that have been deemed appropriate for men and women have affected their participation in American politics.
> 3. explain how the effects of public policies vary by gender, affecting men and women differently.
> 4. take, defend, and evaluate positions on constitutional and public policy issues regarding gender and political participation. (Quigley & Bahmueller, 1991, p. 258)

Overall, *Civitas* examines gender from three frames of reference—conceptual, historical, and contemporary. These suggest directions for sharply defined study. The conceptual frame draws attention to such factors as the basis for past exclusion of women from politics, the role of feminism, arguments for and against changing women's roles in society, women's changing place in politics, and women's relatively small role in the exercise of formal political power. The historical perspective emphasizes the place of women in politics at the founding of the nation, the beginning of women's political activism, the campaign for women's suffrage, and the various phases of the feminist movement. The contemporary perspective looks out on gender issues as they have been articulated in the 1990s. These include wage inequality and job segregation. This view also considers women in politics in present-day America.

Civitas is constructed to be sensitive to the raging controversy over multicultural issues in the social sciences. The writers and editors have tried to respond to critics of other curricula who have argued that too often Western values and European contributions to the United States and to the world have been overstressed. Certainly, the gender section of the curriculum, and other sections, are geared toward change.

Nel Noddings (1984) has argued that society's prevailing conceptions of gender will only be changed by "transforming" what and how children are taught about caring and ethics.

> I have argued for a curriculum aimed at producing people who will not intentionally harm others; a transformed structure of schooling that will encourage the development of caring relations; a moral education that emphasized maternal interests in preserving life, enhancing growth, and shaping acceptable children; and the development of a morality of evil that should help all of us understand and control our own tendencies toward evil. (1992, p. 678)

Noddings (1987), Madeline Grumet (1987), JoAnne Pagano (1988), and others have argued that these attributes of a curriculum are essentially feminist in nature.

Environmental Conservationism

The ozone layer surrounding the earth is disappearing, exposing living things to harmful radiation. Whales and dolphins are endangered by fishermen's nets and by chemicals spilling into the seas, our garbage dumps are full to overflowing with nonbiodegradable materials, the air people breathe is polluted with chemicals and gases, acid rain is killing lakes, streams, and vegetation—the list of environmental hazards goes on, and so, too, do educational efforts to make young people aware of the dangers.

Adults who press this agenda on young people, both inside and outside schools, often assume that while young people used to be initiated into caring about such things by their families, churches, and schools, these influences are no longer present in many students' lives. Adults also worry about the materialism of youth and their unconnectedness or lack of participation in projects that affect the general welfare of society (Lewis, 1988). Environmental problems are many and varied, and they are due in no small measure to ignorance, apathy, and greed—the virulence of which, people argue, might be addressed by greater care given to the curriculum.

From instructional units that teach water conservation in the West, through programs that educate young people about controlling soil erosion in the Midwest, to curriculum aimed at raising consciousness about acid rain in the East, science and social studies teachers work to sensitize young people to the importance of preserving the delicate balance of forces in their environment. Schools regularly encourage student participation in such activities as Arbor Day, recycling programs, and wildlife preservation projects. In so doing, schools play an important but indirect role in educating parents about environmental issues. Figure 9.6 represents points of view about resource management in a Wisconsin curriculum.

Beyond instructional units and programs meant to increase awareness and build knowledge of environmental issues, both school-based and community education curricula encourage volunteer service as a way to stimulate young people's direct involvement in the resolution of environmental problems. It has been estimated that there may be nearly 250,000 opportunities for young people to serve their communities in energy, environmental protection, and urban and rural conservation areas (Slobig & George, 1989).

Family Life Education

Perhaps the most striking and controversial curriculum unabashedly aimed at restructuring society may be that devoted to what is sometimes called *family life education*. Family life education is an integral part of most school programs. It focuses on such topics as personal health and safety, substance abuse prevention, mental health education, human growth and development (including sex education), and HIV-disease prevention. It is probably

FIGURE 9.6

An Issue Web: Wolves in Wisconsin

What are some curriculum goals and learning objectives that an issue web like this would support?

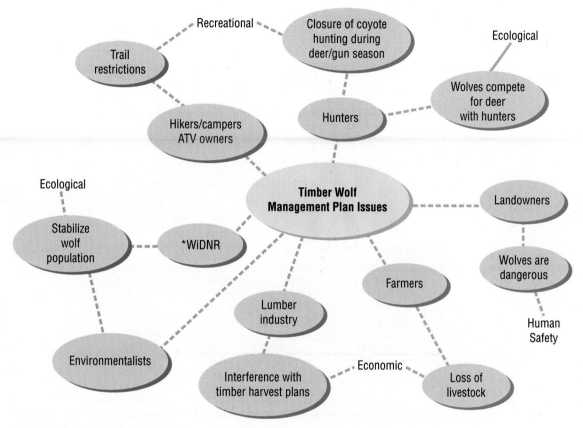

*Wisconsin Department of Natural Resources

Note: From "Science Related Social Issues in the Elementary School: The Extended Case Study Approach" by J. M. Ramsey and M. Kronholm, 1991, *Journal of Science Education, 3* (2), p. 6. Reprinted by permission.

the one area of the curriculum that is most closely scrutinized by the public. Parents must typically sign a permission form in order for their children to participate in family life offerings.

Family life education programs around the country are alike in that they acknowledge the central role of parents in educating their children. How programs in schools are to be carried out, however, may vary greatly from one district to another.

In Fairfax, Virginia, the curriculum for family life education is teacher-centered and highly prescriptive. Those who teach in the program must be selected by their principals and must participate in inservice training "to insure uniform implementation in all schools." (Fairfax County Public Schools, 1991, p. vi). As the following excerpt from the introductory section

FIGURE 9.7

Sex Education Curriculum Materials

Would you use an activity like this in your classroom? Why or why not?

```
A  B  V  I  R  G  I  N  I  T  Y  C  D  E  F  E
G  H  I  J  E  T  A  C  I  N  U  M  M  O  C  G
N  R  L  O  S  E  S  K  F  O  O  L  L  F  M  A
O  E  N  O  P  N  P  E  A  R  R  D  F  L  U  I
I  S  V  W  E  X  R  Y  Z  S  E  P  R  E  H  R
T  P  N  E  C  U  O  W  S  I  V  E  E  S  S  R
A  O  T  S  T  O  P  D  K  D  A  I  D  S  H  A
U  N  M  A  E  Y  N  A  S  A  I  B  N  O  U  M
T  S  M  C  L  R  A  T  I  O  N  A  L  S  M  N
A  I  E  X  I  Y  T  I  R  U  P  T  T  I  A  M
F  B  T  W  T  E  Y  N  O  O  D  A  U  C  N  A
N  I  I  N  R  S  I  G  N  G  L  L  R  W  I  T
I  L  A  D  E  C  I  S  I  O  N  H  L  E  M  E
L  I  W  B  F  E  P  S  V  U  R  E  G  H  N  E
A  T  V  I  R  T  N  E  M  T  I  M  M  O  C  T
G  Y  I  N  N  S  A  X  N  O  T  H  A  N  K  S
```

INFATUATION	WIN	DECISION	SEX
RESPONSIBILITY	LOSE	RISKS	LOVE
VIRGINITY	SELF	STOP	MATURE
FREEDOM	RESPECT	TEENS	RATIONAL
WILL	HUMAN	FOOL	NO
CONTROL	PARENT	FERTILE	WAIT
COMMITMENT	MARRIAGE	PURITY	HERPES
COMMUNICATE	DATING	AIDS	

Note. From *Sex Respect, the Option of True Sexual Freedom* (p.14) by C.K. Mast, 1986, Bradley, IL: Respect, Inc. Copyright 1986 by Respect Incorporated, P.O. Box 349, Bradley, IL 60915. Reproduced by permission.

of the teacher's guide for grades 5 and 6 reveals, teachers are given little leeway in how they present curriculum:

> This teacher's guide specifically designates what must be included in each lesson. . . . To comply with the School Board's commitment to the community, the lessons must be limited to the contents and topics included in this document. No additional activities, media, or materials may be included at the discretion of the teacher. Responses to student questions and oral review of material presented in the media, or on transparencies must be limited to clarification of the topics included in the lessons, and must be answered in an age-appropriate manner. (Fairfax County Public Schools, 1991, p. iii)

In a lesson plan designed for sixth graders as a review of basic facts about socially transmitted diseases, the prescriptiveness of the lesson is evident in the note to the teacher found at the beginning of the lesson plan:

> The sixth grade Human Growth and Development unit does not lend itself to open discussion concerning AIDS. Topics of homosexuality

and the use of condoms for protection are NOT part of this lesson. Do not deviate from this lesson as presented. Preface all statements as to how the human immunodeficiency virus is transmitted by one of the following statements: "'To date scientists believe you cannot get AIDS from . . .'" or "'Studies have shown that . . .'" (p. 65)

The lesson plan offers a step-by-step description of what should occur during the lesson, including what the teacher should say when presenting content to students:

Say: "Today we will see a video called 'I Have AIDS . . . A Teenager's Story,' told by Ryan White, an 18-year-old AIDS victim. We will also learn about some other sexually transmitted diseases. (p. 66)

The plan also makes clear which terms and definitions should be listed on the board, how and at what point in the lesson required instructional materials should be used, and what questions should be asked. A recommended practice for responding to student questions is to ask students to record their questions on 3" x 5" cards and hand them to the teacher. The teacher sorts the questions, answering those relating to information included in the media materials or course outline. For questions about topics not approved for discussion, the teacher is to encourage students to ask their families for answers.

In another example, Shreveport, Louisiana, has adopted a curriculum for sex education that advocates abstinence. The activity in Figure 9.7 is one of several in the student workbook, *Sex Respect: The Option of True Sexual Freedom*, designed for use with junior high or senior high school students.

HOW IS CURRICULUM ASSESSED?

Much of the dialogue of education reform in the 1990s has revolved around concepts of **curricular standards**. Reformers have argued that by establishing national benchmarks against which student performance in a variety of disciplines can be measured, and by setting high expectations, the collective education enterprise will encourage student progress. And, not incidentally, such standards will enable educators to recognize progress when they see it. "In a few short years, the idea that the United States ought to have national standards for what students learn has emerged as one of the most widely discussed options for improving the U.S. education system" (O'Neil, 1993). Table 9.2 lists some of the groups involved in developing standards in the subject areas.

Reformers tend to agree that students need to learn more and often different kinds of science, English, history, mathematics, and foreign languages. They contend that students need to do better in these subjects, too, that is, better compared to some preestablished sets of expectations. Although the logic of developing and applying standards for achievement is seemingly irrefutable, the specifics of what ought to be taught and learned and how success will be judged are more difficult to pinpoint. Moreover, Linda Darling-Hammond (1992) warns that more rigorous achievement standards will not yield better schools unless instructional or delivery standards receive equal attention.

TABLE 9.2   Some Contact Groups for National Standards

Social Studies

National Council for the Social Studies (NCSS)
3501 Newark St. NW
Washington, DC 20016

English

Center for the Study of Reading
174 Children's Research Center
51 Gerty Drive
Champaign, IL 61820

Mathematics

National Council of Teachers of Mathematics (NCTM)
1906 Association Drive
Reston, VA 22091

Science

National Science Education Standards
2101 Constitution Ave. NW, HA 486
Washington, DC 20418

The Arts

Music Educators National Conference (MENC)
1902 Association Drive
Reston, VA 22091

Physical Education

National Association for Sports and Physical Education
1900 Association Drive
Reston, VA 22091

Note. From "Achieving higher standards" by J. O'Neil, 1993, *Educational Leadership*, 50 (5), pp. 4–8. Copyright 1993 by the Association for Supervision and Curriculum Development. All rights reserved. Reprinted by permission of ASCD.

In general, curriculum standards can be thought of as statements about what learning is valued. As such, they can be used to judge the quality of an instructional plan that addresses goals for what students should know, how students are to acquire such knowledge, what teachers should do to help students reach the goals, and in some cases, the educational contexts in which teaching and learning should occur.

Evaluation standards serve as yardsticks against which student performance and curricular programs can be measured. Statements about acceptable indications of success, when taken seriously, shape curriculum and instruction. If educators want their programs and their students to be viewed in a favorable light by those who ascribe to such standards, and they typically do, then curriculum and instruction will bend to fit these publicly stated expectations. Standards can be used to reward and punish, but they can also be used to improve programs and educational practice.

One such example—the Curriculum and Evaluation Standards for School Mathematics, formulated by the National Council of Teachers of Mathematics (1989) or NCTM—is comprised of 54 value statements. Each is couched in three parts that address (a) what mathematics the curriculum should include, (b) a description of the student activities associated with that mathematics, and (c) instructional examples. Experts assert that the NCTM standards are revolutionary because they "remove computation from its reigning role in the mathematics curriculum and make it serve a more important goal—the development of mathematical thinking" (Association for Supervision and Curriculum Development, 1992, p. 3).

The Mathematics Curriculum Standards acknowledge changes in their own and allied fields in some interesting ways. They assume that "knowing" math means "doing" math. They attempt to recognize the revolution in mathematics understanding and applications brought about by computers and calculators. The standards also set out guidelines for core knowledge, or that knowledge common to all students, as well as special requirements for college-bound students. The evaluation standards coupled with the curriculum standards address processes of gathering information about student and program success. As seen in Standard 3, shown below, while the curriculum standards deal with the instructional plan, the evaluation standards are meant to address the ways students integrate their knowledge to demonstrate "mathematical power."

Standard 3: Mathematics as Reasoning

In grades 5–8, reasoning shall permeate the mathematics curriculum so that students can—

- recognize and apply deductive and inductive reasoning;
- understand and apply reasoning processes, with special attention to spatial reasoning and reasoning with proportions and graphs;
- make and evaluate mathematical conjectures and arguments;
- validate their own thinking;
- appreciate the pervasive use and power of reasoning as a part of mathematics. (National Council of Teachers of Mathematics, 1989, p. 81)

The following is one example provided in the discussion section to amplify the standard. Students are given a picture of a roller-coaster track, shown in Figure 9.8. The challenge is to sketch a graph (with no numbers) to represent the speed of the roller coaster versus its position on the track.

The NCTM has also created a companion volume to accompany the standards entitled *Professional Standards for Teaching Mathematics* (National Council of Teachers of Mathematics, 1991). The teaching standards recognize teachers as central to changing mathematics education in the schools. They emphasize, among other factors, the need to shift instruction toward

BENCHMARKS

The Development of National Standards

1989	*Curriculum and Evaluation Standards for School Mathematics* published by the National Council of Teachers of Mathematics (NCTM).
1991	*Professional Standards for Teaching Mathematics* issued by the NCTM, with assessment standards forthcoming.
1992	Content and student performance standards in history drafted by the National Center for History in the Schools and 30 partner groups.
	Outcomes of Quality Physical Education Programs issued by the National Association for Sports and Physical Education.
1993	Standards drafted in the areas of curriculum, teaching, and assessment in science by the National Committee on Science Education Standards and Assessment and the National Research Council.
	Standards drafted for civics by the Center for Civic Education, in cooperation with the National Council for the Social Studies (NCSS).
	Standards drafted for geography by the National Council of Geographic Education and cooperating groups.
	National Task Force for Social Studies Standards convened by the NCSS to develop integrative content across the curriculum, performance standards, and sample assessment tasks and vignettes.
	Standards drafted for art, music, dance, and theatre by the National Oversight Committee for Standards in the Arts, on a grant from the U.S. Department of Education, coordinated by the Music Educators National Conference, the American Alliance for Theatre and Education, the National Art Education Association, and the National Dance Association.
1994	Standards and classroom vignettes illustrating their application drafted by the Standards Project for the English Language Arts, coordinated by the National Council of Teachers of English, the International Reading Association, and the Center for the Study of Reading.

the use of logic and mathematical evidence for verification, away from a reliance on teachers as sources of right answers. They also promote teaching practice that encourages conjecture and problem solving.

In the absence of clearly articulated and widely agreed upon values for curriculum and evaluation, public pronouncements by influential people have the practical effect of establishing themselves as standards. When William Bennett was U.S. Secretary of Education, he announced with great

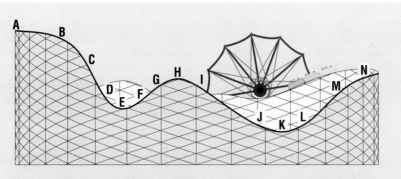

FIGURE 9.8

Sample Problem to Assess Students' Reading Skills

Construct a graph without numbers that depicts the speed of the rollercoaster at various points on the track.

Note. From *Curriculum and Evaluation Standards for School Mathematics* (1989, March), p. 83. Reston, VA: The National Council of Teachers of Mathematics. Reprinted with permission.

fanfare what became known as the "Secretary's Annual Wall Chart." This scorecard of educational performance became a catalyst, particularly at the national and state levels, for stimulating interest in improving what was taught, how it was taught, and how we judged success. The secretary's focus on educational outcomes—measures of what students learn—as indicators of the quality of curriculum and teaching helped to sharpen the debate on reform. The Benchmarks feature lists major ongoing efforts to establish national standards.

To master a curriculum in the fullest sense, as any teacher or student may wish to do, is a formidable challenge. Curricula in public schools are constantly evolving as forces in the community influence what is to be learned, how it is to be learned, and how teaching and learning are to be assessed.

SUMMARY

1. Curriculum is generally thought of as what is taught in school. The development of curricula is driven by a variety of competing values and philosophies about goals, content, and organization of education programs.

2. Arguments about curriculum arise frequently because the population is heterogeneous and rapid socioeconomic change routinely makes curriculum decisions controversial.

3. Because education is a power reserved to the states, states and localities are left to define the curriculum. Thus curriculum can be contextually defined. Beyond some rather vague agreement on the need for students to read, write, and compute, there is considerable variation in people's desires and expectations for what the curriculum should deliver.

4. Curriculum is an operative concept outside school in business, industry, and private organizations, where training and education are important.

5. Curricula can be characterized as explicit (visible or public), implicit (hidden or tacit), null (absent or void), and extra (beyond the required).

6. A variety of forces have shaped curriculum through the years. These include: business, industry, and science; national and international events; government and courts; state agenda; state textbook adoption committees; teachers and students; education industries and publishers; mass media and public opinion; and school boards.

7. Curricula relate to the aims of education in five ways: (a) development of cognitive processes, (b) academic rationalism, (c) personal relevance, (d) social adaptation and social reconstruction, and (e) mastery of learning objectives.

8. Curricula have been planned and organized using linear models of planning, outcomes-based models, processing models, and core curriculum models.

9. Trends in curriculum development in recent years include: character education, minimum competency development, gender sensitivity training, environmental conservation, and family life education.

10. Education reform in the 1990s has revolved around concepts of curricular, instructional, and evaluation "standards," or public statements about what is valued. Reformers hope national standards will raise expectations for performance and enable the measurement of progress.

11. Curricular standards are statements about what learning is valued.

12. Evaluation standards serve as yardsticks against which student performance and curricular programs can be measured.

13. Instructional standards are guidelines for how instruction should be delivered.

14. In the absence of clearly articulated and widely agreed upon values for curriculum and evaluation, public pronouncements by influential people have the practical effect of establishing themselves as standards.

TERMS AND CONCEPTS

behavioral objectives
character education
cognitive behavior
   monitoring
constructivist
   orientation
core curriculum
curricular standards
curriculum

evaluation standards
explicit curriculum
extracurriculum
gender sensitivity
   training
implicit curriculum
literacy
minimum competency

multicultural
   curriculum
null curriculum
outcomes-based
   education
remediation
service learning
teacher-proof curricula

STUDENT ACTIVITIES

Your history as a student has shaped your interpretation of curriculum. Some of the activities below will encourage you to spend a few moments considering curriculum as you have come to understand it from a student's point of view. Some of the other activities will force you to stretch yourself to think about curriculum from other perspectives.

Perceive and Value

Reflect on the curriculum you experienced as a high school student. What beliefs and values about the aims and desirable outcomes of education did your curriculum reflect? What are some concrete examples of explicit, implicit, and null curricula in your experience as a high school student? How did the curriculum affect your future learning and career choices? Write about these experiences or share them with classmates in a small-group discussion.

Know and Act

Choose a subject area and grade level you plan to teach and study the curriculum guidelines or standards for that area and level in any particular state, school district, or school. Who defined this curriculum? In what ways does it reflect each of the following emphases: teacher behavior, outcomes of instruction, student-centered learning, and teacher-centered learning? What aims of education are stated or implied? What specific forces do you think helped shape this curriculum? Does it reflect any of the critical issues, changes, or trends discussed in this chapter?

Evaluate

Assess the subject area curriculum you examined or the high school curriculum on which you reflected. What judgments can you make about the value and effectiveness of that curriculum? What criteria or standards can you apply in assessing its strengths and weaknesses?

Discover

Conduct a public opinion poll on the definition, desirability, and degree of importance of one or more of the following curriculum options (or others of your choice):

    environmental conservationism
    student volunteerism and public service
    citizenship skills
    education in the arts
    education in technology
    family life education (or sex education)
    multicultural education
    gender sensitivity training
    education in ethical conduct
    vocational education
    conflict resolution skills
    religions and religious holidays

Develop a rating form to administer so results can be tallied and compared. What are the implications of your findings?

Foundations

In Action

"It's a problem-solving situation in which they use their higher-order thinking skills."

Teachers are often instrumental in curriculum development. They also have primary responsibility for presenting the curriculum and for finding the teaching methods that best serve students in achieving curriculum goals. What are the curriculum goals and methods in each of the three cases presented here?

Mary Anne Reed-Brown groups students for a problem-solving activity that will help her fifth graders meet curriculum goals in mathematics. She is confident that an activity involving math manipulatives is a good match for these goals. She hands students a box of graham crackers and a cookie sheet and asks them to predict how many crackers will be needed to cover the sheet. She hopes they will apply the strategy of using multiplication to find the area of a surface.

"The whole purpose in a lesson such as this is to give kids manipulatives so they can figure out answers to math problems. It's a problem-solving situation in which they use higher-order thinking skills. They have to predict or hypothesize the number of graham crackers it will take to fill the sheet. In the process they develop different types of strategies for determining the area of a plane.
    Guessing is a good tool when students have an opportunity to follow up by actually proving their guesses. Students can work together placing graham crackers on the sheet and counting or multiplying them to see if their predictions are right and if their problem-solving strategies actually worked."

"This way they gain skill in communicating orally and summarizing stories."

Barbara Shin is principal at Hans Christian Andersen school in Minneapolis, Minnesota. She takes an active role in the classroom.

The teachers at Laura Saatzer's school team to implement an integrated language arts curriculum with students of mixed ability. Saatzer is concerned with reading skills, reading comprehension, oral language skills, thinking skills, cooperative learning skills, and the enjoyment of literature. She also plans for opportunities to present a multicultural curriculum.

"During our language arts block, all the children go to their 'special progress' groups. Each group is led by a different teacher, so the group size remains small and our instruction can be more focused. We feel we can meet the needs of our children better this way than in the traditional way when a teacher has three reading groups and calls up the different groups one at a time.

When the students come into my room, they have assigned books they are reading. I go around and check on their oral reading and reading comprehension. I help with decoding skills and give one-on-one instruction at that time.

I also have them choose a fairy tale or folktale to read with a partner, and then they practice retelling. This way they gain skill in communicating orally and summarizing stories.

After language block, I read to them. For instance, during women's history month I might read interesting biographies about famous women and their contributions to our country."

At Hans Christian Andersen school, classroom teachers and school administrators routinely assess their progress in implementing an innovative multicultural curriculum. Everyone contributes to the discussion and has an opportunity to express ideas and concerns. How do they assess whether or not they are achieving curriculum goals? Principal Barbara Shin explains:

"We spent a whole year planning before we jumped into this. Schools have tended to take a hit or miss approach to multicultural curricula, but we have a plan. We know what we wanted to do and we can go back to that plan to see what we've actually accomplished. We know what lessons and instructional units we provided."

"Kids talk differently to each other now, and they feel proud about our school. 'We are multicultural,' they say. They talk to one another openly about cultural diversity and their cultural heritages. It's really rewarding to hear the kids using those terms and expressing pride. They have a new knowledge base."

"We see academic achievement outcomes here too, especially with our eclectic approach to assessment. We're using nontraditional measures—product reviews, portfolios, performances, participation measures—in addition to the standardized tests."

"Teacher observation and teacher opinion is very important, too, because it is teachers who are developing and transforming the curriculum. How teachers are viewing the children and the new programs makes a big difference."

This chapter explores what teachers need to know and do if they are to establish themselves as professional educators. The chapter describes teaching knowledge, teaching skills, and teaching attitudes that foster continued professional growth. The chapter also examines some perennial issues teachers must face and suggests that teachers are growing increasingly interdependent with others in society who have a stake in the success of schools.

10

Instruction

PROFESSIONAL PRACTICE QUESTIONS

1 Which instructional models have you seen teachers use during their interactions with students?

.... Perceive

2 How do beliefs about the purpose of teaching influence teaching behavior?

.... Value

3 What do effective teachers know about teaching, and from where do they derive their knowledge?

.... Know

4 How might you use knowledge from research on teaching to plan and deliver instruction?

.... Act

5 How do people judge teachers and teaching?

.... Evaluate

HOW IS A GOOD TEACHER LIKE A GOOD STUDENT?

Teachers are students, too. Even the best among them do not always know how or why they are successful. With experience, however, they grow accustomed to not having all the answers and to relying instead on the best information available about teaching and learning—information acquired from successful (and unsuccessful) practice. Because the best have stretched themselves time and again to be creative and technically proficient, they know they can call on their abilities when the need arises. They are not afraid to fail, because they have done that too and have lived to teach and learn another day. A good teacher, like a good student, enjoys the work.

Creative teaching, like creative learning, capitalizes on the inspiration of judgment, sensitivity, and intuitive insight. Stanford professor Elliot Eisner (1991) put it well:

> My work in the arts as a painter made it perfectly clear that cognition, by which I mean thinking and knowing, is not limited to linguistically-mediated thought, that the business of making a picture "that works" is an awesome cognitive challenge, and that those who limit knowing to science are naive about the arts and in the long run injurious to the children whose educational programs were shaped by their ideals. (p. 13)

Technically correct or scientific teaching, like scientific learning, takes advantage of information acquired from careful observation and analysis of phenomena in the surrounding world. This information deals with what goes into teaching and learning, what goes on during the course of instruction, and what results from the delivery of instruction. Social scientists who try to unravel the complexities of teaching and learning often focus on variables such as student characteristics and abilities, teaching behaviors, and measures of students' learning. They seek information that will maximize teachers' chances of being successful.

The ongoing debate about how best to teach reading illustrates well the distinction between technical and creative views of teaching. Some educators advocate the use of phonics, a systematic method of teaching based on the belief that children learn best when taught small components of words (letters) before being taught larger components (sounds, words, sentences). Specialists diagnose students' weaknesses and prepare prescriptions for remediating these deficiencies. Reading specialists in laboratories and carefully designed curricular materials aim to develop hierarchies of skills deemed necessary to master the process of reading.

In contrast, advocates of "whole language" do not think reading should be taught separately from other language arts. Whole language is more an inventive philosophy than a specific method for teaching reading and writing, and whole language advocates contend that teachers should use phonics methods only when they think a child will benefit. Students start with stories and learn sentences, words, and sounds as needed. "The common techniques of whole language teaching—daily journal and letter writing, a great deal of silent and oral reading of real literature, and student cooperation, to name a few—are the philosophy in action" (Gursky, 1991, p. 23).

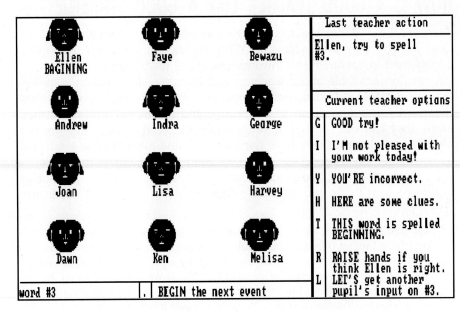

FIGURE 10.1

Computer Simulation for Teaching Practice

Note. From *Teaching Worlds: Simulated Classroom Challenges* (p. 12) by H. R. Strang, 1993, Boston: Allyn and Bacon. Copyright 1993. Reprinted by permission.

Good teachers know that science reveals some simple truths about the connection of teaching to learning, but teachers must apply these principles artfully, and on the run, as they construct knowledge applicable to their own unique situations (Gage, 1977). Attending to both the creative and technical sides of teaching requires that teachers rely on neither creativity nor technical expertise exclusively. Good teachers, like good students, push all their capabilities to the limits to build their knowledge.

One computer simulation allows people to teach "pupils" who appear on a computer screen like the one in Figure 10.1. The teacher practices lesson pacing, manages student misbehavior, promotes active participation in the lesson, and provides constructive feedback to students. "These pupils will not suffer from inexperienced teachers' errors," observes creator Professor Harold Strang (personal communication, November 17, 1993).

WHAT KNOWLEDGE DO EFFECTIVE TEACHERS POSSESS?

Professionals distinguish themselves from nonprofessionals in two important ways: by what they know and by what they know how to do. The formal knowledge base of a profession exists in books, periodicals, and other writings. Beyond providing a rationale for jobs, this knowledge serves as a foundation for teacher education programs, as a basis for licensure and certification examinations, and as a benchmark by which teachers gauge their own practice.

Another more-or-less private, uncodified body of professional knowledge exists in the minds and hearts of those who practice. This personal source of knowledge can be richer and more practically useful for many teachers than the recorded knowledge. Both informal and formal sources of knowledge are important for the successful practice of teaching.

The **formal knowledge base** for teaching consists of two general kinds of knowledge: theory-driven conceptions of effective teaching and actual results from empirical research. The two often complement each other. Theory helps explain logically why teaching and learning occur as they do; research provides results of observations or experiments to help explain relationships between teaching and learning. The most useful theories for educators explain what teachers should do and why (Joyce, Weil, & Showers, 1992).

For example, Jean Piaget formulated a theory of intellectual development that has implications for guiding teachers' actions (see Chapter 8). He described intellectual development in terms of stages (sensorimotor, preoperational, concrete operational, formal operational). The teacher's role, theoretically speaking, is threefold: (a) to create environments where children can spontaneously construct knowledge for themselves in ways that match their stages of cognitive development, (b) to assess children's thinking, and (c) to organize group activities for social interaction among children (Wadsworth, 1978).

TABLE 10.1   Effects of Mathematics Methods

Method	Number of Studies	Effect Size	Graphic Representation of Effect Size
Manipulative materials	64	1.04	.xxxxxxxxxx
Problem solving	33	0.35	.xxxx
New mathematics	134	0.24	.xx

Note. From *Effective Teaching: Current Research* (p. 58) by Hersholt C. Waxman and Herbert J. Wahlberg (Eds.), 1991, Berkeley, CA: McCutchan. Copyright 1991 by McCutchan Publishing Corporation, Berkeley, CA 94702. Permission granted by the publisher.

Such research on children's cognitive development guides specific teaching strategies. Teachers who understand, and can articulate to others, the relationship between educational theory and the research underlying instruction demonstrate an awareness and understanding of the formal knowledge base of teaching.

Harold Mitzel (1960) first described the empirical research on teaching with a set of four **instructional variables**, or concepts that can be used to describe teaching and learning as interrelated activities. These instructional variables deal with presage characteristics, teaching processes, student products, and instructional contexts. Presage characteristics are the characteristics of teachers that are said to "presage" or precede acts of teaching, such as teachers' personalities and their background knowledge. Process variables are those instructional behaviors or processes demonstrated by teachers during the course of a lesson—the questions they ask, the feedback they provide, and the like. Product variables are student outcomes, or learning, measured most often by standardized achievement tests. Context variables are those factors outside the classroom that impinge on teaching and learning, such as school leadership, money spent on education, and children's home environments. Educational researchers conducted experiments to demonstrate causal connections between what teachers do (processes) and student learning (products) (Gage & Needels, 1989).

Herbert Walberg (1991) summarized some 8,000 studies of teaching and learning in elementary and secondary schools to provide an overview of more and less effective educational practices. Using a statistical process of calculating "effect sizes," he revealed the relative power of different instructional behaviors to boost student achievement. For instance, Table 10.1 shows the greater effectiveness of using manipulative materials in the teaching of mathematics over both problem-solving approaches, and the "new math" of the 1960s and 1970s.

To reflect the complexity of life in classrooms, current research on teaching is more methodologically intricate than the bulk of the research summarized by Walberg. As illustrated in Figure 10.2, researchers consider the interactive effects of presage, process, product, and context in a classroom. In doing so, they also consider how teachers and students mediate classroom behavior, or how they think about classroom life.

As Jere Brophy (1992) notes,

current research, while building on findings indicating the vital role teachers play in stimulating student learning, also focuses on the role of the student. It recognizes that students do not merely passively receive or copy input from teachers, but instead actively mediate it by trying to make sense of it and to relate it to what they already know (or think they know) about the topic. Thus, students develop new knowledge through a process of active construction. (p. 5)

Practical knowledge of teaching, constructed through teachers' own experiences, represents yet another valuable source of information about what works with students in classrooms. In many ways, practical knowledge held tacitly by teachers is far ahead of theory and research. Teachers have always constructed their own knowledge by intuiting or learning what it takes to work with others to help them learn. History also teaches, however, that some who have claimed unusual pedagogical insight have been nothing more than charlatans, grifters, and fools. As Gaea Leinhardt (1990) has observed, relying on practical or craft knowledge forces people to consider what or whose knowledge is most useful. Such considerations are accomplished by making implicit knowledge explicit, by communicating it publicly in ways others can understand, and by subjecting it to scrutiny.

Researchers who focus on teachers' and students' thinking make explicit what has previously been hidden from public view. In doing so, they try to explain how teachers make sense out of what they know and how their knowledge influences their actions. Greta Morine-Dershimer (1990, 1992) and her colleagues have used concept maps—ways of organizing ideas about a particular topic so relationships among subtopics can be displayed visually—to describe how teachers construct their own knowledge about effective teaching. As can be seen in Figure 10.3, a teacher's concept map is

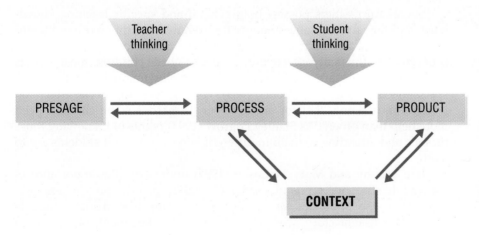

FIGURE 10.2

Model for Describing Research on Teaching

Note. Adapted from "Teacher Effectiveness: Criteria of Teacher Effectiveness" by H. E. Mitzell, 1960. In *Encyclopedia of Educational Research* (3rd ed.) (pp. 1481–1486) by C. W. Harris (Ed.), Copyright 1960, and renewed 1988, by American Educational Research Association. Used by permission of Macmillan Publishing Company.

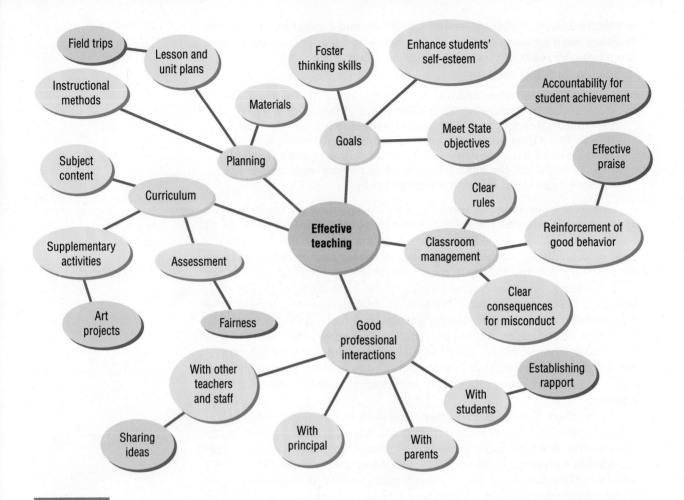

FIGURE 10.3

Construction of Knowledge about Effective Teaching: A Concept Map

What thoughts about planning seemed most important to this teacher?

Note. From "Choosing Among Alternatives for Tracing Conceptual Change" by G. Morine-Dershimer, S. Saunders, A. Artiles, M. Mostert, M. Tankersley, S. Trent, and D. Nuttycombe, 1992, *Teaching and Teacher Education*, 8 (5/6), p. 473. Reprinted with permission from Elsevier Science Ltd., Pergamon Imprint, Oxford, England.

organized in hierarchical fashion. The farther a concept is from the hub, the less central it is to the teacher's thinking about effective teaching (Saunders and Tankersley, 1990).

Successful teachers possess both general and specific teaching knowledge, and they are also able to apply their knowledge differently with students who have special needs. Although some educational programs have proven to be unusually effective with special needs children, most experts suggest that there are no instructional principles uniquely applicable to special needs children (Reynolds, 1989). To be successful, special education teachers must know that for any number of reasons some children need more help than others. As Stanley Pogrow (1993) points out, knowing those reasons and attending to them in different ways is crucial if students are to learn.

Jere Brophy and Mary McCaslin (1992) underscore the importance of teaching to students' needs in a series of studies they did on teachers' perceptions of and strategies for dealing with "problem students" (students exhibiting unsatisfactory achievement, personal adjustment, or classroom behavior). Teachers who had been identified by their principals as more and less successful in dealing with problem students described such students as underachievers, low achievers, aggressive, defiant, distractible, immature, shy, or rejected by peers. Brophy and McCaslin found no magic formula for teaching such problem students, but they did identify some notable differences between successful and unsuccessful teachers. Typically, successful teachers demonstrated more willingness to become personally involved with these students, showed more confidence in their own abilities to help the students improve their behaviors, and were better able to articulate strategies for helping the students.

Do successful teachers have a magic formula for dealing with "problem students?"

What teachers need to know about teaching is closely allied to their disciplines. It is not enough to possess general teaching knowledge at the expense of content knowledge. Nor is it sufficient to know one's content and be ignorant of teaching. To teach mathematics successfully, for example, a teacher must master the subject matter but must also possess the teaching knowledge necessary for creating environments where students can learn mathematics. This blending of content knowledge and teaching knowledge has been called **pedagogical content knowledge** (Shulman, 1986).

HOW DO EFFECTIVE TEACHERS PLAN FOR INSTRUCTION?

Teacher planning has been described as "the thread that weaves the curriculum, or the *what* of teaching, with the instruction, or *how* of teaching" (Frieberg & Driscoll, 1992, p. 22). Among things teachers consider while planning are curriculum, state and local goals and objectives for student learning, instructional strategies for meeting those goals, and methods for assessing students' understanding.

When identifying goals and objectives, teachers determine what it is students should learn or be able to do as a result of instruction (e.g., from examples and nonexamples, students would be able to identify at least four similes in the paragraph provided). Such decisions help teachers clarify their thinking about methods and materials to use during instruction. While objectives are typically influenced by state and local mandates for instruction, they are also shaped by teachers' perceptions of students' needs and abilities before and after instruction.

It is difficult to overestimate the importance of planning how to evaluate the relative success of a lesson. When left to chance, evaluation can be haphazard and yield only partial or misleading information. Such feedback may prompt a teacher to make erroneous decisions about content and methods of instruction most meaningful to students. Teachers' day-to-day

Teachers plan courses, units, and lessons with attention to curriculum, objectives and outcomes, materials, methods, and assessment of student learning.

evaluations of instruction often rely on their perceptions of students' in-class reactions. "Teachers define their primary tasks as successful when other people (usually students) smile, praise, or reward them in some way" (Harootunian & Yarger, 1981, p. 14). As described later in this chapter, there are many other useful ways to evaluate instruction so as to make informed decisions about teaching and learning.

When planning for instruction, teachers also think about classroom management. By establishing clear rules and routines, teachers minimize confusion and maximize instructional time. This aspect of planning is particularly important at the beginning of the year when teachers establish patterns, limits, and expectations that often persist for the remainder of the year (Clark & Dunn, 1991).

Teachers may also consider ways to motivate students when thinking about instruction. According to Jere Brophy (1987), teachers may achieve this goal by: (a) establishing a supportive classroom environment in which students feel comfortable taking intellectual risks, (b) selecting activities that are at the appropriate level of difficulty "that teach some knowledge or skill that is worth learning," and (c) using a variety of motivational strategies (p.208). Such strategies include characterizing the lesson to be taught in familiar, general terms so students can conceptualize what they will be learning and explaining goals and objectives for a lesson and their relevance to students' personal lives.

Lyn Corno (1987) and Philip Winne (1991) contend that when planning academic lessons, teachers should also include on a regular basis activities that will teach students specific and general learning and self-management strategies. This may mean showing students how to take notes from lectures, how to organize their thoughts when writing a paper, or how to monitor and control their concentration during instruction. By providing students with the tools for becoming independent learners, teachers welcome students as "integral, conscious, and rational participants in instructional activities" (Winne, 1991, p. 311). Such skills, in combination with content knowledge, prepare students to continue learning throughout their lifetimes.

Despite all the sage advice on how best to plan, teachers usually plan instruction in ways that make sense to them. Inexperienced teachers tend to pay more attention to students' interests, both in planning and subsequently in teaching, than to students' performances and instructional involvement. Learning how to be a teacher means in part developing one's identity as a teacher. This identity is shaped by social interactions between the teacher and students in the classroom as well as by what a teacher does instructionally with students (Artiles, 1992).

HOW IS THE CURRICULUM DELIVERED?

There is no single best way to teach all people for all purposes. Professional teachers develop a repertoire of teaching strategies or models that can be elicited when conditions warrant; that is, when they are faced with learners who vary in needs and abilities and when striving to accomplish various ends.

Teachers often develop a "style" of teaching that they rely on with most students for most objectives. This style—a manner, a tone, an informal set of practices—reflects their personalities, so much so in some cases that teaching and teacher are virtually inseparable in students' minds. Most likely, these styles also fuel the myths of "Great and Worst" Teachers.

In contrast to a highly personal stylistic approach to teaching, strategies or models are more deliberate, explicit, complete plans for teaching that can be fitted to students and objectives. "The teacher who repeatedly uses the same instructional technique is like the builder who can build only one house. A repertoire of instructional management strategies is necessary to meet the varied needs of learners" (Gunter, Estes, & Schwab, 1995, p. xvi).

Models of teaching explain in broad terms where teachers are going with their students, how they will get there, and how they will know when they have arrived. However, the tactics involved in implementing particular models—the moment-to-moment adaptations of strategy—may vary according to a teacher's reading of student comments and behaviors during the course of instruction. During instruction, for example, teachers might ask themselves a number of questions: Are students attending? Do they understand? Does someone need a question rephrased? A teacher thinks about such matters and makes midcourse corrections in her or his strategy.

Cultural Awareness

Are there particular challenges teachers face when adapting teaching tactics to students' needs? American Sign Language (ASL), one of the most common sign languages, consists of hand movements that represent concepts or words rather than isolated sounds or letters. Learning ASL is much like learning a foreign language. People learn signs for whole words and complete thoughts, build their vocabulary, and improve their speed through practice. As Figure 10.4 suggests, however, hand motions for illustrating concepts may vary from place to place. How does the absence of universal signs put individuals who are deaf doubly at risk? Are there other ways of teaching communication skills to children with severe hearing impairment? What system(s) might you use if one or more of your students was deaf? Why?

FIGURE 10.4

How One Concept is Expressed in Different Areas of the Country

FAINT:
My mother fainted from the ammonia fumes.

1 Alabama, Hawaii

2 Arkansas, Florida, Maine Kentucky, Louisiana, Virginia, North Carolina, South Carolina

3 California, Illinois, Utah

4 Colorado, Texas (1 of 2)

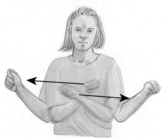

5 Massachusetts

6 Michigan, Ohio

7 Missouri, New Mexico, Washington

8 New York

9 North Dakota

10 Pennsylvania

11 Texas (2 of 2)

12 Wisconsin

Note. Reprinted by permission of the publisher, from E. Shroyer and S. Shroyer, *Signs Across America,* (1984): 79–80. Washington, DC: Gallaudet University Press. Copyright 1984 by Gallaudet University.

Bruce Joyce, Marsha Weil, and Beverly Showers (1992) demonstrate that professional teachers plan for success; they do not leave it to chance. These authors present detailed descriptions of a variety of **instructional models**, explaining the goals for each model, underlying theoretical assumptions, and relevant research supporting the use of a particular model. They also describe the phases of a model, or how a lesson should proceed; teacher and student roles and relationships; recommended ways to respond to what learners say and do during a lesson; and particular materials, personnel, or training necessary for implementing the model.

Joyce and his colleagues have forged two strong conceptual links that make such models of teaching invaluable to teachers. First, they have connected the worlds of theory and practice by translating the work of researchers and theorists into a language that can be applied by teachers in the classroom. In doing so, they demonstrate the validity of Kurt Lewin's (1935) classic observation that there is nothing so practical as good theory. Second, they describe a wide repertoire of models in mutually comparable terms that make sense to teachers. They thus make it possible to decide how best to organize instruction for particular students for certain purposes and to articulate one's reasons for doing so—abilities central to professional practice.

The models described by Joyce and his colleagues serve a variety of purposes and are grouped into four "families" (see Figure 10.5). The Behavioral

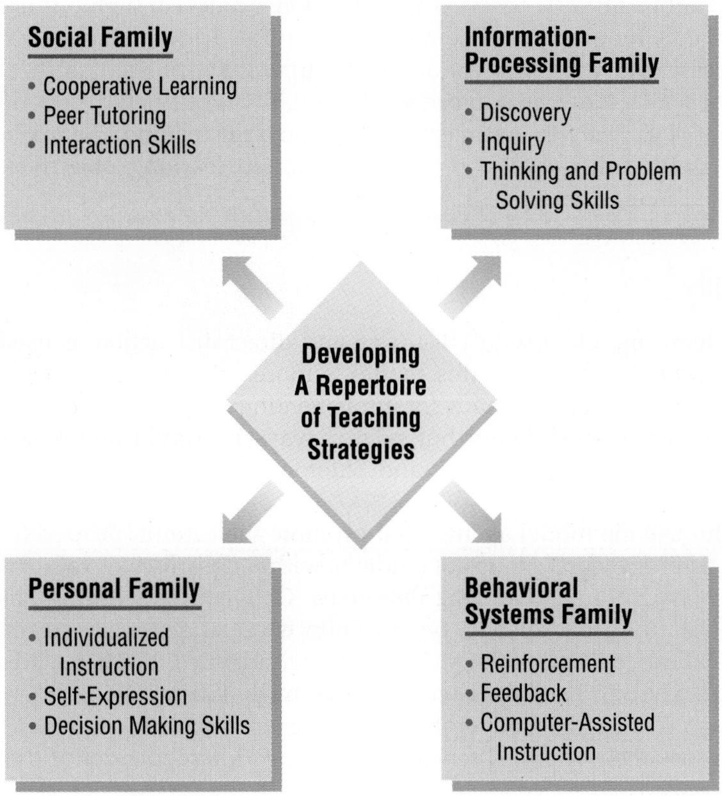

Social Family

- Cooperative Learning
- Peer Tutoring
- Interaction Skills

Information-Processing Family

- Discovery
- Inquiry
- Thinking and Problem Solving Skills

Developing A Repertoire of Teaching Strategies

Personal Family

- Individualized Instruction
- Self-Expression
- Decision Making Skills

Behavioral Systems Family

- Reinforcement
- Feedback
- Computer-Assisted Instruction

FIGURE 10.5

Examples of Teaching Strategies that Contribute to a Teacher's Instructional Repertoire

Effective teachers employ strategies and combinations of strategies from all four "families."

Note. Adapted from *Models of Teaching* (4th ed.) by B. R. Joyce, M. Weil, and B. Showers, 1992, Boston: Allyn and Bacon.

Systems Family uses ideas about manipulating the environment to modify students' behaviors. The Social Family capitalizes on people's nature as social beings to learn and relate to one another. The Information-Processing Family increases students abilities to think—to seek, organize, interpret, and apply information both inductively and deductively. The Personal Family encourages self-exploration and the development of personal identity.

Behavioral Systems Family

Mastery learning, one of several behavioral models that have enjoyed widespread use, was developed through the work of Benjamin Bloom (1971), John Carroll (1971), and their colleagues. The basic strategy suggests that student learning is a function of a student's aptitude, his or her motivation, and the amount and quality of instruction. Instead of defining student aptitude as native ability, proponents of mastery learning define it as the amount of time a student requires to master an objective. Given enough time, the inclination to learn, and instruction fitted to a student's needs, students are thought to be capable of mastering a range of subject matter. Teachers must organize instruction into manageable units, diagnose students' needs with respect to the material, teach in ways that meet those needs, and evaluate progress regularly.

Like mastery learning, **direct instruction** is a highly structured, teacher-centered strategy. It capitalizes on such behavioral techniques as modeling, feedback, and reinforcement to promote basic skill acquisition, primarily in reading and mathematics. Teachers using this model must set high but not unattainable goals for students. The model prescribes classroom organization and processes that maximize the amount of time students spend on academic tasks at which they can succeed with regularity. Policy emphases on the assessment of pupils' minimum competency on basic reading and mathematics objectives, rather than complex or advanced learning objectives, have stimulated interest in direct instruction.

Social Family

Cooperative learning, like mastery learning and direct instruction, is used frequently in schools. However, this model is more social in nature than behavioral systems models. Methods for implementing cooperative learning have been articulated in different but related ways by David and Roger Johnson (1991), Robert Slavin (1991), and Shlomo and Yael Sharan (1989; 1990).

Those who use the model as intended promote the careful, purposeful formation of heterogeneous groups of students within classrooms to accomplish social, personal, and academic objectives. Cooperative learning has grown in popularity because of its positive effects on student self-esteem, intergroup relations, acceptance of students with academic limitations, attitudes toward school, and ability to work cooperatively (Slavin, 1991).

The Johnsons describe cooperative learning as "learning together." Teachers who use their approach encourage positive interdependence (the idea that the group sinks or swims together), face-to-face interaction among students, individual accountability, the development of social skills, and group processing. Teachers serve as facilitators, observing groups, analyzing problems they have working together, offering feedback on their interactive skills, and, when necessary, teaching social skills that promote constructive socialization. That is, students are taught such things as constructive ways to deal with controversy and academic disagreements and ways to keep all members verbally involved in the learning process.

Sharan (1989; 1990) describes cooperative learning as "group investigation." This means having students work in small groups, with each group taking on a different task. Within groups, students decide what information they need and how to organize and present it. Teachers evaluate students in terms of how they apply and synthesize information and how they make inferences.

Slavin advances a variety of cooperative approaches, sometimes coupled with competition among teams. Student Teams-Achievement Divisions (STAD) has the teacher present a lesson and students work in teams on worksheets or other written material. After one or two presentations and one or two sessions of team practice, students complete independently a quiz or test. Individual scores are based on improvement over previous scores, and team performances are recognized. Teams-Games-Tournament (TGT) is similar to STAD, but rather than take a quiz, students compete with classmates of similar achievement from other teams to earn points for their own team. Teachers can use Jigsaw II, a method of teaching which focuses more on concepts than skills, when students are studying material written in narrative form. Students are divided into teams and provided with a common reading to study. Each member of a team becomes an "expert" on one of the topics covered in the reading. Experts from the different teams meet in small groups to master their material and discuss ways to present it to other team members. While such cooperative strategies have been shown to be more successful in elementary and middle grades, they also work with high school students (Newman & Thompson, 1987). In all these instances of cooperative learning, teachers plan team formation carefully to encourage not only mastery of subject matter but understanding and acceptance among students as well.

Cooperative Integrated Reading and Composition (CIRC), the newest of team learning methods, is used for teaching literacy skills in the upper elementary grades. Students are grouped by ability for reading instruction but they are also assigned to small teams with whom they work while the teacher is engaged with a particular reading group. Teams are composed of two pairs of students who represent two different reading groups. For example, one team may have a pair of students from the top reading group and a pair from the low group. During team work time, student pairs may read to one another, summarize stories, work on writing assignments, or practice spelling, decoding, and vocabulary skills. In situations in which teachers do not group by ability for reading instruction, all individuals in a group work as a total group on such concepts as main idea. They may also work together on writing assignments, offering feedback about one another's writing efforts (Slavin, 1991).

Cultural Awareness

Martha Ann Stallings teaches at Gilbert Linkous Elementary School in Blacksburg, Virginia. She and Peter, who has Down's syndrome, worked in the same classroom with 20 nondisabled third graders. They also starred in the Academy Award-winning film, *Educating Peter*, which models successful teacher-student collaboration and cooperative learning.

Martha Ann Stallings and Peter

Note. From "When Peter Came to Mrs. Stallings' Class" by M. A. Stallings, 1993, May, *NEA Today*, p. 22. Copyright 1993 NEA Today/National Education Association. Reprinted by permission.

Information Processing Family

Models in this family stimulate the development of such thinking skills as observation, comparing, finding patterns, and generalizing while also teaching specific concepts or generalizations (Eggen & Kauchak, 1988). Information processing models are built on the ideas of information processing theorists and modern constructivists (see chapters 8 and 9); that is, such models take their cues for instruction from theory that explains how people think. Models in the information-processing family often encourage **inquiry learning** or **discovery learning**—learning whereby students inquire into subjects for themselves, or seek to discover knowledge for themselves rather than being taught more directly by a teacher.

Concept formation, for example, is a model of instruction teachers use when they want students to analyze and synthesize data to construct knowledge about a particular concept or idea. A science teacher using concept formation during a unit on plants would likely ask students to: (a) examine a variety of plant specimens, (b) place the plants into groups based on structural characteristics, and (c) generate labels for each of the plant groups. The teacher might then provide additional

> **Students can be trained to think about their own thinking.**

specimens for students to classify. While most of these plants would probably fit existing classifications, students might have to create new categories to hold some of the plants. In a lesson of this type, students are not passive recipients of information; rather, they are active "creators" or "inventors" of

VOICES

On Student-Centered Instruction

There are many ways for teachers to encourage personal expression, some quite personal. Nancie Atwell—teacher of adolescents, of writing, and of life—makes personal expression central in her classroom.

I confess. I started out as a "creationist." The first days of every school year I created; for the next thirty-six weeks I maintained my creation. My curriculum. From behind my big desk I set it in motion, managed and maintained it all year long. I wanted to be a great teacher—systematic, purposeful, in control. I wanted great results from my great practices. And I wanted to convince other teachers that this creation was superior stuff. So I studied my curriculum, conducting research designed to show its wonders. I didn't learn in my classroom. I tended and taught my creation.

These days, I learn in my classroom. What happens there has changed; it continually changes. I've become an "evolutionist," and the curriculum unfolds now as my kids and I learn together. My aims stay constant—I want us to go deep inside language, using it to know and shape and play with our worlds—but my practices evolve as eighth graders and I go deeper. This going deeper is research, and these days my research shows me the wonders of my kids, not my methods. But it has also brought me full circle. What I learn with these students, collaborating with them as a writer and reader who wonders about writing and reading, makes me a better teacher—not great maybe, but at least grounded in the logic of learning, and growing. . . .

I didn't intuit or luck into this place, and I didn't arrive overnight. I paved the way through writing and reading about writing, through uncovering and questioning my assumptions, through observing kids and trying to make sense of my observations, through dumb mistakes, uncertain experiments, and, underneath it all, the desire to do my best by my kids.

A lot of the time, doing my best hurt. It means looking hard at what I was doing and asking kids to do. It meant learning—and admitting—that I was wrong. And, most painful of all, it meant letting go of my cherished creation.

I learn in my classroom these days because I abandoned that creation. I had to. When I stopped focusing on me and my methods and started observing students and their learning, I saw a gap yawning between us—between what I did as language teacher and what they did as language learners. I saw that my creation manipulated kids so they bore sole responsibility for narrowing the gap, and my students either found ways to make sense of and peace with the logic of my teaching, or they failed the course. In truth, it was I who needed to move, to strike out for some common ground. I learn in my classroom these days because I moved, because the classroom became a reading and writing workshop, a new territory my students and I could inhabit together.

CRITICAL THINKING

What is special about the teaching and learning of writing that might allow teachers and students to learn together? How might teachers and students collaborate with one another in the study of other disciplines?

Source: Atwell, N. (1987). *In the middle: Writing, reading, and learning with adolescents.* Portsmouth, NH: Boynton/ Cook, pp. 3–4. Reprinted by permission.

knowledge. They "think as scientists do as they analyze data and create and test theories and hypotheses" to expand the conceptual system with which they process information (Joyce, Weil, & Showers, 1992, p. 116).

Sometimes teachers actually train students to think about their own thinking, or to become aware of how they process information as they learn. Teachers who use metacognitive strategies such as memory training and cognitive monitoring want students to become independent learners; that is, to learn about their own learning processes and to change them when change is advantageous (Sprinthall & Sprinthall, 1990).

Personal Sources Family

Teachers who use personal models of instruction want to involve students actively in the determination of what and how they will learn. Their ultimate goal is to develop long-term dispositional changes rather than short-term instructional effects (Joyce, Weil, & Showers, 1992). William Glasser's Classroom Meeting model is one systematic teaching strategy used to attain such goals.

When implementing Glasser's model, teachers meet with students for 30 to 45 minutes at least once a week to discuss personal or behavioral problems during an open-ended classroom meeting. Issues to be discussed may be initiated by teachers or students. While the teacher remains nonjudgmental, students make personal value judgments about issues discussed. Together, teachers and students propose alternative courses of action and commit to following the chosen solution. The Classroom Meeting model, then, is aimed at helping students become more responsible for their actions (Glasser, 1986).

WHAT SKILLS MUST TEACHERS DEMONSTRATE TO BE SUCCESSFUL?

The literature on educating teachers is brimming with lists of skills—abilities to use one's knowledge—that one expert or another has advanced as essential components of teachers' repertoires. In the 1970s, a teacher in a single program might have been encouraged to demonstrate upwards of 2,500 "competencies." Burns (1972) described the following types of objectives, or teaching competencies, teachers were expected to master. Some 25 years later, many teacher education programs across the nation still require such competencies:

- terminal behavioral objective: specifies behaviors to be exhibited by teacher at end of learning activity.

- instructional or enabling objective: specifies intermediate behaviors teachers are to acquire on the way to terminal objectives.

- exploratory objective: does not specify behavior but events to be "experienced" by teacher.

- cognitive objective: specifies behavior that will demonstrate teacher's knowledge, understanding, or processing abilities.

- affective objective: specifies behavior that will demonstrate the teacher's possession of a certain attitude.

The following competency represents a cluster of one terminal behavioral objective (TBO) and several instructional objectives (IOs):

TBO: Learners are to develop an understanding of multiple-choice (MC) achievement testing based on a table of specifications, so that they can: (a) create a table of specifications for a 6-7-8 grade unit of their choice, and (b) write a sample of 25 MC items conforming to the table.

IO-5:   Develop a table of specifications.

IO-4:   Write 5 MC items.

IO-3:   When given 25 MC items, locate and classify errors.

IO-2:   Learn types of errors made in MC-item writing.

IO-1:   Learn MC terminology. (Burns, 1972, p. 27)

As knowledge has grown and as philosophies have changed, programs have required that teacher education students demonstrate far fewer yet more complex skills such as those described below. Once teachers distinguish themselves as professionals by applying personal, theoretical, and empirical knowledge, there are some complementary planning and interactive teaching skills, such as those listed in Figure 10.6, that will serve them well. It is possible to be as technical or as creative as one wishes in defining these skills; they are described here only in general terms.

Understanding Students   Good teachers learn about their students. (See Chapter 8 on "Students and Learning.") They use a variety of methods to find out what students know, what they can do, how they think, what they value, what their backgrounds are, and what gets in the way of their learning. The skill of understanding students can be shaped formally by reading and studying student artifacts such as tests and projects and honed informally by observing, talking with, and listening to students and their parents.

Setting Goals   Skillful teachers know how to establish, negotiate, and help students set reasonable goals for learning for themselves. Goals typically relate to the development of students' knowledge, skills, and attitudes. Teachers sometimes select goals from existing curricula and match the goals to a student's needs and abilities; this means teachers must help different students accomplish different goals. Sometimes goals are established within a curriculum, and teachers must help all students accomplish the same goals. At yet other times, teachers need to be able to assist students in setting their own goals.

Creating Learning Environments   Teachers typically create learning environments in two stages: planning for teaching and interacting with

FIGURE 10.6

Teachers' Skills

These skills underlie teachers' abilities to understand students, set goals, create learning environments, evaluate student learning, and communicate.

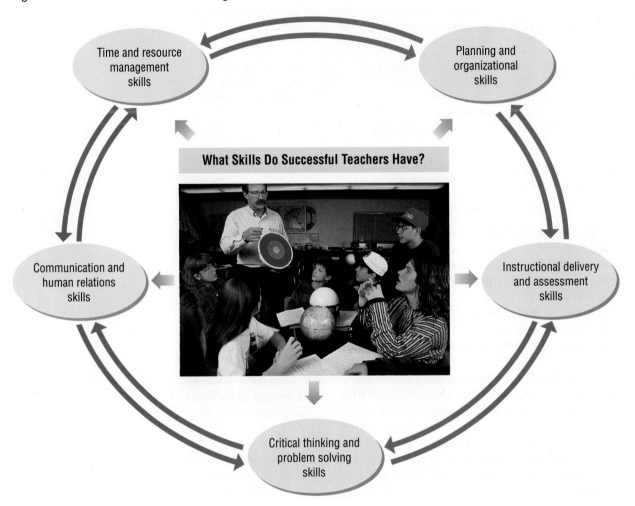

students during the course of instruction. In general, planning means selecting appropriate content, designing activities that maximize opportunities for students to succeed, informing parents and other school personnel (e.g., librarian, fine arts teachers, and other classroom teachers) of curricular plans so they may help in the collection of relevant teaching materials and in the reinforcement of concepts being taught, arranging the classroom and organizing necessary materials, motivating students, reinforcing good work, and managing people, ideas, and resources to inspire students to do their best work.

Evaluating Student Learning   Teachers need to be able to decide what works in teaching and what does not. As we discuss later in this chapter, there are any number of ways to assess student progress and to infer teaching success from informal and formal methods of measurement and evaluation. Good teachers are able to determine what types of student feedback will be most useful when making decisions about curriculum and instruction.

Communicating   At its core, professional teaching is an intellectual enterprise, and thus, good teachers are good communicators. They communicate clearly both verbally and in writing. These communication skills may be applied to transmit information about subject matter. Such skills may also be used to communicate with parents, administrators, and other teachers. But they can just as well be used to communicate expectations for student success, empathy, positive regard, and willingness to help.

HOW DO TEACHERS MANAGE CLASSROOMS FOR EFFECTIVE INSTRUCTION?

Classrooms are "crowded, competitive, contradictory, multidimensional, simultaneous, unpredictable, public . . . [places where] teachers work with captive groups of students on academic agendas that students have not helped to set" (Weinstein & Mignano, 1993, pp. 5–6). Teachers who understand the complexity of classrooms realize the importance of finding ways to gain students' cooperation and involvement in educational activities. Through careful planning, they also take steps to prevent problems from occurring. **Classroom management**, then, deals with how order is established and maintained in classroom environments (Doyle, 1986).

When organizing the physical setting, for example, effective teachers consider ways to organize tables and chairs to minimize congestion and distractions (e.g., avoiding placement of children's chairs near doorways or windows). At the same time, teachers think about ways to arrange furniture to facilitate the types of learning (individualized, cooperative, whole-group) they wish to incorporate during the school day. Regardless of how this is done, effective classroom managers make sure they have easy access to every student. Furthermore, they place students where they can hear and see instructional presentations.

Effective classroom managers also reduce the complexity of the classroom by making explicit their expectations for behavior. To do so, they establish during the first week of school rules for conduct and procedures for carrying out tasks such as pencil sharpening. These guidelines for behavior are age-appropriate, straightforward, and consistent with school rules.

Kounin's classic research (1970) on interactions of teachers and pupils suggests that good classroom managers do not "satiate" students. That is, they prevent boredom by varying learning tasks and by maintaining lesson momentum. They avoid giving too many directions or lengthy explanations, stop activities when students become restless, and make smooth transitions from one activity to the next. The intent is to maximize student involvement and to minimize disruptions.

BENCHMARKS

A Sample of Classic Contributions to the Conceptualization and Study of Teaching

1900–1920	Alfred Binet develops a systematic procedure in France for assessing learning aptitudes. Later, at Stanford University in the United States, Binet's test is revised and a formula for determining IQ added. Research on teaching concentrates on characteristics of learners and on more and less effective teachers.
	In experiments with cats, Edward Thorndike describes the law of effect—that any behavior resulting in satisfaction will tend to be repeated. This and similar work influences development of teaching approaches.
1920–1940	In behavioral experiments with dogs, Russian scientist Ivan Pavlov discovers classical conditioning.
	Swiss psychologist Jean Piaget describes the stages of cognitive development in children from infancy through adolescence.
	Lev S. Vygotsky describes the roles of social learning and language in the cognitive development of children in Russia.
1940–1960	Research on teaching concentrates on what teachers do in classrooms rather than on their personal characteristics.
	Lewis Terman begins a long-term study of 1,528 gifted American children. This classic study is slated to end in 2010.
	In experiments with pigeons and rats, B. F. Skinner develops the concept of operant conditioning, in which learning is based on the consequences of behavior. This work profoundly influences the development of behavioral teaching approaches.
	David Wechsler develops the Adult Intelligence Scale, testing different kinds of aptitude, on which the Wechsler Intelligence Scale for Children (WISC-R) is based. This view of learners' abilities shapes teaching approaches.

When disruptions occur, Kounin suggests a number of things teachers can do to prevent problems from escalating. Among these are use of "with-it-ness" and "overlapping" behaviors. A teacher who is "with it" seems to have "eyes in the back of his or her head." Aware of what is going on, this

1940–1960 (continued)	Humanist psychologists such as Harry Stack Sullivan describe child and adolescent development in terms of interpersonal interaction. Abraham Maslow describes human motivation in terms of the satisfaction of needs. Curriculum and teaching reflect concerns for personal development and interpersonal interactions.
	Benjamin Bloom publishes a taxonomy of educational objectives for the cognitive domain. John Carroll develops the theory of effective instruction on which mastery learning is based.
1960–1990	Research on primate communication advances the study of human language. Noam Chomsky theorizes that children acquire language through transformational grammar and other deep structures of the brain.
	In human development studies, Erik Erikson describes stages requiring resolutions of psychological crises, and Lawrence Kohlberg describes stages of moral development based on children's responses to moral dilemmas. Dilemmas themselves become teaching materials.
	Research on human memory by R. C. Atkinson and others leads to the development of the information processing theory of learning. Robert Gagné, Madeline Hunter, and others develop models of direct instruction based on task analysis and information processing theory.
	Albert Bandura and others describe the behavioral principles of modeling and observational learning. J. Kounin and others describe teacher behaviors that relate to teaching effectiveness and efficacious classroom management.
	Robert Mager proposes behavioral objectives stating precisely what students should know or be able to do at the end of a lesson or unit of study.
	Jerome Bruner and others develop discovery learning and instructional models based on cognitive learning theory.

teacher stops students who are misbehaving and does so in a timely manner. Overlapping, which is a teacher's ability to handle more than one thing at a time, may occur when a teacher who is working with a small group of students also manages a disruption in another part of the room.

HOW DO GOOD TEACHERS EVALUATE STUDENTS?

Teachers have access to a variety of information about students. Using formal measures such as tests and quizzes and informal measures such as questionnaires, interviews, and observations of in-class behaviors, teachers make judgments daily about students' academic performance, their attitudes and interests, and their ability to work with others. Such information enables teachers to: (a) determine what students already know and want to know about topics, (b) plan instruction that is appropriately challenging, (c) motivate student performance, (d) assess progress toward affective and cognitive goals, and (e) communicate progress to others.

When collecting and synthesizing information about students, teachers have a responsibility to use the best information available before making evaluative decisions. This means assessing students frequently using procedures that allow students to demonstrate what they can do. After collecting information, teachers are obligated to "protect its privacy, recognize the limits of its use in decision making, and not use it to demean or ridicule a pupil" (Airasian, 1991, p. 24).

Student Assessment

When their offspring are very young, parents begin to assess informally their potential. Is Andrew going to be a great student or merely a good one? Just exactly how smart is Toyeker? Will Shari be a concert pianist or a track star or both? Should savings be geared toward sending the kids to Harvard or to State University or to trade school? Parents, and soon the children themselves, base their answers on judgments of intellectual capability, artistic sensitivities, athletic prowess, and beyond.

When children enter school, assessment becomes formalized as **measurement**—the collection of data relevant to personal characteristics—and **evaluation**—interpreting and attaching value to the data. Diagnostic tests are used to identify specific problems, needs, or disabilities to be considered when making placement decisions about individual students. For example, there are tests for identifying hearing impairment, visual-perceptual problems, and coordination problems. Academic progress or lack thereof is gauged most often by **standardized tests**—commercially-prepared tests designed to obtain uniform samples of student behavior. These tests are usually but not always multiple-choice, paper-and-pencil tests administered and scored under conditions uniform to all students. Standardized tests do not necessarily measure what should be taught or the levels at which students should perform.

Standardization is important because it helps equalize opportunities to take a test and to make test scores comparable. The scores students acquire on these tests are estimates of what they know or can do; they are, however, imprecise because they are only samples of students' learned behaviors at a particular point in time. Good teachers who interpret standardized test scores are aware that a variety of circumstances, such as testing conditions (e.g., a cold or crowded room), lucky guesses, illness, test anxiety, and disruption at home, may influence how well a child does on a formal assessment (Airasian, 1991). Therefore, when making judgments about a student's achievement or potential for learning, these teachers are careful to consider both informal (e.g., teacher-made tests, observations) and formal measures of learning. Those evaluating test scores must also ask themselves whether students have had an opportunity to learn content included on formal assessments. In school, the consequences of "measuring up" are significant, for results determine the course of one's educational career (U.S. Congress, 1992).

Those who interpret test results have two ways to answer the question, "How well did so-and-so do?" On a **norm-referenced test**, they compare a student's test score to the scores of other students. On a **criterion-referenced test**, a student's performance is judged by comparing it to some clearly defined criterion for mastering a learning task or skill.

To be useful, scores must be reliable; that is, a student's score today must be the same or close to a score he or she would get tomorrow. The score must also generalize to skills similar to those assessed on the test. And if the test is not machine-scored, scorers must be able to agree on their estimates of student performance. Test scores must also be valid; that is, they must measure what they are supposed to measure. For example, if a test claims to assess students' understanding of the workings of an internal combustion engine, it should not be a test of their reading ability.

Authentic Assessment

In recent years, reformers have argued that if schools are to be held accountable for student learning, the instruments of assessment, the tests themselves, must be improved. To many, multiple-choice tests that deemphasize reading, writing, and calculating inhibit learning. Reformers argue that schools need to depend more on **authentic assessment**: assessment concerned less with students' recognition and recall of facts and more with students' abilities to analyze, apply, evaluate, and synthesize what they know in ways that address real-world concerns. Albert Shanker, leader of the American Federation of Teachers, for instance, has argued for the creation of tests that ". . . test for things that are really important: reading, writing, computing, history . . ." ("Shanker Asks," 1989).

More educators are beginning to use portfolios to assess student performances. While there is no standard definition of the term **portfolio**, and thus no consensus on what should be in one, Judith Arter and Vicki Spandel (1992) have offered this working definition:

> A portfolio is a purposeful collection of student work that tells the story of the student's efforts, progress, or achievement in (a) given area(s). This collection must include student participation in selection of portfolio content; the guidelines for selection; the criteria for judging merit, and evidence of student self-reflection. (1990, p. 36)

The popularity of a portfolio approach to evaluation is primarily attributed to its potential for: (a) revealing a range of skills and understandings, (b) encouraging student and teacher reflection, (c) illustrating growth over a period of time, and (d) providing some continuity in a child's education from year to year (Vavrus, 1990). People like the idea of judging students' higher-order thinking and practical skills. Desmond Nuthall's (1992) view of England's experience with the Assessment of Performance Unit is instructive for U.S. educators. He argues that performance assessment can be made to work, and both teachers and students welcome it. It can even improve teaching and broaden the range of skills appraised. But he warns that the cost of performance assessment is immense, both financially and in terms of the time it requires of teachers. Moreover, Nuthall contends, disagreements over assessment standards will mean that some will never view such assessments as rigorous.

> **Assessment is a state of mind, and also a tool-box for teachers. Kidwatching is the key.**

According to Mary Catherine Ellwein (1992, pp. 2, 4), assessment is a process that is "intertwined with the daily life of teachers" and as much a "state of mind as it is a toolbox." In her efforts to understand teachers' typical evaluative behaviors, she has identified two primary activities that teachers use to evaluate; she terms these activities "gathering intelligence" and "kidwatching." By engaging in these activities, teachers learn to understand students in their contexts, determine their strengths and learning strategies, tailor instruction, promote students' awareness of their learning, document their learning and change, and communicate with others connected to the students.

Cultural Awareness

Research on the evaluative behaviors of Asian teachers suggests that they, too, learn much by watching their students. Their learning differs, however, in important ways from that of their American counterparts, particularly when interpreting students' mistakes.

> For Americans, errors tend to be interpreted as an indication of failure in learning the lesson. For Chinese and Japanese, they are an index of what still needs to be learned. These divergent interpretations result in very different reactions to the display of errors—embarrassment on the part of American children, calm acceptance by Asian children. They also result in differences in the manner in which teachers utilize errors as effective means of instruction. (Stigler & Stevenson, 1991, p. 27)

WHAT SPECIAL INSTRUCTIONAL ISSUES MUST TEACHERS FACE?

Some instructional issues are perennial. Teachers must contend with policies that govern classroom behavior and curricula that shape their teaching regardless of when and where they work.

Grading

When assessments are finished, teachers must typically assign grades to students; that is, assignment of grades is usually a job requirement. As we note below, some school systems are beginning to use portfolios—collections of students' work—to describe and report students' progress, but the use of such methods to replace grades entirely is rare. Most school districts continue to use grades to reward students, to report to parents, and to provide estimates of students' potential for post-secondary study.

What do grades mean to students and to teachers?

Grades take various forms: the familiar letter grades (A+, A, A–, B+, etc.); pass/fail (P/F) or satisfactory/unsatisfactory (S/U); and numerical values (90–100 = A; 80–89 = B, etc.). Grades are also frequently supplemented with teachers' comments or estimates of student effort, attitude, work habits, and the like, to provide a fuller representation of students' performances. These comments are often written directly on report cards.

Teachers often feel pulled by opposing desires: to use grades to build students' confidence by rewarding effort and progress or to assign value to students' performances in some "objective" fashion. These sometimes contradictory demands can force teachers to examine their own ethical reasoning with respect to acceptable and unacceptable grading practice. Planning for evaluation and grading early on helps teachers resolve such dilemmas when and if they arise.

Even careful planning, however, does not always prevent problems. On June 22, 1993, Adele Jones, a high school algebra teacher in Georgetown, Delaware, was fired over grades (McCarthy, 1993). Jones had failed 27% of her Algebra II class in 1991–92 and 42% the year before. When the Indian River School Board first announced its decision, some 200-plus students, including some who had failed the course, marched in protest against the dismissal. Jones's colleagues backed her with enthusiasm—43 of 48 signed a letter condemning the board for its action. The Delaware affiliate of the National Education Association paid for a lawyer to take the case to court. Jones claimed to have rebelled against the practice of rewarding students with grades they did not earn; the board interpreted the failure of so many students as an indication of her incompetence.

Cultural Awareness

Some communities are trying to help all their parents understand how to talk with their children about problems with grades.

UNDERSTANDING:
The Most Important Grade

**Tips at
Report Card
Time**

If there is a problem at school:

★ SIT DOWN with your child and look over the report card.

★ PRAISE YOUR CHILD. Find at least one good thing: attendance, no tardies.

★ BE CALM! Let your child tell you about his poor grades.

★ ASK how you can help your child do better.

★ ASK what your child can do to make better grades.

★ MAKE A PLAN with your child's teacher and your child to do better.

If you have questions or need help, please contact your child's teacher, guidance counselor, or principal.

Language: Korean

이해
가장 중요한 점수

성적표에
대한 조언

학교에서 문제가 있으면:

★ 성적표를 같이 보며 차분히 자녀와 애기하십시요

★ 자녀를 칭찬하십시요. 결석, 지각이 없었 던것... 등, 적어도 한가지--.

★ 마음을 가다듬고 댁의 자녀로 하여금 왜 성적이 나빴는지 설명하게 하십시요.

★ 어떻게 하면 성적을 올리는데 부모가 도와줄 수 있는지 물어 보십시요.

★ 어떻게 하면 본인이 성적을 올리는데 도움이될지 물어 보십시요.

★ 교사와 의논하여 학업을 올리도록 같이 계획하십시요.

만약 질문 또는 도움이 필요하시면 담임, 상담지도교사 또는 교장에게 연락하십시요.

Source: Fairfax County Public Schools, Parenting Education Center. Translated and reprinted by permission of SCAN, National Committee for Prevention of Child Abuse.

Retention

Flunking, to use the derisive term for failing a course or repeating grades in school, always an issue of concern, has taken on new urgency as education reformers tout the advantages of setting and maintaining high standards. To prevent mediocrity, they argue, educators must abandon the idea of **social promotion**, or passing children to successive grades to keep them with others of their age. According to folk wisdom, it is only logical, and helpful to both individuals and to the system as a whole, to retain children who do not reach standards (Shepard & Smith, 1989).

VOICES

On Retention

Mary Lee Smith, Professor of Educational Psychology at Arizona State University, an authority on the effects of retention on children's later performance in school and on their feelings of self esteem, sees children and often teachers as at the mercy of the system when it comes to matters of retention.

The decision to retain is often rationalized as the protection of unready or incompetent children from the harsh realities of the higher grade. Kindergarten teachers are confronted with an external standard of performance—to make sure all children are ready to begin reading and figuring on the first day of first grade. The first grade teacher, in turn, is faced with the demand that all children be able readers by the end of first grade. In many districts and states, this common standard is reinforced by the administration and public reporting of accountability tests. To guarantee that promoted kindergartners are ready to read, they must go through a curriculum that achieves a measurable level of reading readiness skills; for example, letter-sound associations, consonant blends, listening and following directions, working independently or with their peers without bothering the teacher unduly, and worksheet skills such as printing their names on the proper line. This is too much for some pupils, who might be more appropriately educated in a kind of kindergarten based on learning through social interactions, natural language development, and guided exploratory play. The now predominant literacy-focused kindergarten curriculum, as described by Weber (1986), defines learning narrowly, assumes that the curricular content to achieve literacy and numeracy is known, can be broken down into small units, sequenced, taught directly, and assessed in standardized ways. The methods of teaching are assumed to be uniform for all pupils, and if a pupil fails to achieve, the same content and methods are repeated and intensified. If necessary, children are recycled through the whole package by retaining them for a second year in kindergarten.

Many teachers reject the view of schooling as inappropriate for young children, yet feel powerless to alter the structure of the school, the externally imposed curriculum and accountability requirements placed on them. The only autonomy still available to them is the recommendation to retain a child who does not fit the structure. The rhetoric of teachers' beliefs about retention regularly places the problem of unreadiness or incompetence in the psychological make-up of the child rather than in the institutional characteristics of the school. The curriculum is left unexamined.

CRITICAL THINKING

Are teachers powerless in the process of retention, or do they only feel powerless? Explain your response. If Smith is correct, and the problem of unreadiness or incompetence is placed on children rather than on the institutional characteristics of the school, where it belongs, how might educators begin to change this situation?

Source: Smith, M. L. (1989). Teachers' beliefs about retention. In L. A. Shepard & M. L. Smith (Eds.), *Flunking grades: Research on policies on retention* (pp. 132-150). London: The Falmer Press, pp. 148–149. Reprinted by permission.

As H.L. Mencken once observed, there is always a simple answer for every problem, and it is usually wrong. Such is the case with retaining students. According to one analysis of the research, flunking students causes more problems than it remedies (Holmes, 1989). Recent studies also suggest that, instead of forcing academically troubled children to mature, to master deficient skills, and to achieve competence in later grades, **retention** makes students feel "sad," "bad," "upset," and "embarrassed" (Olson, 1990). These feelings cause students to exhibit behavioral problems and often eventually to drop out of school.

Like many teachers, Patricia Smith, reading and language arts coordinator at Cypress-Fairbanks School District in suburban Houston, Texas, argues that

> "An extra year gives students a shot at success." "Retention is more merciful," adds Shari Iba, coordinator of child development services in Florida's Broward County. "What is more devastating: to be with my peers and know that I am failing, or to be held back one year?" (Nazario, 1992)

But the facts do not support retention as a viable strategy. Professor Lorrie Shepard of the University of Colorado contends that repeating a grade actually worsens achievement levels in later years for some 70% of students who have been retained. Says Shepard, "If you had a drug that seriously hurt seven of 10 people you gave it to, you shouldn't keep giving it because it helps three of the 10" (Nazario, 1992).

Class Size

One of the more controversial issues in public education—and the one over which teachers exert little or no control—is that of class size. How many children should be placed in a single room with a teacher? What happens to teaching and learning when a group becomes larger or smaller? Should the inclusion of one or more students with disabilities in a class be weighted more heavily in the calculation of class size? How much does it cost to lower class size? How much money can a system save by raising class size? What are the political costs to policy makers of raising and lowering class sizes? Answers to these questions raise the hackles of professionals and nonprofessionals alike, and there is no doubt that the answers greatly influence instruction.

Although research seeks to clarify such questions, not obfuscate them, when it comes to class size, even researchers, or those who claim some expertise, often disagree about the answers. Gene Glass (1988) opened a paper on the subject by summoning the image of Disraeli, who once spoke of three kinds of lies: lies, damned lies, and statistics. More than one scoundrel has relied on statistics to make a point about class size.

In general, the literature supports the value of smaller classes (22 or fewer students), particularly in the early grades. Younger pupils, especially those who are economically disadvantaged and ethnic minority-group students, have benefited from smaller classes as demonstrated in reading and mathematics achievement and in terms of their attitudes and behavior (Finn & Achilles, 1990; Pate-Bain, Achilles, Boyd-Zaharias, & McKenna, 1992). Critics are quick to observe, however, that simply lowering class size does not automatically lead to increases in learning (Robinson, 1990).

Surprisingly to the uninitiated, just measuring class size can cause problems (Glass, 1988). For example, an elementary school may have a principal, a special education teacher, and a counselor in addition to seven classroom teachers. The principal and the counselor do not teach, and the special education teacher works with one student at a time in a resource room. The seven classroom teachers have class sizes that vary from 15 in Mr. Ruiz's kindergarten to 27 in Ms. Rosenblum's sixth grade. The school has a total of 140 students. The usual way to describe class size is to calculate an arithmetic mean. Dividing the 140 students by the 7 general education teachers yields an average class size of 20. When the special education teacher is also considered a teacher, the average drops to 17.5. Counting all the educators as personnel (i.e., adding the principal and the counselor to the mix) lowers the average to 14. Is it surprising that Ms. Rosenblum and her parents are chagrined when average class size is reported in her district under any of these circumstances, especially the last one?

Tracking

Should students be grouped homogeneously or heterogeneously based on estimates of their abilities? The practice of assigning students deemed to have similar abilities to instructional groups, to class sections, and to programs of study—a process referred to most often as tracking—is anathema to many educators and to others the only reasonable way to handle differences among students.

Critics argue that students are tracked on flimsy, often biased evidence. Many assigned to lower tracks may be placed there as much for behavior problems as for academic reasons. Those hurt most severely and most often are poor, minority-group students (Oakes, 1985). Students need offer only passive participation in lower-track classrooms to get by because teachers in lower-track classes may expect little or nothing of students. Students, in turn, tend to develop a poor sense of self. As noted in the chapter on schools, perhaps the most damning charge against tracking is the static nature of the assignments: once a student falls into the lower tracks, he or she seems caught in an academic tailspin from which few pull out (O'Neil, 1992).

Rudolph Ford, former teacher and assistant principal, now a doctoral student, remembers the feeling he had when a teacher helped him break out of the lower track.

> I remember being quietly told in the tenth grade by a blonde, middle-aged guidance counselor that I was college material and would be taken out of the general education track and would be placed in an academic track. . . . I had just been told by a white woman that I was as capable as the white students on the academic track, and that I deserved to be educated among the best students in school. This surprised me, because by tenth grade I had become accustomed to low expectations from school officials for students like myself—black males. I always knew that I was as capable academically as my white schoolmates—to have a white adult confirm this was an uplifting experience. She affected my self-esteem and shaped my later educational development more significantly than anyone else except my parents. (Ford, 1995, p. 161)

Interestingly, promoters of tracking often do not consider themselves as such. When forced to defend their practice of tracking ". . . a chorus of school officials offers the show-stopping line: 'We don't have tracking in our school. All our classes are heterogeneous—except for the advanced placement and remedial ones'" ("The Tracking Wars," 1992, p. 1).

What these officials typically mean is that they do not use test scores or grade point averages to place students in either a straight college preparatory track or a vocational track. Schools offer choices. Counselors and teachers, however, guide students in particular directions, as do prerequisites for upper-level courses. Scheduling also tracks students informally. For example, students who take general mathematics may also be forced to take lower-level English because it is the only course that fits the time slot in their schedule ("The Tracking Wars," 1992).

The privations of the lower tracks make the academic affluence of the upper tracks that much more conspicuous. Those in gifted and talented programs get the best teachers, bright students with whom to associate, and the most interesting classes. What parents of gifted and talented students want and get, argues Patrick Welsh (1990), is "their own private school at taxpayers' expense."

> **Cooperative learning, grouping around curricular themes, cross-age tutoring, and multiage classrooms offer positive alternatives to tracking.**

Should educators interpret this rather grim outlook on tracking as an admonition never to group students by ability? Many would argue that this is neither possible nor desirable in all situations. Instead, educators need to reconsider how "ability" is to be defined, relying less on standardized aptitude and achievement tests and more on constellations of formal and informal assessments that yield a round, full notion of the concept of ability. Also, when students are grouped, good teachers resist permanent assignment of students to groups in favor of periodic review and reassignment. Cooperative learning, grouping around curricular themes, cross-age tutoring, and multiage classrooms offer positive alternatives to tracking.

Homework

For those who do it, for those who help them, and for those who assess it, homework raises lots of questions. How much time should teachers expect students to devote to homework? What types of activities should be assigned? For what purpose is homework to be assigned? How might one tailor homework to fit individual student needs? How much parental involvement in homework is desirable? How should finished homework be judged and weighted in grading schemes?

In the most comprehensive review of research on homework to date, Harris Cooper (1989) asserts:

> The main message of homework research regarding both grade level and content is clear. Teachers should not assign homework to young children with the expectation that it will noticeably enhance achieve-

ment. Nor should they expect students to be capable of teaching themselves complex skills at home. Instead, teachers might assign short and simple homework to younger students, hoping it will foster positive, long-term, education-related behaviors and attitudes. Simple assignments should be given to older students to improve achievement, and complex assignments should be given to generate interest in the subject matter. (p. 82)

Effective teachers know that if some homework is good for students, more is not necessarily better. The relationship between time spent on homework and learning is not linear—that is, spending more time hitting the books can be valuable up to a point, but once this point is reached, an increase in time may actually mean a decrease in learning. This fact would seem to be self-evident to all but the most obtuse: students get bored, and they often have more interesting things to think about and to do.

For teachers, however, the relationship between time spent on homework and learning, indeed time spent on all school activities and learning, is anything but simple to manage. When conceiving homework assignments, good teachers try to take into account their students' propensities to attend, the conditions under which they must study, the demands of the tasks, and the like. Useful homework assignments, like effective interactive instruction, emanate most often from careful planning.

There is one special case of homework that bears mention. Students often fall behind and/or lose opportunities to forge ahead during the summer break. Some schools attempt to avoid these consequences by carefully devising and distributing reading lists to students in the spring. The lists contain good books that are readily available in libraries where students can get them with minimal effort. In the fall, schools make a visible effort to check up on students' summer reading habits.

Inclusion

As discussed in Chapters 7 and 8, recent calls for reform of schools and of general education parallel in time and in intensity calls for reform of special education. Indeed, it has been difficult for people to contemplate restructured schools without thinking about how life after restructuring may be different for all school inhabitants, including special education students.

As John Lloyd and Christine Gambatese (1991) observe, proposed reforms encompass a host of difficult issues. Are regular educators prepared and willing to teach pupils with disabilities? Do they have administrative and institutional support to do so? Do students with disabilities receive a better education when placed with students who do not have disabilities, and vice versa? Are special education categories or labels harmful to children who have them? Are the classification systems by which categories are assigned defensible? Should integration of students depend on the type of disabilities they have? Might the inclusion of special education students in regular classrooms complicate the issue of tracking (National Education Association, 1990)? Is it fair to spend more money on one child than

Proponents of full inclusion argue that self-contained classes such as these understimulate children and isolate them from their peers. Opponents claim that general education teachers are not equipped to teach all students in general education classrooms.

another? Is separate education designed and delivered on the basis of children's learning characteristics inherently unequal? "These are complex questions that cannot be answered with a simple 'yes' or 'no.' A person's answers to some of the questions may conflict with her or his answers to other questions" (Lloyd & Gambatese, 1991, p. 11).

Some parents, educators, and students think that all children with special needs should be included in general or regular education programs because the practice works, educationally speaking, and because it is the right thing to do. At Shawsville, Virginia, Teresa Mills, mother of 9-year-old Toni, who was classified mentally retarded and placed in a regular third grade, said: "She's learning so much more than I ever anticipated" (Viadero, 1992, p. 14). Anne Ryan, one of Toni's nondisabled classmates, says, "I've learned that she's not much different than anybody else" (Viadero, 1992, p. 15).

Dale Margheim, principal: "I taught kids in self-contained classrooms and I thought we were being successful, and I was happy and they were happy. But that lasted about as long as it took them to get out the doorway . . . I was never happy with that." (Viadero, 1992, p. 15)

Johnna Elliott, special education consultant working with the school to help with integration: "Before, we spent a lot of time developing motivation, and we don't have to do that anymore. . . . We spent a lot of time teaching kids to take the top off the toothpaste and brush their teeth, when all we had to do was shove a grooming bag in their hand, send them off to the bathroom, with another student, and say, 'Come back in 10 minutes and you'd better look good.'" (Viadero, 1992, p. 16)

Others contend that decisions about full-inclusion should be made on a case-by-case basis. They recommend looking at a particular child's needs, both educational and emotional, and determining where those needs can best be addressed rather than assuming that there is one place only (the regular classroom) where appropriate education can be provided (Chapman, 1992; Kauffman, 1993).

HOW ARE TEACHERS AND TEACHING ASSESSED?

The distinction between "teachers" and "teaching" in the subhead above is important. To assess *teachers* is to judge the people who are responsible for helping students learn. These judgments are based on such things as a teaching candidate's prior experience with children, his or her area of endorsement, scores on the National Teachers Exam (NTE), and responses during

VOICES

On Parents Opposed to Full Inclusion

The following letter to the editor of *Autism Research Review International* was written by a parent of two children with autism. She raises troubling questions about the practical and financial implications of including all children with special needs in general education.

My husband and I are parents of two children with autism. Both are in non-public schools funded by the School Board. The schools [and class sizes] are very small. One teacher and two trained aides are in each class. . . . The staff knows and deeply cares about my children.

What parent wouldn't want their child in such a school? These schools are, however, very expensive, $20,000 a year per child, plus busing. Therein lies the problem. It is far cheaper to have your child "included" than to send him to a special school. . . . Tremendous pressure [for inclusion] is brought to bear on parents whose dream it is for their children to be in normal schools.

In the late 1970s I was an interpreter for the deaf. We moved children from a residential deaf school to a regular public school. Two of the schools I worked in were rough inner city schools. I was a support person with five or six girls in my case load. To say I was overloaded is to put it mildly. If I became ill, substitutes were difficult to find and often woefully undertrained. The teachers were unable to communicate with the children so they ignored them. This was what was called mainstreaming. Inclusion is a new name for an old idea, an idea that didn't work well 15 years ago.

Tremendous pressure [for inclusion] is brought to bear on parents whose dream it is for their children to be in normal schools. The mere hope that your child can "make it" with regular children is a cruel sales pitch. It does, however, save the school board thousands of dollars while you try it out. Once you're in a regular school it may take years and half a dozen placements to convince the school board that inclusion is not working—years that our kids can't afford to lose. My advice is to look at your child's needs, both educational and emotional, not yours, and certainly not the school board's continual financial woes. (Name withheld by request.)

CRITICAL THINKING

How might other parents of children with disabilities argue against the views expressed in this letter? To what extent is the full inclusion of all children in regular classrooms a matter of protecting people's civil rights?

Source: *Autism Research Review International*. (1993). 7 (2), p. 6.

---

an interview. To assess *teaching* is to judge what transpires once a classroom teaching position is acquired. Judgments in this instance are based on the teacher's ability to create and to maintain environments conducive to learning. As we noted in Chapter 1, people are eager to judge either or both teachers and teaching for several reasons: to improve them, to make decisions about rewarding and punishing teachers (e.g., granting or denying tenure or awarding merit pay), and to aid in personnel decisions (Natriello, 1990).

Teachers are evaluated at several points by different people in various ways throughout their careers. Before they enter teacher education programs, prospective teachers begin a process of self-evaluation to size up their fit with teaching as a career. When they decide to apply to a program, higher education officials evaluate them for admission. During the course of professional preparation, instructors assess preservice teachers' academic abilities and their performances in field experiences (the first attention to processes of teaching). To exit programs, teachers must be judged against graduation requirements and evaluated on the basis of certification or licensure standards. To get a job, teachers must have their potential for success assessed by school administrators. The quality of these assessments varies greatly from place to place.

The National Teachers Examination (NTE) represents an effort to bring some consistency to the assessment of teachers. The NTE consists of a battery of tests used in 33 states to inform teacher certification decisions. The most recent version, the Praxis Series, consists of three parts: academic skills assessment, subject assessment, and classroom performance assessment. Sensitive to criticism that the examinations have measured little more than general ability, the Educational Testing Service has begun to move away from the strict use of multiple-choice, paper-and-pencil formats to include interviewing and observing students. (Information on the Praxis Series appears in Appendix C at the end of the book.)

The **National Board for Professional Teaching Standards (NBPTS)** directs another attempt to use examinations to identify teachers who are truly outstanding. As described in Chapter 1, the NBPTS grew out of the Carnegie Forum on Education and the Economy after the Forum's release of its report *A Nation Prepared: Teachers for the 21st Century*.

Still in the formative stages, the NBPTS is designing a set of examinations that will simulate the jobs that teachers actually perform—jobs in 30 area specialties, such as art, foreign language, special education, physical education, guidance and counseling, library and media, and general education. Certificates of distinction may be earned for specific developmental levels, such as early childhood (ages 3–8), middle childhood (ages 7–12), early adolescent (ages 11–15), and adolescent/young adult (ages 14–18+) or for combinations of the different levels. Whereas the NTE claims only to evaluate beginning teachers for minimal competence, the NBPTS will attempt to evaluate experienced teachers in ways that will identify the truly outstanding.

The formal evaluation of teaching through direct observation, in contrast to the assessment of teachers, is performed far less often and more idiosyncratically. It is extremely difficult and time-consuming to observe teaching, particularly when such information is to be used to make decisions about compensation, status, and tenure. Yet evaluating teaching through direct observation—judging what teachers do in real situations with their own students, instead of judging who teachers are, or what teachers say and do in simulated situations—yields the most valuable information about teachers' ability to apply professional knowledge.

Sometimes supervisors of student teaching, principals, and teachers who work with one another are trained to use a formal system to evaluate teaching. One such example is a process of observation and feedback in which a supervisor does the following: (a) reviews his or her notes about a particular teacher's past performance, (b) meets with the teacher prior to observing a lesson to gather information (e.g., characteristics of the group to be taught or objectives for the lesson), (c) videotapes the lesson and analyzes the data, and (d) meets with the teacher to view and discuss the videotape and to negotiate short-term goals for the improvement of instruction (Herbert & McNergney, 1989; Herbert & Tankersley, 1993).

Some states have developed fairly elaborate, scientific systems to observe teaching to inform certification judgments (McNergney, Medley, and Caldwell, 1988). The Virginia Beginning Teacher Assessment Program (BTAP), for example, framed 14 competencies (e.g., ability to phrase questions and to use them to develop learners' academic knowledge) with accompanying behavioral indicators that could be observed in classrooms. These competencies served as one of the certification requirements for new teachers. The financial and political costs of this and similar systems, however, have made widespread evaluation of teaching through formalized systems of direct observation impractical.

Most evaluation of teaching is less formal and is often conducted by people who have occasion to see and hear teachers in action—supervisors, principals, and teachers themselves. These observations are done for the most part to help teachers improve their performances, not to assemble information upon which to base the reward or punishment of teachers.

According to Philip Winne and Ronald Marx (1979), the most frequent, the most critical, and the most generous evaluators of teaching are students. Students watch what teachers do and listen to what teachers say. They take meaning away from their observations, and they assign meaning to what they see and hear. Good teachers understand that when they help students become discerning, reasonable, compassionate adults, they also encourage students to become perceptive, sensible, considerate evaluators of teachers and teaching.

Winne and Marx (1979) argue that people too often overlook students' perceptions in trying to understand how and why teaching works as it does:

> Sometimes, when we have arranged the most stellar teaching imaginable, students do not get the point. And, fortunately, even when we feel we have botched instruction, they often learn in spite of our failure. Why? . . . neither the teacher nor the educational psychologist can fully explain these mismatches of instructional prowess and instructional effectiveness. Perhaps one reason for this gap in the ability to explain effects of teaching stems from neglecting an essential feature of school learning, namely, how students perceive how to learn from teaching. (pp. 210–211)

Research on students' mental activities during instruction has examined such mediating factors as student motivations, beliefs, perceptions, and learning strategies. In one study, sixth graders were shown a videotape of a mathematics lesson in which they had just participated and asked to recall what they were thinking at various points during the session. One student commented,

"When he [the teacher] was saying, you know, like he was asking people like, What would number seven be? I'm saying it. Like he says . . . I'm saying [it] . . . in my head. And I know they're saying [it] . . . And he [the teacher] would say if it was right so I would see if I'm doing it right." (Peterson, Swing, Stark, & Waas, 1984, p. 28)

This student's recall suggests that he or she is a fairly sophisticated thinker. Besides paying attention to what the teacher was saying, mentally responding to the teacher's question, and hearing what other students were saying, the student was also getting feedback on the correctness of mental responses by listening to the teacher's reaction. There is great variability, even among uniformly able students, in students' ability to demonstrate self-management strategies during instruction (Corno, 1987). Teachers who attempt to understand how students think about learning may be able to fine-tune instruction, teaching strategies as needed and giving students opportunities to practice them so students can become independent learners. Evaluation of teachers and teaching must begin to account for such complexity if it is to reflect accurately the nature of life in classrooms.

HOW CAN EDUCATORS WORK TOGETHER?

Teaching can be a lonely profession. The demands, schedules, curricula, and physical structures of schools themselves sometimes make cooperation among educators difficult. Moreover, the ethos of some school communities encourages competition among educators, or benign neglect, instead of collaboration. "Not only do teachers seldom collaborate, but they are not expected to be either leaders or followers of other teachers" (Maeroff, 1993, p. 514).

How can teaching become a more collaborative process?

There is power in numbers—not just the political power necessary to affect educational and social policies, but also the power of the human capacity to influence daily life in schools. Gene Maeroff (1993) has argued that teachers working together to reform schooling can fuel "team spirit . . . [and] by a common vision and a sense of bonding, can remind other teachers who want to pursue change that they have compatriots" (p. 515).

As described in Chapter 11, "School Governance and Administration," there have been attempts all across the nation to involve teachers in the decision-making process regarding what goes on in schools, and particularly in recent efforts to restructure schools. People both inside and outside the profession have realized that they have a stake in improving education, and that the kind of necessary improvement systems require cooperation that runs from bottom to top, not the kind that is forced from top to bottom.

Sometimes change efforts are organized in a formal way, with teachers being self-selected or selected by others to attend training sessions with their principals. Upon their return to the school, team members share what they learned with colleagues and work collaboratively with them to put new ideas into practice. At other times collaboration occurs informally when teams of colleagues teach together at elementary, middle, and high school levels. Teams may include two or more members from the same or different grade-levels and areas of expertise.

Teams may operate in different ways. Some plan cooperatively and work in the same or different classrooms with a particular group of students; others do not interact with one another's students but plan cooperatively to ensure that students have similar experiences and/or to structure an integrated curriculum. A study of five special education teachers who collaborated with regular education teachers in elementary, middle, and high-school suggests that teachers who plan together, observe one another, and consult with one another over time are likely to increase their knowledge and skills. One teacher, for example, noted,

> "I picked up things in terms of pacing and presentation. I learned ways to assist . . . students, such as how to organize materials, give them clues . . . Also, I learned from Carol to really focus during the lesson on whether the students are getting it . . . Focusing not so much on, 'Did I cover what I said I was going to cover this hour,' but focusing on the students. Now I ask myself, 'Are they really with me?' And I'm doing more adjusting if they aren't." (Nowacek, 1992, p. 274)

Today, teachers are likely to graduate from college, be hired and placed in a mentor program with an experienced colleague for a year or two, meet as teams to plan multidisciplinary units of instruction, guide cadres of parent volunteers, design and participate in their own continuing education, and interact with people all over the world via electronic communications systems. In short, the forces encouraging positive interdependence among professional educators and concerned citizens are gradually winning.

SUMMARY

1. Informal knowledge about teaching is gained through practical experience. This more or less private, uncodified body of professional knowledge that exists in the minds and hearts of those who practice can be a rich resource when planning for and implementing instruction.

2. Formal knowledge of teaching emanates from two sources: theoretical formulations and scientific research. Theory helps explain logically why teaching and learning occur as they do; research provides results of observations or experiments to help explain relationships between teaching and learning.

3. Recent research on teaching has grown more complex and reflective of the complexity of life in classrooms. Besides considering the interactive effects of presage, process, product, and context in a classroom, researchers consider how teachers and students mediate classroom behavior, or how they think about classroom life.

4. Teaching is often conceptualized as a three-part process: planning, interactive teaching, and evaluation. There is no single best way to accomplish this process, but successful teachers attend to all parts in complementary ways.

5. Among things teachers consider while planning for instruction are curriculum, state and local goals and objectives for student learning, instructional strategies for meeting those goals, methods for assessing students' understanding, classroom management, ways to motivate students, and methods for teaching students specific and general learning and self-management strategies.

6. During instruction, successful teachers use a variety of teaching strategies or models to meet the varying needs of learners and to accomplish various ends. Although models of teaching explain in broad terms where teachers are going with their students, how they will get there, and how they will know when they have arrived, teachers make moment-to-moment changes in strategies based on the needs and abilities of students.

7. Successful teachers exhibit skills of understanding students, setting goals, creating environments conducive to learning, judging those environments, and communicating about teaching and learning to others. Successful teachers also manage classrooms to avoid problems and to handle problems when they arise.

8. Teachers use formal measures, such as tests and quizzes, and informal measures, such as questionnaires, interviews, and observations of in-class behaviors, to make judgments daily about students' academic performance, their attitudes and interests, and their ability to work with others.

9. Some issues have and will continue to challenge educators in the near future: grading, retention, class size, tracking, homework, and inclusion of students with special needs in regular classrooms.

10. Teachers and their work are continually assessed both formally and informally by different constituencies. These assessments are meant to improve practice, to reward or punish teachers (e.g., to grant or deny tenure, or to award merit pay), and to inform personnel decisions.

11. It is becoming increasingly important for teachers to be able to work cooperatively with one another and with others who have a stake in schools. Collaboration may occur formally when teams of teachers are self-selected or selected by others to learn new techniques and then to teach them to their peers. At other times, collaboration occurs informally when teams of colleagues teach together at elementary, middle, and high school levels.

TERMS AND CONCEPTS

authentic assessment
classroom management
cooperative learning
criterion-referenced test
direct instruction
discovery or inquiry
    learning
formal knowledge base
instructional models

instructional variables
mastery learning
measurement and evaluation
National Board for
    Professional
    Teaching Standards
    (NBPTS)
norm-referenced test

pedagogical content
    knowledge
portfolio
practical knowledge
    base
retention
social promotion
standardized tests
teacher planning

STUDENT ACTIVITIES

Perceive and Value

Reflect on your classroom experiences as a high school student. Can you recall instances when your teachers used instructional methods that might fit within any of Joyce and Weil's four "families"? What in particular occurred during instruction that leads you to characterize lessons as belonging to the Social, Information-processing, Personal, or Behavioral Systems Families? What were the roles of teacher and students during such lessons? Speculate on the values underlying your teacher's actions. Compare your perceptions of your teacher's values to your own values as a student in that class.

Know and Act

Tracking high school students into college preparatory programs and general or vocational programs is a common practice across the nation. This practice is understandable in some ways and problematic in others.

In groups of three, think about tracking as it existed in your high school. Each individual should respond briefly in writing to each item below in enough detail so the others can understand the answers. The group should discuss the answers.

1. I understand the practice of tracking in my high school to be . . .
2. If I were a teacher in a high school that tracked students and had to explain the system to parents, I would have to talk with the following people (name their roles in the system) to help me understand the process:
3. These other factors might be relevant to the practice of tracking in my high school:
4. If I were a teacher in my high school, and had the power to do so, I would change the following aspect of the tracking system:
5. What forces are at work to change the practice of tracking?
6. What forces are at work to restrain change in the practice of tracking?

Evaluate

Accept or reject the following proposition and explain your reasoning: Student retention in the elementary grades makes sense when children are more than one grade level behind their peers in reading and mathematics, and when their parents agree.

Discover

Go to the library and look for information on criterion-referenced testing (sometimes called domain-referenced testing) and norm-referenced testing. Describe the advantages and disadvantages of each.

Foundations

In Action

"Transitions can be a teacher's nightmare—the worst time bandits of all."

The basic unit of instruction is the lesson, which can be presented through direct instruction, inquiry or discovery learning, or a variety of other instructional approaches. Whatever the approach, all effective lessons have similar characteristics. They reflect organization and planning in relation to both instructional goals and student evaluation. What effects do organization, goals, and evaluation have in the three instances presented here?

Mary Anne Reed-Brown knows that sound classroom management and the effective use of time are organizational prerequisites for effective lessons. Today, however, everything falls apart after she moves her class to the computer lab and discovers that one of the units is down and the program she wants to use is back at her desk. She has 45 minutes with 20 students and 9 functioning machines.

"Okay, everyone just kind of gather around, please. Let's have James go to a computer, also Mehul, Omar, Patricia, Sara, Amanda, Alvi, and Joshua. Excuse me, I would like you all to sit down now so that we can get on with the business of the day. Our lab time is wasted almost every week. Excuse me, you are to take your own diagram and pass the stack down. Now if your name is not there, I don't want you getting up to look for your name. Eric, go back and get my computer box with disks in it, the big one."

Looking back, Reed-Brown regrets losing her patience. "Their lack of immediate cooperation really got to me that day. I was tired and testy. I don't like coming across as impatient with my students. In the past going to the computer lab meant utter chaos, a situation I'm trying to change. Transitions can be a teacher's nightmare—the worst time bandits of all."

"I wanted to come up with creative and enjoyable ways for students to learn concepts and skills."

"It's part of the whole process of modeling, setting up a good example."

Laura Saatzer leads her class in a choral reading of a poem by Shel Silverstein, "The Little Boy and the Old Man." It is part of her literature-based unit on the concept of dialogue and the use of quotation marks. Her measures for assessment are based on students' oral reading skills and their writing skills. Laura also hopes that the theme of the poem will heighten awareness of a relevant topic. Her students participate in a partnership program with an elder home in the community.

"My first year of teaching I participated in a 'writers in the schools' program. I worked with a professional author who came here and helped me to develop some lessons and ways to work with children in writing. Instead of pulling out my language book and saying, 'Open it up and do page 4,' I wanted to come up with creative and enjoyable ways for students to learn concepts and skills.

I learned that a lot can be accomplished through poems. I picked the Silverstein poem because it's one of my favorites and the dialogue in it between an old man and a child is so vivid. I'll ask them to recall this poem when they write dialogues to go with the storyramas they have been creating."

Dr. Barbara Shin, the principal at Hans Christian Andersen, knows that the process of assessment can itself be a lesson, a way to model academic success. She conducts an oral group quiz in each class to support the teacher and reinforce curriculum goals. Preparing for this outside evaluation also motivates students.

"The quiz is an example of some of the learning the children should have. It's part of the whole process of modeling, setting up a good example. I do it in part to give teachers the impetus and also to give them a framework within which to work. And it's my way of working directly with the children as instructional leader."

"All right," Dr. Shin starts, "What does 'multicultural' mean? I see a lot of hands. Good! I'm going to try to give everybody a turn, so don't get disappointed if I don't call on you each time. Okay, Russell, I'll start with you." Russell and the other students respond to each of Dr. Shin's questions. "Thank you, Russell. Class, was he right? Okay, let's give him a hand. That was excellent. Why is multicultural education important? CJ? Yes. I wish everybody knew that. Could you hear him, Daniel? That was a very good answer CJ gave. Now what does 'contributor' mean? What does it mean to be a contributor to our country? Talela?"

The students conclude the session with a recitation of the Chinese proverb that begins, "If there is right in the soul, there will be beauty in the person," and ends, "If there is order in the nation, there will be peace in the world."

This chapter describes federal, state, and local influences on education and draws attention to the characteristics of people who lead and manage public education. Cooperation among levels and organizational units of education is discussed and periodic and continuing management issues with which school leaders must deal are described. This chapter notes the importance of pressure groups on the structure and functions of public schooling. It also considers why change in the conduct of schooling is so difficult to achieve, and yet also why change is inevitable.

School Governance and Administration

PROFESSIONAL PRACTICE QUESTIONS

1 What problems may arise when a school system tries to institute site-based or school-based management?

`Perceive`

....

2 Why may the writers of the Constitution have resisted attempts to provide explicitly for the establishment of a system of public education?

`Value`

....

3 What pressure groups are unusually effective at influencing schooling?

`Know`

....

4 If a school principal wanted to communicate a vision of what schooling should be, what symbols could he or she manipulate to do so?

`Act`

....

5 How could people determine if the schools and the central administrative office in their own system are tightly or loosely coupled?

`Evaluate`

....

WHAT DETERMINES HOW SCHOOLS ARE RUN?

Schools are *managed* or *administered* by school administrators. People tend to use these verbs interchangeably. For some, administration and management have meant decision making (Barnard, 1938; Griffiths, 1959). For others, these actions have been defined ". . . as the process of working with and through others to accomplish organizational goals efficiently" (Sergiovanni, Burlingame, Coombs, & Thurston, 1992, p. 60). Certainly, to administer or to manage schools is to lead others in the fulfillment of a school's mission.

The definition of *leader*, however, is subject to debate. For some a leader is a person who takes on new tasks and pushes for change, someone who is proactive, not reactive (Zaleznick, 1977). For others, a leader is a system-oriented person who is concerned about production and a person-oriented manager who demonstrates consideration for staff members (Stogdill, 1981), or, similarly, a person who is concerned with tasks and people in the organization (Bales, 1954; Bowers & Seashore, 1966). Aristotle believed that leaders are born—people either have the capacity to lead or they do not, and some modern organizational theorists tend to agree. Yet, others think that leadership is largely a function of the situations in which people find themselves (Fiedler, 1967).

These leaders—school board members, superintendents, principals, department heads, and teachers themselves—are responsible for the "governance" of schools: for controlling, directing, and otherwise influencing the actions and conduct of schooling. They do so within a system of institutions, laws, policies, politics, and customs. The leaders are designated and paid to exercise and delegate power to make the schools work.

The power to establish and operate public schools is derived from the Tenth Amendment to the U.S. Constitution: "The powers not delegated to the United States by the Constitution; nor prohibited by it to the States, are reserved to the States respectively, or to the people." The power to educate is one reserved to the states; that is, the states are ultimately responsible for **school governance**, or for establishing and overseeing the structure and functions of public education. That does not mean the states must go it alone; they delegate many educational functions to local education agencies. Indeed, over time, a complex network of formal organizations and informal pressure groups at the state, federal, and local levels has made public education what it is today.

HOW DOES THE FEDERAL GOVERNMENT AFFECT SCHOOLING?

Although there is no specific mention of public education in the Constitution, the federal government has always had a hand in shaping education. James Guthrie, Walter Garms, and Lawrence Pierce (1988) suggest that the federal agenda for education is shaped by the "Iron Triangle"—the combination of education interests in the executive branch, congressional committees, and education interest groups outside government.

> **The federal agenda for education is shaped by the "Iron Triangle."**

In addition to its legislative influence, the federal government has shaped education through decisions made by federal courts and various departments and agencies. The courts have ruled on many civil rights issues as they have emerged in schools. In 1991, 14 federal departments, including the U.S. Office of Education, and more than 25 agencies and programs were involved in the organization of federal programs for education (National Center for Educational Statistics, 1991).

Since 1980, the executive branch has relied heavily on exhortation to draw attention to educational issues. William Bennett, President Ronald Reagan's secretary of education, captured headlines frequently by being outspokenly critical of public education. In 1984, he instituted what became known as the "Secretary's Wall Chart," so named because it was too big to fit on a piece of regular-sized paper and had to be put on the wall. The wall charts were to serve as state by state scorecards on educational production and resources devoted to education.

Secretaries of education in the Bush and Reagan administrations focused attention on states' performances on a variety of educational measures, including standardized achievement and aptitude test scores, graduation rates, and teachers' salaries. Some argued that state by state comparisons filled a void in our knowledge, allowing residents to gauge the quality of education in their own states. Others saw the information as statistically flawed and even misleading (Ginsburg, Noell, & Plisko, 1988).

In the 1990s, state by state progress on resolving education issues has been expressed in relation to the National Education Goals Reports—accounts of the states' progress on addressing the eight National Education goals (See Chapter 1). The goals are an attempt to stimulate education reform on a national level by serving as an annual report card for the governors. Table 11.1 shows how progress in one state was measured in 1991.

TABLE 11.1 One State's Progress on the National Goals

California: Measuring Progress Toward the Goals	
Goal 1: Readiness for School No comparable state data currently available	
Goal 2: High School Completion No comparable state data currently available	
Goal 3: Student Achievement and Citizenship	
1. Percent of public school 8th grade students who are competent in mathematics (1990)	14%
2. Number of Advanced Placement examinations taken in the core subjects (per 1,000 11th and 12th graders enrolled, 1991)	99
3. Number of Advanced Placement examinations taken in the core subjects receiving a grade of 3 or higher (per 1,000 11th and 12th graders enrolled, 1991)	63
Goal 4: Science and Mathematics No comparable state data currently available	
Goal 5: Adult Literacy and Lifelong Learning No comparable state data currently available	
Goal 6: Safe, Disciplined, and Drug-free Schools	
1. Percent of all high school teachers who reported that the following were problems in their schools (1988):	
Physical abuse of teachers	27%
Verbal abuse of teachers	73%
Robbery or theft	76%
Vandalism of school property	83%

Note. From *The National Education Goals Report: Building a Nation of Learners* (p. 84) by National Education Goals Panel, 1991, Washington, DC: U.S. Government Printing Office.

BENCHMARKS

Examples of Government Involvement in Educational Research and Services: 1945–1990

1945	United Nations Educational, Scientific, and Cultural Organization (UNESCO) established.
1948	Fullbright Scholarships founded.
	U.S. Information and Educational Exchange Act.
1950	National Science Foundation established.
1953	U.S. Office of Education founded as a branch of the Department of Health, Education, and Welfare.
1954	Cooperative Research Act.
	National Advisory Committee on Education Act.
1956	Library Services Act.
1958	National Defense Education Act.
1961	Peace Corps established.
1965	National Foundation on the Arts and Humanities Act
1966	U.S. International Education Act.
	Office of Educational Research and Improvement (OERI) established.
	Educational Resources Information Center (ERIC) established.

For example, Goal Three, which calls for students to demonstrate competence in challenging subject matter, has prompted efforts to develop national standards and assessments in various curricular areas. Some oppose this idea because they are concerned that such standards and assessments will shape a national curriculum. Others argue that the information is too politically sensitive to share publicly, especially when it is displayed in a way that permits state by state comparisons. The task of completing the National Education Goals Reports has been complicated by missing infor-

	Research and Development Centers established.
	Regional Educational Laboratories established.
1967	Education Professional Development Act.
1970	Office of Education Appropriation Act.
	Environmental Education Act.
	Drug Abuse Education Act.
	National Commission on Libraries and Information Science Act.
1972	Drug Abuse Office and Treatment Act.
1973	Older Americans Comprehensive Services Amendment.
1974	Juvenile Justice and Delinquency Prevention Act.
	White House Conference on Library and Information Services Act.
1979	Department of Education Organization Act creates a cabinet-level department replacing the former U.S. Office of Education.
1980	Asbestos School Hazard Protection and Control Act.
1989	Presidential Education Summit with Governors.

mation; simply describing what happens in education in 50 states is a massive undertaking.

The New Schools Development Corporation (NSDC), initiated by the Bush administration in the 1990s, has attempted to stimulate school reform by focusing efforts nationally on "break-the-mold schools." The strategy of NSDC has been to issue a request for proposals to create elementary and secondary schools unlike any in existence. In contrast to federal involvement in past times, the architects of NSDC plan to fund the new schools with money from private sector contributions. (For an example, see Chapter 5.)

HOW IS EDUCATION CONTROLLED BY THE STATES?

State governments exercise more influence on public education than does the federal government. They do so in a variety of ways. Figure 11.1 shows a typical organization of public education at the state level.

Powers of the States

State governments influence public education in several ways, most importantly, as we explain in the next chapter ("Education Finance"), through taxation and distribution of revenues. States also set standards for building schools, educating teachers and school administrators, licensing school personnel, and establishing curriculum, the minimum length of the school term, attendance requirements, and school accreditation. They provide a host of other special services. While the structure of state bureaucracies and the relative influence of key officers vary from place to place, the role of the state in public education has become increasingly prominent over the years.

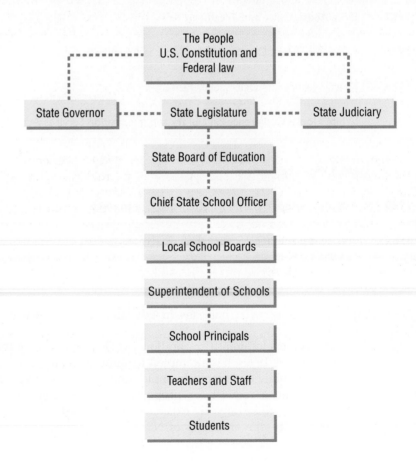

FIGURE II.I

Typical Organization of Public Education at the State Level

The states relate to the federal government in several ways. Education is recognized as a right reserved to the states under the Tenth Amendment to the Constitution. In addition, court cases have defined education as a property right or civil right under the Constitution and thus subject to the Fourteenth Amendment (Section 1: ". . . No State shall make or enforce any law which shall abridge the privileges or immunities of citizens of the United States; nor shall any State deprive any person of life, liberty, or property, without due process of law; nor deny to any person within its jurisdiction the equal protection of the laws."). The Fourteenth Amendment has allowed the Federal government to intervene in ways that influence the education of children at the local level. Passage and implementation of the Education of All Handicapped Children Act (PL 94-142) and its extension through the Individuals with Disabilities Education Act (IDEA or PL 101-476) are two examples of federal connections to the states and to local communities. (For discussion of IDEA, see Chapters 7 and 8.)

State Boards of Education

State boards of education regulate educational practice and advise governors and legislators about the conduct of educational business. Some states have two boards—one for elementary and secondary education, the other for higher education. With the flurry of education reform in recent years, state boards of education have played different roles. Sometimes, board members have behaved as provocateurs pushing for change; at other times, they have counseled caution and lobbied for continuity of valued educational practice.

All states with the exception of Wisconsin have state boards of education. The majority of states, 37 to be exact, allow governors to appoint some or all board members. Table 11.2 describes some characteristics of state board members.

Gene Wilhoit, former executive director of the National Association of State Boards of Education, has recognized many problems before state boards, none more vexing than dealing with issues of equity with regard to race, gender, disabilities, and wealth. He contends that the first challenge all state board members face is to make sense out of many issues and ideas presented to them by people inside and outside the education community. To be true policy-making organizations—proactive instead of reactive—they need to build consensus within their states and to communicate a long-term vision for education (G. Wilhoit, personal communication, January 22, 1992).

State boards of education often find themselves embroiled in controversy. They do such things as establish requirements for homeschooling, and in so doing create possibilities for children to avoid ever setting foot inside a school building. In some states, they establish minimal standards for student performance that are used as hurdles for promotion and failure—hurdles over which some young people trip, embarrassing themselves and those who have purportedly educated them. State boards of education regulate what teachers must do to get and keep their jobs, even though local education authorities may vehemently disagree.

TABLE 11.2 Demographic Characteristics of State Board Members

In January 1992, the National Association of State Boards of Education updated its database on 406 of the 575 state board of education members. Of those on record:

	Number	Approximate %
Sex		
Female	158	40
Male	244	60
Racial/Ethnic Background		
European American	307	80
African American	44	12
Hispanic/Latino American	12	3
Native American	5	1
Asian American	5	1
Hawaiian	1	—
Other	7	1
Age		
20–39	35	10
40–59	193	60
60+	97	30

Source: G. Wilhoit (personal communication, February 19, 1992) National Association of State Boards of Education, Alexandria, VA.

Some state board members make momentous decisions for their own state's schools, decisions that are felt well beyond their own borders. Nowhere is this more obvious than in textbook adoptions. Adoption procedures vary from state to state, but, generally speaking, a state board approves a list of textbooks from which local school districts may select. If local districts expect to receive state funds for textbooks, they must buy from the approved list. State board members in densely populated states, then, wield incredible influence in their own states by anointing some books and shunning others.

These individuals—state board members in Texas, California, and Florida—also influence schools in other states by shaping the content of textbooks that are sold across the nation. For example, when California state board members voice concerns about the lack of literature in elementary reading books, or the sparseness of multicultural examples of family life, textbook publishers take notice. Soon, the reading textbooks contain more samples of literature and focus greater attention on multicultural life. The culture of Montana and Kansas and Vermont can be quite different from that of California, yet the children of these less populous states (smaller text-book markets) will find more literature interspersed in their textbooks and will see more pictures of the many peoples of California (the larger textbook market).

State Education Departments

A **state education department (SED)** is a bureaucracy organized to carry out a state's education business. An SED may administer programs directly, for example, schools for the deaf or blind. SEDs are directed by a state superintendent, a commissioner, or a **chief state school officer**. The organization regulates or oversees, among other things, the elementary and secondary schools' attention to curriculum and colleges' and universities' conduct of teacher and administrator preparation. An SED advises the executive and legislative branches of state government on a variety of issues including school finance. It engages in staff development and public relations work for itself and for other governmental and nongovernmental agencies that have a stake in education. Over the years, SEDs have taken on more and more tasks, but subtracted few. As laws have been passed and regulations established, SEDs have been expected to monitor schools' compliance. This has meant that the number of employees in SEDs has grown steadily.

Some states are trying to alter the way their state education departments are organized and the way they do their work. The Virginia state education department, for instance, has attempted to shift the role of the agency from regulation to research and service:

> "We are going to take the department, put it in a box, wrap a bow around it, and bury it," Superintendent of Public Instruction Joseph A. Spagnolo Jr. told the [state] board shortly before it unanimously approved the department overhaul. . . . the department's current eight layers of bureaucracy are reduced to four and its 22 professional job classifications are reduced to seven. (Schmidt, 1990, p. 18)

The Governor's Influence

Historically, governors have relied on their appointees to formulate and implement educational policy in the states. People who occupy positions such as state superintendent, state commissioner of education, secretary of education, chief state school officer, and the like have run the educational bureaucracies at the state level and taken the point position with respect to the conduct of public education in the states. Only recently have governors themselves become personally involved in education issues.

The leaders of state departments of elementary and secondary education in the 50 states, the District of Columbia, the Department of Defense Dependents Schools, and 5 U.S. extra-state jurisdictions—Virgin Islands, Puerto Rico, Northern Mariana Islands, Guam, and American Samoa—are tied to one another informally by an organization called the **Council of Chief State School Officers**. The organization has functioned since 1927.

The council has no official way to affect policy. It does, however, provide a forum where powerful education leaders edify one another. The council sponsors a series of special programs (international education, technology, national teacher of the year, etc.), a resource center on educational equity, and a state education assessment center. These programs and activities, plus an electronic network, provide opportunities for communication among leaders of state systems of public education, even though such communication rarely leads to consensus on contentious issues.

In recent years, the governors themselves have become major players in education reform via the **National Governors' Association (NGA)**, founded as a coalition of state chief executives called the National Governors Conference in 1908. Many governors have come to believe that good education makes good politics. The problems in education are so intractable and so related to other facets of society that substantive reform virtually demands strong, visible leadership from the very top of state government.

The governors laid out an agenda for reform in 1986 that addressed seven critical issues before the education system: teaching, leadership and management, parent involvement and choice, readiness, technology, school facilities, and college quality. Each year since, they have charted their progress and described their unfinished business.

In the area of leadership and management, for example, there are indications of progress in several states.

> The Colorado State Board of Education and an interim legislative committee are reviewing administrator licensure . . . the state LEAD program is promoting a mentorship program for prospective women and minority administrators. An alliance of the teachers' union and administrator organizations in ten districts interested in restructuring has been developed to provide team training. . . . (National Governors' Association, 1990, p. 10)

The "unfinished agenda" on leadership and management, however, make it clear that the governors have far to go.

> One of the glaring gaps that remains in the area of school leadership is the lack of an administrator corps that represents the racial and gender make-up of the general population. Although the number of qualified female graduates of education administration programs is substantial (larger than the number of minority graduates), few are selected to fill positions as secondary principals or superintendents. School boards appear unwilling to hire female and minority candidates at all levels of administration. . . . (National Governors' Association, 1990, p. 10)

The Influence of State Standards Boards

As Chapter 1 notes, all but two states (Connecticut and South Dakota) now have **state standards boards** or commissions to regulate professional practice in education. These boards may have final authority or they may serve only in advisory capacity to policymakers. In Alabama, for example, the

State Advisory Committee on Teacher Education and Certification is composed of about 30 members appointed by the state superintendent. As its name suggests, the committee advises state policymakers. In contrast, the Minnesota Board of Teaching is charged by law to have seven teachers, one principal, one member of the higher education community, and one lay member. The Minnesota board is autonomous with respect to certification, entry, and exit standards for teachers.

The National Education Association and others have encouraged the establishment of such boards to promote a concept of professionalism. Not until teachers control the state policy- making apparatus, it is argued, will teachers be able to control their own professional destiny. Only five of these boards, however, have teachers as majority members.

Cooperation Among School Districts

Some educational services are so expensive, and both human and material resources so lean, that districts must band together to provide such services. Such joint facilities are most often called **intermediate educational units (IEU)**, educational service agencies (ESA), and boards of cooperative educational services (BOCES). For example, every high school in a state cannot provide the kind of vocational training that students need to make them competitive in the job market. Several districts may join together to construct and maintain a technical training center for their students.

In some cases, the state mandates the creation of special units between the state and local levels and provides special support for the maintenance of these units. Special education services, particularly for children with severe and profound disabilities, represent opportunities for such interdistrict cooperation, or even for statewide cooperation. Some states maintain residential facilities for blind children and for children with hearing impairments.

Trying to count interdistrict collaborative organizations is difficult because state governance systems are changing continuously. Some 36 states report such collaboratives. There are 21 states that report IEUs or BOCES, 9 that have other kinds of legislated collaboratives, 6 with state board of education regulated cooperatives, and 8 with regional collaborative systems to provide special education services (Fletcher, Cole, & Strumor, 1990).

Interorganizational Cooperation

Sometimes organizational units other than school districts cooperate with one another to increase their power, to reduce uncertainty, to increase performance by ensuring a steady flow of resources, and to protect themselves (Stearns, Hoffman, & Heide, 1987). They do so by sharing information, people, funds, and equipment. Schools contract with state and federal governments, universities, and private corporations to conduct research and to operate innovative educational projects. Projects Headstart and Follow

Through are examples of such cooperative arrangements (Hoy & Miskel, 1991).

The National Governors' Association has taken the lead in recent years in creating cooperative educational arrangements among the states. As mentioned previously, the functions of collecting and disseminating information about the states' progress toward the attainment of the National Goals represent such effort.

HOW ARE SCHOOLS MANAGED AT THE LOCAL LEVEL?

Schools' personalities reflect the dispositions of the communities in which they are embedded. Some are dull, lethargic, complacent; others bristle with activity and exude hopefulness. Go to a school board meeting, a gathering of the parent-teacher organization, or a high school sporting event, and citizen participation in and influence on educational matters are demonstrable at these gatherings. People affect the schools, and the schools, in turn, influence constituents both inside and outside their walls.

Spring (1991) notes that communities vary in character and thus exert different types of influences on the schools and those who run them.

> In dominated communities majority power is exercised by a few persons or one person. . . . Factional communities are usually characterized by two factions competing for power. . . . Pluralistic communities have a great deal of competition between a variety of community-interest groups with no single group dominating schools' policies. . . . And in inert communities, there is no visible power structure and there is little display of public interest in the schools. (p. 167)

Paradoxically, while communities are amazingly diverse in character, schools across the country are characterized by some powerful commonalities. People and pressure groups force a certain sameness in schooling. The names and faces, of course, are different from one place to another, but the roles the actors play are familiar: the civic-minded business person who boosts the close connection between good schools and the local economy, the school administrator caught between his or her colleagues' pressures to innovate and the school board's desires to hold down costs, the one-issue taxpayer who monopolizes school board meetings to grind a well-worn ax, the fresh, young face at the

> **Schools' personalities reflect the disposition of the communities in which they are embedded.**

newspaper just starting a career in journalism and assigned to cover education, the harried mothers and fathers with more concern for their children than they have time or money, and a host of others. Stereotypes? Perhaps. But the real individuals who play these roles, and the organizations they represent, shape schools into the kind of places they have become.

Local School Boards

Local school boards are elected or appointed public servants with responsibilities to provide advice and consent on the operation of public schools. Local school boards are one of the most common, visible examples of a republican form of government in action. Because education is a reserved power to the states, local school boards are agents of the states.

Cultural Awareness

Approximately 97,000 American citizens serve on school boards in the United States (Olson & Bradley, 1992). About 95% are elected to represent their constituents while the other 5% are appointed. Following is a profile of a "typical" school board member.

Sex:	Male
Age:	41 to 50 years
Race/Ethnicity:	White
Marital status:	Married
Children in school:	One or more
Education:	Advanced degree
Occupation:	Professional or managerial
Family income:	$40,000 to $49,999
Home:	Homeowner
Community type:	Suburban
School system enrollment:	1,000 to 4,999
Board experience:	One to five years
Board size:	Seven members

Note: From "The Burden School Board Members Bear" by D.M. Seaton, K.E Underwood, and J.C. Fortune, 1992, *The American School Board Journal*, 179 (1), p. 37. Reprinted with permission of the National School Boards Association. All rights reserved.

The local school board is generally recognized as the policy-making body for public schools. For the most part, this means that school board members have the right to establish schools, to select its executive officer (the local **superintendent of schools**), to set rules to insure the smooth running of schools, and to raise and spend tax dollars as they see fit. Although no two school boards function the same, critics claim that too many boards get caught up in management of schools, becoming "so hopelessly enmeshed in the minutiae of running their districts that they fail to see the forest for the trees" (Olson & Bradley, 1992, p. 7). As a random sample of minutes from school-board meetings in West Virginia suggests, some boards deal with a variety of educational issues and problems. Figure 11.2 shows the categories of decisions school board members make.

The majority of school board members learn their jobs by critically examining their actions, reading, talking with others, and/or participating in voluntary training programs offered by school boards associations. Others are required by their respective states to undergo formal training. In West Virginia, for example, board members must participate in 7 hours of training on ways to govern effectively without meddling in administrative matters (Schmidt, 1992, p.19).

Generally, school board members view their schools in much the same way as their constituents do. And most often people think their schools are good. If they perceive problems in education, those problems are usually somewhere else, not in their schools.

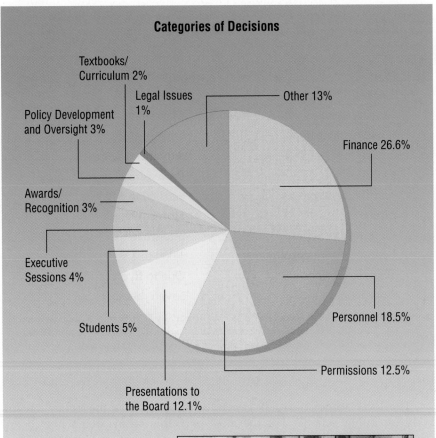

Categories of Decisions

Textbooks/Curriculum 2%
Legal Issues 1%
Other 13%
Policy Development and Oversight 3%
Finance 26.6%
Awards/Recognition 3%
Executive Sessions 4%
Students 5%
Personnel 18.5%
Presentations to the Board 12.1%
Permissions 12.5%

FIGURE 11.2

School Board Decision Making

Do you find any parts of this graph surprising? How do the figures compare with you prior assumptions about what school boards do?

Source: School Boards at a Glance, Categories of Decisions (1992, April 29) *Education Week/Special Report*, p. 6. Used by permission.

Like all representatives in a republic, school board members try to interpret the public will and to exercise their own personal judgment in governing the public education system. On some issues, board members and the people they represent are out of tune with one another. Results from a survey of school board presidents highlight some of these differences (Feistritzer, Quelle, & Chester, 1989):

- About two thirds of school board presidents and superintendents opposed the idea of parents exercising "choice" in where to send their children to school—this is in contrast to three fourths of the general public and parents, who favored the idea.

- The public believed, as they have for many years, that the biggest problems facing schools in their communities were "use of drugs" and "lack of discipline." School board presidents and school administrators overwhelmingly pointed to "lack of financial support" as the biggest problem.

When there is tension between school board members and their constituents, it is more often felt in urban and suburban areas than in rural America, where citizens know school board members personally. The strain is especially strong in areas struggling with societal dilemmas such as increasing drug, alcohol, and sexual abuse; divided and fractious communities; and growing numbers of racial, ethnic, and language minorities. Occasionally, dissatisfaction results in curtailment of power, and in some instances, complete disbandment of school boards. In Chicago, advocacy groups lobbied successfully for the establishment of popularly elected councils of citizens, parents, and teachers at each school who, among other things, were given the right to select principals and to decide how discretionary funds should be spent. In New Jersey, dissatisfaction with the quality of education in the public schools resulted in state takeover of the Jersey City and Paterson districts (Olson & Bradley, 1992).

Sometimes people also seek control of school boards for ideological reasons. For example, Robert Simmonds, an evangelical Christian and former minister, is president of Citizens for Excellence in Education. He is dedicated to restoring Christian values in public schools primarily by electing Christians to school boards (Goldstein, 1992).

A national poll of school board members conducted in 1986 revealed that many were concerned about the erosion of local control, particularly at the hands of state governments. Changes in governance have also been stimulated by the growth of parental choice plans, the prevalence of site-based management, and the delegation of school management to private firms.

School Administration

Despite the fact that there are about 83,000 public schools in the United States, surveys indicate that the superintendents and their associates and assistants who compose the **central office staff**, along with principals, tend to view their worlds in remarkably similar fashion. The demands of their jobs and their training, no doubt, contribute to their common outlook. But administrators share other characteristics as well.

There are more than 14,000 superintendents or superintendents of schools in the United States (Campbell, Cunningham, Nystrand, & Usdan, 1990). The term *superintendent* usually denotes the chief executive officer of a board of education in an operating school district.

Cultural Awareness

Most superintendents are men (96%), and most are European-American (97%). About 75% of the approximately 100,000 principals are men and 90% are European-American. More than 80% of all administrators are over the age of 40. Some would argue that this pool of people represents a convergence of quality in the characteristics of leadership. In contrast, Emily Feistritzer contends that, "Probably nowhere in America is there a larger bloc that gives more credence to the phrase, 'old boys' club' than public school administrators" (Feistritzer, Quelle, & Bloom, 1988, p. 3).

There is considerable variation among the more than 15,000 school districts in the demands of administrative jobs and in the personal and professional characteristics of school leaders. Ernest House (1974) offers one distinction among chief administrators, however, that is particularly useful. Some are "place bound," while others are "career bound." The place-bound superintendent wants to remain within the community as long as possible and eventually retire there. The career-bound superintendent is more interested in winning recognition at either the state or national level and demonstrates less loyalty to the local power structure.

The School Superintendent

School superintendents serve at the pleasure of boards of education. Superintendents administer school systems organized to carry out line and staff functions. The chain of command in the system is organized as a line of authority, with each position holding administrative responsibility over all those below. A staff position, in contrast to a line position, holds no administrative authority. People in staff positions typically advise their superiors but do not give orders to others. When Harry Truman was president, he had a sign on his desk that read, The buck stops here. The same sign could be placed on the desk of any superintendent of schools. The typical line and staff organization of public school systems is shown in Figure 11.3.

The superintendency can be an incredibly demanding job. The issues or challenges facing superintendents are many and varied: financing schools,

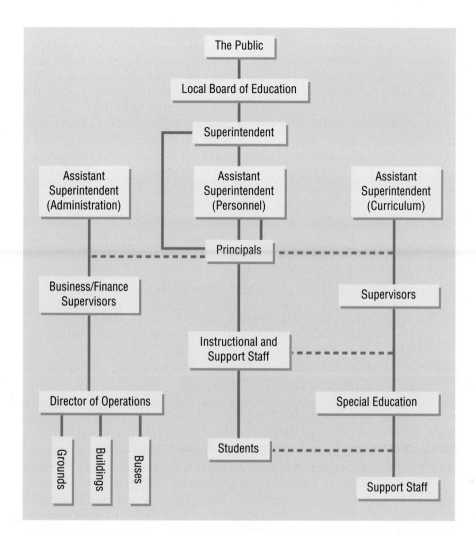

FIGURE 11.3

Typical Line and Staff Organization of Public School Systems

planning and goal setting, assessing educational outcomes, maintaining and enhancing accountability and credibility, evaluating staff and administrators, developing working relations with a school board, administering special education services, obtaining timely and accurate information, negotiating labor contracts, dealing with changing enrollments, and so on (Hansen, 1991).

In large U.S. cities, it has become an embattled position. There are so many problems, so many constituencies with competing interests, and so few resources that city superintendents stay in their jobs about 2.5 years on average, compared to the U.S. average of 5.5 years. Nathan Glazer (1992) has argued that, because the job is so overwhelming and performed so poorly, we should simply abolish the position.

The chancellor of the New York City public schools—a sort of super superintendent—presides over 32 community school district superintendents, 1,000 schools, 100,000 employees, and nearly a million students, about 8% of whom are Asian- or Pacific Islander-American, 35% Hispanic-American, 38% African-American, and 19% European-American (New York City Public Schools, 1990). The New York City public school system is the largest in the nation, and in many ways probably the most complicated. The job description calls on the New York City chancellor to be: (a) an educator well versed in instruction, supervision, and administration; (b) a leader who exhibits decisiveness, shrewdness, powers of consensus building, and a commitment to children; (c) a manager having skills to run a bureaucracy with more than 100,000 employees; and (d) a strategist, good at overcoming institutional barriers (New York City Public Schools, 1992).

No wonder superintendents are often forced out of their jobs, and, while they are there, even the best of them can bend under the pressure. As William Eaton (1990) and his colleagues observe, perhaps better than anyone before or since, Raymond Callahan (1962) described the power of politics in school management as if he were writing in the 1990s:

> I am now convinced that very much of what has happened in American education since 1900 can be explained on the basis of the extreme vulnerability of our schoolmen to public criticism and pressure and that this vulnerability is built into our pattern of local support and control. This has been true in the past and, unless changes are made, will continue to be true in the future. (p. viii)

Many more superintendents work in small communities than in large ones. About 4,000 districts enroll fewer than 300 students; only 16 districts enroll 100,000 or more students. The superintendents in small communities must, however, fulfill many of the same responsibilities of educational leadership. The magnitude of their problems pales in comparison to those of their big-city counterparts, yet their problems can be quite severe. In many instances, for example, their small and declining enrollments make opportunities to offer an intellectually rich, high-powered curriculum virtually impossible. Merely staffing the courses they must have to meet minimal requirements is a major challenge.

Carolyn Tift (1990) contends that for rural school administrators to be successful, they must be a good "fit" with their communities. "Time and again rural administrators have stressed the necessity of understanding their community" (p. 5). In small towns, educational leaders are not nameless, faceless bureaucrats. People know where to go and with whom they can speak if they are unhappy about educational policies and practices.

Over the years, others have emphasized the importance of human relationships in successful school administration and programmatic change. Roland Barth (1990) suggests that schools, be they large or small, rise and fall on the strength of human relationships. Human relationships and **collegiality**, or relationships based on a sharing of power, "allow, energize, and sustain all other attempts at school improvement" (p. 32). People have to talk with and listen to each other or little substantive improvement will ever occur. Principals all perform similar everyday activities, such as visiting or observing classrooms, circulating through the building, and monitoring hallways. As Figure 11.4 suggests, however, the ways principals interpret these activities can make a big difference in their effectiveness as leaders.

FIGURE 11.4

Effective School Leadership

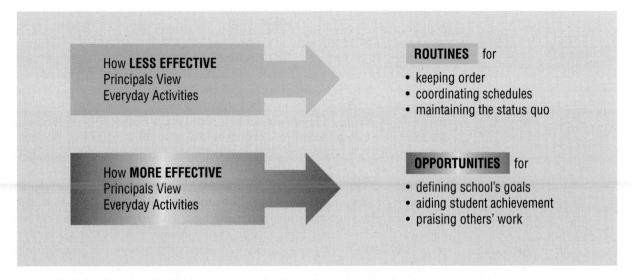

Note. From "How Leaders See What They Do," *National Center for School Leadership Newsletter,* Winter, 1989, 2 (1), p. 3 Adapted by permission.

Principals

If a single individual is key to the everyday operation and tone of a school it is the **principal**—the person responsible for managing a school at the building level. Principals typically administer discipline to students, give guidance to students, deal with staff and faculty on simple to complex issues but rarely on instructional issues, locate substitute teachers, implement rules, conduct surveillance of halls, balance the school's budget, and maintain the building and equipment. High school principals may also spend 10 to 15 hours per week attending sporting events, fine arts performances, faculty socials, parent-teacher meetings, and dances (Hoy & Miskel, 1991).

Terrence Deal and Kent Peterson (1991) have described the job of principal as one of shaping the culture by playing several important roles: symbol, potter, poet, actor, and healer. The cars principals drive, the clothes they wear, the homes they buy, the location of their desks, the way principals spend their time, the memoranda they write, all communicate symbolically what principals value. Whether principals intend to communicate via such symbols may be irrelevant, but the symbols themselves define the public persona of the principal, and thus to a large extent the culture of a school.

Like a potter working a lump of clay, the principal shapes and reinforces the shared values of the school. She or he emphasizes various school rituals—the pep rally, the reading of the honor roll, the stories told at public gatherings—to cultivate a sense of community.

While some dismiss the language principals use as slogans, mindless jargon, or educationese, others interpret it as a critical attribute of a subculture. The acronyms with which principals pepper their speech—PPBS, NAEP, CBE—sound foreign to the uninitiated. The choice of words and phrases, and the tone in which principals utter them, like drama, create vivid images in people's minds.

(Enter, stage left) . . . The principal captures audience attention as any actor might by using a number of theatrical devices—the cheery smile of the good samaritan, the frown of grim determination worn by the heavyweight champ, the expansive gestures of the carnival barker. The script can call for the principal to play a familiar role, for instance, the master of ceremonies at the annual student awards convocation. But the drama that is schooling, filled as it is with random tragedy and triumph, can also force the principal to improvise.

Despite recent educational reforms, surprisingly little has changed in the hiring process since researchers D. Catherine Baltzell and Robert Dentler (1983) described it more than a decade ago. The superintendent and his deputies firmly control the process. Many factors, not always leadership ability, constrain superintendents' choices—the desire to protect and promote good staff, to transfer weak staff, to preserve seniority, to satisfy parents and faculties, and the like. Although there is much rhetoric about picking the best educational leaders, selection criteria are dominated by "fit" and "image" of candidates. Affirmative action has increased the numbers of women and minorities in this position. And in some places where school restructuring is occurring, teachers, parents, and students participate in the hiring process.

How principals become principals, or the process by which they are socialized into their jobs, makes a difference in their professional lives. This fact can seem so obvious that it hardly bears noting. When one looks beyond culture in the United States, however, and assumes an international perspective on principal preparation, the focus on socialization is sharpened. A group of Canadian researchers concluded from a study of 75 principals in Canadian schools, 47 of whom were women, that on-the-job training was the most helpful of all socialization activities (Leithwood, Steinbach, & Begley, 1992).

The principal's relationship with teachers is a critical dimension of the job. The principal is in a position of middle management—between the superintendent and the teachers and school staff. As such, she or he must be able to follow and to lead. To lead the teachers and the support staff (guidance counselors, special education teachers, media specialists, librarians, custodians, bus drivers, and others), the principal must involve others in formulating and implementing ideas without sacrificing authority. Ultimately, the principal is responsible for what occurs in and around the school.

In school-based management, principals, teachers, and parents become directly involved in decision making and the governance of the school.

VOICES

On Collegiality

f educators are to pool their energies in creative ways for the good of students, Catherine Lugg and William Boyd, researchers at Pennsylvania State University, argue that schools must organize themselves to encourage collegial interaction.

We need to restructure our schools, following a "communitarian" rather than a bureaucratic model, if we are to make them better places for making connections between adults and young people. As an antidote to the fragmentation and depersonalization of our traditional "factory model" of schooling, our big schools need to be restructured into schools within schools, with teachers and students organized into "teams" of manageable size that work (and play) together for sustained periods of time—perhaps staying together as teams for two or three years so that strong interpersonal relationships can flourish.

A strong argument can be made that the schools that make such changes are the ones most likely to thrive in systems that adopt some sort of choice plan that enables students and educators to come together in educational communities that share similar values. . . .

Another method of building strong collaboratives within schools is to create structures and processes that increase collegial interaction within schools. These structures should not be restricted to fostering interactions among teachers but should also create ways of collaborating that involve the administrative staff, the custodial staff, and so on. While it is relatively easy to conjure up a vision of a school brimming over with caring adults who easily interact with each other and with students, it is another matter to actually develop such an environment. For administrators, building and maintaining a collegial atmosphere always remains "in process." (p. 256)

CRITICAL THINKING

Think back to your own high school. What could be done there to encourage collegiality among adults and to promote the idea of the school as "community" for all its inhabitants? Are there particularly undesirable organizational structures and functions that could be changed, or especially desirable ones upon which people could capitalize?

Source: Lugg, C.A., & Boyd, W.L. (1993, November). Leadership for collaboration: Reducing risk and fostering resilience. *Phi Delta Kappan, 75* (3), 253–258.

School-Based Management

In the 1980s and 1990s, education reformers have promoted the idea of involving people at the school level more directly in making decisions about teaching and learning, budgeting, and hiring personnel. This relatively new phenomenon in school governance is referred to as **school-based management**, site-based management, **school restructuring**, and/or shared decision making. These innovations are instituted by local school districts.

Reformers encourage these new governance and management strategies for two reasons. First, proponents believe that people who are most affected by educational decisions ought to be involved in those decisions. This belief is driven not only by a concern for fairness but also by a sense that the people most intimately involved may also be most capable of rendering the best decisions. Second, proponents argue that once decisions are made, they are more likely to result in success when those who must live with the decisions help make them. Reformers contend, then, that it makes good sense managerially and politically to involve people when making educational decisions that will affect their lives (American Association of School Administrators and the National Associations of Elementary and Secondary School Principals, undated).

Reforms to institute site-based management have been highly visible in places where the schools have been perceived as in crisis. Chicago, Illinois, Dade County, Florida, and Rochester, New York, have been among the leaders in attempting to move educational decision making and control away from the superintendent's office and toward local schools.

Who could argue with the idea of involving those affected by educational policies in the formation of such policies? The nation's historical commitment to the common school has meant that public education should serve all the people by providing a central core of knowledge and by involving people so as to form a community. School-based management, then, has historical precedent and just seems to make good sense. But what appears reasonable in theory rarely translates smoothly into practice. Moreover, other reform efforts, such as those aimed at professionalizing education, tend to conflict with participatory decision making.

> **Who could argue with the idea of involving those affected by educational policies in the formation of such policies?**

Attempts to use school-based management to change the basic structure of schools have raised serious questions: Do people agree on the purposes and methods of restructuring schools? Are people clear about redefinitions of the roles of teachers, administrators, professional organizations, parents, and policy makers? Who will make what decisions? How will people decide if the changes are improvements over old ways of operating? (Center for Restructuring Educational Issues, 1990).

Like other educational innovations, school-based management must overcome a number of obstacles if it is to succeed. One of the more prominent is inertia. When people are used to behaving in certain ways, it is difficult to change these patterns.

For example, when Chicago began restructuring 32 schools in 1987 to encourage site-based management, teachers and administrators worried about blurring the distinctions between management and labor. And both were concerned about how to involve parents in decision making at the school level. In 1989, the Illinois legislature created local councils in each of Chicago's 595 schools. These councils were composed of six parents, two other community members, two school employees, and a principal. The councils were to govern the schools, managing the budget and hiring and firing employees without regard to seniority. These new working relationships shared authority and accountability among the stakeholders, but none was failsafe.

Despite the excellent intentions of school reformers, some efforts to restructure schools have gone awry. Rosemary Hills Elementary School in Silver Spring, Maryland, received a $10,000 grant, set up a broad-based steering committee of teachers, parents, and administrators, and began to restructure how its children learned math. Eighteen months later the committee voted to kill the experiment.

> "People were intrigued by the idea of having some kind of direct say," said Deborah Litt, a former PTA president who was the project's most active parent. "But it was an inexperienced group doing this. It was very time-consuming and very slow, and people . . . lost steam." (Goldstein, 1991, p. D1)

Another serious obstacle to school-based management is lack of resources. With too little money, no matter how it is shared, even "restructured" schools may remain dismal places. The schools most in need of a new lease on educational life may be least likely to be able to afford it. The ultimate intent of restructuring schools to encourage site-based management is to create environments that motivate and teach students to be successful. But as Jonathan Kozol observes, "In many cities, what is termed 'restructuring' struck me as very little more than moving around the same old furniture within the house of poverty" (Kozol, 1991, p. 4). As long as schools are funded by property taxes, the inequities among schools will continue to reflect differences among communities.

To some degree, school-based management reforms have overlapped with initiatives to encourage "choice" in public schools. As noted in the next chapter ("Education Finance"), "choice" means different things to different people. Chief among the attributes of various choice schemes, however, is the emphasis on local control of schools. Proponent of choice John Chubb puts it this way:

> Those organizational qualities that we consider to be essential ingredients of an effective school—such things as academically focused objectives, pedagogically strong principals, relatively autonomous teachers, and collegial staff relations—do not flourish without the willingness of superintendents, school boards, and other outside authorities to delegate meaningful control over school policy, personnel, and practice to the school itself. (Chubb, 1988, pp. 28–49)

University-Managed Schools

Although few in number, university-managed schools are interesting organizations. In 1989, Boston University and the Chelsea, Massachusetts, public schools signed a contract that called for the university to manage the 3,600 pupil district for 10 years. Chelsea as a community and the schools in particular have long suffered a decline in efficacy (Greer, 1990). The partnership was formed to bring the resources of both organizations to bear collectively on the problems facing children and adults in the public schools.

According to Peter Greer (1990), the management of this partnership was designed to minimize turf battles: "The university's model is simple. It will lead, seek advice before making key decisions, adjust thinking, and

FIGURE 11.5

**Influences on Public
Education**

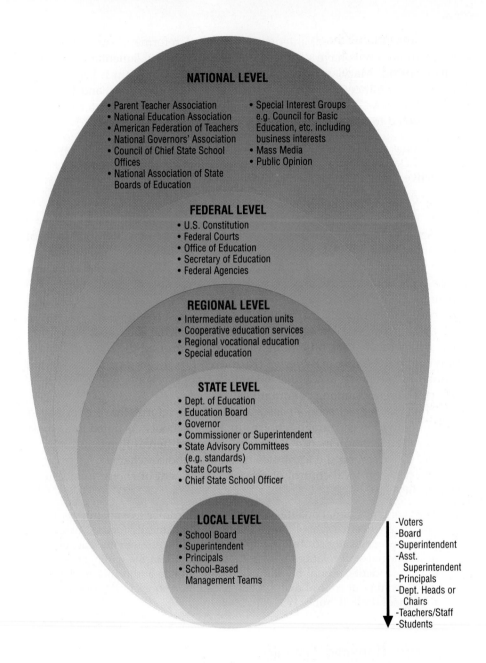

NATIONAL LEVEL

- Parent Teacher Association
- National Education Association
- American Federation of Teachers
- National Governors' Association
- Council of Chief State School
  Offices
- National Association of State
  Boards of Education

- Special Interest Groups
  e.g. Council for Basic
  Education, etc. including
  business interests
- Mass Media
- Public Opinion

FEDERAL LEVEL

- U.S. Constitution
- Federal Courts
- Office of Education
- Secretary of Education
- Federal Agencies

REGIONAL LEVEL

- Intermediate education units
- Cooperative education services
- Regional vocational education
- Special education

STATE LEVEL

- Dept. of Education
- Education Board
- Governor
- Commissioner or Superintendent
- State Advisory Committees
  (e.g. standards)
- State Courts
- Chief State School Officer

LOCAL LEVEL

- School Board
- Superintendent
- Principals
- School-Based
  Management Teams

-Voters
-Board
-Superintendent
-Asst.
  Superintendent
-Principals
-Dept. Heads or
  Chairs
-Teachers/Staff
-Students

make decisions—and allow local officials and community leaders, parents, staff members, and others to do the same" (pp. 37–38).

The optimism with which the partnership was undertaken, however, has dimmed somewhat. In 1992, the Chelsea schools were searching for their third superintendent in as many years (Cohen & Sessler, 1992). In addition, two other key school officials and several principals had left the system. The turnover in personnel did not bode well for the viability of the 10-year management experiment.

Wayne State University began operating a public middle school in Detroit, Michigan, in the fall of 1993. The university opened what is called

University Public School with 330 students in grades 6 through 8 who were selected randomly from more than 5,000 applicants. The academic year ran 190 days in 1993–94, 10 more than at other public schools, and will be 200 days each academic year thereafter. The school day lasts from 8:00 a.m. to 5:00 p.m. Students start the day with a 45-minute advisor-advisee session, and then take four 90-minute classes. There are 20 students per class. "Wayne State President David Adamany wants to prove that the university can provide an exceptional education using innovative techniques while spending no more public money than is spent on each child in the Detroit public schools—$4,308" (National School Boards Association, 1993, p. 5).

Educational reforms, public opinion, and special interest group pressure are among the many factors that influence public education. Figure 11.5 shows some of the forces influencing education at the national, federal, regional, state, and local levels which are taken up in this chapter.

HOW IS SCHOOL INFLUENCED BY PROFESSIONAL ORGANIZATIONS AND PRESSURE GROUPS?

Various individuals, groups, and organizations wield power to shape the course of events in schools. Formal sources of power reside in the organization itself—the person in charge has final authority over salaries, makes staff appointments, and the like. Increasingly, in restructured schools, this formal authority is being redefined to include parents and teachers. Others exercise power informally by virtue of their personalities and/or the constituencies they represent.

In a classic analysis, John French and Bertram Raven (1968) identified five sources of **interpersonal power** that may be brought to bear within organizations. Reward power refers to the ability to reward people for desirable behaviors. Coercive power, in contrast, refers to the power to punish people for undesirable behavior. Legitimate power is that influence which subordinates give to an administrator because they believe they are obligated to comply as members of the organization. Referent power is a person's ability to influence subordinates through respect and admiration. Expert power is based on a person's special knowledge or skill. The first three types of power are tied to positions in organizations while the last two are functions of personal attributes.

School administrators certainly can have the capacity to exercise all five forms of power, and they often do so in various combinations. The results of their actions can be measured in workers' levels of commitment to the organization and to the leaders themselves, in their levels of compliance with administrators' wishes, and in their overt and covert resistance to organizational leadership (Yukl, 1981). But teachers, too, through their unions and professional education associations, can bring significant collective power to bear as educational decisions are made and implemented. In these days of school restructuring and site-based management, teachers' decision-making influence has grown substantially in some localities.

Teachers' Unions

The "unions" as they are often called—the **National Education Association (NEA)** with its 2 million members and the **American Federation of Teachers (AFT)** with its 800,000 members—have influenced the conduct of schooling in many ways. They have articulated visions of childhood, of schools, and of professional practice that have guided educators, policy makers, parents, and children for years. In 1938, the Educational Policies Commission of the NEA set forth the Purposes of Education in American Democracy, which were described in terms of enabling students to develop themselves as people, to practice human relations skills, to learn how to be economically productive citizens, and to be responsible for their community and nation. These purposes were amplified in 1944 and again in 1952. These statements have guided the organization in pursuit of an educational agenda for the nation's youth.

The NEA has developed a rich array of programs and political activities to promote its vision of an educationally viable society. Its publication program includes *Today's Education* and *NEA Today*—monthly offerings that keep all members informed on issues and events that affect their professional lives and the lives of their students. The NEA Professional Library also publishes books of special interest to teachers and parents.

In recent years, the NEA has helped create the National Council for Accreditation of Teacher Education (NCATE)—a national organization that monitors the quality of collegiate teacher education programs. It has participated in developing policies for the establishment of a national certification program for teachers. The NEA has also sponsored the Mastery In Learning Project across the country to encourage faculty-led school reforms, and developed the Team Approach to Better Schools, which guides school-based decision making.

The NEA also sponsors the Student National Education Association (SNEA). The SNEA has about 55,000 members in colleges and universities across the nation. It provides publications to its members, conducts workshops and conferences, and provides liability insurance to students during their student teaching.

Albert Shanker, union leader

Teachers' unions, such as the American Federation of Teachers (AFT), bring educational issues to national attention, lobby the federal government on behalf of education, and sponsor research, publications, and conferences in education.

The NEA is a powerful lobbying organization that takes stands on political issues relevant to education and supports various candidates for election at all levels of government. It entered presidential politics for the first time in 1976, when it supported the Carter-Mondale ticket.

The AFT, too, is a highly influential political organization. It is affiliated with the American Federation of Labor/Congress of Industrial Organizations (AFL/CIO). The AFT has undertaken a variety of initiatives to influence schooling at all levels in society. Its publications program includes, among others, the *American Educator*, *American Teacher*, and *The Reporter*.

In recent years, the AFT has tried to rally public support for public education with a variety of creative projects. The AFT-sponsored program "Focus on Education" was carried on more than 100 PBS stations and on The Learning Channel. The organization has sponsored the telephone homework hotline, Dial-A-Teacher and the Learning Line, a telephone recording of learning ideas for parents. It has supported teacher internship programs, adopt-a-school programs, and national conferences for paraprofessionals and other school personnel. The AFT's Educational Research and Dissemination Project has linked its teachers and research and dissemination coordinators with educational research from schools of education around the country.

The legitimate authority of the unions to bargain for salaries and working conditions has greatly strengthened the hand of teachers and diminished the power of school administration. There is no collective bargaining law at the federal level, but most states allow teachers to bargain to establish their contracts. Even those states that have not formally recognized the power of unions have teachers who have organized themselves collectively to set the conditions of their employment and the conduct of various aspects of schooling.

Teachers actively collaborate to bring their personal and collective skills and knowledge to bear on the resolution of a variety of problems. Like administrators, they put their reputations on the line to advocate the adoption of innovative curricula and new educational programs. Teachers coerce cooperation by withholding their services and sometimes by striking. And teachers reward performance they consider desirable by speaking out for causes they deem admirable and by contributing to Political Action Committees that support candidates for various elected positions. In short, teachers can wield considerable power in the conduct of schooling.

Interest Groups

Public education, it seems, is everyone's business, and some people are more powerful in influencing its direction than others. Some people coalesce around particular interests and try to exert pressure for the advancement of

> **Public education, it seems, is everyone's business.**

their cause, thus the terms **special interest group** and *pressure group*. While many education reforms in recent years have been initiated publicly by authorities at the state level, a variety of organizations and special interest groups have contributed informally to the reforms by working publicly and behind the scenes to shape policy at the local, state, and national levels.

For example, the largest volunteer education organization in the United States—the **National Congress of Parents and Teachers** (commonly referred to as the PTA)—has long supported legislation at the state and national levels designed to benefit children. Professional organizations such as the National School Boards Association, the National Association of State Boards of Education, and the American Association of Colleges for Teacher Education also support in spirit and with funds many education policy initiatives (Campbell, Cunningham, Nystrand, and Usdan, 1990).

Interest groups often attempt to influence schools on ideological grounds. The Council for Basic Education, founded in 1956 by Mortimer Smith and Arthur Bestor, advocates curriculum in the liberal arts, much in keeping with Bestor's essentialist ideas (see Chapter 4, "Philosophical Foundations in Action"). Since the 1960s, African Americans and Native Americans have been increasingly active in demanding that schools respond to their needs and facilitate their participation in school activities. Hispanic Americans, too, have tried to establish *unidos*, or unity, among Spanish-speaking peoples to effect change in public schools. Such groups are often stimulated and sustained by their beliefs about school curricula and issues of social justice.

Interest groups advocate a wide range of activities aimed in one way or another at exerting control over curricular, instructional, and governance issues in public education. Some of the influential groups listed below have defined their educational agendas by advocating a variety of programs and actions.

American Association of University of Women (AAUW) The AAUW's first national study in 1885 was undertaken to dispel the idea that higher education was harmful to women's health. In 1992, the AAUW issued the results of another national study, this one focused on gender bias in schools, or "How Schools Shortchange Girls" (AAUW Educational Foundation and the National Education Association, 1992). As a result of this study, the AAUW made some 40 recommendations for action in public education that include but are not limited to: (a) strengthened reinforcement of Title IX, which prohibits discrimination against women; (b) preparation of teachers, administrators, and counselors to bring gender equity and awareness to every aspect of schooling; (c) inclusion in the formal curriculum of the experiences of women and men from all walks of life, with women and girls valued in the material young people study; (d) encouragement of girls to pursue mathematics and science careers; (e) attention to gender equity in vocational education; and (f) support for students to deal with realities of their sexuality and health.

American Civil Liberties Union For many years, the American Civil Liberties Union (ACLU) has taken public positions on educational issues to defend against what it has perceived as attacks on people's civil liberties. One of its most notable involvements was in the Scopes trial of 1925. In fact, it stimulated the confrontation between Christian fundamentalists and evolutionists. The ACLU offered counsel to any Tennessee teacher who would test the law that forbade teaching in public schools any theory that denied the account of creation in the Book of Genesis. John T. Scopes took them up on the offer and was defended by Clarence Darrow.

Through the years, in addition to supporting direct legal action, the ACLU has tried to influence the conduct of public education in other ways. The group has filed briefs on legal issues as a "friend of the court" for the purpose of educating judges and lawyers. Members of the ACLU have also spoken out publicly on many issues that bear on the protection of civil liberties in schools. For example, the ACLU has endorsed exempting students from the flag salute when their religion suggests refusal is appropriate, but it has opposed the use of vouchers and tuition tax credits that might be used to support students' education in religious schools at public expense. (See Chapter 12 for a discussion of vouchers and tuition tax credits.)

Anti-Defamation League of B'nai B'rith (ADL) The Anti-Defamation League was organized in 1913 to end unjust and unfair discrimination against and ridicule of any sect or body of citizens. The ADL has some 30 field offices in U.S. cities and 400 staff members. Its World of Difference Campaign is a comprehensive educational program for elementary and secondary teachers and students. The program consists of print and video materials that use teacher awareness training, youth training, classroom discussion guides, student after-school programs, and weekend awareness retreats to foster tolerance. According to ADL figures, it has trained some 100,000 teachers and 10 million public, private, and parochial school students.

The Anti-Defamation League of B'nai B'rith (ADL) is one example of the many professional organizations and interest groups that influence education in the United States. The ADL offers anti-discrimination, anti-hate crime education to teachers and students nationwide.

Daughters of the American Revolution (DAR) For more than 100 years, the Daughters of the American Revolution has promoted awards and scholarship programs in both elementary and secondary schools to foster patriotism. It sponsors the Junior American Citizens program to encourage the teaching of good citizenship and gives Good Citizenship Medals to recognize qualities of honor, service, courage, and leadership. It sponsors the American History Essay Contest for the middle grades and rewards essay writers with cash and medals. It gives scholarships to college and university students in the Reserve Officer Training Corps (ROTC) and recognizes outstanding teachers of American history with monetary awards.

National Association of Manufacturers Business organizations have also left their mark on education, among them the National Association of Manufacturers (NAM).

> The NAM believes America's economic well-being and ability to compete in global markets will depend increasingly on the skills of the nation's workforce. The lack of basic skills among workers not only jeopardizes workers' opportunities for employment mobility and success, but also seriously undermines technological advancement, productivity and quality improvements within American companies. (National Association of Manufacturers, 1993, p. 29)

The NAM and the U.S. Department of Labor have formed a partnership to encourage small, medium, and large manufacturers to attend to training, education, and changes in work organizations. They intend to work with organizations who are willing to commit themselves from the top of the management hierarchy to the workers to create high-performance work environments.

As Chapter 12 suggests, business partnerships with schools have flourished in recent years. Whether the connection between education and the nation's economic productivity is as strong as some contend, it is clear that many business leaders are investing their emotions and their money in strengthening education programs on the job and in schools. There is an element of patriotism involved in much of this activity, but such investment is also self-serving: if education can produce more effective and efficient workers, business and industry will boost profits.

National Organization of Women   The Legal Defense and Education Fund (LDEF) of the National Organization for Women (NOW) sponsors a variety of actions to advance women's rights in education systems across the country. In St. Louis, Missouri, for example, the LDEF fought against the board of education policy to transfer pregnant elementary and junior high school girls to a school with a weak academic and extracurricular program—a school "with the bleak air of a penal colony"—when their pregnancies became obvious. The Board changed its policy, allowing girls to remain in regular classes or to transfer (National Organization for Women Legal Defense and Education Fund, 1993, p. 2).

HOW DO PUBLIC OPINION AND THE PRESS AFFECT SCHOOL GOVERNANCE?

One cannot ignore the influence of public opinion on processes of governing and managing public education in the United States. Callahan noted this fact in modern times and Jefferson, Franklin, Webster, and others recognized it in earlier times. The press figures prominently in the public opinion equation both by reporting on the state of the public mind and by running ahead of the people, telling them what they ought to think.

One view, expressed by Juan Williams below, is that the job of the press is to watch governmental and educational leaders so they do not cheat the common people. This is a time-honored position and an important one to remember. When journalists, who have access to information and the means to be heard, fail to keep an eye on the workings of public education, opportunities for mischief abound. The simple act of watching and reporting on leaders can be strongly persuasive. In the nineteenth century, British historians Thomas Carlyle and Thomas Babington Macaulay referred to the press as the fourth estate—a driving force in society almost equal in influence to the clergy, the nobility, and the burghers. The press continues to wield substantial power in modern society.

Williams (1992) described the job of the journalist on the education beat:

> The truth is, reporters and editors and, most important, readers are interested in education only as a function of political power. A major proportion of any jurisdiction's tax dollars goes into schools. Politicians have to make up those school budgets and defend them. The school or university budget has to be both sufficient to the task of educating young people and simultaneously able to withstand charges that it is really a pork-barrel project, wasting the taxpayer's money. Education budgets pay not only for teachers and books but also for construction workers, maintenance people, teachers' aides, administrators, union chiefs, and cooks. In other words, the tax dollars assigned to educate children are a major source of patronage and power in our society. Newspaper editors, as the public's watchdogs, want to know if the taxpayers are being cheated out of their money. (p. 179)

The press performs not only an information function in society but a major educational functional as well. Television, newspapers, radio, and magazines touch more people today than at any time in our history, and they will reach more tomorrow than they do today. Television educates young and old directly through many programs—*The Electric Company, Sesame Street, 3-2-1 Contact, The Brain, College Algebra, French in Action, The Open Mind, NOVA, Connections, The Body in Question, Nature, America, National Geographic Explorer*, and a host of other PBS and other network specials, as well as Channel One.

The print media certainly educate young people indirectly in many ways, but they are also involved in educating young people directly. For example, *Newsweek* magazine also produces *Newsweek-Education Program* and *USA Today* produces and distributes in cooperation with the National Aeronautics and Space Administration a program called *USA Today-Visions of Exploration*. These programs are designed to be used in schools as regular parts of the curriculum.

The power of the press to educate people for life in modern society is only beginning to be understood. But it is already obvious that journalists do much more than simply sway public opinion about the management and governance of our schools. They also edify masses of people about the educational challenges of the day.

WHY IS IT SO DIFFICULT TO CHANGE PUBLIC EDUCATION?

Schools are complicated, subtle organizations that do not always operate rationally. Many work extremely well under difficult conditions with incredible success. But others that function less effectively may also be resistant to change. Meyer and Rowan (1977) argued that even the comparatively weak performances of some schools can become "institutionalized" in people's minds, that is, people come to expect educators to behave in customary ways, even when these ways are less than desirable.

How does this happen? John Meyer and Brian Rowan suggest that there are a set of principles that govern institutionalized organizations such as schools.

1. As our society has grown more elaborate—as rules have arisen and as relationships among people and organizations have grown more complex—schools have incorporated these rules and have taken on more work.

In Chapter 6, we noted that all kinds of social and education problems arise continually in society, and that schools are often called upon to respond. State leaders may, for example, view the disintegration of the family structure as the root cause of teen pregnancy, drug abuse, violence, and any number of other problems. In response, the state may require family life education for all its citizens under the age of 18 who are enrolled in public schools. Where school districts are not already providing family life education, administrators must identify or create a curriculum to meet this requirement. Training must also be provided for teachers who will offer the curriculum, and plans must be made to evaluate the program once it has had a chance to operate.

> **What causes even weak or unsuccessful schools to persist?**

With the requirement, then, come new materials, new personnel, altered instructional procedures and practices, revised school schedules, and different routines for monitoring progress—all of which, if viewed as successful, are acceptable changes in the system.

But once these new programs are established it is difficult to define success. Schools too often rely on inadequate measures to judge program effectiveness. For example, administrators may document the numbers of hours taught, the relatively low cost of instruction, and the number of students who took the new family life program, but avoid examining the pregnancy rate and drug use before and after the program was offered. Pressures to succeed from inside and outside the school are great, so naturally school leaders want to appear successful.

2. Schools that incorporate acceptable ideas are viewed as healthy organizations.

Schools need to innovate to be healthy organizations, but if their leaders get too far ahead of the pack—look too different, behave too radically—schools risk loss of legitimacy and support. To extend the example above, if one school develops and implements a hard-hitting sex education program as part of its family life curriculum, even though sex education may be exactly what is needed, the school may jeopardize its own place in the system. Survival of the school's leaders and the school itself depends not only on being productive but on fitting in or looking like the rest of the schools in the system in which it is embedded.

In their efforts to look good, but not too good, school leaders in relatively weak schools may implement several strategies. First, they can ignore the system and concentrate on being efficient. Second, leaders may go to the other extreme and ignore efficiency and productivity in favor of looking like the other schools in the system. Third, a school's leaders may admit weakness but blame it on somebody else, maybe the central administration. Fourth, they can promise to reform their organization. Each course of action carries a risk.

So how do established schools manage to survive and prosper? Meyer and Rowan assert that they do two things: (a) "decouple" their organizational structure from their activities, and (b) use the logic of confidence to justify their positions in society.

3. Because coordination in school systems can lead to conflicts, units are "decoupled" from activities and from each other.

"Decoupling" happens several ways. First, schools let "professionals" handle activities. There is an elaborate structure in place for certifying different teachers to perform instructional tasks and administrators to perform management tasks. By definition, professionals are trained to do their jobs, so these trained professionals are encouraged to do their jobs with little or no oversight.

Second, goals of schooling are stated in general terms. Process is emphasized over products. For example, teachers offer opportunities for students to learn about healthy family life by reading, participating in discussions, watching movies, etc., but teachers do not guarantee student learning.

Third, classrooms, grade levels, and other organizational units in schools are separated from each other. There is often little communication across units. The evaluation that occurs is largely ceremonial—it does little to improve or condemn inefficient, unproductive teachers and program units.

Finally, a premium is placed on people getting along with each other. Coordination among people and between the structure of the school and its products is minimal. People are left to coordinate their activities on an informal basis.

Decoupling can protect a school from internal conflict by obscuring differences among people and inconsistencies between goals and results. If people inside and outside the school are unaware of the problems, or choose not to confront them, administrators find it easier to win support for the school. People put their faith and confidence in the idea that the school works.

4. The more schools rely on illusions, the more they display confidence, satisfaction, and good faith.

Admitting weakness can be difficult and painful. Sometimes, people overcompensate and try to put the best face on a bad situation.

5. Established educational organizations try to minimize inspection from inside and evaluation from outside.

Despite the best of intentions, principals or other school leaders intent on enhancing productivity can create problems for themselves and for others. By seeking opinions about school needs from staff and from the com-

VOICES

On Bureaucratic Organizations

The influence of Max Weber's thinking about bureaucracy and authority in organizations is felt yet today in the practice and study of school governance and administration. Weber was born in 1864, raised in Berlin, and died in 1920. As a student of history, law, politics, economics, and social systems, Weber conceptualized organizations as complex systems that interacted with their environments. He described three types of "legitimate authority" upon which organizational leaders base the validity of their claims:

1. Rational grounds—resting on a belief in the "legality" of patterns of normative rules and the right of those elevated to authority under such rules to issue commands (legal authority).

2. Traditional grounds—resting on an established belief in the sanctity of immemorial traditions and the legitimacy of the status of those exercising authority under them (traditional authority); or finally,

3. Charismatic grounds—resting on devotion to the specific and exceptional sanctity, heroism or exemplary character of an individual person, and of the normative patterns or order revealed or ordained by him (charismatic authority).

In the case of legal authority, obedience is owed to the legally established impersonal order. It extends to the persons exercising the authority of office under it only by virtue of the formal legality of their commands and only within the scope of authority of the office. In the case of traditional authority, obedience is owed to the person of the chief who occupies the traditionally sanctioned position of authority and who is (within its sphere) bound by tradition. But here the obligation of obedience is not based on the impersonal order, but is a matter of personal loyalty within the area of accustomed obligations. In the case of charismatic authority, it is the charismatically qualified leader as such who is obeyed by virtue of personal trust in him and his revelation, his heroism or his exemplary qualities so far as they fall within the scope of the individual's belief in his charisma.

CRITICAL THINKING

Weber also recognized the power of collegiality to affect decision making in organizations. How might teacher-leaders work together as colleagues to influence the conduct of schooling?

Source: Weber, M. (1947). *The theory of social and economic organization.* (A.M. Henderson & T. Parsons, Trans.). New York: Oxford University Press. (Original work published 1922) p. 328.

munity, by getting involved in instruction, curriculum development, and evaluation, and by seeking information upon which to base school improvement initiatives, leaders create tension in the system.

In some cases, such tension is long overdue. People have become complacent, inefficient, and unproductive. But it is also possible that evaluative activities can damage a strong school. The mere act of looking for problems may actually create more problems than already exist. The maxim that there is always room to improve teaching and learning has been used to dampen more than one person's enthusiasm for their work.

In similar fashion, Douglas McGregor's (1960) "Theory X" describes organizations in terms of their human relations. A Theory X view has important implications for administering and governing schools because it suggests a set of assumptions upon which managers are to operate. The Theory X assumptions about workers in an organization can be summarized as follows:

1. The average person dislikes work and will avoid it if possible.
2. Because people dislike work, they can be coerced, controlled, and punished to exert the effort needed to accomplish organizational goals.
3. People would rather be directed than to take responsibility for their actions. They are lazy and want security.

A bureaucratic or Theory X view of school management has promulgated a set of practices that are evident in varying degrees in schools throughout the land, and even in recent efforts to reform schools (Clark & Astuto, 1994). Jobs are organized to divide work responsibilities among people. Authority is organized so that workers realize who is above, below, and beside them. Salaries are standardized according to schedules. Individual interests are to be subordinated to group interests.

Another view of school administration has emerged in recent years to challenge the bureaucratic, Theory X outlook. This outlook places a high value on the people in the organization. The outlook is similar to what McGregor (1960) calls "Theory Y." Theory Y assumes that people in an organization are motivated to perform, and to be subjects, not objects in the organization. Theory Y assumptions can be summarized as follows:

1. The average person does not dislike work, and, when conditions are right, derives satisfaction from it.
2. Workers will direct and control themselves when they are committed to organizational goals.
3. Workers are committed to goals when they are rewarded for the attainment of these goals.
4. People accept and seek responsibility when conditions encourage them to do so.
5. Lots of people possess the abilities to be creative workers.
6. Most organizations fail to tap the potential of the average worker.

Similarly, William Ouchi (1981) examined corporate culture to determine how and why some corporations were so successful. He argued that the success of corporations in both Japan and the United States was dependent in no small measure on the type of corporate culture they maintained. Successful organizations were characterized by what Ouchi called "Theory Z culture," or an organizational culture that promotes teamwork.

WHY WILL PUBLIC EDUCATION CONTINUE TO CHANGE?

Many factors impede change in the way public schools are organized and managed and in how teaching and learning occur. Visions differ markedly on what change really means and how it should be fostered. But, to be sure, public education is changing. In some places, leaders encourage change school by school, often using "school-based management" as the concept to alter the way schooling occurs. In others, people advocate "systemic change" or change that tries to align the many pieces of an entire education system from the top down to form new organizations that will deliver education creatively and effectively. Some reformers are even trying to work from the top down and the bottom up simultaneously to effect change in public schools (Olson, 1993).

Even the models of governance and administration through which changes occur are changing. A traditional school of thought about school administration is concerned with bureaucratic efficiency. The person most frequently associated with this view is German sociologist Max Weber (1969). He characterized bureaucracies in terms of their hierarchies of authority, divisions of work, rules, and the procedures by which they operated. A bureaucracy was supposed to function like a well-oiled, efficient machine.

More contemporary models of organization promote a Theory Z set of common values that include intimacy, trust, cooperation, teamwork, and egalitarianism. Organizational theorists have extolled the virtues of capitalizing on the capacities of the people in the organization and changing the traditional values with which so many organizations had driven themselves into stagnation. Thomas Peters and Robert Waterman (1982) wrote about those companies that exhibited a set of values that propelled them into prosperity. These organizations demonstrated a bias for action—they were not paralyzed by the complexity or severity of problems. They held their clients uppermost in their minds, for the clients were the ultimate reason the organization existed. Successful organizations demonstrated respect for autonomy and innovation, they did not demand conformity. They put people first, because without people there would be no productivity. Successful organizations were characterized by an achievement orientation—in short, they produced.

The Total Quality Management (TQM) approach to change, developed originally for use in large businesses and industry, is also rapidly becoming part of the educator's lexicon. TQM may best be described as a set of core beliefs about organizations.

> These include a strong focus on customer satisfaction and doing things right the first time, executive-level leadership, and greater investments in employee education and training. In quality companies, empowered workers make decisions based on data that help promote "continuous improvements" in products and services. (Olson, 1992, p. 27)

When TQM is translated for use in schools, leaders often try to capitalize on the idea that teachers and students want to be productive and happy. The task is to help them reconcile their performances with their expectations.

Add to conceptions of school-based management, systemic change, and TQM the burgeoning use of technology, pressures for altering funding for schools, the innovation of whole language instruction, coalitions of parents, educators, and business leaders bent on curricular reform, strategies for promoting cooperative learning, the growing interest in higher order thinking skills, and a veritable smorgasbord of standards and tests and exhortations aimed at making somebody do something differently, and it is difficult to imagine anything but change. Indeed, even a cursory glance at educational history reveals change in American public education wherever the eye can see. The changes have not always played themselves out as people would have hoped, and they may not have lasted long before being supplanted by yet another change.

There is nothing so stable, however, as the constancy of change in American public education, unless perhaps it is the inevitability that, whatever happens, teachers will teach and students will learn. Teacher leaders will help define how teaching and learning will occur in schools of the future by their participation in the system. The more teachers know about how schools are organized, governed, and administered, the better prepared they will be to affect that system.

SUMMARY

1. The power to establish and operate public schools is derived from the Tenth Amendment to the U.S. Constitution: "The powers not delegated to the United States by the Constitution; nor prohibited by it to the States, are reserved to the States respectively, or to the people."

2. The federal agenda for education is shaped by the "Iron Triangle"—the combination of education interests in the executive branch, congressional committees, and education interest groups outside government.

3. State governments influence public education through taxation and distribution of revenues. States also set standards for building schools, educating teachers and school administrators, licensing school personnel, and establishing curriculum, the length of the school term, attendance requirements, and school accreditation processes.

4. State boards of education regulate educational practice and advise governors and legislators about the conduct of educational business.

5. A state education department administers programs, regulates activities of other education agencies, advises other agencies, and engages in staff development and public relations.

6. In recent years, the governors have become major players in education reform via the National Governors' Association. The governors laid out an agenda for reform in 1986 that addressed seven critical issues before their education systems: teaching, leadership and management, parent involvement and choice, readiness, technology, school facilities, and college quality.

7. All but two states (Connecticut and South Dakota) now have state standards boards or commissions to regulate professional practice in education.

8. School districts sometimes cooperate to provide services. Such joint facilities are most often called intermediate educational units (IEUs), educational service agencies (ESA), and boards of cooperative educational services (BOCES).

9. Because education is a reserved power to the states, local school boards are agents of the states. About 95% of local board members are elected to represent their constituents while the other 5% are appointed.

10. School superintendents are hired and fired by boards of education. Superintendents administer school systems organized to carry out line and staff functions.

11. Principals may administer discipline to students, give guidance to students, deal with staff and faculty on simple to complex issues but rarely on instructional issues, locate substitute teachers, implement rules, conduct surveillance of halls, balance the school's budget, and maintain the building and equipment. School principals may also spend 10 to 15 hours per week attending education-related events.

12. Education reformers have promoted the idea of involving people at the school level more directly in making decisions about teaching and learning, budgeting, and hiring personnel. This relatively new phenomenon in school governance is referred to as school-based management, site-based management, school restructuring, and/or shared decision making. These innovations are instituted at the district level.

13. Kinds of power in an education organization include reward power (ability to reward people for desirable behaviors), coercive power (power to punish people for undesirable behavior), legitimate power (subordinates' willing compliance toward administrators), referent power (ability to influence others through respect), and expert power (a person's special knowledge or skill).

14. The National Education Association (NEA) and the American Federation of Teachers (AFT) have instituted many programs and initiatives to influence the conduct of public education. They are among the most visible and powerful interest groups in the education community.

15. Public opinion and the press are powerful factors in the governance and administration of schools, both directly and indirectly.

16. As education practice, indeed any human behavior, becomes institutionalized, it often grows resistant to change. As bureaucratic organizations, schools are also resistant to change. Changes in schools and in education, however, are constant and inevitable.

TERMS AND CONCEPTS

American Federation of
  Teachers (AFT)
central office staff
chief state school officer
collegiality
Council of Chief State
  Officers
intermediate educational unit (IEU)
interpersonal power
local school board

National Congress of
  Parents and Teachers
  (PTA)
National Education
  Association (NEA)
National Governors'
  Association (NGA)
principal
school-based
  management

school governance
school restructuring
special interest group
state boards of
  education
state education departments (SED)
state standards boards
superintendent of
  schools

STUDENT ACTIVITIES

The acts of governing and administering schools frequently look different in practice from how they are described in print. The activities below are designed to encourage an examination of gaps between the theory and the practice of school management and governance.

Perceive and Value

Interview several teachers about their experiences working with school administrators. Keep your questions fairly open ended: for example, ask them to recall the most memorable school administrators with whom they worked and what made them memorable. Share your findings with your colleagues and develop a practical tip sheet for beginning teachers on what to look for in good school leadership. Are there particular actions teachers and administrators might take to foster positive relationships with one another?

Know and Act

Do you know what the state requirements are to become a principal or a superintendent in your state? Do you know which colleges and universities in the state have administrator preparation programs? Contact one of these programs and ask for a description of their program and descriptions of courses within the program. Compare your findings with those of a colleague who investigated a different program. Do you see obvious differences between the two? How do the costs of the two programs compare?

Evaluate

Attend an open meeting of the local school board. As you listen to members' comments, jot brief notes about the content of their remarks. What topics were discussed during the meeting? Which topics got the most attention? Was there a fairly even distribution of talk among school-board members? Did some members dominate discussion? Were any decisions made? If so, what were they? How often, if at all, did board members turn to the superintendent or a member of his or her staff for advice or information? Interview a board member. Ask why she or he got involved in work on the board. Ask what is most rewarding/most frustrating about the job.

Discover

How are school board members chosen in the state where you plan to teach? Does the state have intermediate education units? If so, what are they called, and what services do they provide? How are textbooks selected in the state; that is, who sets the guidelines for selection? How does a company get its books on the approved list?

This chapter examines the forces that have driven funding of public education in the United States. It describes how schools are financed at local, state, and federal levels, noting issues in funding for private schools. The chapter also discusses the concepts of excellence and equity, the role that courts have played in educational finance, and special problems of paying for the educational infrastructure—school buildings. Finally, the chapter explains what the term *choice* has come to mean in public education and describes the increasing interest in developing school/business partnerships.

12

Education
Finance

1 What are some of the forces that have driven patterns of school finance over the years?

.... Perceive

2 Why are there disparities in school funding, and what remedies have been proposed?

.... Value

3 How do states and localities raise money for their public school systems?

.... Know

4 How might a person make a case for and against using lottery money to support public education?

.... Act

5 How might a community decide if the money it spends on education is sufficient?

.... Evaluate

HOW DO ECONOMY AND EDUCATION INTERRELATE?

Since before the founding of the republic, values and money have shaped public education into the system we have today. Values and money trigger all kinds of questions about the conduct of education. Does "equal" educational opportunity mean the "same" level of funding for all students, or must some students and localities be afforded extra resources to put them on equal footing with others in their quest for educational success? Why should and how could low-income communities be helped to provide adequate facilities and programs for educating their children? At what point do providers of money for education cross the line from being efficient to being stingy? Who decides how money will be spent at the school level? Should parents and localities be allowed to choose what schools their children attend and use tax dollars to finance these choices?

As described in Chapter 2, Massachusetts laws of 1642 and 1647 laid the basis for funding public education. When parents and masters were neglectful "in training up their children," the government had the power to levy fines. When towns of 50 or more families failed to appoint a teacher, they too, could be fined, with the proceeds to be used for public education elsewhere in the colony. The parents, masters, or "the inhabitants in general" were to pay the schoolmasters (Benson, 1961).

What values have contemporary local leaders signaled through patterns of financial action? They have been concerned first about enhancing their own community's welfare and concerned second about society at large. Education has contributed to the general welfare or commonweal in a variety of ways. For example, Edward Denison (1983) estimated that between 1929 and 1982 investments in education accounted for almost one quarter of the nation's economic productivity.

Changes in the way corporations do business affect the demand for education. Today, increasing computerization, the proliferation of services offered by businesses, a growing global economy, flatter organizational hierarchies, and decentralization of responsibility necessitate that workers possess a variety of basic and work-related skills (Berryman & Bailey, 1992). Besides learning reading, communication, and mathematical skills, Americans who progress through the educational pipeline have opportunities to reason, to direct their own work, to cooperate with others, and to adapt to change. Armed with such skills, workers are better prepared than the unskilled to understand the requirements of their jobs, to communicate effectively with colleagues, to advance to more challenging positions, and to make decisions on the shop floor. Because they may not need to defer to supervisors in the workplace, such individuals make production more efficient.

Money is Power.

Education has also strengthened national defense. Like industries and businesses, the nation's defense system has been upgraded substantially over time. Highly skilled individuals have contributed to both the creation and refinement of sophisticated weaponry and communication systems. Other skilled individuals have seen to the proper use and maintenance of defense equipment.

As people have increased their levels of educational attainment, they have also increased their work options. The more marketable skills a person has, the more likely he or she is to find a job. High employment rates signal reduced numbers of welfare recipients and possibly more money for education. A repertoire of sophisticated skills also allows many individuals to seek and attain high-paying jobs. High salaries, in turn, increase purchasing power for both goods and services. One service in particular—health care—contributes significantly to general well-being and productivity.

When making a case for education spending, public leaders frequently point to connections between education and success in life and between lack of education and failure. "Would you prefer to pay to help a child learn how to read?" a candidate for public office might ask. "Or would you prefer to house an illiterate prisoner at three or four times the cost?" While these connections have not been established as causal in all situations—that is, illiteracy does not always lead to crime, just as education does not guarantee success—they obviously have some relationship.

Increased educational opportunities have also made democracy run more smoothly. Knowledge of history, geography, and the nation's and a community's cultural heritage enables people to gain a common perspective on current political and social problems. Development of language skills and interpersonal skills prepares people to communicate and work with others in the community and larger world to reach common goals. Education programs convey from generation to generation more and less effective ways for conducting social and political discourse in a free society (Guthrie, Garms, & Pierce, 1988). These outcomes are essential for a democracy and they make efforts to educate people worth the price.

Projections suggest that between 2001 and 2002, the nation will spend $257.7 billion on public elementary and secondary schools, excluding money spent on physical plants (National Center for Education Statistics, 1992). By anyone's standards, this amount represents a substantial investment in our nation's youth—but is it enough to ensure that school and college graduates are prepared to function in an increasingly complex world?

Simply getting information on education spending and payoff presents an imposing problem. Educational systems desperately need good information upon which to base spending decisions. George Strayer and Robert Haig (1923) recognized the problem years ago:

> In 1920 the [New York] State Department of Education called for reports which distributed current expenses among kindergartens, elementary schools [etc.]. . . . It was hoped that these figures would supply the exact information [on such intangible benefits as student learning] desired. Unfortunately, however, a careful check showed that only 18 out of 10,376 school systems submitted reports of the character prescribed. (p. 43)

Chester Finn (1991), education advisor to Republican administrations, argued that acquiring such information continues to be a pressing problem:

> Most of the data we need, we cannot get. Much of what we get, we cannot trust. Of that which we can trust, far too much is obsolete, unintelligible to laymen, or unsuited to crucial analyses and comparisons. So long as this situation endures, we will continue to inhabit a fools' paradise, bereft of the data about individual children and schools that would make possible true choice and accountability, never sure how our daughters and sons are doing, uncertain whether the country is making progress. (p. 263)

Today's economists tend to assess the value of education in terms of both public or social benefits and private returns. Many argue that the social benefits of education—reduced crime rate, inculcation of moral values, economic productivity—are most difficult to assess but also most important to achieve. Society as a whole, they contend, must benefit from money spent on public education because it requires redistribution of resources—taking money away from some to provide services to others.

People also view education as a means of developing human capital, much as businesses acquire and develop physical capital such as buildings and equipment (Becker, 1964; Schultz, 1981). These individuals believe the returns of education must accrue to both students and society. That is, students should have reason to expect that the time, effort, and money they invest in their education will yield some personal benefit, such as increased earnings and greater job satisfaction.

Personal and social gains are not mutually exclusive. Education yields both. When people learn, they become more valuable to their neighbors. When all the neighbors are improving themselves it makes the neighborhood—regardless of whether it is defined locally, regionally, or nationally—a better place for the individual.

Through the years, the challenge for policy makers has been to strike some balance among three dominant values (Guthrie, Garms, & Pierce, 1988). Although the relative importance of these values has waxed and waned at different times and in different locales, all have figured prominently in shaping public education:

- Equality, or equal education opportunity, has typically been defined in terms of providing equal access to schooling, making available to every student educational treatment tailored to his or her strengths and weaknesses, and ensuring that all students acquire at least minimum or basic skills.

- Efficiency connotes getting the maximum benefit from dollars spent on education.

- Liberty or choice implies control over where, how, and for what purposes students are educated.

HOW DO LOCAL COMMUNITIES FUND PUBLIC EDUCATION?

In the majority of states, the local portion of schools' funds is derived almost exclusively from **local property taxes** (mostly taxes on land and improvements). A community's ability to pay for education is dependent on its real assets, that is, on the assessed value of its property. To determine this figure, appraisers estimate the price property would bring if placed on the market. This market value is then converted to an assessed value by using a predetermined ratio, which in the majority of states is now set at 100%.

Property Taxes

Even though most local funds are raised through property taxes, these taxes are widely criticized. One criticism of property taxes is that homeowners shoulder a disproportionate amount of the cost for funding education. Lack of uniformity in schedules for conducting property assessments creates other inequities. While some communities reassess property every year, others reassess every 3rd or 4th year. If the economy fluctuates greatly from year to year, some taxpayers pay more or less than their fair share of taxes because their property assessments remain the same over a long period of time. Furthermore, when localities within a state use different rates of assessment, a rich municipality having a low assessment rate may raise as much revenue or more than a property-poor area having a higher tax rate. Differences in revenue for education lead ultimately to educational inequalities.

Another concern about property taxes is that valuation procedures are inexact. When determining the market value of a house in a subdivision, assessors typically set a value based on what the house would sell for if it were on the market. This value is influenced in large part by recent sales of similar homes in the neighborhood. Such a strategy is difficult to use, however, in neighborhoods where houses vary greatly in age, size, and style. Assessment methods are also problematic in high-priced housing areas where real estate activity is minimal. When there are no benchmarks, some properties may be undervalued, thus masking the wealth of some districts (Cohn & Geske, 1990).

> "[D]istricts that face the toughest challenges are also those [with] the fewest funds to meet their children's needs."

Property taxes, of course, are used to meet other than educational needs. This may be more problematic in some areas than others, particularly in cities where tax-exempt property (e.g., public buildings, churches, government property, and parks) can be a large part of the total. Cities, particularly those in high crime areas, incur many expenses that suburbs either do not face or face on a more modest scale:

> Police expenditures are higher in crime-ridden cities than in most suburban towns. Fire department costs are also higher where dilapidated housing, often with substandard wiring, and arson-for-profit are familiar problems. Public health expenditures are also higher where poor people cannot pay for private hospitals. All of these expenditures compete with those for public schools. So the districts that face the toughest challenges are also likely to be those that have the fewest funds to meet their children's needs. (Kozol, 1991, p. 56)

Cities often provide services funded from property taxes to people who work in the city but live in the suburbs. When it snows, for example, the city must plow the streets so people can get to work. Thus, cities usually have a line item in the annual budget to cover snow removal and other services. While workers who live in the suburbs benefit from the plowing of city streets, they do not support this activity with their own property taxes. The customers who drive from their homes in the suburbs into the city to shop do not pay to plow the streets either. While snow removal benefits many people, it drains the coffers of money that could be earmarked for inner-city schools.

Rural districts, too, can face considerable financial hardship because of higher per pupil costs and other factors (Appalachia Educational Laboratory, 1990; Verstegen, 1990a). When a rural district must build a new school, for example, it is forced to spread the cost of a building over relatively few taxpayers.

To ease such inequities and the burden on property taxes, the trend in recent years has been to replace declining local revenues with state aid to the extent that state aid now surpasses the amount of money raised by local authorities. As illustrated in Figure 12.1, public schools are financed primarily by states (49%), localities (44%), and the federal government (6%).

As of 1991, 11,869 (77%) of the 15,437 school boards in the United States have taxing authority (Szakal & Melton, 1991). In economically troubled times, however, few political leaders, at any governmental level, are willing to risk the ire of voters by raising taxes to raise revenue for the operation of schools. The chances for success of such a maneuver are diminished even further by the fact that more and more taxpayers (because of their advancing age) no longer have children in the public schools. In 1994, however, Michigan legislators bucked conventional wisdom and replaced property taxes as the source of revenue for public schools with a 2% increase in the state sales tax.

Understanding School District Budgets

The best way to understand local finance of public schools is to study a school district budget. Most school boards control such things as the staffing of local schools and types of programs that are offered to students via the

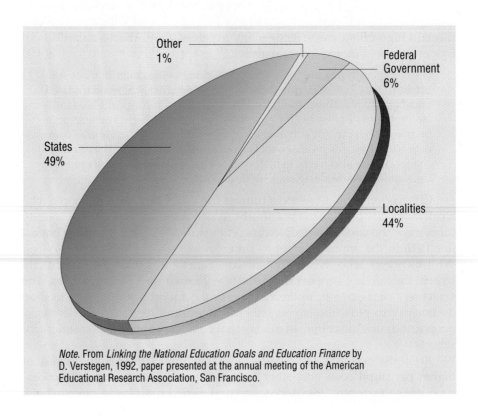

FIGURE 12.1

Sources of Revenues for School Funding

Note. From *Linking the National Education Goals and Education Finance* by D. Verstegen, 1992, paper presented at the annual meeting of the American Educational Research Association, San Francisco.

budget, so the budget represents a concrete statement of local values. To separate rhetoric about educational values from reality, look at a budget.

School districts develop long-term financial plans that represent predictions about the future. District employees craft a new budget for each fiscal year. A **fiscal year** is a 12-month period covered by the annual budget and is set by the school district. The time period can and often does correspond with the state's fiscal year. Unlike an academic year or calendar year, the fiscal year typically begins one summer (e.g., July 1, 1998) and ends the next (June 30, 1999). Once an annual budget is adopted by local officials or approved by the voters, it guides school administrators' actions.

Who makes these plans, and how are they set in place? In most localities, the budget adoption process involves a number of steps:

1. District administrators led by the superintendent analyze needs and costs, set policies for the coming year, and plan an initial draft of the budget.

2. District administrators discuss this draft with the school board in one or more meetings.

3. District administrators publish a proposed budget, which is made available for public study.

4. The school board holds one or more public hearings at which they receive comments from citizens on the proposed budget.

5. The school board adopts an official budget, based on the proposed budget but with amendments it deems necessary.

6. In some districts, the school board vote is the final decision. In other districts, the budget must then be approved by elected officials or by voter referendum.

7. A budget which has received final approval takes effect in the district. (U.S. Department of Education, 1989)

In other areas, such as Chicago, Illinois, where site-based management is the norm, people are experimenting with **school-based budgeting**. In school-based budgeting, as the term implies, responsibility for allocating resources at the building level is fixed at the building level, rather than at the level of central administration (Wohlstetter & Buffett, 1992). Teachers, parents, and principals are often involved in making decisions about how money is spent on hiring staff, on professional development for staff, and on goods and services.

Advocates of school-based budgeting think efficiency will likely improve if decision-making authority is placed close to those who actually do the work (Levin, 1987). Budgeting, then, becomes responsive to the needs of those most immediately affected. School-based budgeting may also make it easier to hold people accountable for spending and for the results they produce, thereby helping to control costs. When William Clune and Paula White (1988) studied 100 school districts undertaking school-based management, they found that budget decisions, in contrast to personnel and curricular decisions, were among those most readily decentralized.

Citizens and taxpayers have a big say in the size and distribution of school budgets. Funding school districts is a complex process of negotiation.

Typically, crafting and adopting school budgets are processes of negotiation. Many people (e.g., taxpayers, teachers, administrators, and special interest groups) have a stake in where the money to run schools comes from and where it goes. A school budget, then, represents a balance of values. It is a political document formed from compromise, one that should provide adequately for the educational needs of its constituents.

When establishing their budgets, school officials sometimes justify only the increase that exceeds the previous year's request. In such instances, what the school district is spending is usually accepted as necessary. On occasion, however, schools have been asked to make a case for their entire appropriation request each year. This process is referred to as **zero-based** budgeting (Pyhrr, 1973). While zero-based budgeting has not gained widespread use, analyzing and reporting of past and budgeted expenditures on a program basis is common among districts (Hentschke et al., 1986).

Once a budget is set, plans for spending may change for a number of reasons: enrollment figures may be higher or lower than projected, unexpected weather may affect utility bills, and unforeseen events (e.g., flooding of a school gymnasium during a heavy rain) may require emergency maintenance. School administrators sometimes have the authority to transfer dollars from one line item to another to take care of unforeseen needs. In other districts, administrators must first consult with the school board before making changes. When changes in budget are made, however, federal regulations prohibit the removal of money from federal grants designed to benefit particular groups of students or programs.

Most school districts use line-item budgets to explain their financial plans. These budgets include a beginning balance for the year, estimates of revenue by source, planned expenditures, and a projected balance at the end of the year. Sources of revenue may include moneys from federal, state, county or parish, and city government; income from local taxes or from the sale of bonds; fees for meals and for use of sports facilities; and private donations expected during the year. Income often is earmarked for use with particular groups of students (e.g., students with disabilities) or special programs (e.g., library support or school nurse programs).

Planned expenditures are the most detailed portion of a school budget. As illustrated in Table 12.1, there are a number of educational expenditures a school system may incur. In some states, regulations dictate which categories are to be listed in a budget; in other states, local districts have the autonomy to create line items as they see fit. Generally, districts categorize expenses in terms of "functions" (broad categories of purposes such as instruction and support to be served by spending) and "objects" (specific things to be paid for, such as personnel salaries and benefits).

TABLE 12.1 A Sample of Actual and Proposed School Budget Items

	Fiscal Year 1990 proposed budget	Fiscal Year 1989 actual budget
Instruction		
Salaries	$2,550,000	$2,350,000
Benefits	200,000	200,000
Purchased services	50,000	50,000
Supplies	100,000	150,000
Property	300,000	300,000
Total instruction	3,200,000	3,050,000
Support		
Salaries	1,100,000	900,000
Benefits	100,000	100,000
Purchased services	150,000	50,000
Supplies	100,000	150,000
Property	150,000	100,000
Total support	1,600,000	1,300,000
Noninstructional services		
Salaries	50,000	100,000
Benefits	5,000	10,000
Supplies	15,000	30,000
Property	40,000	50,000
Total noninstructional	110,000	190,000
Facilities		
Salaries	150,000	120,000
Benefits	15,000	12,000
Supplies	200,000	120,000
Property	135,000	48,000
Total facilities	500,000	300,000
Total expenditures	$5,410,000	$4,840,000

Note. From *Making Sense of School Budgets* (p. 15) by U.S. Department of Education, 1989, Washington, DC: Office of Educational Research and Improvement.

Besides providing line-item budgets for functions and objects, some districts also publish a program budget statement that includes revenues and expenditures for major activities called programs. These budgets may identify separately the amount of money to be spent on special programs for regular elementary and secondary education students, on programs for children with special needs, and on fine arts programs. Program budget statements may also include data relevant to noninstructional programs, such as transportation and food services.

The biggest item in any school budget is personnel. As indicated in Table 12.1, salaries and benefits for both instructional and noninstructional staff (e.g., teachers, administrators, support staff, and maintenance workers) compose the largest portion of planned expenditures. It is not surprising, then, that salaries are often a bone of contention in communities across the country.

Table 12.2 contains information on school administrators' salaries. As the data indicate, salaries tend to vary directly with the size of a system; that is, the larger the school district, the higher the salaries. Disparities in salaries may occur because the demands larger systems place on administrators are potentially greater. For example, there is a marked contrast between the job of chancellor of the New York City public schools (a sort of super-superintendent) and the job of superintendent of public schools in Table Rock, Nebraska. When comparisons are not quite so extreme, however, large differences in salaries are more difficult to understand. They may represent a prestige factor more than account for any real differences in responsibilities or in local revenue available to finance education.

As illustrated in Table 12.2, size of salary also varies directly with the level of schooling—junior high school principals make more than elementary school principals, and high school principals make more than junior high school principals. Superintendents are the most highly paid people in a system.

One could, however, make a convincing case for turning the pay system upside down, or at the very least, equalizing pay among principals. Possibilities for making the greatest educational gains exist in the early grades. If a system invested more heavily in leadership talent in elementary schools than it did in junior high and high schools, it might measure the investment in higher student performance and fewer educational problems later.

As described in Chapter 1, there is considerable regional variation in teachers' salaries. It is important to remember, however, that averages mask considerable variation within states. Wealthy communities having solid tax bases can afford to pay higher salaries to attract and to retain teachers than can low-income districts. At the same time, variation in the cost of living may cancel differences in teachers' salaries from district to district.

The quarterly report by the American Chamber of Commerce Researchers Association (ACCRA) provides some insight about the average cost of living in different parts of the United States. For example, the cost of living index (a composite of the relative costs of groceries, housing, utilities, transportation, health care, and miscellaneous goods and services) is

TABLE 12.2   Mean of Mean Salaries Paid Selected Administrators in Reporting School Systems, by Enrollment Group, 1990–91

Position or Function (Full-time staff)	Size of Enrollment Group				
	25,000 or More	10,000 to 24,999	2,500 to 9,999	300 to 2,499	Total—All Reporting Systems
Superintendents (contract salary)	$100,720	$84,883	$78,436	$67,139	$79,874
Principals					
Elementary School	52,985	51,984	52,457	48,798	51,453
Jr. High/Middle school	56,201	55,472	56,338	51,383	55,083
Sr. High School	61,442	60,717	60,979	53,251	59,106

Note: From ERS Report: Salaries Paid Professional Personnel in Public Schools, 1990–91 (p. 9) by Educational Research Service, 1991), Arlington, VA: ERS. Copyright 1991 by ERS. Reprinted by permission.

130.1% in Long Beach, California, versus 88.3% in Tulsa, Oklahoma (ACCRA, 1992). According to ACCRA's formula for calculating the impact of cost of living differences, a teacher moving from Tulsa to Long Beach would likely have to spend an additional 47.3% of after-tax income to maintain his or her current standard of living (100*[(130.1 − 88.3)/88.3] = 47.3). Although the average teacher salary in California is $15,000 more than it is in Oklahoma, then, cost of living differences would lessen the discrepancy in pay.

As described in Chapter 1, years of experience in a school system and teachers' educational backgrounds also account for some of the variation in teachers' salaries. In Colorado, the average base salary for a teacher with a bachelor's degree and no experience is $17,001 while the average salary for a teacher with a master's degree and no experience is about $18,919. Teachers in Colorado who have master's degrees and at least 20 years experience average $27,169 (National Center for Education Statistics, 1993). In areas of the country where educators reward teachers with incentive income, or merit pay, disparities in teachers' salaries become even larger.

What does the public think about teachers' salaries? Data in Figure 12.2 indicate that half of the people surveyed in 1990 thought teachers' salaries were too low. Asked whether increasing teachers' salaries might improve the quality of education in schools, about 51% responded affirmatively. It is significant that opinions did not vary between those with and without children in school nor between parents of children in public and private schools.

FIGURE 12.2

What Does the Public Think about Teachers' Salaries?

Source: Elam, S.M. (1990, September). The 22nd Annual Gallup Poll of the public's attitudes toward the pubic schools. *Phi Delta Kappan, 72,* 41–55. Used by permission.

Do you think salaries for teachers in this community are too high, too low, or just about right?	National totals %	No children in school %	Public school parents %	Nonpublic school parents %
Too high	5	5	3	1
Too low	50	49	54	54
Just about right	31	31	32	34
No opinion	14	15	11	11

HOW DO STATES FUND PUBLIC EDUCATION?

The major source of funding for public schools is derived from the state. Between 1920 and 1993, state aid to education increased from an average of 16.5% to 47.3% of total spending (National Center for Education Statistics, 1992). Funds earmarked for education are procured from a variety of sources.

State Sales Taxes

Only Alaska, Delaware, Montana, New Hampshire, and Oregon have no sales taxes. (The majority of their educational funds are derived from income or property taxes.) The other 45 states, however, did have general sales taxes, with rates varying from 3% in Colorado and Wyoming to 7% in Rhode Island. Of the 45 states, 31 permitted cities and/or counties to add local sales taxes to state sales taxes. New York City, for example, charged 4.25% in addition to the New York State sales tax of 4% for a total rate of 8.25% (U.S. Advisory Commission on Intergovernmental Relations, 1992).

Sales taxes have great appeal because they are relatively easy and cheap to administer. Retailers collect sales taxes at the point of sale, and the state need only deal directly with retailers instead of collecting from individuals as in the case of personal income taxes. Sales taxes raise large sums of money. The more money people earn, the more they spend, and the more revenue is collected. To ease the burden on the poor and the elderly, some items, such as food and drugs, can be exempt from sales taxes. Sales taxes, particularly on luxury items, are also relatively easy to raise. It can be politically palatable to raise money on so-called sin taxes, or taxes on cigarettes and alcohol. From 1983 to 1987, across the 50 states, taxes on cigarettes were increased 63 times and on alcoholic beverages 32 times (Webb, 1990).

Sales taxes, however, also have drawbacks. As long as the economy expands, and more money is generated from retail sales, people come to expect that there will always be plenty of money. When retail sales decline, however, and there is less money rather than more, the downward adjustment in support for all public services, including education, can be painful. In addition, as more necessities are subject to taxation, sales taxes require people having limited incomes to spend a greater percentage of their income on taxes, particularly on taxes placed on food, than wealthy people spend. This is referred to as **regressive taxation** (Burrup & Brimley, 1982).

State Income Taxes

State income taxes, both personal and corporate, are another source of revenue for education. Unlike sales taxes, income taxes are a form of **progressive taxation**; that is, people pay more as they earn more. But income taxes are only part of a state's education finance system, which is often a hodgepodge of revenue-producing and revenue-spending strategies.

Every state's financial situation is unique in some way, but in the 1990s, the battle over raising taxes and cutting services has been common to most states. Connecticut provides an especially useful example because it did not have an income tax until 1991. Public debate about establishing this tax helped frame the issues. The necessity of balancing the state budget required, in the minds of the governor, the legislature, and many citizens, a stronger source of income to underwrite basic services—education, roads, prisons, and health care.

In 1992, Connecticut had to face the problem that new money raised from the income tax, combined with cuts in public services, was still insufficient to meet the demands for basic services and to reduce its budget deficit at the same time. Unlike the federal government, Connecticut could not print more money with which to pay its bills. Like many other states, it suffered from the economic recession—less business meant less money collected from all its taxes. Connecticut, like other states, also suffered from diminishing federal aid. Yet it had to respond to federally mandated programs, such as Medicaid, which required major commitments of funds. The problem of too much money going out and too little coming in forced state leaders in Connecticut and elsewhere to make difficult choices about where to spend their limited revenues.

State Lotteries and Other Sources

Other sources of state aid for education include estate and inheritance taxes, miscellaneous user fees, licenses, severance taxes—fees for the privilege of extracting natural resources from land or water—and lotteries.

Early attempts to establish state lotteries were cumbersome and largely unsuccessful. New Hampshire, a state that had neither a sales tax nor an income tax, established a state lottery in 1964 to support public education and to hold down property taxes. New York followed in 1967. Neither state raised as much money as it had expected because the lotteries were too costly and burdensome. Tickets cost several dollars each, buyers had to register, and drawings were held only twice a year.

In the 1970s, other states instituted lotteries having streamlined procedures and more frequent payoffs. By 1990, 30 states and the District of Columbia had lotteries that, combined, put billions of dollars into state coffers, but only a small percentage of this money went for state aid to education. In the spring of 1992, Texas became the 35th state to institute a lottery.

> **In twelve states, revenues from state lotteries are used to help support public schools.**

Lotteries have been criticized as being inefficient ways to raise money (Webb, 1990). They are also frowned upon as being an immoral way to raise money, even though the cause may be just. After payoffs, however, the profit margin is immense. An average of about 39% of the money collected ends up in the state treasury.

Funding Formulas

In response to public outcries heard during the early part of the twentieth century, leaders in education finance argued that state aid for education should be given to cities and towns. They reasoned that disparities in local funding denied equal educational opportunities for all students. States now provide financial aid to school districts using variations of the following basic plans (Cohn & Geske, 1990; Verstegen, 1990c).

Flat Grants   **Flat grants** are either uniform or variable in nature. States that provide uniform flat grants usually give equal amounts of money on a per student basis to districts, regardless of district needs or financial capacity. States that use variable flat grants try to compensate for differing classroom needs. Typically, these needs are weighted to give more money to schools having more expensive services. For example, high schools with vocational programs can command more money than elementary schools. More aid may also be given to districts having high demands for bilingual or special education classes.

Foundation Program   When using a **foundation program**, the state guarantees a certain amount of money for educational expenditures (by pupil or by classroom) and determines what proportion of that cost, usually based on a mandated property tax rate, should be shouldered by localities. The required local rate is usually expressed in terms of "mills." A millage rate is the amount of property tax dollars to be paid for each $1,000 of assessed valuation. Foundation funding varies inversely with community wealth; that is, in poorer communities where revenue from property taxes is low the state contributes more money than in affluent communities where revenue is high. Local leeway allows school districts to supplement state contributions with local revenues. It is still possible, however, that inequalities in **per-pupil expenditures**—that is, money allocated for educational services divided by the number of pupils to be served—will vary from district to district.

District Power Equalization   Under a **district power equalization** plan, localities establish the tax rate for educational spending and the state guarantees a set amount of money proportional to local revenue. As in the foundation program, the state augments local revenue if it comes up short of the state guarantee. This program, then, does not attempt to equalize expenditures on education; it merely equalizes access to funds for expenditures.

Full State Funding   Hawaii, operating as a one-district state, provides **full state funding** for its schools. The state pays all educational expenses through a statewide tax. In this plan, then, all funding is equal and all taxation is equal because the source of funds for education comes from statewide taxes. Although this plan is the most egalitarian in nature, the desire for local autonomy causes many districts to reject an option of full state funding.

Because many students have learning needs that require special attention, some states also incorporate weighting schemes in their state aid programs. That is, they assign weighted values to students according to estimated program costs for educating them. For example, regular education students may be weighted 1.0, compared with special education students, who may be weighted 1.5 or more, depending on their educational needs. Students at different grade levels may also carry varying weights. In some districts in Florida, one of 27 states that use weighting schemes, students in grades 1 through 3 are weighted 1.234, in grades 4 through 9 they have an index of 1.00, and in grades 9 through 12 their weight is 1.116 (Cohn & Geske, 1990).

According to James Ward (1992), although the various state funding formulas are intended to provide some standardization of educational quality among communities, formulas are unable to accomplish this goal for at least two reasons: (a) the level of funding from the state is seldom high enough to level the playing field, and (b) localities have discretion in setting local property tax rates for schools. James Ward contends that in many instances, "politics of privilege and exclusion (p. 246)" get in the way of changing inequalities. That is, more affluent school districts that are able to support high levels of education without much assistance from the state are reluctant to shoulder increased state taxes to benefit other districts in the state. Nor do such communities want to give up control of their ability to levy taxes, for to do so potentially reduces their ability to maintain a position of privilege (Ward, 1992, p. 246).

As illustrated in Figure 12.3, per-pupil expenditures vary greatly from state to state. Results from the 25th Annual Phi Delta Kappan/Gallup Poll indicate that people are aware of the differences, and, in contrast to what Ward (1992) contends, are willing to do something to correct the situation. For the first time since 1971, respondents listed "inadequate funding" as number one among the "biggest problems" in the public schools. More specifically, 88% of those polled said that the amount of money allocated in their state should be the same for all students, regardless of whether they live in poor or wealthy school districts. A total of 85% were in favor of taking money from wealthy districts and giving it to poor districts to achieve equality of funding. Furthermore, 68% indicated a willingness to pay more taxes to bring schools in poorer states and communities up to standard (Elam, Rose, & Gallup, 1993).

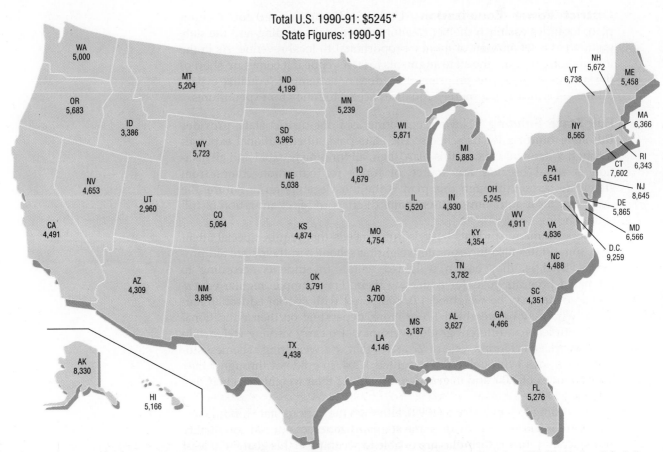

Total U.S. 1990-91: $5245*
State Figures: 1990-91

Note. From *Digest of Education Statistics* (p. 163) by U.S. Department of Education, National Center for Education Statistics, 1993, Washington, D.C.: Author.
*Constant U.S. dollars, based on the Consumer Price Index. Data do not reflect differences in inflation rates from state to state.

FIGURE 12.3

Expenditure Per Pupil in Average Daily Attendance in Public Elementary and Secondary Schools, by State: 1990–1991

Cultural Awareness

A national survey of teachers of fourth-grade students suggests that the amount of instructional materials and resources available for teaching varies according to the economic level of students:

> In schools with the largest percent of poor students, the teachers of 59 percent of the students say they get only some or none of the instructional materials and resources they seek, compared with just 16% in schools without poor students. For schools with *no* children below the poverty line, the teachers of 25 percent of students get *all* the instructional materials they seek. The percentage declines as the proportion of poor students rises. In schools where 30 percent or more of the students are poor, the teachers of just 12 percent of students get all the resources they seek. (Educational Testing Service, 1991, p. 11)

John Augenblick and his colleagues (1990) contend that good tax policy is that which yields a relatively balanced system among the sales, income, and property taxes collected because:

- [I]t helps to keep tax rates low (which is desirable, because high tax rates tend to distort location decisions).

- It often will make the tax system more stable, because when it is diversified it is less subject to swings in particular tax bases.

- It often will be fairer and distort resource use less than an unbalanced tax system because it tends to "average out" the defects of each tax. (Every tax has some undesirable features, but if no tax is used excessively, these bad features are not as serious.) (p. 11)

HOW DOES THE FEDERAL GOVERNMENT FUND PUBLIC EDUCATION?

True or false: The United States spends a larger proportion of its wealth on education, from kindergarten through college, than most other advanced countries.

False. The United States spends a smaller proportion of its wealth on schools than do nearly two thirds of the world's most advanced countries (Nelson, 1991; Verstegen, 1992b). The American Federation of Teachers (1991) reported that the United States spends 5.1% of its Gross National Product (GNP) on education—a consequence that places the United States in 10th position among 15 developed nations. (See Figure 12.4.) Denmark spends 7.6% of its GNP, putting it in first place. West Germany in 15th position spent 4.5% of its GNP. Deborah Verstegen (1992b) concurs, analyzing the results of all major studies available at the time.

Only three countries had larger pupil-teacher ratios than the United States (18.7 students to 1 teacher). The United States had the second largest average elementary school enrollments (352 per school). The 15-country average was 186 pupils per school with a pupil to teacher ratio of 15.8 to 1.

True or false: If people spent more money they could solve their educational problems.

Maybe, maybe not. The same survey revealed that Japan—a frequent point of comparison in recent years because of its favorable connection between productivity and educational expenditures—spent a smaller percentage of its wealth on education than did the United States. Japan also had the largest average school enrollments (412 pupils per school). Educational insiders and outsiders agree that if money is spent inefficiently gain in educational benefits is unlikely to occur.

If there is insufficient money to provide adequately for educational needs, however, it is impossible to solve problems and to be efficient. David Berliner, an educational researcher, has asserted that comparisons with Japan have been used tendentiously to suggest that their educational system is superior to the U.S. system. Instead, he argues that "the evidence is quite clear that the Japanese public school system is a brutal and an enor-

FIGURE 12.4

Government Spending for Education

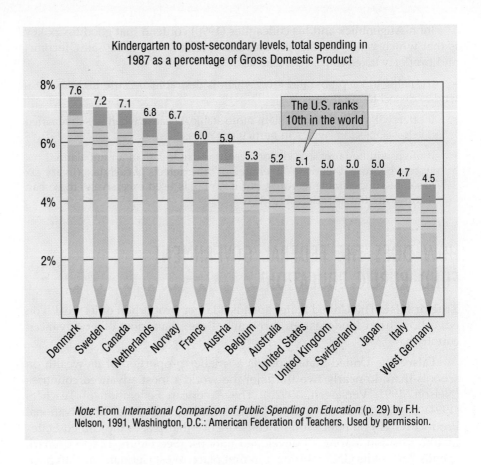

Kindergarten to post-secondary levels, total spending in 1987 as a percentage of Gross Domestic Product

The U.S. ranks 10th in the world

Denmark 7.6, Sweden 7.2, Canada 7.1, Netherlands 6.8, Norway 6.7, France 6.0, Austria 5.9, Belgium 5.3, Australia 5.2, United States 5.1, United Kingdom 5.0, Switzerland 5.0, Japan 5.0, Italy 4.7, West Germany 4.5

Note: From *International Comparison of Public Spending on Education* (p. 29) by F.H. Nelson, 1991, Washington, D.C.: American Federation of Teachers. Used by permission.

mous failure by most of the standards we as a nation have for schooling, save one, achievement in mathematics and science" (Berliner, 1992, p. 2).

Trends in Federal Support for Education

In recent years, there have been fluctuations in spending on education at the federal, state, and local levels. Figure 12.5 illustrates trends in total federal support for education between 1965 and 1993. For elementary and secondary schools, support rose by 1% between 1975 and 1980, declined by 21% between 1980 and 1985, then rose 41% between 1985 and 1993. Federal support for colleges and universities (excluding research) also fluctuated, increasing from $6 billion in 1965 to $18 billion in 1975, dropping to $14 billion in 1991, then increasing to $17 billion in 1993. Funding for university research increased across time while funding for other educational programs remained somewhat constant.

The **National Center for Education Statistics** (1992), an arm of the executive branch responsible for collecting and analyzing education statistics for the nation, reported that the total federal support for education in fiscal year (FY) 1993 was $68.4 billion. As illustrated in Figure 12.6, a substantial

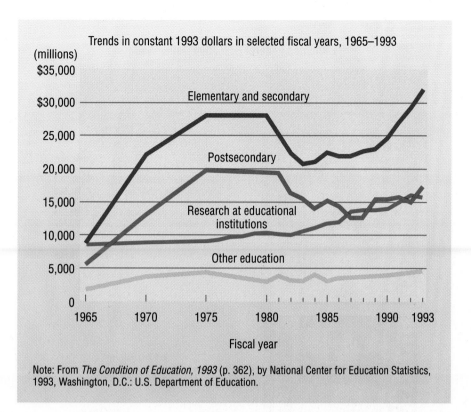

Trends in constant 1993 dollars in selected fiscal years, 1965–1993

FIGURE 12.5

Federal On-Budget Support for Education, by Category

Note: From *The Condition of Education, 1993* (p. 362), by National Center for Education Statistics, 1993, Washington, D.C.: U.S. Department of Education.

portion of that money went to elementary and secondary education programs. Specifically, 46% was allocated to elementary and secondary education, 25% was earmarked to postsecondary expenses, 23% went to research, and 6% went to "other" education programs including libraries, museums, cultural activities, and miscellaneous research. Funds were distributed not only through the Department of Education but also via the Departments of Health and Human Services, Agriculture, Defense, Energy, and Labor, as well as through the National Science Foundation.

In the spring of 1991, President George Bush and his secretary of education presented their vision of the role of the federal government in the form of a report entitled "AMERICA 2000: An Education Strategy." As described in Chapter 5, the plan consisted of four parts: making schools more accountable through the establishment of a new national system of testing, creating at least 545 new schools nationwide, improving adult education, and exhorting communities to adopt the national goals for education. The president requested $690 million for the strategy in the 1992 federal budget, but the proposal was substantially revised by Congress to focus on all schools, not just the 545 new ones, which composed only 1% of the nation's schools.

In President Bill Clinton's proposed 1994 budget, there was evidence of continued interest in the establishment of world class standards in mathe-

FIGURE 12.6

Estimated Federal Education Dollar, 1993

What proportion of the federal budget goes to elementary and secondary education?

Source: The Condition of Education, 1993 (p. 365), National Center for Education Statistics, Washington, DC: U.S. Department of Education.

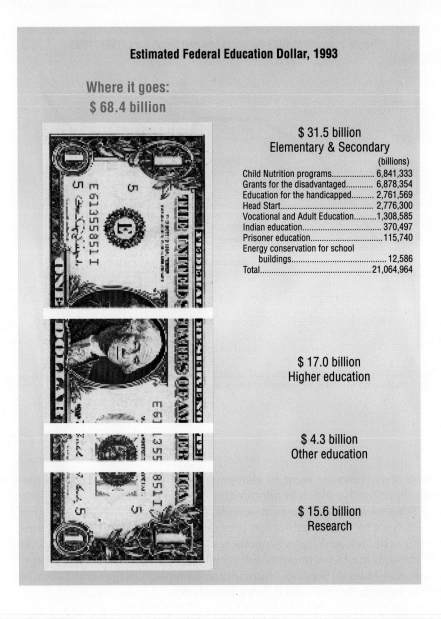

Estimated Federal Education Dollar, 1993

Where it goes:
$ 68.4 billion

$ 31.5 billion
Elementary & Secondary

	(billions)
Child Nutrition programs	6,841,333
Grants for the disadvantaged	6,878,354
Education for the handicapped	2,761,569
Head Start	2,776,300
Vocational and Adult Education	1,308,585
Indian education	370,497
Prisoner education	115,740
Energy conservation for school buildings	12,586
Total	21,064,964

$ 17.0 billion
Higher education

$ 4.3 billion
Other education

$ 15.6 billion
Research

matics and science and other subjects. One line item in Clinton's education-reform bill allocated money for a system of national standards and assessments for grades kindergarten through 12. The budget also included an ambitious plan for increasing participation in Head Start programs. Clinton proposed boosting the Head Start budget by $10 billion over 5 years in order to eventually provide educational services to all eligible preschool children in the nation. Among other programs for which Clinton sought funding were school clinics; school-to-work programs; a national telecommunications network that would link schools, libraries, and other public institutions with individual homes; and educational research, statistics, and assessment (West, 1993; Miller, 1993). When Clinton finally signed the Goals 2000: Educate America Act in March 1994, the centerpiece of the bill was

BENCHMARKS

Federal Government Funding of Education: Patterns and Trends

1785–1887   Northwest Ordinances of 1785 and 1787 and the Morrill Acts of 1862 and 1890 stimulate the establishment of schools through land grants.

1887–1917   The Hatch Act and the Smith-Lever Agricultural Extension Act establish land-grant college extension services across the nation to improve agriculture and industry.

1917–1935   Smith-Hughes Act marks first federal financial aid to public schools below the college level. Funds earmarked for vocational programs, including homemaking. Other acts fund vocational rehabilitation for veterans of foreign wars.

1935–1944   Congressional acts to cope with the Great Depression fund programs that benefit education, such as the Agricultural Adjustment Act, Civilian Conservation Corps, National Youth Administration, Federal Emergency Relief Administration, Public Works Administration, and Federal Surplus Commodities Corporation.

1944–1964   G. I. Bill of Rights assists the education of World War II veterans. Benefits extended to Korean War veterans in 1952 and to Vietnam War veterans in 1966. Federal funding increases for educational programs that contribute to national defense and economic security, such as the Vocational Education Act of 1963, the Manpower Development and Training Act, and the International Education Act. One of the most important is the National Defense Education Act of 1958, which extends financial aid to college students and funds research centers, foreign language study, and experimentation with media.

1964–1994   Congress funds equal educational opportunity programs and services as part of the Civil Rights Movement and War on Poverty. Federal funding also increases for higher education, adult education, elementary and secondary education, special education, teacher education, and for the attainment of the national education goals.

$400 million a year to provide grants to states and districts that adopt education reform plans.

The Nature of Federal Aid

As described in Chapter 11, the federal government first allocated funds for education through the Northwest Ordinances of 1785 and 1787. Since that time, although federal funds compose only a small amount of funding for education, there have been several instances of federal assistance to education. Federal funding for education takes many forms: (a) major grant programs established through legislation such as the Vocational Act of 1963 (more recently the Carl Perkins Vocational Education Act of 1984) and the Education for All Handicapped Children Act of 1975 (more recently the

Individuals with Disabilities Education Act of 1990), (b) aid to localities where there are large federal installations, such as military bases, and (c) **categorical grants** for funding of education programs designed for particular groups and specific purposes. Examples include bilingual education (provided through the Bilingual Education Act of 1972) and compensatory programs for low-income children, such as Project Head Start, which was created in 1964, and Title I (now called Chapter I) of the Elementary and Secondary Education Act of 1965.

Sometimes several education programs are grouped together as a **block grant** to localities. Chapter Two of the 1981 **Education Consolidation and Improvement Act (ECIA)** combined 32 previously enacted education programs under one block grant that state and local education agencies could use for general education purposes. With this particular block grant, funds are allocated to states based on a student population formula. States then prepare a plan for using federal funds based on district enrollment or on measures of student need. Finally, the state gives money to localities for use in whichever programs need additional services (Guthrie, Garms, & Pierce, 1988).

Regardless of what type of federal funding a school district receives, the district is obligated to comply with federal guidelines when spending grant money. In the event a school district does not comply, that is, either does not spend the money the federal government allocates or misspends the money, one of several things can happen: the school system can be forced to return the money, it can be fined, and/or it can be debarred from receiving any federal funds in the future.

HOW ARE PRIVATE SCHOOLS FINANCED?

Using public funds to support private schools has long been a contentious issue. Historically, paying for private schooling has been a private matter. If parents wanted their children to be educated in a certain manner, inculcated with particular values, and associated with certain other children, they paid for these privileges themselves. Those who could afford to send their children to private schools have continued to pay their taxes, which in turn have supported public schools.

While some private schools have developed and maintained their reputations by appealing to the moneyed elite of society, others have attracted people from across the socioeconomic spectrum. The largest alternative school system in the United States, the Catholic schools, has both high- and low-income students. Catholic schools may offer tuition endowments to encourage students from families with low incomes to attend. Other private schools, both religious and nonsectarian, may also do so. Many parents over the years, even those who could least afford to do so, have been willing to sacrifice economically to send their children to private schools.

> Even in the inner cities, Catholic schools have been successful in attracting—and educating—children from poor and minority families willing to bear the cost. The sacrifice is often heavy: high school tuition can approach $4,000 [annually]. Nevertheless, minority enrollment in the Catholic system is now 23% of the total, double what it was 20 years ago. . . . (Allis, 1991, p. 48)

The largest alternative school system in the United States is operated by the Roman Catholic Church. Some services provided to students by Catholic schools are publicly funded, but the debate over using tax revenues to finance private and parochial education continues.

In the 1980s and 1990s, the debate about public support for private elementary and secondary schools has taken on renewed vigor, focusing in part on tuition tax credits, tax deductions, and vouchers. The idea of using **vouchers**, or scrip, to purchase public education was first offered by economist Milton Friedman in 1955. He argued that local government ought to create vouchers that provided parents with a sum of money in the form of scrip to pay for each of their children's education. Parents should be free to spend this money at any school they chose, as long as it met minimum governmental standards. "Such schools would be conducted under a variety of auspices: by private enterprises operated for profit, non-profit institutions established by private endowment, religious bodies, and some even by governmental units" (Friedman, 1955, p. 144). In 1993, the voucher notion appeared on the ballot in California and was a central factor in debate about restructuring education finance in Michigan.

A **tuition tax credit** allows a taxpayer to subtract educational costs from taxes owed. A **tuition tax deduction** allows a taxpayer to subtract educational costs from taxable income before computing taxes. Both credits and deductions are similar to vouchers in that they are designed to give parents at least part of the money they spend on private schooling for their children (Raywid, 1987). The appeal to parents who do so is obvious. The argument from those against such plans is that credits and deductions may encourage people to flee the public schools, leaving the public system—a system for the poor, who cannot afford to pay up front for the cost of education and wait to receive a deduction later.

As we noted in Chapter 11, the Tenth Amendment to the Constitution reserves the power to educate for the states; thus, tuition tax credits, deductions, and vouchers are state matters. If these or other devices are instituted, they must meet with state approval. Even if states adopt new funding mechanisms, they cannot contravene federal law in the process. For example, if a plan were enacted that worked to deny persons their civil rights, the plan would be ruled unconstitutional by federal courts. If vouchers, deductions, and tuition tax credits continue to be part of the public debate on public and private education in the years to come, court challenges will surely ensue. Issues of the separation of church and state and of the possible establishment of a religion by allowing public funds to be spent on private schools will continue to make private schools a focus of public interest.

HOW HAVE THE COURTS INFLUENCED SCHOOL FINANCE?

There are wide variations in expenditures and revenues among school districts across the country and within states. In some instances, the differences between revenues available for education in school districts are so wide that the courts have been involved in settling issues of **funding equity**.

Some schools and school districts have much more money to spend on their students, staffs, and facilities than do others. William Taylor and Diane Piché (1991) report that in 1990, the 100 richest districts in Texas spent $7,233 per pupil, while the 100 poorest districts spent $2,978. Conflicts over education finance have often broken out in state legislatures. When the public pressure educators about rising taxes, they in turn pressure legislators to reform methods of education finance.

The disparities are so great in some parts of the country that those districts poor in property have had to tax themselves three and four times as heavily as rich districts to raise revenue for their schools. Such inequalities, as Arthur Wise (1968) predicted correctly years ago, can result in disputes being settled in the courts.

In the 1960s, people thought that inequities in school finance might be corrected by appealing to the courts. The landmark 1971 case of *Serrano v. Priest* was the first filed in state court (California) that declared unconstitutional a state public school finance system based on taxable wealth. By focusing on the link between educational expenditures and district property wealth, this case stimulated challenges to school district spending inequalities across the nation. William Thro (1990) refers to these cases as the "first wave" of public school finance reform litigation.

The "second wave" of litigation was typified by appeals to the United States Supreme Court on the basis of the equal protection clause of the Fourteenth Amendment. As explained below, early litigation advanced on this theory failed when the Court suggested that disparities in school funding are state issues rather than federal issues.

In *San Antonio Independent School District v. Rodriguez* (1973), a federal district court had ruled that the San Antonio, Texas, school finance system violated the equal protection clause of the Fourteenth Amendment because large disparities in school district expenditures existed across the state. The United States Supreme Court, however, ruled that education was not a fundamental right under the Constitution, and therefore not protected by the Fourteenth Amendment—a major setback for those who sought to reform school finance. The Supreme Court emphasized the importance of local control in educational matters and left such issues to be settled in state courts. This case dampened enthusiasm for court solutions to financial inequalities among districts but did not completely stop complaints. This second wave of school finance reform cases was a mixed success with states finding for and against litigants (Thro, 1990).

Thro (1990) marks the beginning of the "third wave" of school finance reform litigation with three cases reaching the courts in 1989—cases in Montana, Kentucky, and Texas, where school finance systems were invalidated in the same year because school funding disparities had grown dramatically. Thro argues that these cases, relying as they do on education clauses in state constitutions, may stimulate not only school finance reform but general education reform as well. In part, these cases assert that a right to education is fundamental or of extreme importance under state constitutions. Thro describes these developments as having "the potential to cause both a revolution in school finance reform and the development of a greater body of state constitutional law" (p. 250).

Given the number of court cases surrounding issues of funding for schools, it would seem that Thro's predicted "revolution" has begun. The school system in Camden, New Jersey, is a case in point. Here, every student qualifies for free or reduced-price lunch tickets, and 96% of the students are African-American or Hispanic-American. Until 1990, when the New Jersey Supreme Court mandated that the state equalize spending for public education, Camden students had substantially fewer educational resources than did their counterparts in the neighboring, upper-middle class suburb of Cherry Hill. For example, some schools in Camden had no school yard, most had obsolete science labs, and none had computers for student use. Cherry Hill, which spent about $2,000 more per student than Camden schools, was just the opposite. Students attended schools where equipment was up-to-date and accessible.

Since the New Jersey Supreme Court mandate, Camden has received an $80 million increase in state aid while Cherry Hill has lost $5.5 million. Although Cherry Hill still spends $2,215 more per pupil than Camden, increased funding has allowed the Camden school system to make significant improvements in educational offerings. For example, state funds have been used to establish after-school homework centers with free tutoring; to locate medical, psychological, or social service facilities at 10 elementary schools; to purchase computers for reading, writing, and math labs; to update science, technology and music equipment; to start parenting classes; to expand teacher training; to purchase new texts; and to hire consultants to develop new curricula (Lakshmanan, 1993).

More recently, other states, such as Massachusetts, have been cited for wide disparities between their richest and poorest communities. In the past few years, more than 40 states have litigation pending or have recently settled court challenges to school finance systems (Harp, 1993).

WHAT ARE SOME LINKS BETWEEN SCHOOL FUNDING AND EDUCATIONAL SUCCESS?

Public schools have been driven by the idea that a child's future ought not be limited by his or her parents' wealth and influence. Public funds are to be used to establish a public education system that will provide access to education for all children. In a society of limited resources, however, people must decide how much support to provide the schools. Decisions about the amount of funding to provide public education are often couched in terms of educational quality. Funds relate directly to educational opportunities—that is, funds can buy equipment, materials, experiences, and the like. But the relationship between funds and learning as measured by standardized achievement tests and later success in life is less easily explained (Jencks et al., 1972).

> **"On economic grounds, the simultaneous pursuit of excellence and equity is mandatory."**

When education dollars are limited, tradeoffs are made. Sometimes the tradeoffs are described in terms of choices between educational equity and educational excellence. Some believe efforts to promote educational excellence will swamp the poor, the weak, and the minority-group students, while others argue that money spent on equalization could be put to better use capitalizing on the strengths of outstanding students. Allan Odden (1984) contends that such choices are ill-conceived, for there are more connections between excellence and equity than many realize:

> On economic grounds, the simultaneous pursuit of excellence and equity is mandatory. If our national strategy for maintaining a competitive edge in the international market is to increase the per capita productivity of the U.S. work force, then all U.S. workers must have better-developed skills than their counterparts in other countries. In other words, it will not be enough for the top 10% of workers in the U.S. to outperform the top 10% of the workers in Japan . . . The bottom 90% of U.S. workers will have to be better too . . . (p. 316)

Odden's reasoning is compelling, but the press of debt and economic recession began to turn the education reforms of the 1980s into the retrenchment of the 1990s. Even while tax revolt flourished at the state and federal levels in the 1980s, states experimented with a wide range of programs and bureaucratic mechanisms to maximize the effect of the dollars spent on public education. These included site-based management, high-tech classrooms, career ladders for teachers, professional development schools, better and longer training programs for teachers, innovative curricula, restructured school calendars, and new testing for both students and teachers.

But innovations could be expensive, and these would become increasingly difficult for policymakers to justify in the tight economic times of the 1990s. "When many states had expected recent school-improvement experiments to flourish, they instead face a new budget year colored by widespread reports of larger classes, reduced honors and remedial programs, and growing local cynicism about policymakers' commitment to costly school reforms" (Harp, 1991, pp. 1, 26). Most states have faced serious budget problems in the 1990s. For some of the hardest hit, school-reform projects have fallen by the wayside as lawmakers and governors concentrate on ways to pay for basic education services.

The situation has been exacerbated in recent years by declines in students' test scores, in particular declines on the Scholastic Aptitude Test (SAT). Some people argue that money spent on education is being wasted; that is, the public continues to pay for education, but productivity is not forthcoming. If this is so, the argument goes, something must be wrong with teachers and students and educational systems across the board. Surely these problems will not be solved with money, hence the familiar "you can't fix problems by throwing money at them" phrase heard so often.

David Berliner (1992) and others (Bracey, 1991; Carson, Huelskamp, & Woodall, 1991; Verstegen & McGuire, 1991) have taken issue with the position that schools are failing and that funding for education is not connected to success. They argue that test results have been interpreted incorrectly to suggest that student performance and educational quality are declining, moreover, they argue that test results are not the outcomes on which we should concentrate.

> The highest spending states have, on average, eleven times higher percentages of their students taking the SAT than the lowest spending states . . . Working under difficult conditions, with a greater at-risk population, the highest spending states posted a loss of up to ten items or about seven percent of the raw score points on the SAT, but they posted an eleven hundred fifty percent increase in the percent of high school seniors thinking about going to college. (Berliner, 1992, pp. 22–23)

In other words, Berliner and others contend that educational decline, if there really is any, is educationally insignificant. While schools need funds to create opportunities for students to learn and to succeed at a variety of challenges, the schools are doing remarkably well given their circumstances.

The view that money spent on educational quality and student success are related is underscored by Keith Baker (1991). He reexamined research literature on spending and performance and concluded that a good school is like a good hospital in which more resources are devoted to those who need it most—the sickest patients or the least able students. Howard Wainer (1993) of the Educational Testing Service and Larry Hedges (1994) and his colleagues at the University of Chicago have made similar claims for the link between spending and learning.

Critics counter that the available evidence reveals weak or nonexistent links between money spent on public education and student learning.

> One thing mainstream educational reformers can always agree on is that more money—lots more money—needs to be spent. . . . During the 1980s, governments responded to these pressures with handsome increases in funding. The problem is that, common sense notwithstanding, there is no evidence that increases of even this magnitude stand to have important effects on school performance. (Chubb and Moe, 1990, p. 193)

For John Chubb and Terry Moe, the real problem in American education is the liberty or choice that people may exert over their own education and the education of their children.

The Issue of School Choice

The idea that people should be free to choose schools for their children is aired frequently in public forums on education reform. **School choice** has become a rallying cry for political conservatives—a concept, or set of concepts, offered to improve public education or to provide alternatives to public education systems that seem beyond hope. People on both sides of the debate about choice fight for the hearts and minds of the public, and, interestingly, each side often claims to have the public on its side.

While such claims may simply be overheated rhetoric, they may also indicate the lack of care and sensitivity taken when polling the public about school choice. As Figure 12.7 suggests, how questions about school choice are posed can markedly affect how people respond.

Despite difficulties defining *"choice"* and its implications, pollsters have noted growing public support for the idea, particularly for the idea of choice of public schools. In 1979, when asked if they would like to send their eldest child to a public school different from the school that child currently attended, 78% of the parents polled said no. In 1989, 51% of the respondents thought choice would improve some schools and hurt others. Slightly over

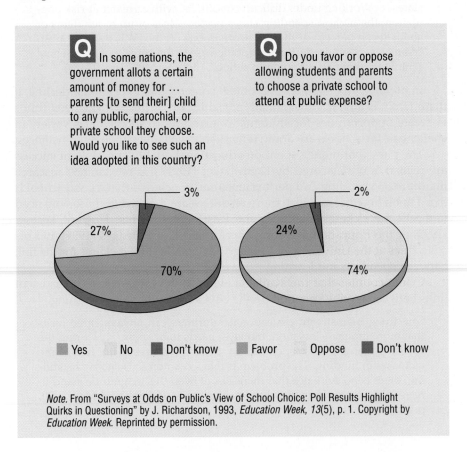

FIGURE 12.7

Two Polls on School Choice

Note. From "Surveys at Odds on Public's View of School Choice: Poll Results Highlight Quirks in Questioning" by J. Richardson, 1993, *Education Week, 13*(5), p. 1. Copyright by *Education Week.* Reprinted by permission.

40% thought choice would not make much difference in student achievement, but 40% thought achievement would increase. About half of the 1989 respondents thought student satisfaction with school would increase with an option for choice (Elam, 1990).

People also oppose concepts of "choice" for many reasons. They believe that if citizens can choose where to send their children to school, schools will become racially segregated, or at the very least the gains made by private schools will exacerbate class distinctions. A central purpose of public education is to prepare people to participate in our democracy, and vouchers will allow people to opt out, thus subverting this goal, they believe (Levin, 1980). Also, they believe, children who most need the involvement of their parents in order to make wise choices will be least likely to get it.

Opponents fear that in a deregulated market—one largely devoid of governmental control—for-profit schools will flourish largely unmonitored, reaping large profits at the expense of consumers (Putka, 1991). Others point out that the money available for most "choice" programs is far below costs—only wealthy individuals who can pay the extra will benefit.

There are various plans at issue for allowing parents to choose schools for their children. These include providing for choices among public schools and between public and private schools. Chubb and Moe (1990) have outlined what they believe are the essential attributes for any choice plan:

- Supply of public schools—the state should set criteria to define a "public school"; any group that meets these criteria must be designated as a public school and be able to accept students and public money. . . .

- Funding of public education—the state should establish and support a Choice Office in each district, and it should maintain records of children and the "scholarship" funding associated with each; the state should maintain the right to specify how much each district must contribute to the support of each child; parents should not be allowed to supplement their scholarships with personal funds; the citizens of each district should be able to add on money to their schools; and scholarships should vary within a district.

- Choice among schools—students should be free to attend any public school in the state, regardless of district; every effort should be made to provide transportation to students who need it; the state should support a parent information center to help parents make choices among schools and require parents to visit the center; the center should handle applications for schools; schools should make their own admissions decisions but adhere to nondiscrimination standards; schools should set their own tuition; each student should be guaranteed a place in a school with a fair chance to get his or her first choice; schools should be free to expel students.

- Governance and organization of public schools—each school should design its own governance; the state should not dictate how schools are organized: statewide tenure laws should be eliminated; teachers should be able to bargain collectively but the bargaining unit should be the school or district; states should continue to certify teachers but criteria should be minimal; the state should hold schools accountable for procedural requirements but not for student achievement or other indicators of school quality. (pp. 219–225)

Professor Henry Levin (1980) warned that any consideration of vouchers or choice must be attuned to differences in plans, for different specifics can yield radically different results.

Clearly a voucher plan with "compensatory" vouchers for the poor, no add-ons [options for parents to purchase more expensive education], an extensive information system, and regulation of admissions to assure participation of the poor will have vastly different consequences than one that provides a uniform voucher with parental add-ons, a poor information system, and a laissez-faire approach to admissions. (p. 247)

The Problem of Infrastructure

School buildings themselves represent a major drain on public coffers. According to a report entitled *Wolves at the Schoolhouse Door*, public education's infrastructure is in a state of disrepair (Education Writers Association, 1989).

Among the report's findings were the following:

During the 1980s and 1990s, Christian academies and Black academies expanded as private school alternatives, especially in states experimenting with school choice plans. Many educators are concerned that choice, vouchers, and tax credits could undermine public education.

- One of every four school buildings is in inadequate condition, 33% are adequate and 42% are in good condition, based on information on one-half of the nation's public school buildings.

- Of the buildings that are inadequate, 61% need maintenance or major repairs, 43% are obsolete, 42% have environmental hazards, 25% are overcrowded, and 13% are structurally unsound.

- The replacement cost of the nation's 88,021 public school buildings is estimated to be $422 billion. States estimate that the education infrastructure needs an investment of $84 billion in new or retrofitting construction and $41 billion for maintenance and repairs.

New Orleans, for example, faces more than one-half billion dollars in capital needs and less than $4 million to spend on repairs (Lindsay, 1994). Capital construction can be a heavy burden for any school district. When considering building a new school, district leaders must engage in an expensive and time-consuming process. This begins with determining the need for a new building by examining other options, such as remodeling existing facilities, searching for other existing facilities, rescheduling instruction, or consolidating with other districts. A decision to build means determining location by studying possible sites for a new building and acquiring land through negotiation or through condemnation (sometimes referred to as eminent domain). When district leaders take the latter course, they are exercising their right to take private property for public use. In this instance, the court sets a price for the property in question.

Building a school also means planning with an architect, which involves setting specifications for the numbers of students and kinds of programs to be housed in the building. School officials must also open bids for construction and negotiate with contractors about various aspects of their work. Once an architect and construction company begin constructing the building, the school is not completed until others can undertake furnishing and preparing it for use (Guthrie, Garms, and Pierce, 1988, pp. 236–256).

Few states provide funding for facilities. Low-income communities that rely only on local revenues to construct buildings face special problems. States are sure to see this issue on their agenda in the coming years.

VOICES

On Choice

J ohn F. Witte, professor of political science and public affairs at the University of Wisconsin, has served as an independent evaluator of the Milwaukee Parental Choice Program. He encourages experimentation with public support for private education, but urges great caution in the process.

Choice in American education, whether it deserves it or not, is the most prevalent reform idea of the 1990s. The idea of using public revenue to support private school options is 35 years old . . . and its advocates believe its time has come. Those advocates include the President, a number of governors and state legislators, and numerous interest groups throughout the country. . . .

This paper has attempted to outline the arguments about whether educational choice would wreak havoc on our current education system, produce great improvement, or generate results somewhere in between. I have argued that there are not clear and definitive answers based on theory, practice, or inferences drawn from research undertaken in existing public and private schools. Because we know little, however, does not mean that we should not experiment with choice; indeed, that may be one of the strongest arguments for experimenting. Does experimentation mean that a state should contemplate completely overturning its existing systems and adopting an amalgamated, deregulated system of choice such as Chubb and Moe advocate? In a democracy, that is up to the citizens and officials of each state. Given the limited knowledge and evidence available to date, I would counsel great caution and prior assessment of educational problems throughout the state. Choice is not without risk or potential damage to education systems that may be functioning adequately.

CRITICAL THINKING

What problems might be solved by using public funds to support private education? What problems might be created?

Source: Witte, J.F. (1991). *Public subsidies for private schools: Implications for Wisconsin's reform efforts* (pp. 3, 25) Madison: Wisconsin Center for Educational Policy, University of Wisconsin.

The Promise of Business-School Partnerships

Many corporations in the United States support education through charitable gifts to higher education, precollege education, and a variety of special programs such as education-related organizations, scholarships, and fellowships. Results from annual surveys conducted jointly by two New York agencies—the Council for Aid to Education and the Conference Board—estimated that corporate gifts to education in 1992 totaled $2.429 billion. Approximately 70% of corporate gifts (about $1.69 billion) went to higher education, 15% ($364 million) to K–12 programs, and another 15% to other education programs. Such figures do not include gifts to higher education for such things as teacher training, nor do they include grants to community, health, and human service programs for school-age children (Sommerfeld, 1993).

Business-school partnerships have existed for years. The New York Alliance for the Public Schools, for example, was established in 1979. It includes business, community, and civic leaders as well as school board members, representatives from the United Federation of Teachers, parents, and others. In the mid-1980s, there were some 35,000 such partnerships (McCormick, 1984). By 1989, the U.S. Department of Education estimated that there were more than 140,000 of them. These associations are typically driven by the idea that good schools make for good citizens and good business.

> "It is time to stop tinkering. We are in a battle . . . that will determine the shape of the future for our children. . . ."

In his keynote address to the Heritage Foundation's conference "Can Business Save Education? Strategies for the l990s," Governor Pierre du Pont of Delaware expressed an idea that often characterizes business-school partnerships:

> I think it is time to stop tinkering. We are in a battle—an international battle—that will determine the shape of the future for our children and our grandchildren. And important from businesses' perspective, the outcome of that battle will determine the quality of the work force of the future and, ultimately, U.S. businesses' ability to compete in a global economy. (Allen, 1989, p. 3)

Business-school partnerships engage in all kinds of activities meant to improve schools. The New York Alliance has sponsored training for school principals and created a data bank to link classrooms with city resources. Houston partnerships are credited with providing career counseling for students and putting science equipment and computers in schools. The Minneapolis Public Academy sponsored by General Mills started a program in the schools that reduced class size, made teachers accountable for students' scores on standardized achievement tests, and put telephones in classrooms so parents could call teachers directly.

Sometimes partnerships take the form of local education funds, or LEFs, that offer money directly to teachers for special projects. Schultz (1990) identified 57 such funds across the nation, mostly in large cities. The LEFs were organized to provide teachers with minigrants ($100 to $900) and to sponsor conferences and workshops for teachers on a variety of subjects.

Multinational corporations have piloted a variety of educational programs. McDonald's U.S.A., for example, has created the McPride program to encourage young people to stay in school. As employees at a McDonald's restaurant, students can earn money if they study for school before they begin their work shift (Reingold, 1992).

Although business-school programs are becoming increasingly visible, they raise questions even in the minds of some believers. As Joan Richardson, an education writer at the *Detroit Free Press*, suggests, there may be good reasons to be skeptical of the business-school connection:

> What problems might be created when Ford Motor Company designs a curriculum aimed at encouraging teenagers' interest in manufacturing as a career? What conflicts exist when a school uses a local company's laboratories for Saturday morning science classes?

Is it appropriate for fourth graders to learn about energy needs from Detroit Edison Company, a company whose profit margin hinges on insuring popular acceptance of nuclear power? . . . Do we want Mazda Corporation footing the bill to take American students to Japan for study programs? Should school districts agree to accept computers from Kroger Company for every $150,000 in Kroger receipts from parents? Do we want Pizza Hut treating first-graders to free pizza if they meet reading goals set by that company? (Richardson, 1992, p. 2)

Public education demands public involvement if it is to succeed. Partnerships, not just between schools and business, but between schools and others, hold the potential to break down barriers between disparate groups of people. When people who have legitimate interests in the success of public education work together to achieve common goals, the schools are bound to benefit.

SUMMARY

1. Public school finance in the United States has been concerned traditionally with balancing issues of equal education opportunity (equal programs tailored to students' needs that allow them to acquire at least minimum or basic skills), efficiency (getting the maximum benefit from dollars spent on education), and liberty or choice (control over where, how, and for what purposes students are educated).

2. People can be seen as representing human capital. That is, the return on educational investment can be characterized in terms of social and personal benefits for students.

3. Localities provide about 44% of the funding for education. In the majority, local tax money is derived almost exclusively from property taxes (mostly taxes on land and improvements). This means that a community's ability to pay for education is dependent on its real assets, that is, on the assessed value of its property. One problem with this strategy is that a rich municipality having a low assessment rate may raise as much revenue or more than a property-poor area having a higher assessment rate.

4. School districts develop long-term financial plans that represent predictions about the future. District employees craft a new budget for each fiscal year. Most school boards control such things as the staffing of local schools and types of programs that are offered to students via the budget. In school-based budgeting, as the phrase implies, responsibility for allocating resources at the building level is fixed at the building level not at the level of central administration.

5. About 49% of funds for local schools come from the state. General sales taxes, state income taxes, and state lotteries are among sources of state aid. To equalize financial aid to school districts, states use some combination of a variety of funding plans.

6. In recent years, the federal government has looked increasingly toward states and localities to provide for the cost of public education. Federal funds may emanate from a variety of sources (e.g., major grants established through legislation, and categorical grants for funding programs designed for particular groups and specific purposes). Sometimes several education programs are grouped together as a block grant to localities.

7. Historically, paying for private schooling has been a private matter. In the 1980s and 1990s, the debate about public support for private elementary and secondary schools has taken on renewed vigor, focusing on tuition tax credits, tax deductions, and vouchers.

8. Decisions about the amount of funding to provide public education are often couched in terms of educational quality. Funds relate directly to educational opportunities—that is, funds can buy equipment, materials, experiences, and the like. But the relationship between funds and learning as measured by standardized achievement tests and later success in life is less easily explained.

9. The idea that people should be free to choose schools for their children is aired frequently in public forums on education reform. In recent years, discussions about citizens' freedom to make decisions about the form and function of public education in their communities have revolved around proposals for vouchers, tuition credits, tax deductions, and the more general notion of choice.

10. The courts tend to view educational matters as state concerns and thus look to authorities at that level of government to settle disputes. In instances when there is wide variation in expenditures and revenues among school districts within states, the courts have been involved in settling issues of equity.

11. Few states provide funding for school buildings. School buildings themselves, many of which are in a state of disrepair, represent a major drain on public coffers.

12. Although business-school partnerships may have various organizational structures and functions, they are becoming increasingly popular. These associations are typically driven by the idea that good schools make for good citizens and good business.

TERMS AND CONCEPTS

block grant	fiscal year	progressive taxation
business-school partnerships	flat grants	regressive taxation
	foundation program	school-based budgeting
categorical grants	full state funding	school choice
district power equalization	funding equity	tuition tax credit
	local property taxes	tuition tax deduction
Education Consolidation and Improvement Act (ECIA)	National Center for Education Statistics	vouchers
	per-pupil expenditures	zero-based budgeting

STUDENT ACTIVITIES

A television interviewer asked Bing Crosby why he always appeared so calm. Bing reached into his pocket and pulled out a wad of dollar bills. "That helps!" he said. Adequate funding has a similar effect on those responsible for the conduct of public education.

In the exercises below, you will explore issues of equity, efficiency, and liberty as they relate to educational finance.

Perceive and Value

Relatively well-funded schools have opportunities to spend money on education in ways that comparatively poorly funded schools do not. Where might differences in expenditures on public education be most noticeable? Least noticeable?

If you were given $25 million in unrestricted funds to create a new school, how would you spend your money? Divide the funds among the categories of facilities, equipment, teachers, administrative support, and other. Be prepared to explain your decisions.

Know and Act

Draw a line from top to bottom down the center of a sheet of paper. Label one side "Pro" and the other "Con." List all the reasons you can think of to encourage the use of public funds for school vouchers that may be spent at public or private schools under the Pro column. List all the arguments you can think of against this position under the Con column. Frame your position on the debate in a paragraph or two.

Evaluate

Your uncle becomes visibly upset at a family gathering when discussion turns to spending on public education. He argues that if schools were run more efficiently, like businesses, the nation would not be in an educational crisis. What questions would you ask him to assess the validity of his position?

Discover

Visit a local school board office in search of information on the school system's annual budget. Most will be able to provide upon request summary information that includes a figure concerning per-pupil expenditures. The National Center for Education Statistics reports in the *Digest of Education Statistics, 1993* that public schools spent $5,334 per pupil in 1992–93 (excluding money spent on buildings and on debt interest) based on average daily attendance. Calculate a 3 to 4% yearly inflation rate since that time. How does the district you studied compare to the national figure?

Also, determine how the district compares on per-pupil expenditures to other nearby districts of about the same size and having similar students. Based on your analysis of the budget summaries, draw conclusions about per-pupil expenditures and discrepancies between comparable districts. What questions would you ask to determine the causes and to make recommendations for budget reform?

This chapter presents some differences of opinion about what ought and ought not be done in public schools. The particular types of disagreements described have at one time or another been played out in courts across the land. Specifically, five categories of rights and responsibilities are considered as they have been elaborated by court actions—those of parents, students, teachers, administrators, and school boards.

This chapter is structured a bit differently from the others. In each general category vignettes or slices of educational life are presented as they might occur in schools. Some of these situations are similar, but not identical, to cases heard in federal and state courts. Issues and problems follow each vignette. In some instances, readers are asked to describe possible teaching actions. This is followed by a response in which attention is drawn to relevant points of law.

The intent of this chapter is to encourage consideration of the relevance of the law as it applies in real situations. It is important to note that points of law discussed in this chapter are illustrative, not definitive. Rulings and legal trends sometimes change quickly, thus making it necessary to stay abreast of courtroom events so as to make informed professional decisions.

13

Education and the Law

PROFESSIONAL PRACTICE QUESTIONS

1 Can you recognize when a teacher's actions run the risk of violating someone's constitutional rights?

`Perceive`

2 Why do you think prayer should or should not be allowed in public schools?

`Value`

3 Do you know what a teacher is supposed to do if he or she suspects child abuse?

`Know`

4 What would you do if you believed your school's policy on the review of library books violated students' rights to read good literature?

`Act`

5 What might happen, legally speaking, if your school does not have a sex education program and you start one?

`Evaluate`

WHAT ARE SOME LEGAL PRINCIPLES THAT AFFECT PUBLIC EDUCATION?

The United States Constitution contains no mention of education. All state constitutions, however, specify that the legislature has the power to establish and maintain public free schools. States' legal control over education is authorized by the Tenth Amendment's provision that "powers not delegated to the United States by the Constitution, nor prohibited by it to the States, are reserved to the States respectively, or to the people." Such control must be exercised in a manner consistent with the Constitution's provisions for the basic rights of individuals.

When disputes arise over educational practices or policies, every effort is made to settle differences at the local level of governance, most always informally before formal entry into the judicial system. Unresolved cases are litigated either by state courts or the federal judiciary system. At the state level, statutes prescribe where cases should be taken and which ones should be heard by the highest court. As Figure 13.1 illustrates, the Supreme Court

FIGURE 13.1

Levels at Which Disputes Are Heard

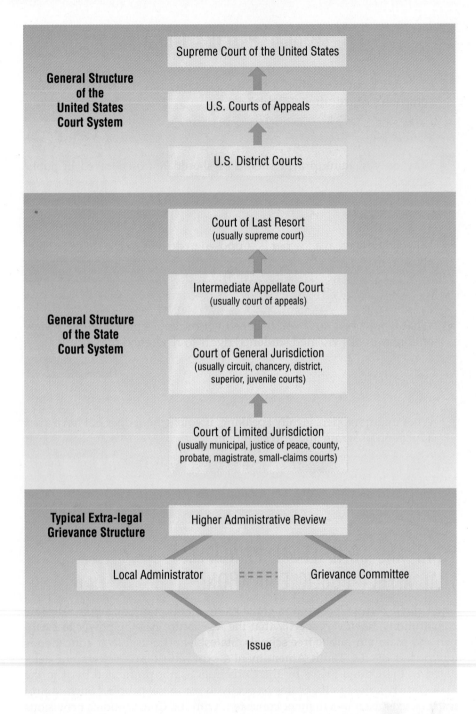

General Structure of the United States Court System

Supreme Court of the United States

U.S. Courts of Appeals

U.S. District Courts

General Structure of the State Court System

Court of Last Resort
(usually supreme court)

Intermediate Appellate Court
(usually court of appeals)

Court of General Jurisdiction
(usually circuit, chancery, district, superior, juvenile courts)

Court of Limited Jurisdiction
(usually municipal, justice of peace, county, probate, magistrate, small-claims courts)

Typical Extra-legal Grievance Structure

Higher Administrative Review

Local Administrator

Grievance Committee

Issue

of the United States is the highest court in the land, beyond which there is no redress. Most cases heard by the Supreme Court are cases in which the validity of a state statute or federal statute is questioned in light of the federal Constitution or cases in which title, right, privilege, or immunity is claimed under the Constitution (Alexander & Alexander, 1992).

There are several statutory and constitutional provisions that the Supreme Court considers frequently when rendering decisions about educational matters. One is the First Amendment to the Constitution, which contains two clauses often cited in lawsuits.

- The First Amendment states that

  Congress shall make no law respecting an establishment of religion, or prohibiting the free exercise thereof; or abridging the freedom of speech, or of the press; or the right of the people peaceably to assemble, and to petition the government for a redress of grievances.

  This amendment is the basis for a number of lawsuits challenging aid to and regulation of nonpublic schools, public school policies that advance or inhibit religion, and actions that impair expression by teachers and students.

- The Fourth Amendment guarantees citizens that the right

  to be secure in their persons, houses, papers, and effects, against unreasonable searches and seizures, shall not be violated, and no warrants shall issue, but upon probable cause, supported by oath or affirmation, and particularly describing the place to be searched, and the persons or things to be seized.

  When a student's bookbag, locker, or person are searched for illegal or dangerous items, this amendment usually serves as the basis for judgments about the legality of such actions.

- The Fourteenth Amendment is the most widely invoked constitutional provision in school-related cases (McCarthy & Cambron-McCabe, 1992). Section 1 states that

  [N]o State shall make or enforce any law which shall abridge the privileges or immunities of citizens of the United States; nor shall any State deprive any person of life, liberty, or property, without due process of law; nor deny to any person within its jurisdiction the equal protection of the laws.

  This clause is often significant in litigation related to school finance, to the expulsion and suspension of students, to the dismissal of teachers, and to discrimination on the basis of race, gender, and disabilities.

When disputes relate to contractual situations, Article I, Section 10 of the Constitution typically comes into play. This article states in part that "no State shall . . . pass any . . . ex post facto law, or law impairing the obligation of contracts. . . ." Interpretations of this constitutional provision enable the courts to determine the validity of contracts and possible breaches of contracts.

As described in Chapter 11, federal legislation also affects public school policies and practices. Categorical legislation such as the 1975 Education for All Handicapped Children Act (in 1990 revised as the Individuals with Disabilities Education Act) and the Bilingual Education Act of 1968 protect citizens' constitutional rights and have general application in the resolution of educational disputes. Figure 13.2 suggests why disputes arise.

In the scenarios that follow, note that disputes are resolved on the basis of constitutional provisions, state and federal legislation, rules and regula-

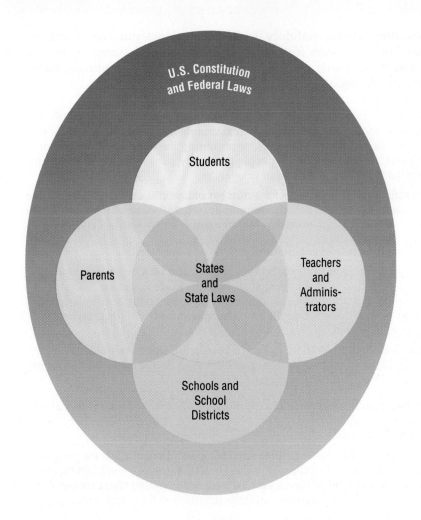

FIGURE 13.2

Groups with Rights and Responsibilities under the U.S. Constitution and Federal Laws

tions of state and local boards, and case law (common law) emanating from the judicial system. Note also that Supreme Court decisions have brought some uniformity to educational practices and policies across the land.

WHAT ARE PARENTS' RIGHTS AND RESPONSIBILITIES?

A number of cases decided by the courts have dealt directly with parents' rights and responsibilities as parents and as guardians of their children. As the following scenarios suggest, knowledge of such rulings is just as important for teachers as for parents themselves.

A Question of Religious Principle

At the end of the school day, Betty Anne Mason fell into stride with three of her ninth grade students weaving their way to the locker room. The students—James, Lashanta, and Miranda—were so engrossed in conversation that they didn't notice Betty Anne until they reached the locker room. Normally friendly and outgoing in class, the students seemed suddenly fidgety and nervous when Betty Anne asked good-naturedly if they planned to attend the ninth grade dance Friday night. Miranda muttered something about having to stay home to "do some stuff," then made a beeline for the front door. As Betty Anne turned toward the other two students, James blushed and whispered something to Lashanta who bobbed her head in agreement. "Hey, what's with you guys today?" asked Betty Anne.

It's a matter of principle!

"Mrs. Mason," said Lashanta, "I don't know if you heard or not, but there is a meeting at 7:00 tonight after the Bible study session at Miranda's house. A bunch of parents who don't like what is going on here at Walden High are getting together to talk about taking their kids out of school and teaching them at home. Miranda's parents have already told her this is her last week at Walden. Can you believe it?"

As she headed for the principal's office, Betty Anne was upset. Miranda was one of her most promising students. Surely her parents wouldn't try to pull something like this. If they did, wouldn't they be violating the compulsory attendance law? By the time she reached the office, Betty Anne's mind was racing. She headed straight for the principal's office, hoping to get some answers to her questions.

Analysis of "A Question of Religious Principle."

If parents have religious or philosophical objections to a school program, can they exempt their children from school? The Supreme Court's 1972 decision in *Wisconsin v. Yoder* allowed members of the Old Order Amish religious community to exempt their children from school attendance beyond eighth grade even though home instruction provided by the Amish was not equivalent to instruction in public schools. (The Amish had argued that compulsory attendance in the upper grades would have a detrimental effect on the established way of life in their farm-based and traditional community.) The Court's decision was based on the religious freedom clause of the First Amendment and evidence that the Amish way of life was an acceptable alternative to formal education (Zirkel & Richardson, 1988).

Litigation since *Yoder* suggests that the "Amish exception" cannot be used by parents who wish to exempt their children from schools for philosophical or religious reasons unless evidence suggests that such schooling might destroy their religion. For those dissatisfied with the public schools, however, compulsory attendance requirements may be fulfilled in private, denominational, or parochial schools. In several states, homeschooling is yet another option. To determine the validity of homeschooling, states look at such things as the educational level of parents and the regularity and time of instruction. In many instances, states also administer achievement tests to monitor home instruction (Alexander & Alexander, 1992).

Besides mandating school attendance, most state agencies also require that students be vaccinated against communicable diseases. Religious groups whose teachings oppose immunizations are sometimes exempted from vaccinations as long as the health of others is not endangered. In the event that students are exempted from school because they pose a threat to others' health, schools must provide some type of home instruction for those students.

You Can't Spank My Child!

Steve Donovan's face was flushed as he escorted Brian's parents to the door. In his role as principal, he suspected there might be some backlash from his actions the day before, but as he had explained to Brian's parents, he had warned Brian several times that if he kept spitting on other students he was going to be spanked. When Brian repeated the offense yesterday, Steve made good on his promise. Brian's parents were furious. "We know Brian has some behavior problems," they said, " but we sent a note to Brian's teacher telling her that spanking was not to be used as a disciplinary measure. Your behavior was an infringement on our rights as parents, and we're going to see that you don't get away with something like this again!"

Analysis of "You Can't Spank my Child!"

Given that Brian's parents requested formally that their child not be spanked, would a court of law support Steve's actions? In *Ingraham v. Wright* (1977), the Supreme Court ruled that the Constitution does not prohibit the use of corporal punishment in the schools. In so ruling, the Court concluded that cases dealing with corporal punishment should be handled at the state rather than the federal level. Whether Brian's parents have a legitimate complaint, then, depends on state and local school board policies.

In states where corporal punishment is allowed, parental objection to the practice does not necessarily prevail. In *Baker v. Owen* (1975), a case challenging a North Carolina state law permitting reasonable corporal punishment, the federal district court recognized parents' basic right to supervise the upbringing of children. The court also recognized the importance of maintaining order in the schools, ultimately deciding that parents' wishes should not interfere with methods chosen by school officials for maintaining discipline.

Some states and localities do have laws requiring written permission from parents before students can be spanked. If there is no state or local regulation to the contrary, however, schools are not required to seek parental permission before administering corporal punishment. As educators, it is important to be aware of state laws and board policies banning or restricting the use of corporal punishment in the classroom.

A common restriction is that principals are the only ones who can use corporal punishment, doing so only in the presence of an adult witness. Educators who violate such policies may face monetary fines, dismissal, and even imprisonment (McCarthy & Cambron-McCabe, 1992). It should also be noted that corporal punishment, though often equated with paddling, is more broadly defined as "any punishment that inflicts bodily pain for disapproved behavior" (Gursky, 1992). Sometimes teachers who have demonstrated excessive force when disciplining a student (e.g., throwing a student against a chalkboard and then pulling him upright by his hair) have been dismissed for cruelty or charged with criminal assault and battery.

Kern Alexander and David Alexander (1992) warn teachers working in school systems where corporal punishment is allowed to avoid excessive force and to adhere to local guidelines when administering it. Corporal punishment is unacceptable in most states. In those that allow it, corporal punishment is a last resort, to be avoided if at all possible.

Cultural Awareness

Daniel Gursky (1992), former editor and writer for *Teacher Magazine*, now a staff member at the American Federation of Teachers, investigated the use of corporal punishment in schools across the nation. Among his findings were:

> Teachers and school officials wield the paddle as often and with as much conviction as ever in many areas, especially the Bible Belt states of the South and Southwest. According to U.S. Education Department figures, more than 1 million students nationwide are spanked each year. (Anti-paddling activists maintain that the true number may be two or three times that.) Texas alone racks up more than 250,000 paddlings per year. Add Alabama, Arkansas, Florida, Georgia, and Tennessee, each with more than 60,000 annual cases, and the number constitutes more than half of the nation's total. Arkansas earns the dubious distinction of leading the country in the proportion of students paddled each year—almost 14 percent. (p. 18).

Do Some Parents Have Special Rights?

Kenneth and Karen Rothschild, deaf parents of non-hearing impaired students, used American sign language as their primary means of communication. When the school system denied their request to hire a sign language interpreter for school-sponsored functions, the Rothschilds were forced to obtain their own interpreter at great personal expense. Subsequently, they brought action against the school district and the superintendent for violating section 504 of the Rehabilitation Act of 1973, which prohibits discrimination on the basis of a handicap. School officials denied the charge, arguing that they had made good faith efforts to accommodate the Rothschilds' needs by providing special seating arrangements at all school-sponsored functions.

Analysis of "Do Some Parents Have Special Rights?"

Must a school system provide special services, such as sign language interpreters, to parents who are disabled? In *Rothschild v. Grottenthaler* (1990), the United States Court of Appeals ruled that a public school system receiving federal financial assistance is obligated to provide a sign language interpreter at school district expense to deaf parents attending school initiated events. In explaining its decision, the court said that, without an interpreter, people like the Rothschilds do not have equal opportunity to participate in activities incidental to their children's education. The court also noted that the Rehabilitation Act specifies that necessary accommodations to permit access to individuals with disabilities should not impose undue financial or administrative burdens on them. Accordingly, the school system was ordered to: (a) reimburse the Rothschilds for monies spent on interpreters, and (b) hire an interpreter to assist the Rothschilds at school-initiated activities directly involving their children's academic or disciplinary progress.

WHAT ARE STUDENTS' RIGHTS AND RESPONSIBILITIES?

In *Tinker v. Des Moines* (1969), the Supreme Court emphasized that students do not lose their rights when they pass through the schoolhouse door. Under the Constitution they continue to be persons "possessed of fundamental rights which the state must respect." Although school authorities are vested with broad powers for the development and implementation of an educational program, then, they must avoid actions that are unreasonable, vague, arbitrary, or in direct conflict with students' constitutional rights and freedoms.

In God Somebody Trusts

Jack Mills was at his desk grading papers late one afternoon when he heard singing down the hall in the direction of the principal's office. He recognized the strains of "Onward Christian Soldiers" being sung by what sounded like a fairly large group of students. It was not uncommon to hear students in the building after the final bell; Omega High had many after-school activities. But it was unusual to hear hymns. When Ellie Ferro, the sophomore English teacher, stormed into his room, Jack was surprised by her anger.

"Jack, the Young Crusaders for Christ are holding a prayer meeting in the auditorium again. Apparently the principal said they could meet there whenever the basketball team was not practicing. It really ticks me off that they get to stay here when nobody else gets to use the building for church meetings. The principal has been cuddling up to those fundamentalists every chance she gets. It isn't fair. I want you to come with me to her office. I think we need to call her on this one."

Analysis of "In God Somebody Trusts"

Jack is discernibly nervous about Ellie's anger, largely because the law on prayer clubs in schools is a mystery to him. Given the number of court cases focusing on the wall of separation between church and state since the mid-twentieth century, Jack's confusion is understandable. In the tug of war over where the lines of separation should be drawn, some argue that the First Amendment's establishment clause prohibits religious observance of any type in schools, while others contend that the Amendment's provisions for free speech, free exercise, and association rights prohibit schools from religious discrimination.

In *Widmar v. Vincent* (1981), the Supreme Court ruled that refusing religious groups access to facilities while allowing other groups use of the same facilities was a violation of students' rights of free speech. Furthermore, college students were deemed less impressionable than high school students, and as adults could be expected to perceive that the university was neutral in granting permission to a prayer club to meet on public property. With passage of the **Equal Access Act (EAA)** in 1984, Congress indicated that secondary-school students were also mature enough to understand that a school does not condone religion by merely allowing prayer clubs on public property.

The EAA stipulates that secondary public schools accepting federal aid must treat student religious groups in the same way as other extracurricular clubs. That is, if a school allows noncurriculum student groups (e.g., the baseball card collecting club or the chess club) to meet on school property during noninstructional time, other student initiated groups, regardless of their religious, philosophical, or political views, must have equal access to school premises. In *Board of Education of the Westside Community Schools v. Mergens* (1990), the Supreme Court upheld the constitutionality of the EAA.

Given the Supreme Court's ruling, the sanctioning of any student club not directly tied to the curriculum prohibits schools from discriminating against other student organizations such as the Young Crusaders for Christ or even groups having little community support, such as satanists or skinheads. If schools do permit noncurriculum student group meetings during noninstructional time, teachers or other school employees may be present only in a nonparticipatory capacity. Furthermore, meetings may not be coordinated or led by nonschool persons (La Morte, 1993).

Rulings on other major cases dealing with separation of church and state are equally instructive for educators:

- *West Virginia State Board of Education v. Barnette* (1943)— It is unconstitutional to require students, who for personal or religious reasons choose not to, to salute/pledge allegiance to the American flag.

- *Goetz v. Ansell* (1973)—Requiring students to stand quietly or to leave the room during the Pledge is unconstitutional. According to the Court, the first action compels an act of acceptance of the Pledge over deeply held convictions, while the latter is a benign form of punishment for nonparticipation.

- *School District of Abington Township v. Schempp* (1963)—Prayer and Bible reading in public school classrooms are unconstitutional. However, study of the Bible as part of a secular program of education focusing on its literary and historic value is permissible.

- *Wallace v. Jaffree* (1985)—A moment of silence for meditation or voluntary prayer is unconstitutional.

- *Lee v. Weisman* (1992)—Prayers at a high school graduation ceremony are unconstitutional. (Since *Weisman*, however, school systems in some states have skirted the ban on prayer at graduation services by allowing students to initiate, plan, and lead invocations.)

Since 1971, Supreme Court justices have often applied the tripartite **Lemon test** (a test emanating from the case *Lemon v. Kurtzman*) when deciding whether particular practices or policies constitute an establishment of religion. Under the Lemon test, each of the following questions must be answered affirmatively to satisfy the Constitution: (a) Does the challenged practice or policy have a secular purpose? (b) Does it have the effect of neither advancing nor inhibiting religious practices? and (c) Does practice or policy avoid an excessive entanglement between government and religion? How much longer the Lemon test will survive as the yardstick for settling establishment clause disputes is questionable, however. As Justice Antonin Scalia noted, there are several problems with the Lemon test:

> . . . It is so easy to kill. It is there to scare us (and our audience) when we wish it to do so, but we can command it to return to the tomb at will. . . . For my part, I agree with the long list of constitutional scholars who have criticized *Lemon* and bemoaned the strange Establishment Clause geometry of crooked lines and wavering shapes its intermittent use has produced. (Bureau of National Affairs, 1993)

> **Constitutional scholars have criticized *Lemon*. Why?**

Playing Fairly

At the end of the school day, Mary Ellen, Joe, and David were called to the office where Anne Jeffrey, the assistant principal, handed each of them a sealed envelope addressed to their parents. "As I understand it," she said, "each of you is suspended for three days. This notice of suspension should be given to your parents."

"Are you kidding?" said Joe. "Nobody said anything to me about this. What are the charges against us?"

"Wait a minute," interrupted Mary Ellen. "Does this have anything to do with what happened during lunch today? If it does, this is a bunch of crap. We weren't the ones who started that fight."

"Yeah," said David. "It was that bunch of rednecks. They're always mouthing off and getting in your face. How come they aren't getting suspended? They cause trouble every day! You guys just never see them!"

"Look, I don't want to hear it," said Anne. "The principal asked me to give you these forms and that's it. Now go get on the bus before you get into any more trouble."

"You mean we don't even to get to tell our side of the story?" asked Joe. "Man, this is really wrong!"

If you were the teacher of these students, how would you respond to their complaints about the way their suspension was handled?

Analysis of "Playing Fairly"

In *Goss v. Lopez*, the Supreme Court addressed the grievances of Dwight Lopez and several of his peers who were suspended by the principal for 10 days without being given a hearing—a practice sanctioned by Ohio law. Because the principal did not follow mandated legal procedures, the Court ruled that the students were denied **due process of law**. Specifically, the Court noted that the principal's actions were in violation of the Fourteenth Amendment and subsequently ordered school officials to remove references to the students' suspensions from school records. The Court held that students facing temporary suspension from school must be given oral or written notice of the charges, an explanation of evidence if they disagree with charges, and an opportunity to present their side of the story. Whenever possible, the notice and hearing is to precede suspension from school (La Morte, 1993).

In instances when student behavior is serious enough to warrant long-term suspension or expulsion, students must be given a written notice describing the charges, time and place of a hearing, and a description of procedures to be followed in the hearing. Students have the right to know what evidence will be presented, who will testify, as well as the substance of such testimony. They also have the right to cross-examine witnesses and to present witnesses to testify on their behalf. Written or taped records of proceedings and the decision of the group conducting the hearing are to be made available to students. Students are also to be made aware of the right of appeal (Fischer, Schimmel, & Kelly, 1991).

Show Me What's in There!

When David Adams, the assistant principal, stepped outside, his attention was drawn to three students walking across the school courtyard. As he moved toward them, he noticed that the boys were looking at a small black bag held by William, one of the students. The bag, a vinyl calculator case, had a suspicious looking bulge in its side.

When he questioned the boys about where they were going and why they were late to class, William, palming the leather case and hiding it behind his back, responded that his classes had ended and he was on his way home. Curious about what William was hiding, the assistant principal insisted to no avail that William show him the object in his hand. "It's nothing," said William. "Leave me alone. You have a search warrant or something?"

After sending the other two boys back to class, David took William to the office and asked an aide to witness his efforts to see the calculator case. When William refused to let him see it, David pried it out of William's hand, unzipped it, and found marijuana and other drug paraphernalia. David called the police, and William was arrested. As he was being escorted out of

Supreme Court rulings give school officials the right to reasonable "search and seizure" of students and their belongings. The guidelines for determining reasonableness give the courts broad powers of interpretation, however, in cases in which students claim their Fourth Amendment rights have been violated.

the office, William turned to David and said, "You haven't seen the end of this. I know my rights. You can't be searching me or anybody else without a warrant!"

Analysis of "Show Me What's in There!"

Does a school official have the right to search students? The scenario of William follows closely the events as they occurred in a California public school. After being convicted in juvenile court, William appealed the decision, saying that the evidence against him had been procured via an illegal search and thus should have been excluded from the hearing. In *In re William G.* (1985), the Supreme Court of California agreed, basing its decision on the reasonable suspicion standard set forth in *New Jersey v. T.L.O.* (1985).

In *New Jersey v. T.L.O.* (1985), the Supreme Court stated that school officials are acting not **in loco parentis** (in place of the parents) but as agents of the state when they search students under their authority. While this means that school officials are subject to the Fourth Amendment, the Court ruled that schools are special settings and thus there should be some "easing of the restrictions" normally placed on public authorities when conducting searches. Accordingly, school officials are not required to obtain a warrant or show "probable cause" when searching a student suspected of violating school rules or the law.

Instead, when determining the legality of school searches, school officials' actions are to be guided by "reason" and "common sense." Tests for determining reasonableness are whether: (a) at the inception of the search there are reasonable grounds for suspecting evidence will be found to prove a student is in violation of the law or school rules; and (b) the scope of the search is reasonably related to the objectives of the search, the age and sex of the student, and the nature of the infraction.

Such guidelines allow for much latitude among courts when interpreting Fourth Amendment rights (McCarthy & Cambron-McCabe, 1992). In the case of William, the court decided that the assistant principal had insufficient grounds for conducting a search. First, the assistant principal had no prior knowledge of use or sale of illegal drugs by William. Second, suspicion that William was late to class and William's attempt to hide the leather object provided no reasonable basis for a search. Third, William's demand for a warrant merely indicated he wanted to preserve his constitutional rights (National Organization on Legal Problems of Education, 1988).

This was considered quite different from the situation in *New Jersey v. T.L.O.* In *T.L.O.*, a student claimed her Fourth Amendment rights were violated when a school official searched her purse. The student (T.L.O.) was one of two girls sent to the office for smoking in the girl's restroom (a violation of school rules). When questioned by the assistant vice principal, T.L.O. denied having smoked at all. However, when T.L.O. complied with the request to open her purse, the assistant vice principal found marijuana and drug paraphernalia, $40.98 in single dollar bills and change, plus a handwritten note to a friend, requesting that she sell marijuana at school. Subsequently, the school official notified T.L.O.'s mother and the police and T.L.O., after being advised of her rights, admitted to selling marijuana at the high school.

When the state brought delinquency charges against T.L.O., she claimed that the assistant vice principal had violated her Fourth Amendment rights and thus evidence from her purse and confession should be suppressed. The Supreme Court disagreed, saying the search met the criteria for reasonableness; that is, a teacher had witnessed T.L.O.'s smoking and thus the school official had a duty to investigate whether a school code had been broken (La Morte, 1993).

Are There Limits on Student Expression?

Students at Kirkwood High School in suburban St. Louis, Missouri, had enjoyed much freedom in the production of the school newspaper. When the students agreed to run an ad for Planned Parenthood, Birthright (an organization concerned with reproductive issues) requested that students run an anti-abortion ad to counteract Planned Parenthood's message. Several parents and local citizens considered such advertisements inappropriate and insisted that principal Franklin McCallie ban the ads from the student newspaper (Conkling, 1991).

Analysis of "Are There Limits on Student Expression?"

Students had reason to cheer when the Supreme Court in 1969 ruled on *Tinker v. Des Moines Independent School District*—a case in which three public school students were suspended for wearing armbands to protest the war in Vietnam. Deciding in favor of the students, the Court declared that public school authorities do not have the right to silence students' political or ideological viewpoints simply because they disagree with students' ideas. Under Tinker, it is only in instances when student behavior could result in disorder or disturbance or interfere with the rights of others that students' verbal or symbolic expression can be restricted.

In 1988, students' First Amendment rights were restricted somewhat when the Supreme Court ruled in *Hazelwood School District v. Kuhlmeier* that principals could censor school-sponsored publications. The basis for the Court's decision emanated from a case involving students in a high school journalism class who claimed that their First Amendment rights were violated when the principal reviewed their material and removed two stories— one on divorce, the other on three students' experiences with pregnancy—from the school-sponsored newspaper. According to the Supreme Court, a student newspaper does not represent a forum for public expression when it is part of the school curriculum. Thus, school officials can censor material considered inconsistent with the educational mission of the school. This includes material that is ungrammatical, poorly researched, biased or prejudiced, vulgar, or inappropriate for an immature audience (Conkling, 1991).

If schools have clearly established either through practice or policy students' rights to control editorial content, the publication is considered an open forum and restrictions under *Hazelwood* do not apply. At Kirkwood High School, principal Franklin McCallie firmly believed that the newspaper should be an open forum for student expression. Thus he allowed student journalists to decide what to do about the controversial ads.

Cultural Awareness

Michael Simpson of the NEA described two Court decisions that allow school officials to limit students' freedom of expression via dress codes:

> The courts have not yet addressed the constitutionality of mandatory uniform policies, but when it comes to the new breed of dress codes, it's fairly clear that most will be upheld under the sweeping standards announced by the Supreme Court in *Fraser* [a Court decision upholding the punishment of a student for including sexual innuendos in his campaign speech] and Hazelwood. Bans on T-shirts promoting drugs, alcohol, cigarettes, or sex, for example, will be sustained on the basis of the schools' interest in discouraging illegal and unhealthy student conduct. Sexually provocative clothing—such as Spandex pants, bustiers, and halter tops—also can be prohibited because of the school's interest in preventing distractions and maintaining proper decorum. (Simpson, 1991, p. 36)

Treating Different Students Differently— Illegal Discrimination?

As Sam Miller's fifth grade class was lining up to leave the gymnasium, Tyrone grabbed Tony's hat and ran to the end of the line. Tony, a mainstreamed student with emotional disturbance, raced after Tyrone, knocked him to the gym floor, and punched Tyrone hard enough to bloody his nose. When Sam pulled Tony away from Tyrone, Tony swung his fist and hit another child in the stomach. Sam wrapped his arms around Tony's waist and carried him to the back of the gym before he could do any more damage, then sent one of his students to get the principal. This wasn't the first time Tony had exploded, but it was the most serious and dangerous of incidents.

Sam was at his wit's end. He had talked with the resource teacher about ways to diffuse Tony's anger, but it was sometimes impossible to intervene before Tony's quick temper caused incidents like the one in the gym. In Sam's mind, Tony was a menace to other students and needed to be disciplined for his misbehavior. Sam decided to ask the principal either to expel Tony or to give him a long-term suspension so Tony's Individual Educational Plan (IEP) team could have sufficient time to rethink Tony's placement.

Analysis of "Treating Different Students Differently— Illegal Discrimination?"

Can students with disabilities be expelled or given long-term suspensions for dangerous conduct? The disciplining of students with disabilities has been a controversial and confusing issue for educators and parents alike. Under the 1975 Education for All Handicapped Children Act (EAHCA), now called the Individualized Disabilities Education Act, students with disabilities are guaranteed a free and appropriate education. In 1988, the Supreme Court ruled in *Honig v. Doe* that expulsion of students with disabilities for behavior attributable to their disability would be a violation of EAHCA provisions (Yell, 1990).

The Court did agree, however, that students with disabilities exhibiting behavior dangerous to self or others may be temporarily suspended for up to 10 days if such punishment is the same that would be used for a non-handicapped student (Bartlett, 1988). During the 10-day period, staff members can review a student's Individualized Education Plan (IEP) and meet with the student's parents to agree on an interim placement. Should parents disagree with a proposed change in placement, the 10-day period also allows school officials to seek court approval of the placement (Beyer, 1989).

Cultural Awareness

A number of court cases have helped to clarify legislation designed to protect the rights of individuals with disabilities. Henry Beyer (1989) cited *Irving Independent School District v. Tatro* (1984) as the more enduring of the Supreme Court's decisions helping families obtain "related services" guaranteed by the 1975 Education for All Handicapped Children Act (Public Law 94-142):

> Amber Tatro was an eight-year-old child with spina bifida and a condition which prevents her from emptying her bladder voluntarily. Every three or four hours she must have a catheter inserted into her urethra to drain her bladder—clean, intermittent catheterization (CIC), a procedure that she was not yet able to perform by herself. Her Texas public school system argued that CIC was a "medical service" and thus not their responsibility. The Supreme Court, however, ruled that it was a "related service" under 94-142 that must be provided by the school. (p. 54)

Would You Check These Papers for Me?

The terse phone call from Amy Aller's mother, a local lawyer, should have alerted Charles Armstrong to the possibility of an unpleasant parent conference, but Amy was a good student, and as far as Charles knew, she had been quite happy in school. Amy had left school that afternoon a little upset by the low score on her math quiz, but her grades in general were so good he couldn't imagine one assignment prompting a parent conference; it had to be something else.

As Charles sat facing Mrs. Aller that afternoon, she explained the reason for her conference. Amy was in fact upset—not so much because of her low math score but because of the "unkind" comments about her paper made by classmates. "How did anyone else know Amy's grade on this quiz?" asked Mrs. Aller. Charles shifted uncomfortably in his chair. "I have student helpers who grade papers for me when they finish their work," said Charles. "I guess one of them must have told the others about Amy's paper today. I'm sorry. This has never been a problem before. I'll be sure to say something to my students tomorrow so this type of thing doesn't happen again."

Is posting grades an invasion of students' privacy?

As she stood to leave, Mrs. Aller said, "I like you, Mr. Armstrong, but I want to tell you I don't think you should use this system anymore. I believe it violates the Buckley Amendment. No student should have knowledge of another student's progress in school."

Later that night Charles pulled out his college textbook, read about the Buckley Amendment, and reflected on his conference with Mrs. Aller. If Mrs. Aller was right, was he also violating students' rights of privacy when he displayed some students' papers as examples of good work? What about when he asked students to raise their hands to indicate whether they got something right or wrong on written assignments? Was he in violation of the law when he had students work problems at the board in front of their peers? Charles made a mental note to call the legal advisor to the teachers' organization the next day to get some answers to these questions.

Analysis of "Would You Check These Papers for Me?"

Is it an invasion of privacy when a student checks or corrects a peer's school work? Charles may very well be in violation of the Buckley Amendment when he allows students to grade classmates' papers. Part of the Family Educational Rights and Privacy Act (commonly referred to as the **Buckley Amendment**) prohibits schools from releasing information about a student to third parties without parental or student permission. This ruling suggests that teacher practices such as permitting students to grade or correct other students' papers, reading aloud or posting grades, and asking students to raise their hands if they responded correctly or incorrectly to a problem violate students' rights to privacy, potentially causing students' embarrassment or shame (Chase, 1976).

WHAT ARE TEACHERS' RIGHTS AND RESPONSIBILITIES?

Teachers enjoy a number of rights also extended to students. For example, they may be excused from saluting or pledging allegiance to the flag if such actions violate their beliefs and commitments. However, as with students, there are times when teachers' constitutional rights must be considered in light of important educational goals. Because of the nature of their jobs, teachers are usually held to higher standards of behavior than ordinary citizens (Imber & van Geel, 1993). The scenarios that follow examine some of the issues decided by the courts in this delicate balance between teachers' rights as citizens and their rights as state employees. Also discussed are some of the responsibilities inherent in teachers' jobs, particularly with regard to student safety.

To Join or Not to Join

Megan was thrilled when she received a contract from the Detroit public schools in July. Although her college advisor had warned her it might be midsummer or later before anyone heard about their job applications, Megan had been on pins and needles since graduation. For as long as she could remember, Megan had wanted to be a teacher. Now she also had school loans to repay, so it was crucial she be employed as soon as possible.

A few days after signing her contract, Megan received a letter from the Detroit Federation of Teachers (DFT) describing benefits of belonging to the professional association and the cost of joining. Megan tossed the letter in the trash, deciding she would wait until she had some financial stability before spending money she didn't have. During the first week of school, a representative of the DFT announced at a faculty meeting that those who had not paid dues to the DFT needed to do so or risk being dismissed from their jobs. Megan was confused. Perhaps she had misunderstood the announcement. Surely nonmembers of the DFT would not be required to pay dues.

Analysis of "To Join or Not to Join"

Can teachers who are not union members be required to pay dues to the organization? Federal law recognizes teachers' constitutional right to advocate, organize, and join a teacher union. In many states, teachers also have the right to engage in collective bargaining, a procedure for resolving disagreements between employers and employees. Teachers negotiate with their school boards, usually through their union representative, about such things as contract hours, salaries, and fringe benefits. There are no constitutional guarantees that school boards must bargain with teachers' unions, however, so restrictions on the scope of bargaining vary greatly from state to state.

By 1991, about 80% of public school teachers belonged to either the National Education Association (NEA) or the American Federation of Teachers (AFT). At the same time, over half of the states had laws requiring nonmembers of unions to pay dues to the union as a condition of employment.

Several Supreme Court rulings uphold the constitutionality of such laws. In a case (*Abood v. Detroit Board of Education*) heard in 1977, Christine Warczak and a number of other teachers challenged a Michigan law requiring teachers who had not become union members within 60 days to pay an amount equal to union dues or to face discharge. The teachers argued that because they did not believe in collective bargaining or agree with union activities unrelated to collective bargaining, such a law violated their right to freedom of association as guaranteed in the First and Fourteenth Amendments. The Supreme Court disagreed, noting that union activities benefit every employee, union member or not, and thus all should share the cost of the union's collective bargaining activities. The Court also decided, however, that it was a violation of First Amendment rights to require public employees to support financially a union's political activities.

In 1984, the Supreme Court clarified this last portion of the *Abood* decision by ruling in *Ellis v. Brotherhood of Railway Clerks* that a union's nonpolitical publications, conventions, and social activities are sufficiently related to the union's work in collective bargaining to justify the charging of nonunion members for such services. Litigation expenses not involving the negotiation of agreements or settlement of grievances, or charges for general organizing efforts, however, cannot be charged to dissenting employees. In its 1986 ruling in *Chicago Teachers Union, Local No. 1 AFL-CIO v. Hudson*, the Supreme Court also stated that unions must explain the basis for the dues amount, allow a prompt opportunity to contest the fee before an impartial decision maker, and hold in escrow disputed amounts until consensus is reached (Fischer, Schimmel, & Kelly, 1991).

There's Got to be a Way to Keep This Job!

Sandra Allen, a 2nd-year teacher, loved her teaching job. With the exception of two or three students who had difficulty controlling their actions, her class was well-behaved and motivated to learn. Most students consistently completed assignments on time, and their work was accurate and neat. Sandra knew parents had been ambivalent about their children having the "new" teacher at school, but their comments during parent conferences indicated that they, too, were pleased with the academic progress of their children.

When Sandra was given notice in May that she would not be rehired for the upcoming academic year, she was shocked and angry. Because her principal's midyear evaluation rated Sandra as "above average" or "outstanding" on all categories, Sandra had assumed her contract would be renewed. She needed only 1 more year of teaching in the system to earn tenure. Surely the school board could not force her out of the system without giving her reasons for doing so, or could it?

Analysis of "There's Got to be a Way to Keep This Job!"

Sandra's story is much like that of David Roth, an assistant professor of political science at Wisconsin State University-Oshkosh who was hired for a fixed term of 1 academic year. When Roth was notified at the end of the academic term that he would not be rehired for the following year, he went to court, claiming that the decision infringed on his Fourteenth Amendment rights. In ruling on *Board of Regents of State Colleges v. Roth* (1972), the Supreme Court disagreed with Roth's charge, explaining that a probationary teacher does not have the same rights as a tenured teacher.

According to the Court, tenured teachers may not be removed from their positions without specific or good cause, nor may they be dismissed for capricious or arbitrary reasons (e.g., political beliefs and activities). Thus, tenured teachers have a property interest meriting due process protection. In most states, however, the contract of a teacher with probationary status may be terminated at the end of the year (state statute generally specifies a date by which teachers must be notified of such action) without cause. This means a probationary teacher's property interest is only for the duration of a 1-year term. However, if the probationary teacher can present evidence to suggest nonrenewal is in retaliation for exercise of constitutional rights (e.g., freedom of speech), due process is required (Fischer, Schimmel, & Kelly, 1991).

Should the school board resort to **dismissal** (removing a probationary or tenured teacher before the completion of his or her contract), a notice, hearing, or notification of reasons for dismissal is required by law. State statutes typically list broad causes for dismissal, such as incompetency, immorality, unprofessional conduct, and neglect of duty. Lack of funding and a decline in student enrollment may also be just cause for the midyear dismissal of both tenured and nontenured teachers (La Morte, 1993). Many state laws also stipulate that nontenured teachers must be dismissed before tenured teachers, and, among tenured teachers, the least experienced must be dismissed first.

A Line Between Personhood and Professionalism

Jason O'Hara was one of the most popular teachers at Baker Middle School. Students, parents, and colleagues alike respected him for his innovative ideas, sharp wit, and ability to interest students in learning. Now in his 4th year of teaching, Jason had tenure in the school system and was chair of the English department.

Can a teacher be dismissed for private conduct?

When Jason received a note from John Wright, the principal, requesting that he come to the office that afternoon, Jason thought nothing of it. Mr. Wright had been very supportive of Jason and his efforts to upgrade the English curriculum. As he stepped through the office door, however, Jason knew something was amiss. Mr. Wright, a grim look on his face, handed

Jason a two-page letter addressed to the superintendent. The letter, written by a teacher with whom Jason had had a brief homosexual relationship the year before, made explicit the nature of their relationship. Jason read it in stunned silence.

"Jason," said Mr. Wright, "this letter was also mailed to members of the school board. Several of them are really uptight about this. They want to dismiss you for immoral behavior. I think this is going to be an ugly battle. I'll do everything I can to help you, but I think you also need legal assistance. Do you have a good lawyer?"

Analysis of "A Line Between Personhood and Professionalism"

Can a teacher be dismissed for private conduct? As noted in Chapter 2, teachers in early times were held to rigid codes of conduct. Those who crossed the line between "moral" and "immoral" behavior resigned or were dismissed immediately from their teaching duties. In recent times, however, the line of demarcation has blurred because it is often difficult to get community consensus about what constitutes immoral conduct. Moreover, many educators believe that when the school day ends, what occurs in the privacy of their homes is their own business and should not affect negatively their status as professionals. Those who disagree argue that being a private person does not relieve educators of their duty to serve as role models for children (Sendor, 1992).

Ambiguity about what constitutes moral and immoral behavior is reflected by court decisions in different states. In making employment decisions based on a teacher's sexual orientation, courts usually consider "the adverse effect on students or fellow teachers, adversity anticipated within the school system, surrounding circumstances, and possible chilling effects on discipline" (Alexander & Alexander, 1992, p. 586).

Depending on public reaction to Jason's case, then, he may or may not be dismissed from his teaching position. In 1969, the California Supreme Court heard a case (*Morrison v. State Board of Education*) involving a teacher, Marc Morrison, whose circumstances were much like those of Jason. When the superintendent received a letter from a male teacher who had been involved sexually with Morrison the year before, the school board voted to dismiss Morrison on grounds of immoral and unprofessional behavior. The court disagreed with the school board's actions, saying that the board's definition of "immoral" behavior was dangerously vague and could implicate many educators. Ruling in favor of Morrison, the court also stated that disapproval of an educator's private conduct was insufficient reason for dismissal, particularly when there was no proof that the educator's professional work was affected negatively by the conduct.

Eight years later in a case (*Gaylord V. Tacoma School District No. 10*) heard by the Supreme Court of Washington, however, the court upheld the dismissal of a teacher who admitted his homosexuality to the vice principal of the school. Based on the fact that at least one student and several teachers and parents had challenged the teacher's fitness to teach, the court held that the teacher's continuance in the system would likely disrupt the educational process.

VOICES

On Teachers' Freedom of Expression

Court cases such as *Pickering v. Board of Education of Township High School District 205*, heard in 1968, have helped define teachers' rights of freedom of expression on matters of "public" concern. Marvin Pickering, a tenured teacher, published a letter in a local newspaper that was critical of the school board's efforts to raise new revenue. The Board dismissed Pickering on the basis that numerous statements in the letter were false, that he damaged the reputations of board members and administrators, and that such comments would be disruptive to the workplace. The Illinois Circuit and Supreme Courts upheld the Board's decision on the grounds that Pickering's letter was "detrimental to the interests of the school system." When the case reached the United States Supreme Court, the courts' judgments were reversed. Justice Thurgood Marshall delivered the Court's opinion:

What we . . . have before us is a case in which a teacher has made erroneous public statements upon issues then currently the subject of public attention, which are critical of his ultimate employer but which are neither shown nor can be presumed to have in any way either impeded the teacher's proper performance of his daily duties in the classroom or to have interfered with the regular operation of the schools generally. In these circumstances we conclude that the interest of the school administration in limiting teachers' opportunities to contribute to public debate is not signif-

icantly greater than its interest in limiting a similar contribution by any member of the general public. The public interest in having free and unhindered debate on matters of public importance—the core value of the Free Speech Clause of the First Amendment—is so great that it has been held that a State cannot authorize the recovery of damages by a public official for defamatory statements directed at him except when such statements are shown to have been made either with knowledge of their falsity or with reckless disregard for their truth or falsity. . . . (p. 1737)

In sum, we hold that, in a case such as this, absent proof of false statements knowingly or recklessly made by him, a teacher's exercise of his right to speak on issues of public importance may not furnish the basis for his dismissal from public employment. (p. 1738)

CRITICAL THINKING

The courts have refused to lay down a general standard against which all public statements made by teachers might be measured for protection by the First Amendment. Why would the courts be reluctant to do so? Why do the courts try to balance the need for protecting free speech with the need to ensure harmony among coworkers in the workplace?

Source: Pickering v. Board of Education of Township High School District 205, Will County, Illinois, 391 U.S. 563 (1968).

Such cases are decided differently by different localities because the Supreme Court has not yet recognized a constitutional privacy right to engage in homosexual behavior. Based on the 1984 ruling in *National Gay Task Force v. Board of Education of Oklahoma City*, however, teachers do have the right to advocate publicly for legalization of homosexuality as long as such activity is not disruptive to the educational process. As indicated in the 1984 ruling in *Rowland v. Mad River Local School District*, advocacy does not include talking with coworkers about personal sexual preferences or those of students.

In this particular instance, an Ohio guidance counselor who had been dismissed by the school board for admitting her bisexuality to several members of the staff argued that her First and Fourteenth Amendment rights had been violated. The Court disagreed, saying that the guidance counselor's statements were not protected by the First Amendment because they were not made as a citizen on matters of public concern. Rather, the counselor's statements were a matter of private concern. Furthermore, the court held that, absent evidence that heterosexual employees had been or would be treated differently for discussing sexual preferences, nonrenewal of the counselor's contract was not in violation of the Fourteenth Amendment (Morin, 1991).

What Do You Mean I'm Violating Copyright Laws?

During summer vacation, Robert Wells—newly appointed chair of the mathematics department at Central High—videotaped a two-part series on "Mathematics in Today's Workplace" and added it to his growing collection of tapes. Robert's students had responded well to his occasional use of a videotape to illustrate concepts being taught in class. He was sure these newest tapes would be especially effective in the spring, when math analysis students planned projects showing real-life applications of mathematics.

As he thought about the upcoming inservice program he would conduct for department members, Robert also realized that his videotapes might be an excellent tool for helping others think about ways to vary instruction. Excited by the prospect, Robert contacted Dorothy James at the media center to see if she would make copies of his videotapes and place them on reserve in the school library. When Dorothy asked Robert if he had permission to videotape the copyrighted television programs, he was caught off guard. "What do you mean?" Robert said. "I'm using these tapes for teaching purposes. Lots of people do that. What's the big deal?"

"I used to think it was okay myself," said Dorothy, "but now I'm not so sure. I'll call central office and see what I can find out. Until we know, we'd better not copy any of those videotapes."

Analysis of "What Do You Mean I'm Violating Copyright Laws?"

Can teachers videotape television programs and use them for educational purposes? Although the Supreme Court has not decided whether it is illegal for teachers to tape television broadcasts on home video recorders for later classroom use, 1981 Congressional guidelines for off-the-air taping suggest that such activities may in fact constitute copyright infringement. Guidelines specify that copyrighted television programs may be videotaped by nonprofit educational organizations but that videotapes must be destroyed or erased after 45 calendar days if the institution has not obtained a license for such videotaping. Teachers may use the videotapes with students at school, or with students receiving homebound instruction, one time during the first 10 school days after recording occurs. One additional showing is allowed during the 10-day period, but only for instructional reinforcement. Additional use is limited to evaluation of the videotape's usefulness as an instructional tool (Copyright Information Services, 1987).

In *Encyclopedia Britannica Educational Corporation v. Crooks*, a New York federal district court found a school system guilty of violating fair use standards by engaging in extensive off-the-air taping and replaying of programs broadcast on public television. Such taping was deemed to interfere with the marketability of producers' films. In 1984, in *Sony Corporation of America v. Universal City Studios*, the Supreme Court ruled that personal videorecording for the purpose of "time shifting" (recording of a program for later viewing), however, did not harm the television market (Fischer, Schimmel, & Kelly, 1991).

Until the Supreme Court decides whether home taping for broader viewing by students in your classrooms constitutes fair use of copyrighted materials, you are well-advised to adhere to Congressional guidelines for off-the-air taping (see Appendix D at the end of the book). Another option, of course, is to seek written permission from copyright owners to videotape programs for classroom use.

Maybe She Is Just a Sickly Child

She chose a desk near the back of the room, not near anyone in particular. She was quiet and somewhat plain in her dress, but her long brown hair was striking. Joan Mason didn't know much about 8-year-old Theresa because Theresa had just moved to town in August. Her permanent records indicated that she was above average in ability. While she had missed a lot of school last year, her grades were about average, but maybe a little low in math.

Another parent told Joan that Theresa's mother had been divorced last year and had moved here, at least in part, to get away from her former husband. The family—Theresa's mother, younger sister, a man she called Jim, whom she described as her mother's friend, and Jim's 17-year-old son—lived in a small ranch house in a nice neighborhood on the outskirts of town.

As Joan worked with Theresa the first few weeks of school, Theresa seldom missed a day of school and kept up with daily assignments. By mid-October, however, things had begun to change. Theresa's attendance became sporadic, and Joan noticed that Theresa was often passive and uncommunicative, both with her and with classmates. During seatwork, Theresa chewed her fingernails, her constant gnawing sometimes drawing blood. When Joan talked with Theresa's mother during a parent conference, she did not seem overly concerned by Joan's observations. She indicated that Theresa's behavior at home had not changed and attributed Theresa's recent absences and withdrawn manner to her tendency to be a "sickly child." After the conference, Joan was still worried about Theresa, but she didn't know what to do.

What about this situation concerns you? What, if anything, would you do if you were Theresa's teacher?

Analysis of "Maybe She is Just a Sickly Child"

Educators, unlike physicians, social workers, and law enforcement officers, have a unique opportunity to monitor students' social behaviors, academic progress, and attitudes over time. Some patterns of behavior, especially sudden, dramatic changes, can be a warning sign of something gone awry in a child's life. Teachers need to be particularly alert to patterns of behavior that could indicate that a child is the victim of abuse or neglect.

As defined by the Child Abuse Prevention and Treatment Act, child abuse and neglect include physical or mental injury, sexual abuse or exploitation, negligent treatment, or maltreatment: (a) of a child under 18 years of age (unless state law specifies a younger age), (b) by any person responsible for a child's welfare, (c) under circumstances that harm or threaten a child's health or welfare.

Sexual abuse is defined as:

> [(1)] the use, employment, persuasion, inducement, enticement or coercion of any child to engage in, or assist any other person to engage in, any sexually explicit conduct (or any simulation of such conduct) for the purpose of producing any visual depiction of such conduct, or (2) rape, molestation, prostitution, or other form of sexual exploitation of children, or incest with children. (U.S. Department of Health and Human Services, 1992, pp. 1–2)

As noted in Chapter 6, abuse can occur at any socioeconomic level to both males and females. In every state, educators are required by law to report cases of abuse or neglect resulting in physical injury to a child, and, in the majority of states, educators are also required to report instances of emotional, mental, or sexual abuse. Failure to report suspected abuse and neglect in most states is a misdemeanor and, with a few exceptions, teachers are identified among professionals required to make such reports. Certain behaviors or signs occurring repeatedly or in combination may cue an educator that child abuse is present in a family (see Appendix E at the end of the book).

Procedures for reporting child abuse or neglect are specified in state statutes. Many localities also have school board policies and procedures to encourage effective reporting of suspected child abuse. Under the Child Abuse and Neglect Act, educators are assured immunity from civil liability if reports of abuse and neglect are made in good faith.

You Should Have Known Better

Two teachers organized a trip to a museum of natural history for a group of about 50 students ranging in age from 12 to 15 years. When they arrived at the museum, students were allowed to divide into small groups to tour the museum without supervision. One student, Roberto Mancha, of his own volition joined a group and proceeded with them to the various exhibits. While out of his teacher's sight, Roberto alleged that he was accosted by a group of youths not connected with the school, beaten by them, and as a result, suffered serious injuries. In *Mancha v. Field Museum of Natural History*, Roberto's father initiated action against the school district, the two teachers, and the museum for the injuries suffered by his son at the museum.

Were the teachers negligent? Should they have been expected to supervise students at all times?

Analysis of "You Should Have Known Better"

Suits brought by students injured during school-related activities are the most common type of litigation in education (Imber & van Geel, 1993). A teacher who demonstrates **negligence** (failure to exercise reasonable care to protect students from injury), may be held liable for damages if an injured student can prove the following: (a) the teacher had a legal duty to offer a standard of care that would have prevented the injury from occurring, (b)

> **When can a teacher be sued for negligence?**

the teacher did not live up to the standard of care, (c) the teacher's carelessness resulted in harm to the student, and (d) the student sustained an actual injury that could be measured in monetary terms (Imber & van Geel, 1993).

When accused of negligence, a teacher may try to prove that a student's injury was a mere accident, that his or her action or inaction was not the cause of such injury, and that some other act intervened and was the cause of the injury. Other rejoinders against negligence include contributory negligence, comparative negligence, and assumption of risk (Alexander & Alexander, 1992).

Contributory negligence is failure of the student who was injured to exercise the required standard of care for his or her own safety. When this condition exists, depending on such things as a child's age and mental maturity, the teacher may be absolved from liability. A high school student, for example, who has been taught how to use a power saw and observed to determine that she can operate the machine safely may be guilty of contributory negligence if injured while removing a piece of wood from the machine with her hands—a violation of safety practices students have been taught.

In situations in which teacher and student are both held liable for an injury, there may be a charge of **comparative negligence**. Generally, this means that a teacher is held accountable for a proportion of damages commensurate with the degree to which he or she contributed to the injury. **Assumption of risk**, rarely applicable except in cases of competitive athletics, means that people who are aware of possible risks involved in an activity voluntarily participate, thus agreeing to take their chances.

Teachers cannot be everywhere at once during recess, but they are expected to protect students from foreseeable risks of harm. This means being aware of what students are doing and stopping them from acting in ways that could result in injury, such as rock-throwing, hanging upside down on the jungle gym, or pushing and shoving.

In *Mancha v. Field Museum of Natural History* (1972), charges of negligence brought against the school, museum, and teachers were dismissed by an Illinois court. Although the courts viewed the teachers' action of letting students tour the museum in an unsupervised group as an intentional act, given the nature of the environment (a museum), it was not an act that teachers should have anticipated would result in harm to a student. In explaining their verdict, the court argued that a museum is very different from a factory, a stone quarry, or a place where there might be dangerous machinery, or a place where there might be a shooting or an assault:

> The Museum in question is itself a great educational enterprise which enables teachers, parents, and children to learn much that could be learned at school...To say that the teachers had a duty to supervise and discipline the entire Museum trip would be to ignore the realities of the situation and to make such trips impossible. (*Mancha v. Field Museum of Natural History*, 1972, p. 902)

However, there have been several cases in which students were injured and educators were found to have breached duty of care:

- A group of students with mental retardation were left unattended for a half hour, and a student received an eye injury when another pupil threw a wooden pointer (*Gonzalez v. Mackler*, 1963).

- A student who was permitted to wear mittens fell while climbing on a jungle gym (*Ward v. Newfield Central School District No. 1*, 1978).

- A student was burned when she and her peers were working on a project for the science fair. The accident occurred when the students tried to light a defective burner that had gone out and alcohol exploded. Although the teacher had set up the experiment and checked to see that it worked properly, the teacher was not in the room when students lit the burner. Because the students were not advised to wait until the teacher's return to light the fire and were not personally supervised, the teacher was held liable for negligence (*Station v. Travelers Insurance Co.*, 1974).

WHAT ARE THE RIGHTS AND RESPONSIBILITIES OF SCHOOL DISTRICTS?

Although the courts have consistently asserted that the authority for public education resides in the state legislature, schools for the most part are locally administered. As mentioned in Chapter 11, school boards deal with a variety of educational issues and problems. A number of court cases, in conjunction with federal and state statutes, have clarified the special responsibilities and rights of local school boards.

Balancing Academic Freedom

The school board meeting was an angry one. Three English teachers from the high school and a number of parents voiced their opinions about the list of texts used in elective high school literature courses. When the board voted to eliminate 10 texts from the diverse list of 1285 books, the teachers were enraged. They believed that all the books were necessary components of a curriculum designed to stimulate debate and broaden student knowledge. Viewing the board's action as an invasion of their First Amendment right to academic freedom, the three English teachers decided to seek legal counsel. They could not believe that a local school board had ultimate authority to determine what textbooks would be used in schools.

Analysis of "Balancing Academic Freedom"

Since the U.S. Supreme Court ruling in *Hazelwood School District v. Kuhlmeier* (1988), the U.S. Supreme Court has indicated a willingness to allow local school boards the final decision regarding the curriculum and the availability of books, films, and materials in elementary and secondary classrooms. However, if school boards' actions have the effect of contracting rather than expanding knowledge, judicial intervention is not uncommon (Alexander & Alexander, 1992). When deciding individual cases, the courts usually consider the educational relevance of controversial material, teaching objectives, and the age and maturity of the intended audience.

In *Virgil v. School Board of Columbia County, Florida* (1989), the Supreme Court upheld a local school board's right to remove two readings from the curriculum because of objections to the material's vulgarity and sexual explicitness. Although the Court did not endorse the decision, stating that they seriously questioned how young people could be harmed by reading the "masterpieces" of Western literature, the Court acknowledged that the school board's decision was reasonably related to "legitimate pedagogical concerns." That is, as in *Hazelwood*, school officials considered the emotional maturity of the intended audience when determining the appropriateness of readings dealing with potentially "sensitive" topics (Alexander & Alexander, 1992).

How much freedom does a teacher have in the selection of material for his or her students? In 1989, a Fifth Circuit Court of Appeals ruling held that teachers cannot assert a First Amendment right to replace an official supplementary reading list with their own list of books without first getting administrative approval. Nor may a teacher delete parts of the curriculum if they conflict with personal beliefs. A kindergarten teacher, for example, who refuses to teach a unit on patriotic topics may be dismissed by the school board for not covering prescribed material (McCarthy & Cambron-McCabe, 1992).

Such restrictions do not mean that teachers have no freedom in the selection of teaching strategies, however. Teachers who want to assign controversial materials may usually do so as long as selected materials are relevant to the topic of study, appropriate to the age and maturity of students, and unlikely to cause disruption. When a high school psychology teacher in a conservative Texas community was fired for having her students read a masculinity survey from *Psychology Today*, the court ruled that the school violated the teacher's constitutional rights. In the eyes of the court, there was no evidence that the material caused substantial disruption, and there was no clear, prior prohibition against the use of such materials (Fischer, Schimmel, & Kelly, 1991).

Equal Treatment

Fifteen African-American preschool and elementary students living in a low-income housing project in Ann Arbor, Michigan, brought suit against the board of education for practices they claimed denied them equal educational opportunities. According to the students, their language (African-American English) differed from standard English that was spoken by teachers and used in written materials of the school. The students claimed a violation of Title 20 of the U.S. Code which provides that no state can deny individuals educational opportunities due to their race, gender, or national origin by failing to overcome language barriers that might inhibit learning (*Martin Luther King, Jr., Elementary School Children v. Michigan Board of Education* (1979).

Analysis of "Equal Treatment"

Are school boards legally obligated to make special provisions for students who speak "black English"? In its 1954 landmark decision *Brown v. Board of Education of Topeka*, the Supreme Court addressed for the first time issues of educational inequality when it repudiated the "separate but equal" doctrine, attempting to put an end to racial segregation in schools. As the courts worked, and continue to work, to effect unitary school systems, many have questioned the quality of educational opportunities for minority-group students in such settings. One area of concern has been classification of students for special services. Sometimes courts and legislatures have directed attention to discriminatory classifications of minority-group students; in other situations, such as those involving linguistic minority-group students, the courts have addressed the absence of student classifications.

In *Lau v. Nichols* (1974), the only Supreme Court decision involving English-deficient students, the Court held that a school district receiving federal aid must provide special instruction for non-English-speaking students whose opportunities to learn are restricted because of language barriers. This particular case centered around the plight of about 1,800 Chinese-American students in San Francisco public schools who spoke little or no English yet were offered no remedial English language instruction or other special compensatory program by the school system. According to the Court, such treatment of students violated Title VI of the **Civil Rights Act of 1964**, which specifies that no one, regardless of race, color, or origin, can be discriminated against or denied participation in programs receiving federal assistance (Wadlington, Whitebread, & Davis, 1988).

Following *Lau*, Congress offered further protection to students when it passed the **Bilingual Act of 1974**, amended in 1988. This act calls for parental involvement in the planning of appropriate educational programs for children with limited English-speaking ability. It should be noted, however, that neither the Bilingual Act nor Title VI specifies what types of programs are appropriate for addressing the needs of students with limited

VOICES

Prince Edward County Closes Its Schools

In many communities across the United States, school desegregation focused public attention directly on the concept of equal treatment as no event had before. One of the most stubbornly resistant communities in the nation was Prince Edward County, Virginia. Rather than desegregate its public schools, the board of supervisors closed them. During the school crisis, Bob Smith, associate editor of the *Norfolk Virginian-Pilot*, covered the story of race relations that "touched on the lives of ordinary people and sometimes forced them to make painful or even dangerous decisions."

On June 2, 1959, without a great deal of ado, the board of supervisors of Prince Edward County announced its intention not to appropriate money to operate public schools for the coming year. The board issued a statement meant to cover its action:

> "The action taken today . . . has been determined upon only after the most careful and deliberate study over the long period of years since the schools in this county were first brought under the force of federal court decree. It is with the most profound regret that we have been compelled to take this action. . . . [It] is the fervent hope of this board . . . that we may in due time be able to resume the operation of public schools in this county upon a basis acceptable to all people of the county."

In other words, the supervisors were closing the schools rather than agreeing to operate them integrated; they would open them only if and when they could operate them, once again, segregated. The schools were closed for five years.

CRITICAL THINKING

Why do you think our society has come to believe that separate education for children of different races is undesirable?

Source: Smith, B. (1965). *They closed their schools: Prince Edward County, Virginia, 1951–1964.* Chapel Hill: The University of North Carolina Press, p. 151.

English-speaking abilities. There is thus much variation state to state in the types of assistance offered to students who have difficulty understanding standard English.

Since the *Lau* ruling, many cases have been heard by the courts, one of which was *Martin Luther King, Jr., Elementary School Children v. Michigan Board of Education* (1979). As described above, this suit was brought by African-American students who protested the use of standard English as the sole medium of instruction.

In ruling on the case, the Court acknowledged that Michigan schools had provided special assistance to these and other students through learning consultants, a speech therapist, a psychologist, a language consultant, tutors, and parent helpers. There was thus evidence of good faith efforts to meet the needs of students who spoke black English. The Court noted, however, that teachers seemed to lack knowledge about black English and thus were restricted in their ability to educate African-American students. To remedy this, the court did not order the establishment of a bilingual program, as was done in the *Lau* case. Instead, the Court required the school board to develop a plan whereby teachers would learn to recognize the home language of students and to use that knowledge to teach reading skills and standard English more effectively.

How Could You Let This Happen to a Student?

When Peter graduated from high school, he sought $500,000 in damages from the San Francisco Unified Schools for failing to provide him with an adequate education. According to Peter, the school system was at fault for his poor skills because it had: (a) failed to apprehend his reading disabilities, (b) assigned him to classes in which curricular materials were not geared to his reading level, (c) allowed him to pass from grade to grade without seeing that he mastered basic skills necessary for success at succeeding levels, (d) assigned him to teachers who did not know how to meet his learning needs, and (e) allowed him to graduate without being able to read at the eighth-grade level as required by the Education Code. Moreover, Peter said that his mother had been told that his reading ability was not much below the school's average.

Given the sequence of events, can the school system be held liable for educational malpractice?

Analysis of "How Could You Let This Happen to a Student?"

Although teachers and educational institutions have historically been exempt from legal responsibility and accountability, increasing numbers of educational malpractice claims have forced the courts to deal frequently with issues of academic negligence. A precedent-setting case occurred in California in 1976 when Peter W., the high-school graduate described above, accused the school system of negligently and intentionally depriving him of basic skills.

The state appellate court dismissed Peter W.'s suit, contending that there were no explicit "standards of care" by which schools or classroom teachers could be judged negligent in their duties. Besides conflicting ideas about the best way to educate students, the Court noted that there were a variety of physical, neurological, emotional, cultural, and environmental factors that influenced learning yet were beyond a classroom teacher's control. In addition, the Court reasoned that attempts to hold school districts to a "duty of care" in academic matters would likely result in a flood of malpractice suits that would only inhibit their ability to discharge their academic functions (*Peter W. v. San Francisco Unified School District*, 1976).

For the most part, the California court's decision has been followed in educational-malpractice litigation. However, in instances when educators have maliciously or intentionally caused injury to children by furnishing false information about a child's learning problems and altering information to cover their actions (*Hunter v. Board of Education of Montgomery County*), or placing a child in a program despite scores showing a placement to be inappropriate (*B.M. v. Montana*), courts have allowed parents to bring action against school officials (Fischer, Schimmel, & Kelly, 1991).

Somebody Will Pay!

Christine Franklin, a 10th-grade student, was uncomfortable around Andrew Hill, a sports coach and economics teacher at her high school in suburban Atlanta. According to Christine, Hill sexually harassed her by doing such things as asking if she would be willing to have sex with an older man, calling her at home to ask her out, and forcibly kissing her on the mouth in the school parking lot. During Christine's junior year, things got much worse; on at least three occasions, Hill allegedly pressured her into having sex. When Christine reported Hill's actions to school officials, no immediate steps were taken to curtail Hill's behavior. By the time Christine had lodged a complaint with the U.S. Education Department's office for civil rights, however, Hill had resigned and the school had adopted a grievance procedure to avoid future violations.

Can students who are victims of sexual harassment . . . sue for monetary damages?

Still angry about the abuse she had suffered at the high school, Christine decided to sue the school district for monetary damages. Her argument was that Hill's behavior toward her was a violation of Title IX (a law prohibiting schools supported with federal monies from discriminating on the basis of gender). In school officials' eyes, Christine didn't stand a chance in court; they had resolved the problem and it was unlikely to occur again.

Can students who are victims of sexual harassment and other forms of sex discrimination sue for monetary damages?

Analysis of "Somebody Will Pay!"

In 1992, when the Supreme Court heard Christine Franklin's case (*Franklin v. Gwinnett County Public Schools*), the Court ruled unanimously that Christine was indeed the victim of sexual harassment. Furthermore, the Court stated for the first time that schools supported by federal funds were susceptible to lawsuit and, in instances of sexual harassment and other forms of sex discrimination, liable for monetary damages to victims of such mistreatment. What this means for school systems is that more lawsuits will likely be filed against them by individuals alleging discrimination in employment and athletics. Legal experts also predict that this court case will clear the way for monetary damages to victims of race and disability discrimination in schools (Walsh, 1992).

What Kind of Choice Is This?

When the special education teacher and Anita Leopold met at the end of second grade to construct Miranda Leopold's IEP, they agreed that Miranda was at a point where she could benefit academically and socially from interactions with regular education students. Accordingly, they created a plan that would allow Miranda to be mainstreamed into a regular third grade classroom. With the exception of daily tutorial sessions with a resource teacher, Miranda would experience the regular curriculum for third grade students.

Anita was pleased with her daughter's new placement. However, when she learned that Miranda also qualified for the Milwaukee Parental Choice Program, she didn't know what to think. One of the private schools on the choice list was one focusing on art and music, both of which Miranda loved. The idea of sending Miranda to such a school was very appealing. When she phoned the school for information about the program, however, Anita learned that the choice school had no resource teacher to help Miranda with her reading skills. Anita was perplexed. Didn't choice schools have to offer the same services to students with disabilities as the public schools? How could state taxes be used for educational programs that, in a sense, discriminated against certain students?

Are choice schools held to the same standards as public schools?

Analysis of "What Kind of Choice is This?"

On March 3, 1992, the Wisconsin Supreme Court voted 4 to 3 to overturn a court of appeals ruling that the Milwaukee Parental Choice Plan was unconstitutional. Established in March 1990, the Choice Plan allowed up to 1,000 low-income students in Milwaukee to receive a voucher worth $2,500 each year to attend certain private, nonsectarian schools in the city. According to Shirley S. Abrahamson, one of the dissenting Justices, the majority opinion on this issue "permits the legislature to subvert the unifying, democratizing purpose of public education by using public funds to substitute private education for public education without the concomitant controls exerted over public education" (*Davis v. Grover*, 1992).

Participating private schools do not have to meet the same standards as public schools in the Milwaukee Parental Choice Plan. That fact has been troubling to many. Julie Underwood (1991) noted that "quality assurances" in the Choice Plan ensure that participating schools be operating as private schools and that one of the following occur: at least 70% of the student body should advance one grade level per year, average attendance rate should be at least 90%, at least 80% of the pupils should show "significant" educational progress; or at least 70% of the pupils' parents should meet school criteria for active involvement in the program.

Such criteria omit requirements for the provision of services to students, such as Miranda, who may have special learning needs. According to Underwood (1991), minimal standards for participating private schools mean that "there are no assurances that the severe problems facing disadvantaged youth will in any way be closer to being solved by merely changing either vendor or delivery systems" (p. 9).

Since *Davis v. Grover*, the Supreme Court has ruled unanimously that parents of students with learning disabilities may be eligible for tuition reimbursement if they send their children to private schools for special help, even if the schools are not approved by the local school district (*Florence County School District Four v. Carter*, 1993). Such litigation will surely redefine the relationship between "public" and "private" schools in the years ahead.

BENCHMARKS

Selected Supreme Court Cases on School-Related Issues

1943	*West Virginia State Board of Education v. Barnette.* Requiring students to salute or pledge to the American flag becomes unconstitutional.
1963	*School District of Abington Township v. Schempp.* Prayer and Bible reading in public school classrooms become unconstitutional.
1969	*Tinker v. Des Moines Independent School District.* Students do not lose their constitutional rights and freedoms when they pass through the schoolhouse door.
1971	*Lemon v. Kurtzman.* States may not provide direct aid for secular services to parochial schools, including teacher salaries and instructional materials.
1974	*Lau v. Nichols.* School districts receiving federal aid must provide special instruction for non-English-speaking students whose opportunities to learn are restricted because of language barriers.
1975	*Goss v. Lopez.* Students may not be suspended from school without a hearing.
1977	*Ingraham v. Wright.* The U. S. Constitution does not prohibit the use of corporal punishment in the schools. *Abood v. Detroit Board of Education.* It is constitutional for states to require nonmembers of unions to pay union dues as a condition of employment.
1981	*Widmar v. Vincent.* Refusing religious groups equal access to public facilities while allowing access to other groups is a violation of students' freedom of speech.
1984	*National Gay Task Force v. Board of Education of Oklahoma City* and *Rowland v. Mad River Local School District.* Teachers can advocate publicly the legalization of homosexuality unless the activity disrupts the educational process. Advocacy does not include telling coworkers about one's own or students' sexual orientation.
1985	*New Jersey v. T.L.O.* School officials are not required to obtain a warrant or show probable cause when searching a student suspected of violating school rules or the law.
1988	*Hazelwood School District v. Kuhlmeier.* School principals can censor school-sponsored publications.
1990	*Rothschild v. Grottenthaler.* Public school systems receiving federal funds must provide a sign-language interpreter to deaf parents attending school events directly relating to their children's academic program.
1992	*Franklin v. Gwinnett County Public Schools.* Schools supported by federal funds can be sued for sex discrimination and sexual harassment.
1993	*Florence County School District Four v. Carter.* Parents who unilaterally withdraw their child from a public school that fails to provide appropriate education under IDEA and place the child in a private school that offers such education are entitled to state reimbursement of expenses.

SUMMARY

1. Past precedents and milestones—important decisions rendered in pivotal cases—should guide teachers' actions, but few situations that will arise in the field will exactly match those dealt with in past cases.

2. In many states, parents may exempt their children from attending school if they meet certain requirements for providing education at home.

3. The legality of corporal punishment varies from state to state and district to district.

4. Students categorized as having special learning needs must be afforded special educational assistance.

5. As long as the school building is available for use by other noncurriculum clubs, and as long as the school does not sponsor or conduct club meetings, religious clubs are permissible on school grounds.

6. Students cannot be suspended or expelled without due process.

7. School searches must be guided by "reason" and "common sense"; that is, at the inception of the search, there must be reasonable grounds for suspecting evidence will be found to prove a student is in violation of the law or school rules; and the scope of the search must be reasonably related to the objectives of the search, the age and sex of the student, and the nature of the infraction.

8. School officials can censor school-sponsored student- produced material that is considered inconsistent with the educational mission of the school.

9. Schools can institute dress codes.

10. Schools should not release information about a student to third parties without parental or student permission, except in the event of an emergency.

11. Teachers may be required to share in the cost of the union's collective bargaining activities even though they do not belong to the union.

12. Tenured teachers cannot be dismissed without specific or good cause. Teachers with probationary status, however, generally have no constitutional right to due process when their contract is terminated at the end of the school year.

13. The Supreme Court has not yet recognized a constitutional privacy right to engage in homosexual behavior. Teachers do have the right to advocate publicly or encourage homosexual activity as long as such activity is not disruptive to the educational process. Advocacy does not include talking with coworkers about sexual preference.

14. Until the Supreme Court decides whether home videotaping for broader viewing by students in your classrooms constitutes fair use of copyrighted materials, you are well-advised to adhere to Congressional guidelines for off-the-air taping. Another option is to seek written permission from copyright owners to videotape programs for classroom use.

15. Educators are required to report cases of abuse or neglect resulting in physical injury to a child, and, in most states, educators are also required to report instances of emotional, mental, or sexual abuse.

16. Educators are expected to demonstrate care that a reasonable and prudent person would take when supervising students. When unusual dangers exist, special caution must be employed to prevent injury or harm to students.

17. Public school teachers do not have the right to determine curriculum to be taught.

18. School districts receiving federal aid must provide special instruction for non-English-speaking students whose opportunities to learn are restricted because of language barriers.

19. Educational-malpractice suits do not fare well in the courts. However, educators cannot maliciously or intentionally injure children by furnishing false information about a child's learning problems and alter information to cover their actions, or place a child in a program despite scores showing a placement to be inappropriate.

20. Public schools can be sued for sexual harassment and other forms of discrimination.

21. The relationship between public and private schools may be redefined in the future in cases involving the funding of school choice programs.

TERMS AND CONCEPTS

assumption of risk	contributory negligence	establishment clause
Bilingual Act of 1974	dismissal	free exercise clause
Buckley Amendment	due process of law	in loco parentis
Civil Rights Act of 1964	Equal Access Act (EEA)	Lemon test
comparative negligence	equal protection clause	negligence

STUDENT ACTIVITIES

Perceive and Value

What are the tenure laws in your state? What are the pros and cons of granting tenure?

Know and Act

If you wanted your social studies class to read sections of the Bible, how might you justify such action? Describe in writing some of the activities you might use that would indicate you were teaching about religion rather than instilling religious tenets.

Discover

Read the "De Jure" section of a current issue of the *Phi Delta Kappan* and a "School Law" article in *The American School Board Journal*. (Both journals will likely be on the reference shelves in the education library.) In 25 words or fewer, describe pertinent issues in each of the articles. Are there common themes (e.g., instructional issues, student classification practices, classroom management, or conditions of employment) in the two articles?

Evaluate

What questions do these issues raise in your mind? What implications do they have for teachers and students? Compare your perceptions with one or two other students in your class.

Education Futures in a Changing World

14

Only soothsayers predict the future with assurance, but one eventuality is almost certain: Professional educators of tomorrow will know where and how to connect with others at home and around the world who share interests in educating young people. Educators will depend on each other and on people with special knowledge and talents in ever increasing ways. They will work together, interact, cooperate, collaborate, interrelate, and in all manner of ways influence each other. They will do so because they cannot solve educational problems alone, and because together they can create new educational opportunities.

Educators of the future cannot become interdependent and remain private or hidden from public view. On the surface they may look like educators of today and yesterday, but they will be evolving into a new kind of professional who will be seen and heard by people inside and outside the traditional educational establishment. Stanley Aronowitz and Henry Giroux (1991) call this kind of educator a "public intellectual"—a person who resists the idea that knowledge is fixed, who engages in discussions to redefine what it means "to learn," and who displays the moral courage to face pressing problems and to capture opportunities to educate themselves and others when such opportunities arise. This chapter speculates about the futures of public intellectuals whoever and wherever they may be.

1 What kinds of problems may coalitions and collaborative networks of education professionals and interested people in this country and around the world be best suited to address?

.... Perceive

2 Why might educators want to work with other professionals to address problems rather than merely acquire more resources and address the problems themselves?

.... Value

3 How is the structure of the American public school similar to and different from the structures of schools in other countries? What might we learn about schools abroad that will help us think more creatively about schooling in this country?

.... Know

4 How might an educator reach out to others who do not live in the community to link them with his or her school?

.... Act

5 How might the establishment of national standards pull people closer together by affecting curricula of public schools, the practice of teaching, and the assessment of students?

.... Evaluate

HOW MIGHT AMERICANS BENEFIT FROM STUDYING EDUCATION IN OTHER COUNTRIES?

Foundations of American education are becoming less nationalistic with each passing day. Technological advances in communication and transportation systems have made the world smaller, more immediate, and less remote than ever before. People are connected around the globe by the images and words of one another etched in their minds by modern technology. We can no longer afford, if we ever could, to view American education in strictly American terms. International comparative education has become a foundational area for all teachers.

The concept of **international comparative education** suggests (a) that problems of educational development are common in many societies; and

(b) that by studying education in different societies, educators develop new insights into these societies, and they derive innovative understanding of their own society as well (Thomas, 1990).

Because U.S. culture is so different from cultures in many other parts of the world, American attempts to mimic education in other countries are often ill-advised. For example, even though school choice (see Chapter 12) has long been an option in other nations, their models cannot automatically be fitted to educational practice in the United States (Glenn, 1989). We can, however, learn much about ourselves by studying life in other cultures and by listening to and working with colleagues from other cultures. In many instances, the problems Americans face are not unique to U.S. society. Others face them too, often with considerable success. Their experiences can help us reflect on our own assumptions and actions in ways that would be impossible without a point of comparison.

> **International comparative education has become a foundational area for all teachers.**

Harold Stevenson and James Stigler (1992) demonstrate this idea vividly in their study of Chinese, Japanese, and American cultures. They asked fifth graders and their mothers in each country to determine the degree to which they believed the following factors influenced children's success: effort, ability, difficulty of the task, and luck. Generally, they found that American children and their mothers placed much greater emphasis on innate ability than did Asian children and their mothers, who assigned most importance to children's efforts. These socially constructed views, Stevenson and Stigler argue, have direct implications for education:

> Under an "ability" model, motivation to try hard depends to a great extent on the individual child's assessment of whether he has the ability to succeed. By contrast, an "effort" model, such as the Chinese and Japanese tend to hold, portrays learning as gradual and incremental, something that almost by definition must be acquired over a long time. (p. 102)

We Americans might also learn much about concepts of multicultural education, and about ourselves in relation to these concepts, by studying other countries. In recent years, various approaches to multicultural education in the United States have focused attention on similarities and differences among cultures (see Chapter 7). Public schools have helped sustain that attention and have reinforced the importance of fostering connections among people across cultures.

The discourse on multicultural education in this country, however, has been framed in purely American terms. International comparative perspectives have largely been missing. This is unfortunate, because the United States is not the only country that is experiencing or has experienced the phenomenon of being home to a diversity of cultural groups within its national borders. Nor is the United States the only country addressing problems that arise from close interaction among diverse cultural groupings. With the advent of the North American Free Trade Agreement (NAFTA), the European Community (EC), and other multinational pacts, multicultural understanding becomes increasingly important. As Plutarch, the ancient Greek biographer argued, those who are willing to learn from others stand to gain by strengthening their own character, by avoiding others' pitfalls, and perhaps even by tipping the powers of fate in ways that will benefit all people.

What might a child or a teacher in the United States have in common with a child or a teacher in Europe, Africa, or Asia? People are only beginning to realize that children and teachers in the United States are tied to people in other countries throughout the world by a set of emerging themes that characterize formal education wherever it occurs. These include conceptions of choice, reform, control, literacy, and responsibility, to mention but a few. Such themes, or patterns of thinking and behavior, are salient in many cultures and therefore influential in students' and teachers' lives.

Elise Boulding (1988) demonstrated how some themes reveal themselves daily. For example, children in different countries learn to maximize their capacity for making judgments and for choosing when choices are possible, despite the oppressive conditions of their circumstances.

Fifteen-year-old Indira in India had never attended school. She worked for hire on a nearby farm, but she noticed she could do some things better than the children who went to school. The older women in her family taught her, and she did not think she needed formal schooling. "I can count," she says proudly (Boulding, 1988, p. 81).

A 9-year-old girl worked on garbage heaps in Nagpur, India, seeking salable scrap. "I would like to go to school. I like to see small girls going to school with books and slates. I don't know why I want to go with them. . . . Life will be better when I am older. I will work on building sites and earn money" (Boulding, 1988, p. 81).

As Boulding notes, there is no comparison between the hardness of life for a child in the developing world and a child in the United States. Both, however, have a "common down-to-earth knowledge of their environment and its physical and social complexities . . ." (p. 82). They possess knowledge, and they know how to use it to meet their needs and the needs of adults around them. When children go to school, no matter where they may be, their world expands dramatically. "They quickly discover how to link what they know from firsthand experience with the secondary data they acquire in the classroom and from books." (p. 82)

Education in India

India, a nation of nearly 900 million people, in addition to being the world's largest democracy, may be the most culturally and ethnically diverse country in the world. It is in a region known historically for its tolerance of diversity; nonetheless, regional and ethnic tension continue. Because the language of commerce and language of instruction in India is English while more than a dozen regional languages (such as Hindi, Urdu, and Tamil) and local dialects are used in everyday speech in all but the major cities, the nation offers unique opportunities to educate others about diversity. Bilingualism is the norm and trilingualism is common.

The Indian constitution set forth in 1950 directs the government to provide free and compulsory education for all children up to age 14. It also provides for equal educational opportunity and protection of religious and linguistic minority groups. The school system, which varies from state to state, is generally organized as 2 to 3 years of private kindergarten (beginning about age 3), followed by 10 years of private or public basic education, perhaps followed by 2 years of private or public higher secondary education, and then perhaps followed by 3 years of tuition-free higher education. School holidays include 20 religious festivals from Hindu, Muslim, Christian, Sikh, Parsi, and Jain traditions.

In 1986, the federal parliament adopted its National Policy for Education and Policy of Action which have served as the bases for the development of the National Curriculum for Elementary and Secondary Education. The intent of the common core is to cut across subject areas and to promote "India's common cultural heritage, egalitarianism, democracy and secularism, equality of the sexes, protection of the environment, removal of social barriers, observance of the small family norm, and the encouragement of a scientific outlook" (Bordia, 1988, p. 351).

Changes in Indian teaching methods, however, are difficult to effect, in part because classes often have more than 50 students, many of whom are plagued by poverty (some 45% of the country lives below the poverty line and another 20% barely above it). ". . . [T]he young teacher inevitably succumbs to the advice of older colleagues and settles into a pattern of delivering sermons and a stylized catechism of question-and-answer exchanges" (Taylor, 1991, p. 331).

The KATHA school was founded in a New Delhi, India slum by Geeta Dharmarajan in 1990. She believes that children's mothers can help their children succeed by becoming empowered themselves—through her teacher education program and built-in opportunities to earn money.

Education in the United Kingdom

The United Kingdom, which is increasingly ethnically and culturally diverse, offers an array of educational approaches. London, with its 10 million-plus inhabitants, is a city of great diversity. Immigrant settlement has not been limited to London; many have settled in other cities, towns, and small communities. The British education system has conducted a variety of schemes to address the needs of students and society caused by this rapid change in the country's ethnic and cultural composition. There is a long history of dealing with diversity in schools.

Children in the United Kingdom must attend school between ages 5 and 16. The British publicly supported school system is organized into two or three tiers. The two-tier system is composed of primary schools (ages 5–11), occasionally subdivided into infant (5–7) and junior (7–11), and secondary schools (ages 11 to 16 or 18) that resemble American comprehensive high schools. The three-tier system, used only in England, consists of first schools (ages 5 to 8 or 9), middle schools (ages 8–12 or 9–13), and upper schools that are usually nonselective (ages 12 or 13 to 16 or 18). Churches help operate some primary and secondary schools even though these schools are supported by public funds (Booth, 1988). Religious instruction is required in all British schools.

Until recently, the British educational system had a long tradition of noninterference by the central government. In 1988, however, the Education

Reform Act emphasized two themes in the education of all students in the British system: back to the basics and the link between education and the economy (Judge, 1989). The Act has been followed by pressure for a national curriculum and teacher accountability (i.e., the alignment of teaching performance with the curriculum). It has also promoted the idea of giving parents a greater voice in the management of schools and stimulated the creation of a new system of national compulsory and universal examinations. These are to be designed by the central government and given to 7, 11, 14 and 16-year-old students. As Liz Bondi (1991) observed, the shift in mood in the British system from expansion and optimism to one of retrenchment and redefinition has mirrored a similar occurrence in the United States. The reasons for this shift have largely to do with demographic changes, public disenchantment, and a shortage of public funds for the support of education.

One creative educational response to the changing culture in the United Kingdom can be found in the work of the Association of Science Educators Multicultural Education Working Party, chaired by Kabir Shaikh (Thorp, 1991). This group identified a range of teaching methods designed to incorporate issues of race and equality in science teaching. They did so to emphasize the "potential of science to enhance the curriculum by drawing on the richness and diversity of cultures and on the practice of science, now and throughout history . . . (and) the powerful role of science teaching for combatting racism and prejudice in society" (Thorp, 1991, p. 5). Figure 14.1 shows an activity that is part of this new curriculum.

Education In Denmark

Denmark offers an interesting contrast to the United Kingdom. It is small and has a homogeneous population of slightly over 5 million. Danish citizens exhibit open, liberal politics and sentiments. They have one of the most highly developed social welfare systems in the world. Immigration is a relatively recent phenomenon in Denmark. Since about 1970, most immigrants have come from Turkey and the Indian subcontinent. Recently, however, people have come to Denmark from virtually all over the world.

The Danish Ministry of Education takes an activist, interventionist approach to educational and social problems. Yet schools in Denmark have an exceptionally high degree of local control, similar to the United States. While Danish is the first and most important language, English is widely spoken, and at a very high level by the well-educated professional classes. Classes taught in English are common at the upper secondary level.

Education in Denmark is free and compulsory for students from 7 to 16 years of age. Approximately 90% of the students go to the Folkeskole, or public school as it is called in the United States, and the remainder to "private" schools supported by the government. Most 3- to 6-year-olds go to kindergartens. For the first 7 years, the Folkeskole teaches all subjects. In grades 8 through 10, the Folkeskole is comprehensive except in mathematics, English, German, physics, and chemistry; students in these courses are separated into basic and advanced courses. Grade 10 in the Folkeskole is optional, after which students enter various forms of vocational/technical

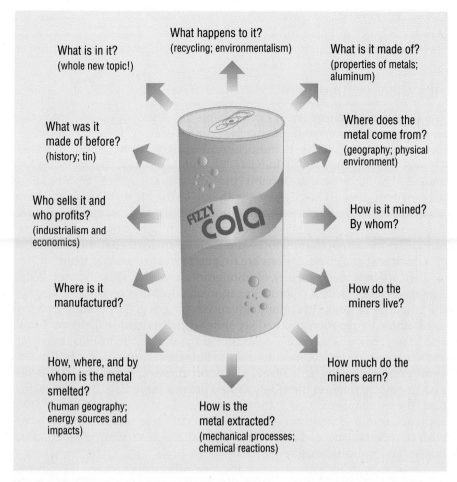

What happens to it?
(recycling; environmentalism)

What is in it?
(whole new topic!)

What is it made of?
(properties of metals; aluminum)

What was it made of before?
(history; tin)

Where does the metal come from?
(geography; physical environment)

Who sells it and who profits?
(industrialism and economics)

How is it mined? By whom?

Where is it manufactured?

How do the miners live?

How, where, and by whom is the metal smelted?
(human geography; energy sources and impacts)

How is the metal extracted?
(mechanical processes; chemical reactions)

How much do the miners earn?

FIZZY cola

FIGURE 14.1

Activity from the "Cola Can Curriculum"

What science instruction could be planned on the basis of this activity? How might issues of race and ethnicity enter into such a plan? What do you think are some advantages and disadvantages for teachers and students working in this way?

Note. From *Race, equality and science teaching: An active INSET manual for teacher educators* (p. 125) by Thorp S. (Ed.) (1991) London: The Association for Science Education. Adapted by permission.

education and commercial training programs or attend a gymnasium—a "higher preparatory" course of study. Students from the highest social group have the highest probability of going to college (Orum & Hansen, 1975). The relatively casual nature with which examinations are given and used ensures the promotion of most students. The world of work, however, is still widely viewed as desirable to higher education. There is a heavy emphasis on remedial education (Florander, 1988).

The Ministry of Education sets school objectives, but local schools decide how to meet them. Individual schools determine their own curricula, and teachers teach however they please. Highly experienced teachers write the learning materials. There is no control over the scope, sequence, and content of textbooks. Like other Westerners, the Danes are seeking to prepare students to be qualified technically to function effectively in society and to socialize young people to the importance of common moral concepts and social solidarity (Florander, 1988). Also, like other Western countries,

Denmark has lost many unskilled jobs in recent years. As a consequence, the Danes are eager to boost the knowledge and skills of their people so as to remain economically competitive in the emerging European Community.

Education in Singapore

The Republic of Singapore, a city-state on the southern tip of continental Southeast Asia, is considered the world's laboratory for experiments in social engineering. It is a multicultural society, comprising people of Chinese (77%), Malay (14%), Indian (7%), and Eurasian (2%) ancestries. Just under 3 million people inhabit the 231 square miles of Singapore (Gopinathan, 1994). The city-state, with one of the highest living standards in Asia, bills itself as the Switzerland of Asia, the Gateway to the Future. Singapore is a city of business opportunity and a hub of high-tech development. The government tries to assure that, no matter what their ethnic or cultural background, all citizens are first and foremost Singaporean.

Singapore consists mainly of immigrants and their descendants. While Singapore was a British colony, Singaporean education required English as the language of government and advanced schooling. The system also fostered ethnic segregation and had separate schools taught in Chinese, Tamil, and Malay. Since Singapore's establishment as a republic in 1965, however, life has changed. Today, most tourists to Singapore know that it is illegal to chew gum (not really; it is illegal to import chewing gum) and that extinguishing a cigarette on the sidewalk can draw a large fine. But few realize that the Singaporean educational system has developed innovative approaches to multicultural education. The nation is sometimes characterized as paternalistic and authoritarian, but it is also viewed as efficient, honest, and radically interventionist.

Even though Singapore maintains four official languages, the government has unified the English- and non-English-speaking schools (Chinese, Malay, and Tamil) into a single educational system. The unification of schools has been viewed by leaders as an essential ingredient in their strategy to build a nation with its own unique identity.

By 1968, as a result of a strong family planning program and large investment in school facilities and teacher education, all children of primary school age were enrolled in school. In 1973, educational authorities required all students to know English as either their first or second language and one other major language of the community. In the 1980s, authorities backed off this overly ambitious goal. Most students now try to become bilingual, and many seek the English track as a first choice for the access it offers to jobs and higher education (Thomas, 1988).

Primary school teaches basic skills for 6 years. The curriculum of the first 2 years of secondary

Singaporean teachers from Anderson Secondary School work together to develop multicultural curricula for students in their diverse society in Southeast Asia. Curriculum and instruction are also multilingual, serving students who speak Chinese, Tamil, Malay, and English.

VOICES

On the Bond Between Schools and Society

Professor Saravanan Gopinathan (1994) of the National Institute of Education, Nanyang Technological University, points to the influence of Singapore's first prime minister, Lee Kuan Yew, on the formation of the present school system. Lee Kuan Yew served as prime minister for almost 4 decades, and he foresaw early in his tenure the importance of the bond between schools and society.

If in the four different languages of instruction, we teach our children four different standards of right and wrong, four different ideal patterns of behavior, then we will produce four different groups of people and there will be no integrated coherent society. What is in the balance is the very foundation of our society. For if we are not to perish in chaos caused by antagonisms and prejudices between watertight cultural and linguistic compartments, then you have to educate the right responses amongst our young people in school.

CRITICAL THINKING

Is Lee Kuan Yew's view as expressed here appropriate only for a nation that is just beginning to define itself, or do such "right responses" also exist in stable, enduring democracies such as the United States? If there are such right responses in the United States, what might they be? If there are no right responses, on whom or what do American educators rely for guidance? Do you know what right responses Lee Kuan Yew might have had in mind? How could you find out?

Source: Yew, L.K. (1959, December 9). Speech. *Straights Times*, p. 1.

school is the same for all students and varies only slightly in the last 2 years. At the end of the 4th year, examinations screen students for a preuniversity course of study, and are followed by more examinations to screen for admission to postsecondary education. Students are tracked as early as the third grade. The schools operate multiple language streams in the same building to encourage interaction among students and to promote a feeling of national unity (Thomas, 1988).

Unlike the United States, there is a close relationship among government, industry, and secondary and postsecondary education in Singapore. Annual surveys estimate workforce needs, and the schools and informal educational organizations respond with programs to fulfill those needs. These connections are especially important to a country that has no natural resources of its own and so must depend on the talents of its people for its place in the world.

Education in South Africa

South Africa is one of the most multicultural societies in the world. Since 1949, the structure of society has been shaped by an official policy of apartheid (pronounced "a·par·tate" or "a·par·tite"), or separation of the

TABLE 14.1 Composition of the Total South African Population*

	Number	Percent
Whites	4,979,000	16.5
Coloureds (of mixed white and black descent)	3,168,000	10.5
Asians	941,000	3.1
Blacks	21,105,000	69.9
Total	30,193,000	100.0

*Mid-year estimates, excluding Republics of Transkei, Bophuthatswana, Venda, and Ciskei.

Note. From "Educational Renewal in South Africa: Problems and Prospects" by E. M. Lemmer, 1993, Compare, 23 (1), p. 54. Copyright 1993 by Compare. Adapted by permission.

races. This has meant that blacks have lived in "homelands," "black states," and segregated "townships" outside the major cities. Under apartheid, whites were not allowed to enter the townships without permission and nonwhites were not permitted to stay overnight in white urban areas without special permission. People had to carry passes at all times so that authorities could control movement throughout the country. The white minority has held political and economic power.

While the United States is marked by a history of slavery, it is difficult for most Westerners to imagine how a policy such as apartheid could ever be justified in recent history anywhere in the world. The former language of apartheid in South Africa, however, must sound hauntingly familiar to western ears: The ultimate goal of apartheid was to create "a mosaic of peoples, each with a separate national identity. They will be politically independent but economically interdependent" (King, 1988, p. 600).

South Africa's repeal of apartheid laws in 1991 spells dramatic restructuring of the education system.

The apartheid legislation was repealed in 1991, initiating what promises to be a dramatic restructuring of society, including a restructuring of the segregated education system which has supported it. The challenge is to make a new country out of the same people on the same land.

A new constitution was adopted in 1993, opening the door to free elections in which all South Africans may participate. In daily life, however, segregation continues to be reinforced by great disparities in wealth, personal attitudes, and historically separate and unequal education systems. The open challenge to segregated education began in 1976–77 with riots in Soweto, a black township outside Johannesburg (Lemmer, 1993). This revolt was triggered by an attempt to impose instruction in Afrikaans (an amalgam of Dutch, French, German, African, and Malay) instead of English (King, 1988).

Almost all South African school systems are organized with 4 years of junior primary, 3 of senior primary, 3 of junior secondary, and 2 of senior secondary. Schools have been oriented toward the western view of a liberal education, that is, students are to be well-grounded in history, languages, mathematics, the sciences, and the arts. Teaching is typically teacher-centered, and learning is passive with a heavy emphasis on rote and academics. As such, education has been perceived as irrelevant to black children, who generally live bleak lives. School is compulsory for whites until age 16, Asians until 15, coloreds until age 14. School attendance is not yet compulsory for black South Africans.

For the past 10 years or more, in protest against the apartheid-supporting education system, black South Africans in large numbers have boycotted schools and destroyed school property. The morale and authority of black teachers have been seriously damaged. Many black students have literally forgotten how to learn and how to study. Influential black leaders fear that the crisis in education may have cost the nation a generation of young people (Hartshorne, 1990).

In Cape Town, South Africa, students leave racially integrated Queen's Park High School. The anti-apartheid movement has called for government action to reform the educational system so that black South Africans gain the same opportunities as Anglo-Europeans, Asians, and "Coloureds."

Cultural Awareness

Often lost in the struggle between black and white South Africans are the so-called coloured South Africans. Mostly of Indian descent, they constitute about 10% of the population. They, too, have gone to their own schools. And they, too, have been caught in the troubled times that have characterized their country's recent history. Considered neither white nor black, they have been trapped in a political limbo. As this 1993 report from a student on the Student Representative Council at Garlandale High School in Cape Town reveals, the frustration of young coloured South Africans is often apparent in schools.

1985 . . . The Year of rebellion in schools throughout the country and the start of our school's Student Representative Council (SRC).

Because of an element of conservatism and the political climate at the time, the establishment of the SRC was surrounded with controversy. However, they managed to get it off the ground and the SRC served mainly as a vehicle for protest against the government, who clamped down severely on all student protests. There are some who still remember Spine Road Secondary in Mitchell's Plain where the beating up of school children was shown on SATV . . .

Garlandale also had its fair share of protests right here on the premises.

A huge rally, attended by the pupils of approximately six schools was held at the school, there were placard demonstrations and, to some extent, examinations were disrupted. The unrest and boycotts culminated in September when the then Minister of Education, Mr. Carter Ebrahim, decreed that all schools falling under the jurisdiction of the House of Representatives be closed.

Throughout all this, the SRC functioned. Tribute is paid to the pupils who served as chairpersons of the SRC during those turbulent eighties: 1985: Shamiela Francis, 1986: Bayiesha Solomons, 1987: Eleanor Mocke, 1988: Nathan Diedericks, 1989: Clinton Mocke.

The political climate took a dramatic turn during the 90's and schools settled down to some sort of normality. Chairpersons were: 1990: Elaine Sacco, 1991: Cheree Dyers, 1992: Zurina Hoosain, 1993: ?

In the past we always chose our representative at the beginning of the year. However this year it was felt that new pupils are unaware of the responsibilities attached to being a class representative on the SRC nor do they really know the candidates who they have to vote for. We are now in the process of changing our traditions and we will choose the Student Representative Council during the following term.

So, please don't think that we are invisible—we are yet to prove ourselves.

Rushdia Omar (Omar, 1993, p. 2)

WHY IS GLOBAL AWARENESS IMPORTANT?

Our connections to the countries and the people of the world grow closer and more numerous by the day. The extent to which we recognize these connections constitute an estimate of our **global awareness**. As Barbara Tye and Kenneth Tye (1992) observe, the welfare of the United States is tied to the welfare of other countries by economics, the environment, politics, culture, and technology. When there is unusual activity on the New York stock market, people watch to see what effect it will have in Tokyo, Bonn, and London. Acid rain, depletion of the ozone layer, ocean pollution, and disposal of nuclear waste are multinational concerns. The fall of the Soviet Union and reorganization of Eastern Europe have had reverberations in military spending, labor policies, capital investment, and, most immediately, in the immigration of children into the classrooms of the world.

As more people travel and work in countries other than those in which they were born, and as more people employ the dramatic advances in communications technology, the interplay of cultures increases. In some instances, increased contact leads to competition and conflict. In other cases, familiarity breeds cooperation, for different people realize that they must work together if they are to survive and prosper. Everywhere, people call upon schools to promote technical skills to communicate and wisdom to use these technological skills for enhancing mutual understanding. Schools around the world must help tomorrow's adults learn languages, understand cultures, and use a host of electronic communication systems in order to be present in today's world. A global society is no longer the pipedream of the futurist but an idea people define each day as they reach around the world with their computers and fax machines.

Unfortunately, it is difficult to discuss global challenges and the potential of modern education without using grandiose language—the kind that glazes people's eyes. The simple truth is, however, as Marvin Cetron and Owen Davies (1992) suggest, that the implications of joining education and technology on a global scale are nothing short of breathtaking. Think of it this way: Literacy remains a fundamental goal in developing societies. An illiterate population means a population burdened by health problems, low labor productivity, weak or no economic growth, and social fragmentation. The proportion of children not enrolled in school worldwide will fall from 26% in 1985 to 18% by the year 2000. Most developed countries have literacy rates of 95% or above. But as the developed world forges ahead, many sub-Saharan countries fall further behind in terms of everything that supports life. Yet, as some gaps between rich and poor countries widen, some also narrow. Technology brings the developed and developing countries closer together and makes them more aware of one another than ever before. Technology promises to deliver education to even the most remote locations and to transport the minds of people and the people themselves from those locations to new worlds.

> [T]he implications of joining education and technology on a global scale are . . . breathtaking.

Tye and Tye (1992) argue that a global perspective, aided by technology, forces people to consider problems that cut across national boundaries. Educators who think about the world also cultivate students' abilities to decenter and to view the world from others' perspectives. Elise Boulding (1988) noted that this process has occurred naturally for years through voluntary associations referred to as international nongovernmental organizations, or **INGOs**. These transnational associations—groups such as churches, scouts, farmers, chambers of commerce, physicians, athletes, educators—have grown from 176 in 1909 to more than 18,000 in the mid-1980s. They all advance agenda that focus on problems and issues of common interest, regardless of national borders.

But if educators are to think globally and to encourage their students to do so, basic curricular and instructional change in most schools is required. A number of obstacles or competing demands must be overcome for this to occur (Tye & Tye, 1992). School leaders have not historically considered global perspective to be very important. Teachers' limited amounts of time have already been captured by their attention to existing curricula, to standardized testing, and to accreditation demands. Moreover, leadership is essential if people are to attend to global issues, and in many districts there is no such leadership.

When a critical mass of educators think globally, however, they can make global thinking come alive for students. For example, in one school, along with regular activities such as use of library materials and speakers, teachers and students instituted five special projects: (a) the study of folk literature, poetry, and music from around the world for grades 1 and 2; (b) a collection of books dealing with cultural commonalities among families of the world for grades 7 and 8; (c) an endangered species unit for the middle grades; (d) a special global education section in the school library; and (e) an all-school display of "Our Earth" that represents interdisciplinary work at all grade levels (Tye and Tye, 1992). Activities such as these help make global education a viable part of the curriculum.

Not surprisingly, money and jobs fuel interests in global and international issues. Business leaders have been among the more vocal in encouraging schools to think globally, for they view the schools as vital to the production and maintenance of the workforce that will be called upon to compete in a wider world.

An example of one state's commitment to the connection between schooling and competitiveness in the global marketplace can be found in South Carolina. The state has established "special schools" to train workers free of charge for any company that agrees to create new jobs in the state.

> The state trains workers with no experience in using things like the metric system or computers or blueprints. That has given South Carolina a big edge, especially in attracting internationally owned outfits . . . which makes parts for windows and radiators. . . . [T]he Greenville-Spartanburg corridor, known as the I-85 Autobahn, is dotted with international companies, half of them German. The latest big catch is BMW, which is building a thousand-acre plant to build cars for worldwide export, including exports to the fatherland. . . . Eventually, BMW will employ at least 2,000 people. That should mean another 8,000 jobs for South Carolina. (Cochran, 1993, p. 7)

The real challenge for American public education is to educate workers today for careers and jobs they will fill tomorrow. In other words, educators must identify and teach knowledge and skills now, in hopes of preparing students for a future they can only vaguely imagine. If you were asked to identify knowledge and skills deemed critical for today's students to master, what would you say?

WHAT ARE SOME COOPERATION-BUILDING TRENDS IN EDUCATION?

When people look carefully, they find signs everywhere in education of the interconnectedness of people, ideas, and events. No one seems to have recognized the complexity of these educational relationships across society and over time better than Lawrence Cremin (1990):

> Education has always served political functions insofar as it affects, or at least is believed and intended to affect, the future character of the community and the state. Aristotle explicated the relationship in the classic discussion of education he included in the *Politics*. Recall his

argument there: it is impossible to talk about education apart from some conception of the good life; people will inevitably differ in their conceptions of the good life, and hence they will inevitably disagree on matters of education; therefore the discussion of education falls squarely within the domain of politics. In more recent times, commentators from Thomas Jefferson to Horace Mann to John Dewey have applied these Aristotelian doctrines to the American experience, arguing the inescapable connection between education and the character of the American polity. (p. 85)

The debate about public education in the United States and about the place of our education system in a global context sometimes sounds fractious. But it is also possible to perceive the debate as a legitimate and healthy interaction that refocuses public attention on our varying conceptions of the good life. Although the debate can sound discordant, participation links people to the idea that public education is important and worth improving. Participation also connects people to others who share those beliefs, even though they may not see eye to eye on what is to be done. The debate itself, then, represents the first and a necessary step toward building consensus for action.

To work well, education, like politics and like democracy, needs players—people who do not simply sit on the sidelines observing the wrangles of others but who are willing to grapple intellectually and emotionally with the problems. That is not to say that everyone has to be connected to public education in the same way or to the same degree; but people must be aware of problems and opportunities, and must care, if education systems are to serve society. Maybe because good leaders, regardless of their political persuasions, recognize this fact, they fall unknowingly into the use of crisis rhetoric; they rouse public concern by using emotionally "hot" language about educational success and failure to keep people involved. Sometimes, when the volume is up, the harmony suffers.

It is increasingly possible, however, to hear concordance in the debate about public education. From different philosophical quarters, many people agree on a number of issues: Public education in the United States has problems, but they are not unsolvable. The problems cannot be fixed with money alone, but they will not be fixed without money. People in poverty and members of minority groups are especially vulnerable when public education is weak; their vulnerability threatens everyone. The status of education professionals is inextricably bound to the conditions of schools and must improve for the long-term health of society. Education systems must be unified in ways that allow communications to flow smoothly between and among those who need information. In many ways, people are much more alike than they are different from one another.

Incentives and Experiments

The 8 National Education Goals represent one of the most visible indications of governmental cooperation on educational matters (see Chapter 1). The 6 goals, established in 1989 by President George Bush and the 50 governors, and the 2 goals added by President Clinton in 1994, serve as targets for educational achievement. The goals have focused attention on critical education needs and have stimulated cooperation between the Federal and state governments.

The Federal Coordinating Council for Science, Engineering, and Technology (FCCSET) and the Committee on Education and Human Resources (CEHR) represent one initiative at the federal level that has emanated from the Goals. The FCCSET and CEHR initiative is meant to eliminate duplication of efforts, that is, to prevent the creation and maintenance of different unrelated programs meant to address essentially the same problem and to focus the resources of 16 federal agencies on educating people in mathematics, engineering, and technology at all levels of society.

The plan calls for three tiers of action: (a) revitalization of undergraduate education, the evaluation of all federal science, mathematics, engineering, and technology education programs, and a redefinition of what students are expected to learn beginning at the earliest grades; (b) increasing the participation of individuals from groups underrepresented in these

FIGURE 14.2

School-Linked and Other Integrated Service Activities of the U. S. Department of Education

America 2000	Implementing the AMERICA 2000 Education Strategy. Seeking through legislation to maximize program flexibility in order to better serve students and families with fewer categorized requirements for eligibility and resource utilization. Promoting community-wide strategies to improve education, some of which may include service integration.
Interagency Collaborations	Participating in the White House Empowerment Task Force's Work Group on Services Integration. Carrying out a joint study of school-based and non-school-based, comprehensive service models for at-risk children and their families (joint project with the Department of Health and Human Services). Providing technical assistance to new collaborative efforts in the state of West Virginia and the cities of Memphis and Cincinnati.
Research Centers	Funding several research centers that are actively investigating the integrated service approach. Examples are the National Research Center on Families, Schools, Communities, and Children's Learning (Boston), which is carrying out an evaluation of New Jersey's statewide comprehensive service program; the National Research Center on Education in Inner Cities (Philadelphia); and the National Research Center on the Study of Organization and Restructuring of Schools (Madison, Wisconsin).
Family Literacy Programs	Funding of 123 Even Start family literacy projects, many of them school-linked, to provide adult literacy training, appropriate developmental early childhood education for the children of these adults, and to encourage parents to reinforce their children's learning.

Note. From "Current Activity at the Federal Level and the Need for Service Integration," by M. H. Gerry and N. C. Certo, 1991, *The Future of Children: School Linked Services, 2* (1), p. 125. Reprinted by permission.

VOICES

On America's Neglect of Children

Janet Reno's years as a prosecutor in Florida educated her about the connection between children and adults. Since her appointment as U.S. Attorney General, Reno has spoken frequently and forcefully on the strong connection between public education and a healthy, safe society.

It is clear to me . . . that the violence we are seeing in America, particularly among our youth, is the symptom of a deeper problem in society. Drugs, teen pregnancy, youth gangs, dropouts, the increasing number of children who are in the ranks of the homeless, are evidence of the single greatest problem that has faced America since World War II. It is that we have too often forgotten and neglected our children.

When 21 percent of American children live in poverty—a far greater percentage than any other age group—you begin to see the dimension of the problem. We must understand that there is no single key intervention point where you can more effectively prevent violence than any other. But we have got to reduce teen pregnancy. We've got to make sure that every child in American has safe, constructive education. We've got to make sure that we provide adequate medical care in preventative terms for our children, including immunizations. When a significant number of two year olds in Washington, D.C., are not receiving immunizations, that is one of the most stupid cost-cutting measures possible. For every dollar spent for immunization we save ourselves from epidemics and the costs associated with it.

No child development specialist or reporter that I've ever talked to has questioned the fact that the most formative time in a person's life is from birth to age three when a child learns the concept of reward and punishment and develops a conscience. Fifty percent of all learned human response is learned in the first year of life. What good is it going to do to build prisons 18 years from now unless we give that child a structure, an environment in which he can learn reward and punishment and develop a conscience so that he knows not to hurt people?

We've got to develop programs for our children after school and in the evenings to keep them occupied. We've got to focus on truancy prevention programs. We've got to make our educational system fit with our job training and placement system. Right now, you might see a kid with a summer job chipping paint on a curb. That summer job in no way ties into what he might anticipate in terms of career goals. We should take seventh graders, or whatever age the educators suggest, and do thorough evaluations of aptitudes and interests. Then, we could have a counselor link summer job programs with schoolwork experience and education programs, so if the child follows that track, he knows that he will graduate with a skill that can enable him to earn a living wage. (pp. 22–24)

CRITICAL THINKING

Why does Reno's view of links between education and society also support the idea of building closer ties between home and school?

Source: Reno, J. (1993). First impressions, future plans. *Aspen Institute Quarterly*, 5 (4), 13–30.

areas, for example, racial minorities and women, and broadening the use of educational technologies across the board in education; and (c) improving public understanding of science and developing partnerships between 2-year colleges and other education institutions (Federal Coordinating Council for Science, Engineering, and Technology and Committee on Education and Human Resources, 1992). It is too early to determine if this strategy will yield better communication, better programs, and better learning, but it is a visible recognition of the need to help people work together.

Many people have recognized that education problems are related to other problems in society, and thus require coordinated responses. Attorney General Janet Reno, for example, continually draws attention to children's problems caused by the irresponsibility of adults. As a prosecutor in Florida, Reno established a one-stop child-support center with counselors, police, and medical staff to help children and their parents. She advocated shorter workdays so parents could be home to supervise their children after school. She vigorously prosecuted spouses for failure to pay child support (Gibbs, 1993).

New Links Between Technology and Education

People have often learned the hard way, through experience with innovative programs like the ones Reno describes, that the programs themselves are not good or bad, it is how people implement them that makes the difference. The same can be said of technology. Technology is neither good nor bad. People attach value to technology by how they use it. Teachers, now more than at any time in history, have the power to make technology a force for good in students' lives, and in so doing, to change their conceptions of teaching and teachers.

As schools develop capacities to deliver video, audio, data, and text to classrooms, teachers face multiple challenges beyond the problems of operating the machinery. They must use technology as a means of direct instruction that focuses students on key ideas. But they must also use technology to help students construct their own knowledge and develop a deep understanding of their subjects. As Robert DeVillar and Christian Faltis (1991) observe, many computers sit unused in classrooms. Or, when they are used, too frequently it is for purposes of drill and practice or as a reward for students who finish their "real work" early. In some schools, lack of funds make simply acquiring a computer a daunting task. The challenge of getting a computer, however, may pale in comparison to the challenge of using it intelligently.

Most experts agree that some basic conditions need to exist if computers are to be used effectively to link students with a larger world. Computers must be available in sufficient number so that work stations can be provided for every two or three students. Teachers need training and opportunities to use computers if they are going to help students use them. Teachers also need time to restructure their curricula around computers if the machines are going to be used for anything other than drill and practice. While teachers must help students learn about technology, they cannot sacrifice their responsibilities to teach basic skills of literacy and numeracy.

Teachers need to begin to use technology to learn how students learn. As students gather, analyze, and display data, teachers can learn much

BENCHMARKS

Today's Classroom: A Chronology of Technological Developments

c. 1800	Lead pencil devised by an American woman who removed the pith from twigs and filled them with a mixture of pounded lead, gum arabic, and glue.
1800–1850	Photography, color offset lithography. electric clock, principle of the analog computer, calculator, telegraph.
1850–1900	Batteries, linoleum, fluorescent light, typewriter, telephone, phonograph, electric light bulb, fountain pen, microphone, linotype, celluloid film, Kodak camera, ballpoint pen, motion pictures, discovery of the electron.
c. 1900	Human speech first transmitted by radio waves. The vacuum tube on which radio technology is based invented in 1904. The first radio program of voice and music broadcast in the U. S. in 1906.
1900–1950	Color photography, plastic, cellophane, transcontinental telephone, self-winding wristwatch, sound movies, color movies, television, quartz crystal clock, ballpoint pen, polyethylene, electronic computer, digital computer, magnetic recording tape, xerography, transistor, long-playing record.
c. 1950	Color television introduced in U.S. in 1951. Black-and-white-compatible color television became commercially available in 1953.
1950–1995	Transatlantic cable telephone, stereophonic recording, laser technology, communications satellite dish, acoustic tile, overhead projector, personal microcomputer, computer network, cable television, VCR, digital recording disc, CD-ROM, videodisc, fiber optics.

from evaluating students' thinking during these processes. Some people believe that as students use technology, they reveal how they think about problems and possibilities in the disciplines, and thus provide clues to alert teachers about how best to teach. Others contend that the technology which allows virtually simultaneous interaction with print and video and audio media constitutes the most dramatic advancement in civilization since the Gutenberg Bible—an advancement that will actually change how students think. For example, symbolic representations work best for some algebraic analyses while graphical representations are better for others. The computer permits the use of either or both, as they might appear designed and redesigned by experts and students. As teachers watch and listen to students think, both will learn to make technology work with curriculum.

With a computer and access to the **Internet**, an electronic network having the capacity to span the globe, that curriculum is sure to expand exponentially. The Center for Technology in Education at the Bank Street College of Education found that 48% of the teachers they surveyed had access to Internet, and, of those, some 46% got on the system through a university computer. Teachers and their students use this information superhighway to communicate via electronic mail, to read news or bulletin boards, to hook up to other computers, to access databases, and to transfer files from place to place. (See Figure 14.3.)

Technology can help teachers work with students, but it can also serve directly to join teachers together into mentoring relationships. For example, G. Robert Moore (1991) described how his relationship with preservice teachers at the University of Nevada, Las Vegas, had been altered and strengthened by the use of electronic mail, or **e-mail**—messages sent and received via computers. After he began reading student writing assignments posted on e-mail, both he and students took advantage of the greater potential for contact. Students wrote: "We take time to reflect on what we are actually learning; often we don't do this because everything seems so overwhelming," and "It makes me stop and reflect on what I'm doing and how I'm improving on my teaching in my practicum" (Moore, 1991, p. 40). The technology created more opportunities for students and instructor to talk with one another about teaching.

Televised instruction has been a fact of life for decades, but new technology designed to promote **distance learning** provides possibilities for teachers and students and teachers and teachers to connect with each other and to make rather staid courses come alive by communicating interactively over long distances. In its most advanced form, the phenomenon of distance learning allows people to interact with one another as if they were in the same room. Students can see and hear teachers, and teachers can answer students' questions and react to students' comments instantaneously (Pease, 1991). These features are especially useful when students are located in geographically remote areas.

FIGURE 14.3

How the Internet Is Used

Why might teachers have to learn how to use the Internet when they already have a telephone at their fingertips and a library nearby? ▼

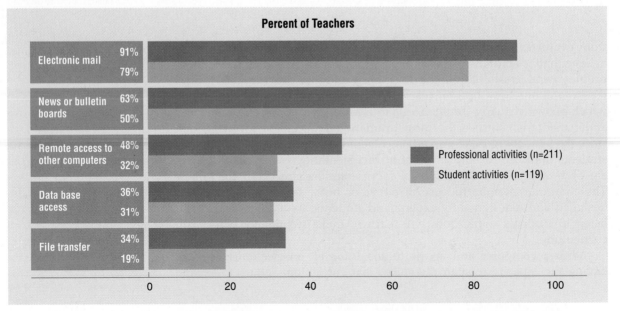

Percent of Teachers

Electronic mail	91% / 79%
News or bulletin boards	63% / 50%
Remote access to other computers	48% / 32%
Data base access	36% / 31%
File transfer	34% / 19%

Professional activities (n=211)
Student activities (n=119)

0   20   40   60   80   100

Note. From "How the Internet is Used," 1993, *Education Week, 12* (4), p. 3. Copyright 1993 by *Education Week.* Reprinted by permission.

The Star Schools Program, established in 1988 and funded with nearly $50 million from the U.S. Department of Education, has allowed distance learning to take a giant step forward. By the early 1990s, more than 100,000 students in 45 states had enrolled in courses in math, science, foreign language, and many other subjects funded in part by Star School grants. In addition, some 20,000 teachers had taken courses and participated in staff development programs offered through the Star Schools Program. Regional partnerships in San Antonio, Texas, Cambridge, Massachusetts, Columbia, South Carolina, and Stillwater, Oklahoma, have, in turn, collaborated with one another to share resources and to strengthen their offerings (Jordahl, 1991).

Links between computers, television sets, satellite dishes, and the information superhighway are transforming schools and redefining education.

Distance learning projects are especially important for many small, isolated school districts that, because of cost constraints, have had to exclude all but basic level courses from their curriculum. As financial support goes down and state education standards go up, distance learning offers attractive possibilities for making connections with people and ideas.

Cultural Awareness

The Radio Language Arts Program (RLAP) in the East African nation of Kenya demonstrates how simple technology, reasonably applied, can serve the learning needs of many children in remote areas. The RLAP was designed to teach English to primary school students to prepare them for secondary school, where English is the language of instruction.

> Radio has been adopted in preference to television, not only because of the very limited availability of TV receivers and production facilities, but also because radio represents a continuation of the oral tradition in Africa. Each day a 30-minute lesson is broadcast as the pupils' major instruction in language arts, with the programs focusing on improving students' oral skills. Instead of directly importing foreign materials, the program planners developed their own lessons that assist the student in learning skills related to needs and interests in their rural environments. The daily broadcasts also engage classroom teachers in preparing their pupils for each lesson and, following every broadcast, in providing pupils with additional language exercises, both oral and written. Thus, RLAP has offered quality instruction in English at lower cost to a greater number of students than would be possible with direct classroom teaching. (Howard, 1990, pp. 79–80)

New Links Between Education and Human Services

There is a long history in the United States of linking social services with public schools (Tyack, 1992). Since the early twentieth century, physicians and dentists have volunteered their services in schools, volunteer and governmental organizations have served meals for children who might not have had them otherwise, and law enforcement agencies have come to school to educate children about drugs and crime and to change their own image in the minds of young people.

In the 1960s, Congress passed legislation to establish Head Start as well as the Elementary and Secondary Education Act; both stimulated school involvement in health care, nutrition, and job training. As David Tyack (1992) notes, schools have long assimilated reforms meant to address all sorts of human needs and made them part of the regular school operation. Some people think that linking social services to schools is a good idea; others believe that emphasizing social services detracts from the schools' primary educational mission.

Some people think that linking social services to schools is a good idea. Others don't.

Kentucky's Parent and Child Education (PACE) program, which began in 1986, assumes that a child's chances for educational and economic success are directly related to the parent's level of education (Weiss, 1992). Thus PACE tries to promote positive attitudes toward academic achievement in both parents and children. The program operates in 30 school districts and serves more than 1,800 parents and children, the majority of whom are European-American.

To qualify for PACE, 50% or more of a district's parents must not have graduated from high school. PACE runs a preschool program in each site for 3- and 4-year old children based on the High/Scope Educational Foundation or the Perry Preschool Program (see Chapter 6). The program also offers literacy tutoring, adult basic education, and GED coaching for parents. Each site also conducts support groups for parents on personal, academic, and vocational issues.

The New Jersey School-Based Youth Services Program (SBYSP) also links schools and social services, but does so for older children (Levy & Shepardson, 1992). The New Jersey Department of Human Services initiated the SBYSP in or very near high schools in every county in the state and in most low-income areas. The state does not impose a single program design but instead requires each site to offer a core of services during and after school hours, on weekends, and during vacations.

Core services of SBYSP include mental health, family counseling, primary and preventive health, substance abuse counseling, employment counseling, summer and part-time job placement, and academic counseling. The sites also offer recreation activities to encourage young people to become involved. Some sites offer day care, vocational programs, family planning, transportation, and hotlines. SBYSP is open to all students in participating schools. The intent is to encourage participation in the program's activities by many children, not just those with identified problems, so as to avoid the stigma of association with a center designated for "problem" cases.

Sidney Gardner (1992) argues that school-linked integrated services depend heavily on the cooperation of key players for their success. Coequals must plan details of implementation and work toward the same goals. This can only occur when no single agency "owns" the planning process. The planning team must address issues of whom to serve, governance, financing, evaluation, and sharing information. In addition, Gardner contends that planners should include community representatives, neighborhood groups, those workers who would deliver services, and parents. A widely representative planning group boosts the chances that people with various interests will "buy into" the program.

The examples noted above represent only a few of the kinds of programs that integrate educational and social services. Many others exist across the country; for instance, as we noted in Chapter 6, some communities have instituted school-based health clinics. No doubt new models of integrated services will be developed as people search for ways to address the needs of children in the context of society.

New Links Between Schools and Universities

Policymakers and education leaders have recognized that too many teachers feel overworked, lacking in support, and isolated from their colleagues—a set of conditions not conducive to professional and/or school reform. Evidence of the existence of these kinds of problems can be found in many schools, but the problems have been acute in urban areas.

Collaborative Networks to Advance the Study of Mathematics

Collaborative networks are groups of people who have come together voluntarily to help each other explore and advance particular educational issues. In 1985 and 1986, the Ford Foundation targeted more than $6 million at 11 cities across the United States to establish collaborative networks of mathematics teachers, school administrators, and mathematicians from colleges, universities, and industry. These cities were Cleveland, Durham, Los Angeles, Memphis, Minneapolis-St. Paul, New Orleans, Philadelphia, Pittsburgh, St. Louis, San Diego, and San Francisco. Since 1990, four more cities have been added to the group—Dayton, Ohio, Columbus, Georgia, Worcester, Massachusetts, and Milwaukee, Wisconsin. Figure 14.4 shows various types of collaborative networks.

The networks "have attempted to break teacher isolation and encourage professionalism by providing such activities as industrial internships for teachers, symposiums, workshops, dinner meetings and site visits" (Wisconsin Center for Education Research, 1992). They also funded trips to conferences and professional meetings for teachers.

Evaluation of the collaboratives' activities suggest that of the approximately 3,000 high school mathematics teachers in the original sites, about

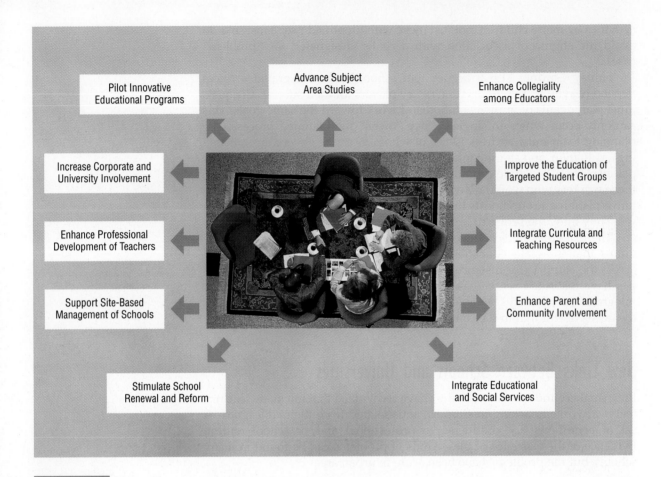

Pilot Innovative
Educational Programs

Advance Subject
Area Studies

Enhance Collegiality
among Educators

Increase Corporate and
University Involvement

Improve the Education of
Targeted Student Groups

Enhance Professional
Development of Teachers

Integrate Curricula and
Teaching Resources

Support Site-Based
Management of Schools

Enhance Parent and
Community Involvement

Stimulate School
Renewal and Reform

Integrate Educational
and Social Services

FIGURE 14.4

Uses of Collaborative Networks

20% have become frequent participants in activities offered at their sites. More than 80% of those teachers thought the network had enriched their professional lives and that they were valued by a larger community (Webb & Romborg, in press).

Collaborative Networks to Enhance Collegiality Among Educators John Goodlad and his colleagues at the University of Washington have led another attempt to institutionalize some new opportunities for teachers to assemble as colleagues around common interests and to function cooperatively. They have established the National Network for Educational Renewal, consisting of some 15 universities and 50 to 60 partner schools (R. Soder, personal communication, August 24, 1993). As Goodlad notes ". . . these are in an exploratory, embryonic stage; few of the problems of control, funding, division of labor, and the like have been worked out" (1990, p. 281).

The intent of this network is to seek the simultaneous renewal of schools and the education of educators. This means shifting the focus of reform from the management aspects of teaching and learning to the moral and political dimensions of the profession itself (R. Soder, personal communication, August 24, 1993). Goodlad (1988) has described such a shift as concentrating

VOICES

On Accelerated Schools

Henry Levin talks with Ron Brandt, editor of *Educational Leadership*:

We move from taking stock to developing a deep vision of the future. This is not just a one-day inservice; it typically takes weeks or months and involves reflection, deep thinking. We work around two key questions. . . . "Design as fully as possible the dream school you would want for your own child or your grandchild, a child very dear to you." We ask them to portray it in artistic ways; they get very excited about that. And they write a vision statement—but that's really the least important part. Because in the research some of us did in the early '80s, we saw hundreds of schools with mission statements but no mission, and vision statements with no vision. So our concern is whether they have a vision in their hearts and a set of beliefs that drive their daily behavior. . . . Around each priority we ask people to select working cadres, typically no more than eight or nine people. And the real work goes on when these small groups start to do research. . . .

The first school I worked in—this is a school with 600 kids, 90 percent minority, very poor—they had 17 parents come to back-to-school night—and 7 of them left after they ate. If you ever saw teachers who had no faith in parents, there they were. The next year, as they were planning another back-to-school night they said, "We don't agree with you—we don't believe we can get parents interested—but we'll test it by adding to our notice for back-to-school night that there will be a short presentation on 'How to Help Your Child Succeed with Homework.'" Well, 175 parents showed up. We had to run out for more coffee and doughnuts.

CRITICAL THINKING

Why do you think parents are willing/unwilling to be involved in their children's schools? What does the phrase "be involved in their children's schools" mean to you?

Source: Brandt, R. (1992). On building learning communities: A conversation with Hank Levin. *Educational Leadership, 50* (1), 19–23.

on "the ways some people—both within and outside the schools—benefit from keeping things the way they are" (p. 110).

The members of the National Network for Educational Renewal have agreed to address three goals:

> (1) to promote exemplary performance by universities in their role of educating educators; (2) to promote exemplary performance by schools in their role of educating the nation's young people; and (3) to promote constructive collaboration between schools (and their districts) and universities in assuring exemplary performance of overlapping mutual self-interests. (Goodlad, 1990, p. 324)

Collaborative Networks to Improve the Education of Children At Risk Another innovative effort to form "learning communities" is the brainchild of Stanford professor Henry Levin (see Chapter 5). His idea is simple. Provide children with rich experiences and connect their schools with their experiences, their culture, and their community, and these children will enter the mainstream of American life.

Levin calls his approach Accelerated Schools. Instead of trying to remediate perceived deficiencies in children's learning abilities, Levin encourages educators to capitalize on students' strengths. He has worked against the grain by giving at-risk students the kind of rich and challenging instruction typically reserved for gifted and talented children.

For Levin, collaboration in the process of transforming a school into an Accelerated School is indispensable: 80% of the entire staff must agree before he will work with them. He encourages them to "take stock" of what they are doing and to form a "deep vision" for the future (Brandt, 1992). Always, the adults who run schools must ask themselves, "Is this what we would want for our own children?" The answer to the question can spur people to behave in new and creative ways.

Collaborative Networks to Transform High School Teaching and Learning Theodore Sizer of Brown University organized the Coalition of Essential Schools to build and maintain viable networks of parents, students, and educators that can transform high schools into better places to teach and learn. (See Chapter 5 for a discussion of Boston's Fenway Middle College High School.) By 1991, about 200 schools in 23 states were involved in the Coalition. Most of the schools were public and 18 were private. Each defines for itself what constitutes a "good school," but the coalition of all schools expresses allegiance to nine common principles (Sizer, 1992).

These principles can be summarized as follows: (a) The school should focus on helping adolescents learn to use their minds well. Schools should not attempt to perform too many functions if they detract from the central intellectual purpose—less is more; (b) the school's mission should be a simple one, requiring students to master essential skills and knowledge; (c) all students should strive for the same goals, but means may vary according to students' needs; (d) teaching and learning should be personalized; (e) the metaphor that guides a school should be student as worker, not teacher as deliverer of instruction; (f) students who enter high school should be prepared adequately in language and mathematics—to graduate, students should "exhibit" their knowledge and skills; (g) school tone should communicate expectations, trust, and decency—incentives should be part of the program and parents should be collaborators; (h) staff should think of themselves first as generalists and next as specialists; (i) budget should provide for planning time, competitive salaries, and per-pupil costs of no more than 10% above traditional schools.

One challenge for essential schools is to link or integrate everything from curricula to people. In their effort to live up to the motto Less Is More, essential schools encourage high school teachers who view themselves as subject-matter specialists to think about stripping down their own discipline to essentials and linking instruction among the disciplines. Coalition members advocate taking some simple steps in this direction—"adopting common themes or aligning parallel courses either separately or in teams" (Cushman, 1993b, p. 4). These might be followed by combining content of two or more courses—for instance, linking history, literature, government, and the arts in an American Studies course (Cushman, 1993a).

Strategies for involving parents and community members in an essential school run the gamut of possibilities: sponsor evening study groups in which adults explore the same educational issues, hold public exhibitions of student work, pay parents as classroom aides, organize parent advisory groups, hold small-group sessions with the principal, publish a newsletter, encourage the newspaper to cover educational issues, and so forth. "The more schools work to know their communities in non-adversarial ways, it seems, the more trusting people will be" (Cushman, 1993b, p. 7).

In late 1993, Sizer and his colleagues were among several groups to receive a portion of a $500 million grant from philanthropist Walter Annenberg. In bestowing the gift, Annenberg noted their efforts to stimulate school reform and encouraged them verbally as well as materially to continue their work.

Collaborative Networks to Transform Teachers' Professional Development The Holmes Group, an association of education deans from 93 research universities, has concentrated on reforming teacher education (see Chapter 1). Chief among its initiatives has been a call for the establishment of "professional development schools," discussed in Chapter 5. A professional development school (PDS) is to "be the place where university faculty and novice teachers learn from the experiences that many teachers bring to successful work with diverse learners" (Holmes Group, 1990, p. 40).

William Johnson (1990) has described the Holmes notion of a professional development school as one constructed in the language of Dewey; that is, the image of the teacher promoted in the concept is that of "interpreter of culture to active children, not the scientific classroom manager guiding children through hierarchically organized curricula" (p. 584). Paul Dixon and Richard Ishler (1992) call the professional development school movement ". . . the inventing of a new institution mixing the best of theory, research, and practice at the precollege level and among teacher preparatory programs" (p. 28). The concept of a professional development school is very similar to what others have called a professional practice school (Levine, 1992).

Texas Tech University, five schools in the Lubbock Independent School District, and Texas's Region 17 Education Service Center formed a professional development school in 1991. The PDS melds ideas from the Holmes Group and Levin's Accelerated Schools model. The PDS houses student teachers and students participating in other field experiences. Some elementary preservice courses are taught in one of the participating elementary schools. Public school teachers have helped teach such courses. Cadres of professors, school faculty, and service unit representatives are organized to address the PDS goals, ranging from changing "family and health services as a natural extension of the school" to altering the "organizational structure and culture of the school" (Holmes Group, 1992, pp. 12, 13).

Researchers at the Center for Research on the Context of Teaching at Stanford University suggest that "teachers' professional communities—be they academic departments, schools, or teacher networks—are powerful mechanisms for stimulating innovation, reflection, experimentation, and reform" (McLaughlin & Talbert, 1993, p. 3). Despite many encouraging and highly visible attempts to foster collaboration between universities and public schools, however, people are probably more likely to read about such efforts than to experience them. When John Goodlad and his colleagues attempted to assess the developmental status of professional development schools and related types of organizations, "the gap between rhetoric and reality was found to be great" (1990, p. 400).

Trends Toward National Goals and Standards

Interdependence. Cooperation. Interaction. Collaboration. All well and good, but to what end? Education reformers of the 1980s and 1990s began to refocus the nation's collective attention more on student outcomes and less on the processes of education. Their argument was simple: If the nation cannot systematically assess student progress, that is, evaluate student progress in ways that can be compared across locales and over time, people will have no way of knowing (a) how well or how poorly students are performing, (b) what might best be done to improve weak showings, and (c) whether various reform measures actually affect students' performances.

Comprehensive Assessment Concerns about student progress have prompted educators to rethink time-honored practices of student assessment. The trend in student assessment is toward measuring not only what students know but also what they can do and how they reason. Tests that yield information on students' abilities to pick "right" and "wrong" answers promise to diminish in importance in the years ahead. Instead, educators want to develop a comprehensive assessment of student progress that will provide information on students' capacities for divergent thinking and creative problem solving.

If it is to be useful, such a comprehensive assessment will reflect more accurately the kinds of challenges students will face in real life than do paper-and-pencil, multiple-choice tests of knowledge acquisition. A truly comprehensive assessment will provide estimates of students' abilities to complete a variety of life's tasks and to function effectively in many societal contexts. To develop such an assessment for a future that is at best difficult to predict is in itself a challenging task.

Outcomes-Based Learning Reformers, chief among them those from the business community, frequently voice concern about the need to demonstrate results in education—they want outcomes, some kind of product emanating from students' engagement in processes of education. This desire is not new. Concern about educational outcomes or products reached its zenith in the 1920s with efforts to apply scientific principles to education problems and to assess these applications by examining students' products. The word *accountability* is often associated with demands to demonstrate competence via some palpable piece of evidence—a test score, a composition, a time on a race, or the like.

Typically, the more complex and highly developed a society becomes, the more it demands from its schools and students. Schools in developing countries and in earlier times in the United States have focused on building literacy. As the world grows more interdependent and more technologically demanding, the outcomes students are expected to demonstrate have advanced accordingly.

Standards for Professional Practice Should the United States have national tests similar to those in other countries? This question arises frequently when policymakers discuss educational standards. Lynne Cheney (1991) notes that other countries may help U.S. educators rethink testing.

> . . . [O]nly those [tests] of the Japanese make extensive use of multiple choice. For the most part, national achievement tests assess mastery by having students write. Some examining systems—the one used in the European Schools, for example—also require students to respond to questions orally. Others, such as the German *Abitur*, require students to give practical demonstrations in subjects such as music and the natural sciences. (Cheney, 1991, p. 4)

Student assessment, more particularly the **National Assessment of Educational Progress (NAEP)**, has become a fulcrum in the reform process in the United States. The NAEP is a Congressionally mandated set of tests operated by the Educational Testing Service. It is not national, however, in the sense that it is linked to a national curriculum. For 20 years, the NAEP has taken national samples of students in grades 4, 8, and 12, measuring their ability to read, write, and compute at different levels of sophistication.

Will the United States have a national curriculum?

The NAEP is viewed as one part of a comprehensive assessment system by which political and education leaders can leverage change in teaching so as to encourage progress toward accomplishment of the National Education Goals (see chapter 1). As it stands, however, the NAEP has been criticized as useful only for assessing trends in students' performance over time and as virtually worthless as a means of determining students' absolute abilities in mathematics (Glaser & Linn, 1992). An improved NAEP system will presumably eventually include local and state assessments, international comparisons, and explicit links among assessments, curricula, teaching, and professional development for teachers (Technical Subgroup for the National Education Goals Panel, 1992).

Other countries have national examination systems—driven by national standards and national curricula—which are often criticized by Americans as restrictive sorting devices. But Marc Tucker, president of the National Center on Education and the Economy, has argued that our own system is far more restrictive and inflexible than those of other countries.

> We have different standards for different kids because we have different expectations. . . . We decide on those expectations very early and close off options with a finality that European systems cannot match. . . . An examination system . . . properly designed and embedded in the right

policy system, can be an extremely powerful motivator to kids. It can elicit effort in school in a way that almost nothing else can match. (Gursky, 1991, 53–56)

Past reforms have typically dealt with the inputs and processes of schooling—human and material resources, curriculum, and instruction— not with the outcomes of schooling, in other words, student learning. Arguments for the most recent round of reforms have been based heavily on American students' test scores—classic outcome measures. Critics have asserted, however, that these arguments are misleading for two reasons. First, American students' test scores are not nearly so poor as people have made them out to be (Bracey, 1991; Carson, Huelskamp, & Woodall, 1991). And second, the real differences between and among students in various countries is not explained so much by differences in curriculum and instruction as by economic factors and family structure and stability (Jaeger, 1992).

Standards for education will drive the formation of new and revised tests which, in turn, will stimulate the production of new and revised curricula. Does this mean the United States will have a "national curriculum"— one to which local education authorities will be compelled to conform? If so, what might happen to less affluent communities and students compared to the more affluent? How might provisions for deviations from a national curriculum be arranged, if at all? Even if new standards, tests, and curricula do not assume a national cast, will they make a difference in teachers' and students' behaviors on a day-to-day basis? These questions will demand answers in the years ahead.

Lauren Resnick, director of the New Standards Project for the federal government, describes standards not simply as benchmarks for gauging tests but as a means to improve student outcomes:

We believe that the American education system has to begin to deliver on its rhetoric and see to it that all students are educated to high standards. The development of standards and assessments is a critical piece of reforming the entire educational system so that it is much more coherent and is driven by much higher standards. (O'Neil, 1993, p. 17)

Elliott Eisner (1993) views the development of standards in a somewhat different light.

The current emphasis on standards will provide no panacea in education. Paying close attention to how we teach and building institutions that make it possible for teachers to continue to grow as professionals may be much more effective educationally than trying to determine through standard means whether or not our students measure up. (p. 23)

HOW CAN EDUCATORS PREPARE THEMSELVES FOR THE FUTURE?

It would be natural for educators to be overwhelmed by the complexity and pace of our rapidly changing world. There is so much to know, so much to do. Faced with the diversity of interests that contend for attention in public education, it would be easy to slip into one of two roles: the Pollyanna who leaps headfirst into the maelstrom of problems or the cynic who throws up his or her hands in despair. Is there no reasonable way to mature and prosper as a professional?

We have tried to fashion a general response to this urgent question in the preceding chapters—in a sense to introduce a strategy for early and continuing development as an educator. One cannot implement this strategy naturally or easily, however. It demands professional behavior—behavior rooted in some old values that professionals, regardless of their stripe, have found useful.

Good professionals perceive problems and opportunities, because they are awake—they are mentally alert to what is going on around them. If physicians or lawyers or business people were oblivious to problems and opportunities in their fields, there would be nothing germane to be said or done. The same holds true for educators.

It is very unlikely that educators will become professionally competent or highly respected without being able to articulate their own values in relation to the values of others they hope to serve. If this is to happen, educators must be able to make their own values explicit and to do likewise for their communities' values. Values drive actions. And when professionals' values dictate actions outside the latitude of acceptance of others, they must be prepared to deal with the differences in constructive ways.

If a person wishes to claim professional status, he or she must possess some special knowledge that other nonprofessionals do not possess. Professional educators know their content, and they know how to communicate in ways that students will be likely to understand and accept. They know much subject matter, and they possess much knowledge about teaching and learning. Exceptionally strong teachers also frequently know when they do not know what might be important to know.

Acting, performing, behaving, applying what one knows are the bread and butter of professional life. Good professionals can do things nonprofessionals cannot do.

If not for the power of hindsight, professionals might never be able to evaluate their actions with any reasonable sense of efficacy. Looking backward at what has happened is one of the most useful ways of seeing what might lie ahead.

Although there is much to be learned from our professional forebears, sometimes intellectual tools that have been useful at one time in one place can be inappropriate for another time and another place. Sometimes people must invent or **discover** new ways of thinking and behaving, and not necessarily in that order. They need to do something, and then they can think about what went right and what went wrong, so they can do better next time. In all likelihood, the most frequent errors in professional life, and those that cannot be set straight later, are the missed opportunities for learning and for taking pleasure from action. People who continue to learn and to enjoy doing important work as best they can turn jobs into careers.

SUMMARY

1. The concept of international comparative education suggests (a) that problems of educational development are common in many societies; and (b) that by studying education in different societies, educators develop new insights into these societies while deriving innovative understanding of their own society.

2. A careful examination of other cultures may yield new insights into American culture. Such seems to be the case when studying how other English-speaking countries deal with issues of multiculturalism.

3. People around the world appear to be tied to one another by some common themes, including but not limited to choice, reform, control, literacy, and responsibility.

4. The welfare of the United States is tied to the welfare of other countries by economics, the environment, politics, culture, technology, and education. Concerns that cut across national borders demand global awareness.

5. Disagreement about educational matters is evidence of interest and participation—prerequisites for consensus.

6. Consensus on the education reform agenda is emerging on several points: education problems can be solved; money is a necessary part of a solution but not sufficient by itself; poverty threatens everyone in society; professional status is tied to school improvement; education must flow within and across education systems; people have many common needs and abilities.

7. Government can and must coordinate its own activities to serve people if problems are to be addressed successfully.

8. Many formal education networks appear to be based on the dual assumption that education problems cannot be solved by educators alone and that providing opportunities for involvement early in the formation of networks encourages people to work together.

9. Technology may actually change how people think. Teachers need the time and support to merge technology and curricula if students are to maximize the potential of both.

10. Distance learning holds the potential for conducting interactive teaching and learning between developed and remote areas in cost effective ways.

11. Interest in linking educational and social services appears to be increasing.

12. Standards for education will drive the formation of new and revised tests which, in turn, will stimulate the production of new and revised curricula. It is too early to determine how effective these efforts will be.

TERMS AND CONCEPTS

collaborative networks	INGOs	Internet
distance learning	international	National Assessment of
e-mail	comparative	Educational Progress
global awareness	education	(NAEP)

STUDENT ACTIVITIES

It may be hyperbole to say you either control your own future or are controlled by it. Truth probably lies somewhere in between. Nonetheless, you can do much to shape your professional destiny by allowing yourself to learn from others.

Perceive and Value

Compare and contrast the educational systems described in this chapter in terms of the way schooling is structured, the aims of education, and approaches to cultural diversity and language instruction. What differences stand out in contrast to the American educational system? How may the differences be accounted for? Identify different policies, aims, or practices in other countries that you think could benefit American education, and give reasons to support your arguments.

Know and Act

What kinds of education coalitions, collaboratives, and networks similar to the ones described in this chapter are operating in your state? What educational and social concerns do they address? As a teacher, which would you like to participate in, in what ways, and why?

Evaluate

What are the advantages and disadvantages of creating and implementing a national curriculum and national standards of performance for students? For teachers? For school districts and states? For the nation?

Discover

Access Internet, e-mail, or other electronic networks through your school and initiate communication with preservice and inservice teachers. Ask them for tips on how to go about reconfiguring curriculum to match computer capabilities for direct instruction in the classroom. Share, collect, and jointly publish tips with classmates.

Talk with education faculty and/or people at your local computer center to determine if you presently have or can get access to the Society for Technology and Teacher Education's (STATE) Teacher Education Internet Server. The Teacher Education Server was designed for teacher education faculty and students. Among other features, it contains hypermedia modules on various subjects in instructional technology, a forum to submit articles, and opportunities to participate in on-line discussions about teaching and learning with other educators around the world. (For more information, contact: Bernard Robin, STATE Server Curator, Department of Curriculum & Instruction, University of Houston, (713) 743-4952, Internet e-mail: brobin@uh.edu)

APPENDIX A

Professional Organizations

American Alliance for Health, Physical Education, Recreation and Dance (AAHPERD)

1900 Association Drive
Reston, VA 22091
Phone: (703) 476-3400

Students and educators in physical education, dance, health, athletics, safety education, recreation, and outdoor education. Purpose is to improve its fields of education at all levels though such services as consultation, periodicals, and special publications, leadership development, determination of standards, and research. Operates information and Resource Utilization Center devoted to physical education and recreation for the handicapped and programs for senior citizens. Maintains biographical archives; sponsors placement service, bestows awards.

American Counseling Association (ACA)

5999 Stevenson Avenue
Alexandria, VA 22304
Phone: (703) 823-9800

Counseling professionals in elementary and secondary schools, higher education, community agencies and organizations, rehabilitation programs, government, industry, business, and private practice. Maintains special library of 5000 books and pamphlets. Provides placement service for members; conducts professional development institutes and provides liability insurance. Maintains Counseling and Human Development Foundation to fund counseling projects.

American School Counselor Association (ASCA)

c/o American Counseling Association
5999 Stevenson Avenue
Alexandria, VA 22304
Phone: (703) 823-9800

A division of the American Counseling Association. School counselors; professionals engaged in school counseling or related activities at least 50% of the time; students; other interested individuals. Promotes human rights, children's welfare, healthy learning environments, and positive interpersonal relationships; fosters academic, occupational, personal, and social growth among members. Works to improve professional standards in school counseling and in other student personnel services; seeks to further public awareness of such services. Develops and promotes career development

programs; sponsors interprofessional activities and leadership development programs. Represents members' interests in governmental and public relations. Serves as liaison among members and counselors in other settings; disseminates education, professional, and scientific materials.

American Schools Association (Counseling) (ASA)

3069 Amwiler Road, Suite 4
Atlanta, GA 30360
Phone: (404) 449-7141

Coordinates educational counseling and consultation; administers national scholarship programs. Conducts GED, PSAT, ACT, and SAT preparation courses; offers remedial tutorial assistance, and continuing education on a home-study basis for license/certificate maintenance for Rehabilitation Professionals nationwide.

American Vocational Association (AVA)

1410 King Street
Alexandria, CA 22314
Phone: (703) 683-3111

Teachers, supervisors, administrators and others interested in development and improvement of vocational, technical, and practical arts education. Areas of interest include: secondary, post secondary, and adult vocational education; education for special population groups, cooperative education. Works with such governmental agencies as: Bureau of Apprenticeship in Department of Labor: Office of Vocational Rehabilitation in Department of Health and Human Services; Veterans Administration; Office of Vocational and Adult Education of the Department of Education. Maintains hall of fame; bestows awards.

Association for Education and Rehabilitation of the Blind and Visually Impaired (AER)

206 N. Washington Street
Suite 320
Alexandria, VA 22314
Phone: (703) 548-1884

Educators, rehabilitators, administrators, parents, agencies, schools, and others interested in the education, guidance, vocational rehabilitation, or occupational placement of the blind and partially sighted. To expand the opportunities for the visually handicapped to take a contributory place in society. Cooperates with colleges and universities in conferences and workshops. Presents awards; conducts certification programs; maintains job exchange services and speaker's bureau.

Association for the Education of Teachers in Science (AETS)

5040 Haley Center
Auburn University
Auburn, AL 36849
Phone: (205) 844-6799

Science education faculty and college science teachers with a special interest in teacher education; supervisors and administers of science programs in school systems; chairpersons of science departments in secondary schools; elementary and secondary schools science consultants. Presents Outstanding Science Educator, Implications of Research for Educational Practice, Honorary Emeritus Membership awards annually.

Council for Exceptional Children (CEC)

1920 Association Drive
Reston, VA 22091-1589
Phone: (703) 620-3660

Teachers, school administrators, teacher educators, and others with a direct or indirect concern for the education of handicapped and gifted, defined as those children and youth whose instructional needs differ sufficiently from the average to require special services and teachers with specialized qualifications. Council is concerned with children who are mentally gifted, mentally retarded, visually handicapped, hearing impaired, physically handicapped, and those with behavioral disorders, learning disabilities, and speech defects. Champions the right of exceptional individuals to full educational opportunities, career development, and employment opportunities. Provides information to teachers, parents, and others concerning the education of exceptional children. Sponsors workshops, academies, and symposia on special education topics; provides technical assistance to legislators, state departments of education, and other agencies; disseminates information, Coordinates political action network to support the rights of exceptional people. Conducts special projects in areas such as special education technology and software and training educators. Maintains 63,000 volume library. Operates ERIC Clearinghouse on Handicapped and Gifted Children.

Council for Learning Disabilities (CLD)

PO Box 40303
Overland Park, KS 66204
Phone: (913) 492-8755

Professionals interested in the study of learning disabilities. Works to promote the education and general welfare of individuals having specific learning disabilities by improving teacher preparation programs and local special education programs and by resolving important research issues. Sponsors educational sessions; bestows awards.

International Reading Association (IRA)

800 Barksdale Road
PO. Box 8139
Newark, DE 19714-8139
Phone: (302) 731-1600

Teachers, reading specialists, consultants, administrators, supervisors, researchers, psychologists, librarians, and parents interested in promoting literacy. Seeks to improve the quality of reading instruction at all education levels; stimulates and promotes lifetime reading habits and an awareness of the impact of reading; encourages the development of every reader's proficiency to the highest possible level. Disseminates information pertaining to research on reading, including information on adult literacy, computer technology and reading, early childhood and literacy development, international education, literature for children and adolescents, and teacher education and effectiveness. Gives awards, sponsors competitions, and maintains placement service.

National Art Education Association (NAEA)

1916 Association Drive
Reston, VA 22091-1590
Phone: (703) 860-8000

Teachers of art at elementary, secondary and college levels; colleges, libraries, museums, and other educational institutions. Studies Problems of Teaching art: encourages research and experimentation. Serves as clearinghouse for information on art educational programs, materials, and methods of instruction. Presents annual awards; sponsors special institutes and workshops. Cooperates with other national organizations for the furtherance of creative art experiences for youth. Maintains placement services and library on art education.

National Association for Bilingual Education (NABE)

Union Center Plaza
810 1st Street NE, 3rd Fl.
Washington, DC 20002
Phone: (202) 898-1829

Educators, administrators, paraprofessionals, community and lay people, and students. Purposes are to recognize, promote, and publicize bilingual education. Seeks to increase public understanding of the importance of language and culture. Utilizes and develops student proficiency and ensures equal opportunities in bilingual education for language-minority students. Works to preserve and expand the nation's linguistic resources. Educates language minority parents in public policy decisions. Promotes research in language education, linguistics, and multicultural education. Coordinates development of professional standards, organizes conferences and workshops; supports state and local affiliates; and establishes contact with national organizations. Bestows awards for Bilingual Teacher of the Year and Bilingual Instructional Assistant of the Year; sponsors nationwide writing contest for bilingual students.

National Association for Research in Science Teaching (NARST)

c/o Dr. John R Staver
Kansas State University
219 Bluemont Hall
Manhattan, KS 66506
Phone: (913) 532-6294

Science teachers, supervisors, and science educators specializing in research and teacher education. Promotes and coordinates science education research and interprets and reports the results. Presents five awards annually: for contributions to research in science education, significant contributions to research for best article published in a journal, for best doctoral dissertation, and best research report given at annual meeting.

National Association of Biology Teachers (NABT)

11250 Roger Bacon Drive
No. 19
Reston, VA 22090
Phone: (703) 471-1134

Professional society of biology and life science teachers and others interested in teaching biology at all educational levels. Works to achieve scientific literacy among citizens. Promotes professional growth and development; fosters regional activities for biology teachers; confronts issues involving biology, society, and the future; provides a national voice for the profession. Sponsors summer biology updates. Bestows Outstanding Biology and Student Science Fair awards.

National Association of Classroom Educators in Business Education (NACEBE)

c/o Janet H. Auten
Watauga High School
Highway 105 South
Boone, NC 28607
Phone: (704) 264-2407

Secondary, post secondary, and adult educators, coordinators, and department chairmen involved in business education programs who are members of the American Vocational Association. Objectives are to: promote, develop, and upgrade business education in the U.S.; cooperate with state supervisors, teacher educators, and city supervisors; develop leadership in educational programs for business occupations.

National Association of Elementary School Principals (NAESP)

1615 Duke Street
Alexandria, VA 22314
Phone: (703) 6840-3345

Professional association of principals, assistant or vice principals, and aspiring principals; persons engaged in educational research and in the professional education of elementary school administrators. Sponsors National Distinguished Principals Program., Presidential Academic Fitness Program, American Student Council Association, and National Fellows Program.

National Association of School Psychologists (NASP)

8455 Colesville Road
Suite 1000
Silver Spring, MD 20910
Phone: (301) 608-0500

School psychologists. Serves the mental health and educational needs off all children and youth; encourages and provides opportunities for professional growth of individual members; informs the public on the services and practice of school psychology; advances the standards of the profession. Operates national school psychologist certification system. Maintains library and placement service. Conducts workshops and symposia.

National Association of Secondary School Principals (NASSP)

1904 Association Drive
Reston, VA 22091
Phone: (703) 860-0200

Secondary school principals and assistant principals; other persons engaged in secondary school administration and/or supervision; college professors teaching courses in secondary education. Sponsors National Association of Student Councils, National Honor Society, and National Junior Society.

Nationals Association of Vocational Home Economics Teachers (NAVHET)

c/o Bonnie Claycomb
811 E. Main Street
Horse Cave, KY 42749
Phone: (502) 786-2796

Professional society of home economics teachers who are members of the American Vocational Association. Presents annual awards.

National Council for Geographic Education (NCGE)

Indiana University of Pennsylvania
16A Leonard Hall
Indiana, PA 15705
Phone: (412) 357-6290

Teachers of geography and social studies in elementary and secondary schools, colleges, and universities; geographers in governmental agencies and private businesses. Encourages the training of teachers in geographic concepts, practices, teaching methods, and techniques; works to develops effective geographic educational programs in schools and collages and with adult groups; stimulates the production and use of accurate and understandable geographic teaching aids and materials. Bestows annual Distinguished Service Awards for meritorious service to geographic education; also honors exceptional geographical articles published each year.

National Council for History Education (NCHE)

c/o Elaine Wrisley Reed
26915 Westwood Road, Ste. B2
Phone: (216) 835-1776

Elementary and secondary school teachers of history, academic historians, education curriculum policymakers and developers, and historical and museum personnel. Promotes the formal and Informal study of history in schools and society. Maintains speakers' bureau, archives, and library or reference books, periodicals, and audiovisual material.

National Council for Languages and International Studies (NCLIS)

2300 Eye Street, N. W., Suite 211
Washington, DC 20002
Phone: (202) 546-7855

Language and international education associations, and organizations concerned with foreign language education, international studies, international exchanges, and global affairs. Primary goal is to maintain contact with legislators and policymakers in order to sensitize them to concerns of the language and international studies communities, and to acquire and disseminate information. Objectives are: to broaden and improve the learning and teaching of languages and other international studies; to increase cooperation and dialogue among foreign language, classical, English-as-a-second-language, bilingual, and international studies associations; to inform others of the importance and value of language and international studies to the political, economic, and intellectual security of the U.S.; to foster international exchange and foreign study programs that stress development of full proficiency in languages and international studies. Supports legislation and policies that promote languages and international studies. Conducts political action workshops.

National Council for the Social Studies (NCSS)

3501 Newark Street, NW
Washington, DC 20016
Phone: (202) 966-7840

Teachers of elementary and secondary social studies, including instructors of civics, geography, history, economics, political science, psychology, sociology, and anthropology; interested others. Promotes the teaching of social studies to the best advantage of the students. Bestows awards.

National Council of Teachers of English (NCTE)

1111 Kenyon Road
Urbana, IL 61801
Phone: (217) 328-3870

Teachers of English at all school levels. Works to increase the effectiveness of instruction in English language and literature. Sponsors conference on College Composition and Communication, Conference of English Education, and Conference of English Leadership. Presents achievement awards for writing to high school juniors and students in the eighth grade, and awards for high school literacy magazines. Provides information and aids for teachers involved in formulating objectives, writing, evaluating curriculum guides, and planning in-service programs for teacher education.

National Council of Teachers of Mathematics (NCTM)

1906 Association Drive
Reston, Virginia 22091-1593
Phone: (703) 620-9840

Teachers of mathematics in grades K–12, two-year colleges, and teacher education personnel on college campuses.

National Science Teachers Association (NSTA)

1742 Connecticut Avenue, NW
Washington, DC 20009-1171
Phone: (202) 328-5800

Teachers seeking to foster excellence in science teaching. Studies students and how they learn, the curriculum of science, the teacher and his/her preparation, the procedures used in classroom and laboratory, the facilities for teaching science, and the evaluation procedures used.

Note: From *Encyclopedia of Associations 1994,* 28th Edition, vols. 1 & 2. P.K. Daniels and C.A. Schwartz, Editors. Detroit, MI: Gale Research Inc.

Teacher-Interstate Agreement Contracts (October 1, 1991—September 30, 1996)

	AL	AK	AR	AZ	CA	CO	CT	DE	FL	GA	HI	ID	IL	IN	IA	KS	KY	LA	ME	MD	MA	MI	MN	MO	MS	MT	NE	NV	NH	NJ	NM	NY	NC	ND	OH	OK	OR	PA	PR	RI	SC	SD	TN	TX	UT	VT	VA	WA	WV	WI	WY	DC	DOS
AL	■																																																					
AK		■																																																			
AR			■																																																		
AZ				■	X		X	X		X	X	X					X		X	X	X	X							X	X		X	X		X			X		X	X		X		X	X	X	X	X			X	
CA	X			X	■		X	X	X	X	X	X		X		X			X	X	X	X				X			X	X			X		X		X	X		X	X		X	X	X	X	X	X	X			X	
CO	X			X		■	X	X	X	X	X	X		X		X			X	X	X	X							X	X			X		X		X	X		X	X		X		X	X	X	X	X				
CT	X			X	X	X	■	X	X	X	X	X		X		X	X	X	X	X	X	X				X			X	X		X	X		X		X	X		X	X		X	X	X	X	X	X	X			X	
DE	X			X	X	X	X	■	X	X	X	X		X		X	X	X	X	X	X	X				X			X	X		X	X		X		X	X		X	X		X	X	X	X	X	X	X			X	
FL	X				X	X	X	X	■	X	X	X		X		X	X	X	X	X	X	X				X			X	X		X	X		X		X	X		X	X		X	X	X	X	X	X	X			X	
GA	X			X	X	X	X	X	X	■	X	X		X		X	X	X	X	X	X	X				X			X	X		X	X		X		X	X		X	X		X	X	X	X	X	X	X			X	
HI	X			X	X	X	X	X	X	X	■	X		X		X	X	X	X	X	X	X				X			X	X		X	X		X		X	X		X	X		X	X	X	X	X	X	X			X	
ID	X			X	X	X	X	X	X	X	X	■		X		X	X		X	X	X	X				X			X	X		X	X		X		X	X		X	X		X	X	X	X	X	X	X			X	
IL													■																																								
IN	X			X	X	X	X	X	X	X	X	X		■		X			X	X	X	X							X	X		X	X		X		X	X		X	X		X		X	X	X	X	X			X	
IA															■																																						
KS	X			X	X	X	X	X	X	X	X	X		X		■			X	X	X	X				X			X	X		X	X		X		X	X		X	X		X		X	X	X	X	X			X	
KY	X			X			X	X	X	X	X	X					■	X	X	X	X								X	X		X	X		X		X	X		X	X		X	X	X	X	X	X	X			X	
LA							X	X	X	X	X						X	■	X	X	X								X	X		X	X					X		X	X		X		X	X	X	X	X				
ME	X			X	X	X	X	X	X	X	X	X		X		X	X	X	■	X	X								X	X		X	X		X		X	X		X	X		X		X	X	X	X	X			X	
MD	X			X	X	X	X	X	X	X	X	X		X		X	X	X	X	■	X	X							X	X		X	X		X		X	X		X	X		X		X	X	X	X	X			X	
MA	X			X	X	X	X	X	X	X	X	X		X		X	X	X	X	X	■	X				X			X	X		X	X		X		X	X		X	X		X	X	X	X	X	X	X			X	
MI				X	X	X	X	X	X	X	X	X		X		X				X	X	■							X	X		X	X		X		X	X		X	X		X		X	X	X	X	X			X	
MN																							■																														
MO																								■																													
MS																									■																												
MT					X		X	X	X	X	X	X				X					X					■				X					X		X			X			X		X	X	X	X	X			X	
NE																											■																										
NV																												■																									
NH	X			X	X	X	X	X	X	X	X	X		X		X	X	X	X	X	X	X				X			■	X		X	X		X		X	X		X	X		X	X	X	X	X	X	X			X	
NJ	X			X	X	X	X	X	X	X	X	X		X		X	X	X	X	X	X	X				X			X	■		X	X		X		X	X		X	X		X	X	X	X	X	X	X			X	
NM																															■																						
NY	X			X			X	X	X	X	X	X		X		X	X	X	X	X	X	X							X	X		■	X		X		X	X		X	X		X	X	X	X	X	X	X			X	
NC	X			X	X	X	X	X	X	X	X	X		X		X	X	X	X	X	X	X							X	X		X	■		X		X	X		X	X		X	X	X	X	X	X	X			X	
ND																																		■																			
OH	X			X	X	X	X	X	X	X	X	X		X		X	X	X	X	X	X	X				X			X	X		X	X		■		X	X		X	X		X	X	X	X	X	X	X			X	
OK																																				■																	
OR				X	X	X	X	X	X	X	X	X		X		X			X	X	X	X				X			X	X		X	X		X		■	X		X	X		X		X	X	X	X	X			X	
PA	X			X	X	X	X	X	X	X	X	X		X		X	X	X	X	X	X	X				X			X	X		X	X		X		X	■		X	X		X	X	X	X	X	X	X			X	
PR	X																																						■													X	
RI	X			X	X	X	X	X	X	X	X	X		X		X	X	X	X	X	X	X				X			X	X		X	X		X		X	X		■	X		X	X	X	X	X	X	X			X	
SC	X			X	X	X	X	X	X	X	X	X		X		X	X	X	X	X	X	X				X			X	X		X	X		X		X	X		X	■		X	X	X	X	X	X	X			X	
SD																																										■											
TN	X			X	X	X	X	X	X	X	X	X		X		X	X	X	X	X	X	X				X			X	X		X	X		X		X	X		X	X		■	X	X	X	X	X	X			X	
TX				X	X		X	X	X	X	X	X					X				X					X			X	X		X	X		X			X		X	X		X	■	X	X	X	X	X			X	
UT	X			X	X	X	X	X	X	X	X	X		X		X	X	X	X	X	X	X				X			X	X		X	X		X		X	X		X	X		X	X	■	X	X	X	X			X	
VT	X			X	X	X	X	X	X	X	X	X		X		X	X	X	X	X	X	X				X			X	X		X	X		X		X	X		X	X		X	X	X	■	X	X	X			X	
VA	X			X	X	X	X	X	X	X	X	X		X		X	X	X	X	X	X	X				X			X	X		X	X		X		X	X		X	X		X	X	X	X	■	X	X			X	
WA	X			X	X	X	X	X	X	X	X	X		X		X	X	X	X	X	X	X				X			X	X		X	X		X		X	X		X	X		X	X	X	X	X	■	X			X	
WV	X			X	X	X	X	X	X	X	X	X		X		X	X	X	X	X	X	X				X			X	X		X	X		X		X	X		X	X		X	X	X	X	X	X	■			X	
WI																																																		■			
WY																																																			■		
DC	X			X	X		X	X		X	X	X		X		X	X		X	X	X	X				X			X	X		X	X		X		X	X	X	X	X		X	X	X	X	X	X	X			■	
DOS																																																					■

Note: Used by permission of Audrey Huggins, Chair of Interstate Certification Agreement Contract Administrators Association, NASDTEC.

560

APPENDIX C

The Praxis Series: Professional Assessments for Beginning Teachers™

From Preparation Through Performance

The Praxis Series offers assessments for each stage of the beginning teacher's career, from entry into teacher education to actual classroom performance.

Praxis I tests skills in reading, writing, and mathematics that all teachers need, regardless of grade or subject taught.

Praxis II measures candidates' knowledge of the subjects they will teach.

Praxis III judges teaching skill in the classroom through the use of local assessors.

Praxis I	Praxis II	Praxis III
Academic Skills Assessments	Subject Assessments	Classroom Performance Assessments

Designed with State Licensing Requirements in Mind

The Praxis Series provides nationally available tests in a choice of formats. The series built-in flexibility helps states meet specific licensing requirements for beginning teachers and other educational professionals.

The series integrates current tests with newly developed assessments to measure key areas of competence.

Research-Based

Each assessment is founded on extensive research, including analyses of tasks considered important for beginning teachers. These job analyses involved thousands of teachers, teacher educators, administrators, and educational policy makers.

Source: Educational Testing Service. (1992). *21st Century Teacher Assessments.* Princeton, NJ: Educational Testing Service.

Innovative Assessment Formats

In addition to multiple-choice questions, many tests in the series feature *candidate-constructed-response* questions, requiring examinees to produce their own answers.

The computer-based assessments introduce *adaptive testing.* The computer creates a unique test geared to the test-takes performance level. The computer-based assessments also allow candidates to use *built-in calculators and word processors.*

The Classroom Performance component recognizes the unique nature of every teacher and every teacher situation. It uses an *integrated framework of criteria* reflecting the complex nature of teaching. This component includes a training program to prepare local assessors to make informed judgments about beginning teachers' performance.

Cost-Saving Validation Procedures

Before new tests are assembled, ETS submits all questions to multistate validation panels. Because ETS underwrites the cost of these studies, states save both time and money. Since only questions validated by these panels of practicing professionals are assembled into tests, states can be confident that all questions in all tests have been approved for use.

A closer look . . .
PRAXIS I: Academic Skills Assessments

Should entry-level teachers be able to determine the main point of the reading selection? Organize ideas clearly and effectively? Interpret tables and graphs?

ETS analyzed surveys from almost 3,000 teachers, teacher educators, administrators and other professionals to determine what skills they considered important for beginning teachers.

Based on their comments and extensive research, ETS has created Academic Skills Assessments in reading, writing, and mathematics.

These tests, designed to be taken early in the candidate's college career, determine that prospective teachers have the enabling skills they need for their profession.

Praxis I offers two testing formats, both of which are linked to a new, computer-delivered instructional package.

Computer-Based Academic Skills Assessments

- Computer delivered—expands range of question types to include multiple response, highlighting, fill-ins, reordering, and candidate-constructed response
- Computer adaptive—tailors tests to suit candidates' performance
- Technologically advanced—includes built-in calculator and word processor
- Flexible administration—scheduled to accommodate candidates' needs.

Pre-Professional Skills Tests (PPST)

- Paper-and-pencil format requires no special equipment
- Convenient scheduling, administered eight times a year
- Revised and linked to job analysis

LearningPlus™—Computer-Delivered Instructional Package

To help teacher candidates who may need to improve certain basic academic skills and to help increase access to the profession, ETS has developed a new computer-delivered instructional package—

LearningPlus™: Computer-Based Learning of Skills and Strategies.

Based on contemporary learning theory and research identifying important enabling skills for entry-level teachers, LearningPlus™ is individualized to match each student's needs:

- Covers skills in reading, writing, and mathematics tested in Praxis I
- Leads candidates to specific lessons through diagnostic skills profiles
- Provides 20 to 30 hours of instruction in each subject
- Focuses on strategies for learning, ways of organizing knowledge, and development of skills
- Links instruction to both the revised Pre-Professional Skills Tests and the new Computer-Based Academics Skills Assessments.

Here's How It Works . . .

1. A familiarization program introduces students to computer and mouse functions and to the built-in assistance of a calculator and word processor.
2. Students then take a diagnostic skills profile.
3. Students are directed to computer-delivered lessons in specific areas as needed. They are led through learning programs that gradually remove instructional assistance as students' skills improve.
4. Immediate feedback lets students decide if they're ready for the actual test or need to review certain skills.
5. Students may receive between 20 to 30 hours of instruction in each of the three areas—reading, writing, and mathematics.
6. Lessons are modular. Students take only those identified by diagnostic skills profile.
7. Many different examples are included. Candidates can review one skills area a number of times without repeating material.
8. Materials may be used in learning lab.
9. Practice test help candidates decide when they are ready for the actual test.

More than 70 subjects covered . . .
PRAXIS II: Subject Assessments

ETS offers states new modular Subject Assessments for measuring teaching candidates' understanding of the subjects they will teach.

These tests give states great flexibility in meeting their individual licensing requirements.

- Before beginning development of these new tests, ETS considered state licensing content area requirements.
- Teachers, teacher educators, and other professionals were involved throughout the evolution of the individual assessments.
- Test developers were guided by results of extensive job analyses.
- Constructed-response modules target skills and knowledge difficult to assess through multiple-choice tests. They allow candidates to demonstrate in-depth understanding and reinforce the importance of writing within the teaching profession.

- Modular subject-area tests give states maximum flexibility.

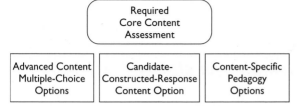

For example:

The Spanish Assessment features a two-hour multiple-choice core and two optional candidate-constructed response modules—productive language skills and pedagogy.

In the Mathematics Assessment, the two-hour multiple-choice core is supported by four optional modules—multiple-choice advanced content; proofs, models, and problems (level 1 and 2); and pedagogy.

The optional modules in each area give states maximum flexibility in tailoring their assessments to meet their specific licensure requirements.

- The content core is central to each nationally available subject assessment.
- Optional modules focus on particular aspects of the subject or on ways of teaching the subject.
- Modular options differ from test to test. For example, in addition to a two-hour multiple-choice core in social studies, a state might choose one or more candidate-constructed-response modules covering analysis, interpretation, and how to teach the subject.
- ETS is underwriting the costs of multistate validity studies for these new assessments.
- Expanded and improved study guides will offer test-taking tips, test-content specifications, and sample questions.

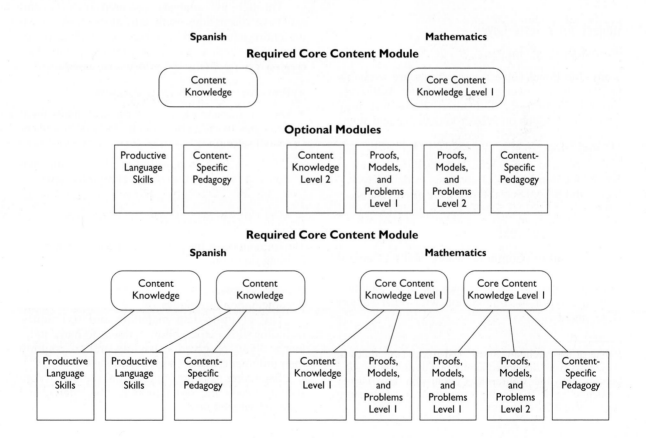

Modular Subject Assessments* Available for Adoption:

- Art
- Biology
- Chemistry
- Elementary Education
- English Language, Literature, and Composition
- French
- General Science
- Mathematics
- Music
- Physical Education
- Physical Sciences
- Physics
- Principles of Learning and Teaching
- Spanish
- Social Studies

Combinations of assessments—for example, Biology and General Science—are also possible.

Subject Area Tests Cover a Wide Range of Topics

Many additional subject assessments are available for adoption. Covering subjects from Audiology through Technology Education, these test may combine questions on subject knowledge and items covering content-specific pedagogy.

Specialties, such as Teaching English as a Second Language, and non-teaching specialties, including School Guidance and Counseling, School Psychologist, and School Social Worker are also available.

Core Battery Tests

Tests covering Communication Skills, General Knowledge and Professional Skills are available. These multiple choice tests may be used together, individually, or in combination with other subject Assessments.

---

*Some of the candidate constructed response modules in these tests were developed jointly by Educational Testing Service and the California Commission on Teacher Credentialing (CTC) in the Content Area Performance Assessment (CAPA) project.

ETS Field Marketing Representatives will work with state licensing boards to create a system of tests suite to state licensing requirements.

Teaching for student learning . . .
Praxis III: Classroom Performance Assessment

ETS has responded to increasing state emphasis on teachers' performance in the classroom and one criterion for licensing.

The development of the performance assessment has been guided by a conception of teaching that reflects the complexity of the classroom environment, sensitivity to individual student needs, awareness of multicultural issues, differing requirements for different subjects, and an understanding of teaching. The assessment recognizes the need for teachers to be judged on their ability to make thoughtful decisions, then put them into action.

Through job analysis, research reviews, and extensive discussions with educators drawn from the entire educational spectrum, the ETS development team and a group of practicing educators created a comprehensive performance assessment.

- Provides training for local assessors

- Uses a framework of criteria and assessment strategies to judge beginning teachers in and in-school setting.

- Combines in-class assessment with documentation and pre-and post- observation interviews.

Training Local Assessors

The foundation of the performance assessment is the training program.

ETS training program introduces local assessors to state-accepted criteria, assessment methods, and documentation techniques.

Use of up-to-date materials and techniques, including video-tapes, allow trainees to make judgments about observed behaviors and to conform their judgments against expert critiques.

Beginning teachers benefit from the use of consistent framework, orientation to the criteria, and state-determined feedback.

National Scope . . . Adapted for Individual States

ETS has spent more than five years developing this comprehensive system for the testing and licensing of beginning teachers. Advisory committees of teachers, teacher educators, administrators, professional organizations, and many other constituencies offered their candid evaluations of current testing programs and their ideas about teacher licensing assessments.

The methodologically advanced test formulas are based on the latest research. The participation of thousands of teaching professionals in extensive job analysis has ensured assessments that accurately reflect the skills required of beginning teachers.

What this means for the states . . .

- Assessments based on job-relevant knowledge and skills
- Test-development expertise of seasoned teachers and key educators
- Flexibility, with options designed to fit the licensing needs of states concerned with the competence of entry-level teachers
- Commitment to minority representation at every stage of development and validation
- Ongoing review by external committees
- A new academic skills instructional package that opens doors to those who may need additional preparation
- Cost savings through ETS-conducted multistate validity studies.

The Praxis Series Users Chart (as of April 30, 1993)

The Praxis Series is responsible for the development, administration, scoring, and reporting of tests. Policies regarding their use or the setting of qualifying scores are established by the score users or score recipients. Questions about the development and administration of the Praxis Series tests should be addressed to The Praxis Series office.

Questions regarding admission, certification, or other requirements should be addressed to the appropriate state agency, association, or organization office. Please note that the requirements are periodically revised. The requirements of individual colleges and school districts may differ from state requirements.

	AR	CA	CT	DE	DC	HI	ID	IN	KS	KY	LA	ME	MD	MN
NTE CORE BATTERY TESTS														
General Knowledge (10510)						•	•	•		•	•	•	•	
Communication Skills (20500)						•	•	•		•	•	•	•	
Professional Knowledge (30520)	•					•	•	•	•	•	•	•	•	
MULTIPLE SUBJECTS ASSESSMENT FOR TEACHERS														
Content Knowledge (10140)		•												
Content Area Exercises 1 (20150)		•												
Content Area Exercises 2 (30160)		•												
PRAXIS I: ACADEMIC SKILLS ASSESSMENTS														
Pre-Professional Skills Tests: Mathematics (10730)	•			•	•					•		•		•
Pre-Professional Skills Tests: Reading (10710)	•			•	•					•		•		•
Pre-Professional Skills Tests: Writing (20720)	•			•	•					•		•		•
Computer-based Test: Mathematics	*			*	X					*				X
Computer-based Test: Reading	*			*	X					*				X
Computer-based Test: Writing	*			*	X					*				X
PRAXIS II: SUBJECT ASSESSMENTS & NTE SPECIALTY AREA TESTS														
Accounting (10960)														
Accounting (PA) (10791)														
Agriculture (10700)										○				
Agriculture (CA) (10900)		•												
Agriculture (PA) (10800)				•										
Art Education (10130)	•	•	•			•		•		•			•	
Art Making (20131)		•												
Audiology (10340)														
Biology (10230)			•			•		•					○	
Biology: Content Essays (20233)		•												
Biology: Content Knowledge, Part 1 (10231)					•									
Biology: Content Knowledge, Part 2 (10232)					•									
Biology: Pedagogy (20234)					•									
Biology & General Science (10030)	•	•				•		•		•	•		•	
Business Education (10100)	•	•	•			•		•		•	•		•	
Chemistry (10240)			•			•		•					○	
Chemistry: Content Essays (30242)			*											
Chemistry: Content Knowledge (20241)					•									
Chemistry, Physics, & General Science (10070)	•	•				•				•	•		•	
Communication (10800)														
Composition, Literature, & English Language (PA) (10820)			*											
Computer Literacy/Data Processing														
Content, Traditions, Aesthetics, & Criticism of Art (20132)		•												
Cooperative Education (10810)														
Data Processing (PA) (10792)														

MS	MO	MT	NE	NV	NJ	NM	NY	NC	OH	OK	OR	PA	RI	SC	TN	VA	WV	WI	ASHA	CAE	DODDS	NASP	NASW
●		●			●	●	●	●	●		●	●	●		●	●				●			
●		●				●	●	●			●	●	●		●	●				●	●		
●	●	●		●		●	●	●	●		●	●	●	●	●	●					●		

MS	MO	MT	NE	NV	NJ	NM	NY	NC	OH	OK	OR	PA	RI	SC	TN	VA	WV	WI	ASHA	CAE	DODDS	NASP	NASW

MS	MO	MT	NE	NV	NJ	NM	NY	NC	OH	OK	OR	PA	RI	SC	TN	VA	WV	WI	ASHA	CAE	DODDS	NASP	NASW
			●	●						●					●		●	●		●	●		
			●	●						●					●		●	●		●	●		
			●	●						●					●		●	●		●	●		
			x	*						*					*		x	x					
			x	*						*					*		x	x					
			x	*						*					*		x	x					

MS	MO	MT	NE	NV	NJ	NM	NY	NC	OH	OK	OR	PA	RI	SC	TN	VA	WV	WI	ASHA	CAE	DODDS	NASP	NASW
															○								
												○											
	○														○	○							
											●												
												○											
●	●				●			●	●		●	○	●	●	●	●							
●								●	●									●					
●	●							●	●						●	○							
											*												
											*												
											*												
			●		●			●	●		●	○	●			●							
●	●				●			●	●		●		●	●		●							
●	●							●	●		●	○		●		○							
											*												
											*												
●					●			●	●		●	○		●		●							
												○											
												●											
○																							
												○											
												○											

PRAXIS II: SUBJECT ASSESSMENTS & NTE PROGRAMS SPECIALTY AREA TESTS	AR	CA	CT	DE	DC	HI	ID	IN	KS	KY	LA	ME	MD	MN
Early Childhood Education (10020)	●				●			●		●	●		●	
Earth/Space Science (10570)			●					●						
Economics (10910)								●						
Education in the Elementary School (10010)	●					●		●		●	●		●	
Education of Students with Mental Retardation (10320)								●			●			
Educational Leadership: Administration & Supervision (10410)	●									●	●			
Elementary Educ: Content Area Exercises (10011)					●	*								
Elementary Educ: Curriculum, Instruction, & Assessment (10011)					●	*								
English Language & Literature (10040)	●	●				●		●		●	●		●	
English Language, Lit., & Composition: Content Knowledge (10041)			*		●	*								
English Language, Lit., & Composition: Essays (20042)		●	●			*								
English Language, Lit., & Composition: Pedagogy (30043)					●									
Environmental Education (10830)														
Foreign Language Pedagogy (10840)														
French (10170)	●	●	●		●	●		●		●	●		●	
French: Linguistic, Literary, & Cultural Analysis (30172)		●												
French: Productive Language Skills (20171)		●	*		●									
General Science (10430)			●					●						
General Science: Content Essays (20433)		●												
General Science Content Knowledge, Part 1 (10431)					●									
General Science Content Knowledge, Part 2 (10432)					●									
Geography (10920)								●						
German (20180)		●	●			●		●		●	●		●	
Government/Political Science (10930)								●						
Health & Physical Education (10120)														
Health Education (10550)	●		●					●						
Home Economics Education (10120)	●	●	●			●		●		●	●		●	
Introduction to the Teaching of Reading (10200)	●	●						●						
Italian (10620)			●											
Japanese (10660)														
Latin (10600)			●											
Library Media Specialist (10310)	●					●		●		●	●		●	
Marketing Education (10560)	●													
Marketing (PA) (10793)														
Mathematics (10060)	●	●	●			●		●		●	●		●	
Mathematics: Content Knowledge (10061)					●	*								
Mathematics: Pedagogy (20065)					●									
Mathematics: Proofs, Models, and Problems, Part 1 (20063)		●			●	*								
Mathematics: Proofs, Models, and Problems, Part 2 (30064)		●				*								
Music Education (10110)	●	●	●			●		●		●	●		●	
Music: Analysis (20112)		●												
Music: Concepts & Processes (30111)		●												
Office Technology (10980)														
Office Technology (PA) (10794)														
Physical Education (10090)	●	●	●			●		●		●	●		●	
Physical Education: Content Knowledge (10091)						*								
Physical Education: Movement Forms— Analysis & Design (30092)		●				*								

MS	MO	MT	NE	NV	NJ	NM	NY	NC	OH	OK	OR	PA	RI	SC	TN	VA	WV	WI	ASHA	CAE	DODDS	NASP	NASW
●								●	●		●	●		●	●								
	●							●				○			●	○							
															○								
●	●			●				●	●			●		●	●	●							
●								●	●		●			●		●							
●				●	●			●	●		●			●									
●	●			●	●			●			●			●	●	●							
											✳												
											✳												
												○											
												○											
●	●			●	●			●	●		●	✳		●	●	●							
				●					●		●				●								
											✳												
											✳												
											✳												
															○								
●	●				●			●			●	✳				●							
															○								
												●											
	●			●				●	●		●	○		●	●	○							
●	●			●	●			●	●		●	○		●	●	●							
				●	●			●	●					●									
												✳				○							
											●												
											✳	✳			○								
●								●	●		●	○		●	●								
●	●							●	●		●			●	●	●							
												○											
●	●			●	●			●	●		●	●		●	●	●							
											✳												
											✳												
											✳												
●	●				●			●			●	●		●	●	●							
															○								
												○											
●	●				●			●	●		●			●	●	●							
											✳												
											✳												

PRAXIS II: SUBJECT ASSESSMENTS & NTE PROGRAMS SPECIALTY AREA TESTS	AR	CA	CT	DE	DC	HI	ID	IN	KS	KY	LA	ME	MD	MN
Physical Education: Movement Forms—Video Evaluation (20093)		●				*								
Physical Education: Pedagogy (30094)														
Physical Science: Content Essays (20482)		●												
Physical Science: Content Knowledge (10481)					●									
Physical Science: Pedagogy (20483)					●									
Physics (10260)			●			●		●					○	
Physics: Content Essays (30262)														
Physics: Content Knowledge (20261)														
Pre-Kindergarten Education (10530)								●						
Psychology (10390)								●						
Reading Specialist (10300)	●													
Russian (20670)														
Safety/Driver Education (10860)														
School Food Service Supervisor (10970)														
School Guidance & Counseling	●					●								
School Psychologist (10400)	○									●				
School Social Worker (10210)														
Secretarial (PA) (10795)														
Social Studies (10080)	●	●	*			●		●		●	●		●	
Social Studies: Analytical Essays (20082)		●				*								
Social Studies: Content Knowledge (10081)			*		●	*								
Social Studies: Interpretation of Materials (20083)		●				*								
Social Studies: Pedagogy (30084)					●									
Sociology (10950)								●						
Spanish (10190)	●	●	●			●		●		●	●		●	
Spanish: Content Knowledge (10191)					●	*								
Spanish: Linguistic, Literary, & Cultural Analysis (30193)		●				*								
Spanish: Pedagogy (30194)					●									
Spanish: Productive Language Skills (20192)		●			●	*								
Special Education (10350)	●		●		●	●				●			●	
Special Education: Preschool/Early Childhood (10690)														
Speech Communication (10220)	●							●		●			●	
Speech-Language Pathology (10330)	●													
Teaching Emotionally Disturbed Students (10370)								●						
Teaching English as a Second Language (20360)					●	●								
Teaching Hearing Impaired Students (10270)	●							●						
Teaching Learning Disabled Students (10380)								●						
Teaching Minimally Mentally Handicapped Students (10540)								●						
Teaching Orthopedically Impaired Students (10290)														
Teaching Speech to the Language Impaired (10880)														
Teaching the Physically & Mentally Handicapped (10870)														
Teaching Visually Handicapped Students (10280)	●													
Technology Education (10050)	●	●	●			●		●		●			●	
Theatre (10640)														
U.S. History (10580)								●						
Vocational General Knowledge (10890)														
World & U.S. History (10940)														
World Civilization (10590)								●						

MS	MO	MT	NE	NV	NJ	NM	NY	NC	OH	OK	OR	PA	RI	SC	TN	VA	WV	WI	ASHA	CAE	DODDS	NASP	NASW
											*												
●	●							●			●	○			●	○							
											*												
											*												
				●										●	●								
								●			●	○											
											●												
												○											
															○								
●				●				●	●		●			●	●								
●								●	●		●			●	●							●	
															○								●
●	●			●	●			●	●		●	●		●	●	●							
											*												
											*												
											*												
															○								
●	●			●	●			●	●		●	*		●	●	●							
●	●			●				●			●			●	●								
															○								
●	●			●	●			●			●				●	●							
●	●			●	●			●	●		●			●				●					
●								●	●					●		○							
								●	●														
●								●			●	○		●	●								
								●	●					●		○							
														●									
												○											
												●											
								●	●		●	○		●	○								
●	●				●			●			●	○		●	●	●							
															○								
												○											
				○											●								

APPENDIX D

Signs of Physical Abuse

Consider the possibility of physical abuse when the child:

- has unexplainable burns, bites, bruises, broken bones, or black eyes;
- has fading bruises or other marks noticeable after an absence from school;
- seems frightened of the parents and protests or cries when it is time to go home from school;
- shrinks at the approaches of adults; or
- reports injury by a parent or another adult caregiver.

Consider the possibility of physical abuse when the parent or other adult caregiver:

- offers conflicting, unconvincing, or no explanation for the child's injury;
- uses harsh physical discipline with the child; or
- has a history of abuse as a child.

Signs of Neglect

Consider the possibility of neglect when the child:

- is frequently absent from school;
- begs or steals food or money from classmates;
- lacks needed medical or dental care, immunizations, or glasses;
- is consistently dirty and has severe body odor;
- lacks sufficient clothing for the weather;
- abuses alcohol or other drugs; or
- states that there is no one at home to provide care.

Consider the possibility of neglect when the parent or other adult caregiver:

- appears to be indifferent to the child;
- seems apathetic or depressed;
- behaves irrationally or in a bizarre manner; or
- abuses alcohol or other drugs.

Signs of Sexual Abuse

Consider the possibility of sexual abuse when the child:

- has difficulty walking or sitting;
- suddenly refuses to change for gym or to participate in physical activities;
- demonstrates bizarre, sophisticated, or unusual sexual knowledge or behavior;
- becomes pregnant or contracts a venereal disease, particularly if under age 14;
- runs away; or
- reports sexual abuse by a parent or another adult caregiver.

Consider the possibility of sexual abuse when the parent or other adult caregiver:

- is unduly protective of the child, severely limits the child's contact with other children especially the opposite sex;
- is secretive and isolated; or
- describes marital difficulties involving family power struggles or sexual relations.

Signs of Emotional Maltreatment

Consider the possibility of emotional maltreatment when the child:

- shows extremes in behavior, such as overly compliant or demanding behavior, extreme passivity or aggression;
- is either inappropriately adult (parenting other children, for example) or inappropriately infantile (frequently rocking or head-banging, for example);
- is delayed in physical or emotional development;
- has attempted suicide; or
- reports a lack of attachment to a parent.

Consider the possibility of emotional maltreatment when the parent or other adult caregiver:

- constantly blames, belittles, or berates the child;
- is unconcerned about the child and refuses to consider offers of help for the child's school problems; or
- overtly rejects the child.

Note: From *Educators, Schools, and Child Abuse* (pp. 6–7) by D.D. Broadhurst, 1991, National Committee for Prevention of Child Abuse, Chicago, Illinois. Copyright 1986. Reprinted by permission.

APPENDIX E

Summary of Fair Use Guidelines[1]

Print and Audio Recordings

A teacher may make singly copies of the following to use for research or preparation for class:

- a book chapter
- an article from a newspaper or periodical
- a short story, essay, or poem
- a chart or figure from a published book
- sound recordings of copyrighted music owned by the teacher or school (unless prohibited by other copyrights on the recording itself) to be retained for aural exercises or explanations.
- recordings of students' performances made and retained for purposes of evaluation or instruction.

When producing multiple copies of materials (not to exceed one copy per student) for instructional purposes, teachers may not copy the same item term to term or charge students any more than the cost of reproduction. Each copy must include a *notice of copyright*. Copies must also meet the test of **brevity**, **spontaneity**, and **cumulative effect**. The chart on page 574 summarizes the criteria of the test of **brevity**—in other words, the length or proportion of material that can be copied without violating the test of brevity.

To meet the test for **spontaneity**, copying should be initiated by the teacher rather than a supervisor and should occur in situations where there is insufficient time between the decision to use the material and the moment of use to obtain permission. Definitional criteria for **cumulative effect** put specific limitations on uses of photocopied materials. Except for newspaper articles or current news periodicals, copies of books and periodicals are restricted to use in one class per term and may not include more than one complete work (or two excerpts) from the same author

or more than three pieces from a collective work or periodical volume. During the class term, multiple copies may not be used on more than nine occasions. Neither is it permissible to use copies as substitutes for anthologies or collective works or as replacements for consumable materials such as workbooks and test booklets.

Software

The guidelines for copying software suggest the following:

- Create back-up copies of software for use only when original disks are dysfunctional.
- Do not load a single disk into multiple computers at one time (unless the school has a license to do so).
- Unless you have written license agreement from the copyright holder, do not load a software program onto a local area network.

Off-The-Air Videotaping

The guidelines for copying television programs suggest:

- Programs are to be videotaped at the teacher's request, not in anticipation of request.
- No program, no matter how often broadcast, is to be recorded more than once for an individual teacher.
- Videotapes may be shown to students twice within the first ten days following recording, with the second showing being for reinforcement purposes only. If off-the-air recordings are shown during the 10-day period, they may be retained for additional 35 school days and used only for making evaluative decisions about the place of the videotape in the curriculum.

[1] These guidelines, which suggest minimum standards for fair- use, are subject to change. They are based on *The Official Fair-use Guidelines*, 4th Ed. (1989). If the school library does not contain a current version of fair-use guidelines, one can be purchased from Copyright Information Services, AECT Publication Sales, 1025 Vermont Avenue, NW, Suite 820, Washington, DC 20005.

SATISFYING THE TEST OF BREVITY

Poetry	Prose	Illustration (chart, graph, diagram, drawing, cartoon, or picture)	Special Works (combination of illustrations with text)	Music
entire poem (if fewer than 250 words printed on not more than 2 pages)	complete article, story, or essay if fewer than 2,500 words	one per book or periodical		excerpt of less than 10%, not constituting a performable unit
excerpt from longer poem, not to exceed 250 words	excerpt, if at least 500 words long and no more than 1,000 words, or 10% (whichever is less)		excerpt of not more than 2 pages containing not more than 10% of prose	entire performance unit, only in an emergency situation (e.g., copies of purchased works needed for an imminent performance are missing), with the understanding that replacement copies will be purchased in a timely manner[2]

[2]It should be noted that editing or simplifying printed copies of music which has been purchased is permissible if the fundamental character of the work is not destroyed or lyrics changed or added.

GLOSSARY

A

Accelerated schools movement: a national movement for speeding up the learning of economically disadvantaged students based on the work of Henry Levin.

Accreditation: the review and approval of education programs by outside experts.

Aesthetics: the branch of philosophy concerned with beauty.

Afrocentric curriculum: educational program that places African culture and history at the center of what students are expected to learn, illustrating the important role that Africa has played in the development of Western civilization.

Alternative certification: approval to teach without having participated in a traditional, state-approved teacher education program.

Alternative school: any school operating within the public school system that has programs addressing the specific needs or interests of targeted student groups.

America 2000 schools: experimental schools designed to achieve the National Goals of Education.

American Federation of Teachers (AFT): political organization of 800,000 members devoted to the advancement of educational issues and affiliated with the American Federation of Labor/Congress of Industrial Organizations (AFL/CIO). The organization has sponsored such projects as Dial-A-Teacher and Learning Line. It has also supported teacher internship programs, adopt-a-school programs, and national conferences for paraprofessionals and other school personnel.

Apprenticeships: practical work experiences under the supervision of skilled workers in the trades and the arts.

Assimilation: the process of educating and socializing a population or group to make it similar to the dominant culture.

Assumption of risk: people who are aware of possible risks involved in an activity voluntarily participate, thus agreeing to take their chances.

At-risk students: children who are unlikely to complete high school; have failed one or more grades; are enrolled in special education classes; speak a language other than English; and/or are affected adversely by life- and health-threatening factors such as poverty, disease, abuse and neglect, substance abuse, teenage pregnancy, and physical violence.

Authentic assessment: assessment concerned less with students' recognition and recall of facts and more with students' abilities to analyze, apply, evaluate, and synthesize what they know in ways that address real-world concerns.

Axiology: a branch of philosophy that seeks to ascertain what is of value.

B

Behavioral objectives: objectives that describe conditions for teaching and learning, what is to be learned, and criteria for success.

Behaviorism: a philosophical orientation based on the belief that human behavior is determined by forces in the environment that are beyond human control rather than by the exercise of free will.

Bilingual Act of 1974: a law requiring parental involvement in the planning of appropriate educational programs for children with limited English-speaking ability.

Bilingual education: instruction in both English and a student's native language.

Black codes: conduct codes established by southerners that allowed African Americans to hold property, to sue and be sued, and to marry, but forbade them to carry firearms, to

testify in court in cases involving European Americans, or to leave their jobs.

Block grant: money provided in a lump sum for several education programs in a locality.

Blue-Backed Speller: Webster's *American Spelling Book*, first published in 1783.

Brown v. Board of Education: the Supreme Court case that determined that segregation of students by race is unconstitutional and that education is a right that must be available to all Americans on equal terms.

Buckley Amendment: part of the Family Educational Rights and Privacy Act that prohibits schools from releasing information about a student to third parties without parental or student permission.

Bureau of Indian Affairs (BIA): a governmental agency established to, among other activities, oversee education programs for Native Americans.

Business-school partnerships: partnerships in which businesses and institutions set up and run public schools to try to meet the needs of students who are struggling in traditional schools or who have already dropped out.

C

Career Academies: schools for troubled students that combine the disciplined environment of the military with academic and vocational requirements of schools.

Career ladder: incentive program designed to acknowledge differences in the skills of teachers.

Categorical grant: funding for an education program designed for a particular group and a specific purpose (e.g., bilingual education).

Central office staff: superintendents and their associates and assistants.

Certification: recognition by the state that a teacher has met minimum standards for competent practice.

Chapter 1: one of the largest federally funded education programs for at-risk elementary and secondary students; begun in 1965 as the first bill of President Johnson's War on Poverty.

Character education: a curricular approach driven by personal relevance that focuses on clarifying or teaching values.

Charter schools: independent public schools supported by state funds but freed from many regulations and run by individuals who generally have the power to hire and to fire colleagues and to budget money as they see fit.

Chautauqua movement: an adult education movement that began in the late 1800s and led to the establishment of civic music associations, correspondence courses, lecture-study groups, youth groups, and reading circles.

Chief state school officer: the chief administrator of the state department of education and the head of the state board of education, sometimes referred to as the state superintendent or the commissioner of education.

Child Abuse Prevention and Treatment Act: passed by Congress in 1974 to provide financial support to states that implemented programs for identification, prevention, and treatment of instances of child abuse or neglect.

Civil Rights Act of 1964 (Title VI): a law which specifies that no one, regardless of race, color, or origin, can be discriminated against or denied participation in programs receiving federal assistance.

Classroom management: methods of gaining and maintaining students' cooperation and involvement in educational activities.

Coalition for Essential Schools: alternative high schools serving targeted students through school-based educational reform initiatives; based on Theodore Sizer's work.

Cognitive behavior monitoring: the use of self-assessment strategies to monitor and to improve one's own attending behaviors.

Cognitive development: changes in children's mental functioning over time.

Cognitivism: a philosophical orientation based on the belief that people actively construct their knowledge of the world through experience and interaction rather than through behavioral conditioning.

Collaborative networks: groups of people who have come together voluntarily to help each other explore and advance particular educational issues.

Collective bargaining: the negotiation of the professional rights and responsibilities of workers (e.g., teachers) as a group.

Collegiality: relationships based on a sharing of power.

Committee of Fifteen: a committee that addressed the curriculum of elementary schools in 1895. Its curriculum focused on "the five windows of the soul"—grammar, literature and art, mathematics, geography, and history. It believed the role of school to be an efficient transmitter of cultural heritage through a curriculum that was graded, structured, and cumulative.

Committee of Ten on Secondary School Studies: a committee established by the NEA in 1892 to standardize high school curricula.

Common schools: tax-supported schools established in colonial times to allow all boys and girls to have 3 free years of education focused on reading, writing, arithmetic, and history—predecessors of public schools.

Compensatory education program: a program that provides children from low-income families with additional education opportunities beyond those offered in a school's standard program to compensate for factors (e.g., teachers, curricula, time, and materials) missing in young people's lives.

Conflict resolution/mediation: teachers provide opportunities for students to practice skills in negotiating and mediating differences among themselves. Students learn to state what they want; state how they feel; state the reasons for their wants and feelings; summarize their understanding of the other person's wants, feelings, and reasons; invent three optional plans to resolve the conflict; and choose one plan and shake hands.

Constructivist orientation: a view of knowledge as constructed or built up by individuals acting within a social context that molds knowledge but does not determine absolutely what constitutes knowledge.

Contributory negligence: failure of a person who is injured to exercise the required standard of care for his or her own safety.

Comparative negligence: situations in which teacher and student are both held liable for an injury.

Cooperative learning: a teaching model that encourages heterogeneous groups of students to work together to achieve such goals as mastery of subject matter and understanding and acceptance of one another.

Core curriculum: courses of study based on the idea that all students should be exposed to the same selective knowledge.

Council of Chief State School Officers: a non-policy-making organization composed of leaders of state departments of elementary and secondary education in the 50 states, the District of Columbia, the Department of Defense Dependents Schools, and 5 U.S. extra-state jurisdictions—Virgin Islands, Puerto Rico, Northern Mariana Islands, Guam, and American Samoa.

Criterion-referenced test: a test by which a student's performance is judged by comparing it to some clearly defined criterion for mastering a learning task or skill. The quality of a student's performance is measured against an absolute standard.

Cross-age tutoring: the practice of older students assisting younger students with academic tasks.

Cultural literacy: shared information or common knowledge of a culture supposedly needed to function fully in that culture.

Cultural pluralism: a state in which people of diverse ethnic, racial, religious, and social groups maintain autonomous participation within a common civilization.

Culture: the sum of the learned characteristics of a people (e.g., language, religion, social mores, artistic expression, sexual behavior), which may be tied to geographical region. Culture can also be used in a "micro" sense to describe more conceptually discrete groups of people—cultures within cultures, subcultures, or microcultures.

Curricular standards: benchmarks against which student performance in a variety of disciplines can be measured.

Curriculum: what is taught inside and sometimes outside school.

D

Dame schools: educational programs for boys and girls run by local women in a colonial community that typically focused on rudimentary reading skills.

Department of Defense Dependent Schools (DoDDS): schools operated by the U.S. federal government primarily for dependents of Americans working or serving abroad.

Developmentally appropriate instruction: instruction geared to the needs and abilities of students.

Direct instruction: highly structured, teacher-centered strategy which capitalizes on such behavioral techniques as modeling, feedback, and reinforcement to promote basic skill acquisition, primarily in reading and mathematics.

Discovery or inquiry learning: learning that occurs from students' efforts to seek to discover knowledge for themselves rather than from being taught more directly by a teacher.

Discrimination: differential treatment associated with labels.

Dismissal: removing a probationary or tenured teacher before the completion of her or his contract.

Distance learning: the capacity for teachers and students and teachers and teachers to communicate interactively with one another over long distances.

District power equalization: localities establish the tax rate for educational spending and the state guarantees a set amount of money proportional to local revenue.

Due process of law: mandated legal procedures designed to protect the rights of individuals.

E

Early intervention: providing care and support form the prenatal period through the first years of life to enable children to enter school ready to learn.

Education Consolidation and Improvement Act (ECIA): the 1981 act of Congress that consolidated many education programs into two major programs (Chapter One and Chapter Two).

Education for All Handicapped Children Act (Public Law 94-142): Federal law that requires all states to provide a free and appropriate public education to children with disabilities between the ages of 5 and 18. Education is to be planned through an individualized education program (IEP) and carried out in the least restrictive environment.

Elementary and Secondary Education Act (ESEA) of 1965: the single most comprehensive extension of federal involvement in education, which resulted in policy-making power shifting to the federal level. The Act provided funds to alleviate the effects of poverty through a variety of programs. It supported school libraries, the purchase of textbooks and other instructional materials, guidance, counseling, and health services, and remedial instruction. It also established research centers and laboratories to advance educational practice.

E-mail: messages sent and received via computers.

English Academy: a school established in Philadelphia in 1749 by Benjamin Franklin that emphasized the acquisition and application of knowledge thought to be most useful to the modern man.

English as a Second Language (ESL): an instructional program designed to teach English to speakers of other languages.

Epistemology: a branch of philosophy concerned with the nature of knowledge or how we come to know things.

Equal Access Act: a 1984 law passed by congress that recognizes that secondary-school students are mature enough to understand that a school does not condone religion by merely allowing prayer clubs on public property.

Equal educational opportunity: access to the resources, choices, and encouragement each student needs to achieve his or her fullest potential through education, regardless of race, color, national origin, gender, disability, or socioeconomic status.

Equal protection clause: Section 1 of the Fourteenth Amendment, which prevents states from making or enforcing laws which abridge the privileges or immunities of citizens of the United States; deprive people of life, liberty, or property without due process of law; or deny equal protection of the laws.

Essentialism: a philosophical orientation that acknowledges the existence of a body of knowledge that all people must learn if they are to function effectively in society.

Establishment clause: the clause in the First Amendment prohibiting Congress from making laws respecting the establishment of religion or prohibiting the free exercise of religion.

Ethics: a branch of philosophy concerned with issues of morality and conduct.

Ethnicity: a term for describing a group of people with a common tradition and a sense of identity that functions as a subgroup within the larger society; membership is largely a matter of self-identification.

Ethnocentrism: the inability to see and understand society from points of view different from one's own.

Eurocentric: curriculum and/or teaching that depict Europe as the cradle of western culture.

Evaluation standards: yardsticks against which student performance and curricular programs can be measured.

Exceptional learners: children who have special abilities or disabilities that set them apart from other children.

Exclusion acts: acts based on race passed by Congress to stop unwanted immigration.

Existentialism: a philosophy that emphasizes the subjectivity of human experience and the importance of individual creativity and choice in a nonrational world.

Explicit curriculum: curriculum contained in policy statements, manuals of procedure, instructional materials, books, and other printed matter that explicate what and how students are to learn.

Extracurriculum: non-credit-bearing activities, such as debate club and cheerleading, that are over and above the required curriculum.

F

Fiscal year: a 12-month-period covered by the annual budget.

Flat grant: a uniform or variable grant provided by the state to the school districts.

Formative assessment: evaluation conducted for the purpose of shaping, forming, and improving knowledge and performance.

Formal knowledge base: theory-driven conceptions of effective teaching and actual results from empirical research in classrooms.

Foundation program: a program by which the state guarantees school districts a certain amount of money for educational expenditures and determines what proportion of that cost should be shouldered by localities.

Free exercise clause: a clause in the First Amendment prohibiting Congress from making laws abridging the freedom of speech or of press or the right to peaceably assemble or to petition the government for a redress of grievances.

Freedman's Bureau: a government-sponsored organization established 1 month before the end of the Civil War to provide food, medicine, and seed to destitute southerners.

Full inclusion: teaching students with disabilities in regular classrooms throughout the day in their neighborhood schools.

Full-service school: a school that attempts to meet basic needs of students by providing such things as food, clothing, showers, medical care, and family counseling.

Full state funding: the state pays all educational expenses of school districts through a statewide tax.

Funding equity: equal amounts of financial support for students regardless of where they live.

G

Gender bias: discriminatory treatment, often subtle or unconscious, that unfairly favors or disfavors individual because they are females or because they are males.

Gender sensitivity training: use of curricula that avoid sex role stereotyping and the creation of educational opportunities for females to take advantage of all their possibilities for education.

Giftedness: the potential for high performance due to strengths in one or more of the following areas: general intellectual ability, specific academic aptitude, creative or productive thinking, leadership ability, ability in the visual or performing arts, and psychomotor ability.

Global awareness: the recognition of people's connections to other countries and peoples of the world

H

Habits of mind: the shared skills, attitudes, and values transmitted by custom or convention from one generation to the next.

Head Start: the first major early childhood program subsidized by the federal government, it provides comprehensive services to low-income 3- and 4-year-olds and their families.

Hearing impairment: degree of deafness; uncorrectable inability to hear well.

Hidden passage: educational activities that provided slaves with the intellectual power to escape bondage and to make lives for themselves after the Civil War.

Hispanic: having Spanish colonial origins or being Spanish-speaking.

Holding power: the ability to keep students in school until they receive a high school diploma or an equivalency certificate.

Humanism: a philosophy that, in terms of education, calls for respect and kindness toward students and developmentally appropriate instruction in liberal arts, social conduct, and moral principles.

I

Idealism: a philosophy that suggests that ultimate reality lies in consciousness or reason.

Implicit curriculum: the unvoiced and often unintended lessons influenced by teachers' value orientations.

Incentive programs: programs that offer outside incentives for good attendance and good grades.

Indian Self-Determination and Educational Assistance Act: the decision by Congress in 1975 to terminate federal reservations for Native Americans.

Individualized education program (IEP): a plan approved by parents or guardians that spells out what teachers will do to meet students' individual needs.

Individuals with Disabilities Education Act (IDEA): a 1990 Act of Congress that amended the Education for All Handicapped Children Act by changing the term *handicapped* to *with disabilities* and by extending a free and appropriate public education to every individual between 3 and 21 years of age, regardless of the nature or severity of his or her disability.

Information processing theory: theory about how people think (what kinds of strategies they use to approach tasks and the mental effort that goes into the tasks).

INGOs: international nongovernmental organizations that advance agenda focused on problems and issues of common interest, regardless of national borders.

In loco parentis: a term meaning "in place of the parent" that suggests that educators possess a portion of a parent's rights, duties, and responsibilities.

Institution: an established organization having an identifiable structure and a set of functions meant to preserve and extend social order.

Instructional models: deliberate, explicit, complete plans for teaching that can be fitted to students and objectives.

Instructional variables: concepts such as characteristics of teachers, instructional behaviors, student outcomes, and factors outside the classroom that affect teaching and learning.

Intelligence quotient (IQ): score calculated by dividing an individual's mental age by his or her chronological age and multiplying the result by 100.

Intermediate educational units (IEUs): collaborative organizations maintained by separate districts to provide educational services (e.g., joining together to construct and maintain a technical training center for students.)

International comparative education: the study of education in different societies to develop new insights into these societies and to derive innovative understanding of one's own society.

Internet: an electronic network having the capacity to span the globe.

Interpersonal power: the ability to influence others due to one's position in an organization or one's personal attributes (e.g., possession of special knowledge or skills).

L

Land-grant colleges: public colleges of agriculture and mechanical or industrial arts established by federal funds guaranteed through the Morrill Act of 1862.

Language disorders: receptive, expressive, or language processing problems; and/or difficulty with the meaning of words (semantics), the sequential organization of words according to their relationship to each other (syntax), and/or the purpose or uses for language.

Latchkey children: children who are without adult supervision for several hours each day.

Latin grammar school: first formal type of secondary school in the colonies, established in Boston in 1635 for boys from 9 to 10 years of age who could read and write English.

Learning disability: a disorder in one or more of the basic psychological processes involved in understanding or in using language, spoken or written, which may manifest itself in an imperfect ability to listen, think, speak, read, write, spell, or to do mathematical calculations.

Lemon test: a tripartite test used to decide whether particular practices or policies are an establishment of religion.

License: a certificate that indicates a teacher has demonstrated minimal teaching competence.

Limited English Proficient (LEP): a categorization of students who are qualified for instruction in English as a Second Language.

Literacy: one's ability to read and write.

Local property taxes: taxes on land and improvements firmly attached to the land (e.g., fences, barns) and on personal property such as automobiles.

Local school board: the primary policy-making body for public schools, composed of elected or appointed public servants.

Lyceums: out-of-school programs, such as reading circles and debating clubs, designed to improve the education of children and adults.

M

Magnet schools: alternative schools within a public school system that draw students from the whole district instead of drawing only from their own neighborhoods and that offer a curriculum based on a special theme or instructional method.

Marxism: a philosophy based on Karl Marx's belief that the human condition is determined by forces in history that prevent people from achieving economic freedom and social and political equality.

Mastery learning: one of several behavioral models that suggest that, given enough time, the inclination to learn, and instruction fitted to a student's needs, students are capable of mastering a range of subject matter.

McGuffey readers: books first produced in 1836 by William Holmes McGuffey to teach literacy skills and to advance the Protestant ethic through stories and essays.

Measurement and evaluation: the collection and interpretation of data about individual students from a variety of sources (e.g., tests and quizzes, interviews, questionnaires, observations of in-class behaviors).

Mental retardation: "significantly subaverage intellectual function [an IQ standard score of 70 to 75 or lower], existing concurrently with related limitations in two or more of the following applicable adaptive skills areas: communication, self-care, home living, social skills, community use, self-direction, health and safety, functional academics, leisure, and work."

Mentoring programs: support systems aimed at enhancing academic success and self-esteem of at-risk students; also programs to help new teachers.

Merit pay: an incentive program designed to encourage teachers to strive for outstanding performance by rewarding such practice.

Metacognitive skills: methods for monitoring and controlling one's own thinking; thinking about thinking.

Metaphysics: the branch of philosophy that focuses on the study of reality.

Minimum competency: a minimum level of learning expected from a learner.

Minority status: a term that carries both a quantitive meaning (e.g., groups or subgroups in society who are identifiably fewer in number than another group) and/or a political connotation (e.g., the relative political power or influence that perceptions of a group exerts in society).

Mission schools: schools established by priests to convert Native Americans to Catholicism.

Monitorial method: a method devised by Lancaster for teaching large groups of students by which a master teacher instructed monitors, and they, in turn, instructed younger children.

Moral development: changes relating to age and intelligence in the an individual makes reasoned judgments about right and wrong.

Multicultural education: "reform movement designed to bring about educational equity for all students, including those from different races, ethnic groups, social classes, exceptionality, and sexual orientations."

Multiple intelligences: a large number of cognitive abilities, each slightly different from the next, that constitute one's intellectual ability.

N

National Assessment of Educational Progress (NAEP): a congressionally mandated battery of achievement tests operated by the Educational Testing Service to assess the effects of schooling.

National Association for the Advancement of Colored People: established in 1934, this was the first nationwide special interest group for African Americans.

National Association for the Education of Young Children (NAEYC): one of the largest professional associations for early childhood educators.

National Board for Professional Teaching Standards (NBPTS): a nonprofit organization charged with the task of creating a national system of certification to be used to designate truly outstanding teachers.

National Center for Education Statistics: an arm of the executive branch responsible for collecting and analyzing education statistics for the nation.

National Congress of Parents and Teachers (PTA): the largest volunteer education organization in the United States; it has long supported legislation at the state and national levels designed to benefit children.

National Defense Education Act (NDEA): a federal law passed in 1958 to provide funds for upgrading the teaching of mathematics, science, and foreign languages, and for establishing guidance services.

National Education Association (NEA): organization having 2 million members who are guided by the vision of enabling students to develop themselves as people, to practice human relations skills, to learn how to be economically productive citizens, and to be responsible for their community and nation. It was instrumental in creating the National Council for Accreditation of Teacher Education (NCATE), a national organization that monitors the quality of collegiate teacher education programs.

National Education Goals: national goals established by President George Bush and the 50 governors in 1989 to insure readiness for school, high school completion, student achievement and citizenship, excellence in science and mathematics, adult literacy and lifelong learning, and safe, disciplined, and drug-free schools. Extended by President Clinton in 1994 to include teacher education and parental involvement.

National Governors' Association: a coalition of state chief executives.

National Teacher Examinations (NTE): Examination constructed and marketed by the Educational Testing Service; a test of teacher competency before the granting of initial certification.

Negligence: failure to exercise reasonable care to protect students from injury.

Nongraded classroom: a classroom in which children are grouped heterogeneously by ability, sometimes with students of various ages.

Normal schools: educational programs established in the 1800s dedicated solely to training teachers so that they could perform according to high standards, or "norms."

Norm-referenced tests: a test used to compare the quality of a student's performance to that of other students.

Null curriculum: the curriculum that is not taught in schools.

O

Outcome-based education: eduction that concentrates first on what it is that students are to acquire or to be able to do as a result of the activities in which they engage.

P

Parochial schools: schools established by various religious groups to inculcate their beliefs and ideas in children.

Pedagogical content knowledge: the particular teaching knowledge necessary to impart content knowledge.

Perennialism: a philosophy that exalts the great thoughts and accomplishments of the past for their own sake and for what they can offer to future generations.

Per-pupil expenditures: money allocated for educational services divided by the number of pupils to be served.

Philosophy: a set of ideas about the nature of reality and about the meaning of life.

Plessy v. Ferguson: the 1896 Supreme Court case that legalized separate but equal public facilities and served to legalize school segregation.

Portfolio: "a purposeful collection of student work that tells the story of the student's efforts, progress, or achievement in (a) given area(s)."

Practical knowledge: knowledge constructed through teachers' own experiences about what works with students in classrooms.

Pragmatism: a philosophical method that defined the truth and meaning of ideas according to their physical consequences and practical value.

Praxis: an examination battery that purports to assess skills and knowledge at each stage of a beginning teacher's career from entry into teacher education to actual classroom performance.

Primers: textbooks for children designed to impart rudimentary reading skills that also reflected the religious values of the colonies.

Principal: the person responsible for managing a school at the building level.

Private schools: nonprofit, tax-exempt institutions governed by boards of trustees and financed through private funds, such as tuitions, endowments, and grants; sometimes called for-profit schools.

Professional development school: a school where university and public school people work together to explore problems of teaching and learning.

Professional teachers: people who possess specialized knowledge about education.

Progressive taxation: taxes, such as income taxes, that require people to pay more as they earn more.

Progressivism: a movement aimed at using human and material resources to improve the American's quality of life as an individual; in schools this meant focusing on the needs and interests of students rather than on those of teachers. The movement was characterized by a willingness to experiment with methods of teaching and learning.

Psychometric perspective: the belief that intelligence can be measured with tests.

Psychosocial development: changes relating to age and intelligence in the way an individual's social and emotional needs are met through relationships with others.

Pull-out programs: programs in which individual students are removed from regular classes for a period of time each day for special instruction.

R

Race: a classification that is not typically chosen but instead assigned by others; defined most often by physical characteristics.

Realism: a philosophy that suggests that objects of sense or perception exist independently of the mind.

Reciprocity agreement: a pact by which professional licensure for educational practice in one state makes one eligible for licensure in another state.

Regressive taxation: methods of taxing citizens that require those with limited incomes to spend a greater percentage of their income on taxes than wealthy people spend.

Remediation: curriculum designed to correct students' weaknesses.

Retention: nonpromotion from one grade to the next at the expected time because of school failure.

S

Scaffolding: teacher provides assistance, guidance, and structure to enhance student learning and self-regulation.

School-based budgeting: allocating resources at the building level rather than at the level of central administration.

School-based health centers: clinics in schools that allow schools to coordinate health care with health curricula emphasizing preventive care.

School-based management: involving people at the school level directly in making decisions about teaching and learning, budgeting, and hiring personnel.

School choice: the idea that people should be free to choose schools for their children.

School district: a state-defined geographical area assigned responsibility for public instruction within its borders.

School governance: establishing and overseeing the structure and functions of public education.

School restructuring: efforts to encourage site-based management.

Self-esteem: the value or sense of worth an individual places on his or her own characteristics, abilities, and behaviors.

Seminaries: academies for girls that were the primary means for advancing the educational skills of future teachers.

Service learning: learning that results from volunteer work performed outside school hours.

Settlement houses: houses, the first of which was established in 1886 in New York, located in poor neighborhoods to offer educational services to new immigrants adjusting to life in a new country.

Social promotion: passing children to successive grades to keep them with others of their age regardless of their past performances or academic abilities.

Social reconstructionism: a philosophy based on the belief that people are responsible for social conditions and can improve the quality of human life by changing the social order.

Socioeconomic status: a combination of one's income, occupation, values, education, and lifestyle.

Socratic method: teaching through inquiry and dialogues in which students discover and clarify knowledge.

Special interest group: people who coalesce around particular interests and try to exert pressure for the advancement of their causes.

Speech impairments: fluency disorders (such as stuttering), articulation disorders (abnormality in the production of sounds), voice disorders (such as hoarseness or hypernasality—too many sounds produced through the nose), and/or delayed speech.

Standardized tests: assessment through tests, often multiple-choice, paper-and-pencil tests, administered and scored under conditions uniform to all students.

State boards of education: regulatory agencies that control standards for educational practice in most states and advise governors and legislators about the conduct of educational business.

State education department (SED): a bureaucracy that acts as an advisor to the executive and legislative branches of a state government. An SED is organized to carry out a state's education business, including regulating or overseeing elementary and secondary schools and colleges' and universities' conduct of teacher and administrator preparation.

State standards boards: commissions established to regulate profession practice in education that either have final authority or serve only in advisory capacity to policymakers.

Strike: a walkout from school, designed to halt operations.

Summative assessment: assessment designed to inform a summary decision. For example, an assessment of a teacher's strengths and weaknesses to be used to make decisions about such matters as tenure and termination of contract.

Superintendent of Schools: executive officer of the local school board, appointed by the board.

T

Teacher planning: consideration of such things as curriculum, state and local goals and objectives for student learning, instructional strategies for meeting those goals, and methods for assessing students' understanding.

Teacher portfolio: a compilation of products displaying a teacher's knowledge and skills, such as teacher-created tests and videotapes of one's own teaching.

Teacher-proof curricula: curricula that minimize the role of those who transmit them to students.

Teacher union: a confederation of educators joined politically to advance their cause.

Tenure: a continuing contract that guarantees a teacher's employment unless it can be demonstrated that there is just cause for termination.

Thomism: a philosophy based on the writings of Saint Thomas Aquinas that suggests that reality is an ordered world created by God that humans can come to know. Life is temporary, and humans strive for eternity with God.

Tracking: a process of segregating students by ability.

Tuition tax credit: a provision that allows a taxpayer to subtract educational costs from taxes owed.

Tuition tax deduction: a provision that allows a taxpayer to subtract educational costs from taxable income before computing taxes.

U

Universal schooling: educating all citizens for the common good.

V

Visual impairment: degree of blindness; uncorrectable inability to see well.

Voucher: scrip used to purchase education for one's child.

W

Women's Educational Equity Act (WEEA): a 1974 law that expanded programs for females in mathematics, science, technology, and athletics; mandated nonsexist curriculum materials; implemented programs for increasing the number of female administrators in education and raising the career aspirations of female students; and extended educational and career opportunities to minority-group, disabled, and rural women.

Y

Year-round schools: educational programs that run through the summer months as well as during the academic year.

Z

Zero-based budgeting: a process of budgeting that requires all expenditures to be justified each fiscal year.

REFERENCES

Chapter I

A new voice for teachers. (1992, May/June). *Teacher Magazine*, p. 10.

American Association of Colleges for Teacher Education (AACTE). (1990a). *Teacher education pipeline II: Schools, colleges, and departments of education enrollments by race and ethnicity*. Washington, DC: Author.

American Association of Colleges for Teacher Education (AACTE). (1990b). *Teacher education policy in the states: A 50-state survey of legislative and administrative actions*. Washington, DC: Author.

American Association of Colleges for Teacher Education (AACTE). (1985). *A call for change in teacher education*. Washington, DC: Author.

American Federation of Teachers. (1993). *Survey and analysis of salary trends*. Washington, DC: Author.

Ashton, P.T., & Webb, R.B. (1986). *Making a difference: Teachers' sense of efficacy and student achievement*. NY: Longman.

Association of Teacher Educators (ATE). (1986). *Visions of reform: Implications for the education profession*. Reston, VA: Author.

Bacharach, S.B., Conley, S.C., & Shedd, J.B. (1990). Evaluating teachers for career awards and merit pay. In J. Millman & L. Darling-Hammond (Eds.), *The new handbook of teacher evaluation: Assessing elementary and secondary school teachers* (pp. 133–146). Newbury Park, CA: Sage Publications, Inc.

Barber, L.W. (1990). Self-assessment. In J.Millman & L. Darling-Hammond (Eds.), *The new handbook of teacher evaluation: Assessing elementary and secondary school teachers* (pp. 216–228). Newbury Park, CA: Sage Publications, Inc.

Brandt, R.M. (1990). *Incentive pay and career ladders for today's teachers: A study of current programs and practices*. Albany, NY: State University of New York Press.

Bureau of the Census. (1990). *Statistical abstract of the United States: 1990* (110th ed.). Washington, DC: U.S. Government Printing Office.

Carnegie Forum on Education and the Economy, Task Force on Teaching as a Profession. (1986). *A nation prepared: Teachers for the 21st century*. New York: Author.

Choy, S.P., Bobbitt, S.A., Henke, R.R., Medrich, E.A., Horn, L.J., & Lieberman, J. (1993). *America's teachers: Profile of a profession*. Washington, DC: U.S. Department of Education.

Clark, D.L., & McNergney, R.F. (1990). Governance of teacher education. In W.R. Houston, M. Haberman, & J. Sikula (Eds.), *Handbook of research on teacher education: A project of the Association of Teacher Educators* (pp. 101–118). NY: Macmillan.

Deck, S.L. (1991, November 14). A young teacher corps faces old battles. *The Declaration—A Weekly Newsmagazine*, pp. 6–7.

Dilworth, M.E. (1990). *Reading between the lines: Teachers and their racial/ethnic cultures*. Washington, DC: ERIC Clearinghouse on Teacher Education and American Association of Colleges for Teacher Education.

Dimensions: The teacher's work week. (1990, February 7). *Education Week*, p. 3

Ducharme, E.R. (1993). *The lives of teacher educators*. New York: Teachers College Press.

Duke, D.L., & Stiggins, R. J. (1990). Beyond minimum competence: Evaluation for professional development. In J. Millman & L. Darling-Hammond (Eds.), *The new handbook of teacher evaluation: Assessing elementary and secondary school teachers* (pp. 166–132). Newbury Park, CA: Sage Publications, Inc.

Feistritzer, C.E. (1990). *Profile of teachers in the U.S.* Washington, DC: National Center for Education Information.

Fenstermacher, G.D. (1990). Some moral considerations on teaching as a profession. In J.I. Goodlad, R. Soder, & K.A. Sirotnik (Eds.), *The moral dimensions of teaching* (pp. 130–151). San Francisco: Jossey-Bass.

Freudenberger, H.J. (1975). The staff burnout syndrome in alternative institutions. *Psychotherapy: Theory, Research, and Practice, 12,* 73–82.

Gerard, D.E., & Hussar, W.J. (1991). *Projections of education statistics to 2002*. Washington, DC: National Center for Education Statistics.

Gold, Y., & Roth, R.A. (1993). *Teachers managing stress and preventing burnout: The professional health solution*. London: The Falmer Press.

Gursky, D. (1992, April 1). Separating the 'stars' from the 'quitters,' professor predicts urban teachers' success. *Education Week*, pp. 6–7.

Herbert, J.M., & Keller, C.E. (1989, March). *A case study of an effective teacher in an inner-city mainstreamed classroom*. Paper presented at the annual meeting of the American Educational Research Association, San Francisco, CA.

Holmes Group. (1986). *Tomorrow's teachers*. East Lansing, MI: Author.

Lach, M.C. (1992). Essay: An inner-city education. *Scientific American, 266* (1), 151.

Lawton, M. (1991, July 31). Teach for America: Salvation or 'disservice'? *Education Week*, pp. 26–27.

Lortie, D.C. (1975). *School teacher: A sociological study*. Chicago: The University of Chicago Press.

Louis Harris and Associates, Inc. (1991). *The Metropolitan Life Survey of the American teacher 1991. The first year: New teachers; expectations and ideals, a survey of new teachers who completed their first year of teaching in the public schools in 1991*. New York: Metropolitan Life Insurance Company.

Macrorie, K. (1984). *20 teachers*. New York: Oxford University Press.

McCarthy, M.M., & Cambron-McCabe, N.H. (1992). *Public school law: Teachers' and students' rights* (3rd ed.). Boston: Allyn and Bacon.

Meier, D. (1992). Reinventing teaching. *Teachers College Record, 93* (4), 594–609.

National Association of State Directors of Teacher Education and Certification (NASTEC) Joint Standards and Middle Level Committee. (1992). *Promoting systemic change in teacher education and certification: NASDTEC outcome-based standards and portfolio assessment*. Dubuque, IA: Kendall-Hunt.

National Council for Accreditation of Teacher Education. (1992). *NCATE standards, procedures, and policies for the accreditation of professional education units*. Washington, DC: Author.

National Education Association. (1991). *The organization of state government units responsible for teacher licensure: An NEA survey of state affiliates*. Washington, DC: Author.

National Education Association. (1992). *The status of the American public school teacher, 1990-91*. Washington, DC: Author.

National Governors' Association. (1986). *Time for results: The governors' 1991 report on education*. Washington, DC: Author.

Ogle, L.T., Alsalam, N., & Rogers, G.T. (1991). *The condition of education 1991: Volume 1, elementary and secondary education*. Washington, DC: U.S. Department of Education, National Center for Educational Statistics.

Porter, A. (1993). *Opportunity to learn* (Brief to policymakers No. 7). Madison: University of Wisconsin-Madison, School of Education, Wisconsin Center for Education Research.

Raquepaw, J., & de Haas, P.A. (1984, May). *Factors influencing teacher burnout*. Paper presented at the 56th annual meeting of the Midwestern Psychological Association, Chicago.

Romer, R. (1991). Foreward. In National Education Goals Panel, *Executive summary: The national education goals report* (p. 1). Washington, DC: National Education Goals Panel.

Roth, R., & Pipho, C. (1990). Teacher education standards. In W.R. Houston, M. Haberman, & J. Sikula (Eds.), *Handbook of research on teacher education* (pp. 119–135). New York: Macmillan.

Stinnett, T.M. (1969). Teacher education, certification, and accreditation. In E. Fuller & J.B. Pearson (Eds.), *Education in the states: Nationwide development since 1900* (pp. 381–438). Washington, DC: National Education Association of the United States.

Teachers of the world unite. (1993, March). *Teacher Magazine,* p. 10.

Terkel,S. (1974). *Working.* New York: Ballantine Books.

Tomlinson, T. M. (1988). *Class size and public policy: Politics and panaceas.* Washington, DC: OERI, U.S. Department of Education.

Tryneski, J. (1991). *Requirements for certification of teachers, counselors, librarians, administrators for elementary and secondary schools* (56th ed.). Chicago: The University of Chicago Press.

U.S. Department of Education. (1993). *Fifteenth annual report to Congress on the implementation of The Individuals with Disabilities Education Act.* Washington, DC: Author.

U.S. Senate-House Conference Report 103-446 Goals 2000 Educate America Act, March 21, 1994.

Warren, D. (Ed.). (1989). *American teachers: Histories of a profession at work.* New York: Macmillan.

Chapter 2

Barman, J., Hebert, Y., & McCaskill, D. (1986). *Indian education in Canada* (Vol. I). Vancouver: University of British Columbia.

Barnard, H. (1857, March). The public high school. *The American Journal of Education,* pp. 185–189.

Berlin, I. (1974). *Slaves without masters: The free negro in the antebellum south.* New York: Vintage Books.

Best, J.H. (Ed.). (1962). *Benjamin Franklin on education.* New York: Teachers College Press, Columbia University.

Blum, J.M., McFeely, W.S., Morgan, E.S., Schlesinger, A.M., Jr., Stampp, K.M., & Woodward, C.V. (1989). *The national experience: A history of the United States* (7th ed.). San Diego: Harcourt Brace Jovanovich.

Boyd, W. (Ed.). (1962). *The Emile of Jean Jacques Rousseau.* New York: Bureau of Publications, Teachers College, Columbia University.

Bullock, H.A. (1967). *A history of Negro education in the South: From 1619 to the present.* Cambridge, MA: Harvard University Press.

Caplan, N. (Ed.). (1965). Some unpublished letters of Benjamin Coleman, 1717–1725, *Massachusetts Historical Society Proceedings,* 77 (pp. 101–142).

Cohen, S. (Ed.). (1974). *Education in the United States: A documentary history.* New York: Random House.

Coleman, M.C. (1993). *American Indian children at school, 1850–1930.* Jackson: University Press of Mississippi.

Cremin, L.A. (1970). *American education: The colonial experience, 1607–1783.* New York: Harper & Row.

Cremin, L.A. (1980). *American education: The national experience, 1783–1876.* New York: Harper & Row.

Cross, B.M. (1965). *The educated woman in America: Selected writings of Catharine Beecher, Margaret Fuller, and M. Carey Thomas.* New York: Teachers College Press, Columbia University.

Deighton, L.C. (Ed.). (1971). *The encyclopedia of education* (Vol. 9). New York: Macmillan Company and The Free Press.

Dolan, J.P. (1985). *The American Catholic experience: A history from colonial times to the present.* Garden City, NY: Doubleday.

Douglass, F. (1882). *Life and times of Frederick Douglass.* Hartford, CT: Park.

Douglass, F. (1974). Frederick Douglass describes his self-education (c. 1830). In S. Cohen (Ed.), *Education in the United States: A documentary history* (Vol. 3) (pp. 1624–1625). New York: Random House.

Downs, R. B. (1978). *Friedrich Froebel.* Boston: Twayne Publishers.

Edwards, P. (Ed.). (1972). *Encyclopedia of philosophy* (Vol. 7). New York: The Macmillan Company and The Free Press.

Elsbree, W.S. (1939). *The American teacher: Evolution of a profession in a democracy.* New York: American Book Company.

Emerson, R. W. (1884). *Lectures and biographical sketches.* Cambridge, MA: The Riverside Press.

Flynn, G. (1971). *Sor Juana Ines De La Cruz.* New York: Twayne.

Fogel, D. (1988). *Junipero Serra, the Vatican, and enslavement theology.* San Francisco, CA: Ism Press.

Ford, P.L. (Ed.). (1899). *The New England primer.* New York: Dodd, Mead.

Franklin, B. (1842). *Memoirs of Benjamin Franklin* (Vol. 1). New York: Harper & Brothers.

Gay, P. (Ed.). (1964). *John Locke on education.* New York: Bureau of Publications, Teachers college, Columbia University.

Gutek, G. L. (1968). *Pestalozzi and education.* New York: Random House.

Hahner, J. (1976). *Women in Latin American history.* Los Angeles: University of California.

Hallahan, D.P., & Kauffman, J.M. (1994). *Exceptional children: Introduction to special education* (6th ed.). Boston: Allyn and Bacon.

Hewett, F.M., & Forness, S.R. (1984). *Education of exceptional learners* (3rd ed.). Boston: Allyn and Bacon.

Jefferson, T. (1931). Report of the Commissioners Appointed to Fix the Site of the University of Virginia. In R.J. Honeywell (Ed.), *The Educational Work of Thomas Jefferson* (pp. 248–260). Cambridge, MA: Harvard University Press.

Kaestle, C.F. (1983). *Pillars of the republic: Common schools and American society, 1780–1860.* New York: Hill and Wang.

Kauffman, J. (1981). Introduction: Historical trends and contemporary issues in special education in the United States. In J.M. Kauffman & D.P. Hallahan (Eds.), *Handbook of special education* (pp. 3–23). Englewood Cliffs, NJ: Prentice-Hall.

Krug, E.A. (1964). *The shaping of the American high school, 1880–1920.* New York: Harper & Row.

Lannie, V.P. (1968). *Public money and parochial education: Bishop Hughes, Governor Seward and the New York school controversy.* Cleveland, OH: Press of Case Western Reserve.

Mann, H. (1974). On the employment of female teachers, 1884. In S. Cohen (Ed.), *Education in the United States: A documentary history* (pp. 1315–1317). New York: Random House.

Mann, L. (1979). *On the trail of process: A historical perspective on cognitive processes and their training.* New York: Grune & Stratton.

Manuel, H.T. (1965). *Spanish-speaking children of the Southwest: Their education and the public welfare.* Austin: University of Texas Press.

Pestalozzi, J.H. (1898). *How Gertrude teaches her children* (2nd ed.). Syracuse, NY: C.W. Bardeen.

Reigart, J.F. (1969). *The Lancasterian system of instruction in the schools of New York City.* New York: Arno Press & The New York Times.

Riesman, D. (1954). *Individualism reconsidered.* Glencoe, IL: The Free Press.

Rury, J.L. (1989). Who became teachers?: The characteristics of teachers in American history. In D. Warren (Ed.), *American teachers: Histories of a profession at work* (pp. 9–48). New York: Macmillan.

Steinhardt, M.A. (1992). Physical education. In P.W. Jackson (Ed.), *Handbook of research on curriculum* (pp. 964–1001). New York: Macmillan.

The Sun. (1833a, December 19). New York, p. 2.

The Sun. (1833b, December 20). New York, p. 3.

Tocqueville, A. (1840). *Democracy in America: Part the second, the social influence of democracy* (H. Reeve, Trans.). New York: J. & H.G. Langley.

Tyack, D. (1967). *Turning points in American educational history.* Lexington, MA: Xerox College.

Ulich, R. (1968). *History of educational thought.* New York: D. Van Nostrand.

Zitkala-Sa. (1921). *American Indian stories.* Washington, DC: Hayworth Publishing House.

Chapter 3

Alba, R.D. (1991). *Ethnic identity: The transformation of white America.* New Haven, CT: Yale University Press.

Agee, J., & Evans, W. (1960). *Let us now praise famous men* (2nd ed.). NY: Ballantine Books.

Bates, P. (1990, September). Desegregation: Can we get there from here? *Phi Delta Kappan,* pp. 8–17.

Bennett, C. I. (1990). *Comprehensive multicultural education* (2nd ed.). Boston: Allyn and Bacon.

Blum, J.M., McFeely, W.S., Morgan, E.S., Schlesinger, A.M., Jr., Stampp, K.M., & Woodward, C.V. (1989). *The national experience: A history of the United States* (7th ed.). San Diego: Harcourt Brace Jovanovich.

Bond, H.M. (1934). *The education of the Negro in the American social order*. New York: Prentice-Hall.

Bossert, S.T. (1985). Effective elementary schools. In R.J. Kyle (Ed.), *Reaching for excellence* (pp. 39–53). Washington, DC: U.S. Government Printing Office.

Brinkley, D. (1988). *Washington goes to war*. New York: Alfred A. Knopf.

Brown, C.L., & Pannell, C.W. (1985). The Chinese in America. In J.O. McKee (Ed.), *Ethnicity in contemporary America: A geographical appraisal* (pp. 195–216). Dubuque, IA: Kendall/ Hunt.

Callahan, R.E. (1962). *Education and the cult of efficiency*. Chicago: The University of Chicago Press.

Carlson, R.A. (1975). *The quest for conformity: Americanization through education*. New York: John Wiley and Sons.

Carnegie, D. (1936). *How to win friends & influence people*. New York: Simon and Schuster.

Carnegie Forum on Education and the Economy (1986). *A nation prepared: Teachers for the 21st century, the report of the task force on teaching as a profession*. New York: Carnegie Corporation.

Cole, J.Y. (1979). *For Congress and the nation: A chronological history of the Library of Congress*. Washington, DC: Library of Congress.

Commission on the Reorganization of Secondary Education (1918). *Cardinal principles of secondary education* (Bulletin No. 35). Washington, DC: U.S. Government Printing Office.

Cooper, K.J. (1991, January 27). For Alexander, schooling in education began at home. *The Washington Post*, pp. A1, A9.

Cremin, L.A. (1988). *American education: The metropolitan experience*. NY: Harper & Row.

Cuban, L. (1984). *How teachers taught: Constancy and change in American classrooms 1890–1980*. New York: Longman.

Dabney, C.W. (1969). *Universal education in the South* (Vol.II). New York: Arno Press & the New York Times.

Decker, L.E. (1972). *Foundations of community education*. Midland, MI: Pendall.

Degler, C.N. (1959). *Out of our past: The forces that shaped modern America*. New York: Harper & Row.

Du Bois, W.E.B. (1904). *The souls of black folk*. Chicago: A.C. McClurg.

Ebenstein, W. (1954). *Today's ISMS*. Englewood Cliffs, NJ: Prentice-Hall.

Edwards, J. (1991). To teach responsibility, bring back the Dalton Plan. *Phi Delta Kappan, 72* (5), 398–401.

Efron, S. (1990, April 29). Few Viet exiles find U.S. riches. *Los Angeles Times*, p. 1.

Elsbree, W.S. (1939). *The American teacher: Evolution of a profession in a democracy*. New York: American Book Company.

Franklin, J.H. (1967). *From slavery to freedom* (3rd ed). New York: Alfred A. Knopf.

Fuchs, L.H. (1990). *The American kaleidoscope: Race, ethnicity, and the civic culture*. Middletown, CT: Wesleyan University Press.

Goodman, J.M. (1985). The Native American. In J.O. McKee (Ed.), *Ethnicity in contemporary America: A geographical appraisal* (pp. 195–216). Dubuque, IA: Kendall/Hunt.

Gould, J.E. (1961). *The Chautauqua movement*. Albany: State University of New York Press.

Halberstam, D. (1979). *The powers that be*. New York: Alfred A. Knopf.

Harris, K.A. (1984). *Profiles of Detroit's high schools: 1975 to 1984*. Detroit: Detroit School District, U.S. District Court Monitoring Commission.

Jackson, H.H. (1977). *A century of dishonor: A sketch of the United States government's dealings with some of the Indian tribes*. St. Clair Shores, MI: Scholarly Press. (Original work published 1880).

Jencks, C., Smith, M., Acland, H., Bane, J.J., Cohen, D., Gintis, H., Heyns, B., & Michelson, S. (1972). *Inequality: A reassessment of the effect of family and schooling in America*. New York: Basic Books.

Kauffman, J.M. (1981). Historical trends and contemporary issues in special education in the United States. In J.M. Kauffman & D.P. Hallahan (Eds.), *Handbook of Special Education*. Englewood Cliffs, NJ: Prentice Hall.

Kliebard, H.M. (1986). *The struggle for the American curriculum, 1893–1958*. Boston: Routledge & Kegan Paul.

Koerner, J.D. (Ed.). (1959). *The case for basic education*. Boston: MA: Atlantic Monthly Press.

Kohn, A. (1988, April). Home schooling. *The Atlantic*, pp. 20–25.

Lazarus, E. (1888). *The Poems of Emma Lazarus* (Vol. 1). Boston: Houghton, Mifflin.

Link, A.S., & Catton, W.B. (1963). *American epoch: A history of the United States since the 1890s*. New York: Alfred A. Knopf.

Lodge, H.C. (1891). The restriction of immigration. *The North American Review*, pp. 27–36.

Massachusetts Commission on Industrial and Technical Education. (1906). *Report of the Commission on Industrial and Technical Education*. Boston, MA: Wright & Potter Printing.

McCorry, J.J. (1978). *Marcus Foster and the Oakland public schools: Leadership in urban education*. Berkeley: University of California Press.

Minzey, J.D., & LeTarte, C. (1979). *Community education, from program to process to practice: The schools' role in a new educational society*. Midland, MI: Pendell.

Murphy, J. (1990). The educational reform movement of the 1980s: A comprehensive analysis. In J. Murphy (Ed.), *The educational reform movement of the 1980s* (pp. 3–55). Berkeley, CA: McCutchan.

Orfalea, G. (1988). *Before the flames: A quest for the history of Arab-Americans*. Austin: University of Texas Press.

Painter, N.I. (1977). *Exodusters: Black migration to Kansas after reconstruction*. New York: Alfred A. Knopf.

Parkhurst, H. (1922). *Education on the Dalton Plan*. New York: Dutton.

Peabody, E.P. (1886). *Sara Winnemucca's practical solution of the Indian problems: A letter to Dr. Lyman Abbot of the "Christian Union"*. Cambridge,MA: John Wilson and Son.

Powell, A.G., Farrar, E., & Cohen, D.K. (1985). *The shopping mall high school: Winners and losers in the educational marketplace*. Boston: Houghton Mifflin.

Raven, S., & Weir, A. (1981). *Women in history*. London: Weidenfeld and Nicolson.

Ravitch, D. (1983). *The troubled crusade: 1945-80*. New York: Basic Books.

Reed, S., & Sautter, C. (1990). *Children of poverty: The status of 12 million young Americans*. Bloomington, IN: Kappan Special Report.

Riis, J.A. (1890). *How the other half lives*. New York: Charles Scribner's Sons.

Television Bureau of Advertising. (1989). *TVB a research trend report: Trends in viewing*. New York: Author.

Travers, R.M. (1983). *How research has changed American schools: A history from 1840 to the present*. Kalmazoo, MI: Mythes Press.

Tyack, D., & Hansot, E. (1982). *Managers of virtue*. New York: Basic Books.

U.S. Bureau of Indian Affairs. (1974). Government schools for Indians (1881). In S. Cohen (Ed.), *Education in the United States: A documentary history* (Vol. 3, pp. 1754–1756). New York: Random House.

U.S. Bureau of the Census. (1975). *Historical statistics of the United States: Colonial times to 1970* (Part 1). Washington, DC: U.S. Government Printing Office.

U.S. Bureau of the Census. (1990). *Statistical abstract of the United States* (110th ed.). Washington, DC: U.S. Government Printing Office.

U.S. Department of Education, Office of Educational Research and Improvement. (1988). *Youth Indicators, 1988*. Washington, DC: U.S. Government Printing Office.

U.S. Department of Education, Office of Educational Research and Improvement. (1989). *Digest of education statistics* (25th ed.). Washington, DC: U.S. Government Printing Office.

U.S. Department of Education, Office of Educational Research and Improvement. (1990). *The condition of education, 1990* (Vols. 1–2). Washington, DC: U.S. Government Printing Office.

U.S. Department of Education,. (1991). *The condition of education, 1991: Volume 2. Postsecondary education*. Washington, DC: Author.

Washington, B.T. (1907). *The future of the American negro*. Boston, MA: Small, Maynard.

Chapter 4

Achebe, C. (1968). *Things fall apart.* London: Heinemann Educational Books Ltd.

Adler, M. (1982). *The Paideia proposal: An educational manifesto.* New York: Macmillan.

Apple, M. (1982). *Education and power.* Boston: Routledge and Kegan.

Asante, M.K. (1987). *The Afrocentric idea.* Philadelphia, PA: Temple University Press.

Asante, M.K. (1992). Learning about Africa. *Executive Educator, 14* (9), 21–23.

Banks, J.A. (1994). *Multiethnic education: Theory and Practice* (3rd ed.). Boston: Allyn and Bacon.

Bestor, A. (1985). *Educational wastelands: The retreat from learning in our public schools* (2nd ed.). Urbana: University of Illinois Press.

Bloom, A. (1987). *The closing of the American mind.* New York: Simon and Schuster.

Brameld, T. (1950). *Patterns of educational philosophy: A democratic interpretation.* New York: World Book Company.

Brown, R.G. (1991). *Schools of thought.* San Francisco: Jossey-Bass.

Buber, M. (1970). *I and thou* (W. Kaufman, Trans.). New York: Charles Scribner's Sons. (Original work published 1937)

Clark, C.M., & Peterson, P.L. (1986). Teachers' thought processes. In M.C. Wittrock (Ed.), *Handbook of research on teaching* (3rd ed.) (pp. 255–296). New York: Macmillan.

Clive, J. (1989). *Not by fact alone: Essays on the writing and reading of history.* Boston: Houghton Mifflin.

Cohen, S., & Hearn, D. (1988). Reinforcement. In R.F. McNergney (Ed.), *Guide to classroom teaching* (pp. 43–66). Boston: Allyn and Bacon.

Corbin, H. (1993). *History of Islamic philosophy.* London: Kegan Paul International.

Counts, G.S. (1928). *School and society in Chicago.* New York: Harcourt, Brace.

Durant, W. (1961). *The story of philosophy: The lives and opinions of the great philosophers.* New York: Simon and Schuster.

Eisner, E.W. (1992). Curriculum ideologies. In P.W. Jackson (Ed.), *Handbook of research on curriculum* (pp. 302–326). New York: Maxwell Macmillan International.

Ewert, G.D. (1991). Habermas and education: A comprehensive overview of the influence of Habermas in educational literature. *Review of Educational Research, 61* (3) 345–378.

Fakhry, J. (1983). *A history of Islamic philosophy* (2nd ed.). New York: Columbia University Press.

Fenstermacher, G. D. (1986). Philosophy of research on teaching: Three aspects. In M.C. Wittrock (Ed.), *Handbook of research on teaching* (3rd ed.) (pp. 37–49). New York: Macmillan.

Friere, P. (1970). *Pedagogy of the oppressed.* New York: The Seabury Press.

Fukuyama, F. (1992). *The end of history and the last man.* New York: The Free Press.

Gerber, P.J. (1992). Being learning disabled and a beginning teacher and teaching a class of students with learning disabilities. *Exceptionality, 3* (4), pp. 213–231.

Green, T. (1976). Teacher competence as practical rationality. *Educational Theory, 26,* 249-258.

Haberman, M. (1987). *Recruiting and selecting teachers for urban schools.* New York: ERIC Clearinghouse on Urban Education, Institute for Urban and Minority Education; Reston, VA: Association of Teacher Educators.

Hirsch, E.D., Jr. (1987). *Cultural literacy: What every American needs to know.* Boston: Houghton Mifflin.

Hirsch, E.D., Jr., Rowland, W.G., Jr., & Stanford, M. (Eds.). (1989). *A first dictionary of cultural literacy: What our children need to know.* Boston: Houghton Mifflin.

Holtom, D.C. (1922). *The political philosophy of modern Shinto: A study of the state religion of Japan.* Chicago: University of Chicago Libraries.

Hunt, D.E. (1987). *Beginning with ourselves: In practice, theory, and human affairs.* Cambridge, MA: Brookline Books.

Hutchins, R.M. (1936). *The higher learning in America.* New Haven: Yale University Press.

James, W. (1899). *Talks to teachers on psychology: And to students on some of life's ideals.* New York: Henry Holt.

James, W. (1907). *Pragmatism and four essays from the meaning of truth.* New York: Longmans, Green and Co.

James, W. (1955). *Pragmatism, and four essays from The Meaning of Truth.* New York: Meridan Books.

King, M.L., Jr. (1964). *Stride toward freedom: The Montgomery story.* New York: Harper and Row.

Kneller, G.F. (1971). *Introduction to the philosophy of education* (2nd ed.). New York: Wiley.

Lesko, N. (1988). *Symbolizing society: Stories, rites, and structure in a Catholic high school.* New York: Falmer Press.

Morine-Dershimer, G. (1990, April). To think like a teacher. Vice-presidential address presented at the annual meeting of the American Educational Research Association, Boston.

Nietzsche, F. (1924). *On the future of our educational institutions.* New York: Macmillan.

Nietzsche, F. (1961). *Thus spake Zarathustra: A book for everyone and no one.* (R. J. Hollingdale, Trans.). New York: Penguin Books. (Original work published 1883)

Noddings, N. (1984). *Caring: A feminine approach to ethics & moral education.* Berkeley: University of California Press.

O'Neill, W. F. (1981). *Educational ideologies: Contemporary expressions of educational philosophy.* Santa Monica, CA: Goodyear.

Organ, T.W. (1974). *Hinduism: Its historical development.* Woodbury, NY: Barron's Educational Series.

Paley, V. (1979). *White teacher.* Cambridge: Harvard University Press.

Rambachan, A. (1992). *The Hindu vision.* Delhi: Motilal Banarsidass.

Rickover, H.G. (1963). *American education—a national failure: The problem of our schools and what we can learn from England.* New York: E.P. Dutton.

Robinson, F. (1990, November 18). Learning the new age way. *The Washington Post Education Review,* pp. 9–11.

Rorty, R. (1991). *Objectivity, relativism, and truth: Philosophical papers, volume 1.* Cambridge: Cambridge University Press.

Sartre, Jean-Paul (1947). *Existentialism.* New York: Philosophical Library.

Schön, D. A. (1987). *Educating the reflective practitioner: Toward a new design for teaching and learning in the professions.* San Francisco: Jossey-Bass.

Shulman, L. S. (1987). Knowledge and teaching: Foundations of the new reform. *Harvard Educational Review, 57,* 1–22.

Skinner, B.F. (1971). *Beyond freedom and dignity.* New York: Alfred A. Knopf.

Sleeter, C.E., & Grant, C.A. (1993). *Making choices for multicultural education: Five approaches to race, class, and gender* (2nd ed.). New York: Merrill.

Snelling, J. (1987). *The Buddhist handbook: A complete guide to Buddhist teaching and practice.* London: Century.

Westbrook, R. B. (1991). *John Dewey and American democracy.* Ithaca, NY: Cornell University Press.

Winkler, K.J. (1994). An African writer at a crossroads. *The Chronicle of Higher Education, XL* (19), A9, A12.

X, Malcolm. (1965). *The autobiography of Malcolm X.* New York: Grove Press.

Chapter 5

American Political Network. (1992, September 15). *Daily Report Card,* Note 8 of 8, p.13.

Appalachia Educational Laboratory. (1992, Spring). Dialogue: News from AEL's colleges and schools program. *The Link,* supplement.

Bainbridge, W. L., & Sundre, S.M. (1992, October 14). What parents really look for in a school. *Education Week,* p. 27.

Barnes, H. (1991, October). Learning that grows with the learner: An introduction to Waldorf education. *Educational Leadership,* pp. 52–54.

Berliner, D.C. (1992, February). *Educational reform in an era of disinformation.* Paper presented at the annual meeting of the American Association of Colleges for Teacher Education, San Antonio, TX.

Bracey, G.W. (1991). Why can't they be like we were? *Phi Delta Kappan, 73* (2), 104–112.

Bradley, A. (1992, November 18). Reforming Philadelphia's high schools from within. *Education Week*, pp. 1, 17–19.

Bredo, E., & Henry, M. (1989). Alternatives to the one best system: Patterns of value, curriculum, and pedagogy in private schools. Unpublished manuscript, University of Virginia, Charlottesville.

Brown, S.M. (1992, Fall). The choice for Jewish dayschools. *Educational Horizons*, pp. 45–52.

Bryant, D. M., Clifford, R.M., & Peisner, E.S. (1991). Best practices for beginners: Developmental appropriateness in kindergarten. *American Educational Research Journal, 28* (4), 783–803.

Bryk, A., Holland, P., Lee, V., & Carriedo, R. (1984). *Effective Catholic schools: An exploration.* Washington, DC: National Catholic Education Association.

Carson, C.C., Huelskamp, R.M., & Woodall, T.D. (1991, May 10). *Perspectives on education in America.* Annotated briefing, third draft. Albuquerque, NM: Systems Analysis Department, Sandia National Laboratories.

Center on Organization and Restructuring of Schools (1992). *Estimating the extent of school restructuring* (Brief No.4). Madison: School of Education, Wisconsin Center for Education Research, University of Wisconsin.

Cohen, D. L. (1992, November 25). Preschools in Italian town inspiration to U.S. educators. *Education Week*, pp. 1, 12, 13.

Commission on Jewish Education in North America. (1991). *A time to act.* Lanham, MD: University Press of America.

Cuban, L. (1992). What happens to reforms that last? The case of the junior high school. *American Educational Research Journal, 29* (2), 227–251.

Cushman, K. (1990, Summer). The whys and hows of the multi-age primary classroom. *American Educator*, pp. 28–32.

Dentler, R.A. (1991, February). The national evidence on magnet schools. Occasional paper series. Available from Southwest Regional Laboratory for Educational Research and Development, Los Alamitos, CA.

Department of Defense Dependents Schools. (1991). *Department of Defense Dependents Schools: Providing a quality education overseas.* Washington, DC: U.S. Government Printing Office.

Dolan, J.P. (1985). *The American Catholic experience: A history from colonial times to the present.* Garden City, NY: Doubleday & Company.

Editors of the Chronicle of Higher Education. (1993). *The almanack of higher education, 1993.* Chicago: University of Chicago Press.

ERIC Clearinghouse on Urban Education. (1991, August). Improving urban education with magnet schools. *ERIC/CUE Digest*, p. 1

Fichter, F. H. (1958). *Parochial school: A sociological study.* Notre Dame, IN: University of Notre Dame Press.

Figueroa, D.L. (1992, December 2). Federal joint venture offers job training to troubled students. *Washington Post*, pp. 3.

Flanigan, P. M. (1991, February 12). A school system that works. *The Wall Street Journal*, p. 6.

Goldstein, A. (1991, February 24). Gentle guidance for courageous children: National Institutes of Health school lets seriously ill youngsters continue to learn. *Washington Post*, p. C1.

Goodrich, C. (1993, April 4). Learning in uniform. *Education Review*, pp. 1, 27–29.

Grubb, W.N. (1991, February). The challenge to change. *Vocational Education Journal*, pp. 24–26.

Gursky, D. (1992, September 16). Where school's spirit is a "sense of community." *Education Week*, pp. 1, 14–15.

Gutiérrez, R., & Slavin, R. E. (1992). Achievement effects of the nongraded elementary school: A best evidence synthesis. *Review of Educational Research, 62* (4), 333–376.

Harp, L. (1993, February 24). Advocates of year-round schooling shift focus to educational advantages. *Education Week*, pp. 1, 17.

Hill, D. (1993, February). Teach your children. *Teacher Magazine*, pp. 16–23.

Hostetler, J. A., & Huntington, G. E. (1992). *Amish children: Education in the family, school, and community* (2nd ed.). Orlando, FL: Holt, Rinehart and Winston.

Hunt, T., & Kunkel, N. (1984). Catholic schools: The nation's largest alternative school system. In J. Carper & T. Hunt (Eds.), *Religious Schooling in America* (pp. 1–34). Birmingham, AL: Religious Education Press.

Jordan, M. (1992, August 14). More adults are hooking up to higher education: Technology-delivered courses turn homes and work sites into college classrooms. *Washington Post*, pp. A1, A17.

Koepke, M. (1992, March). All in the family. *Teacher Magazine*, pp. 21–23.

Kolman, S. (1992, July 2). The forgotten years: The middle grades. *Richmond Times Dispatch*, p. A2.

Lawton, M. (1991, November 13). For working students, New York high school opens doors after others have closed theirs. *Education Week*, pp. 6–7.

Leight, R. L., & Rinehart, A. D. (1992, Winter). Revisiting America: One-room school in retrospect. *The Educational Forum*, pp. 133–151.

Lesko, N. (1988). *Symbolizing society: Stories, rites, and structure in a Catholic high school.* New York: Falmer Press.

Levine, D. (1991). Creating effective schools: Findings and implications from research and practice. *Phi Delta Kappan, 72* (5), 389–393.

Mansnerus, L. (1992, Noverber 1). Should tracking be derailed? *New York Times*, Sect. 4A, pp. 14–16.

Martin, D. (1991, November 16). At New School, passion for many ages but old. *New York Times*, p. 23.

National Association for the Education of Young Children & the National Association of Early Childhood Specialists in State Departments of Education (NAECS & SDE) (1991). Guidelines for appropriate curriculum content and assessment in programs serving children ages 3 through 8. *Young Children, 46* (1), 21–38.

National Center for Education Statistics. (1989). *Characteristics of the 55 largest public elementary and secondary school districts in the United States: 1987–88.* Washington, DC: U.S. Department of Education, Office of Educational Research and Improvement.

National Center for Education Statistics. (1991). *The Condition of Education* (Vol. 1). Washington, DC: U.S. Department of Education, Office of Educational Research and Improvement.

National Center for Education Statistics. (1992). *Digest of education statistics, 1992.* Washington, DC: U.S. Department of Education, Office of Educational Research and Improvement.

National Center for Education Statistics (1993a). *Profile of preschool children's child care and early education program participation.* Washington, DC: U.S. Department of Education, Office of Educational Research and Improvement.

National Center for Education Statistics (1993b). *Announcement: New report.* Washington, DC: Office of Educational Research and Improvement.

Newman, M. (1992, November 1). Mix, don't match. *New York Times*, Sect. 4A, p. 17

Northwest Regional Educational Laboratory. (1992, Spring). Northwest Partnership reaches 400 schools. *Northwest Report*, pp. 1–3.

Odden, A. (1985). State level policies and practices supporting effective school management and classroom instruction. In R.M.J. Kyle (Ed.), *Reaching for excellence: An effective schools sourcebook* (pp. 131–142). Washington, DC: U.S. Government Printing Office.

Office of Job Corps. (1992). *Job Corps in brief.* Washington, DC: U.S. Department of Labor.

Olson, L. (1992a, October 7). New approaches blurring the line between public and private schools, *Education Week*, p. 1.

Olson, L. (1992b, November 25). A matter of choice: Minnesota puts "charter schools" idea to test. *Education Week*, pp. 1, 10.

Olson, L. (1993, January 20). Winning NASDC project takes flight in Md. *Education Week*, pp. 1, 24–25.

Penkowsky, L.B. (1991, winter/1992, spring). Teacher feature: Real life examples of integrating academic skills in vocational education. *The Journal of the National Association of Vocational Education Special Needs Personnel*, pp. 66–69.

Phelan, P., Davidson, A.L., & Cao, H.T. (1992). Speaking up: Students' perspectives on school. *Phi Delta Kappan, 73* (9), 695–704.

Rothman, R. (1991, October 30). Schools stress speeding up, not slowing down. *Education Week*, pp. 1, 15.

Sargent, K. J. (1993). *The handbook of private schools: An annual descriptive survey of independent education* (74th ed.). Boston: Porter Sargent.

Schmidt, P. (1993, January 13). Mass. leads mounting charge against ability grouping. *Education Week*, pp. 1, 22, 24.

Schweinhart, L. J. (1992, April). How much do good early childhood programs cost? *Early Education and Development*, pp. 115–127.

Smith, M.L., & Shepard, L.A. (1989). Flunking grades: A recapitulation. In L.A. Shepard & M.L. Smith (Eds.), *Flunking grades: Research and policies on retention* (pp. 214–236). New York: Falmer Press.

Sommerfeld, M. (1992, December 2). "Micro-society" schools tackle real-world woes. *Education Week*, pp. 1, 14.

Suro, M.D. (1992, November 1). Selecting the smart set. *New York Times*, Sect. 4a, p. 18.

Survey tracks Catholic high school changes. (1993, July 15). *Education Daily*, p. 4.

Til, W.V., Vars, G.F., & Lounsbury, J.H. (1967). *Modern education for the junior high school years* (2nd ed.). Indianapolis: Bobbs-Merrill.

Toch, T. (1991, October 20). Lost in class: How oversize schools fail our students. *Washington Post*, pp. C1, C2.

Wagner, M.B. (1990). *God's schools: Choice and compromise in American society*. New Brunswick, NJ: Rutgers University Press.

Walsh, D. J., Ellwein, M.C., Eads, G.M., & Miller, A. (1991). Knocking on kindergarten's door: Who gets in? Who's kept out? *Early Childhood Research Quarterly*, 6, 89–100.

Washington, V., & Oyemade, U.J. (1987). *Project Head Start: Past, present, and future trends in the context of family needs*. New York: Garland.

Williams, L.R., & Fromberg, D.P. (1992). *Encyclopedia of early childhood education*. New York: Garland Publishing.

Willis, S. (1991, March). Breaking down grade barriers: Interest in nongraded classrooms on the rise. *ASCD Update*, pp. 1, 4.

Chapter 6

Appalachia Educational Laboratory. (1991, Spring). New Kentucky program getting positive results. *The Link*, pp. 1, 6–7.

Asante, M.K. (1991). The Afrocentric idea in education. *The Journal of Negro Education*, 60 (2), 170–180.

Ascher, C. (1991). *School programs for African American male students*. New York: ERIC Clearinghouse on Urban Education.

Beardsley, L. (1990). *Good day bad day: The child's experience of child care*. New York: Teachers College, Columbia University.

Bratt, H.M. (1992, October 26). Students outfitted with fashionable incentive program. *Detroit News*, p. B2.

Buckley, W.E, Yesalis, C.E., & Friedl, K.E. (1988). Estimated prevalence of anabolic steroid use among male high school seniors. *Journal of the American Medical Association*, 3441–3445.

Buckley, S. (1991, October 24). Sex is on the minds of students and parents in Howard County. *Washington Post*, p. D2.

Bureau of the Census. (1990, October). School enrollment: Social and economic characteristics of students (Table 4). In *Current population reports, Series P20 No. 460*. Washington, DC: U.S. Department of Commerce, Author.

Cantrell, R.P., & Cantrell, M.L. (1993, November). Countering gang violence in American schools. *Principal*, pp. 6–9.

Children's Defense Fund. (1992). *The state of America's children 1992*. Washington, DC: Author.

Centerwall, B.S. (1992). Television and violence: The scale of the problem and where to go from here. *Journal of the American Medical Association*, 267 (22), 3059–3063.

Cohen, D.L. (1990, June 20). Counselors in elementary schools: Children's "prevention specialists." *Education Week*, pp. 1, 14.

Cohen, D.L. (1993a, April 14). Rewards, penalties for attendance said to benefit teenage parents. *Education Week*, p. 15.

Cohen, D.L. (1993b, April 21). Perry Preschool graduates show dramatic new social gains at 27. *Education Week*, pp. 1, 16–17.

Comer, J.P. (1986). Parent participation in the schools. *Phi Delta Kappan*, 67 (6), 442–446.

Cooper, K. (1991, October 28). Innovations in education: Florida principal seeks to instill "sense of family." *Washington Post*, pp. A1, A12-13.

Creighton, L.L. (1991, December 16). Silent saviors. *U.S. News and World Report*, pp. 80–89.

Cuban, L. (1991, November 20). All-male African-American public schools: Desperate remedies for desperate times. *Education Week*, pp. 36, 30.

Davis, J.M., & Sandoval, J. (1991). *Suicidal youth: School-based intervention and prevention*. San Francisco: Jossey-Bass.

Department of Health and Human Services. (1990). *Health United States 1990* (DHHS Publication No. PHS 91-1232). Washington, DC: U.S. Government Printing Office.

Fingerhut, L.A., Ingram, D.D., Feldman, J.J. (1992). Firearm and nonfirearm homicide among persons 15 through 19 years of age: Differences by level of urbanization, United States, 1979 through 1989. *Journal of the American Medical Association*, 267 (22), 3048–3053.

Finn, C.E., Jr. (1991). *We must take charge: Our schools and our future*. New York: The Free Press.

Flax, E. (1991, November 27). 90 percent of homeless children in school, but many face disadvantages, studies find. *Education Week*, p. 5.

Flaxman, E., & Inger, M. (1991). Parents and schooling in the 1990s. *The Eric Review*, 1 (3), 2–6.

Gallup Organization, Inc. (1991). *Teenage suicide study executive summary*. Princeton, NJ: Author.

Garbarino, J., Dubrow, N., Kostelny, K., & Pardo, C. (1992). *Children in danger*. San Francisco: Jossey-Bass.

Goldstein, A.P., Harootunian, B., & Conoley, J.C. (1994). *Student aggression: Prevention, management and replacement training*. New York: Guilford Publications.

Green, J. (1991, October 13). This school is out: At Harvey Milk, a high school for gay students, lessons are taught in grammar, algebra and survival. *The New York Times Magazine*, pp. 32, 33, 36, 59, 60, 68.

Groopman, J.E. (1993, March 8). T.B. or not T.B.? *The New Republic*, pp. 18–19.

Hewlett, S.A. (1991). *When the bough breaks: The cost of neglecting our children*. New York: Basic Books.

Hispanic students gain under a plan. (1990, June 6). *New York Times*, p. B7.

Kaufman, P., & McMillen, M.M. (1991). *Dropout rates in the United States: 1990*. Washington, DC: U.S. Government Printing Office.

Koop, C.E., & Lundberg, G.D. (1992). Violence in America: A public health emergency. *Journal of the American Medical Association*, 267 (22), 3075–3076.

Langer, J.A., Applebee, A.N., Mullis, I.V., & Foertsch, M.A. (1990). *Learning to read in our nation's schools: Instruction and achievement in 1988 at grades 4,8, and 12*. Princeton, NJ: Educational Testing Service.

Lawton, M. (1993, May 5). Program found curbing children's violent behavior. *Education Week*, p. 14.

Lee, M.T. (1992, April). Greensville's parent resource center delivers. *Virginia Journal of Education*, pp. 12–13.

Marriott, M. (1991, January 30). As students come to class less healthy, school clinics try to offer more. *New York Times*, p. B6.

Mathews, J. (1991, June 3). Dropout prevention: Human touch helps. *Washington Post*, pp. A1, A4.

McCarthy, M.M., & Cambron-McCabe, N. (1992). *Public school law: Teachers' and students' rights* (3rd ed.). Boston: Allyn and Bacon.

Merina, A. (1993, February). Stopping violence starts with students. *NEA Today*, pp. 4–5.

Mitchell, E. (1991, May 20). One man's Taylor-made tuition. *Time*, p. 62.

National Center for Education Statistics. (1990). *Eighth graders' reports of courses taken during the 1988 academic year by selected student characteristics*. (In NELS 88, NCES 90-459). Washington, DC: U.S. Department of Education, Office of Educational Research and Improvement.

National Center for Education Statistics. (1991). *Quality of the responses of eighth-grade students in NELS: 88* (NCES 91-487).

Washington, DC: U.S. Department of Education Office of Educational Research and Improvement.

National Commission on Children. (1991a). *Beyond rhetoric: A new American agenda for children and families.* Washington, DC: Author.

National Commission on Children. (1991b). *Speaking of kids: A national survey of children and parents.* Washington, DC: Author.

National Education Association. (1990). After-school care. *NEA Today, 8* (9), 26.

National Education Association. (1991). *Federal funding: The cost of excellence.* Washington, DC: Author.

Office of Educational Research and Improvement. (1991). *Youth indicators, 1991.* Washington, DC: U.S. Department of Education.

Panel on High-Risk Youth, Commission on Behavioral and Social Sciences and Education, National Research Council. (1993). *Losing generations: Adolescents in high-risk settings.* Washington, DC: National Academy Press.

Phelps, L., & Bajorek, E.(1991). Eating disorders of the adolescent: Current issues in etiology, assessment, and treatment. *School Psychological Review, 20* (1), 9–22.

Portner, J. (1993a, May 19). Rural students learn about hazards to health in "culturally relevant" program. *Education Week,* pp. 6–7.

Portner, J. (1993b, June 16). Prevention efforts in junior high found not to curb drug use in high school. *Education Week,* p. 9.

Presseisen, B.Z. (1988). Teaching thinking and at-risk students: Defining a population. In B.Z. Presseisen (Ed.), *At-risk students and thinking: Perspectives from research* (pp. 19–37). Washington, DC: National Education Association of the United States Research for Better Schools.

Reed, S., & Sautter, R.C. (1990, June). Children of poverty: The status of 12 million young Americans. *Kappan Special Report,* pp. K1–K12.

Reynolds, B. (1993, June 12). Throwaway children are nation's secret scandal. *USA Today,* p. 11A.

Rosenberg, M., O'Carroll, P., & Powell, K. (1992). Let's be clear: Violence is a public health problem. *Journal of the American Medical Association, 267* (22), 3071–3072.

Russell, R. (1991, March 25). Good attendance at Western High is money in the bank. *Detroit News,* pp. B1–B2.

Sanderson, C.A., & Wilson, S.N. (1991). Sexuality education in schools: Planning the future. *Curriculum Review, 30* (5), 3–7.

Sarkees-Wircenski, M. D. (1991). The school at-risk team. In Lynda L. West (Ed.), *Effective strategies for dropout prevention of at-risk youth* (pp. 191–218). Gaithersburg, MD: Aspen Publishers.

Schorr, L.B., & Schorr, D. (1988). *Within our reach: Breaking the cycle of disadvantage.* New York: Doubleday Dell.

Slavin, R. E., Madden, N.A., Karweit, N. L., Dolan, L.J., & Waski, B.A. (1992). *Success for All: A relentless approach to prevention and early intervention in elementary schools.* Arlington, VA: Educational Research Service.

Steiner, D.D. (1990). *AEL minigrant report No.16: The Broadway project.* Charleston, WV: Appalachia Educational Laboratory.

Stout, H. (1991, April 18). Firms help set up, run public schools. *The Wall Street Journal,* p. B1.

Taylor, P. (1991, June 3). Children in poverty: Who are they? *Washington Post,* p. A7.

Teenagers & AIDS: Are you at risk? (1991, February 22). *Scholastic Update (Teacher's Edition),* pp. 12–13.

Tonks, D. (1992, December/1993, January). Can you save your students' lives? Educating to prevent AIDS. *Educational Leadership,* pp. 48–54.

U.S. Department of Education. (1993). *Reinventing Chapter 1: The current Chapter I program and new directions, final report of the National Assessment of the Chapter I Program.* Washington, DC: Author.

Walsh, M. (1993, March 24). Ga. district backs separate classrooms for black pupils. *Education Week,* p. 24.

Waxman, H.C. (1992). Introduction: Reversing the cycle of educational failure for students in at-risk environments. In H.C. Waxman, J. Walker de Felix, J.E. Anderson, & H.P. Baptiste, Jr. (Eds.), *Students at risk in at-risk schools: Improving environments for learning* (pp. 1–9). Newbury Park, CA: Corwin Press.

Wetzel, J.R. (1989). *American youth: A statistical snapshot.* Washington, DC: The William T. Grant Foundation Commission on Work, Family, and Citizenship.

Wheeler, L. (1991, November 6). No-cut policy prompts a lot to cheer about. *New York Times,* p. A18.

WHO. (1991). WHO predicts up to thirty million world AIDS cases by year 2000. *The Nation's Health,* 1, 1.

Zigler, E.F., & Lang, M.E. (1991). *Child care choices: Balancing the needs of children, families, and society.* New York: The Free Press.

Chapter 7

Across the nation: Districts. (1992, May 20). *Education Week,* p. 3.

Alba, R.D. (1990). *Ethnic identity: The transformation of white America.* New Haven, CT: Yale University Press.

Asayesh, G. (1992). Baltimore, MD: Aching to do better. In *Listening to mothers' voices: A reporter's guide to family literacy* (pp. 17–24). Washington, DC: Education Writers Association.

Baltzell, E.D. (1964). *The Protestant establishment: Aristocracy and caste in America.* New York: Random House.

Banks, J.A. (1992, Fall). It's up to us. *Teaching Tolerance,* pp. 20–23.

Banks, J.A. (1993). Multicultural education: Characteristics and goals. In J.A. Banks & C.A. McGee Banks (Eds.), *Multicultural education: Issues and perspectives* (2nd ed.) (pp. 3–28). Boston: Allyn and Bacon.

Banks, J.A., & Banks, C.A. (Eds.). (1993). *Multicultural education: Issues and perspectives* (2nd ed.). Boston: Allyn and Bacon.

Bernstein, R. (1990, October 14). In U.S. schools: A war of words. *The New York Times Magazine,* pp. 44–47.

Bourdieu, P., & Passeron, J.C. (1977). *Reproduction: In education, society, and culture.* Beverly Hills, CA: Sage.

Bullivant, B.M. (1993). Culture: Its nature and meaning for educators. In J.A. Banks & C.A. McGee Banks (Eds.), *Multicultural education: Issues and perspectives* (2nd ed.) (pp. 29–47). Boston: Allyn and Bacon.

Caplan, N., Choy, M.H., & Whitmore, J.K. (1991). *Children of the boat people: A study of educational success.* Ann Arbor: University of Michigan Press.

Chira, S. (1991, October 23). Educators ask if all-girl schools would make a difference in inner cities. *New York Times,* p. B5.

Cooper, K.J. (1990, December 5). Three Rs and role model in Baltimore third grade: Single-sex class harnesses boys' instincts. *Washington Post,* pp. A1, A33.

Cooper, K.J. (1992, November 27). Broadening horizons: Afrocentrism takes root in Atlanta schools. *Washington Post,* p. A1.

Edwards, A., & Polite, C.K. (1992). *Children of the dream: The psychology of black success.* New York: Doubleday.

Elam, S.M. Rose, L.C., & Gallup, A. (1992). The 24nd Annual Gallop/Phi Delta Kappa poll of the public's attitudes toward the public schools. *Phi Delta Kappan, 74* (1), 41–53.

Gardner, H. (1993). *Multiple intelligences: The theory in practice.* New York: Basic Books.

Gartner, A., & Lipsky, D.K. (1989). *The yoke of special education: How to break it.* Rochester, NY: National Center on Education and the Economy.

Gorski, L.J. (1992, November/December). What are you doing November 4? *The Disability Rag,* pp. 15–16.

Grant, C.A., & Sleeter, C.E. (1993). Race, class, gender, and disability in the classroom. In J.A. Banks & C.A. McGee Banks (Eds.), *Multicultural education: Issues and perspectives* (2nd ed.) (pp. 48–68). Boston: Allyn and Bacon.

Green, J. (1991, October 13). This school is out: At Harvey Milk, a high school for gay students, lessons are taught in grammar, algebra and survival. *New York Times Magazine,* pp. 32, 33, 36, 59, 60, 68.

Hallahan, D.P., & Kauffman, J.M. (1994). *Exceptional children: Introduction to special education.* Boston: Allyn and Bacon.

Highet, G. (1954). *Juvenal the satirist, a study.* Oxford: Clarendon Press.

Hill, D. (1990, June/July). A theory of success and failure. *Teacher Magazine,* pp. 40–45.

Hodgkinson, H.A. (1992). *A demographic look at tomorrow.* Washington, DC: Institute for Educational Leadership.

Hollins, E. (1982). The Marva Collins story revisited: Implications for regular classroom instruction. *Journal of Teacher Education, 33* (1), 37–40.

Hunt, D.E., & Sullivan, E.V. (1974). *Between psychology and education.* New York: Holt, Rinehart and Winston.

Jackson, K.T. (1991). A dissenting comment. In New York State Social Studies Review and Development Committee, *One nation, many peoples: A declaration of cultural interdependence* (pp. 80–81). Albany: New York State Education Department.

Jetter, A. (1993, February 21). Mississippi learning. *New York Times,* Section 6, pp. 28–72.

Johnson, D.W., Johnson, R.T., Dudley, B., & Burnett, R. (1992, September). Teaching students to be peer mediators. *Educational Leadership,* pp. 10–13.

Kamen, A. (1991, August 12). The Cambodians: A temple anchors community. *Washington Post,* p. A9.

Kauffman, J.M. (1990). Restructuring in sociopolitical contest: Reservations about the effects of current reform proposals on student with disabilities. In J.W. Lloyd, N.N. Singh, & A.C. Repp (Eds.), *The regular education initiative: Alternative perspectives on concepts, issues, and models* (pp. 57–66). Sycamore, IL: Sycamore Publishing.

Kleinfeld, J. (1995). Critical perspective on the case of Hans Christian Andersen School. *Guide to foundations in action: Videocases: Teaching and learning in multicultural settings* (pp. 191–208). Boston: Allyn and Bacon.

Kleinhuizen, J. (1991, May 7). Tribal colleges combine academics and heritage. *USA Today,* p. 4D.

Marshall, S. (1992, December 24). Louisiana ruling draws fire. *USA Today,* p. A3.

Matute-Bianchi, M.E. (1991). Situational ethnicity and patterns of school performance among immigrant and nonimmigrant Mexican-descent students. In M.A. Gibson & J.U. Ogbu (Eds.), *Minority status and schooling: A comparative study of immigrant and involuntary minorities* (pp. 205–248). New York: Garland.

McDonnell, L.M., & Hill, P. (1993). *Newcomers in American schools: Meeting the educational needs of immigrant children.* Washington, DC: RAND Corporation.

Meek, M. (1992, Fall). The peacekeepers: Students use mediation skills to resolve conflicts. *Teaching Tolerance,* pp. 46–52.

Mosle, S. (1993, August 1). Scissors, not sermons. *Washington Post Education Review,* p. 5.

Myers, S.L. (1992, December 2). Queens School Board suspended in fight over gay-life curriculum. *New Tork Time,* p. A1.

(NASBE) National Association of State Boards of Education Study Group on Special Education. (1992). *Winners all: A call for inclusive schools.* Alexandria, VA: The National Association of State Boards of Education.

National Education Association. (1993, February). Stopping violence starts with students. *NEA Today,* pp. 4–5.

New York State Social Studies Review and Development Committee. (1991). *One nation, many peoples: A declaration of cultural interdependence.* Albany, NY: New York State Education Department.

Nieto, S. (1992). *Affirming diversity: The sociopolitical context of multicultural education.* New York: Longman.

Office of Federal Statistical Policy and Standards. (1978). *Statistical policy handbook.* Washington, DC: U.S. Department of Commerce.

Ogbu, J.U. (1991). Immigrant and involuntary minorities in comparative perspective. In M.A. Gibson & J.U. Ogbu (Eds.), *Minority status and schooling: A comparative study of immigrant and involuntary minorities* (pp. 3–36). New York: Garland.

Percell, C. H., & Cookson, P. W. (1990). Chartering and bartering: Elite education and social reproduction. In P.W. Kingston & L. S. Lewis (Eds.), *The high-status track: Studies of elite schools and stratification* (pp. 25–49). New York: State University of New York Press.

Pratt, R.A. (1992). *The color of their skin: Education and race in Richmond Virginia 1954–89.* Charlottesville: University Press of Virginia.

Quality Education for Minorities Network. (1991, March 4). *Multicultural education.* Washington, DC: QEM Network.

Raspberry, W. (1993, January 6). Performance at school begins at home. *Daily Progress,* p. A4.

Ravitch, D. (1990, November 29). We can teach cultural history—or racial hate. *New York Daily News,* p. 30.

Ray, D. (1992). Integration of recent immigrants throughout schooling: An introduction. In D. Ray & D.H. Poonwassie (Eds.), *Education & cultural differences: New perspectives* (pp. 413–418). New York: Garland.

Schlesinger, A.M. (1991). *The disuniting of American: Reflections on a multicultural society.* Knoxville, TN: Whittle Direct Books.

Schlesinger, A.M. (1991). Report of the social studies syllabus review committee: A dissenting opinion. In New York State Social Studies Review and Development Committee, *One nation, many peoples: A declaration of cultural interdependence* (pp. 89–93). Albany, NY: New York State Education Department.

Schmidt, P. (1990, May 2). 5-year study faults placement practices for L.E.P. students. *Education Week,* pp. 1, 11.

Southern Poverty Law Center. (1992, Fall). *Teaching Tolerance.* Montgomery, AL: Southern Poverty Law Center.

Steele, S. (1990). *The content of our character: A new vision of race in America.* New York: Harper Perennial.

Terkel, Studs. (1992). *Race: How blacks and whites think and feel about the American obsession.* New York: The New Press.

Theodorson, G.A., & Theodorson, A.G. (1970). *A modern dictionary of sociology.* London: Methuen.

Thornton, J., Whitman, D., & Friedman, D. (1992, November 9). Whites' myths about blacks: Though some white views have softened, mistaken beliefs persist. *U.S. News & World Report,* pp. 41–44.

Trillin, Calvin (1983). *Uncivil liberties.* Garden City, NY: Anchor Books.

U.S. Department of Commerce, Census Bureau. (1991). *Statistical abstract of the U.S.* (111th ed.). Washington, DC: Author.

U.S. Department of Education. (1992). *Fourteenth annual report to Congress on the implementation of the Individuals with Disabilities Education Act.* Washington, DC: Author.

U.S. Department of Education. (1993). *Fifteenth annual report to Congress on the implementation of the Individuals with Disabilities Education Act.* Washington, DC: Author.

Viadero, D. (1992, November 25). Deaf student allowed to enter speech contest. *Education Week,* p. 4.

Villegas, A. M. (1991). *Culturally responsive pedagogy for the 1990s and beyond.* Princeton, NJ: Educational Testing Service.

Vobejda, B. (1991, September 23–29). The changing face of America: Racial and ethnic shifts are remixing the melting pot. *Washington Post,* pp. 6–7.

Chapter 8

AAUW Educational Foundation and the National Education Association. (1992). *The AAUW report: How schools shortchange girls: A study of major findings on girls and education.* Washington, DC: Authors.

Abramowitz, R.H., Petersen, A.C., & Schulenberg, J.E. (1984). Changes in self-image during early adolescence. In D.Offer, E. Ostrov, & K. Howard (Eds.), *Patterns of adolescent self-image* (pp. 19–28). San Francisco: Jossey-Bass.

American Association on Mental Retardation. (1992). *Mental retardation: Definition, classification, and systems of support* (9th ed.). Washington, DC: Author.

Ansley, L., & McCleary, K. (1992, August 21–23). Do the right thing. *USA Weekend,* pp. 4–7.

Ashe, A., & Rampersad, A. (1993). *Days of grace: A memoir.* New York: Alfred A. Knopf.

Athletic Footwear Institute. (1990). *American youth and sports participation.* North Palm Beach, FL: Author.

Avery, P. G., & Walker, C. (1993,). Prospective teachers' perceptions of ethnic and gender differences in academic achievement. *Journal of Teacher Education, 44* (1), 27–37.

Bempechat, J., London, P., & Dweck, C. S. (1991). Children's conceptions of ability in major and experimental study. *Child Study Journal, 21* (1), 11-35.

Berg, C.A. (1992). Perspectives for viewing intellectual development throughout the life course. In R.J. Sternberg & C.A. Berg

(Eds.), *Intellectual development* (pp. 1–15). Cambridge: Cambridge University Press.

Bouchard, J.J., Jr., Lykken, D.T., McGue, M., Segal, N., & Tellegen, A. (1990). Sources of human psychological differences: The Minnesota study of twins reared apart. *Science, 250,* 223–228.

Brindis, C. D., Irwin, C. E., Jr., & Millstein, S. G. (1992). United States profile. In E.R. McAnarney, R. E. Kreipe, D.P. Orr, & G.D. Commerci (Eds.), *Textbook of adolescent medicine* (pp. 75–111). Philadelphia: W.B. Saunders.

Brooks-Gunn, J., & Petersen, A.C. (Eds.). (1983). *Girls at puberty: Biological and psychological perspectives.* New York: Plenum.

Ceci, S. J., & Ruiz, A. (1993). Transfer, abstractness, and intelligence. In D. Detterman & R. J. Sternberg (Eds.), *Transfer on trial: Intelligence, cognition, and instruction* (pp. 168–191). Norwood, NJ: Ablex.

Children's Defense Fund. (1992). *The state of America's children 1992.* Washington, DC: Author.

Clark, C.M. (1990). The teacher and the taught: Moral transactions in the classroom. In J.I. Goodlad, R. Soder, & K.A. Sirotnik (Eds.), *The moral dimensions of teaching* (pp. 251–265). San Francisco: Jossey-Bass.

Clifford, M. M. (1975). Physical attractiveness and academic performance. *Child Study Journal, 5,* 201–209.

Cohen, D. L. (1993, April 7). New study links lower I.Q. at age 5 to Poverty. *Education Week,* p. 4.

Cremin, L.A. (1957). *The republic and the school.* New York: Teachers College Press.

Elliott, E., & Dweck, C. S. (1988). Goals: An approach to motivation and achievement. *Journal of Personality and Social Psychology, 54,* 5–12.

Erikson, E.H. (1980). *Identity and the life cycle.* New York: Norton.

Finkel, D. (1993, June 13). The wiz. *Washington Post Magazine,* pp. 8–13, 22–27.

Gardner, H. (1993). *Multiple intelligences: The theory in practice.* New York: Basic Books.

Gardner, H., & Hatch, T. (1989). Multiple intelligences go to school: Educational implications of the theory of multiple intelligences. *Educational Researcher, 18* (8), 4–10.

Gilligan, C. (1982). *In a different voice: Psychological theory and women's development.* Cambridge, MA: Harvard University Press.

Gilligan, C., & Attanucci, J. (1988). Two moral orientations: Gender differences and similarities. *Merrill-Palmer Quarterly, 34,* 223–237.

Guilford, J.P. (1988). Some changes in the structure-of-intellect model. *Educational and Psychological Measurement, 48,* 1–4.

Hallahan, D.P., & Kauffman, J. M. (1994). *Exceptional children: Introduction to special education* (5th ed.). Englewood Cliffs, NJ: Prentice-Hall.

Hammill, D.D., Leigh, J.E., McNutt, G., & Larsen, S. (1988). A new definition of learning disabilities. *Learning Disability Quarterly, 11* (3), 217–232.

Hartshorne, H., May, M.A., & Shuttleworth, F.K. (1930). *Studies in the organization of character.* New York: Macmillan.

Henry, S. L., & Pepper, F. C. (1990). Cognitive, social, and cultural effects on Indian learning style: Classroom implications. *Journal of Educational Issues of Language Minority Students, 7,* 85–97.

Hilliard, A. G., III. (1990). Back to Binet: The case against the use of IQ tests in the schools. *Contemporary Education, 61* (4), 184–189.

Jenkins, J., Zigmond, N., Fuchs, L., Fuchs, D., & Deno, S. (in press). Special education in restructured schools: Findings from three multi-year studies. *Phi Delta Kappan.*

Kuralt, C. (1992, May 29). Sunday morning. (CBS). Transcript from: Livingston, NJ: Burrelle's Information Services.

Leff, L. (1992, April 5). The learning curve: Inside an American high school. *Washington Post,* pp. A1, A22, A23.

Lerner, J.W., & Lerner, S.R. (1991). Attention deficit disorder: Issues and questions. *Focus on Exceptional Children, 24* (3), 1–17.

Lerner, R. M., & Lerner, J. V. (1977). Effects of age, sex and physical attractiveness on child-peer relations, academic performance and elementary school adjustment. *Developmental Psychology, 13,* 585–590.

Lyons, N.P. (1993). Luck, ethics, and ways of knowing: Observations on adolescents' deliberations in making moral choices. In A.Garrod (Ed.), *Approaches to moral development: New research and emerging themes* (pp. 133–154). New York: Teachers College Press.

Mullis, I., Owens, E., & Phillips, G. (1990). *Accelerating academic achievement: A summary of findings from 20 years of NAEP.* Washington, DC: U.S. Department of Education.

Mwamwenda, T.S. (1992). Comment: Universality of formal operational thought. *Perceptual and Motor Skills, 78* (2), 78.

Orlansky, M.C. (1981). *Voices, interviews with handicapped people.* Columbus, OH: C.E. Merrill.

Page, R. M. (1990, September/October). Loneliness and adolescent health behavior. *Health Education,* pp. 14–17.

Palmer, J. M., & Yantis, P. A. (1990). *Survey of communication disorders.* Baltimore, MD: Williams & Wilkins.

Phelan, P., Davidson, A.L., & Cao, H.T. (1992). Speaking up: Students' perspectives on school. *Phi Delta Kappan, 73,* 695–704.

Power, F.C., Higgins, A., & Kohlberg, L. (1989). *Lawrence Kohlberg's approach to moral education.* New York: Columbia University Press.

Renzulli, J.S. (1982). Dear Mr. and Mrs. Copernicus: We regret to inform you . . . *Gifted Child Quarterly, 26,* 11–14.

Rierdan, J., & Koff, E. (1991). Depressive symptomology among very early maturing girls. *Journal of Youth and Adolescence, 20,* 415–25.

Rosenbaum, M., & Leibel, R. (1989). Obesity in childhood. *Pediatric Review, 11* (2), 43–55.

Rosso, J. (in press), The impact of pubertal and asocial events upon girls' problem behavior. *Journal of Youth and Adolescence.*

Rutherford, F.J., & Ahlgren, A. (1990). *Science for all Americans.* New York: Oxford University Press.

Sadker, M., & Sadker, D. (1993, March). Fair and square? *Instructor,* pp. 45, 46, 67, 68.

Schmidt, P. (1993, May 26). Seeking to identify the gifted among L.E.P. students. *Education Week,* pp. 1, 12–13.

Seefeldt, V., Ewing, M., & Walk, S. (1991). *An overview of youth sports programs in the United States.* Washington, DC: Carnegie Council on Adolescent Development.

Shaywitz, S. E., Shaywitz, B. A., Fletcher, J.M., & Escobar, M.D. (1990). Prevalence of reading disability in boys and girls: Results of the Connecticut longitudinal study. *Journal of the American Medical Association, 264,* 998–1002.

Shore, D. (1992, November/December). Thinking out loud. *Teacher Magazine,* pp. 22–25.

Sockett, H. (1992). The moral aspects of the curriculum. In P.W. Jackson (Ed.), *Handbook of research on curriculum* (pp. 543–569). New York: Macmillan.

Spearman, C. (1927). *The abilities of man.* New York: Macmillan.

Sprinthall, N.A., & Sprinthall, R.C. (1990). *Educational psychology: A developmental approach* (5th ed.). New York: McGraw-Hill.

Sternberg, R.J. (1988). *The triarchic mind: A new theory of human intelligence.* New York: Viking.

Sternberg, R.J., & Detterman, D.K. (Eds.). (1986). *What is intelligence? : Contemporary viewpoints on its nature and definition.* Norwood, NJ: Ablex.

Sutherland, P. (1992). *Cognitive development today: Piaget and his critics.* London: Paul Chapman.

U.S. Department of Education. (1992). *Fourteenth annual report to Congress on the implementation of The Individuals with Disabilities Education Act.* Washington, DC: Author.

U.S. Department of Education, Office of Educational Research and Improvement. (1991). *National education longitudinal study (NELS: 88) on gifted and talented education.* Unpublished study. Washington, DC.

U.S. Department of Education, Office of Educational Research and Improvement. (1993). *National excellence: A case for developing America's talent.* Washington, DC: Author.

U. S. Department of Health, Education, and Welfare. (1977, August 23). *Federal Register, 42* (163), 42478.

Viadero, D. (1992, April 29). Education data seen bypassing disabled youths: Measures' reliability is called into question. *Education Week,* pp. 1, 25.

Walker, L.J. (1989). A longitudinal study of moral reasoning. *Child Development, 60,* 157–166.

Walker, L.J., de Vries, B., & Trevethan, S.D. (1987). Moral stages and moral orientations in real-life and hypothetical dilemmas. *Child Development, 58,* 842–858.

Wolf, B., Pratt, C., & Pruitt, P. (1990). *Human exceptionality: Society, school and family* (3rd ed.). Boston: Allyn and Bacon.

Youth sports: Kids are the losers. (1992, July/August). *Harvard Education Letter,* pp. 1–3.

Ysseldyke, J.E., Christenson, S.L., & Thurlow, M.L. (1993). *Final report: Student learning in context model project.* Minneapolis: University of Minnesota College of Education.

Yussen, S.R., & Kane, P. T. (1985). Children's conception of intelligence. In S.R. Yussen (Ed.), *The growth of reflection in children* (pp. 207–241). Orlando, FL: Academic Press.

Chapter 9

Apple, M.W. (1993). *Official knowledge.* New York: Routledge.

Apple, M.W., & Beyer, L.E. (1988). Social evaluation of curriculum schooling. In L.E. Beyer & M.W. Apple (Eds.), *The curriculum: Problems, politics, and possibilities* (pp. 334–349). Albany: State University of New York Press.

Applebee, A.N. (1991). Environments for language teaching and learning. In J.Flood, J.Jensen, & J.R. Squire (Eds.), *Handbook of research on teaching the English language arts* (pp. 549–558). New York: Macmillan.

Applebee, A.N., & Purves, A.C. (1992). Literature and the English language arts. In P.W. Jackson (Ed.), *Handbook of research on curriculum* (pp. 726–748). New York: Macmillan.

Armstrong, D.G. (1989). *Developing and documenting the curriculum.* Needham Heights, MA: Allyn and Bacon.

Association for Supervision and Curriculum Development. (1992, January). What the NCTM standards say. *Curriculum Update,* p. 3.

Banks, J. A. (1988). *Multiethnic education: Theory and practice* (2nd ed.). Boston: Allyn and Bacon.

Berk, L.E. (1992). The extracurriculum. In P.W. Jackson (Ed.), *Handbook of research on curriculum* (pp. 1002–1043). New York: Macmillan.

Bloom, B. (Ed.) (1956). *Taxonomy of educational objectives: The classification of educational goals, handbook I: Cognitive domain.* New York: David McKay.

Blum, J.M., McFeely, W.S., Morgan, E.S., Schlesinger, A.M., Jr., Stampp, K.M., & Woodward, C.V. (1989). *The national experience: A history of the United States* (7th ed.). San Diego: Harcourt Brace Jovanovitch.

Bobbitt, F. (1918). *The curriculum.* Cambridge, MA: Riverside Press.

Boyer, E.L. (1991). Foreword. In C.N. Quigley & C.F. Bahmueller (Eds.), *Civitas: A framework for civic education* (pp. xv–xvii). Calabasas, CA: Center for Civic Education.

Buser, R.L., & Humm, W.L. (1975, March). *Curriculum/instructional change through state education agencies.* Paper presented at the annual meeting of the American Educational Research Association, Washington, DC. Reported in ERIC #ED 103 971.

Butts, R.F. (1991). A personal preface. In C.N. Quigley & C.F. Bahmueller (Eds.), *Civitas: A framework for civic education* (pp. xix–xxvi). Calabasas, CA: Center for Civic Education.

Clandinin, D.J., & Connelly, F.M. (1992). Teacher as curriculum maker. In P.W. Jackson (Ed.), *Handbook of research on curriculum* (pp. 363–401). New York: Macmillan.

Cremin, L. A. (1961). *The transformation of the school.* New York: Vintage Books.

Cuban, L. (1992). Curriculum stability and change. In P.W. Jackson (Ed.), *Handbook of research on curriculum* (pp. 216–217). New York: Macmillan.

Darling-Hammond, L. (1992). *Standards of practice for learner-centered schools.* New York: Teachers College, Columbia University.

DeBoer, G. E. (1991). *A history of ideas in science education: Implications for practice.* New York: Teachers College Press.

Doll, R.C. (1986). *Curriculum improvement: Decision making and process* (6th ed.). Boston: Allyn and Bacon.

Education Writers Association. (1987). *Covering the education beat: A current guide for editors and writers.* Washington, DC: Author.

Eisner, E. W. (1985). *The educational imagination: On the design and evaluation of school programs* (2nd ed.). New York: Macmillan.

Eisner, E. W. (1992). The misunderstood role of the arts in human development. *Phi Delta Kappan, 73* (8), 591–595.

Eisner, E. W., & Vallance, E. (1974). *Conflicting conceptions of curriculum.* Berkeley: McCutchan.

Elmore, R., & Sykes, G. (1992). Curriculum policy. In P.W. Jackson (Ed.), *Handbook of research on curriculum* (pp. 185–215). New York: Macmillan.

Fairfax County Public Schools. (1991). *Family life education: Human growth and development, grades 5–6.* Fairfax, VA: Office of Curriculum Services, Fairfax County Public Schools.

Finn, C.E., Jr. (1991). *We must take charge: Our schools and our future.* New York: The Free Press.

Gifford, V.D., & Dean, M.M. (1990). Differences in extracurricular activity participation, achievement, and attitudes toward school between ninth-grade students attending junior high school and those attending senior high school. *Adolescence, 25* (100), 799–802.

Grobman, H. (1970). *Developmental curriculum projects: Decision points and processes.* Itasca, IL: Peacock.

Grumet, M. (1987). Women and teaching: Homeless at home. *Teacher Education Quarterly, 14* (2), 39–46.

Gudmundsdottir, S. (1991). Values in pedagogical content knowledge. *The Journal of Teacher Education, 41* (3), 44–52.

Harp, L. (1993, September 22). Pa. parent becomes mother of "outcomes" revolt. *Education Week,* pp. 1, 19–21.

Hirsch, E.D. (1987). *Cultural literacy: What every American needs to know.* Boston: Houghton Mifflin.

Jackson, P.W. (1990). *Life in classrooms.* New York: Teachers College Press.

Hunt, D.E., & Sullivan, E.V. (1974). *Between psychology and education.* Hinsdale, IL: Dryden Press.

Kliebard, H. M. (1979). The drive for curriculum change in the United States, 1890–1985. I—The ideological roots of curriculum as a field of specialization. *Journal of Curriculum Studies, 19* (3), 191–202.

Kliebard, H.M. (1986). *The struggle for the American curriculum, 1893–1958.* Boston: Routledge and Kegan Paul.

Langer, J.A., & Applebee, A.N. (1986). Reading and writing instruction: Toward a theory of teaching and learning. In E.Z. Rothkopf (Ed.), *Review of research in education: Vol. 13* (pp. 171–194). Washington, DC: American Educational Research Association.

Lerner, B. (1991, March). Good news about American education. *Commentary,* pp. 19–25.

Lewis, A. (1988). *Facts and Faith: A status report on youth service.* Washington, DC: The William T. Grant Foundation Commision on Work, Family, and Citizenship.

Littell, J., & Wynn, J. (1989). *The availability and use of community resources for young adolescents in an inner-city and a suburban community.* Chicago: Chapin Hall Center for Children at the University of Chicago. Cited in What did you learn outside of school today? (1991, July/August). *The Harvard Education Letter,* p. 8.

Lloyd, J.W., Landrum, T.J., & Hallahan, D.P. (1991). Self-monitoring applications for classroom interventions. In G.Stoner, M.R. Shinn, & H.M. Walker (Eds.), *Interventions for behavior and academic problems in regular class settings* (pp. 201–213). Stratford, CT: National Association of School Psychologists.

Madaus, G.F., & Kellaghan, T. (1992). Curriculum evaluation and assessment. In P.W. Jackson (Ed.), *Handbook of research on curriculum* (pp. 119–156). New York: Macmillan.

Magee, M. (1992). *On television: Teach the children, study guide & transcript.* Kent, OH: PTV Publications.

Mager, R. F. (1962). *Preparing instructional objectives.* Palo Alto, CA: Fearon.

McConaghy, T. (1992). A witch hunt bedevils a Canadian reading series. *Phi Delta Kappan, 73* (8), p. 649.

McNergney, R., & Haberman, M. (1987, April). Extracurricular activities: Shattering the myth. *NEA Today,* p. 21.

McNergney, R., & Haberman, M. (1990, May/June). Doing good by doing good. NEA Today, p. 27.

McNergney, R.F., Hallahan, D.P., Keller, C.E., & Crowley, E.P. (1992). Improving communication between educational researchers and journalists. In R.F. McNergney (Ed.) *Education, research, policy, and the press: Research as news* (pp. 75–88). Boston: Allyn and Bacon.

Morrison, G.S. (1993). *Contemporary curriculum K–8.* Boston: Allyn and Bacon.

National Council of Teachers of Mathematics. (1989). *Curriculum and evaluation standards for school mathematics.* Reston, VA: Author.

National Council of Teachers of Mathematics. (1991). *Professional standards for teaching mathematics.* Reston, VA: Author.

New York State Social Studies Review and Development Committee. (1991). *Executive summary of the report of the New York State social studies review and development committee.* New York: State Education Department and the University of the State of New York.

Noddings, N. (1984). *Caring: A feminine approach to ethics and moral education.* Berkeley and Los Angeles: University of California Press.

Noddings, N. (1987). Do we really want to produce good people? *Journal of Moral Education, 16* (3), 177–188.

Noddings, N. (1992). Gender and the curriculum. In P.W. Jackson (Ed.), *Handbook of research on curriculum* (pp. 659–686). New York: Macmillan.

Oliva, P.F. (1992). *Developing the curriculum* (3rd ed.). New York: Harper Collins.

O'Neil, J. (1993). Achieving higher standards. *Educational Leadership, 50* (5), 4–8.

Ornstein, A.C., & Hunkins, F.P. (1988). *Curriculum: Foundations, principles, and issues.* Englewood Cliffs, NJ: Prentice Hall.

Pagano, J.A. (1988). The claim of Philia. In W.F. Pinar (Ed.), *Curriculum theory discourses* (pp. 414–420). Scottsdale, AZ: Gorsuch Skarisbrick.

Putka, G. (1992, February 12). Readers of latest U.S. history textbooks discover a storehouse of misinformation. *The Wall Street Journal,* p. B1.

Quigley, C.N., & Bahmuller, C.F. (Eds.). (1991). *Civitas: A framework for civic education.* Calabasas, CA: Center for Civic Education.

Schubert, W.H. (1986). *Curriculum: Perspective, paradigm, and possibility.* New York: Macmillan.

Schwartz, J. L. (1989). Intellectual mirrors: A step in the direction of making schools knowledge-making places. *Harvard Educational Review, 59* (1), 51–61.

Simon, S.B., Howe, L.W., & Kirschenbaum, H. (1972). *Values clarification: A handbook of practical strategies for teachers and students.* New York: Hart.

Sleeter, C.E., & Grant, C.A. (1991). Race, class, gender, and disability in current textbooks. In M.W. Apple & L.K. Christian-Smith (Eds,), *The politics of the textbook* (pp. 78–110). New York: Routledge.

Slobig, F., & George, C. (1989). *A policy blueprint for community service and youth employment.* Washington, DC: Roosevelt Centennial Youth Project.

Sobol, T. Memorandum to members of the New York Board of Regents, June 13, 1991.

Spady, W.G. (1986). *Defining components of outcome-based education.* Unpublished manuscript.

Squire, J.R., & Morgan, R.T. (1990). The elementary and high school textbook market today. In D.L. Elliott & A. Woodward (Eds.), *Eighty-ninth yearbook of the National Society for the Study of Education* (pp. 107–126). Chicago: National Society for the Study of Education.

Tyler, R.W. (1949). *Basic principles of curriculum and instruction.* Chicago: University of Chicago Press.

USA Today. (1992, April 23). *News for release.* Arlington, VA: Gannett.

Vallance, E. (1983). Curriculum as a field of practice. In F.W. English (Ed.), *Fundamental curriculum decisions, 1983 yearbook* (pp. 37–56). Alexandria, VA: Association for Supervision and Curriculum Development.

Viadero, D. (1990, November 28). Battle over multicultural education rises in intensity: Issue is what kind, not whether. *Education Week,* pp. 1, 11, 13.

Viadero, D. (1992, November 25). Survey finds young people more likely to lie, cheat, steal. *Education Week,* p. 5.

Weiss, C.H., & Singer, E. (1988). *Reporting of social science in the national media.* New York: Russell Sage Foundation.

William T. Grant Foundation Commission on Work, Family, and Citizenship (1988). *The forgotten half: Pathways to success for America's youth and young families.* Washington, DC: Author.

Wilson, S. (1991). *Making the case for arts education in the schools: Research/case statement summaries, arts education publication list.* Richmond: Virginia State Department of Education.

Chapter 10

Airasian, P. W. (1991). *Classroom assessment.* New York: McGraw-Hill.

Arter, J.A., & Spandel, V. (1992). NCME Instructional Module: Using portfolios of student work in instruction and assessment. *Educational Measurement, 11,* 36–44.

Artiles, A.J. (1992, April). *Patterns of classroom interaction associated with alternative perspectives on teacher planning.* Paper presented at the annual meeting of the American Educational Research Association, San Francisco.

Bloom, B. (1971). Mastery learning. In J.H. Block (Ed.), *Mastery learning: Theory and Practice* (pp. 13–28). New York: Holt, Rinehart & Winston.

Brophy, J. (1987). On motivating students. In D. C. Berliner & B.V. Rosenshine (Eds.), *Talks to teachers* (pp. 201–245). New York: Random House.

Brophy, J. (1992). Probing the subtleties of subject-matter teaching. *Educational Leadership, 49* (2), 4–8.

Brophy, J., & McCaslin, M. (1992). Teachers' reports of how they perceive and cope with problem students. The *Elementary School Journal, 93* (1), 3–68.

Burns, R.W. (1972). The central notion: Explicit objectives. In W.R. Houston & R.B. Howsam (Eds.). *Competency-based teacher education: Progress, problems, and prospects* (pp. 17–33). Chicago: Science Research Associates.

Carroll, J.B. (1971). Problems of measurement related to the concept of learning for mastery. In J.H. Block (Ed.), *Mastery learning: Theory and practice* (pp. 29–46). New York: Holt, Rinehart & Winston.

Chapman, J. W. (1992). Learning disabilities in New Zealand: Where kiwis and kids with LD can't fly. *Journal of Learning Disabilities, 25,* 362–370.

Clark, C. M., & Dunn, S. (1991). Second-generation research on teachers' planning. In H. C. Waxman & H. J. Walberg (Eds.), *Effective teaching: Current research* (pp. 183–201). Berkeley, CA: McCutchan.

Cooper, H. (1989). *Homework.* New York: Longman.

Corno, L. (1987). Teaching and self-regulated learning. In D. C. Berliner & B.V. Rosenshine (Eds.), *Talks to teachers* (pp. 249–266). New York: Random House.

Doyle, W. (1986). Classroom organization and management. In M.C. Wittrock (Ed.), *Handbook of research on teaching* (3rd ed.) (pp. 392–431) New York: Macmillan.

Eggen, P.D. , & Kauchak, D.P. (1988). *Strategies for teachers: Teaching content and thinking skills* (2nd ed.). Englewood Cliffs, NJ: Prentice Hall.

Eisner, E.W. (1991, September). What the arts taught me about education. *Art Education,* pp. 11–19.

Ellwein, M.C. (1992). Research on classroom assessment meanings and practices. *Commonwealth Center News, 5* (1), 2, 4.

Finn, J.D., & Achilles, C.M. (1990). Answers and questions about class size: A statewide experiment. *American Educational Research Journal, 27* (3), 557–577.

Ford, R. (1995). Critical perspective on the case of Hans Christian Andersen School. *Guide to foundations in action: Videocases: Teaching and learning in multicultural settings* (pp. 161–174). Boston: Allyn and Bacon.

Freiberg, H. J., & Driscoll, A. (1992). *Universal teaching strategies.* Needham Heights, MA: Allyn and Bacon.

Gage, N.L. (1977). *The scientific basis of the art of teaching.* New York: Teachers College Press.

Gage, N.L., & Needels, M.C. (1989). Process-product research on teaching: A review of criticisms. *Elementary School Journal, 89* (3), pp. 253–300.

Glass, G.V. (1988). *At last—A better way to measure class size: A step-by-step guide for local associations.* Washington, DC: National Education Association.

Glasser, W. (1986). *Control theory in the classroom.* New York: Harper and Row.

Gunter, M.A., Estes, T.H., & Schwab, J.H. (1995). *Instruction: A models approach* (2nd ed.). Boston: Allyn and Bacon.

Gursky, D. (1991, August). After the reign of Dick and Jane. *Teacher Magazine,* pp. 22–29.

Harootunian, B., & Yarger, G.P. (1981). *Teachers' conceptions of their own success.* Washington, DC: AACTE.

Herbert, J. & McNergney, R. F. (1989). Evaluating teacher evaluators using a set of public standards. *Journal of Personnel Evaluation in Education, 2,* 321–333.

Herbert, J.M., & Tankersley, M. (1993). More and less effective ways to intervene with classroom teachers. *Journal of Curriculum and Supervision, 9* (1), 24–40.

Holmes, C.T. (1989). Grade level retention effects: A meta-analysis of research studies. In L.A. Shepard & M.L. Smith (Eds.), *Flunking grades: Research and policies on retention* (pp. 16–33). London: The Falmer Press.

Johnson, D., & Johnson, R. (1991). *Learning together and alone* (3rd ed.). Englewood Cliffs, NJ: Prentice-Hall.

Joyce, B.R., Weil, M., & Showers, B. (1992). *Models of teaching* (4th ed.). Boston: Allyn and Bacon.

Kauffman, J. M. (1993). How we might achieve the radical reform of special education. *The Council for Exceptional Children, 60* (1), 6–16.

Kounin, J. S. (1970). *Discipline and group management in classrooms.* New York: Holt, Rinehart and Winston.

Leinhardt, G. (1990). Capturing craft knowledge in teaching. *Educational Researcher, 19* (2), 18–25.

Lewin, K. (1935). *The meaning and measurement of personality.* New York: McGraw-Hill.

Lloyd, J.W., & Gambatese, C. (1991). Reforming the relationship between regular and special education: Background and issues. In J.W. Lloyd, N.N. Singh, & A.C. Repp (Eds.), *The regular education initiative: Alternative perspectives on concepts, issues, and models* (pp. 3–13). Sycamore, IL: Sycamore.

Maeroff, G. (1993). Building teams to rebuild schools. *Phi Delta Kappan, 74* (7), 512–519.

McCarthy, C. (1993, July 3). Firing the messenger. *Washington Post,* p. A23.

McNergney, R.F., Medley, D.M., & Caldwell, M.S. (1988). Making and implementing policy on teacher licensure. *Journal of Teacher Education, 39* (3), 38–44.

Mitzel, H.E. (1960). Teacher effectiveness. In C.W. Harris (Ed.), *Encyclopedia of educational research* (3rd ed.) (pp. 1481–1486). New York: Macmillan.

Morine-Dershimer, G. (1990, October). *Choosing among alternatives for tracing conceptual change.* Paper presented at the annual meeting of the Northeast Educational Research Association, Ellenville, NY.

Morine-Dershimer, G. (1992, April). *Patterns of interactive thinking associated with alternative perspectives on teacher planning.* Paper presented at the annual meeting of the American Educational Research Association, San Francisco.

National Education Association (1990). *Academic tracking: Report of the NEA executive committee subcommittee on academic tracking.* Washington, DC: Author.

Natriello, G. (1990). Intended and unintended consequences: Purposes and effects of teacher evaluation. In J. Millman & L. Darling-Hammond (Eds.), *The new handbook of teacher evaluation: Assessing elementary and secondary school teachers* (pp. 35–45). Newbury Park, CA: Sage Publications.

Nazario, S.L. (1992, June 16). Move grows to promote failing pupils. *Wall Street Journal,* p. B1.

Newman, F.M., & Thompson, J.A. (1987). *Effects of cooperative learning on achievement in secondary schools: A summary of research.* Madison, WI: National Center on Effective Secondary Schools.

Nowacek, E. J. (1992). Professionals talk about teaching together: Interviews with five collaborating teachers. *Intervention in School and Clinic, 27* (5), 262–276.

Nuthall, D.D. (1992, May). Performance assessment: The message from England. *Educational Leadership,* pp. 54–57.

Oakes, J. (1985). *Keeping track: How schools structure inequality.* New Haven, CT: Yale University Press.

Olson, L. (1990, May 16). Education officials reconsider policies on grade retention. *Education Week,* pp. 1, 13.

O'Neil, J. (1992). On tracking and individual differences: A conversation with Jeannie Oakes. *Educational Leadership, 50* (2), 18–21.

Pate-Bain, H., Achilles, C.M., Boyd-Zaharias, J., & McKenna, B. (1992). Class size does make a difference. *Phi Delta Kappan, 74,* 253–256.

Peterson, P.L., Swing, S.R., Stark, K.D., & Waas, G.A. (1994). Students' cognitions and time on task during mathematics isntruction. *American Educational Research Journal, 21,* 487–515.

Pogrow, S. (1993, May 26). The forgotten question in the Chapter 1 debate: Why are the students having so much trouble learning? *Education Week, 12* (35), 26, 36.

Reynolds, M.C. (1989). Students with special needs. In M.C. Reynolds (Ed.), *Knowledge base for the beginning teacher* (pp. 129–142). Oxford: Pergamon Press.

Robinson, G.E. (1990, April). Synthesis of research on the effects of class size. *Educational Leadership,* pp. 80–90.

Saunders, S., & Tankersley, M. (1990). *En route to conceptions of effective teaching: Preservice teachers; concept maps.* Paper presented at the annual meeting of the Northeast Educational Research Association, Ellenville, NY.

Shanker asks end to some standard tests. (1989, October 29). *Washington Post,* p. A13.

Sharan, S. (1990). Cooperative learning and helping behavior in the multi-ethnic classroom. In H.C. Foot, M.J. Morgan, & R.H. Shute (Eds.), *Children helping children* (pp. 151–176). New York: John Wiley & Sons.

Sharan, Y., & Sharan, S. (1989). Group investigation expands cooperative learning. *Educational Leadership, 47* (4), 17–21.

Shepard, L.A., & Smith, M.L. (1989). *Flunking grades: Research and policies on retention.* Philadelphia, PA: The Falmer Press.

Shulman, L.S. (1986). Paradigms and research programs in the study of teaching. In M.C. Wittrock (Ed.), *Handbook of research on teaching* (3rd ed.) (pp. 3–36). New York: Macmillan.

Slavin, R.E. (1991). Synthesis of research on cooperative learning. *Educational Leadership, 48* (5), 71–82.

Sprinthall, N.A., & Sprinthall, R.C. (1990). *Educational psychology: A developmental approach* (5th ed.). New York: McGraw-Hill.

Stigler, J.W., & Stevenson, H.W. (1991, Spring). How Asian teachers polish each lesson to perfection. *American Educator,* pp. 20–30.

Strang, H.R. (1993). *Teaching worlds: Simulated classroom challenges.* Boston: Allyn and Bacon.

The tracking wars: Is anyone winning? (1992). *The Harvard Education Letter, 8* (3), 1–4.

U.S. Congress, Office of Technology Assessment. (1992). *Testing in American schools: Asking the right questions* (OTA-SET-519). Washington, DC: U.S. Government Printing Office.

Vavrus, L. (1990). Put portfolios to the test. *Instructor, 100* (1), 48–50.

Viadero, D. (1992, November 18). Va. hamlet at forefront of "full inclusion" movement for disabled. *Education Week,* pp. 1, 14–16.

Wadsworth, B. (1978). *Piaget for the classroom teacher.* New York: Longman.

Walberg, H.J. (1991). Productive teaching and instruction: Assessing the knowledge base. In H.C. Waxman & H.J. Walberg (Eds.), *Effective teaching: Current research* (pp. 33–62). Berkeley, CA: McCutchan.

Weber, E. (1986). *Ideas influencing early childhood education.* New York: Teachers College Press.

Weinstein, C.S., & Mignano, A.J. (1993). *Elementary classroom management: Lessons from research and practice.* New York: McGraw-Hill.

Welsh, P. (1990, September 16). Fast-track trap: How "ability grouping" hurts our schools, kids and families. *Washington Post,* p. B1.

Winne, P. H. (1991). Motivation and teaching. In H. C. Waxman & H. J. Walberg (Eds.), *Effective teaching: Current research* (pp. 210–230). Berkeley, CA: McCutchan.

Winne, P. H., & Marx, R. W. (1979). Perceptual problem solving. In P. L. Peterson & H. J. Walberg (Eds.), *Research on teaching: Concepts, findings, and implications* (pp. 210–230). Berkeley, CA: McCutchan.

Chapter 11

AAUW Educational Foundation and the National Education Association. (1992). *The AAUW report: How schools shortchange girls: A study of major findings on girls and education.* Washington, DC: Authors.

American Association of School Administrators and the National Associations of Elementary and Secondary School Principals. (undated). School-based management: A strategy for better learning. Arlington, VA: Author.

Bales, R.F. (1954). In conference. *Harvard Business Review, 32,* 41–49.

Baltzell, D.C., & Dentler, R.A. (1983). *School principal selection practices: Five case studies.* Cambridge, MA: Abt Associates. (ERIC document No. ED 319 107)

Barnard, C.I. (1938). *The function of the executive.* Cambridge, MA: Harvard University Press.

Barth, R.S. (1990). *Improving schools from within: Teachers, parents and principals can make the difference.* San Francisco: Jossey-Bass.

Bowers, D.G., & Seashore, S.E. (1966). Predicting organizational effectiveness with a four-factor theory of leadership. *Administrative Science Quarterly, 11,* 238–264.

Callahan, R.E. (1962). *Education and the cult of efficiency: A study of the social forces that have shaped the administration of the public schools.* Chicago: University of Chicago Press.

Campbell, R.F., Cunningham, L.L., Nystrand, R.O., & Usdan, M.D. (1990). *The organization and control of American schools* (6th ed.). Columbus, OH: Merrill.

Center for Restructuring Education Issues. (1990). *Information packet on school-based management/shared decision-making.* Washington, DC: American Federation of Teachers.

Chubb, J.E. (1988, Winter). Why the current wave of school reform will fail. *The Public Interest,* pp. 28–49.

Clark, D.L., & Astuto, T.A. (1994). Redirecting reform: Challenges to popular assumptions about teachers and students. *Phi Delta Kappan, 75* (7), 513–520.

Cohen, M., & Sessler, A. (1992, May 3). Turnover burdens Chelsea schools. *Boston Globe,* p. 29.

Deal, T.E., & Peterson, K.D. (1991, June). *The principal's role in shaping school culture.* Washington, DC: U.S. Department of Education.

Eaton, W.E. (Ed.). (1990). *Shaping the superintendency: A reexamination of Callahan and the cult of efficiency.* New York: Teachers College Press.

Feistritzer, C.E., Quelle, F., & Bloom, I. (1988). *Profile of school administrators in the U.S.* Washington, DC: National Center for Education Information.

Feistritzer, C.E., Quelle, F., & Chester, D.T. (1989). *Profile of school board presidents in the U.S.* Washington, DC: National Center for Education Information.

Fiedler, F.E. (1967). *A theory of leadership effectiveness.* New York: McGraw-Hill.

Fletcher, R., Cole, J.T., & Strumor, A. (1990). *State governance systems for interdistrict collaboratives: What makes a difference? A report of a national study.* Washington, DC: U.S. Department of Education, Office of Educational Research and Improvement. (ERIC Document Reproduction Service No. ED320328)

French, J.R., & Raven, B.H. (1968). Bases of social power. In D. Cartwright & A. Zander (Eds.), *Group dynamics: Research and theory* (pp. 259–270). New York: Harper & Row.

Ginsburg, A.L., Noell, J., & Plisko, V.W. (1988). Lessons from the wall chart. *Educational Evaluation and Policy Analysis, 10* (1), 1–12.

Glazer, N. (1992, March 18). Do we need big-city school superintendents? *Education Week,* p. 36.

Goldstein, A. (1991, 10 June). Opting out of democracy: Md. teachers vote to end school-based plan. *Washington Post,* pp. D1, D13.

Goldstein, S. (1992, November/December). Christian soldier. *Teacher Magazine,* pp. 18–21.

Greer, P.R. (1990, November). University management of schools: First lessons. *Education Digest,* pp. 36–39.

Griffiths, D.E. (Ed.). (1959). *Administrative theory.* New York: Appleton.

Guthrie, J.W., Garms, W.I., & Pierce, L. (1988). *School finance and education policy: Enhancing educational efficiency, equality, and choice* (2nd ed.). Englewood Cliffs, NJ: Prentice Hall.

Hansen, E.M. (1991). *Educational administration and organizational behavior.* Boston: Allyn and Bacon.

House, E. (1974). *The politics of educational innovation.* Berkeley, CA: McCutchan.

Hoy, W.K., & Miskel, C.G. (1991). *Educational administration: Theory, research, and practice.* New York: McGraw-Hill.

Kozol, J. (1991). *Savage inequalities: Children in America's schools.* New York: Crown.

Leithwood, K., Steinbach, R., & Begley, P. (1992). Socialization experiences: Becoming a principal in Canada. In F.W. Parkey & G.E. Hall (Eds.). *Becoming a principal: The challenges of beginning leadership* (pp. 284–307). Boston: Allyn and Bacon.

McGregor, D. (1960). *The human side of enterprise.* New York: McGraw-Hill.

Meyer, J.W., & Rowan. B. (1977). Institutionalized organizations: Formal structure as myth and ceremony. *American Journal of Sociology, 83,* (2) 340–363.

National Association of Manufacturers. (1993). *Tap your workers' potential.* Washington, DC: Author.

National Center for Educational Statistics. (1991). *Digest of educational statistics 1991.* Washington, DC: U.S. Department of Education Office of Educational Research and Improvement.

National Governors' Association. (1990). *The governors' 1991 report on education, results in education: 1987, 1988, 1989, 1990.* Washington, DC: Author.

National Organization for Women Legal Defense and Education Fund. (1993, Fall). *NOW LDEF challenges St. Louis board of education.* NOW Legal Defense and Education Fund, p. 2.

National School Boards Association. (1993, September 28). University operates public middle school in Detroit. *School Board News,* p. 5.

New York City Public Schools. (1992, February 10). *Qualities of the New York City schools chancellor.* Facsimile of an "unofficial document."

New York City Public Schools, Division of Strategic Planning/Office of Educational Data Services. (1990, October 31). *Annual pupil ethnic census city-wide by school level.*

Olson, L. (1992, May/June). Quality is job one. *Teacher Magazine,* pp. 27–31.

Olson, L. (1993, April 21). Off and running. *Education Week,* pp. 4–12.

Olson, L., & Bradley, A. (1992, April 29). Boards of contention. *Education Week/Special Report,* pp. 2, 3, 5, 7, 9, 10.

Ouchi, W. *Theory Z.* Reading, MA: Addison-Wesley.

Peters, T.J., & Waterman, R.H. (1982). *In search of excellence.* New York: Harper & Row.

Schmidt, P. (1990, September 19). Va. overhauls department to shift focus from regulation to research and service. *Education Week,* p. 18.

Schmidt, P. (1992, April 29). "Minimal" training may not fit boards' needs. *Education Week/Special Report,* p. 19.

Seaton, D.M., Underwood, K.E., & Fortune, J.C. (1992, January). The burden school board members bear. *The American School Board Journal,* p. 37.

Sergiovanni, T.J., Burlingame, M., Coombs, F.S., & Thurston, P.W. (1992). *Educational governance and administration.* Boston: Allyn and Bacon.

Spring, J. (1991). *American education: An introduction to social and political aspects* (5th ed.). New York: Longman.

Stearns, T.M., Hoffman, A.N., & Heide, J.B. (1987). Performance of commercial television stations as an outcome of interorganizational linkages and environmental conditions. *Academy of Management Journal, 30,* 71–90.

Stogdill, R.M. (1981). Traits of leadership: A follow-up to 1970. In B.M. Bass (Ed.), *Stogdill's handbook of leadership* (pp. 73–97). New York: Free Press.

Tift, C. (1990, June). *Rural administrative leadership handbook.* Portland, OR: Northwest Regional Educational Laboratory.

Weber, M. (1969). Bureaucracy. In J. Litterer (Ed.), *Organizations: Structure and behavior* (pp. 29–30). New York: John Wiley. Reprinted from H.H. Gerth & C.W. Mills (Eds. and Trans.), *Essays in sociology.* London: Oxford University Press.

Williams, J. (1992). The politics of education news. In R.F. McNergney (Ed.), *Education research, policy, and the press: Research as news* (pp. 177–200). Boston: Allyn & Bacon.

Yukl, G. A. (1981). *Leadership in organizations.* Englewood Cliffs, NJ: Prentice-Hall.

Zaleznick, A. (1977). Managers and leaders: Are they different? *Harvard Business Review, 55* (3), 67–78.

Chapter 12

Allen, J. (Ed.). (1989). *Can business save education? Strategies for the 1990s.* Washington, DC: The Heritage Foundation.

Allis, S. (May 27, 1991). Can Catholic schools do it better? Yes, with less money, more selectiveness and rigor, they produce better students—and now want to sell that fact. *Time,* pp. 48–49.

American Chamber of Commerce Researchers Association (ACCRA) (1992). *ACCRA cost of living index, third quarter 1992.* Louisville, KY: Author.

American Federation of Teachers. (1991). *International comparison of public spending on education* (research report). Washington, DC: Author.

Appalachia Educational Laboratory. (1990). Rural school finance, fiscal policies for rural schools, a conference summary [Special issue]. *The Link, 9* (4).

Augenblick, J., Gold, S.D., & McGuire, K. (1990). *Education finance in the 1990s.* Denver: Education Commission of the States.

Baker, K. (1991, April). Yes, throw money at schools. *Phi Delta Kappan, 72,* (8), 628–631.

Benson, C.S. (1961). *The economics of public education.* Boston: Houghton Mifflin.

Becker, G.S. (1964). *Human capital: A theoretical and empirical analysis, with special reference to education.* New York: Columbia University Press.

Berliner, D.C. (1992, February). *Educational reform in an era of disinformation.* Paper presented at the annual meeting of the American Association of Colleges for Teacher Education, San Antonio, TX.

Berryman, S. E., & Bailey, T. R. (1992). *The double helix of education and the economy: Executive summary.* New York: The Institute on Education and the Economy, Teachers College, Columbia University.

Bracey, G.W. (1991). Why can't they be like we were? *Phi Delta Kappan, 73* (2), 105–117.

Burrup, P. E., & Brimley, V. (1982). *Financing education in a climate of change.* Boston: Allyn and Bacon.

Carson, C.C., Huelskamp, R.M., & Woodall, T.D. (1991). *Perspective on education in America* (3rd draft). Albuquerque, NM: Sandia National Laboratories.

Chubb, J.E., & Moe, T.M. (1990). *Politics, markets, and America's schools.* Washington, DC: The Brookings Institute.

Clune, W.H., & White, P.A. (1988). *School-based management: Institutional variation, implementation, and issues for further research* (Rep. No. RR-008). New Brunswick, NJ: Rutgers University, Consortium for Policy Research in Education.

Cohn, E., & Geske, T.G. (1990). *The economics of education* (3rd ed.). Oxford: Pergamon Press

Denison, E. F. (1983). *Trends in American economic growth, 1929–1982.* Washington, D.C.: Brookings Institute.

Education Writers Association. (1989). *Wolves at the schoolhouse door: An investigation of the condition of public school buildings.* Washington, DC: Author.

Educational Testing Service. (1991). *Policy information report: The state of inequality.* Princeton, NJ: Author.

Elam, S.M. (1990). The 22nd Annual Gallop Poll of the public's attitudes toward the public schools. *Phi Delta Kappan, 72* (1), 41–55.

Elam, S. M., Rose, L. C., & Gallup, A. M. (1993). The 25th annual Phi Delta Kappan/Gallup Poll of the public's attitudes toward the public schools. *Phi Delta Kappan, 75* (2), 137–152.

Finn, C.E. (1991). *We must take charge: Our schools and our future.* New York: The Free Press.

Friedman, M. (1955). The role of government in education. In R.A. Solo (Ed.), *Economics and the public interest* (pp. 123–144). New Brunswick, NJ: Rutgers University Press.

Guthrie, J.W., Garms, W.I., & Pierce, L.C. (1988). *School finance and education policy: Enhancing educational efficiency, equality, and choice.* Englewood Cliffs, NJ: Prentice Hall.

Harp (1991, June 19). States slashing reform programs as funding basics becomes harder. *Education Week,* pp. 1, 26.

Harp, L. (1993, September, 22). Momentum for challenges to finance systems still seen strong. *Education Week,* p. 22.

Hedges, L.V., Laine, R.D., & Greenwals, R. (1994). Does money matter? A meta-analysis of studies of the effects of differential school inputs on student outcomes. *Educational Researcher, 23* (3), 5–14.

Hentschke, G.C., Dembowski, F.L., Faux, J.H., Hansen, S.J., Kehoe, E., Meno, L., Murphy, M.J., Vigilante, R.P., & Yagielski, J. (1986). *School business administration: A comparative perspective.* Berkeley, CA: McCutchan.

Jencks, C., Smith, M., Acland, H., Bane, M.J., Cohen, D., Gintis, H., Heyns, B., & Michelson, S. (1972). *Inequality: A reassessment of the effect of family and schooling in America.* New York: Basic Books.

Kozol, J. (1991). *Savage inequalities: Children in America's schools.* New York: Crown.

Lakshmanan, I. A. R. (1993, June 20). N.J. schools offer omen for Mass. *Boston Sunday Globe,* p. 1.

Levin, H.M. (1980). Educational vouchers and social policy. In James W. Guthrie (Ed.), *School finance: Policies and practices* (pp. 235–263). Cambridge, MA: Balinger.

Levin, H.M. (1987, June). *Finance and governance implications of school-based decisions.* Paper presented at the National Advisory Committee of the Work in American Institute, New York.

McCormick, K. (1984). These tried-and-true alliances have paid off for public schools. *The American School Board Journal, 10,* 24–26.

Miller, J. A. (1993, April 21). Budget greeted with mixed reviews, predictions Congress will change it. *Education Week,* p. 23.

National Center for Education Statistics. (1992). *Digest of education statistics, 1992.* Washington, DC: U.S. Department of Education.

National Center for Education Statistics. (1993). *America's teachers: Profile of a profession.* Washington, DC: U.S. Department of Education.

Nelson, H.F. (1991). *International comparison of public spending on education.* Washington, DC: Research Department of the American Federation of Teachers.

Odden, A. (1984). Financing educational excellence. *Phi Delta Kappan, 65* (5), 311–318.

Putka, G. (May 15, 1991). Whittle develops plan to operate schools for profit. *Wall Street Journal,* p. B8.

Pyhrr, P. A. (1973). *Zero-base budgeting: A practical management tool for evaluating expenses.* New York: John Wiley & Sons.

Raywid, M.A. (1987). Public choice, yes; vouchers, no! *Phi Delta Kappan, 68* (10), 762–769.

Reingold, E.M. (1992, June 29). America's hamburger helper: McDonald's gives new meaning to "we do it all for you" by investing in people and their neighborhoods, *Time,* pp. 66–67.

Richardson, J. (1992, May). Who benefits? School/business partnerships. *Education Reporter,* pp. 1, 2, 7.

Schultz, E. (1990, October). Money for the asking. *Teacher Magazine,* pp. 33–41.

Schultz, T.W. (1981). *Investing in people: The economics of population quality.* Berkeley: University of California Press.

Sommerfeld, M. (1993, September 29). Corporate gifts to K–12 Education up 13% in 1992. *Education Week,* p. 10.

Strayer, G.D., & Haig, R.M. (1923). *The financing of education in the state of New York: A report reviewed and presented by the Educational Finance Inquiry Commission.* New York: The Macmillan Company, pp.42–43.

Szakal, N. E. & Melton, M. A. (1991). *Characteristics of local school boards: Selection methods and taxing authority.* Commonwealth of Virginia: Division of Legislative Services.

Taylor, W.L., & Piché, D.M. (1991, March 20). Fiscal equality and national goals. *Education Week,* p. 26.

Thro, W.E. (1990). The third wave: The impact of the Montana, Kentucky and Texas decisions on the future of public school finance reform litigation. *Journal of Law & Education, 19* (2), 219–250.

U.S. Advisory Commission on Intergovernmental Relations. (1992). *Significant features of fiscal federalism, budget processes and tax systems* (Vol. 1). Washington, DC: U.S. Government Printing Office.

U.S. Department of Education. (1989). *Making sense of school budgets.* Washington, DC: Office of Educational Research and Improvement.

Verstegen, D. (1990a). Efficiency and economies-of-scale revisited: Implications for financing rural school districts. *Journal of Education Finance, 16,* 159–179.

Verstegen, D. (1990b, winter). Fiscal policy in the Reagan administration, *Educational Evaluation and Policy Analysis, 12* (4), 355–374.

Verstegen, D. (1990c). *School finance at a glance.* Denver, CO: The Education Commission of the States.

Verstegen, D. (1992a). *Linking the national education goals and education finance.* Paper presented at the annual meeting of the American Educational Research Association, San Francisco.

Verstegen, D. (1992b). International comparisons of education spending: A review and analysis of reports. *Journal of Education Finance, 17* (4), 257–276.

Verstegen, D., & McGuire, C.K. (1991). The dialectic of reform. *Educational Policy, 5* (4), 386–411.

Wainer, H. (1993). Does spending money on education help? A reaction to the Heritage Foundation and the Wall Street Journal. *Educational Researcher, 22* (9), 22–24.

Ward, J.G. (1992). Schools and the struggle for democracy: Themes for school finance policy. In J.G. Ward & P. Anthony (Eds.), *Who pays for student diversity?* (pp. 241–250). Newbury Park, CA: Corwin Press.

Webb, L.D. (1990). New revenues for education at the state level. In J.K. Underwood & D.A. Verstegen (Eds.), *The impacts of litigation and legislation on public school finance: Adequacy, equity, and excellence* (pp. 27–58). New York: Harper & Row.

West, P. (1993, April 21). Educators say technology program comes up short. *Education Week,* p. 25.

Wise, A. (1968). *Rich schools, poor schools.* Chicago: University of Chicago Press.

Wohlstetter, P., & Buffett, T.M. (1992). Promoting school-based management: Are dollars decentralized too? In A.R. Odden (Ed.), *Rethinking school finance: An agenda for the 1990s* (pp. 128–165). San Francisco: Jossey-Bass.

Chapter 13

Alexander, K., & Alexander, M. D. (1992). *American public school law* (3rd ed.). St. Paul, MN: West.

Baker v. Owen, 395 F. Supp. 294 M.D.N.C. (1975).

Bartlett, L. (1988, January). Disciplining handicapped students: Legal issues in light of *Honig v. Doe. Exceptional Children,* pp. 357–366.

Beyer, H. A. (1989, September). Education for All Handicapped Children Act: 1975-1989 a judicial history. *Exceptional Parent,* pp. 52–54, 56, 58.

Board of Education of the Westside Community Schools v. Mergens, 496 U.S. 226 (1990).

Board of Regents v. Roth, 408 U.S. 564 (1972).

Bureau of National Affairs. (1993). Lamb's Chapel and John Seigerwald, petitioners v. Center Moriches Union Free School District et al. *The United States Law Week, 61* (46), 4549–4554.

Chase, C.I. (1976). Classroom testing and the right to privacy. *Phi Delta Kappan, 58,* 331–332.

Conkling, W. (1991, November/December). The big chill. *Teacher Magazine,* pp. 46–53.

Copyright Information Services. (1987). *The official fair-use guidelines: Complete texts of four official documents arranged for use by educators* (3rd ed.). Friday Harbor, Washington: Author.

Davis v. Grover, 480 N. W. 2d 460, (Wis. 1992).

Fischer, L., Schimmel, D., & Kelly, C. (1991). *Teachers and the law* (3rd ed.). White Plains, NY: Longman.

Florence County School District Four v. Carter, U.S. Lexis 7154, 62 U.S L.W. 4001 (S.C., 1993).

Goetz v. Ansell, 477 F.2d 636 (2nd Cir. 1973).

Gonzalez v. Mackler, 241 N.Y.S.2d 254 (N.Y. App. Div. 1963).

Goss v. Lopez, 419 U.S. 565, 95 Ct. 729, 42 L.Ed.2d 725 (1975).

Gursky, D. (1992, February). Spare the child? *Teacher Magazine,* pp. 17–19.

Hazelwood School District v. Kuhlmeier, 484 U.S. 260 (1988).

Imber, M., & van Geel, T. (1993). *Education law.* New York: McGraw-Hill.

Ingraham v. Wright, 430 U.S. 651, 97 S.Ct 1401, 51 L.Ed.2d 711 (1977).

In re William G., 221 Cal. Rptr. 118 (1985).

Irving Independent School District v. Tatro, 468 U.S. 883, 104 S.Ct. 3371, 82 L.Ed.2d 664 (1984).

La Morte, M. W. (1993). *School law: Cases and concepts* (4th ed.). Boston: Allyn and Bacon.

Lau v. Nichols, 414 U.S. 563 (1974).

Lee v. Weisman, 69 U.S.L.W. 4723 (1992).

Lemon v. Kurtzman, 403 U.S. 602, 91 S.Ct. 2105, 29 L.Ed.2d 745 (1971).

Mancha v. Field Museum of Natural History, 283 N.E.2d 899 (Ill. App. 1972).

Martin Luther King, Jr., Elementary School Children v. Michigan Board of Education, 473 Federal Supplement, 1371 (1979).

McCarthy, M. M., & Cambron-McCabe, H. (1992). *Public school law: Teachers and students' rights* (3rd ed.). Boston: Allyn and Bacon.

Morin, C.M. (1991). *Summary of cases relating to the rights of gay/lesbian public employees.* Washington, DC: National Education Association.

National Organization on Legal Problems of Education (1988). *Education Law Update 1987–1988.* USA: Author.

New Jersey v. T.L.O., 221 Cal. Rptr. 118 (1985).

Peter W. v. San Francisco Unified School District, 131 Cal.Rptr. 854 (1976).

Rothschild v. Grottenthaler, 907 F. 2nd, 286, (1990, June 27).

School District of Abington Township v. Schempp, 374 U.S. 203, 83 S.Ct 1560, 10 L.Ed.2d 844 (1963).

Sendor, B. (1992, January). The teacher as a private person. *American School Board Journal,* p. 18.

Simpson, M. (1991, November). Dress codes uncovered in schools. *NEA Today,* p. 36.

Station v. Travelers Insurance Co., 292 So.2d 289 (La. Ct. App. 1974).

Tinker v. Des Moines Independent Community School District, 393 U.S. 503, 89 S.Ct. 733, 21 L.Ed.2d 731 (1969).

Underwood, J. K. (1991). *Choice Wisconsin style.* Madison: Wisconsin Center for Educational Policy.

U.S. Department of Health and Human Services. (1992). *Child abuse and neglect: A shared community concern.* Washington, DC: Clearinghouse on Child Abuse and Neglect Information.

Virgil v. School Board of Columbia County, 862 F.2d 1517 (1988).

Wadlington, W., Whitebread, C. H., & Davis, S. M. (1988). *Cases and materials on children in the legal system.* Mineola, NY: The Foundation Press.

Wallace v. Jaffree, 427 U.S., 38 (1985).

Walsh, M. (1992, March 4). Students claiming sex harassment win right to sue: Ruling holds schools to workplace standard. *Education Week,* pp. 1, 24.

Ward v. Newfield Central School District No. 1, 412 N.Y.S.2d 57 (N.Y. App.Div. 1978).

West Virginia State Board of Education v. Barnette, 319 U.S. 624; 642 (1943).

Widmar v. Vincent, 454 U.S. 263 (1981).

Wisconsin v. Yoder, 406 U.S. 205 (1972).

Yell, M. L. (1990, September). Honig v. Doe: The suspension and expulsion of handicapped students. *Exceptional Children,* pp. 60–69.

Zirkel, P. A., & Richardson, S. N. (1988). *A digest of Supreme Court decisions affecting education* (2nd ed.). Bloomington, IN: Phi Delta Kappa Educational Foundation.

Chapter 14

Bondi, L. (1991). Choice and diversity in school education: Comparing developments in the United Kingdom and the USA. *Comparative Education, 27* (2), 125–134.

Booth, C. (1988). United Kingdom. In T.N. Postlethwaite (Ed.), *The encyclopedia of comparative education and national systems of education* (pp. 691–698). Oxford: Pergamon Press.

Bordia, A. (1988). India. In T.N. Postlethwaite (Ed.), *The encyclopedia of comparative education and national systems of education* (pp. 350–358). Oxford: Pergamon Press.

Boulding, E. (1988). *Building a global civic culture: Education for an interdependent world.* Syracuse, NY: Syracuse University Press.

Bracey, G.W. (1991). Why can't they be like we were? *Phi Delta Kappan, 73* (2), 104–117.

Brandt, R. (1992). On building learning communities: A conversation with Hank Levin. *Educational Leadership, 50* (1), 19–23.

Carson, C.C., Huelskamp, R.M., & Woodall, T.D. (1991). *Perspectives on education in America* (3rd draft). Albuquerque, NM: Sandia National Laboratories.

Cetron, M., & Davies, O. (1992). Trends shaping the world. In R.M. Jackson (Ed.), *Global issues 92/93* (pp. 21–29). Guilford, CT: Dushkin.

Cheney, L. (1991). *National tests: What other countries expect their students to know.* Washington, DC: National Endowment for the Humanities.

Cochran, J. (1993, June 28). *NBC Nightly News,* transcript, p. 7.

Cremin, L.A. (1990). *Popular education and its discontents.* New York: Harper & Row.

Cushman, K. (1993a, March). What's essential? Integrating the curriculum in essential schools. *Horace,* pp. 1–8.

Cushman, K. (1993b, May). Essential collaborators: Parents, school, and community. *Horace,* pp. 1–8.

DeVillar, R.A., & Faltis, C. (1991). *Computers and cultural diversity: Restructuring for school success.* Albany, NY: State University Press.

Dixon, P.N., & Ishler, R.E. (1992). Professional development schools: Stages in collaboration. *Journal of Teacher Education, 43* (1), 28–34.

Eisner, E.W. (1993). Why standards may not improve schools. *Educational Leadership, 50* (5), 22–23.

Federal Coordinating Council for Science, Engineering, and Technology and Committee on Education and Human Resources. (1992). *Pathways to excellence: A federal strategy for science, mathematics, engineering, and technology education—U.S. science, mathematics, engineering, and technology education strategic plan, FY 1994–FY 1998.* Washington, DC: National Aeronautics and Space Administration.

Florander, J. (1988). Denmark: System of Education. In T. Husen & T.N. Postlewaite (Eds.), *The international encyclopedia of education: Research and studies,* Vol. 3 (pp. 1354–1360). New York: Pergamon Press.

Gardner, S.L. (1992). Key issues in developing school-linked integrated services. In R.E. Behrman (Ed.), *The future of children: School-linked services* (pp. 85–94). Los Altos, CA: Center for the Future of Children, The David and Lucile Packard Foundation.

Gibbs, N. (1993, July 12). Truth, justice and the Reno way. *Time,* pp. 20–27.

Glaser, R., & Linn, R. (1992). *Assessing achievement in the states: The first report of the National Academy of Education Panel on the Evaluation of the NAEP Trial State Assessment—1990 trial assessment.* Stanford, CA: National Academy of Education.

Glenn, C.L. (1989). *Choice of schools in six nations: France, Netherlands, Belgium, Britain, Canada, West Germany.* Washington, DC: U.S. Government Printing Office.

Goodlad, J.I. (1988). Studying the education of educators: Values-driven inquiry. *Phi Delta Kappan, 70* (2), 105–111.

Goodlad, J.I. (1990). *Teachers for our nation's schools.* San Francisco: Jossey-Bass.

Gopinathan, S. (1994). Education and development: The Singapore experience. In P. Morris & A. Sweeting (Eds.), *Education and development: The East Asian experience* (pp. 1–25). New York: Greenwood Press.

Gursky, D.H. (1991). Ambitious standards. *Teacher Magazine,* pp. 49–56.

Hartshorne, K. (1990). Post-apartheid education: A concept in process (opportunities within the process). In R. Schrire (Ed.), *Critical choices for South Africa: An agenda for the 1990s* (pp. 168–185). Oxford: Oxford University Press.

Holmes Group. (1990). *Tomorrow's schools: Principles for the design of professional development schools.* East Lansing, MI: Author.

Howard, J.Z. (1990). Instructional methods and materials: How are decisions made about which teaching procedures are most appropriate? In R.M. Thomas (Ed.), *International comparative education: Practices, issues, & prospects* (pp. 59–86). Oxford: Pergamon Press.

Jaeger, R.M. (1992). World class standards, choice, and privatization: Weak measurement serving presumptive policy. *Phi Delta Kappan, 74* (2), 118–128.

Johnson, W.R. (1990). Inviting conversations: The Holmes Group and tomorrow's schools. *American Educational Research Journal, 27* (4), 581–588.

Jordahl, G. (1991). Breaking down classroom walls: Distance learning comes of age. *Technology and Learning, 11* (5), 72–78.

Judge, H. (1989). Is there a crisis in British secondary schools? *Phi Delta Kappan, 70* (10), 813–815.

King, E.J. (1988). South Africa. In T.N. Postlethwaite (Ed.), *The encyclopedia of comparative education and national systems of education* (pp. 600–605). Oxford: Pergamon Press.

Lemmer, E.M. (1993). Educational renewal in South Africa: Problems and prospects. *Compare, 23* (1), 53–62.

Levine, M. (Ed.). (1992). *Professional practice schools: Linking teacher education and school reform.* New York: Teachers College Press.

Levy, J.E., & Shepardson, W. (1992). A look at current school-linked service efforts. In R.E. Behrman (Ed.), *The future of children: School-linked services* (pp. 44–55). Los Altos, CA: Center for the Future of Children, The David and Lucile Packard Foundation.

McLaughlin, M.W., & Talbert, J.E. (1993). *Contexts that matter for teaching and learning.* Stanford, CA: Center for Research on the Context of Secondary School Teaching.

Moore, G.R. (1991). Computer to computer: Mentoring possibilities. *Educational Leadership, 49* (3), 40.

Omar, R. (1993). Student representative council report. *The Garland.* Cape Town, South Africa: Garlandale High School.

O'Neil, J. (1993). On the new standards project: A conversation with Lauren Resnick and Warren Simmons. *Educational Leadership, 50* (5), 17–21.

Orum, B., & Hansen, E.J. (1975). *Illusions about education.* Copenhagen: Fremad.

Pease, P.S. (1991). Preparing your facility for distance learning. *American School & University, 63* (10), 37–38.

Sizer, T.R. (1992). *Horace's school: Redesigning the American high school.* Boston: Houghton Mifflin.

Stevenson, H.W., & Stigler, J.W. (1992). *The learning gap: Why our schools are failing and what we can learn from Japanese and Chinese education.* New York: Summit Books.

Taylor, W.H. (1991). India's national curriculum: Prospects and potential for the 1990s. *Comparative Education, 27* (3), 325–334.

Technical Subgroup for the National Education Goals Panel. (1992). *Gauging high performance: How to use NAEP to check progress on the National Education Goals.* Washington, DC: Author.

Thomas, R.M. (Ed.). (1988). *Oriental theories of human development.* New York: Peter Lang.

Thomas, R.M. (Ed.). (1990). *International comparative education: Practices, issues, & practices.* Oxford: Pergamon Press.

Thorp, S. (Ed.). (1991). *Race, equality, and science teaching.* London: The Lavenham Press.

Tyack, D. (1992, Spring). Health and social services in public schools: Historical perspectives. In R.E. Behrman (Ed.), *The future of children: School-linked services* (pp. 19–31). Los Altos, CA: The David and Lucile Packard Foundation.

Tye, B.B., & Tye, K.A. (1992). *Global education: A study of school change.* Albany: State University of New York Press.

Webb, N.L., & Romberg, T.A. (in press). *Collaboration as a process of reform: The urban mathematics collaborative project.* New York: Teachers College Press.

Weiss, H. (1992). *Pioneering states: Innovative family support and education programs: Connecticut, Kentucky, Maryland, Minnesota, Missouri* (2nd ed.). Cambridge, MA: Harvard Family Research Project, Harvard Graduate School of Education.

Wisconsin Center for Education Research. (1992, Winter). Collaboration breaks mathematics teacher isolation and builds professionalism. *WCER Highlights,* pp. 1–2.

NAME INDEX

SUBJECT INDEX